A BRITISH FRO

Dedicated to the memory of my mother, Davina J. Meikle, who helped and encouraged all my doctoral research and the subsequent creation of this book

A BRITISH FRONTIER?

LAIRDS AND GENTLEMEN IN THE EASTERN BORDERS, 1540–1603

Maureen M. Meikle

TUCKWELL PRESS

First published in Great Britain in 2004 by
Tuckwell Press Ltd
The Mill House
Phantassie
East Linton
East Lothian, Scotland

Copyright Maureen M. Meikle 2004

ISBN 1 86232 261 9

British Library Cataloguing-in-Publication Data

A catalogue record of this book is available
on request from the British Library

Published with the assistance of the Marc Fitch Fund

Typeset by Hewer Text Ltd, Edinburgh
Printed and bound by Bell & Bain Ltd., Glasgow

Contents

Preface

Comparative history was not fashionable in the 1980s, but became so in the 1990s due to the interest in the multiple kingdoms approach to early modern British history. Gaining knowledge of how local societies functioned in both sixteenth-century Scotland and England was time consuming and complex. However, this background enabled me to look at the micro history of the Eastern Borders before the Union of the Crowns of 1603 with a fully Anglo-Scottish perspective. *A British Frontier?* began life as a doctoral thesis completed at the University of Edinburgh as long ago as 1988. My supervisors, Professor Michael Lynch and Professor Tony Goodman gave me the benefit of their combined experience in Scottish and English history. I am grateful to them for their continuing encouragement and kindness. Thanks are also due to the many excellent archivists who assisted my searches. These include the staff of Archives and Special Collections of the University of Durham Palace Green Library (formerly the Department of Palaeography), Mr Roger Norris of Durham Chapter Library, the National Archives of Scotland (formerly the Scottish Record Office), the National Register of Archives (Scotland), the National Library of Scotland and the National Archives (formerly the Public Record Office). I should point out that many of the archive collections I visited have been reorganised and changed location since the 1980s, but most record classifications remain the same. This is particularly the case with Alnwick Castle, the University of Durham and the Public Record Office. I was also allowed privileged access to the manuscript collections of the late Lord Home of the Hirsel and the late duke of Northumberland. Amongst other private manuscript collections, I would particularly like to thank Mrs Dorothy Pringle of Torwoodlee and Lady McEwen of Marchmont for their kind hospitality. Since completing my thesis the Walter Mason trust has been formed, providing most welcome extra documentation for my book. I would like to thank Mr Ian Brown and Mr Walter Elliot for letting me see advanced copies of transcriptions of protocol books preserved by the trust in the early 1990s.

Since 1988, I have benefited from various temporary employment opportunities at the Open University in Scotland, Heriot-Watt University, Warwick University, Bristol Polytechnic (now the University of the West of England), Stirling University and the University of Edinburgh. Teaching and lecturing duties were good experience, but they ultimately distracted me from my research and writing. Nevertheless, the help and advice I received from early modern colleagues at the Department of History at Warwick

University have focused many of my postdoctoral ideas and arguments. I thank them all, but especially Professor Bernard Capp for being my 'mentor' as a new lecturer. My original thesis has now been comprehensively reworked, updated, rewritten and adapted to ever-improving technology. Much of this was accomplished whilst I was the Fulbright Visiting Professor of British History at Westminster College, Fulton, Missouri, U.S.A., during 1993–95. I would like to thank the College for giving me a light teaching load and the use of a good computer to accomplish this task. I am also grateful to Professor William Palmer of Marshall University who has encouraged and discussed my more recent Border research and writing via e-mail. I would also like to acknowledge the stability that a permanent lectureship at the School of Arts, Design, Media and Culture at the University of Sunderland has given me for updating my original Border research and allowing me to begin other research projects on Anna of Denmark and sixteenth-century Scotland. My Sunderland colleagues Dr Gwenda Morgan and Dr Peter Rushton deserve much credit for discussing my research over many pleasurable lunches. Furthermore, I wish to thank Professor Tony Pollard and my fellow committee members of the 'Time, Space and Boundaries' strand of the AHRB Centre for North-East England History. They have shown great interest in and given me helpful feedback on the findings of my Anglo-Scottish Border research.

Lastly I must thank my parents, Roy and the late Davina, for all their moral and financial support during my student days. My parents' care and devotion also saw me through the dark months of 1990 when serious illness set me back. I will always be grateful for this and for their giving me a permanent base during my many temporary teaching contracts. My only regret is that my mother did not live to see this book finally in print, but it is dedicated to her memory with love and affection.

Maureen M. Meikle

Conventions

1. Placenames are as the Ordnance Survey, or *RSS* if the location is now lost.

2. Personal names have been modernised. Scottish surnames conform to G. F. Black, *The Surnames of Scotland,* New York 1946, with the exception of Aitchison, Hangingside, Mow, Robson and Spottiswoode.

3. All dates have been modernised e.g. 2 March 1560, not 2 March 1559/ 60, or 2 March 1559.

4. Transcriptions are given as in the original documentation, with contractions expanded. Quotations from printed primary sources are given as published.

5. Currency is in pound sterling, unless specified as pound Scots. The English mark and Scots merk were both worth 13s 4d in their respective currencies.

6. Printed primary sources are referred to by number. Page references are only used when numbers are unavailable.

7. North Northumberland will always be lower case 'n' to avoid confusion with North Durham, an outpost of the county palatine of Durham.

8. Titles are lower case with the exception of Lord, e.g. Lord Home, but earl of Northumberland.

Glossary

Scots	English
Bairns	Children
Bailie	Bailiff
Depute	Deputy
Escheat	Forfeited property
Feuars	Holders of land be feu charter
Fiar	Owner of the fee-simple of a property
Horning	Outlawing
Justice ayre	Circuit court
Kirkland	Glebe
Merk (13s 4d)	Mark (13s 4d)
Overman	Supervisor
Poind	Impound
Sheiling	Summer pasture
Tacksman	Tenant
Tailzie	Entail
Teind	Tithe
Tocher	Dowry
Tutors Testamentars	Overseers *in loco parentis*
Wadset	Mortgage
Wappinshaw	Muster

Abbreviations

AA.	*Archaeologia Aeliana* (Newcastle-upon-Tyne, 1822–).
ADCP.	*Acts of the Lords of Council in Public Affairs, 1501–1554* (Edinburgh, 1932).
ALN MS.	Duke of Northumberland, Alnwick Manuscripts, Alnwick Castle.
APC.	*Acts of the Privy Council of England* (London, 1890–1907).
APS.	*Acts of the Parliaments of Scotland* (Edinburgh, 1814–75).
Bannatyne Misc.	*The Bannatyne Miscellany* (Bannatyne Club, 1826–55).
BIHR.	Borthwick Institute of Historical Research, York.
BL.	British Library, Department of Manuscripts.
BRO.	Berwick Record Office.
BUK.	*(Booke of the Universall Kirke), Acts and Proceedings of the General Assemblies of the Kirk of Scotland from 1560 to 1618* (Bannatyne Club, 1839–45).
Calderwood, *History*.	*History of the Kirk of Scotland by Mr. David Calderwood* (Wodrow Society, 1842–49).
CBP.	*Calendar of Letters and Papers relating to the affairs of the Borders of England and Scotland* (London, 1894–96).
CPR.	*Calendar of the Patent Rolls Edward VI, Philip and Mary and Elizabeth I* (London, 1924–).
CRS.	*Catholic Record Society* (London, 1905–).
CSPDom.	*Calendar of State Papers Domestic* (London, 1856–72 & 1992–).
CSPDom Add.	*Calendar of State Papers Domestic Addenda* (London 1870–72).
CSPFor.	*Calendar of State Papers Foreign* (London, 1861–1901).
CSPScot.	*Calendar of the State Papers relating to Scotland and Mary, Queen of Scots* (Edinburgh, 1898–1969).
CSPSpain.	*Calendar of State Papers, Spanish* (London, 1862–1954).

Carey, *Memoirs.*   *The Memoirs of Sir Robert Carey,* ed. F. H. Mares
                               (Oxford, 1972).
Cliffe, *Yorkshire*   J. T. Cliffe, *The Yorkshire Gentry* (London, 1969).
   Gentry.
D & Ch. Reg.   Durham Chapter Archives, 5 The College,
                               Durham, Dean and Chapter Registers.
DDR.   University of Durham Library, Archives and
                               Special Collections, Durham Diocesan Records.
DPRW.   University of Durham Library, Archives and
                               Special Collections, Durham Probate Records:
                               Wills.
DPRW Reg.   University of Durham Library, Archives and
                               Special Collections, Durham Probate Records:
                               Register of Wills.
EHR.   *The English Historical Review.*
ER.   *The Exchequer Rolls of Scotland* (Edinburgh,
                               1878–1908).
Fraser, *Annandale.*   W. Fraser, *The Annandale Family Book of the
                               Johnstones* (Edinburgh, 1894)
Fraser, *Buccleuch.*   W. Fraser, *The Scotts of Buccleuch* (Edinburgh,
                               1878).
Fraser, *Douglas.*   W. Fraser, *The Douglas Book* (Edinburgh, 1885).
Godscroft, *De Familia.*   D. Home of Godscroft, *De Familia Humia
                               Wedderburnensi Liber* (Abbotsford Club, 1839).
Godscroft, *History.*   D. Home of Godscroft, *The History of the House
                               and Race of Douglas and Angus* (London, 1657).
Hamilton Papers.   *The Hamilton Papers: Letters and papers
                               illustrating the political relations of England and
                               Scotland* (Edinburgh, 1890–92).
Hatfield MS.   Marquess of Salisbury's MS, Hatfield House.
HMC, 3rd Report.   *Reports of the Royal Commissioners of the
                               Historical Manuscripts Commission,* Third Report
                               (London, 1872).
HMC, 4th Report.   *Reports of the Royal Commissioners of the
                               Historical Manuscripts Commission,* Fourth
                               Report (London, 1874).
HMC, 6th Report.   *Reports of the Royal Commissioners of the
                               Historical Manuscripts Commission,* Sixth Report
                               (London, 1877–78).
HMC, 9th Report.   *Reports of the Royal Commissioners of the
                               Historical Manuscripts Commission,* Ninth Report
                               (London, 1883–4).
HMC, Bath.   *Reports of the Royal Commissioners of the
                               Historical Manuscripts Commission,* Manuscripts

	of the marquis of Bath, preserved at Longleat (London, 1904–80).
HMC, Hastings.	*Reports of the Royal Commissioners of the Historical Manuscripts Commission,* Manuscripts of Reginald Hastings (London, 1928–47).
HMC, Home.	*Reports of the Royal Commissioners of the Historical Manuscripts Commission,* Manuscripts of the earl of Home. Twelfth Report, appendix viii (London, 1891).
HMC, Laing.	*Reports of the Royal Commissioners of the Historical Manuscripts Commission,* Laing Manuscripts, University of Edinburgh (Edinburgh, 1914–25).
HMC, Marchmont.	*Reports of the Royal Commissioners of the Historical Manuscripts Commission,* Manuscripts of H. Hume Campbell, Fourteenth Report, appendix iii (London, 1894).
HMC, Milne-Home.	*Reports of the Royal Commissioners of the Historical Manuscripts Commission,* Manuscripts of David Milne Home of Wedderburn (London, 1902).
HMC, Pepys.	*Reports of the Royal Commissioners of the Historical Manuscripts Commission,* Pepys Manuscripts, Magdalen College, Cambridge (Cambridge, 1911).
HMC, Roxburghe.	*Reports of the Royal Commissioners of the Historical Manuscripts Commission,* Manuscripts of the duke of Roxburghe, Fourteenth Report, appendix iii (London, 1894).
HMC, Rutland.	*Reports of the Royal Commissioners of the Historical Manuscripts Commission,* Manuscripts of the duke of Rutland (London, 1888–1905).
HMC, Salisbury.	*Reports of the Royal Commissioners of the Historical Manuscripts Commission,* Manuscripts of the marquess of Salisbury (London, 1883–1930).
HMC, Talbot.	*Reports of the Royal Commissioners of the Historical Manuscripts Commission,* Talbot Manuscripts, College of Arms (London, 1971).
HBNC.	*History of the Berwickshire Naturalists' Club.*
IR.	*The Innes Review.*
JED JM.	Roxburgh District Council, Jail Museum, Jedburgh Castle.
KAO.	Centre for Kentish Studies, Maidstone.

Laing Chrs.	*Calendar of the Laing Charters 854–1837* (Edinburgh, 1899).
LAMB MS.	Lambeth Palace Library, Talbot & Shrewsbury MS.
Lesley, *History.*	*The Historie of Scotland, wrytten in Latin by the most reverend and worthy Jhone Leslie, Bishop of Rosse*, ed. E. G. Cody & W. Murison (Scottish Text Society, 1888–95).
L&P. Hen VIII.	*Letters and Papers, Foreign and Domestic, of the Reign of Henry VIII* (London, 1862–1932).
L&I.	Public Record Office, *List and Index Society.*
MacGibbon & Ross, *Architecture.*	D. MacGibbon & T. Ross, *The Castellated and Domestic Architecture of Scotland* (Edinburgh, 1887).
Mary of Lorraine. Corresp.	*The Scottish Correspondence of Mary of Lorraine* (Scottish History Society, 1927).
Meikle, 'Thesis'.	Maureen M. Meikle, 'Lairds and Gentlemen: a study of the landed families of the Eastern Anglo-Scottish Borders, c. 1540–1603'. unpubl. PhD diss, Edinburgh 1989.
Melville, *Memoirs.*	*Memoirs of his own life by Sir James Melville of Halhill* (Bannatyne Club, 1827).
Mingay, *Gentry.*	G. E. Mingay, *The Gentry: The Rise and Fall of a Ruling Class* (London, 1976).
Moysie, *Memoirs.*	*Memoirs of the Affairs of Scotland by David Moysie, 1579–93* (Bannatyne Club, 1830).
NAS.	National Archives of Scotland (formerly the Scottish Record Office).
NCH.	*A History of Northumberland* (London, 1893–1940).
NH.	*Northern History.*
NLS.	The National Library of Scotland.
NRAS.	National Register of Archives, Scotland.
O'Day, *Education.*	R. O'Day, *Education and Society, 1500–1800* (London, 1982).
Palliser, *Age of Elizabeth.*	D. M. Palliser, *The Age of Elizabeth* (London, 1983).
P&P.	*Past and Present.*
Pitcairn, *Trials.*	R. Pitcairn, *Criminal Trials in Scotland, 1488–1624* (Edinburgh, Maitland Club, 1833).
Pitscottie, *Historie.*	*The Historie and Chronicles of Scotland by Robert Lindsay of Pitscottie*, ed. J. G. Mackay (Scottish Text Society, 1899–1911).
Pollard, *Wars of the Roses.*	A. J. Pollard, *North-Eastern England during the Wars of the Roses* (Oxford, 1990).

PRO.	Public Record Office (now the National Archives).
Rae, *Scottish Frontier.*	T. I. Rae, *The Administration of the Scottish Frontier, 1513–1603* (Edinburgh, 1960).
Raine, *North Durham.*	J. Raine, *The History and Antiquities of North Durham* (London, 1852).
RMS.	*Registrum Magni Sigilli Regum Scotorum* (Edinburgh, 1882–1914).
RPC.	*The Register of the Privy Council of Scotland* (Edinburgh 1877–).
Retours.	*Inquisitionum ad Capellam Domini Regis Retornatum, quae in publicis archivis Scotiae adhuc servatur, Abbreviato* (Edinburgh 1811–16).
RSCHS.	*Records of the Scottish Church History Society.*
RSS.	*Registrum Secreti Sigilli Regum Scotorum* (Edinburgh, 1908–).
Sadler Papers.	*The State Papers and Letters of Sir Ralph Sadler,* ed. A. Clifford (Edinburgh, 1809).
Sanderson, *Rural Society.*	M. H. B. Sanderson, *Scottish Rural Society in the Sixteenth Century* (Edinburgh, 1982).
Scot Antiq.	*Scottish Antiquary (Northern Notes and Queries)* (Edinburgh, 1886–1903).
Selkirk Protocol Books.	*Selkirk Protocol Books 1511–1547,* ed. T. Maley & W. Elliot (Stair Society, 1993).
SHR.	*Scottish Historical Review.*
SP.	*The Scots Peerage* (Edinburgh, 1904–14).
Sharp, *Memorials.*	C. Sharp, *Memorials of the Rebellion* (London, 1840).
SS.	*The Surtees Society.*
Stat.	*Statutes of the Realm* (London, 1810–28).
Stone, *Open Elite?*	L. & J. C. F. Stone, *An Open Elite? England 1540–1880* (Oxford, 1984).
Summerson, *Medieval Carlisle.*	H. Summerson, *Medieval Carlisle: The City and the Borders from the late eleventh to the mid-sixteenth century,* 2 vols (The Cumberland and Westmorland Antiquarian and Archaeological Society, Kendal, 1993).
SYON MS.	Duke of Northumberland, Syon Manuscripts, Alnwick Castle.
Thirsk, *Agrarian History.*	J. Thirsk, ed. *The Agrarian History of England and Wales* (Cambridge, 1967).
Tough, *Last Years.*	D. L. W. Tough, *The Last Years of a Frontier* (Oxford, 1928).
TA.	*Accounts of the Lord High Treasurer of Scotland* (Edinburgh, 1877–1916).

TRHS.	*Transactions of the Royal Historical Society.*
Tranter, *Fortified House.*	N. G. Tranter, *The Fortified House in Scotland* (Edinburgh, 1962).
T&WAS.	Tyne and Wear Archives Service, Newcastle-upon-Tyne.
WMT.	The Walter Mason Trust, Selkirk.
Warrender Papers.	*The Warrender Papers,* ed. A. I. Cameron (Scottish History Society, 1931–32).
Watts, *Border to Middle Shire.*	S. J. Watts, *From Border to Middle Shire: Northumberland 1586–1625* (Leicester, 1975).
Wormald, *Community.*	J. Wormald, *Court, Kirk and Community, 1470–1625* (London, 1981).
Wormald, *Lords and Men.*	J. Wormald, *Lords and Men in Scotland: Bonds of Manrent, 1442–1603* (Edinburgh, 1985).

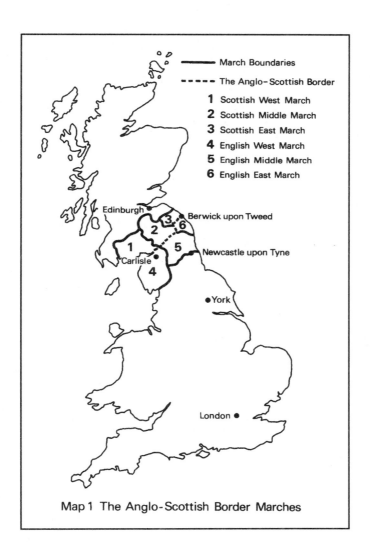

Map 1 The Anglo-Scottish Border Marches

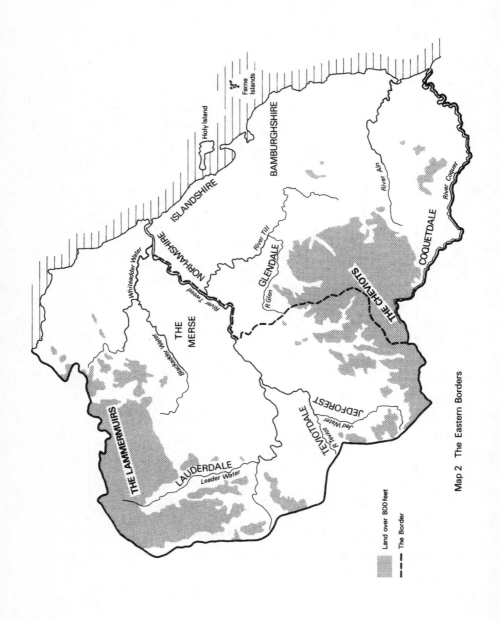

Map 2 The Eastern Borders

Land over 800 feet

--- The Border

THE LAMMERMUIRS

LAUDERDALE

Leader Water

Blackadder Water

Whiteadder Water

THE MERSE

River Tweed

NORHAMSHIRE

ISLANDSHIRE

Holy Island

Farne Islands

BAMBURGHSHIRE

River Till

GLENDALE

R Glen

THE CHEVIOTS

COQUETDALE

River Aln

River Coquet

JEDFOREST

TEVIOTDALE

R Teviot

Jed Water

Map 3   The Eastern Scottish Borderland

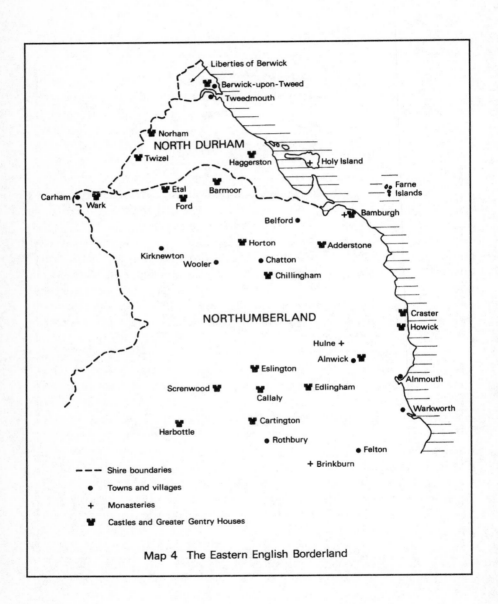

Map 4 The Eastern English Borderland

Introduction: A British Frontier?

Did the Eastern Anglo-Scottish Borders constitute a 'British' frontier between 1540 and 1603? This question arose from the 1990s debate about the formation of a British State[1] and forced a rethink of my original research on landed families in the Eastern Borders.[2] Although the British approach is controversial, the question of whether this frontier contributed to the creation of Britain cannot be ignored. The answer is far from straightforward as frontiers can be social, economic, linguistic, religious, geophysical or cultural as well as political, military and administrative. The frontier was only recognised by Eastern Borderers when it suited them for it could be highly visible in political or religious terms, yet invisible in a social, economic and military context. Nor is there a typical Border society or culture from which to draw conclusions about its relationship with central governments. There was, for example, an entrenched east-west social, economic and cultural divide on this Border which has not been explored before. Moreover, some would argue that the policies of sixteenth-century monarchs were inconsistent as far as their boundaries were concerned,[3] thus the existence of a 'British' mentality or polity here is difficult to determine.

The debate about the formation of Britain 'may well fade in time' and 'runs the risk of presupposing parallels where there is in fact nothing but coincidence, distinction or divergence.'[4] It is certainly still being challenged by historians in the early-twenty-first century. Some question whether there was a British policy in the sixteenth century, believing rather that there was an English policy 'to keep foreign powers out of the British periphery.' England and Scotland were arguably still forming their own states in the sixteenth century, so discussion of British state formation appears premature. There is also the conundrum of why the state forming English government regarded Ireland and Scotland differently, with policies of 'conquest and colonisation' for Ireland and 'alliance and union' for Scotland.[5] Even the term 'British' is controversial and increasingly complex.[6] Indeed the 1603 Union of the Crowns may well be 'as much the consequence of Tudor/Stewart dynastic roulette as of any conscious British state-building.'[7] In reality if any state building was being attempted on the Anglo-Scottish frontier prior to 1603 it was more from an English imperialist basis and not a truly British foundation.

The shift away from Anglocentricity in the historical study of what is now termed the 'Atlantic archipelago' is nevertheless commendable for its use of comparative history. As Ronald Asch noted in 1993 'if nothing else the

British perspective can certainly teach us to be more cautious in taking for granted the time-honoured framework of the various national histories.'[8] In his *Tudor Frontiers and Noble Power: the making of the British State* and elsewhere, Steven Ellis emphasised how the Irish and English frontiers interacted with a centralizing government that had a British polity in mind. He also noted how different these peripheries were from the English Lowlands. Whilst it is useful to demarginalize the Tudor borderlands in mainstream political history, this viewpoint fails to be convincing for the Anglo-Scottish Borders – particularly during the period 1540–1603. The geography, politics and society of the Irish Pale do not necessarily compare with the entire Anglo-Scottish frontier. This study will show, for example, that the sixteenth-century English north-east frontier cannot be described as part of a 'desolate, sparsely populated landscape of isolated farmsteads, large parishes and manors' with 'few substantial gentry or major towns.'[9] As the basis of his argument for the sixteenth-century north in *Tudor Frontiers and Noble Power*, Ellis concentrated on one magnate family in the English West March and ended this analysis around 1535. Since many changes in English regional government were instigated from 1534 onwards,[10] stopping such a research project in 1535 is questionable. This is clearly too narrow a framework upon which to draw major conclusions about the state of this gentry-dominated frontier during the alleged formation of the British state. To study one noble family in only one (of six) Border Marches, is merely to scratch the surface of complex pre-union Anglo-Scottish Border history.

Nearly seven decades of the century before 1603 are largely unaccounted for in *Tudor Frontiers and Noble Power*. Not all the events of 1540–1603 in the Eastern Borders contradict Ellis's argument that 'the problem of the borderlands was in many ways a good deal more fundamental to the development of British political culture and the Tudor state'. Nevertheless, this study will show that there are important distinctions to be made for the Eastern frontier and there are many problems with these 'British' polity assertions.[11] Henry VIII's attempts at centralization worked well for aspiring local gentry who sidelined the traditional influence of the Percy, earls of Northumberland. A change in the local power structure was also evident on the Scottish side with the demise of the Lords Home. However, the Borderers co-operation with their respective crowns was never certain in an arena of self-interested landed society. John Guy has noted that 'despite the apparent resilience of this continued policy of centralization, it may be illusory to suppose that, at the level of the northern grass roots, the state had triumphed by 1603.' Sandy Grant and Keith Stringer have also reminded us that 'historians should beware of Whiggishly reading history backwards.'[12]

Landed opinion in the Eastern Borders would not have considered any kind of 'British' context until the last years of Elizabeth I's reign and even then they would probably have only thought along Anglo-Scottish lines. The idea mooted after 1603 by King James VI & I that there was one British monarch and nation, rather than a united sovereignty of independent states, was overwhelmingly rejected by both Scots and English.[13] Identity, in reality, was far more complex, for in the sixteenth-century Eastern Borders the lairds and gentlemen tended to be Borderers first and foremost and Scots or English second. By studying 454 landed families in the Eastern Borders, especially those below the ranks of the nobility, a clearer picture of their frontier ideology emerges. These families project an alternative image of relative peace and sophistication, far removed from the much written about endemic cross-border violence that more properly belongs in the Western Anglo-Scottish Borders. They have often been falsely associated with those Borderers who lived beyond the law.[14] All too often their violence and negligence have been exaggerated by Elizabethan officers who were eager to receive their salaries on time and therefore deliberately overstated their dangerous working conditions. The trend towards exaggeration continued with the Border Ballads collected by Sir Walter Scott in the nineteenth century and twentieth-century writers such as George McDonald Fraser, who failed to realise that many original reports were fabrications. The truth surely lies between the lines of these reports as edited calendars of state papers can omit important information.[15] Similarly those writers who use the more plentiful material from the 1580s and 1590s to explain the events of earlier decades have also falsified the image of the Anglo-Scottish Borders. The area changed rapidly with every decade of the sixteenth century being markedly different to the preceding one.[16] Modern day tourism has further encouraged a false image by concentrating too much upon the reivers, rather than the genuine achievers who lived in the region. The Tullie House Museum in Carlisle, for example, has a good representation of the violence of the West March reivers, but this is far from the whole story of the Anglo-Scottish frontier in the sixteenth century.[17]

This book is not intended as a study of Border administration, reiving and military activities, for these have been the focus of other solidly-researched works.[18] Rather it is a thematic, comparative micro history of landed society along part of a political frontier, encompassing important decades leading up to the Union of the Crowns in 1603. The focus will be on the social structures of landed communities on both sides of the Border, their politics, wealth, education and culture, the effects of the Reformations in both countries, their disorder and cross-border relations. This approach will hopefully revise previously held opinion about this frontier, though the recorded lifestyle of these families cannot answer every question about sixteenth-century British frontiers.

The Eastern Anglo-Scottish Borders had a large population of landed families, a reasonable proportion of whom were relatively substantial. From 1540 to 1603 there were at least 307 separate laird families and 147 gentry families. The overall population of the region in 1603 was probably around

24,000 on the Scottish side and 33,000 on the English,[19] gainsaying the
sparsely populated scenario advocated by Ellis. Indeed parts of the upland
Western Borders, which had a poor soil and climate, were arguably over-
populated at this time.[20] It is interesting to note where these landed families
emerged from. They were in part the descendants of former Douglas and
Percy squires who began to emerge in their own right during the fifteenth
century. In the Scottish Borders the fall of the powerful 'Black' Douglases in
the mid-fifteenth century heralded the rise of the Home, Ker and Pringle
kindreds. During the later-fifteenth century the English monarchy's deter-
mination to subvert the power of over-mighty magnates in the North began
a similar process of change.[21] This culminated with some local gentry acting
independently of the Percies from the 1520s and 1530s onwards. By looking
closely at one locality the complex influence of central politics on local
society can be deciphered and more easily understood. The opinion of W. K.
Boyd, who once thought Border matters were of little historical value can no
longer be justified.[22]

Contrary to popular opinion the Eastern Anglo-Scottish Border was
neither a backwater, nor a constant war zone. Landed families here were
no more violent than any other gentry community in Scotland and England.
Furthermore their cultural appreciation made them appear to be on the
fringes of civilised society, rather than miles from it. They were arguably not
part of perceived Western Border *mores*. The majority did not indulge in
cross-border feuding and reiving activities, that were often linked more to
poverty than malice. The Eastern Borderers were able to derive a sufficient
living from their more fertile lands and thus did not raid unless it was part of
an official Anglo-Scottish war. Even when they were in financial difficulties
they did not resort to the barbarous customs practised by Western Borderers. Neither were they ignorant of politics for though the gentry were
remote from the centre of English government and communications were
slow, they knew of central events. The lairds were much closer to their
government and had speedier communication with their crown, privy
council and parliament, but this was probably due more to the personalised
nature of sixteenth-century Scottish government than specific Border problems.[23]

The landed families of the Eastern Border shared broadly similar social
structures, kinship, wealth patterns, problems with younger sons and reiving
from the Western Borders. The River Tweed was not an impenetrable
barrier to communication, so the shared interests of landed families were
cemented by sociable activities.[24] The Eastern Borders were, in fact, a
microcosm of the political state of Scotland and England from 1540 to
1603, though it would be controversial to call this British as both nations
viewed their Borders and Borderers differently. Distinctions were also made
by these families between civilised lowlanders and troublesome uplanders,
with many preferring landed friendships across the frontier to association

with thieves of their own nationality. Though this might appear British, it was, in reality, friendship amongst like-minded Borderers who chose to ignore the frontier when it suited them; much to the alarm of non-local English officials.

Primary sources for the Eastern Borders are quite good, though there are technical difficulties in interpreting the language, law, religion, economics and customs of two realms. There are some inevitable gaps in family papers and local legal records on both sides of the frontier. It may surprise some to know that the Scottish records were more plentiful than the English, though there were sufficient government and legal documents in both countries to satisfy the aims of this study. For example, the surviving probate material for both countries is an excellent source of social history. The sheer volume of state papers from the 1580s onwards led to the curtailing of my original project at 1603 instead of 1625. None the less the period 1540–1603 is significantly longer than some other works on the Borders.[25]

The best contemporary family history is *De Familia Humia Wedderburnensi* by David Home of Godscroft. Later historians concentrated on the administration of the East, Middle and West Marches of Scotland and England.[26] Others have discussed the incessant activities of Border reivers. There were, in fact, few reivers within the Eastern Borders, yet it is this image that dominates much Border history and folklore. In the eighteenth century Ridpath, Nicolson and Burn published reasonable histories of the Borders.[27] They were followed by the nineteenth-century romanticism of Sir Walter Scott who portrayed the Borders unrealistically. He unfortunately influenced much subsequent Border history. Other nineteenth-century historians such as Raine, Hodgson and Armstrong were more perceptive, if a little inaccurate.[28] There are a number of family histories and the detailed Northumberland County History volumes that straddle the nineteenth and twentieth centuries. These vary from highly inaccurate storybooks to well-researched genealogical texts, such as the Carr, Ormiston, Pringle and Rutherford histories.[29] The twentieth-century historians Batho, Bean, James, Rae, Reid, Tough and Watts have helpfully re-appraised Border history using modern methodology and perspective.[30] Other works have pushed this process further in the late-twentieth century[31] and new millennium books have added further insights.[32] This book will now revise both traditional and recent 'British' opinions about Anglo-Scottish Border *mores* and ideology.

Notes

1 *Cf.* R. G. Asch, ed. *Three Nations – a common history? England, Scotland, Ireland and British History c. 1600–1920* (Bochum, 1993), S. J. Connolly, ed. *Kingdoms United? Great Britain and Ireland Since 1500* (Dublin, 1999), S. G. Ellis, *Tudor Frontiers and Noble Power. The Making of the British State* (Oxford, 1995), S. G. Ellis & S. Barber, eds. *Conquest and Union, Fashioning a*

6   *A British Frontier?*

British State 1485–1725 (Harlow, 1995), A. Grant & K. J. Stringer, eds. *Uniting the Kingdom? The Making of British History* (London, 1995) and B. Bradshaw & J. Morrill, eds. *The British Problem, c. 1543–1707* (Basingstoke, 1996).

2 Meikle, *Thesis.*

3 W. Palmer, 'High Officeholding, Foreign Policy, and the British Dimension in the Tudor Far North, 1525–1563', *Albion* 29 (1998), 581.

4 P. Gaunt, *The British Wars 1637–1651* (London, 1997), 4. M. Nicholls, *A History of the Modern British Isles 1529–1603* (Oxford, 1999), xv.

5 M. Braddick, *State Formation in Early Modern England c. 1550–1700* (Cambridge, 2000). J. Goodare, *State and Society in Early Modern Scotland* (Oxford, 1999). H. Morgan, 'British Policies before the British State', in Bradshaw & Morrill, *The British Problem,* 66.

6 J. G. A. Pocock, 'British History: A Plea for a New Subject', *Journal of Modern History,* 47 (1975), 601–28, *The Limits and Divisions of British History -* Studies in Public Policy 31 (Strathclyde, 1979), 'The Limits and Divisions of British History: in search of the unknown subject', *American Historical Review,* 67 (1982), 311–36, 'Two Kingdoms and Three Histories? Political Thought in British Contexts', in R. A. Mason, ed. *Scots and Britons: Scottish Political Thought and the Union of 1603* (Cambridge, 1994), 293–312 and 'British History: the pursuit of the expanding subject', in W. Prest, ed. *British Studies into the 21st Century. Perspectives and practices* (Melbourne, 1999), 58–72. M. J. Stoyle has argued that the mid-seventeenth century should now be studied as 'a war of five peoples: English, Irish, Scottish, Welsh – and Cornish' in his 'The Last Refuge of a Scoundrel: Sir Richard Grenville and Cornish Particularism, 1644–6', *Historical Research,* lxxi (1998), 51.

7 A. Grant & K. Stringer, quoting J. Morrill and M. Merriman in 'The enigma of British History' in their *Uniting the Kingdom?* 7.

8 Asch, *Three Nations,* 19.

9 S. G. Ellis, 'Tudor state formation and the shaping of the British Isles', in Ellis & Barber, *Conquest and Union,* 43.

10 John Guy, ed. *The Tudor Monarchy* (London, 1997), 280.

11 Ellis, *Tudor Frontiers and Noble Power,* 271. S. G. Ellis 'Tudor Northumberland: British History in an English County', in Connolly, ed. *Kingdoms United?* 29–42 and 'The English State and its Frontiers in the British Isles, 1300–1600', in D. Power & N. Standen, eds. *Frontiers in Question. Eurasian Borderlands 700–1700* (Basingstoke, 1999), 153–81.

12 J. Guy, ed. *The Tudor Monarchy* (London, 1997), 281. A. Grant & K. Stringer, 'The enigma of British History' in their *Uniting the Kingdom?* 7.

13 A. D. Nicholls, *The Jacobean Union. A Reconsideration of British Civil Policies Under the Early Stuarts* (Westport, 1999), 16–17.

14 G. M. Trevelyan, 'The Middle Marches,' in *Clio, A Muse and Other Essays* (London, 1930), 19–41, R. Robson, *The English Highland Clans* (Edinburgh, 1989), vi and M. H. & R. Dodds, *The Pilgrimage of Grace 1536–7 and the Exeter Conspiracy 1538* (Cambridge, 1915), i, 210; ii, 227 refer incorrectly to mosstroopers. This term is relevant to mid-seventeenth century Border raiders and not the sixteenth-century surname groups. P. Williams, 'The Northern Borderland Under The Early Stuarts', in Bell & Ollard, *Historical Essays Presented To David Ogg* (London, 1963), 2. G. M. Fraser, *The Steel Bonnets* (London, 1974), 23, 43, 47–8, 91–3, 96–101, 153–5. J. Speed, *The Theatre of*

the Empire of Great Britaine (London, 1611), 89. P. J. Bradley, 'Social Banditry on the Anglo-Scottish Border during the late Middle Ages', *Scotia*, xii (1988), 27–43.

15 *CBP., CSP Scot., CSP Dom., CSPDom Add., CSP For.,* etc.

16 P. G. Boscher, 'Politics, Administration and Diplomacy: the Anglo-Scottish Border 1550–60'. unpubl. Ph.D diss. Durham 1985, 14, 18 (who uses *CBP* material from 1580, 1583, 1586, 1596 and 1601 for a thesis confined to the 1550s) and G. M. Fraser whose story of the reivers, *The Steel Bonnets,* is heavily drawn from *CBP*, which really only begin in the 1580s.

17 See the Tullie House 'In Search of the Border Reivers' – http://www.reivers.com

18 Cf. G. Phillips, *The Anglo-Scots Wars 1513–1550* (Woodbridge, 1999). Rae, *Scottish Frontier*. Tough, *Last Years*. Watts, *Border to Middle Shire.*

19 Cf. Tough, *Last Years,* 26–8. Watts, *Border to Middle Shire,* 40.

20 For example R. P. Sanderson, ed. *Survey of the Debateable and Border Lands, 1604* (Alnwick, 1891).

21 A. J. Pollard, *North-Eastern England During the Wars of the Roses* (Oxford, 1990), 404.

22 *CSP Scot*, v, p. xxvi.

23 *CSP Scot*, xiii, pt 1, 211. G. H. Thomson, *Some Influences of the Geography of Northumberland upon it's History* (London, 1912). R. Newton, *The Northumberland Landscape* (London, 1972), ch. i. Wormald, *Community,* 18–26.

24 *HMC,* Salisbury, xv, 353.

25 Cf. Boscher, 'Politics and Diplomacy', Merriman, 'The Struggle', and Watts, *Border to Middle Shire.*

26 See map one. For example, G. W. S. Barrow, 'The Aftermath of War', *TRHS*, 5th ser, xxviii (1978), 103–126. R. L. Storey, 'The Wardens of the Marches of England towards Scotland, 1577–1489', *EHR*, lxxii (1957), 593–616. Rae, *Scottish Frontier*. Tough, *Last Years.*

27 G. Ridpath, *The Border History of England and Scotland* (Edinburgh, 1776). W. Nicolson, *Leges Marchiarum or Border Laws* (London, 1747). J. Nicolson and R. Burn, *The History of Westmorland and Cumberland* (London, 1777).

28 W. Scott, *The Minstrelsy of the Scottish Border* (Edinburgh, 1802); *The Border Antiquities of England and Scotland* (London, 1814), 2 vols. Raine, *North Durham*. J. Hodgson, *A History of Northumberland* (Newcastle, 1820–58). R. B. Armstrong, *History of Liddesdale, Eskdale, Ewesdale, Wauchopedale and the Debateable Land* (Edinburgh, 1883).

29 R. E. and C. E. Carr, *The History of the Family of Carr* (London, 1893–99). K. R. Davis, *The Rutherfords in Britain* (Gloucester, 1987). T. L. Ormiston, *The Ormistons of Teviotdale* (Exeter, 1951). A. Pringle, *The Records of the Pringle Family* (Edinburgh 1933).

30 R. R. Reid, *The King's Council in the North* (London, 1921). M. E. James, 'The Concept of Order and the Northern Rising', *P&P*, lx (1973), 49–63, etc. G. R. Batho, 'The Percies and Alnwick Castle 1557–1632', *AA*, 4th ser, xxxv (1957), 48–63. J. M. W. Bean, *The Estates of the Percy Family, 1416–1537* (London, 1958). Pollard, *Wars of the Roses*. Tough, *Last Years*. Watts, *Border to Middle Shire*. Rae, *Scottish Frontier.*

31 B. W. Beckingsale, 'Characteristics of the Tudor North', *NH*, iv (1969), 67–83. M. L. Bush, 'The Problems of the Far North and the Crisis of 1537', *NH*, vi (1971), 40–63. Ellis, *Tudor Frontiers and Noble Power*. A. Goodman, 'The

Anglo-Scottish Marches in the Fifteenth Century: A Frontier Society?' in R. A. Mason, ed., *Scotland and England, 1286–1815* (Edinburgh, 1987), 16–33. R. Lomas, 'The Impact of Border Warfare: The Scots and South Tweedside, c. 1290–c. 1520', *SHR*, lxxv (1996), 143–67. C. J. Neville, *Violence, Custom and Law. The Anglo-Scottish Border Lands in the Later Middle Ages* (Edinburgh, 1998). W. Palmer, 'High Officeholding'. A. A. Cardew, 'A Study of Society in the Anglo-Scottish Borders. 1455–1502', unpubl. PhD diss. St Andrews 1974. S. M. Keeling, 'The Church and Religion in the Anglo-Scottish Border Counties, 1534–1572', unpubl. PhD diss. Durham 1976. C. M. F. Ferguson, 'Law and Order on the Anglo-Scottish Border, 1603–1707', unpubl. PhD diss. St Andrews 1981. P. G. Boscher, 'Politics, Administration and Diplomacy: The Anglo-Scottish Border 1550–1560', unpubl. PhD diss. Durham 1985.

32 A. J. MacDonald, *Border Bloodshed. Scotland, England and France at War, 1369–1403* (East Linton, 2000). M. Merriman, *The Rough Wooings Mary Queen of Scots 1542–1551* (East Linton, 2000).

I

The Social Structure of Landed Society in the Eastern Anglo-Scottish Borders

I. Landed communities and a definition of the Eastern Borders

The Eastern Borders have no exact geographical definition or political boundary. For this study they are based on the location of landed communities that were distinct from those of the Western Borders.[1] The lairds resided in the counties of Berwickshire, Roxburghshire, Selkirkshire and Midlothian, between the Border and the Lammermuir Hills. This included the river valley districts of Jedforest, Teviotdale and Lauderdale, as well as the lowland agricultural basin known as the Merse. In the sixteenth century Scots often identified themselves more with these districts than with a politically defined county. In the Eastern Borders they also counted themselves as Borderers – a definition still in use today.[2] The gentry lived in the area to the north of the river Coquet in Northumberland, which included Norhamshire and Islandshire (North Durham) and the local government wards of Bamburghshire, Coquetdale and Glendale (Northumberland).[3] The gentry also had a multi-layered identity as they were part of a gentry community, as well as being Northumbrians, Borderers and Englishmen. They had no particular adherence to the counties of Northumberland or North Durham, though these were necessary parameters for legal, fiscal and military matters. Like other landed communities they often confusingly referred to their county as their 'country', perhaps to reinforce their social dominance of a particular area.

Society was therefore predominantly localised on both sides of the frontier, yet there were still pronounced differences between the Eastern and Western Border lairds that emerged in the composition of major bloodfeuds. In the Ker and Scott, and Pringle and Elliot feuds the majority of the Scott and Elliot support came from the Western Borders, whilst the Ker and Pringle following came from the Eastern Borders.[4] The lairds of the East also disassociated themselves from the notorious reivers of the Western Borderland. There were a few Eastern Border reivers in east Teviotdale and Jedforest, but the majority of the Eastern Borderers were peaceable. The Mersemen, for example, were known to 'manure justice' and 'studie to politike affairs'.[5] Furthermore in 1561 David Home of Wedderburn refused to sign a bond of loyalty to the Queen because known Jedforest reivers were also signatories. He remembered a Douglas taunt from 1556 that 'we of the

Forest will teach you of the Merse to fight' and would not associate with 'such men with whom he would not enter into any societie, fellowship or combination'. A similar incident occurred in 1573 when the Homes' stance was then chastised by the regent 'that it is not fit or possible to observe those school-rules precisely in Politik affairs'.[6] However, a Scottish Act of 1587 to keep better order in the Borders omitted the East March as there was so little trouble there. The Homes' actions were similar to those of the Eastern Border gentry who disowned the infamous reivers of Tynedale and Redesdale.[7]

A distinct 'county community' within the vast area of Northumberland and north Durham[8] would have been almost impossible to achieve, as the topography, poor communications and proximity to the frontier enhanced localism. Furthermore, as independent gentry rose at the expense of traditional aristocratic leadership, the area to the north of the river Coquet has been studied as a strong gentry community rather than a 'county community'.[9] It will henceforth be referred to as north Northumberland and North Durham. The Coquet is a recognised geographical and linguistic divide within the county of Northumberland and only the greater and middle gentry transcended this boundary by travelling outwith the area for government, business or social matters.[10]

The concept of a 'county community' in early modern England was first explored by Alan Everitt in the 1960s and was revised in the 1970s by Alfred Hassell Smith and Diarmaid MacCulloch, amongst others.[11] In the 1980s historical opinion about 'county communities' questioned their whole concept. County community studies tended to concentrate on greater gentry families, so studying all levels of landed society within a smaller area can be illuminating.[12] Smaller clusters of gentry are also evident in other regions. Regionalism and individual gentry families over several generations have become a focus of recent English and Welsh studies. Sixteenth-century Eastern Border gentry belonged to many areas such as their parish, landed community, the Borders and their nation, though contemporary references to a country meant England, not Britain, reinforcing the non-Britishness of this area before 1603. Even in regions where union had taken place there was a lack of Britishness. For example the gentry of south-west Wales refused to adapt or change their Welshness, despite the Anglo-Welsh Union of 1536–43.[13]

Thus far there has been no equivalent of the English county community in Scotland, though comparisons are possible as broadly-based Scots kinship created strong communities of lairds. As in England there could be several communities within one county or even across a shire boundary, proving once again how artificial these boundaries are. Gordon Donaldson unwittingly analysed the various Scottish shires as county communities, whilst discussing the followers of Mary Queen of Scots, but apart from several Reformation studies there have, until now, been few thorough studies of a rural locality as a social, political, economic and religious unit in the sixteenth century.[14] They have rarely been compared and contrasted across the Anglo-Scottish frontier, but this study now reverses this trend.

II. Who were the landed families?

There is no easy definition of Scottish landed gentlemen in the sixteenth century as the terminology of 'laird' was confusing. There was also an invisible divide between some greater lairds and the Scottish nobility, for Lord Home was a greater laird, surname chief and part of the nobility before 1600.[15] By contrast the stratification of the English gentry was rigid and separate from the nobility. They were recognisable as knights, esquires or gentlemen, often with registered armorial bearings to prove their gentility. There were various types of middling people who could be classified as landed men or lairds in Scotland, yet as a coat of arms was not an essential feature of gentility or nobility in sixteenth-century Scotland strict classification is impossible.[16] To try to make sense of this complicated group, I have opted to classify them as greater, lesser, lesser or bonnet, and bonnet lairds.

There were four dominant kin communities in the Eastern Scottish Borders led by greater laird kin chiefs.[17] The Kers of Cessford were based in the area around Kelso, whilst the Kers of Ferniehirst drew their strength from the Jedforest area, and the Pringles centred on the area around Galashiels. The Pringle power base defied shire boundaries as it occupied the counties of Roxburghshire, Selkirkshire and Midlothian. The Homes dominated Berwickshire, but were also quite strong in East Lothian. Kinship, marriages, friendships and petty quarrels existed between these groups, but they drew the majority of their support from their own patronage networks. They also kept to their own territories as they seem to have had a mutual respect for their fellow kin chiefs' spheres of influence. The only exception to this were the Kers of Littledean, kinsmen and allies of the Kers of Cessford. Sir Andrew Ker of Littledean was rewarded with lands belonging to Coldstream Priory for reporting the 1542 victory at Haddenrig to James V. Ker decided to live at the Hirsel in the Home heartland, which caused friction on several occasions. Despite marriage to a Home, these Kers never integrated with the xenophobic local population. When this marriage turned sour they had to summon support from their native Teviotdale and property disputes had to be settled by non-local arbiters to avoid bias in favour of the Homes.[18]

A laird was literally the 'lord' of his lands with greater lairds having most wealth, power and status and bonnet lairds the least. The diversity of lairds evolved with fundamental changes in sixteenth-century Scottish society. Lairds who were traditionally the backbone of rural society as barons, sheriff deputes, jurors and arbitrators began demanding a role in central government.[19] The common factor shared by all these men was that they were landed, whether they held land directly from the crown or indirectly through a nobleman, the church, a monastic foundation or from another laird. They were inevitably referred to as the laird of a particular property and were often called by this placename rather than their surname. This was a practice peculiar to Scotland as the English gentry always used their surnames.

The feuing of Scottish church and crown land turned some landholders into lairds, but this only compounded the problem of determining who the lairds were. Both English and Scottish correspondents were clearly bemused by the term. The derivations 'lord', 'laird' and 'gentlemen' were all used to describe lairds. The Scottish parliament and privy council referred to 'landit men', 'lordis, baronis and uther gentlemen of the Merse and Teviotdale', 'barons, landit men, gentilmen and utheris' and 'landlordis, baillies and landit men' in the sixteenth century. These leading institutions add to the complexity by not using the term 'lairds'.[20] One Scottish commentator referred to the 'meanest sort of gentlemen called lairds', but this was blatantly untrue for lairds encompassed a wide cross-section of landed people.

Scottish surname groups included lairds and non-lairds alike, but English Border officials thought them separate from gentlemen in 1583.[21] The 'separate' gentlemen listed in this report included Homes, Trotters, Brounfields, Dicksons, Craws and Cranstons in the Scottish East March, and Kers, Youngs, Pringles, Burns, Rutherfords and Taits in the Scottish Middle March. These families were not exclusively lairds, but they did have a substantial number of gentlemen in their ranks. Another English survey of the Scots carried out a few years later recorded Border surnames of those who were 'not landed' and proceeded to list most of the above names. This list does not regard the chiefs of the surname groups as lairds, although the majority of them ranked as lesser lairds and were certainly landed. Another list of 1590 has omissions and mistakes, but at least tried to note who the actual lairds were. These reports reflect English foreign policy interest in the Scots dating back to the troubled 1540s when captured Brounfields and Dicksons were referred to as gentlemen.[22]

There were at least 307 traceable laird families in the Eastern Scottish Borderland. A laird normally held a minimum of two husbandlands of land, or fifty-two acres.[23] The Teviotdale surname of Hall has been excluded from table I.1 as there are no surviving records of their landholding to prove or disprove their status. The sixth Lord Home certainly had no respect for the Halls as lairds as he tortured Hall of Heavyside in 1604 for his infamous reiving activities. The Burns were equally notorious, yet there is enough evidence to identify two of them as lairds. The Robsons had one identifiable laird who left his core group of kinsmen in the Jedforest area to settle near Dryburgh Abbey.[24] The kin groups of Home, Ker and Pringle dominate all the laird strata listed in table I.1, but there were many sub-groupings and independent lairds as well.

TABLE 1.1.
THE STRATIFICATION OF THE LAIRDS[25]

Greater Lairds. (40)

Bennet of Chesters.
Cairncross of Colmslie.
Chirnside of East Nisbet.
Cockburn of Choicelee.
Cockburn of Langton.
Cockburn of that Ilk.
Cranston of Corsbie.
Cranston of Thirlestane Mains.
Douglas of Bonjedward.
Douglas of Melrose.
Edmonston of that Ilk.
Hepburn of Whitsome.
Home, Lord and laird of Home.
Home of Ayton.
Home of Cowdenknowes.
Home of Eccles.
Home of Huttonhall.
Home of Manderston.
Home of Polwarth.
Home of Spott.

Home of Wedderburn.
Ker of Ancrum.
Ker of Cessford.
Ker of Faldonside.
Ker of Hirsel.
Ker of Ferniehirst.
Ker of Primsideloch.
Lauder of that Ilk.
MacDougal of Makerstoun.
Maitland of Thirlestane
Nisbet of that Ilk.
Ormiston of that Ilk.
Pringle of Galashiels.
Pringle of that Ilk.
Ramsay of Dalhousie.
Renton of Billie.
Rutherford of Hundalee.
Rutherford of Hunthill.
Seton of Greenknowe.
Swinton of that Ilk.

Lesser Lairds. (219)

Ainslie of Falla.
Ainslie of Thickside.
Aitchison of Slighhouses.
Angus of Hoprig.
Auchinleck of Cumledge.
Bennet of Grange.
Bog of Burnhouses.
Borthwick of Collielaw.
Brounfield of Eastfield.
Brounfield of Gordon Mains.
Brounfield of Greenlawdean.
Brounfield of Hardacres.
Brounfield of Nether Mains.
Brounfield of Pittlesheugh.
Brounfield of Tenandry.
Brounfield of Todrig.
Brounfield of Whitehouse.
Burn of Elisheugh.

Cairncross of Allanshaws.
Cairncross of Calfhill.
Carmichael of Edrom.
Chirnside of Whitsomelaws.
Cockburn of Caldra.
Cockburn of East Borthwick.
Cockburn of Stobswood.
Cockburn of the Woodhead.
Cranston of Falwoodshiel.
Craw of Flemington-Fluris.
Cranston of Kirkhill.
Craw of Gunsgreen.
Craw of East Reston.
Craw of Swinwood.
Davidson of Samieston.
Dickson of Belchester.
Dickson of Bughtrig
Dickson of Herdrig.

Table I.1.—contd
Lesser Lairds—contd

Dickson of Kames.
Dickson of Overmains.
Dickson of the Peel.
Dickson of Whitrig.
Douglas of Mordington.
Douglas of Timpendean.
Duns of Grueldykes.
Edgar of Flass.
Edgar of Wedderlie.
Edington of that Ilk.
Edington of Harcarse.
Ellem of Butterdean.
Ellem of Bassendean or of that Ilk.
Ellem of Renton.
Erskine of Shielfield.
French of Thornydykes.
Frissell of Overton.
Galbraith of Easter Windshiel.
Gladstone of Cocklaw.
Graden of Earnslaw.
Graden of Langrig.
Grahamslaw of Newton.
Haig of Bemersyde.
Haitlie of Broomhill.
Haitlie of Hurdlaw.
Haitlie of Lambden.
Haitlie of Mellerstain.
Haitlie of Sneep.
Haliburton of Mertoun.
Haliburton of Muirhouselaw.
Haliburton of Newmains.
Hamilton of St John's Chapel.
Hangingside of that Ilk.
Hepburn of Fairnington.
Hepburn of Rollandstoun.
Heriot of Trabrown.
Home abbot of Jedburgh.
Home commendator of Jedburgh.
Home of Bassendean.
Home of Bellitaw.
Home of Blackadder East.

Home of Blackadder West.
Home of Blacksmill.
Home of Broomhouse.
Home of Carolside.
Home of Cheeklaw.
Home of Cranshaws.
Home of Crossrig.
Home of Crumstane.
Home of Edrom.
Home of Fairnieside.
Home of Fans.
Home of Fishwick.
Home of Framepath.
Home of Godscroft.
Home of Hardiesmill.
Home of Hilton.
Home of Hutton Bell.
Home of Hutton.
Home of Lauder.
Home of Ninewells.
Home of Prenderguest.
Home of Reidheuch.
Home of Renton.
Home of the Law.
Home of West Reston.
Home of Rollandstoun.
Home of Slegden.
Home of Tinnis.
Home of Whitchester.
Hunter of Williamlaw.
Ker of Broomlands.
Ker of Cavers.
Ker of Chatto.
Ker commendator of Coldstream.
Ker of Corbethouse.
Ker of Dalcove.
Ker of Gateshaw.
Ker of Graden.
Ker commendator of Kelso.
Ker of Kippilaw.
Ker of Lintalee.

Table I.1.—contd
Lesser Lairds—contd

Ker of Linton.
Ker of Lochtower.
Ker of Mainhouse.
Ker of Maisondieu.
Ker of Mersington.
Ker of Middlemist Walls.
Ker of Milnrig.
Ker of Newhall.
Ker of Little Newton.
Ker of Newton.
Ker of Ormiston.
Ker of Oxnam.
Ker of Raperlaw.
Ker of Redden.
Ker of Old Roxburgh.
Ker of Shaws.
Ker of Shielstockbraes.
Ker of Sunderlandhall.
Ker of Whitmuir.
Ker of Whitmuir Hall.
Ker of Yair.
Kirkton of Stewartfield.
Lauder of Burngrange.
Lauder of Edington.
Lauder of Muircleugh.
Lauder of Whitslaid.
Lauder of Newbigging.
Linlithgow of Drygrange.
Lumsden of Blanerne.
Lumsden of Rikilside.
MacDougal of Manorhill.
MacDougal of Stodrig.
Mow of that Ilk.
Mow of Mow Mains.
MacDougal of Floors.
Newton of Graden.
Nisbet of Raashill.
Nisbet of Spital.
Nisbet of Swansfield.
Ormiston of Easter Muirdean.
Ormiston of Grahamslaw.

Ormiston of Old Melrose.
Ormiston of Westhouses.
Pringle of Blindlee.
Pringle of Buckholm.
Pringle of Charterhouse.
Pringle of Clifton.
Pringle of Craigleith.
Pringle of Hownam.
Pringle of Langmuir.
Pringle of Muircleugh.
Pringle of Muirhouse.
Pringle of Nether Blainslie.
Pringle of Slegden.
Pringle of St John's Chapel.
Pringle of Stitchill.
Pringle of Torquhan.
Pringle of Torwoodlee.
Pringle of Trinlyknowe.
Pringle of Westhousebyre.
Pringle of Whytbank.
Pringle of Wrangholm.
Purves of Purvishaugh.
Ramsay of Wyliecleuch.
Redpath of Angelraw.
Redpath of Crumrig.
Redpath of Greenlaw.
Redpath of Rowchester.
Redpath of that Ilk.
Redpath of Todrig.
Renton of Cockburnspath Shiels.
Riddall of that Ilk.
Rutherford of Chatto.
Robson of Gledswood.
Rule of Peelwalls.
Rutherford of Edgerston.
Rutherford of Grundiesnuke.
Rutherford of Longnewton.
Rutherford of Littleheuch.
Scott of Haughhead.
Seton of Gordon.
Shoreswood of Bedshiel.

Table I.1.—contd
Lesser Lairds—contd

Sinclair of Blainslie.
Sinclair of Longformacus.
Sleigh of Birkinside.
Rutherford of the Grange.
Sleigh of Otterburn.
Sleigh of Cumledge.
Spence of Chirnside Mains.
Spottiswoode of Quhitlie.
Spottiswoode of that Ilk.
Spottiswoode of Whinrig.

Stewart of Eildon.
Tait of Cherrytrees.
Trotter of Catchelraw.
Trotter of Chesters.
Trotter of the Overhall of Sisterpath.
Trotter of Printonan.
Trotter of Ryslaw.
Young of Otterburn.
Young of Feltershaws.

Lesser or bonnet Lairds. (33)

Brounfield of Farnyrig.
Brounfield of Howlawhead.
Brounfield of Whiteside.
Burn of Coate.
Cairncross of Birksneep.
Davidson of Easter Fowmerton.
Douglas of Bankend.
Fala of Wells.
Frissell of Quarrelbush.
Hog of Old Roxburgh.
Home of Chirnside East Mains.
Home of Crumiecruke.
Home of the Fleurs of Coldingham.
Home of Simprim.
Home of Whiterig.
Ker of Kerchesters.
Ker of Lauder.

Ker of Melrose.
Nisbet of Nether Raecleugh.
Paxton of Auchencrow.
Pringle of the Bents.
Pringle of Tanlaw.
Purves of that Ilk.
Pyle of Millheugh.
Rutherford of Cleethaugh.
Rutherford of the Know of Nisbet.
Rutherford of the Walls of Nisbet.
Tait of the Stankford.
Trotter of Fogo.
Trotter of Fogorig.
Trotter of Foulshotlaw.
Trotter of Harcarse.
Trotter of the Netherhall of Sisterpath.

Bonnet Lairds. (15)

Birgham of Birgham.
Craw of Renton.
Craw of Upsettlington Shiels.
Davidson of Harden.
Davidson of the Kaims.
Davidson of Marchcleuch.
Davidson of Wooden.
Dickson of the Loanhead.

Duns of East Borthwick.
Fairbairn of West Gordon.
Home of Middlethird.
Ker of Bloodlaws.
Ker of Softlaw.
Ker of Templeland.
Pringle of Fans.

Bonnet lairds were the most humble type who usually worked their own land, rather than sublet it to tenants. The term 'bonnet' laird was first used by Sir Walter Scott in 1816.[26] A bonnet laird's holding could be as small as fifty-two acres and they did not normally hold any offices. Adam Birgham of Birgham held only two husbandlands but as he held them directly from the crown, he went to the expense of registering his charter under the Great Seal of Scotland.[27] The 'lesser or bonnet' designation indicates that there is no evidence of whether they farmed their own land or sublet. They include a peculiar category of 'alias' lairds who were nevertheless landholders in their own right. These lairds typify the confused middle order of Scottish society at this time. For instance James Hog 'alias laird Hog' had at least three husbandlands in Old Roxburgh and Town Yetholm in 1545, William Paxton 'alias laird Paxton' had six husbandlands at Auchencrow in 1576 and Alexander Purves 'alias laird Purves' held four ploughgates (416 acres) and sixteen husbandlands (also 416 acres) in Earlston in 1553. William Broun 'alias Laird Broun' in Eyemouth had only one husbandland and has therefore been discounted as this is below the bonnet laird qualification of two husbandlands. In 1583 a social sneer may have been intended by 'callit laird Spens' for Richard Spence of Chirnside Mains as it was written by an irate minister owed five years' teinds.[28]

Lesser lairds can be classified as small barons, small landholders, portioners, wadsetters, and dependent lairds.[29] They did not usually hold high-ranking offices, but were often jurors or deputies. Their wealth, landholding and local power put them above the rank of the bonnet lairds. Wadsetters and portioners are rather vague descriptions for lairds of all strata who could be mortgaged, and a portioner was the holder or co-heir of a small or a large portion of land. Wadsetters as a separate class of landholders really belong to the seventeenth century, but portioners were commonplace in the sixteenth century. For example, the Homes of Black-adder were consistently called 'portioners' as joint proprietors of the sizeable Blackadder estate.[30] They were undoubtedly lesser lairds, but were never called 'of Blackadder', only portioners thereof. A portioner should thus not be rejected as a laird until there is proof of landholding below two husbandlands.

Small barons were few, but there were many dependent lairds. The small barons such as the Ellems of Butterdean, Edingtons of that Ilk and Ruther-fords of Edgerston were holders of geographically small baronies that yielded status rather than power. Dependent lairds have not really been identified before as this concept of a laird seems anomalous. Many of the Border lairds belonged to this category as they were linked to greater lairds by bonds of kinship or through the political bond of manrent. Their holdings were generally large enough to give them the status of a lesser laird. The Davidsons of Samieston, for instance, held land from greater lairds worth forty shillings a year of 'old extent'. This was a medieval tax assessment worth far more than forty shillings in real terms by the sixteenth century. The dependent Brounfields of Hardacres held land worth four pounds a year of old extent from Lord Home, whilst the Kers of Gateshaw and the Rutherfords of the Grange held lands from their respective kinsmen the Kers of Cessford and Rutherfords of Hundalee.[31]

The remaining lesser lairds were all small landholders holding land in chief or in feu from monasteries, the church or the crown. They include four lay commendators of religious houses who held part of their monasteries' lands in their own right. Lesser lairds' wealth ranged from that of the Brounfields of Greenlawdean, who were very substantial lesser lairds, to the Homes of Hardiesmill who probably only held land as servants of Lord Home. The Scotts of Haughhead held a feu charter from Jedburgh Abbey worth only £4–6s–8d Scots a year. Feuars were particularly well represented amongst small landholders, owing to the burgeoning grants of feu charters in this century.[32] Although feuars came from all levels of Scottish society a proportion of them entered into the laird communities. There was no precedent for this, but their charters gave them legal entitlement to lands sufficient to merit the title of laird in return for paying an annual feu duty. Many held these lands as unsecured kindly tenants before being granted a feu charter, yet there is much confusion about who qualified as feuing lairds. Both Margaret Sanderson and Craig Madden refer to feuars designated 'of' a property as being of laird status, whilst those designed 'in' as being below the class of laird.[33] However, this can be misleading as lairds could be described as being both 'in' or 'of' a property, particularly before 1550.[34] Madden notes that Pringle of Torwoodlee was a substantial feuar of land in Ettrick Forest in the 1540s, but was not a laird because he was 'in Torwoodlee'. The *Register of the Privy Seal* disproves this by calling Pringle 'of Torwoodlee' in 1548. Pringle of Blindlee is equally confusing as he was termed 'in Blindlee' in 1543, 1555 and 1578, but was 'of Blindlee' in 1558.[35] Both men had landholding enough to qualify as lairds and it would be ridiculous to omit them when a man with a mere two husbandlands could call himself a laird. Moreover John Stewart, feuar of the Melrose Abbey lands of Eildon, subinfeudated to no fewer than twenty-one tenants in 1570.[36] The feuing system had thus overturned the traditional niches of landed society and forced the accommodation of newly-risen lairds.

'In' and 'of' derivatives also caused confusion amongst established lairds, for Alexander Brounfield of Eastfield, Robert Dickson of Bughtrig, Alexander Trotter of Chesters and Bartholomew Spence of Chirnside Mains were called 'in' and then 'of' their respective properties within the space of a few years.[37] Their landholding identifies them as lairds, just as Lancie Ker of Little Newton held too much land to be a non-laird. Confusion over his title may have stemmed from multiple ownership of Little Newton by other lairds such as Ker of Dalcove, Lord Home, Hangingside of that Ilk and

Henry Haliburton of Mertoun.[38] The anomalous term 'goodman', once thought to pertain only to feuars, was applied at various times to Alexander Home of Huttonhall and Andrew Pringle of Galashiels, who clearly held greater laird status within their communities with large landholdings.[39] As with portioners, this term should be interpreted from a broad basis when identifying lairds.

Greater lairds are easily identified as they held extensive tracts of land in chief. They would have leased most of their property, leaving only a small demesne or home farm in their own hands to supply provisions for their household. Their wealth varied according to their success in the political stakes of the period, though it was greater than that of most lesser lairds. Greater lairds were more likely to hold important offices and knights were chosen exclusively from their rank. Scottish knighthoods were usually bestowed as a personal honour at coronations and royal baptisms. A knight's wife was entitled to call herself 'Dame' and 'Lady' was usually reserved for daughters of noblemen, but there are instances of noblemen's wives being called 'Dame'. At the lower end of the stratum were families such as the Swintons of that Ilk, who had failed to take advantage of sixteenth-century opportunities to enlarge their estates, but could still attend parliament by individual summons. At the top of this rank were the surname chiefs of Home, Ker and Pringle. Cockburn of Langton was a chief as well, though he lacked the wealth of the others.[1] These kin chiefs each had a wide power base that made them the elite of the Scottish lairds, but like the most humble bonnet laird they held land of the King either in chief or in feu from a noble, laird, church or monastery.

TABLE I.2. LAIRD FAMILIES, 1540–1603

Year	No of Families[41]	Families	
1540	148	Died out in the male line	29
1570	268	Lost or sold their estates	4
1603	268	New families to the area	3
Total 1540–1603	307	Cadet branches established	50

Table I.2 confirms that approximately eleven per cent of laird families died out or sold out. This was more than compensated for by expanding branches and newly-established families, who confirm the vibrancy of the lairds in sixteenth-century Scottish society. The sample years were chosen at random, yet their numbers seem to have been maintained in 1570 and 1603. There were only three noticeable differences between the lairds and gentlemen. Firstly, there were proportionally fewer new families in Scotland. Secondly, more cadet branches formed in Scotland and thirdly, fewer lairds lost or sold their estates. This is probably explained by the political dominance of Home and Ker laird communities that could make local heiresses unavailable to fortune hunters, whilst the feuing movement and the prosperity of many lairds enabled younger sons to form independent branches. However, during the ascendancy of Regent Morton in the 1570s two heiresses were stolen from the clutches of the xenophobic Homes. He married them to favourites in an attempt to improve his political power in the Merse, creating the new families of Auchinleck of Cumledge and Carmichael of Edrom.[42] That fewer lairds than gentlemen sold or lost their lands is probably due to the complicated mortgaging system in Scotland that seemed never-ending with frequent renewals being granted.[43]

Downward mobility resulted when lairds died out in the male line, but it occurred less than in England and was normally due to premature death, childlessness or misfortune. The circumstances of the Grahamslaws of Newton are poignant as they lost all eight sons during a bloodfeud with the Western Border family of Turnbull. With one daughter remaining John Grahamslaw decided to dispose of his estates in a dignified manner. He sold his lands to Robert Ker a political ally and younger son of Robin Ker of Ancrum and arranged the marriage of his daughter, Helen, to Robert. This measure ensured that his ancestral lands would not be overrun by the avaricious Turnbulls.[44] Another example of kinship assistance through marriage occurred in 1600 when Andrew Brounfield of Pittlesheugh turned to his uncle, Robert Dickson of Buchtrig, to pay off his debts and rescue the estate for his cousin David Dickson.[45] Other downwardly mobile lairds were in financial difficulties such as the Haitlies of Mellerstain or politically-weakened lairds like the Haigs of Bemersyde who, despite ancient lineage, were now subservient to the Homes of Cowdenknowes.[46]

Upwardly mobile lairds were typified by the Homes whose wealth, power and prestige had been rising since the fifteenth century. They capitalised on court favour and their younger sons benefited from this by establishing themselves as independent lairds. Even dependent lesser lairds such as the Brounfields of Todrig and Whitehouse could be interpreted as being upwardly mobile on a smaller scale. However the majority of extant lairds were static during the sixteenth century.

Across the frontier at least 147 separate gentry families lived in north Northumberland and North Durham. Knights were seen as greater gentry, esquires as middle gentry and ordinary gentlemen as lesser gentry.[47] Gentlemen were supposed to have a coat of arms, but this required eighty years' lineage and a fee for registration with the heralds of the College of Arms. Northumberland has a few surprising registrations and omissions, as the Rutherfords of Middleton were listed, despite being a relatively unimportant family, whereas the office-bearing Selbies of Twizel were not properly recorded.[48] Although a minimum landholding acreage cannot be found owing to a scarcity of source material, the identification of poorer gentry is not quite as confusing as the lairds. In 1539 the Border gentry were disparagingly described as like 'a petty gentleman, who have no right to that name by ancestry lands or the like'. Nevertheless Northumberland's poor gentry believed themselves to be gentlemen and gave themselves this title in their wills. The probate court at Durham was particular about titles and could strike out references to gentility in a testament if they thought the testator unworthy of the distinction 'gentleman' as in the case of John Harbottle of Rugley. 'Petty gentlemen' were therefore accepted as part of the lowest stratum of the gentry community.[49] Other gentlemen are mentioned in several gentry lists or as jurors at *Inquisitions Post Mortem*.[50] The higher a gentleman's status the more likely he was to hold office and be noticed, but this was not a concrete rule. Successful younger sons could be high sheriff of Northumberland or an Exchequer commissioner whilst remaining a plain gentleman.

TABLE I.3. GENTRY FAMILIES, 1540–1603[51]

Year		No of Families	Gentry population movements	No of Families
1540		72[52]	Died out in male line	13
1570		115	Disappeared without trace	6
1600		118	Lost or sold estates	12
			New families to area	6[53]
Total	1540–1603	147	Cadet branches established	12

Several cadet branches were formed, but in comparison to counties further south new families were rare in this area. This was probably because of the assumed lack of economic prosperity and restrictions on land sales near the Border. A few were tempted by heiresses' fortunes or office in the Berwick garrison, but they did not make up the shortfall. The overall loss of thirty-one families (twenty-one per cent) is ten per cent higher than in Scotland, but this was not remarkable amongst English gentry families.[54] Vincent Rutherford of Middleton Hall sold his land willingly, but the downwardly mobile Roger Fowberry of Fowberry lost his estate through mortgaging. Overall the majority of the gentry families were either upwardly mobile or static during 1540–1603. Table I.4 has stratified the gentry as greater gentry (who were often knights), middle gentry (esquires) and lesser gentry (gentlemen). This stratification is typical of other northern counties such as Yorkshire, where the gentry had similar interests in land, office, kinship, and marriage.[55] The powerful surname groups of Collingwood, Gray and Selby appear to mirror the Home, Ker and Pringle kindreds in Scotland.

TABLE I.4. THE STRATIFICATION OF THE GENTRY

Greater Gentry Families. (10)

Collingwood of Eslington.
Ellerker of Hulne.
Forster of Adderstone.
Forster of Bamburgh.
Gray of Chillingham.

Gray of Horton.
Horsley of Screnwood.
Radcliffe of Cartington.
Reed of Holy Island.
Selby of Twizel.

Middle Gentry Families. (19)

Armorer of Belford.
Beadnell of Lemmington.
Bradford of Bradford.
Carr of Ford.
Clavering of Callaly.
Craster of Craster.
Haggerston of Haggerston.
Ilderton of Ilderton.
Lawson of Rock.
Lisle of Felton.

Muschamp of Barmoor.
Ogle of Eglingham.
Ord of Ord.
Roddam of Roddam.
Selby of Shoreswood.
Strangeways of Cheswick.
Strother of Kirknewton.
Swinburne of Edlingham.
Swinhoe of Cornhill.

Lesser Gentry families. (118)

Alder of Hobberlaw.
Alder of Prendwick.
Beadnell of Low Buston.
Burrell of Howtel.
Carr of Boulmer.
Carr of Hetton.
Carr of Lesbury.
Carr of Newlands.
Clennell of Clennell.
Clerk of Wark.
Collingwood of Abberwick.
Collingwood of Barton.
Collingwood of Bewick.
Collingwood of Branton.
Collingwood of Broome Park.
Collingwood of East Ditchburn.
Collingwood of Etal.
Collingwood of Farnham.
Collingwood of Great Ryle.
Collingwood of Ingram.

Collingwood of Kimmerston.
Collingwood of Little Ryle.
Collingwood of Shipley.
Collingwood of Thornton.
Collingwood of Thrunton.
Collingwood of Titlington.
Doxford of Doxford.
Elwick of Elwick.
Elwick of Humbleton.
Felton of Great Felton.
Fenwick of Brinkburn.
Finch of Twizell.
Forster of Brunton.
Forster of Fleetham.
Forster of Lucker.
Forster of Newham.
Forster of Overgrass.
Forster of Tughall.
Fowberry of Fowberry.
Gallon of Alnwick.

Table 1.4—contd
Lesser Gentry Families—contd

Gallon of Cawledge Park.
Gallon of Trewhitt.
Gray of Berwick.
Gray of Doddington.
Gray of Heaton.
Gray of Howick.
Gray of Kyloe.
Gray of Outchester.
Gray of Spindelston.
Harbottle of Preston.
Harbottle of Cawledge.
Harbottle of Tughall.
Hazlerig of Swarland.
Hepburn of Hepburn.
Hering of Howick.
Heron of Crawley.
Holburn of Holburn.
Hoppen of Hoppen.
Horsley of High Farnham.
Horsley of Newton.
Horsley of Outchester.
Lilburn of Middleton.
Lisle of Dunstanburgh.
Lisle of Hazon.
Manners of Cheswick.
Manners of Longframlington.
Manners of Newton.
Manners of Ord.
Middleham of Alnmouth.
Morton of Murton.
Morton of Unthank.
Muschamp of Lyham Hall.
Muschamp of Middleton.
Ogle of Burradon.
Ogle of Holy Island.
Ogle of Trewhitt.
Ord of East Newbiggin.
Ord of Horncliffe.
Ord of Longridge.

Ord of West Ord.
Park of Warton.
Proctor of Shawdon.
Radcliffe of Thropton.
Reveley of Ancroft.
Reveley of Berrington.
Reveley of Chatton.
Reveley of Humbleton.
Reveley of Tweedmouth.
Rutherford of Middleton Hall.
Rutherford of Middleton Tower.
Salkeld of Alnwick West Park.
Salkeld of Hulne.
Scott of Earle.
Selby of Beal.
Selby of Biddlestone.
Selby of Burton.
Selby of Cornhill.
Selby of Grindon.
Selby of Grindonrig.
Selby of Hulne Park.
Selby of Longhoughton.
Selby of Pawston.
Selby of South Charlton.
Selby of Tillmouth.
Selby of Tweedmouth.
Selby of Weetwood.
Strother of Abberwick.
Strother of East Duddo.
Swinhoe of South Charlton.
Swinhoe of Berrington.
Swinhoe of Mousen.
Unthank of Unthank.
Wallis of Akeld.
Wallis of Coupland.
Wallis of Nesbit.
Weetwood of Weetwood.
Wetwang of Dunstan.
Widdrington of The Friars.

This total of 147 families north of the Coquet contradicts Lawrence Stone's figures for the whole county of Northumberland in the sixteenth century.[2] Stone assumes there were only sixty gentry households from 1550–99 as he does not recognise county squires before 1610. His survey of gentry houses in 1610 has oversights and mistakes as it was based on the Northumberland County History volumes which, although informative, lack sixteenth-century detail and show bias towards their gentry subscribers.[57] S. J. Watts consulted a much wider range of sources than Stone, yet still underestimated the numbers of gentry families at eighty-nine in 1615. The original probate records at Durham verify the existence of many previously unmentioned gentlemen, yet these have often been overlooked by historians interested in Northumberland.[58]

III. Patterns of Landholding

TABLE 1.5. LAIRD LANDHOLDING, 1540–1603

Principal lands held[59]	No of lairds
In chief	87
In feu from the crown	23
In feu from the church or a monastery	49
From another laird	97
From a non-resident noble[60]	8
From Lord Home	33

The majority of lairds held land indirectly of the crown, but the pattern of landholding is intricate. When compared to England there were far more dependent lairds than gentry as feudal subservience was rare in Scottish landholding.[61] The sharp division between lord and tenant in England was an anathema to the Scottish lairds who had strong feelings of paternalism and mutual respect for blood-related kinsmen, their surname group and allies (who were not necessarily related to the laird or even called by his surname).[62] The significant proportion of feuars in the table reflect the general trend towards feuing both crown and church lands in the sixteenth century. The small number of lairds holding land from non-resident nobility is a reminder of medieval land grants in the Eastern Borders. The earls of Angus still expected loyalty from laird tenants, such as the Homes of Wedderburn. Other tenants may only have given sufficient loyalty to these noblemen to ensure the renewal of a charter whilst they were really allied to a local greater laird. For example, the Kers of Linton held land from the Lords Somerville, yet gave allegiance to the Kers of Cessford.

The chief Kers and Homes had a high number of lairds dependent on them because of strong kinship in the Borders, but their laird tenants included non-kinsmen who were not related by blood, marriage or surname. Therefore Kers, Burns and Youngs of East Teviotdale were 'friends and servants of the laird (Ker) of Cessford' as well as being his tenants and political allies.[63] Lesser lairds had dependants as well, for Dand Ker in Linton called Ker of Linton 'his master' in 1582.

TABLE 1.6. GENTRY LANDHOLDING, 1540–1603

Of whom held	Numbers
In chief	35
Crown lease. (Rutland lands, Duchy of Lancs, Monastic Leases)[64]	17
Earls of Northumberland. (Baronies of Alnwick, Beanley and Mitford, Lordship of Ditchburn, Bailiffs and Keepers)	54
Gray. (Barony of Wark-on-Tweed, Manor of Wooler)	11
Ogle. (Barony of Hepple)	2
Dean and Chapter of Durham	4
From other gentry	24
Total	147

Gentry families were dependent on other gentlemen for their leases, but to a lesser extent than in Scotland. Lands were granted by greater gentry to their kinsmen, making kinship important within the local gentry community though not quite as widely interpreted as the lairds' notion of kinship. Robert Collingwood of Eslington, for example was noted as chief of his widespread kin in 1543 with nine Collingwood gentlemen dependent upon him for land.[65] The Forsters also had a broad kin group, with Sir John Forster superseding his brother Thomas as head of their kin owing to his spectacular ascendancy. The variety of landholding in this area proves that the earls of Northumberland did not predominate, though the overall pattern was more feudalistic than in Scotland.

IV. Kinship: Employment, Entail and Marriage

Kinship, in its broadest interpretation, permeated all aspects of landed families' lifestyles in the Eastern Borders. It was only ever as strong as the lairds and gentlemen wanted it to be, but it had more advantages than disadvantages. It helped lesser lairds seeking employment or security and it was fundamental to testaments or wills. Nor should kinship links through marriage be underestimated as they could lead to interesting patterns of friendship or alliance.

Cross-border meetings relied upon the visible support of kinsmen and allies to show force to the opposite side. In 1560 Lord Home had 300 horsemen with him at a meeting, the majority of whom were kinsmen, dependent lairds such as the Brounfields, Dicksons and Trotters and their tenants. The Kers of Ferniehirst could draw good support from Jedforest lairds and were able to exploit bonds of manrent for additional support.[66] Manrent usually tied men of lesser rank to a more powerful laird or nobleman to assist him if needed. In return they were assured of maintenance by him. For this reason the Rutherfords of Hunthill signed bonds of manrent to the Kers of Ferniehirst in 1544, 1560 and 1586 and the Rutherfords of Hundalee did likewise in 1544.[67] The Rutherfords and Kers were all of the rank of greater laird, but Ferniehirst was recognised as the more powerful laird in the Jedforest locality.[68] Richard Rutherford of Edgerston, a lesser laird, gave a 'sufficient leitre of manrent' to John Stewart of Traquair to secure his lands.[69] Furthermore as bailie of Coldstream Priory the fifth Lord Home was entitled to receive manrent from the tenants and they expected him to protect them from attack.[70]

Other types of bonds signed by the lairds included those of friendship and mutual assistance. Bonds of friendship were used to end property feuds by the Homes of Blackadder and Wedderburn and by Lord Home with Maitland of Thirlestane. Bonds of mutual assistance or maintenance could be used for the same purpose. The Rutherfords on one part and the Kers of Littledean, Mow of that Ilk and Haitlie of Mellerstain on the other signed a bond of this type to ease tensions between them. A more usual use of this bond was the mutual desire of Lord Home and the earl of Bothwell to oppose the English invasion of Southern Scotland in 1545. Neither party was subservient to the other in this type of bond.[71]

English kinship may not have been as wide, but it was important and the term 'cousin' could be used to address both a nephew or a distant relative.[72] Kinship through marriage was noticeable amongst the greater and middle gentry. Kinship for the lesser gentry implied political and social allegiance to the head of their surname or a powerful family just as it did for the lesser lairds. It could extend beyond blood relations, yet there was no equivalent of the Scottish bonds of manrent. It was the Grays' wealth and status that ensured them a wide following from kinsmen and tenants. The Selbies included very distant relatives in an elaborate entail deed of 1591, but it is difficult to trace families like the Forsters as many of their branches descend from illegitimate offspring. In a letter of 1590 to a London 'cousin' (actually a second cousin), Sir John Forster referred to a great-grandfather having twenty-two sons. Though they had never met, Sir John offered 'if ther be any thing in this country wherin I may stand you in steed, I pray you charge me therwithall, and thee shall find me willing to accomplish the same'. Sir John was helpful to more immediate kinsmen as well for he obliged his brother Thomas with a mortgage.[73] Forster and Sir Cuthbert Collingwood sold or gave land to kinsmen, as well as granting them leases.[74]

Gentry leaders also gave kin employment within their household for Sir

Thomas Gray of Horton employed a full cousin, Thomas, son of Lionel Gray of Berwick; Sir Thomas Gray of Chillingham had a household servant called Matthew Gray and William Haggerston of Haggerston had a well educated servant called Henry Haggerston.[75] Kinsmen were sometimes employed as trusted bailiffs as Peter Gray was bailiff of Doddington for his 'master' Sir Thomas Gray of Chillingham.[76] Further up the social scale Thomas Forster of Adderstone, junior, and John Carr of Hetton were deputy sheriffs to their respective kinsmen Ralph Gray (1582–3) and Sir Cuthbert Collingwood (1581–2).[77]

In Scotland there was much preferential employment of kinsmen as well, for Mark Home of Hardiesmill and David Home of Ninewells were bailies at Hume and Chirnside respectively for Lord Home, whilst John Pringle of Smailholm had a bailie in Lauder called William Pringle. George Ker of Linton also employed two Kers as bailies in his barony of Linton. John Cranstoun of that Ilk's bailie for his Border lands was Thomas Cranstoun and Thomas MacDougal of Makerstoun's bailie was Patrick MacDougal. Other examples include Sir Andrew Ker of Ferniehirst's household steward Michael Ker, William Cockburn of Langton's servant George Cockburn and William Home of Ayton employed a Robert Home. John Haitlie of Mellerstain had a servitor named John Haitlie and James Home, a younger son of Carolside, was servitor to Alexander Home of Huttonhall.[78] Bailies were usually the highest-ranking administrators of estates, yet servitor seems to have been a rather nondescript title for a secretarial manservant. Ninian Chirnside of Whitsomelaws was a servitor to the earl of Bothwell, yet he employed a servitor of his own called Nisbet. The terms of employment are mostly unknown, except for the survival of a bond between Steven Rutherford, a younger son of Hunthill, and Andrew Ker of Ferniehirst in 1589, whereby Rutherford bound himself in service to Ker for twenty-three bolls of victual a year. This may well have been the result of previous bonds of manrent between the two parties' families, which demonstrates Ferniehirst's understanding of *noblesse oblige.*[79]

Passing lands to future generations sometimes required deeds of tailzie, so kinsmen needed a broad knowledge of their ancestry to correctly entail property or rebut claims made against their estates. The Kers of Cessford were obsessive about their lands remaining in kinsmen's hands and thus made repeated tailzies that entailed to the Kers of Newbattle, Faldonside, Littledean, Primsideloch, Mersington, Linton and Gateshaw in descending succession of importance. The Kers of Littledean recorded their own tailzie that included the Kers of Cessford, Faldonside and Graden, and the Pringles of Galashiels did likewise in 1586, mentioning Pringle of Whytbank and a Pringle burgess of Peebles. The Kers of Ferniehirst entailed their lands to fewer kinsmen than their rivals the Kers of Cessford, as they only listed the Kers of Ancrum and Cavers. Tailzies could work up or down the social scale as Alexander Home of Huttonhall reinforced his kinship to Lord Home by including him in his tailzie of 1587.[80] In England the Selbies of Twizel and the Strothers of Kirknewton also made elaborate entails to their kinsmen.[81] The kin-conscious Horsleys of Outchester, Carrs of Hetton and Lisles of Felton fell back on relations when in financial difficulties. They chose to mortgage their properties to distant kinsmen, namely Henry Horsley of Lynn, (Norfolk), Robert Carr of Sleaford, (Lincolnshire) and Thomas Lisle of Stannington and John Lisle of Acton in Northumberland.[82] The Fowberries of Fowberry also kept in contact with their remote kinsmen, the Fowberries of Holm in Yorkshire, though this time the gambit did not pay off as these 'uncles' refused to rescue the Fowberry estate.[83]

Tailzies could also be incorporated into marriage arrangements to prevent extinction. In 1580 the Cranstons of that Ilk chose a very distant kinsman, Mr William Cranston, a younger son of John Cranston of Morriston to be both their son-in-law and heir.[84] This arrangement was nearly scuppered by the birth of an heir to Cranston of that Ilk after the marriage, but the child cannot have survived infancy as William Cranston did inherit the Cranston lands. A similar situation faced Sir Thomas Gray of Horton in Northumberland as he had six daughters and no legitimate son. To keep his estates in Gray hands, he chose to entail his entire estates to his grandson and ward Ralph Gray, second son of Sir Ralph Gray of Chillingham. Entails were becoming popular, but they suffocated the common law rights of co-heiresses. With the exception of the eldest daughter Dorothy, who had married Sir Ralph Gray of Chillingham, Gray's other daughters and their husbands were disinherited and much angered by this preponderance with kin survival.[85] They must have made their opposition known during his lifetime as Sir Thomas ignored them in his will, leaving many personal items to the Chillingham branch including his most treasured gold chain for Ralph. Sir Thomas could not have anticipated that his action would lead to the eventual unification of the Horton and Chillingham estates when Ralph's elder brother Sir Thomas died without heirs in 1590. Ralph Gray then became the head of these vast Gray lands. A less confrontational example of kinship and inheritance occurred when the Homes of Blackadder East and West agreed to reunite the Blackadder estate that had been divided between two heiresses in 1541. David Home of Blackadder West had only three daughters so in 1598 he agreed to sell his portion of land to John Home of Blackadder East, in return for payment of £3000 Scots to each daughter.[86]

TABLE 1.7. GENTLEMEN'S FIRST MARRIAGES

Stratification	In Community	Ex Community
Greater Gentry	13	12
Middle Gentry	34	4
Lesser Gentry	78	4
Total	125	20

Ralph Gray's good fortune continued when he married a Yorkshire Catholic bride, Jane Arthington of Arthington. Her father held Ralph in high regard and left him in charge of his estates after his death in 1585, as well as bequeathing a horse to Sir Thomas Gray.[87] Greater gentry marriages outwith the county often had such recusant connections as the Catholic William Haggerston of Haggerston married Margaret Butler from Lancashire.[88] The two families maintained friendship for intercepted letters show that William Haggerston's son Thomas was staying with his grandfather Henry Butler in Lancashire and had been ill with smallpox.[89] Sir Thomas Gray married Lady Katherine Neville, daughter of the rebellious Catholic earl of Westmorland, in Yorkshire. This was not just an arranged match for Sir John Forster noted that they had a liking for one another. Ironically Forster fought the earl during the Northern Rebellion, though he approved of his kinsman's marriage to a noblewoman as this was socially advantageous.[90]

TABLE I.8. ALL GENTRY MARRIAGES, 1540–1603[91]

Married down a stratum	33
Married within 10 miles	100
Married in the same stratum	128
Married up a stratum	36
Married endogamously	14
Married merchant families	11
Married Scots	4
Total marriages	197

Middle-ranking gentry had fewer resources than the greater gentry, but they did sometimes marry outside the community. The marriage between Lancelot Strother and Eleanor Conyers of Sockburn, in Durham was unusual as Lancelot was from a middling gentry family. The Conyers were greater gentry, but the Strothers were evidently upwardly mobile.[92] The ratio of in community marriages amongst the lesser gentry was typical of many landed communities where marriages within the same stratum were common. The Selbies of Biddlestone and Clennells of Clennell typify marriages within a particular neighbourhood as they lived four miles apart and intermarried over two generations.[93] Fifty per cent of the marriages in table I.8 were within a ten mile radius, yet the rate of endogamous marriages was low in comparison to upland areas with poor communications. This surely signifies another difference between the East and West Borders.

The only new gentlemen in the community were younger sons from outwith the area who sought heiresses, military positions or lands. They did

not experience opposition, unlike the 1570s interlopers in the Merse.[94] The
Percies married three heiress tenants to outsiders as a means of rewarding
loyalty in their other spheres of influence. So Thomas Armorer of Ulgham
married Elizabeth Lilburn to found the Armorers of Belford; William
Proctor of Craven in Yorkshire married Elizabeth's sister Isabel to found
the Proctors of Shawdon and Robert Lawson of Little Usworth in Durham
married Margery Swinhoe of Rock forming the Lawsons of Rock. Ironically
it would be the local marriage of Thomas Carr, a younger son of John Carr
of Hetton, to Elizabeth Heron of Ford that created the most bitter gentry
feud of the century.[95] Other newcomers included Sir Ralph Ellerker, an
ambitious younger son from Yorkshire, who was granted Hulne Priory and
Border offices in the 1530s and 1540s. He settled in the community after
marrying the widow of Sir Edward Gray of Chillingham. Sir William Reed
was another ambitious military man who worked his way up in the Berwick
garrison and made his fortune from monastic grants. Thomas Salkeld from
Cumbria may have come up to Alnwick to serve the Percies, but defected to
the ranks of the Forsters for employment.

Contemporary opinion was against gentlemen marrying merchants'
daughters, and lairds mostly avoided these unions.[96] The Eastern Scottish
Borders did not experience the strong lure of Newcastle, as the only recorded
laird marriage with a merchant family was Brounfield of Greenlawdean with
Alison MacGill. The burghs were not overlooked by lairds, however, when
it came to placing younger sons in apprenticeships.[97] However Newcastle's
prosperity could not be ignored by the gentry, nor by merchants seeking
respectability. There were eleven marriages between gentry families and
mercantile families, nine being with Newcastle merchants including the
powerful families of Anderson, Brandling, Mitford and Selby.[98] Berwick
was a less enticing source of mercantile wealth, but its geographical con-
venience attracted lesser gentry such as William Burrell of Howtel, who
married Elizabeth Morton of Murton. The Mortons were seeking accept-
ability among the local Norhamshire gentry after buying local estates.[99]
There were few cross-border marriages between landed families probably
because they accepted that these unions were contrary to Border law.[100]
Most gentry marriages ended in death, rather than divorce, which was very
difficult to obtain in England until modern times.

TABLE 1.9. LAIRDS' FIRST MARRIAGES

Stratification	Within the E. Borders	Outwith the E. Borders
Greater lairds	51	45
Lesser lairds	149	58
Lesser/bonnet lairds and bonnet lairds	3	1

TABLE I.IO. ALL LAIRD MARRIAGES, 1540–1603[101]

Married down a stratum	31
Married in the same stratum	241
Married up a stratum	64
Married within 10 miles	96
Married endogamously	48
Married merchants' daughters	1
Married Englishwomen	1
Total marriages recorded	336

Marriage patterns amongst the lairds are very similar to those of the gentry, with wealthier lairds arranging more external marriages than poorer lairds, who tended to marry locally and within their own stratum. However, there were proportionally fewer marriages within a ten mile radius and far more endogamous marriages. As surname kinship was more powerful in Scotland, this would account for the greater proportion of endogamous unions. This was easier after the Scottish Reformation, when it was no longer necessary to apply to Rome for papal dispensation to marry within the fourth degree of consanguinity. The last known request for dispensation was sent in 1556 when Thomas Pringle of that Ilk wanted to marry Isabel Pringle of Torwoodlee.[102] Marriage links between the Ker, Home and Pringle laird communities were fairly commonplace, but there were very few between the East and West Borderland, again reflecting their sharp social divide. Weddings between the friendly Homes and Pringles included William Home of Bassendean to Marion Pringle of Whytbank, Katherine Home of Polwarth to Robert Pringle of Blindlee and Sir David Home of Wedderburn to the widow of James Pringle of Whytbank, Margaret Ker of Linton. Some marriages were arranged between the Kers and Scotts to pacify their feud, but most failed. The exception was Sir Thomas Ker of Ferniehirst's second marriage to Janet Scott of Buccleuch. Marriage did not guarantee military support in a feuding situation, yet kinship by marriage was important enough for English observers to try to list laird and noble kinship.[103]

Amicable Ker and Home links were typified by the marriage of Margaret Ker of Cessford to the fifth Lord Home and that of Robert Ker of Ancrum to Isabel Home of Wedderburn. The first marriage seemed a downward step as the Scottish nobility normally married within their own rank, but the Borderers saw it differently. These were two local kin chiefs cementing their friendship and mutual respect for each other in a marriage. It did not matter that one was a nobleman and the other a laird as both men were equally powerful in their own localities. Later on, the marriage of their daughter to the Earl Marischal was thought to benefit both Homes and

Kers. The Kers of Ferniehirst also intermarried with the nobility as one of their daughters married Lord Hay of Yester in 1559. Again this drew no adverse comment as the Kers were nobility in all but title. There were rumours that the sixth Lord Home would marry a Ker of Cessford cousin in 1584, but this came to nothing as political marriages were then in vogue.[104] Powerful figures of central government such as the earl of Arran and Maitland of Thirlestane dabbled in Border affairs and married Andrew Ker of Ferniehirst to Anna Stewart of Ochiltree in 1584 (Arran's niece) and Robert Ker of Cessford to Margaret Maitland in 1587 (Maitland's niece). The latter marriage gave Maitland more trouble than he could have anticipated as Robert Ker turned out to be an untypical Eastern Borderer. He was the epitome of a delinquent juvenile, murdering William Ker of Ancrum in 1590 and continually causing trouble across the Border. Young Cessford's wedding ceremony had to be postponed for two days owing to his antagonism to English Borderers. This had greatly offended James VI, who put Cessford into ward the day after his wedding.[105] The lack of cross-border marriage here is again probably due to the its illegality and the fact that there was no shortage of available Scotswomen. Although divorce was obtainable in Scotland, very few lairds sought to end their marriages this way.[106]

V. The strength of Border kinship

Scottish kinship was generally broader than English family ties as it encompassed a mutual respect for blood-relationships, endless cousinage and surname. It also included landholding, political alliances, money-lending, employment, cautioning, refuge from justice and care of children. This is probably why distinctions between social strata were more blurred in Scotland.[107] Lesser lairds and their tenants knew the importance of being loyal to greater lairds and surname chiefs, particularly if they held land or offices from them. Some Home greater lairds were disloyal to the Lords Home on political grounds, but their kinship links never disappeared. Kin ties were exploited by the Scottish government in the second half of the sixteenth century. They made leading kinsmen cautioners under financial penalty for their kinsmen's action or misdeeds. John Haitlie of Mellerstain, as cautioner, brought two troublesome Haitlies before the Privy Council in 1597. He believed that his obligation to the council had been fulfilled, yet they tried to make him responsible for all the attempts made by these Haitlies even before he became their cautioner. As a kin chief Haitlie was obliged to his kinsmen, but as a private individual he must have found kinship a tiresome business.[108] In 1602 Ker of Cessford (as Lord Roxburgh) tried to shirk his responsibilities by claiming that wrongdoers in Morebattle were not his direct tenants. Cessford held the land directly from the King which he then feued to Ker of Corbethouse, who sublet to Mark Ker in

Morebattle.[109] Kinship could therefore have some limitations as Cessford expected loyalty from Corbethouse when necessary, but did not want to be held responsible for any of his subtenants' misdeeds. Cautioning could also be used to break kinship bonds for in 1572 the Ainslies had to find caution of 1,000 merks to burn the house of their kinsman and rebel, William Ainslie of Falla. They had previously been reluctant to carry out this action against a kinsman.[110]

The system of cautioning was not exclusively kin-based for friends, neighbours or kinsmen by marriage could also be sureties, though kinsmen usually took priority. For lesser lairds it was advantageous to appeal to the social conscience of a greater laird or wealthy kinsman. There are numerous examples of kinsmen acting as cautioners for kin to keep the peace in a feud or to enter a rebel. Kinsmen cautioners could be remotely related like Robert Ker, portioner of Duddingston and second-generation burgess of Edinburgh, who was cautioner for John Ker of Kerchesters in 1593. The Homes of Blackadder had marriage links with the more powerful Homes of Cowdenknowes and used them as cautioners in 1582 and 1591. The Homes of Ninewells made use of their kinsman and neighbour Alexander Home of Huttonhall in 1589 and as kin chiefs the Pringles of that Ilk helped their kinsmen Blindlee and Galashiels in 1591 and 1597 respectively.[111] Cautioners could also be found lower down the social scale as Home of Huttonhall stood surety for his kinsman the sixth Lord Home on many occasions in the later-sixteenth century.

Acts of caution were also required for securing loans, debts, tochers and wadsets. The lairds made good use of this aspect of cautioning as there are thousands of references in the Register of Deeds to friends, neighbours and kinsmen obliging each other. A few examples are Thomas Ramsay of Wyliecleuch as financial surety for Triamor Redpath of Crumrig in 1563, George Pringle of Wrangholm and Thomas Haitlie of Sneep for Henry Haitlie of Mellerstain in 1569, David Edington of that Ilk for his cousin David Home of Ninewells in 1571 and Robert Haig of Bemersyde and Nicol Cairncross of Calfhill for their neighbour William Linlithgow of Drygrange in 1595.[112]

Another bonus of kindred was informal money-lending amongst themselves. John Home of Huttonhall and William Home of Ayton both borrowed money from David Home of Ninewells. The non-Border George Home, portioner of Gullane (and prosperous younger son of Patrick Home of the Law), lent money to kinsmen over a wider geographical area, including Andrew Home commendator of Jedburgh and Lord Home. The Kers also borrowed from kinsmen; James Ker of Corbethouse, William Ker, a younger son of Linton and Lancie Ker of Little Newton all owed money to James Ker of Middlemist Walls in 1595. On a more domestic level, Oliver Edgar of Flass and Alexander MacDougal of Stodrig borrowed money from their brothers.[113]

Kinship was advantageous to Mr Thomas Cranston of Morriston when he was forfeited and declared a rebel in 1592. He had intrigued with the traitorous earl of Bothwell, yet was still uncaptured in 1600 because his kinsman John Cranston of that Ilk had sheltered him for long periods. This was illegal, but the power of kinship was far stronger than respect for the law in this instance. Cranston's estates were fortuitously granted to Lord Home, who regarded him as a kinsman through allegiance. Home would not have exploited his misfortune as Cranston's father had given good service to the Lords Home.[114] William Ker of Ancrum was similarly sheltered by the Homes of Wedderburn in 1573, as they were his kin by marriage and they also hid a rebellious younger son of theirs, John Home of Crumstane. Regent Morton, who was normally unforgiving, tolerated Wedderburn's protectionism as he was a distant kinsman. Crumstane went to Tantallon Castle to apologise in person, but hid at first until Morton had gone to bed

> ... he fell to cards with the servants in the hall. The Regents Chamber was hard by, and he, not resting well arose and came forth to the hall in his night gowne to look on their gaming. By chance John sate next to him and he was leaning with his hand on his shoulder a long time, without knowing who he was, at last going away to bed again, he perceived it was he, and smiling said to him GOD make you a good man, and so he went away.[115]

Some greater lairds seem to have differed from lesser lairds in their kin loyalties. Self-interest could disrupt kinship when lairds were willing to break their traditional bonds of kinship to further their careers. The Home lairds were guilty of disloyalty to their kin chiefs from the 1560s to the 1580s. Although Camden called them 'a noble and faire spred familie', their ascendancy at court during the sixteenth century had given them a certain independence from the Lords Home. These 'sondrey gentlemen of goode power and lyving' were bolstered by deliberate crown and factional inter-ference in the localities, but overall this was an effective policy that guaranteed their support if their Lord and kin chief was disloyal.[116]

Home lairds had devotedly followed the fourth Lord during his brave resistance against English aggression in the 1540s, refusing to assure to England when many other lairds gave into English pressure. However this loyalty was shattered by the political and religious upheavals of the late 1550s, when Scotland generally became divided between pro-French and pro-English factions. The fifth and sixth Lords Home would fail to com-mand the respect held by the fourth Lord Home because of factionalism. Inconsistent leadership by the fifth Lord in the 1560s saw him fighting against his own kinsmen with only a few lairds such as Broomhouse supporting him. He was finally deserted by all his kinsmen in 1569 when he made a decision to rejoin the Marian party.[117]

The Lords Home lacked the territorial magnitude of the earls of Huntly, yet until 1560 they had been able to rally their kinsmen to dominate the Merse. Huntly was deserted by his kinsmen at the battle of Corrichie in 1562, but he quickly managed to recoup his kin domination whilst Home did not. The Homes of Manderston and Cowdenknowes were openly hostile to Lord Home in the early 1570s while other Home lairds were more subdued in their opposition to him by simply refusing to join him. An erroneous English report of 1570 stated that 'my lord Hume and almost all the gentlemen in Tevydale Marsh and Lowdyan were knitt together in such frendship'.[118] In truth Home had very few friends at this time, especially amongst his own kinsmen, as he had made a major political blunder.

The Homes of Wedderburn were reluctant to admit disloyalty to their chief and probably used David Home of Godscroft, a younger son of this branch to cover their tracks. He wrote a family history, *De Familia Humia Wedderburnensi,* that pledged loyalty to Lord Home, but then idolised the earls of Angus in his *History of the House and Race of Douglas and Angus*.[119] During the mid 1560s David Home of Wedderburn fought on the opposite side to Lord Home though Godscroft insists that his father did not accept any of Lord Home's property when he was forfeited in 1573. This may be true yet Godscroft's assertion that his brother George did not take any gains from Lord Home's teinds of Greenlaw is dubious for teinds were profitable in an era of inflation.[120] Wedderburn was absent in 1573 when Lord Home needed financial sureties though Polwarth, North Berwick, Huttonhall and even the previously antagonistic Manderston obliged their Lord. Furthermore when their Lord was under threat of execution in 1573 it was the unlikely duo of Manderston and Cowdenknowes, along with North Berwick who pleaded for his life, not Wedderburn. By 1575 Lord Home had probably discovered the treachery of Manderston and Cowdenknowes for in his will he asked the lairds of Wedderburn, Ayton and Polwarth to protect his son.[121]

Wedderburn took credit for the restoration of the sixth Lord Home in 1578 despite opposition from Regent Morton who told him

> You never got any good of that house . . . you will get but small thanks for your pains: Sir George answered that the Lord Home was his chief, and he could not see his house ruined . . . he thought himself bound to do, and for his own part, whatsoever their carriage were to him, he would do his duty to them, if his chief should turne him out at the foredoore, he would come in again at the back-doore.[122]

Godscroft wrote this in 1625, nearly fifty years after these events took place. Amongst his many talents, Godscroft was a poet and poetic licence was certainly adopted here. Wedderburn may have been party to Lord Home's restoration, but he was still allied to the nefarious Morton at this time and had no hesitation in accepting Home's office of warden of the East

March and a grant of his own ward and marriage. He then married Jean Haldane of Gleneagles, a kinswoman of the ascendant earl of Mar. Godscroft overlooked a feud between his father and Lord Home in 1567 and actually feuded with the sixth Lord Home himself in 1590. The evidence against the absolute loyalty claimed by Godscroft is overwhelming. In reality, they were no different to other Home greater lairds who took political, social and economic advantage of Lord Home's misfortune.[123]

The thirteen-year-old Lord Home faced a daunting task in 1578. English reports surmised his situation correctly noting that 'although his surname and power upon the Borders is very greate' they 'all follow him not'.[124] He quickly took responsibility as kin chief for he was settling an internal Home feud in 1580. Although his family had come close to ruination with the 1573 forfeiture he managed to rally his kinsmen around him by 1600. This revival may have been caused by the more moderate opinions of a new generation of greater Home lairds. Their loyalty was made easier after 1591 by Lord Home's unswerving loyalty to James VI and they were all favoured by the king. Another more cynical reason for this loyalty was probably Lord Home's barrenness. His wife had children from her first marriage, but none from Home and this caused marital friction. According to court gossip, there was 'appearance of a seperacon between my Lord Home and my Lady who hathe taken the platte and beste stuffe at Dunglass and caryed with her to fife to her lyving there'.[125]

The Homes of Cowdenknowes had the nearest descent from Lord Home, and a marriage between Isobel Home, sister of Lord Home, and James Home, commendator of Eccles and younger son of Cowdenknowes, cemented their kinship. In 1599 the Homes of Cowdenknowes were officially declared heirs apparent to Lord Home and other Home lairds took note. Even Sir George Home of Spott, the supremely-ascendant younger son of the Homes of Manderston saw the advantage of this tailzie and arranged the marriage of his infant daughter Anne to the young son and heir of Cowdenknowes.[126] Alexander Home of North Berwick was similarly childless in the 1590s and was consequently feted by his outwardly-pious Home of Polwarth nephews, of whom John became his heir. The other Polwarth Homes were not forgotten in his will.[127]

The Homes of Manderston likewise revived their kinship links to Lord Home in the 1590s. Sir Alexander Home of Manderston succeeded his father in 1593 and shook off past grudges when he signed a bond of manrent to 'my verie gude lord and chieff' Lord Home in 1595. Sir Alexander may well have been genuinely sorry for his father's ill-treatment of the fifth Lord, but Lord Home was now commendator of Coldingham Priory, a possession once held by the Homes of Manderston. This leads to speculation that he may have been trying to regain some of these lands. If this was so, he failed, but Lord Home did grant him a new charter of Manderston.[128] When Lord Home tangled with Maitland of Thirlestane over the teinds of Lauder in

1593, the Homes of Cowdenknowes, Ayton, Polwarth, Manderston, Blackadder, Huttonhall and North Berwick all rallied to his aid. This revival was miraculous after the political complexities of the 1560s and 1570s. It would probably have been envied by the Percy earls of Northumberland who never recovered their gentry following before 1603.[129]

The Kers of Cessford and Ferniehirst had a slightly different problem with their kinship as they fought to be head of the Ker surname. In typical Border fashion they could bind together to oppose the Scotts in their long-running bloodfeud whilst they each built up powerful kin groups in East Teviotdale and Jedforest. Pacification attempts for this bloodfeud listed their kin groups separately, with neither dominating the other. The problem of who held the more ancient lineage was contentious even amongst nineteenth-century historians as it was within one generation during the fifteenth century.[130] A marriage between the two branches in 1540 created only a temporary truce. Sir Walter Ker of Cessford settled a local feud in 1582, claiming to speak for the 'remanent surname of Kerris', but in reality this meant his own Ker allies of Littledean, Faldonside, Linton, Primsideloch, Yair, Newhall, Maisondieu, Whitmuir and Kippilaw. None of Ferniehirst's allies, such as Ker of Ancrum or Cavers, were mentioned and in 1593 reference was made to 'Farniherst and his Kers', so the divisions were as deep as ever.[131]

Feuding within a kindred was uncommon across the frontier for 'most of the principall houses in the countrey are so neere comoyned together by bloud or alliance that there is verie few or almost none but are on the one side within the 3 degree'.[132] The Gray of Chillingham kinship included most of the greater gentry families of Northumberland with marriages to the Widdringtons of Widdrington, Delavals of Seaton Delaval, Radcliffes of Cartington, Forsters of Adderstone, Collingwoods of Eslington and Herons of Chipchase. They were also allied to important families in Norfolk and Yorkshire. Like the lairds they often obliged each other by standing surety or accepting mortgages. Ralph Gray of Chillingham may have regretted his kinship to the Delavals as they were slow to repay him for loans. However, Francis Radcliffe was more useful by standing surety for Ralph in 1602.[133] In 1577 Ralph and his brother Sir Thomas obliged Sir George Radcliffe with a mortgage and Ralph himself mortgaged his lands in 1593 to Sir John Forster, Robert Delaval and Francis Radcliffe amongst others.[134]

The Grays' wide kindred included lesser gentry neighbours as friends and allies, rather than relations. The Hepburns of Hepburn were regarded as neighbouring kinsmen and Sir Thomas Gray pitied the widow of a friend, leaving her a £5 pension.[135] Sir Thomas hunted regularly with a group of friends that included his kinsman Thomas Forster of Adderstone, junior, and the husband of the aforementioned widow, Thomas Ilderton of Ilderton. Gray's gift was motivated by knowledge that Ilderton valued his hounds more than his wife. As well as hunting together the gentry must have visited friends and kinsmen's houses. Thomas Carr of Ford is recorded visiting his mother-in-law Lady Selby in Berwick and Robert Beadnell of Lemmington died whilst staying at Eslington, his mother's childhood home.[136]

The Forsters and Grays were kinsmen through a second marriage. Dorothy Ogle married Sir Thomas Forster of Adderstone in the early sixteenth century and had four sons and five daughters. She then remarried Sir Thomas Gray of Horton in 1529 and had the six daughters subsequently disinherited by their father. Sir John Forster, although at first reticent about his mother's remarriage, was very proud to be a stepbrother of the Grays and protected Dorothy's children after the death of Sir Ralph Gray. They affectionately referred to him as 'uncle'. Even in the 1590s when difficulties arose through differences in religion and politics, Sir John hoped they would be resolved as Ralph Gray was 'my sister's son'.[137] The only noticeable lack of kinship through marriage was between the Selbies and Grays, and the Selbies and Collingwoods. These parties feuded as part of a local power struggle in the 1580s and 1590s. The Selbies did, however, tend to marry locally or endogamously, with the exceptions of a Scottish match and a political marriage arranged by Sir Francis Walsingham for William Selby to Dorothy Bonham of Kent.[138] As in Scottish feuds, the gentry could find allies amongst their kinsmen. For instance, the Collingwoods of Etal were helped by their brothers-in-law Henry and Edmund Craster of Craster when fighting Ralph Selby of Weetwood.[139]

Bonds of kinship were only as strong as the gentry families wanted them to be, but probate records reveal how effective kinship was in practice. The supervisors of wills were frequently kinsmen, for Robert Collingwood of Eslington's supervisors were all Collingwoods, those of Thomas Forster of Adderstone senior were all Forsters and John Selby of Branxton's consisted of two brothers-in-law and a son-in-law.[140] Supervisors could, however, just be unrelated neighbours as Francis Armorer of Belford nominated Henry Haggerston of Haggerston and Thomas Forster of Adderstone. Presumably they were just friends who thought of themselves as being like kinsmen, though they were all linked by their Catholicism in an officially Protestant country.[141] Another anomaly is the inclusion of powerful men as supervisors, who were not necessarily kinsmen or of the same religion. Robert Clavering of Callaly, for example, made Protestant Sir John Forster a supervisor alongside his Catholic kinsmen Sir Thomas and Ralph Gray to ensure his will was honoured. William Collingwood of Barton, a Protestant, made his Catholic kin chief Sir Cuthbert Collingwood of Eslington a supervisor.[142] Durham wills prove how wide kinship could be for Thomas Collingwood of Eslington referred to his 'brother' Francis Radcliffe though they were only connected by marriage to daughters of Sir Ralph Gray. Ursula Brandling made her son Sir Cuthbert Collingwood sole executor of her will in 1592, even though she had been widowed from his father forty-five years previously.[143] Perhaps this was not so unusual as executors were normally members of the immediate family.

There are innumerable examples of kinsmen as lairds' executors, overmen and tutors testamentars, which point to the strength of Border kinship. In 1576 Cuthbert Home in Duns, a very remote kinsman of the Homes of Ayton, asked 'the laird of aittoun his derrest cousing' to be overman to the executors' of his will and protect his wife and bairns 'as unto his maist special freind'. As in England the term cousin implied a blood relationship that could be third or fourth cousinage, if not more.[144] In 1565, when Margaret Ker of Cessford first wife of the fifth Lord Home died as a result of childbirth at her mother's house, (Holydean, near Melrose), her executors were her husband and mother. Margaret died young so she depended on her own family, but older ladies tended to appoint their sons; for example Katherine Pringle, first wife of David Spottiswoode of that Ilk named her son Ninian. Ninian himself appointed a step-uncle Adam Brounfield of Hardacres, a kinsman James Spottiswoode of Whinrig and his uncle Mr John Spottiswoode (an outstanding minister of the reformed church), as his executors.[145] Andrew Brounfield of Pittlesheugh asked his kinsmen Adam Brounfield of Hardacres and Robert Dickson of Bughtrig, to be overmen of his will. William Pringle of Torwoodlee made his wife and children executors along with his brother-in-law James Heriot of Trabrown as tutor testamentar. Kinship examples continued with Andrew Pringle of Galashiels naming fellow Pringles John of Buckholm and Mr Robert Pringle as his executors; and Mr Thomas Cranston of Corsbie appointing his uncle, father-in-law and brother-in-law (Alexander Home of North Berwick, Patrick Home of Polwarth and Patrick Home of Polwarth younger) as tutors testamentars to his children. As the century progressed, the position of overman was overtaken by the increasingly-important office of tutor testamentar.[146]

VI. Social provision for children[147]

The exact size of the landed families in the Eastern Borders is difficult to determine with few parish records surviving and widespread illegitimacy. Wills and testaments are therefore useful for identification.[148] Their size appears typical for landed families in early modern society, though these appear quite large by modern standards. They were smaller if a parent died and infant mortality was high. Remarriages were common amongst the lairds and gentlemen and this made some families large. For instance, John Renton of Billie had twelve surviving children from his three marriages, whilst Sir James Cockburn of Langton had twenty-one children from two marriages. Both Sir Cuthbert Collingwood of Eslington and Dorothy Ogle, Lady Gray of Chillingham, had fifteen children from two marriages. Conversely, Steven Brounfield of Greenlawdean had only one son before he was murdered in 1564.[149]

Tutors testamentars and supervisors of children could be important lairds or gentlemen for reasons of prestige or protection. The long-running feud between the Carrs and the Herons made William Carr of Ford ask Lord Hunsdon, cousin of Queen Elizabeth, to be guardian to his children. This was a great personal sacrifice as William was a church papist and knew this wardship would lead to his family being brought up as Protestants.[150] Robert Lauder of that Ilk's father had been murdered by the Homes of Cowdenknowes so he nominated Sir Robert Ker of Cessford to protect his children against any future Home action.[151] Tutors testamentar had no legal rights over the children in their care, so their status was more akin to that of an English godfather or honorary father. This restriction did not undervalue their influence as they could voice opinions and give visible support or protection to their charges until they were beyond minority at fourteen if male, or twelve if female. However it was left to tutors and curators to provide for children's education and executors to pay out their bairns' portions.

For landed families in Scotland a tutor dative and curator were appointed by a court of law. This proceedure overrode normal rules about the legal age of minors. Their names were suggested and if they accepted the nomination they were then empowered as administrators of the minors. However if a guardian had been appointed as well, he would have the overriding right of ward and marriage of the tutee. Tutors and curators were often kinsmen, such as Andrew Home commendator of Jedburgh to the sixth Lord Home, his nephew, or William Cockburn of that Ilk who had an uncle and great-uncle in these roles.[152] A tutor had to satisfy three directives: he had to be over twenty-five years of age, prudent in his own affairs and not be the immediate successor of his charge. Andrew Home satisfied all three counts which enabled him to look after Lord Home until he was sixteen. He must have been a respected tutor of this Lord as other laird families such as French of Thornydykes, involved him in the overseeing of their children as well.[153]

When an elite Scottish youth reached sixteen he or she was deemed to be beyond the age of tutory and had then to choose curators for the rest of his or her minority. This ended at twenty-one for men and eighteen for women unless they had married. Lord Home went to the Court of Session in 1581 to select curators, but lesser lairds went to their local sheriff court. Home chose his guardian William Lord Ruthven, James Lord Ogilvy, his former tutor Andrew Home commendator of Jedburgh, John Lord Herries, his stepfather Mr Thomas Lyon of Baldukie and Sir Lewis Bellenden of Auchnoule. Alexander Home of Huttonhall and John Cranston of Morriston were additionally designated advisers to the sixth Lord Home until he was twenty-one. They were resident kinsmen on hand to give advice *in loco parentis*, whereas his official curators lived at great distances from their charge, with the exception of Andrew Home of Jedburgh. Curators were only required on formal occasions, such as the drawing up of marriage contracts or land transactions when consent was required. These curators were representative of the high social status of Home. Further down the social scale James Ker of Middlemist Walls chose Ker of Primsideloch and Lochtower at Jedburgh Sheriff Court.[154]

When a guardian had not been appointed, tutors administered minors' estates.[155] The title of tutor was used by several lairds such as Robert Pringle, tutor of Blindlee, Patrick Cockburn, tutor of Langton and Gilbert Home, tutor of West Reston. They were all younger sons and thus uncles of their charges, wielding great power whilst in office. They would have been demoted when the heir came of age, but all three tutors died before this happened. Gilbert Home clearly relished his appointment as it gave him access to wealth and power normally denied a younger son. His inventory was worth over £3,700 Scots in 1581 and he gave generous endowments to his own son and sisters from money that was probably not his to bestow. Patrick Cockburn left his charges with debts of over £1,000 Scots in 1602, whilst Robert Pringle left his nephews and nieces £3,250 Scots in credit in 1588. The competence of tutors as administrators therefore varied.[156]

Home of Godscroft charged his stepmother with mishandling the family's estate. She also quarrelled with Godscroft's grandmother over gold, silver and jewels.[157] Godscroft adored his own mother and extolled her pious virtues at length in his family history, despite being no more than four years old when she died of a miscarriage. His father remarried Margaret Ker, widow of James Pringle of Whytbank, who had children by her previous marriage. Godscroft portrays her as a wicked stepmother who indulged her own children at the expense of the Home offspring. It was the Homes' misfortune that she outlived David Home of Wedderburn by fourteen years and continued to wreak havoc with the family's finances. The situation was apparently so bad that Godscroft, along with his brothers and sisters, refused to claim their bairns' portions to assist the family's fortunes, but this may have been an exaggeration.

A legal guardian had the right to determine the marriage of his or her ward. Lord Ruthven (later earl of Gowrie) offered Lord Home the marriage of either Dorothy or Lilias Ruthven, his daughters. Home declined and would have incurred a financial penalty as a result had it not been for the friendship between Ruthven and Home's late father.[158] In 1532 Andrew Ker of Primsideloch charged 100 merks 'for his favour and lack of obstruction' when his ward Thomas MacDougal of Makerstoun married Janet Scott of Howpasley, yet he made Elizabeth Fawlaw sell him half of her lands of Softlaw after she married John Brydin, burgess of Selkirk.[159] Janet Newton the heiress of Dalcove, was not so fortunate. James Ker of Mersington exploited his legal right to determine Janet's marriage in the most brutal manner possible during the 1530s. Janet fell in love with Adam Ker of Shaw, but James Ker objected despite their mutual surname. James offered Janet the right to 'mary quhat partey she plesis', and be infeft in her late father's lands providing she pay him a £2,000 Scots penalty. Janet was given less than a month to comply with this, but she decided none the less to marry Adam Ker and sold a third of her lands to her guardian as well as wadsetting the remaining two-thirds to pay the fine. This was a heavy price to pay for love, but the methods used by the unscrupulous Mersington were legitimate and probably not deemed unreasonable in a patriarchal society.[160]

There was some compensation for the above in grants of male wardship made to politically-favoured women. Isabel Home of Wedderburn gained that of John Haldane of Gleneagles in 1574 and Isobel Home of Cowdenknowes bought Henry Haitlie of Mellerstain in 1547. Both women subsequently married their wards. As a mark of favour, wardship could also be granted to the minors themselves as happened with Andrew Douglas of Timpendean, George Home of Wedderburn, Andrew Ker of Yair, Richard Spence of Chirnside Mains and Ninian Spottiswoode of that Ilk. They were free to chose their own brides, but guardians were not necessarily ill-intentioned as they could be close relatives. Robert French of Thornydykes had his mother, whilst Marie Hepburn of Fairnington and George Pringle of Torwoodlee had their grandfathers. William Ker of Cessford's guardian was his father and Robert Lauder of that Ilk had an uncle. The Homes of Manderston and the Kers of Littledean were exceptionally lucky as they all reached their majority before their fathers died and thus avoided wardship.[161]

Occasionally guardians could be appointed whilst the father or grandfather of a ward was still alive. This anomaly arose when the custom of infefting an heir in lands as a fiar, before his father died, backfired with the premature death of the heir. The lands then went to a brother or son, whichever was the deceased's heir, rather than reverting to the father. There were no real problems when this happened to the Kers of Cessford in 1563 as a brother became the ward of his own father, but the Haitlies of Mellerstain were not so fortunate. The ward of John Haitlie was granted to Walter Ker of Littledean, which caused endless wrangles between Ker and his ward's grandfather John Haitlie. Alexander Dickson of Herdrig was perhaps another resentful ward as he was cautioned not to harm his former guardian's son thirty years after he had been a ward of Alexander MacDougal of Stodrig. The wardship of John Mow of that Ilk also caused a feud in the 1540s.[162]

Across the Border children mentioned in wills were often left to the guardianship of friends, godparents and kinsmen if they were not the subject of wardship. English wardship has been described as 'a grossly inhuman method of taxation' and was probably more ruthless than the treatment of Scottish minors holding land in chief. Wardship gave control of all the estates belonging to minor heirs, as well as their marriages if they were not precontracted. It usually lasted until the heir reached the age of twenty-one, or sixteen if female. Girls over fourteen when their father died were not subject to wardship.[163] Fortunately Northumbrian wards were not exploited by their guardians who either purchased their wardship direct from the Court of Wards and Liveries, or from the successful buyer of a wardship. Guardians were often kinsmen, which was unusual in England. John Swinburne of Edlingham's wardship was bought by Sir Cuthbert Collingwood, a family friend, from Nicholas Errington who had in turn bought it from the Court of Wards. Thomas Swinburne had wanted his son John to marry a daughter of Sir Cuthbert's and arranged this before his death, so there was no enforced marriage obligation by the guardian on his ward.[164] Robert Collingwood of Eslington was guardian to his nephew John Collingwood of Etal, as were Thomas Craster to Edmund Craster of Craster and Ralph Gray of Chillingham to Robert Collingwood of Eslington. When the Percy estates were not under crown control the earls of Northumberland were guardians to several minors including Roger Fowberry of Fowberry and William Lawson of Rock. The Grays of Chillingham as feudal superiors of the barony of Wark were guardian of John Weetwood of Weetwood.

If children were not the subjects of wardship then kinship and allegiance came to the fore. Several lesser gentlemen left their sons to the custody and service of the earls of Northumberland, but this was a diminishing practice and reflected the meagre Percy-dependent estates of George Harbottle of Cawledge and Odnel Selby of Hulne Park. Sir Robert Ellerker of Hulne also left a son to the Percy household as his lease of Hulne was unlikely to be renewed by the crown.[165] Straightforward kinship was a more usual source of protection for minors. Thomas Weetwood of Weetwood, favouring his Forster kinship, left his son Alexander to the governance of Hugh Forster, a younger (illegitimate) son of Adderstone, and Alexander's great-uncle. Thomas Forster of Adderstone senior asked his brother Sir John to look after the interests of their niece Elizabeth, daughter of their deceased brother Rowland Forster of Lucker.[166] Thomas Manners of Cheswick chose a combination of friends and kinsmen for his children in 1593 as he had no great patron. Agnes was left to Henry Gray of Kyloe (brother-in-law), Isobel to Thomas Ord of West Ord (distant kinsman), Margaret to George Morton of Murton (merchant friend) and Elizabeth to Gilbert Scott of Earle (friend). Manners's son Henry was left to George Carleton of the Berwick garrison, perhaps to give him a military future.[167] Another method of ensuring minors' security was to leave them to their brothers and sisters who had already attained majority, or to brothers or sisters of the testator. Thus Isabel Selby of Twizel was left to her brother William's care in 1595 and Beyll Gallon of Alnwick was given to the care of 'the old good wife of Newham', her aunt Margaret Forster of Newham.[168]

The high mortality rate amongst the adult population could completely wreck plans envisaged for minors, but the gentry concerned just passed their wards onto other kinsmen. For example, George Carr of Lesbury was left the tuition of the children of Robert Manners of Newton and of Lucy Hering of Dunstan, but he had to pass them onto other Carr kinsmen. A later generation of Carrs of Lesbury had similar problems when George Middleham of Alnmouth left his daughter Anna to his father-in-law, John Carr of Lesbury in 1587. Carr died in 1588 so Anna was left to John Carr of Hetton's protection.[169] The gentry took their responsibilities as guardians seriously and probably discussed future plans whilst the will was being drawn up. Thomas Holburn of Holburn valued his friendship with the Selbies of Twizel so he arranged for Sir John to look after his illegitimate son John. Thomas died in 1581, whilst Sir John Selby was at the Newcastle assizes, so his son William took his place by riding to Holburn's house at Buckton to sort out John's portion and make an immediate inventory of goods including 'all his papers and evidence'.[170]

The choice of children's names often reflected godparentage, kinship and status amongst the gentry.[171] The role of godparents was probably less important than that of guardians, unless the two were combined. Small gifts or remembrances appear in wills such as Thomas Holburn of Holburn leaving six silver spoons to a son of Thomas Forster of Adderstone junior, 'whom I kersned'. Thomas Lilburn of Middleton-by-the-Sea left an orphaned god-daughter four nobles and hoped that Henry Haggerston of Haggerston would look after her as she was called Helen Haggerston.[172] Nicholas Forster, illegitimate son of Sir John Forster, had four godparents at his 1543 baptism: Sir Reginald Carnaby his uncle, who was responsible for his education, Cuthbert Mitford of Mitford, Nicholas Forster of Newham and Florence Wharton his aunt, the wife of Sir Thomas Forster of Adderstone.[173]

Illegitimate children were certainly not uncommon in sixteenth-century England, yet unusually in Northumberland some inherited property as heirs of greater gentlemen. Nicholas Forster was allowed his father's surname and was treated like a legitimate son even though bastards were normally excluded from inheritance and had to take their mother's name. It was not until the 1590s that a hearing took place in the Durham Consistory Court concerning Nicholas's baptism and legitimacy. Illegitimate offspring could only be legitimated if the parents subsequently married or if the crown granted legitimacy, but Nicholas Forster did not qualify on either account.[174] The Forsters were notorious for having illegitimate children and mistresses. Sir John Forster even fronted mortgages through his mistress Isabel Sheppard, though he later married her and thus legitimised his daughter Mary.[175] Sir John's nephew Thomas Forster of Adderstone junior had an illegitimate heir, Matthew, but he was probably legitimised by his parents' marriage as Thomas married a local woman from a non-gentry family.

The Forsters may have regarded their illegitimate children as legitimate, but other greater gentry families overlooked their bastard offspring. Peter Gray, son of Sir Thomas Gray of Horton, was excluded from inheriting by his father (along with his six legitimate sisters) in favour of Ralph Gray of Chillingham. The progeny of the bigamous marriage of Thomas Rutherford of Middleton Hall battled against the claim of their uncle John to their lands, but a gentry jury upheld his right to the estate. Thomas Forster senior was, ironically, a juror deciding this case. However, the most audacious case of illegitimacy concerned the Reeds of Holy Island.[176] Sir William Reed was a thoroughly ambitious Puritan in public and a Don Juan in private. In his will he left an illegitimate daughter £50 and gave her tuition to Myra Matthew. There was nothing untoward in this bequest as bastards were sometimes left a small bequest, but Myra Matthew was the wife of Tobie Matthew, the outwardly pious bishop of Durham. Reed was illegitimate himself and despite marrying three times he managed to father a large number of bastards, including his heir William who was conceived whilst both parents were married to other partners, though they subsequently married. Amongst the lesser gentry there were similar mixtures of illegitimate heirs and forgotten bastards as Lancelot Manners of Longframlington inherited, but John Holburn of Holburn did not.[177]

There was a fairly high proportion of illegitimacy amongst the lairds' offspring before 1580. After this morality preaching by the reformed church seems to have accounted for a slight decline in the number of illegitimate births. The Homes of Wedderburn and Kers of Ancrum were part of this decline, but the Homes of Cowdenknowes and Kers of Littledean legitimised bastards in 1586 and 1582, respectively. Alexander Home of Huttonhall was illegitimate before being legitimised by the crown in 1541. Legitimising in Scotland normally did not entitle the child to any title or heritable property, but Huttonhall seems to have been an exception to this rule. David and George Home, illegitimate sons of Sir George Home of Wedderburn, were legitimised in 1543 but did not inherit. The fourth and fifth Lords Home copied the actions of James V by exploiting the availability of monastic land to endow their 'natural' sons with lands and offices at Jedburgh Abbey. As lay clerics John Home, abbot of Jedburgh and later Andrew, commendator of Jedburgh had illegitimate families themselves. Andrew Home's daughter Elizabeth became prioress of Abbey St Bathans, another Home sinecure.[178]

The kinship networks, marriages and families of the Eastern Borders are therefore complex, yet the most salient feature of these landed communities was the strength of kinship through blood, marriage, landholding, and even illegitimacy. The diversity of landed families on both sides of the frontier has rarely been explored before, yet their kinship permeated most social relationships from the humblest bonnet laird or lesser gentleman to the greater lairds. An understanding of the intricate nature of this kinship is therefore vital to any study of the sixteenth-century Borders. However, this level of kinship was not unique to the Borders; any landed community in early modern Scotland or England would have had comparable kinship networks.

Notes

1 In Scotland the western Borders are west of Selkirk and Jedburgh, comprising West Teviotdale, Liddesdale, the 'Debateable Ground', Dumfriesshire. Pitscottie, *History*, 33.

2 S. Smith, 'Bordering on Identity', *Scotlands*, iii (1996), 18–32. See map two.

3 See maps two and four. *CBP*, i, 972. *CSP Scot*, x, 156; xi, 26. G. Johnson, *The Natural History of the Eastern Borders* (London, 1853), 1.

4 See ch. vii.

5 Lesley, *History*, i, 10.

6 Godscroft, *History*, 276, 323. *HMC, Milne-Home*, 86.

7 *APS*, iii, 461–6.

8 North Durham was incorporated into Northumberland in 1844, but survived as petty sessions until 1974. K. Emsley, 'North Durham', *Tyne & Tweed*, 46 (1991–92), 17–23. See map four.

9 P. Dixon, 'The Deserted Medieval Villages of North Northumberland', unpubl. PhD diss. University of Wales 1985, 58–61. P. A. Johnson, 'A Synchronic and Historical View of Border Area Bimoric Vowel Systems', unpubl. Ph.D diss. Edinburgh 1985, 13–14.

10 Watts has looked at the whole county of Northumberland in *Border To Middle Shire*, but he failed to look at the original probate material at Durham; a vital source of information on families.

11 A. Everitt, *The Community of Kent and The Great Rebellion, 1640–60* (Leicester, 1966). A. Hassell Smith, *County and Court, Government and Politics in Norfolk 1558–1603* (Oxford, 1974). Dairmaid MacCulloch, *Suffolk and the Tudors* (Oxford, 1986).

12 P. Williams, 'The Crown and the Counties', in C. Haigh, ed. *The Reign of Elizabeth I* (London, 1985), 126–46. See map four.

13 *Cf.* J. Thirsk, 'The Fashioning of the Tudor-Stuart Gentry', *Bulletin of the John Rylands Library*, lxxii (1990), 73. P. Fleming, A. Gross & J. R. Lander, eds. *Regionalism and Revision. The Crown and its Provinces in England 1200–1650* (London, 1998). J. G. Jones, *The Wynn Family of Gwydir: origins, growth and development c. 1490–1674* (Aberystwyth, 1995) and *The Welsh Gentry 1536–1640. Images of Status, Honour and Authority* (Cardiff, 1998). V. Larminie, *Wealth, Kinship and Culture. The seventeenth-century Newdigates of Arbury and their world* (London, 1995). H. A. Lloyd, *The Gentry of South-West Wales, 1540–1640* (Cardiff, 1968).

14 G. Donaldson, *All The Queen's Men* (London, 1983), 102–112. F. D. Bardgett, 'Faith families and faction: the Scottish Reformation in Angus and the Mearns'. unpubl PhD thesis. Edinburgh 1987. A. J. White, 'Religion, Politics and Society in Aberdeen, 1543–93.' unpubl PhD thesis. Edinburgh 1985. M. Lynch, *Edinburgh and the Reformation* (Edinburgh, 1981). D. Baptie, *A Lairdship Lost. The Mowats of Balquholly, 1309–1736* (East Linton, 2000) only discusses one family, mostly in the seventeenth century.

15 M. M. Meikle, 'The Invisible Divide: The Greater Lairds and the Nobility of Jacobean Scotland', *SHR* lxxi (1992), 70–87.

16 J. Wormald, 'Lords and Lairds in Fifteenth Century Scotland: Nobles and Gentry', in M. Jones, ed. *Gentry and Lesser Nobility in Late Medieval Europe* (Gloucester, 1986), 182–200. A register of Scottish Arms is not extant before 1672 and it was not until the Restoration period that a coat of arms became a requisite for those claiming to be Scottish gentry.

17 See map three. For further explanation of chiefs see F. Adam, *The Clans, Septs and Regiments of the Scottish Highlands* (Edinburgh, 1952), 154–9.

18 NAS RH9/17/1/2. *RMS*, iii, 2801; v, 533. Calderwood, *History*, i, 144. Godscroft, *De Familia*, 78–80.

19 *CSP Scot*, ix, 631. J. Wormald, *Community*, 32–3.
20 *APS*, ii, 346, 461; iii, 462. *CSP Scot*, viii, 45; xiii, pt 1, 189. *L & P. Hen VIII*, xvii, 1143; xx, pt 1, 244. *RPC*, i, 282.
21 *CBP*, i, 166. *HMC*, Salisbury, iii, 295.
22 *Hamilton Papers*, ii, 745. *RPC*, iv, 783–4. C. H. Hunter Blair, 'Scottish Borderers of the Sixteenth Century', *HBNC*, xxvii (1932–4), 90–4, incorrectly puts the Youngs, Davidsons, Pringles, Taits and Burns in the East March instead of the Middle March and the Rutherfords in Liddesdale instead of the Middle March. See ch. ii.
23 52 acres are equivalent to 21.05 hectares.
24 *RPC*, vi, 186, 604.
25 This table is based on Meikle, 'Thesis', ch. i. app.
26 C. Thornton-Kennedy, *Bonnet Lairds* (Montrose, 1972), 11–12. H. Fenwick, *Scottish Baronial Houses* (London, 1986), 96.
27 *RMS*, v, 1817.
28 NAS CC8/8/14 fo. 236. *RMS*, iv, 1613, 2128.
29 Adapted from the table in C. Larner, *Enemies of God* (London, 1981), 45.
30 NAS GD267/31/24. *RMS*, iv, 1290, 2357.
31 NAS RD1/28 fo. 405. *Retours*, ii, Roxburgh, 23. A. Stevenson, 'Taxation in medieval Scotland', in P. G. McNeill & H.L. McQueen, eds. *Atlas of Scottish History* (Edinburgh, 1996), 298–305.
32 See ch. iv. M. H. B. Sanderson, *Scottish Rural Society in the Sixteenth Century* (Edinburgh, 1982), 78–105.
33 *Cf.* Sanderson, *Rural Society*, 78–9. C. Madden, 'The Feuing of Ettrick Forest', *IR*, xxvii (1976), 79–81.
34 Many documents in the Walter Mason Trust have 'in' and 'of ' derivations for the same lairds. For example Cuthbert Cranston of Thirlestane East Mains called himself 'in', whilst the notary present in 1550 called him 'of '. WMT, *Protocol Book of Robert Wedderop*, 24.
35 *RSS*, iii, 299, 2676; iv, 2905; v, 537; vii, 1624.
36 NAS CS7/45 fo. 253. GD55/607. RD1/15 fo. 166. SC62/2/1. *RMS*, iv, 1624. G. Mackenzie, *The Works of Sir George Mackenzie of Rosehaugh* (Edinburgh, 1716), ii, 583 who states that feuars who held directly from the crown were rendered noble.
37 NAS CC8/8/33 CC8/8/40 fo. 176. *RMS*, iv, 1689, 1738; v, 954, 2343; vi, 1674. *HMC*, Marchmont, 63, 65.
38 NAS CC8/8/6 fo. 75, CC8/8/25 fos 311–13. SC62/2/5. NRAS 859/112/2. *RMS*, v, 914. *RPC*, v, 586, 650.
39 NAS CC8/8/16 fos 345–7, CC8/8/26 fos 179–81. CS7/39 fo. 36. GD157/385. NRAS 859/13/7. *RMS*, iv, 887, 1344, 2929; v, 916, 1264–5. *RSS*, v, 3211, 3506. *SS*, xiv (1834), 289. *cf.* Mackenzie, *Works*, ii, 583 makes comments about goodmen from an eighteenth-century perspective, which are unhelpful for the very different world of sixteenth-century Scotland. W. C. Dickinson repeats this misinterpretation in 'Freehold in Scots Law', *Juridical Review* (1945), 140–1., though he does note one exception.
40 *L & P. Hen VIII*, xviii, pt 1, 12.
41 Based on all the families listed in Meikle, 'Thesis', ch. i. app. Sources are not as plentiful for 1540 as they are for 1570 and 1603.
42 NAS CS7/42 fo. 44. CS7/63/2 fo. 387. RD1/50 fo. 814. *RPC*, iii, 227–8, 387, 758, iv, 27–8, 596. Godscroft, *History*, 336. See note 94 below.

43 See ch. iv.

44 NAS RD1/24/1 fos 182, 183. *CBP*, ii, 218. Pitcairn, *Trials*, ii, 370–5, 378–81, 421, 445. *RPC*, ii, 117, 266–71.

45 Edinburgh University Library, Laing MS: La. Add1, fo. 14; La. Add2, fo. 69.

46 NAS CC8/8/7 fos 11–13. *CSP Scot*, xiii, pt 1, 299.

47 G. Mingay, *The Gentry*, 1–3.

48 J. Forster, *Pedigrees Recorded at the Herald's Visitation of Northumberland* (London, 1891), 108. *AA*, 4th ser, xxiii (1945), 108, xxiv (1946), 75–6, xxviii (1950), 72.

49 DPRW 1602. *L&P. Hen VIII*, xiv, pt 2, 7. J. Cooper, *Land, Men and Beliefs* (London, 1984), 62–77. J. Sharpe, *Early Modern England* (London, 1987), 153. K. Wrightson, 'The Social Order of Early Modern England: Three approaches', in Bonfield, Smith and Wrightson, eds. *The World We Have Gained* (Oxford, 1986), 177–202.

50 PRO SP15/4/30. *L & P. Hen VIII*, add. vol i, pt 1, 618, 828. *HMC*, Rutland, i, 38–9. *Sadler Papers*, ii, 19.

51 Based on Meikle, 'Thesis', ch. ii. app. All established families, younger son branches that were given land in perpetuity and new families to the area are listed.

52 This figure is incomplete owing to a lack of source material.

53 This figure includes those fortune hunters from outside the region who married local heiresses.

54 F. Heal & C. Holmes, *The Gentry in England and Wales 1500–1700* (Basingstoke, 1994), 40–42. *cf.* M. Havinden, 'The Increase and Distribution of the Resident Gentry of Somerset, 1500–1623', *Southern History*, xx-xxi (1998–99), 68–107.

55 B. G. Blackwood, *The Lancashire Gentry and the Great Rebellion, 1640–60* (Manchester, 1978). J. T. Cliff, *The Yorkshire Gentry* (London, 1969). J. E. Hollinshead, 'The gentry of south-west Lancashire in the later-sixteenth century', *NH* xxvi (1990), 82–99. J. S. Morrill, 'The Northern Gentry and the Great Rebellion', *NH*, xv (1979), 66–87. M. J. Sayer, *English Nobility* (Norwich, 1979), 3–11.

56 L. Stone, *An Open Elite?, England 1540–1880* (Oxford, 1984), 39, 48. E. Spring, *Law, Land and Family,* (Chapel Hill, 1993), 13–14 also disputes Stone's figures for Northumberland.

57 *Cf.* Stone, *Open Elite?*, 433–5. Bamburgh Abbey was part of the Canon's house, whilst Bamburgh Friars was a separate holding. Alnwick Abbey, Fenham and Edlingham are all omitted, though they were substantial houses and Longridge was near Berwick, not Rothbury.

58 *Cf.* Watts, *Border to Middle Shire*, 60–1, 68, 251–3. He records only one family leaving the county between 1586–1615, but table I.3 shows that there were more than this. Also the Selbies of Grindon were gentlemen, not yeomen.

59 To avoid repetition only the largest portion of an individual laird's lands have been considered, as many lairds held land in chief as well as from a monastery or in feu. The statistics are based on Meikle, 'thesis' ch. i. app and only include known landholding.

60 Excludes the Lords Home.

61 See table I.6.

62 Rae, *Scottish Frontier*, 7–8.

63 *APC*, xxvi, 560. *CSP Scot*, viii, 351; xiii, pt 2, 724. *HMC*, Salisbury, vii, 240.

64 Excludes the crown acquisition of the Percy estates 1537–57. That 54 families were Percy tenants shows how poor their loyalty was in the 1569 rising.

65 *L&P. Hen VIII*, xviii, pt 1, 761. The dependent gentry were the Collingwoods of Barton, Bewick, Branton, Broome Park, East Ditchburn, Shipley, Thornton, Thrunton, and Titlington.

66 *CSP For*, 1560–1, 1. *RMS*, v, 1382. *TA*, xiii, 348–81. Wormald, *Lords and Men*, 52–75.

67 NAS GD40/1/370/1, GD40/2/9/7, GD40/2/9/36, GD40/2/78.

68 NAS CC8/8/11 fos 100–01. *CSP Scot*, xii, pt 2, 526.

69 NLS Acc 7676/A/IV/12.

70 *RMS*, iv, 1709. Fraser, *Douglas*, iii, 213, 218, 219. *cf.* Wormald, *Lords and Men*, 176, 280, 284.

71 NAS CS6/26 fo. 129. GD267/31/24. NRAS 832/78. *HMC*, Home, 19, 20.

72 NRO ZHG1/14. R. A. Houlbrooke, *The English Family 1450–1700* (London, 1984), 40. D. Cressy, 'Kinship and Kin Interaction in Early Modern England', *P&P*, xiii (1987), 38–69.

73 PRO CP25/2/192/ 30 Eliz/ HIL. Raine, *North Durham*, 308–09.

74 Thomas Collingwood bought Little Ryle from Sir Cuthbert and Richard Forster of Tughall was given land by Sir John. PRO WARD7/88. NRO ZCE2/1.

75 *SS*, cxxi (1912), 60; xxxviii (1860), 174. *CBP*, ii, 1496.

76 DPRW Reg iv, fo. 100.

77 PRO STAC5 K6/40. WARD9/442.

78 *Selkirk Protocol Books*, 30–31, 38. *RPC*, iii, 737; iv, 194; vi, 797. Pitcairn, *Trials*, ii, 378. J. Anderson & W. Angus, eds. *Protocol Book of Sir William Corbet 1529–1555* (Scottish Record Society, vol xxxix, 1911), nos 52, 68.

79 NAS GD40/5/4/5. NRAS 859/8/2. *RMS*, v, 1862, 1962. *RPC*, iv, 414, 614. *HMC*, Milne-Home, 174. P. J. Murray, 'The Lay Administrators of Church Lands in the Fifteenth and Sixteenth Centuries', *SHR* lxxiv (1995), 26–44.

80 *RMS*, iii, 2649, 2784; iv, 489, 912, 2213; v, 916, 1265, 1889.

81 PRO CP25/2/192/23 & 24 Eliz/MICH. NRO ZHGI/14. *Laing Chrs*, 401.

82 PRO ADM75/101 (9 August 1593). NRO ZAN M15/c/3. *NCH*, xiv, 233.

83 PRO REQ2 270/67, REQ2 64/70. *Laing Chrs*, 1183. *SS*, xxxviii (1860), 159–60n.

84 NAS RD1/19 fo. 175. *RMS*, v, 353, 2107. *RSS*, v, 1268; viii, 1541.

85 PRO WARD7/13 fo. 46. C3/71/11. C142/158/19. *SS*, cxxi (1912), 59–61. *cf.* Spring, *Law, Land and Family*, 27–30.

86 NAS GD362/36/3, GD362/36/7/2.

87 BIHR PR 23a, fo. 122. *SS*, xxxviii (1860), 175. The horse was mentioned in Sir Thomas's will of 1590 as 'Gray Arthington' and was left to his brother-in-law, Sir Cuthbert Collingwood of Eslington.

88 William was originally betrothed to a local recusant, Katherine Collingwood of Eslington, but she married Lancelot Carnaby instead. PRO C142/432/134.

89 *CBP*, ii, 1496, 1497.

90 *CSPDom Add*, 1580–1625, 177.

91 Includes first, second and third marriages and the marriages of any children, when recorded. Again I do not agree with L. Stone's results, *cf. Open Elite?*, 39 (Table 2.2).

92 *Laing Chrs*, 1195, 1214.

93 *NCH*, xv, 429–32. *cf.* Forster, *Pedigrees*, 29, 110.

94 See note 42 above.

95 M. M. Meikle, 'Northumberland Divided; Anatomy of a sixteenth-century bloodfeud', *AA* 5th ser. xx (1992), 79–89.

96 J. Ferne, *The Blazon of Gentrie*, (London, 1586), 9–10.

97 See ch. v. NAS RD1/10 fo. 43. *RSS*, v, 1689. The Brounfields of Greenlawdean undoubtedly benefited from their marriage to a burgess's daughter who also happened to be a niece of the powerful clerk register, James MacGill of Nether Rankeillor.

98 Fortune Collingwood of Eslington married Henry Anderson of Newcastle. Jane Craster of Craster married Bartram Anderson, Ursula Buckton, widow of John Carr of Hetton married Henry Brandling and Margaret Selby of Twizel married Sir George Selby, a distant kinsman.

99 The other burgess/gentry families were Morton of Unthank, Ord of Longridge and Beadnell of Low Buston.

100 Cross-border marriages will be discussed in ch. viii.

101 Includes all known first, second and third marriages.

102 NRAS 482/Add/30/14.

103 PRO SP52/51/80. *CSP Scot*, x, 53. *Sadler Papers*, i, 636–7. C. Rogers, Estimate of the Scottish Nobility, *Grampian Club*, vi (1873). *cf.* Wormald, *Lords and Men*, 79 and 'Bloodfeud, Kindred and Government in Scotland', *P&P*, lxxxvii (1980), 67–8 dismisses the role of marriage in kinship too readily.

104 *CSP Scot*, vii, 26; x, 35. *CBP*, i, 70. See Meikle, 'Invisible Divide'.

105 NAS GD40/2/10/57. *CBP*, i, 574. *CSP Scot*, vii, 498; x, 507; xii, pt 1, 124. *HMC*, Salisbury, iii, 73.

106 See ch. vii.

107 J. Fergusson, *Lowland Lairds* (London, 1949), 14–15. Kinship was equally strong in the Scottish Gaidhealtachd.

108 *RPC*, v, 404.

109 *RPC*, vi, 387. For similar examples see *RPC*, iv, 69–70, 211, 789; vi, 406–07.

110 *RPC*, ii, 127–8.

111 NAS RD1/17 fo. 183, RD1/20/1/2 fo. 370, RD1/24/1 fo. 165, RD1/36 fo. 206, RD1/37 fo. 405. *RPC*, iv, 414, 810; v, 66, 681.

112 NAS CC8/8/2 fos 302–03. RD1/6 fo. 193, RD1/10 fo. 81, RD1/17 fo. 221, RD1/29 fo. 47, RD1/50 fo. 97.

113 NAS CC8/8/4 fo. 30, CC8/8/15 fos 44–5, CC8/8/27 fo. 123, CC8/8/29 fos 8–9, CC8/8/40 fos 42–4. *HMC*, Laing, i, 76. For more detail on loans see ch. iv.

114 *APS*, iii, 528. *RMS*, vi, 699. *RPC*, v, 114; vi, 73. Pitcairn, *Trials*, ii, 125–7. See note 84 above.

115 Godscroft, *History*, 338. David and John's father had married Alison Douglas, sister of the sixth earl of Angus and therefore an aunt of Regent Morton.

116 PRO SP52/27 fo. 51. Camden, *Britannia*, London 1586, 10.

117 NRAS 2177/2690. Godscroft, *History*, 295–6, 311. Calderwood, *History*, iii, 100–01.

118 *Sadler Papers*, ii, 114.

119 *Cf.* Wormald, *Lords and Men*, 176. There is a contemporary manuscript copy of Godscroft's family history in NAS GD267/2/4. The manuscript of the history of the Douglases has been rediscovered after a lengthy search instigated by the author. It had been lost since the 1920s, but is now available as NRAS 2177/2690.

120 NAS RD1/15 fo. 403. Godscroft, *De Familia*, 67; *History*, 52–3.

121 NAS RD1/17 fo. 183. *HMC*, Milne-Home, 540; Salisbury, ii, 303. Melville, *Memoirs*, 256

122 Godscroft, *History*, 344; *De Familia*, 72–4. *cf.* Wormald, *Lords and Men*, 77, 82 and Sanderson, *Rural Society*, 171.
123 NRAS 859/7/9. *HMC*, Home, 284. *RPC*, iv, 530–1. *RSS*, vii, 425, 429, 1228. *SP*, v, 609. Godscroft, *De Familia*, 68, 70–2.
124 *Bannatyne Misc*, i, 68. *HMC*, Fourth R, 537.
125 PRO SP52/57/37. Melville, *Memoirs*, 348. Home had children from his second marriage, post 1606.
126 *CSP Scot*, xiii, pt 1, 299, 837. The son of this Cowdenknowes marriage later became the third earl of Home, so Spott was indeed far-sighted.
127 NAS GD110/28. *RMS*, v, 1492, 1866.
128 NAS RD1/22 fo. 177. NRAS 859/6/1. *RSS*, vi, 1163. *HMC*, Home, 288, 316.
129 NAS RD1/44/2 fos 365–7. See ch. iii.
130 NAS GD40/9/3, GD40/15/2/2. RD1/7 fo. 131. *SP*, v, 50–2, 452; vii, 323–4. *Herald and Genealogist*, vii, 125–7.
131 *CSP Scot*, xi, 122. *HMC*, Laing, i, 33.
132 BL MS Cotton, Caligula, C, iii, fo. 120.
133 Edward Gray married Katherine Le Strange of Norfolk as he had been placed in the household of the duke of Norfolk by his father. PRO C142/141/31. NRO 650/B/1602, 1DE/1/162, 1DE/4/11. Hatfield MS C.P.Petitions 991.
134 These mortgages were often a cover up for evasion of wardship. See ch. iv. PRO CP25/2/192/19 Eliz/EAST & 35 Eliz/ HIL.
135 *SS*, ii (1835), 404; xxxviii (1860), 173n. M. Hicks argues that fifteenth-century kinship amongst the Nevilles was less widespread in 'Cement or Solvent? Kinship and Politics in Late Medieval England: The Case of the Nevilles', *History*, 83 (1998), 31–46.
136 PRO C142/208/190. NRO ZHG1/17. *CBP*, ii, 1434.
137 PRO C66/1238 m. 6–7. DPRW 1595 (Sir Thomas Gray). *CSPDom Add*, 1566–79, 321; 1580–1625, 118, 367–8. *CSP For*, 1560–1, 735; 1562, 289; 1564–5, 955, 1195. See note 85 above and ch. vi.
138 PRO SP59/33 fos 78–83. STAC8/261/20. NRO ZHG1/14. *CBP*, i, 556, 646; ii, 111. *Laing Chrs*, 627. *HMC*, Salisbury, iii, 290–1; iv, 188; v, 477.
139 PRO STAC5 L8/40 & S80/21. Morpeth Records Centre QS1/1 fo. 22.
140 DPRW 1589 (1) Thomas Forster. *SS*, ii (1835), 148, 326.
141 *SS*, ii (1835), 404. Catholic supervisors are noted in ch. vi. as vital evidence for post-Reformation Catholicism in Northumberland.
142 DPRW 1583, Reg vi, fos 300–01.
143 *SS*, xxxviii (1860), 234–5, 268n.
144 NAS CC8/8/4 fos 368–9. See note 72 above.
145 NAS CC8/8/1 fos 144–5, CC8/8/3 fo. 454. CS7/76 fo. 220.
146 NAS CC8/8/5 fos 80–1, CC8/8/6 fos 291–3, CC8/8/16 fos 345–7, CC8/8/20 fos 37–8.
147 For the economic problems associated with younger children see chs. iv. and v.
148 In Scotland only Kelso has a register pre-1603 and it starts in 1598. Of the Northumbrian parish records only Berwick and Holy Island were available.
149 See Meikle, 'Thesis', ch. i. app.
150 PRO C142/227/195. *APC*, vi, 254–5. *cf.* Meikle, 'Northumberland Divided', 86–7.
151 NAS CC8/8/33. *CSPFor*, 1566–8, 1289. *RSS*, vi, 2254.
152 NAS RD1/45 fo. 299. NRAS 859/5/7.
153 NAS CC8/8/13 fo. 368.

154 NAS RD1/24 fo. 48, RD1/45 fo. 153. SC62/2/1, SC62/2/5. *RMS,* v, 1862. *RSS,* vii, 1611; viii, 1254. *HMC,* Home, 34, 37.

155 This may be why C. H. Hunter Blair confuses tutors with guardians in *HBNC,* xxviii (1932–4), 91n.

156 NAS CC8/8/10 fos 131–3, CC8/8/12 fos 78–9, CC8/8/19 fos 159–161, CC8/8/3.

157 NAS GD150/1471/a & c. *HMC,* Milne-Home, 104. Godscroft, *De Familia,* 53–6, 63–4.

158 NRAS 859/5/7. *CSP For,* 1564–5, 1620. *HMC,* Home, 40.

159 *Selkirk Protocol Books,* 79, 81–82, 97. Primsideloch was also guardian of Helen Fawlaw, *RSS,* ii, 1375. *RMS,* iii, 1518.

160 NAS GD239/1/2, GD239/2/1/2, GD239/2/1/8. *Selkirk Protocol Books,* 118–19. *RMS,* iii, 1364, 2033. *RSS,* iii, 2330. They were still buying back land in 1550. *Protocol Book of Sir William Corbet,* no. 56.

161 NAS RD1/14 fo. 7. *RSS,* vii, 425. Godscroft, *History,* 357–8. Godscroft wrongly attributes the grant of the Haldane marriage to 1581. *RSS,* iii, 2132. See note 123 above. See also Meikle, 'Thesis', ch. i. app.

162 NAS RD1/20/2/2 fo. 89. SC62/2/2 (June 1542). *RPC,* iii, 299–300; iv, 676. *RSS,* v, 540; vii, 710, 714; viii, 1759.

163 H. E. Bell, *An Introduction to the History and Records of the Court of Wards and Liveries* (Cambridge, 1953), 69, 79. J. Hurstfield, *The Queen's Wards* (London, 1958), xv, 70, 80, 137–40, 157.

164 NRO ZSW1/193. ZSW1/194.

165 *SS,* ii (1835), 408, xxxviii (1860), 135, cxii (1906), 32. It was not just the gentry who looked for this type of patronage. Richard Strother a yeoman of Coldmartin left his heir to his 'master' Sir Thomas Gray of Chillingham and his three other sons to Ralph, Edward and Arthur Gray, brothers of Sir Thomas.

166 DPRW 1589 (1). *SS,* xxxviii (1860), 160–1.

167 DPRW 1593. *SS,* xxxviii (1860), 218–19.

168 DPRW 1595. *SS,* xxxviii (1860), 256–8; cxii (1906), 95n.

169 DPRW 1587 (3), 1588 (1).

170 PRO E134/26 & 27 Eliz/MICH 20. *SS,* xxxviii (1860), 48–9.

171 S. Smith-Bannister, *Names and Naming Patterns in England 1538–1700* (Oxford, 1997).

172 DPRW 1589 (2). *SS,* xxxviii (1860), 49.

173 DDR iii 5, unfoliated (9 July 1596). His mother was Janet Buickes.

174 *Cf.* Ferne, *Blazon,* 282–7. H. Swinburne, *A Treatise of Testaments and Last Wills, 1591* (London, 1743), 368, 373.

175 PRO CP25/2/192/34 & 35 Eliz/MICH. *Laing Chrs,* 1194. M. M. Meikle, 'A Godly Rogue; The Career of Sir John Forster, an Elizabethan Border Warden', *NH* xxviii (1992), 136–7.

176 NRO Delaval MS/Waterford Chrs 97.

177 *SS,* cxlii (1929), 2. *CBP,* ii, 1433. Meikle, 'Thesis', ch. ii. app.

178 *RMS,* iii, 2416, 2900; v, 477, 924. Meikle, 'Thesis', ch. i. app.

2

The Eastern Border Lairds:
Their Administration and Politics

I. A Rise of the Lairds?

The Eastern Scottish Borders were governed at local, national and international levels. Lairds were involved with these offices according to their power, status and allies, but there can be no doubt that they were the backbone of local administration. The political strengths of the surname chiefs may have appeared independent in 1540, yet from the mid-sixteenth century onwards faction and court politics were never far away. Lairds seeking advancement dabbled with allegiances to major courtiers and to the crown itself, with mixed results for their locality. They never let a major politician dominate them for long, but some kin loyalties were stretched to breaking point by these figures and their factions. By 1600 there had been a remarkable turnaround as Border lairds at court rather than outsider nobility were then directing local policy. This was partly due to James VI's careful establishment of a safety net of local Border lairds, but it owed much to the tenacity of these lairds and their younger sons. Like other Scottish lairds, they never missed an opportunity for political advancement in the fast-changing decades of the later-sixteenth century. Any patronage offered was readily accepted and the rise of some lairds was spectacular, challenging previously-held opinion that the Borders were a backwater. Whether these changes were consciously British is debatable, for only a handful would succeed in England after 1603. None the less, when James VI and I went south he knew that there were many reliable lairds in this region to keep good order and administer justice.

II. The Administration

i. Domestic office
The principal domestic officer was the sheriff, though his duties differed from that of English sheriffs in several ways. In some shires the office had become unintentionally hereditary, unlike the annual appointments system in England, and was now dominated by powerful local families. Scottish sheriffs appointed lesser laird kinsmen as their deputes and they performed most of the everyday administration such as serving writs or making arrests. As the Eastern Scottish Borders did not have any working Justices of the

Peace before 1603, sheriff deputes had wider powers than English deputies. Adam and John Cockburn, younger sons of Langton and William Trotter of Falwoodshiel, were all noted as able sheriff deputes. They would have been assisted by sheriff's officers and clerks when making arrests or poinding goods.[1] The sheriff or his deputes presided over sheriff courts where the majority of jurors were lairds. They were supervised by justiciars on itinerant justice ayres to hear serious criminal cases and appeals. The justiciar could be the warden of the March for Lord Home held a justice court in the Merse in 1595 assisted by Home of Wedderburn and Home of Ayton. A justiciar could also be specially commissioned, such as Sir James Home of Cowdenknowes in 1588. The only limitation on a sheriff's power were baronies and regalities. These were private jurisdictions that neither he nor his officers could officially enter.[2]

The shrievalty of Berwickshire was normally held in conjunction with the office of bailie of Lauderdale, but political upheavals interfered with these posts. They went from the Hepburn earls of Bothwell to the fifth Lord Home in 1567 by forfeiture. Then in 1573 Home forfeited them to the eighth earl of Angus, who lost them in 1581. After this the offices were probably split up as the sixth Lord Home became sheriff, whilst the fifth earl of Bothwell became bailie of Lauderdale. Bothwell resigned his office to Maitland of Thirlestane in 1587. Home also lost his office to the duke of Lennox during 1591–92 when he was absent from Scotland, though he was reinstated as sheriff upon his return. Another exile in 1599–1600 saw Sir George Home of Spott as temporary sheriff. The importance of these offices to the government probably lies behind all these changes, for they were never left vacant and justice was maintained. By contrast, the shrievalty of Roxburghshire had been held by the Douglases of Cavers as a hereditary office since the fifteenth century.[3]

The sheriff courts of Roxburghshire were usually held at Jedburgh. Some diet books survive from the sixteenth century, showing that most of the transactions were financial and heard before one of the deputes. The sheriff usually sat for more important matters such as *Inquisitionum Retornatarum*, the Scottish equivalent of an *Inquisition Post Mortem*. There are no surviving records of the Berwickshire sheriff courts and bailie courts of Lauderdale, but obscure references to these courts confirm that they were held at Langton Church, the mercat cross of Duns and at Lauder's Courthouse or mercat cross.[4] There were few complaints about the Scottish sheriffs before 1600, unlike the much berated Northumbrian shrievalty. The Scots may have submitted their accounts to the Exchequer on a more regular basis than the English sheriffs and thus avoided the wrath of central authority. Scottish sheriffs were latterly accused of negligence and discriminating in favour of their kinsmen, but this was only to be expected in a community dominated by kinship.[5] Kinship could, of course, work both for and against the office, but in the Borders the system worked well.

Once the heir of a tenant-in-chief had procured a Chancery writ to hold an *Inquisitionum Retornatarum* it was the sheriff who convened it. There was no equivalent of the English Court of Wards in Scotland and neither were there feodaries or escheators (who usually began the process of an *Inquisition Post Mortem* in England). As this was the heir's responsibility in Scotland the speed of retours varied. For instance, Sir Robert Ker of Cessford, John Haliburton of Mertoun and John Edgar of Wedderlie all obtained the necessary writs within months of their fathers' deaths, but William Linlithgow of Drygrange and Andrew Ker of Newhall delayed for over thirty years.[6] This was perhaps indicative of the value of the lands concerned as Cessford and Mertoun had lands of greater worth than Drygrange or Newhall. For the inquest the sheriff summoned a jury of fifteen men, most of whom were lairds. They then declared under oath that the claimant was rightful heir to the lands in question. Their decision was then 'retoured' back to Chancery as either a general retour establishing the claim only, or a special retour listing the lands and their valuation. Lairds who were not tenants-in-chief were infeft of their lands by their feudal superior. They would have received a precept of *clare constat,* a specialised sasine that recognised the grantee as heir. Retours are a good source for identifying landed men as the juries are listed. A few jurors were non-resident, such as Richard Maitland of Lethington, though the majority were neighbours, kin and friends of the deceased.[7] Lairds were also called upon by the sheriff to act as jurors in land disputes and criminal cases.[8]

Lesser lairds were probably content to act as jurors, but greater lairds were more ambitious and sought parliamentary representation. Before 1587 lairds who were already barons had an automatic right to be summoned to parliament, though they did not necessarily attend every sitting. Lairds who were also commendators of religious houses were summoned as spiritual lords. Other lairds were effectively denied representation, but at the exceptional 1560 parliament, known as the Reformation Parliament, over 160 lairds lobbied for a right to participate. Other lairds sporadically attended the less powerful conventions of estates that met more often than parliament. Lairds were clearly an ascendant social group, but they had to wait until an 1587 Act of Parliament that revived a lapsed 1428 statute. This allowed each county to convene freeholders and elect two parliamentary or shire commissioners.[9] Even this emancipation was not far-reaching as parliaments sat intermittently and shire elections were infrequent. The property qualification of forty shillings of old extent for the freeholders still excluded many feuars, lesser lairds and bonnet lairds.[10] Whether they were personally bothered by this is uncertain, but the enfranchisement of some had the disadvantage of increased taxation for all lairds and this was unpopular. It led to accusations that representation had been bought rather than freely granted.[11] None the less records show that some Eastern Border greater lairds did attend both conventions and parliaments after 1587 as commissioners for small barons.[12]

Shire commissioners were summoned individually to parliament in the tradition of the barons and Lords of Parliament. For example, the Homes of Cowdenknowes attended previous parliaments as barons of Earlston and the Swintons of that Ilk came as barons of Cranshaws. It is not clear if all the eligible barons were summoned to every Parliament as they were not always present. They may have been unable to attend or perhaps could not afford to, as Ellem of Butterdean and Redpath of Greenlaw were barons of slender means.[13] The Lords Home were summoned to parliament as Lords of Parliament and both the fifth and sixth Lords were elected as one of the Lords of the Articles. The Committee of the Articles became increasingly important as it prepared all parliamentary business. Lairds called to parliament, whether as barons or shire commissioners, were from the dominant local families of their shires. In 1594 Berwickshire was represented by the Homes of Cowdenknowes, Huttonhall, Manderston and Wedderburn. Roxburghshire was represented largely by lairds from East Teviotdale, such as the Kers of Cessford and Littledean, MacDougal of Makerstoun and Douglas of Bonjedward, with Scott of Buccleuch the sole member from West Teviotdale. There were various offices attached to parliament, which are not well documented in the Eastern Borders. They were held by lairds such as George Home of Wedderburn as collector of taxes of the small barons in 1588. Other commissioners were appointed against the Armada in 1588, against Jesuits in 1588 and 1590, or as commissioners for wappinshaws.[14]

Many lairds held important local franchises that were relatively detached from central government. Chief amongst these local positions were barons who could attend parliament, but whose role in the locality was more fundamental to rural society. Originally a baron had the right to hold a court within his barony to settle civil disputes and try cases of theft and slaughter without the sheriff's interference. The advancing importance of the Court of Session rather sapped these powers from the barons, so their baron courts' function was mostly financial with tenants paying their rent and renewing leases. Occasional property disputes within the barony were also settled. Baron courts were convened at a 'head' place within the barony several times a year and were thus called head courts. At Ancrum and Jedburgh there were three head courts a year.[15] The barons of the Eastern Borders were a mixture of lairds and non-resident nobility. Their jurisdictions varied in geographical size from regalities, which were in effect large baronies such as Jedforest, to the tiny barony of Butterdean. There were twenty-six baronies and one regality in Berwickshire and thirty-one jurisdictions in the parts of Roxburghshire that encompassed the Eastern Borders, consisting of twenty-nine baronies and two regalities.

TABLE 2.1. BERWICKSHIRE JURISDICTIONS

Name	Jurisdiction	Barons
Bunkle and Preston	Regality	Earls of Angus
Cockburnspath	Barony	Douglases
Dryburgh	Barony	Erskines
Foulden	Barony	Ramsays of Dalhousie
Gordon	Barony	Earls of Huntly
Haliburton	Barony	Lord Haliburton, then divided into thirds for Lord Ruthven, Lord Home and Ker of Faldonside
Hutton	Barony	Logans of Restalrig and Ogilvies of Dunlugus
Lambden	Barony	(as Haliburton)
Mordington	Barony	Douglases
Whitsome	Barony	Earls of Bothwell
Blackadder	Barony	Homes
Coldingham	Barony	Homes (1570–82, 1592–1603)
Duns	Barony	Homes
Earlston	Barony	Homes
Eyemouth	Barony	Homes
Hilton	Barony	Homes
Hume	Barony	Homes
Horndean	Barony	Homes
Ladykirk	Barony	Homes
Redbraes (Polwarth)	Barony	Homes
Blythe	Barony	Maitland of Thirlestane
Boon	Barony	Cranston of Corsbie
Butterdean	Barony	Ellem of Butterdean
Cranshaws	Barony	Swinton of that Ilk
Edington	Barony	Edington of that Ilk, then sold to Ramsay of Dalhousie
Greenlaw-Redpath	Barony	Redpath of Greenlaw, then sold to Sir George Home of Spott
Langton	Barony	Cockburn of Langton

Greater lairds dominated these jurisdictions, though they were not always resident in the locality. Of the twenty-seven jurisdictions in Berwickshire ten belonged to non-residents, another ten baronies belonged to the Homes and the remaining seven baronies were held by independent lairds. In Roxburghshire the thirty-one jurisdictions were divided into four baronies belonging to the church, nine and a half to non-residents and nine to the Kers. The Rutherfords held another five and a half baronies, which

left three independent baronies. Another barony that belonged to an
Eastern Border laird was Galashiels in Selkirkshire with Pringle of Galashiels as the baron.[16]

TABLE 2.2. EAST ROXBURGHSHIRE JURISDICTIONS

Name	Type of jurisdiction	Barons
Ancrum and Lilliesleaf	Barony	Archdiocese of Glasgow
Ulston	Barony	Jedburgh Abbey
Bowden	Barony	Melrose Abbey
Melrose	Barony	Melrose Abbey
Bonjedward	Barony	Earls of Angus
Broxfield	Barony	Lords Home
Hownam	Barony	Half Lords Home and half Rutherfords
Ednam	Barony	Edmonstons of that Ilk
Jedforest	Regality	Earls of Angus
Linton	Barony	Lords Somerville
Longnewton	Barony	Douglases
Maxwell	Barony	Lords Maxwell
Stitchill	Barony	Gordon of Lochinver
Yetholm	Barony	Earls of Bothwell
Cessford	Barony	Kers
Ferniehirst	Barony	Kers
Kelso	Regality	Kers/commendators of the Abbey
Maxton	Barony	Kers
Old Roxburgh (incorporated into Cessford)	Barony	Kers
Ormiston (after 1567)	Barony	Kers
Oxnam	Barony	Kers
Primside	Barony	Kers
Roxburgh	Barony	Kers
Edgerston	Barony	Rutherfords
Grubbit	Barony	Rutherfords
Scraesburgh	Barony	Rutherfords
Rutherford	Barony	Rutherfords
Makerstoun	Barony	MacDougal of Makerstoun
Riddell	Barony	Riddall of that Ilk
Smailholm	Barony	Cranston of that Ilk

Baronies as jurisdictions were never static. They could simply lapse, be newly created or become amalgamated with older ones. The nineteen and a half baronies held by non-resident men did not create unwelcome interference in the local politics as they appointed local lairds to be their bailies. A bailie could deputise at all times for the baron and was therefore a very important local officer. Bailies were similarly appointed to oversee regalities, monastic lands and crown lands. The appointees varied from non-landed men to lesser and greater lairds depending upon the size of the jurisdiction. For instance the sixth Lord Home was a bailie of Coldstream and Coldingham priories, yet he employed Mark Home of Hardiesmill as his bailie of Hume. The Homes were bailies for several of the non-resident barons, such as David Home of Ninewells (Hutton) and Patrick Home of Polwarth (Bunkle and Preston). In Roxburghshire the Kers of Cessford were bailies of Ancrum, Kelso and Lilliesleaf and the Kers of Ferniehirst were hereditary bailies of Jedforest. Before the Scottish monasteries were dissolved Robert French of Thornydykes and Robert Dickson of Hassington Mains were recorded as bailies to Dryburgh Abbey and Eccles Priory respectively.[17]

Barony records for the Eastern Borders are scarce, but precepts of sasine are an excellent source for identifying bailies. Their duties encompassed collecting rents, delivering sasines and holding the barony courts in the absence of the baron. A bailie was therefore a skilled administrator, though mundane duties in the barony would have been carried out by a clerk or sergeant. The obligations of the Kers of Cessford as bailies of the regality (Abbey) of Kelso were more bizarre than mundane. In 1593 Presbyterian zeal impacted upon their duties for these included enforcement of church attendance, reporting fornicators and banning harlots, passion plays, bonfires and religious feasts from the regality. They were also to fine absentees from kirk session meetings and make sure that the grass in the kirkyard was mown and not eaten by livestock. All this was in addition to the more usual task of collecting rents and enforcing legislation about middings, paving and defence. The influence of the zealous post-Reformation commendator (Maitland of Thirlestane) was clearly dominating this regality in a stronger way than the medieval abbey did.[18]

Barony and regality court juries had some lairds as jurors, but the proportion of unlanded men was far higher in these courts as they dealt with very localised matters. An exception to this occurred at the Jedforest court in 1554, when all the jurors were non-local, to settle a property feud between Ker of Ferniehirst as hereditary bailie and the earl of Angus as lord of the regality. There was an uneasy working relationship between the Kers and Angus over this jurisdiction as trouble flared on many occasions, including a ban being imposed on Ker holding the court in 1566. The Oxnam barony court was more normally administered as it had a mixture of lairds and small tenants on its jury in 1602.[19] The barony court of Coldingham met in the parish church. As bailie, Lord Home dealt with small local matters such as the tenants of Coldingham and Eyemouth's evading the mill of William Home of Prenderguest and the annual riding of the barony's common grazing bounds. As the barony was geographically widespread, Home had two deputy bailies to assist him. In 1583 they were his kinsmen, Alexander Home of Huttonhall and David Home of Nine-wells.[20]

The powers of the bailies were localised, yet they were an indisputable asset to local land administration and alongside sheriff deputes could justifiably be called the spine of local government. With their apparent enthusiasm for administration these lairds may have sought participation in the government of the reformed church by administering poor relief or enforcing discipline through kirk sessions. Unfortunately no kirk session records are extant in the Eastern Borders before 1622 and the seventeenth century records reveal no participation by the lairds. The only exception is the Kers of Cessford and their aforementioned duties at Kelso. In pre-Reformation times the election of James Home, a younger son of Alexander Home of Carolside, to succeed his father as clerk of the parish of Earlston in 1549 is intriguing. However it is probably not indicative of general laird interest in this parish office.[21]

Lairds were involved with the administration of some burghs with the assistance of central government. For instance the office of the provost of Jedburgh was contested by local lairds in the later-sixteenth century, with the backing of central factions. Friction arose as Jedburgh rejected a provost imposed on them through crown favour or court faction. The locally dominant family of Rutherford were frequently elected to the office of provost of Jedburgh, such as Adam (1541–5), Nicol of Hundalee (1559–65), Richard (1569–81) and William (1592).[22] There were tensions within the Rutherford kindred as the burgesses, many of whom were Rutherfords, unsuccessfully opposed Nicol Rutherford of Hundalee's appointment in 1559. When he later demanded that a kinsman be elected to replace him in 1565 they refused to comply. Hundalee's nominee Richard Rutherford was later elected in 1569, but the Rutherfords' support for the disgraced earl of Angus cost them this office in 1581. It was given to Sir Thomas Ker of Ferniehirst by the earl of Lennox, despite objections from the 155 voting burgesses. The Rutherfords were bound to Ferniehirst in manrent as he was a powerful local landholder, but this did not endear him to the Jedburgh burgesses. He remained in office until his fall from grace in 1585. This political appointment was typical of the 1580s when many burghs were being subjected to central interference on an unprecedented scale. This was invariably in favour of a court-connected local laird.[23]

At Jedburgh there was a short truce between the burgesses and central government until 1590 when the Kers of Cessford entered their claim to the provostry. There is some confusion about this as the Kers of Cessford had not previously held this office, contrary to the claims made by Archbishop

Spottiswoode and others. Nor was the office held by William Ker of Ancrum, whose murder in 1590 was part of an entirely different feud.[24] James VI wanted to bolster William Ker of Cessford's power base as warden of the Middle March by giving him the office. The Rutherfords, remembering their kinship obligations to Cessford's rival Ker of Ferniehirst, disregarded this appointment and elected William Rutherford as provost. For once the burgh was victorious as Cessford was discredited by his son's slaying of Ancrum. William Rutherford remained in office and was sheltered by an exemption granted to Ferniehirst and his kindred from Cessford's jurisdiction of the Middle March. The king sought revenge for this rejection in 1592 by appointing the duke of Lennox as provost, followed by Walter Ker of Littledean in 1593. He exploited the outlawing of the Rutherfords and Kers of Ferniehirst for associating with the rebel earl of Bothwell during these years. By 1603 the situation had seemingly reverted to a Rutherford/ Ferniehirst candidate as Robert Ker of Ancrum was provost. The laird provosts of the later sixteenth century sought these offices for power and local prestige, therefore they would have delegated most of their routine duties to a deputy provost such as David Moscrop, deputy provost of Jedburgh in 1586.[25]

Aside from the Border burghs, lairds such as the Homes and their younger sons also proved adept at gaining court favour. Sir George Home of Spott, a younger son of Manderston, rose from stabler in 1585 to treasurer in 1600. Another successful younger son, Alexander Home of North Berwick, provost of Edinburgh, was ambassador to England in 1567, 1580 and 1596 and a gentleman of the bedchamber in 1580. Others, such as William Home of Bassendean (lieutenant of the King's Guard) and William Home of Whitelaw (captain of the King's Guard and master stabler) had to be content with smaller court offices. Greater lairds such as the Homes of Cowdenknowes, Manderston elder and younger and Ker of Cessford received prestigious appointments as gentlemen of the bedchamber, or captains of royal castles, such as Home of Cowdenknowes at Edinburgh (1585) and Home of Polwarth at Tantallon (1592–5). The sixth Lord Home gained many offices such as grand master stabler and captain of the King's personal guard, when he abandoned allegiance to the treacherous earl of Bothwell in the early 1590s. However none of these court offices was hereditary or held for any length of time. The only exception to this was the office of Usher of the White Rod held by the Cockburns of Langton since the late-fourteenth century.[26] Many high officeholders were politically advantaged and received remuneration, but they had to tread carefully.

The financial post of comptroller of the royal household should have been profitable to Sir George Home of Wedderburn. However, during his 1597–9 appointment there were repeated claims that he was not furnishing the royal household adequately. Wedderburn blamed a poor return on the king's lands, devaluation of the coinage, unpaid customs and even the expense of

the king's horses. In April 1599 he was deprived of the office for incompe-
tence and was made surety of a wadset of crown lands necessary to make up
the shortfall in income. Wedderburn was later cleared of all charges against
him and even received a £9,000 Scots refund. He had been the victim of
inflation and corruption amongst other royal officials like the king's
brewster who took more of the king's grain than he should.[27] Wedderburn
was forgiven, though he never received any other court office as his
reputation had been tarnished. The shame he felt must have been pronounced as his brother, Godscroft, makes no mention of this unfortunate
episode in the family history.

Court offices tended to draw lairds away from their locality, though their
influence persisted there and was undoubtedly increased by the acquisition
of high office. These lairds were fortunate that they could rely on the support
of fellow lesser lairds who dominated the local administration. There was,
however, another source of office for the lairds to exploit in the administration of the Borders.

ii. Border office

Scottish Border administration has been extensively researched by Ian Rae,
but not from the point of view of individual lairds. Sixteenth-century
wardens were local greater lairds appointed annually, unlike the English
wardens who were rarely local and held office for long periods. Scottish
wardenships appeared to be hereditary as the office was dominated by
Maxwells, Kers and Homes, but this was misleading. The English disapproved of Scottish wardens believing them 'extraordinarilye adicted to
parcialities, favoure theire blood tenantes and followers'.[28] It was true that
kinship played an important part in all Scottish office-holding, but this
remark was not applicable to the Scottish East March where the Homes kept
good order in comparison with the Middle and West Marches. The wardens
of the Middle March were guilty of partiality as the Kers of Cessford and
Ferniehirst allowed their personal feud to dominate the office. In 1564
Cessford complained that Ferniehirst and his allies would not co-operate
with him as warden. During 1570–73 Ferniehirst falsely claimed to be
warden of the Middle March, though in 1584 he was exempted from
Cessford's jurisdiction owing to political favour from the powerful earl
of Arran.[29] The complexity of this wardenship continued with another
exemption granted to Ferniehirst in 1590–91 and the practical division of
Teviotdale between the two sides in 1593–95 and 1600–03. A division like
this had previously occurred in 1576–78 along the Roman road, Dere Street,
as part of an experiment by Regent Morton to favour his kinsman Douglas
of Bonjedward.[30] These changes must have confused the English wardens,
who disliked dealing with two Middle March wardens and thus complained
with some justification about partiality.

Wardens were directly answerable to the crown unless there was an appointed lieutenant, in which case the wardens reported to him. Lieutenants were latterly less important as James VI appointed the earl of Angus lieutenant of only the Middle and West Marches in 1599. When Cessford objected Angus was left with only the West March.[31] The office of warden was prestigious, yet poorly funded and burdensome. Wardens, like sheriffs and bailies, were assisted by deputies, clerks and sergeants. As well as dealing with international Border law they were expected to be justiciars within their Marches, exercising the power of a justice ayre in their warden courts. The fifth and sixth Lords Home conveniently combined the offices of East March warden and sheriff of Berwickshire.[32] Typical duties included holding regular warden courts, Border meetings or 'days of truce' with opposite wardens and providing escorts for strangers travelling through their Marches. Deputy wardens were mostly lairds and kinsmen of the warden. Information about deputies is scarce as no formal records of warden courts survive. Nevertheless it is known that the sixth Lord Home employed Alexander Home of Huttonhall from 1582–94 and Home of Manderston in 1598 and 1599–1600 during Home's absences. In the Middle March Sir Robert Ker had Andrew Ker of Primsideloch as a deputy and he likewise was warden during Cessford's absence in 1602.

The Scottish Borders were not as militarised as the English Borders, so the only military positions open to the lairds were at court or overseas with the Scots Guard of the kings of France. The lairds were much closer to their court than the Northumbrian gentry and this made offices more available. The only other Border office that concerned the lairds were Border commissions that examined Border bills and tried to secure redress of grievances on a much grander scale than a warden's meeting. Although they were really international meetings of great importance, the local knowledge of lairds and gentlemen allowed them representation on these commissions.[33] The Kers of Cessford, Faldonside, and Ferniehirst along with the Homes of Cowdenknowes, Huttonhall and Wedderburn were all members of these commissions in the second half of the sixteenth century. There were unsubstantiated reports that they were biased in favour of their kinsmen, though these are somewhat improbable as Home of Wedderburn was accused of being both pro-and anti-Cessford within a three-month period. Overall, they appear to have been efficient commissioners.[34] Most appointments, whether domestic or Border, were made for complex political reasons that need explanation.

III. The Political Scene

Laird politics were rarely stable as there was little political continuity in Scotland between 1540 and 1603. Every decade saw differing politics and faction fights in which many lairds were devious enough to play one faction against another for personal interests, or as part of feuds. In the 1540s and

1550s pro-English and pro-French factions split the laird communities, whilst in the 1560s court politics began to filter into the locality and remained there for the remaining decades of the century. Interference by courtiers enabled a rise of some lairds at the expense of traditional leaders like the Lords Home, just as the gentry in north Northumberland rose at the expense of the earls of Northumberland. There was a turnaround in the 1590s and 1600–03 when the Border lairds and their kinsmen became influential courtiers themselves and thus influenced local politics in their own areas. Localised political power was synonymous with Lord Home and the Home lairds in the Merse and with the Kers of Cessford and Ferniehirst in Teviotdale and Jedforest. Their control was periodically challenged by non-resident noblemen such as Maitland in Lauderdale, Bothwell in the Merse and Angus in Teviotdale, but the lairds never failed to respond to these challenges and would ultimately remain in overall control of the Eastern Borders.

i. The 1540s

International relations between Scotland, England and France dominated local politics in the 1540s. This decade of 'rough wooing' centred around protracted negotiations, bribery, threats, warfare and the garrisoning of Southern Scotland by English imperialist soldiers to force the marriage of the infant Mary, Queen of Scots, to Prince Edward of England. The Border lairds were always in the front line of Anglo-Scottish warfare and they naturally turned this situation to their advantage by being Borderers first rather than Scots, English or even British. The desperate English offered lairds money in return for their allegiance during the wooing. This treasonable practice was known as 'assuring' to England, for which the Scot had to 'wear a red cross sewed to his coat', pay his rent to England and assist their soldiers' attacks on non-assured men.[35] This was clearly English imperialism at work rather than a 'British' alliance, but devious lairds exploited every move, including the implied commitment to help the spread of Protestantism in an officially Catholic country. How convincing the Border lairds were in this pursuit is questionable as they were 'feigning themselves favourers of the word of God more for . . . pleasour than for Godes sake'.[36]

Without bribery or intimidation it is doubtful if belligerent lairds would have assured to their traditional enemy. In October 1541 several young Kers had raided into England 'minding to provoke war between the realms', but by 1544 they were assuring.[37] The lure of money must have been persuasive, yet the persistent and brutal harrying of those who had not capitulated would have pushed many into assuring or fleeing. There was also the temptation to use English forces to attack feud rivals, like the Kers against the non-assured Scotts. The Kers as true Borderers mischievously gave allegiance to both England and Scotland simultaneously. Sir Andrew Ker of Ferniehirst was 'so crafty an old fox and beareth himself so uprightly that it is hard to know unto what party he bendeth.'[38] Ker of Littledean secretly communicated with England while attending the Scottish court in July 1543, without revealing his true allegiance. George Ker of Linton was awarded the escheats of several assurers by the Scottish government who thought him loyal, though he too had assured to England. The Pringles were reported to be ready to assure at this time, but as one of their kinsmen was under sentence of death in England they had to capitulate. Sandy Pringle, a younger son of the laird of Torwoodlee, saved his kinsman by offering himself as a spy to the English. They found Sandy to be a trusted servant who went further than they anticipated by genuinely betraying Scottish activities throughout the 1540s. He was the only real turncoat of the laird communities whose outright betrayal of the Scots led to English denization and fortuitous property grants, but social isolation from Scotland.[39]

There is no doubting the ferocity of these times and the dangers posed by English artillery. In June 1544, when the earl of Hertford attacked Jedburgh, the Rutherfords of Hunthill and Hundalee submitted as the burgh was their stronghold. In July Ker of Ferniehirst and his son were captured and probably forced to assure as Ker left his son as a hostage. By November the Kers of Cessford and Primsideloch, Douglas of Bonjedward and Kirkton of Stewartfield were also being paid for assuring, but this money dried up in February 1545. The lairds naturally complained and were 'like to revolt to the Scottish faction unless aid be the rather provided for them'. They duly reneged on their obligations of assurance and assisted the Scottish victory at Ancrum Moor in March 1545.[40] The devastation inflicted by Hertford's invasion in September 1545 led these lairds to re-assure, but they were loath to assist Hertford as 'the Borderers will not most willingly burn their neighbours'. Janus-like they attended the Scottish parliament in October 1545, but they were cannily keeping their options open.[41] However the English garrisons planted in the Scottish Borders after the Hertford raids ensured that lairds kept their assurance. Resident English soldiers were, after all, more threatening than raiding parties from across the Border. The Kers, Rutherfords and Pringles therefore remained assured until 1549, though they were subsequently pardoned for their treasonable activity.[42]

The lairds of the Merse behaved rather differently from those of Teviot-dale and Jedforest. The Home lairds bravely followed Lord Home's loyalty to Scotland (and France), by refusing to assure to England throughout the 1540s, with Home of West Reston being the only exception. Other Merse lairds like the Rentons of Billie chose to flee rather than face trouble, yet some did assure.[43] The pressures to assure were the same as in Teviotdale, but English raids were more persistent here owing to the Homes' refusal. This defiance of the Home kindred led to a specific attack against Lord Home in September 1543, 'considering his malice to the King and realm.' An erroneous report in October 1543 stated that the master of Home along with the Homes of Wedderburn, Cowdenknowes, Ayton and Blackadder had assured. This was only wishful thinking as none of these lairds would ever assure, even in the wake of atrocities committed by Hertford in 1544 and 1545. Scott of Buccleuch held a similar resolve and refused to assure even 'if all Tividall were brent in ashes to the bottom of Hell.' It should be remembered, however, that loyal Scots as well as the assured Scots received remuneration. The Homes of Polwarth, for example, had the placement of one of their daughters as prioress of North Berwick confirmed and this led to many advantageous land grants.[44]

The Homes' situation appeared grave by the autumn of 1547 when it seemed that French help was never coming. Even Dame Mariota Haliburton, Lady Home, seems to have given a kind of assurance in person to Protector Somerset, formerly the earl of Hertford, without her husband's knowledge. Lady Home held out for as long as possible and bravely negotiated in person with Somerset, but with her husband injured and her son and heir, Alexander, in English captivity she had little bargaining power. Hume was therefore handed over without bloodshed on 22 September, but Lady Home knew that she had betrayed her lord. She wrote 'I dare not let my lord my husband see your last writing about the rendering of Home and the pledges'. Shortly afterwards the Homes were forced to retreat to their East Lothian properties to await help from France. When French forces arrived in 1548 they helped them reconquer southern Scotland, including Hume Castle. The Homes received gifts of escheats and pensions from the French crown for their efforts, but much of this would have been used for repairing damaged property and replacing destroyed crops.[45] Still, in the face of adversity the Homes' patriotism to Scotland and the Borders was courageous.

Other Merse lairds lacked the Homes' fortitude. Alexander Cockburn of Caldra assured, but promptly left for France to serve in the Scots Guard. Haitlie of Mellerstain, Haliburton of Mertoun, Spottiswoode of that Ilk, French of Thornydykes and even Lord Home's adherents the Dicksons of Belchester and Bughtrig assured to protect themselves from attack. There were two traitors amongst the Merse lairds, not of the calibre of Sandy Pringle, but damaging nonetheless to the loyal Scots. Both James Cockburn of Langton and Ninian Chirnside of East Nisbet spied for England. Chirnside advocated a stronger English policy even when their cause was lost writing 'the moir gentylle we be handyllyt the moir wyld be we. Quhen your grace sendis oni power in Scotland, haiff the heift (handle) and blaid in your awyn handis . . .'[46] This statement could also be interpreted as a warning about the Borderers' reluctance to hurt each other. Of fifty lairds who are known to have assured very few were prosecuted. This was due to the 1548 general amnesty that was designed to win back assured Scots. Those who were not part of this agreement were pardoned in the 1550s, including the treacherous Cockburn of Langton.[47]

ii. 1550–69

1550s politics were much the same with pro-French and pro-English factions, yet the years leading up to the Scottish Reformation of 1560 proved to be particularly tense. The Home lairds' political independence became evident when Home of Manderston was summoned to the division of the Debateable Ground in 1551. Home of Cowdenknowes had been the first laird to break from the Borders when he became a keeper of Holyrood Park in 1544. Cowdenknowes' ascendancy protected him from prosecution in 1552 for murdering Sir Walter Scott of Buccleuch who had earlier killed his father-in-law Sir Andrew Ker of Cessford in 1526. It was the Kers, rather than the Homes who were subsequently threatened with banishment in France, but this was not carried out. The government may not have wanted to jeopardise the auld alliance by foisting bloodthirsty Borderers on the French.[48]

When the pro-English faction in Scotland, known as the Lords of the Congregation threatened to topple the pro-French party in 1559, the Homes and Kers remained neutral. That Lord Home did not immediately support the French faction is surprising. He had visited France in 1551, held a French pension of 2000 livres and had the gift of his own ward and marriage by the dowager Queen Mary of Guise. Home was, however, just displaying the janus-faced deviousness that many Borderers had adopted in the 1540s.[49] The Reformation led to many *politique* actions by lairds who switched between the nominally pro-English support for the Reformation and the pro-French opposition, more for political expediency than religious fervour. The Kers of Cessford and Ferniehirst came out in favour of the Protestant Lords as they appeared genuine supporters of the Reformation, but the Kers of Littledean and Primsideloch swayed. Home of Blackadder joined the Protestant party, but Lord Home kept everyone guessing. Home was belatedly paid his French pension that had not been forthcoming for five years, yet he remained neutral and then surprisingly joined the Protestants. He was not trusted by William Cecil who believed 'Hume would be caught with a hook of a few ducats'. Perhaps he was just being a typical Borderer, but by October 1560 there were rumours of new French pensions on offer and Lumsden of Blanerne travelled to France.[50]

When news arrived in December 1560 that Francis II, husband of Mary Queen of Scots, had died, many of the Border lairds had second thoughts about their allegiance to the Protestant cause and met at Dunbar to discuss their predicament. The English faction, remembering the tactics of the 1540s, hoped that bribery would keep the Homes and Kers in their allegiance, but when Mary arrived back in August 1561 they reverted to her side.[51] The early years of Mary's personal reign proved relatively harmonious after the Reformation upheavals of 1559–60. The ascendant James Home of Cowdenknowes became a servant of Lord Darnley and was knighted by Mary in 1565, but there were a few dissenters. For example

Adam Home, a younger son of Polwarth, found his adherence to Protestantism conflicted with loyalty to a Catholic monarch. Nevertheless the Homes, Kers and Rutherfords all supported Mary during the Chaseabout Raid of 1565. The position of the Pringles is unclear though they probably accepted the *status quo*. Local tensions remained in the Borders with ill-feeling between the MacDougals of Stodrig and the Kers. Such was his distrust of the Kers that Stodrig appointed the earl of Morton, Douglas of Cavers and Dickson of Buchtrig as overmen of his will, despite living in a Ker heartland.[52] Morton was thus displaying his skill for meddling in Border factions that would only increase during the next thirteen years.

The murder of William Ker, commendator of Kelso, by his kinsmen was a local event proven to be connected to central politics. The unfortunate William was an ally of the earl of Bothwell and there was a general enmity between the Kers and the earl in 1566. Ker of Faldonside, for instance, was party to both William's murder and the murder of David Rizzio the queen's secretary.[53] Lord Home was still loyal to the queen in March 1566, but as a territorial rival of Bothwell he deserted her when she married Bothwell. There is very little foundation in the pro-Bothwell rhyme 'Hume and Hebron (Hepburn) hald you togidder an ye dissever ye will rew it for ever'. The Homes were not allies of Bothwell and were better off without his skulduggery. If Bothwell fell from grace the Homes knew they would be well placed to benefit, but they were not united over this. A significant division of the once-solid Home kindred occurred after the royal marriage, with Wedderburn, Blackadder and Broomhouse following the queen, whilst Manderston, Cowdenknowes, Fishwick, Huttonhall and Lord Home defected.[54] Cockburn of Langton and Lumsden of Blanerne were amongst other Merse lairds who stayed loyal to Mary in 1567–68. In Teviotdale the Kers of Ferniehirst, Littledean, Shielstockbraes, Primsideloch and Faldonside, the Ainslies of Falla and Mow of that Ilk all fought for Mary at the battles of Carberry and Langside. As with the Homes there were divisions within the Kers, for Cessford fought against the queen. This pattern of loyalty was complex enough, yet in 1568–69 it changed again after Mary's defeat at Langside. Faldonside, Wedderburn and Blackadder left Mary's allegiance, but Lord Home made an ill-advised return to the queen's party.[55]

Home had been a strong supporter of the king's party and Regent Moray until November 1569 when he disagreed with the regent and began provisioning Hume Castle in anticipation of trouble. Home's infant son had even been granted a pension by Moray, in respect of their alliance. Home had been wounded fighting, with the support of 600 of his kinsmen and allies, at the battle of Langside against the queen. His reversion to the queen's side may be linked to his reconversion to Catholicism, for he was never a very convincing Protestant. However, he harboured grudges against England and therefore supported the ostensibly Catholic rebellion by the English earls of Northumberland and Westmorland that was then breaking out.[56]

Sir Thomas Ker of Ferniehirst never left Mary's allegiance and was a regular correspondent with her during her English exile. He anticipated her return after the rebellion in northern England and Mary's letters asked him to 'be reddy for our service quhen we sall mak you advertisment'. In another letter she hoped to deliver her next instructions in person so 'have yourself and frins [friends] in readynes'.[57] Ferniehirst's friends included Sir Andrew Ker of Littledean, Thomas Ker of Cavers and James Ormiston of that Ilk. When the 1569–70 rising collapsed the earls of Northumberland and Westmorland sheltered at Ferniehirst and Hume Castles. Ferniehirst could rely on the support of his kinsmen in this troubled time, but Lord Home found himself isolated from his kinsmen. The Kers allied to Cessford did not give the exiles any assistance as the old feud between them and the Kers of Ferniehirst interceded. Lord Home's total alienation from his kinsmen was a departure from the loyalty his family commanded in the past. This division would dominate the local politics of the Merse in the 1570s.[58]

iii. The 1570s

In April 1570 an erroneous report stated that 'In the Mers and Lauderdale newir man wilbe against the Quene except a few nombre that depends on Mortoun'. This was presumably based on the knowledge that rebel Lord Home and Maitland of Lethington, who held land in Lauderdale, would rely on their kinsmen and tenants for support. The noted 'few' who followed the perverse Regent Morton were more of a crowd and Lord Home's 'best friends in the Merse' had refused him. Instead of sensibly yielding to the pressures of this widespread desertion Home became more resolute in his support for the Marian cause and let the battered Hume Castle be surrendered to English forces.[59] The English who garrisoned the castle were a reminder of the 1540s, but this time Lord Home had no grass-root support to recapture it. They gathered Home's crops for their own profit without being challenged and ignored pointless negotiations for the castle's return in 1570 and 1572.[60] Home, ironically, gained the sympathy of Lord Hunsdon, his opposite warden in the English East March. Hunsdon was a staunch Protestant and cousin of Elizabeth I, yet he could see how Home's kinsmen were usurping his position. Hunsdon's reasons for backing Home must have been based on cross-border friendship as his support for a rebellious Catholic Marian would otherwise appear disloyal.

Alexander Home of Manderston was the principal target of Hunsdon's wrath; 'Alexander looks to govern all the Marches, for which reason he desires so much that Home and Fast Castles be delivered into the hands of the King, for then he would sit down there'. Hunsdon determined that Manderston should not be granted Hume Castle and wrote to him threatening that neither 'you nor any other shall intermeddle with it'.[61] Home of Godscroft launched a similar attack on Manderston's arrogance in his family history. His family of Wedderburn were Merse rivals to Manderston in the 1570s and 1580s vacuum created by Lord Home's downfall. As Manderston was a descendant of the Wedderburn Homes, Godscroft may have resented a junior kinsman's success. Manderston duly acquired some of Lord Home's property after his forfeiture and (with the backing of Morton) probably wanted to go much further than this to equal, if not exceed, the wealth of the Lords Home.[62] Eastern Border society had potentially entered a new era akin to the fall of the Douglases in the previous century.

After the Marian rebels had surrendered Edinburgh Castle to Morton's English-assisted forces in 1573, Lord Home was apparently only saved from execution by the intercessions of the Homes of Manderston, Cowden-knowes and North Berwick.[63] This account seems incredible considering the hostility between Lord Home and Manderston. Cowdenknowes also benefited from Home's fall, so North Berwick was more likely to have been Home's saviour along with the Homes of Polwarth and Huttonhall and his kin the Kers of Cessford and Faldonside. None of them could prevent the forfeiture of Lord Home, yet Faldonside did his former curator a good turn by leasing many of his forfeited lands to prevent them being devastated by Morton. Lord Home's 1575 testament clearly states his revulsion for Cowdenknowes and Manderston, as he asked Regent Morton to 'tak sik offices as sumtyme appertenit to me, sik as the wardanrie and bailzeries, furth of the handis that presentlie occupyis thame and put thame in the handis of thame that hes nocht schawin thame selffis manifest oppressouris of me and my puir decayit hous'.[64] Hume Castle had been handed over to Morton in November 1573, who promptly gave it to Cowdenknowes as his new warden of the East March. That Manderston was made commendator of Coldingham, where Home had been bailie, only added to his anger.

Home was perhaps unaware that Morton, his former ally in the 1560s, was deliberately trying to ruin him by bolstering Manderston and Cow-denknowes. Manderston grasped every opportunity he could to attack Lord Home's remaining influence in the Merse. This is why he feuded with Cranstons of Thirlestane Mains, who were amongst the minority of lairds still loyal to Lord Home. Morton also tried to increase his influence in the Merse by marrying two of his allies to heiresses, but this manoeuvre alienated local lairds who normally supported him.[65] Patrick Cockburn of East Borthwick even tried, unsuccessfully, to hide the heiress Jane Sleigh of Cumledge from Morton's officers. The lairds opposed interference in their domain if there was no advantage to be gained from it, but when Morton offered patronage to them they had responded.[66]

The conduct of Cowdenknowes and Manderston was reminiscent of the Northumbrian gentry who took full advantage of the absence of the earls of Northumberland in the sixteenth century.[67] It is therefore ironic that these usurping lairds were criticised rather than praised by the gentry. Sir John Forster and Lord Hunsdon were sympathetic to Lord Home and Sir Thomas

Ker of Ferniehirst, despite their participation in the burning of Ferniehirst and Hume Castles as rebel strongholds. Forster even sheltered Sir Thomas Ker of Ferniehirst in the English Middle March during 1572–74, though Ker returned briefly in November 1573 to survey English damage to his property near Jedburgh. Cross-border friendship must surely have prevailed over international politics, but why Forster did not condone newly-risen men in a power vacuum remains a mystery.[68] Perhaps he recognised the consequences of such a power struggle only too well, having risen in the same manner himself.

Ferniehirst was less unfortunate than Lord Home as he had not participated in the siege of Edinburgh Castle. Nevertheless he was forfeited, suffered losses at the hands of English soldiers and was forced into exile in both the English Middle March and France. Morton bestowed Ferniehirst's lands on his Douglas kinsmen to undermine his local influence just as he had attempted to reduce Home's power base in the Merse. Morton also bolstered Ferniehirst's rival, Ker of Cessford, by granting him a 650 merk pension to assist him as warden of the Middle March.[69] Cessford received an additional 500 merks from Morton, who even tried to lure Ferniehirst's immense grass-root support by pardoning hundreds of them in 1576. Fortunately, Ferniehirst's followers proved not to be turncoats like the Homes. When he returned from exile in 1581, his kinship network was still intact.[70]

Other lairds either accepted Morton's power or tolerated it. Ker of Cessford was superficially loyal to Morton and thus remained as warden of the Middle March. Cockburn of Langton, Home of Ayton, Home of Wedderburn and Swinton of that Ilk were all pro-English and Protestant in 1570 and Langton openly supported Morton in 1574. John Cranston of Morriston was the only laird to join Lord Home in Edinburgh Castle during 1572–73. The pseudo-loyal Wedderburn and Pringle of that Ilk were pledged to England in 1573 and Home of Huttonhall was superficially loyal to Morton. Edmonston of that Ilk, Pringle of Galashiels and MacDougal of Makerstoun were probably more convinced followers of Morton.[71] It is difficult to judge how supportive these lairds were to Morton or England as the turbulence of the period saw lairds allying to four separate regents whilst dallying with English (not British) factionalism.

Morton's Border supporters were as fickle as their 1540s counterparts when he did not show them favour. The support for Morton began to fall off in 1567 when he snubbed both Home of Cowdenknowes and Ker of Cessford. Cowdenknowes was angered at having to pay a £5,000 Scots fine for not keeping the Brounfields peaceable whilst he was surety for their good behaviour. As a Morton supporter he had expected the fine to be rescinded. Other reasons for Cowdenknowes' defection proffered by George Hewitt are inconclusive as the Home kinship was fragmentary in the 1570s.[72] Cowdenknowes did, none the less, lose the wardenship of the

East March to Wedderburn in September 1578. Ker of Cessford had also been annoyed by Morton's experimental division of his Middle March, so the Kers were generally 'malcontent' with the regent. Morton also managed to alienate his greatest Merse ally, Home of Manderston, by marrying his illegitimate son James Douglas to Anne Home. She was the heiress of Spott in East Lothian and niece of Manderston by marriage. Manderston had arranged Anne's marriage to his younger son George so, incensed, he looked for an opportunity for revenge. The loss of a Home heiress was such a serious matter for the Homes that it was even lamented by Manderston's rival, Home of Godscroft. Godscroft's brother Wedderburn remained a Morton supporter, but he was increasingly isolated in this allegiance and was warded for six months as punishment after Morton's downfall.[73]

Morton had gone too far and lost the regency in 1578, but remained head of the Scottish administration for a further two years. Hostility from the Home lairds may have persuaded him to allow the restoration of the sixth Lord Home to his near-ruinous estates for £10,000 Scots (though this bribe was never paid).[74] The restoration of Ferniehirst was not so straightforward. He courted the favour of Morton and the earl of Angus in 1579, to bring about his restoration, unaware that Morton was losing power and that both lords were trying to gain his attainder for themselves. Ferniehirst hoped that they would influence a pardon for him in return for manrent and the gift of the marriage of his heir. Fortunately he was not obliged to keep these promises as both Morton and Angus were forfeited in 1581.[75]

iv. The 1580s

Ferniehirst was licensed to return from France in 1580 and he arrived back in Scotland to witness yet more upheavals in Scottish politics. The 1580s saw a definite rise of lairds to power, such as Maitland of Thirlestane, who followed the success of his father and brother at court. There was increasing court interference in the localities as well that emerged within local feuding. Morton had been executed in 1581, to the satisfaction of many of his enemies. Lord Home had escorted him to his execution and Ferniehirst 'stood in a shott over against the scaffold, with his large ruffes, delyting in this spectacle.' The forfeiture of both Morton and Angus effectively checked Douglas interference in the Merse and Jedforest during the 1580s. The Kers of Ferniehirst and their allies the Rutherfords were thus no longer obliged to Angus in manrent, though the Rutherfords remained loyal to Angus when he was temporarily restored in 1582. This created local frictions in the Jedforest area that were more reminiscent of the Homes in the 1570s, but it may have been Ferniehirst's reported arrogance that alienated the normally loyal Rutherfords. The problem resolved itself with Angus's fall from grace in 1583 and Ferniehirst's full restoration. The Homes and Kers, with some exceptions, backed the ascendant earl of Lennox in 1580 and it was Lennox who really masterminded the full restoration of Ferniehirst, Home and Maitland.[76]

Lord Home faced a much harder task than Ferniehirst in reclaiming his lands and offices from the ascendant Home lairds. Central government's interference in the Merse had been much more intrusive. The privy council even had to order the Homes of Cowdenknowes, Manderston and Reidheuch to restore him to 'quhatsumevir landis, rowmes, offices and possessionis' they declared, which is a clear indication that these lairds were putting up resistance to their young kinsman's restoration. Cowdenknowes insisted that he would not return the teinds of Eccles Priory until Home was twenty-one, which was not for another five years.[77] One English reporter noted Lord Home as 'of no very good government or hope', but this was an unkind remark. Lord Home had much ground to recover at a relatively young age, but he would succeed in achieving this near impossible task by 1600.[78]

At the centre, the Ruthven Raid of 1582 saw the return of a Protestant regime to Scotland, but the raiders were ousted in 1583 by the ascendant earl of Arran. Many Protestant lairds followed the raiders, though none actively participated. The Catholic Ferniehirst went back to France in disgust and Lord Home only superficially supported the raiders.[79] The Kers of Cessford and Faldonside as well as the Homes of Cowdenknowes and Wedderburn all supported the new regime until the raiders' regime collapsed. Only Ferniehirst was in a position to take advantage of their fall so he quickly returned from his French exile in 1584 and became a close associate of Arran. His first victim was his old rival Cessford, whom he unfairly engineered out of the office of warden of the Middle March.[80] Ferniehirst's appointment as warden in place of Cessford had disastrous consequences. In July 1585 Lord Russell was killed in mysterious circumstances during a day of truce between Ferniehirst and Sir John Forster. Godscroft noted that 'whether by chance or of set purpose is uncertain'. Shortly before this Border meeting there had been a large-scale English raid into the Scottish Middle March, but this would hardly have provoked the murder as cross-border raids were commonplace. Contemporary descriptions of the events of 27 July are unhelpful, as they are full of contradictions and exaggerations. Forster, despite being the father-in-law of Russell, did not immediately blame his friend Ferniehirst and only hinted that he could not keep his men under control. Forster significantly made no mention of the suspected complicity of Arran in the killing in his first report. Neither did he think Ferniehirst's forces excessive for a Border meeting. The Borders now became the focus of brief international attention with political points to be won or lost.

The force that Ferniehirst assembled that fateful day did outnumber the English contingent, but they were not 'ranged in order of battell' as later reports suggested. Ferniehirst was, after all, a pompous man known to like a large garrison around him.[81] Russell was 'slaine in the myddest of his owne men', which suggests a prearranged plan to kill him. However after the murder both Forster and Ferniehirst 'stood together and made a quietnes' then took order over pledges and prisoners and 'parted quietly oute of the feeld'.[82] The next day Forster was a signatory to a divergent report that clearly suspected foul play and described a tumult that ended with a foray four miles into England. Forster's first report made no mention of this foray and even taking his shock into account he could not have missed witnessing such an event. Elizabeth I and her spymaster Sir Francis Walsingham focused their blame on Ferniehirst, to attack Arran's political power. Walsingham with his accustomed guile, determined to gather evidence against Ferniehirst regardless of its authenticity.[83]

James VI, who was now showing himself to be an adult monarch, warded both Arran and Ferniehirst. As investigation witnesses contradicted each other the king rejected Walsingham's claim that Ferniehirst was guilty. James refused to hand Ferniehirst over to England, but suspicion remained with his kinsmen; the Kers of Ancrum, Lintalee and Primsideloch and Rutherford of Hunthill. There may have been some enmity between Ferniehirst and Russell as it was suggested that Russell had annoyed Ferniehirst by intercepting letters. Russell called him half lunatic in May 1585 perhaps as a result of his pomposity, yet for Ferniehirst to order his kinsmen to murder Russell is dubious. Ferniehirst 'would rather the blood of one of his own friends had been shed'. It took Scottish Border commissioners, who included the normally pro-English lairds of Cowdenknowes, Huttonhall and North Berwick to settle the matter. This allegiance was overridden as they did not want to see a fellow laird being used as an English scapegoat. They therefore declared that England had started the trouble.[84]

The death of Russell remains an enigma. Elizabeth I sought revenge in October 1585 by letting the banished Lords Angus, Mar and Glamis return to Scotland. They subsequently toppled Arran's regime after being welcomed into the Borders by Bothwell, Home (whose mother had remarried a kinsman of Glamis), and Cessford. Also present were the Homes of Cowdenknowes, Huttonhall and Wedderburn (a kinsman of Mar by marriage). Ferniehirst fell with Arran and died ignominiously at Aberdeen in 1586. His kinsmen were declared rebels for participating in the murder, though they went unpunished as this was merely a manoeuvre to appease Elizabeth (who was paying James a lucrative pension at the time).

As a result of Arran's fall, Bothwell and Home rose to prominence yet it was Maitland of Thirlestane, ironically a former secretary to Arran, who became leader of the new order. The Homes of Cowdenknowes and Polwarth advanced in the rearguard of their success, changing the political spectrum of the Eastern Borders once more. Cowdenknowes became both captain of Edinburgh Castle and a privy councillor, whilst Polwarth entered and progressed through court circles. Even Polwarth's heir would become a gentleman of the chamber to Queen Anna of Denmark in 1590. Cowdenknowes was already a gentleman of the bedchamber and his ascendancy was further helped by Bothwell who successfully petitioned for his release from ward in 1584 and married his half-sister to Cowdenknowes' son and heir.[85] Bothwell's rise was a problem for the Homes of Manderston who had profited from the forfeiture of the earl of Angus in 1581. They had gained Coldingham Priory, but it was now the subject of a triangular contest between themselves, Bothwell and Maitland (whose kinsmen had previously held the Priory). Bothwell's claim had caused friction with these Homes since his restoration in 1581. This was highlighted in 1584 when Bothwell's men murdered David Home of Cranshaws, a younger son of Manderston. Cranshaws and the Manderstons had also been allies of Bothwell's enemy, the earl of Arran.[86] The Manderstons found little compassion from their ally Arran, or from their kin chief Lord Home in this matter. Home was intriguing with Bothwell at the time and was still bitter about the Manderston Homes' treatment of his father in the 1570s. The Manderstons therefore turned against Arran in a rare moment of unanimity with other Home lairds. Coldingham Priory was eventually yielded to Bothwell by the Manderstons' bowing to crown pressure and Maitland was diplomatically compensated by an exchange agreement over Kelso Abbey which was held by Bothwell. The Manderston ascendancy at the expense of Lord Home ended with this surrender, but their younger sons remained successful buffers against Bothwell at court with the spectacular success of Sir George Home and the Homes of Tinnis and Whitelaw.[87]

Along with a rise of the lairds, the second half of the 1580s also witnessed the beginning of the personal reign of James VI. He independently meddled with local politics and promoted lairds' younger sons at court. He visited the Eastern Borders on hunting trips, such as in 1588 when he was careful to stay with both the Kers of Cessford and Ferniehirst so as not to inflame their feud. He also visited Cockburn of Langton and Lord Home in the Merse.[88] James deliberately set about cultivating a 'safety net' of loyal lairds in the Eastern Borders in case Lord Home followed the rebellious behaviour of the earl of Huntly, Lord Maxwell and latterly Bothwell. Huntly and Maxwell normally had an impenetrably loyal kin group, but Lord Home's kinsmen now had a record of disloyalty that could be manipulated. James therefore bestowed patronage on the lairds on an unprecedented scale and took a personal interest in all their major feuds. For instance, when he was about to embark for Denmark to bring home his bride in 1589, he halted Court of Session actions against the feuding Homes of Blackadder, Cowdenknowes and Tinnis to ensure fair play upon his return. He probably cultivated 'safety-net' lairds in other regions as well.[89]

Maitland of Thirlestane also interfered with local politics in Lauderdale and the Merse. He subdued his pro-Bothwell neighbours, the Homes of Cowdenknowes, by forcing them to hand back forfeited property 'in friendship'. Maitland also tried to wrestle the teinds of Lauder from Lord Home. He scored a victory over Bothwell by forcing him to hand over the office of bailie of Lauderdale in 1587 and he deliberately incited Bothwell's feud with the Homes of Manderston. Lord Home was initially jealous of Maitland's rise to power and thus quarrelled with Maitland's brother-in-law Lord Fleming in 1587. He later realised that Bothwell was more of a threat in his locality so he sided with Maitland against Bothwell.[90]

During the 1580s the power struggle between Home and Bothwell would eclipse all other battles in the Merse. There had been initial friction between the earl of Angus as sheriff of Berwickshire and Andrew Home, commendator of Jedburgh. Andrew tried to hold a sheriff court on Lord Home's behalf in 1580, but this was nullified. When Lord Home became sheriff in 1581 upon the forfeiture of Angus, this problem was resolved. Lord Home was simultaneously warden of the East March, which gave him and his kinsmen a commanding position in the Merse. An anonymous 1589 report stated 'this shire is divided in two partes, the weste governed by the Lord Home and hys followers, and the easte governed by the prior of Coldingham, who is nowe the earle Bothwell and followe him.'[91] The Merse was not really divided between Home and Bothwell, yet Bothwell's charismatic leadership meant the he was not without support. Bothwell's landholding in the area was not large enough to give him real power and even with the acquisition of Coldingham Priory he was not a prominent Merse laird for his power base was located in neighbouring East Lothian. To emphasise this James VI ordered Home to stay in the Scottish East March and Bothwell to remain in Edinburgh and the Lothians during his 1589–90 sojourn to Denmark.[92]

Home and Bothwell were friends except for periods of interpersonal violence that persisted into the 1590s. Bothwell's Border following included Thomas Cranston of Morriston who was normally a Home ally, his servitor Ninian Chirnside of Whitsomelaws, his tenant William Craw of Swinwood and William Ker of Ancrum who needed support against Cessford and James Ker of Middlemist Walls. The enmity between Home and Bothwell was not a territorial rivalry, so it could have been caused by inherited prejudice or by the memory of Morton being Bothwell's tutor.[93] Home and Bothwell first quarrelled in 1586 when Home backed the Homes of Manderston in their feud with Bothwell. They argued anew in 1587 over the teinds of Greenlaw and Hume.[94] By August 1589 Home and Bothwell were feuding again, owing to the deviousness of Maitland who had separate quarrels with both men. Maitland half-heartedly offered to arbitrate, whilst deliberately engineering a fracas between them and their retainers on the road to Thirlestane. Maitland wanted Home to continue feuding with Bothwell as they were court rivals.[95] Home and Bothwell discovered Maitland's plot whilst he was away in Denmark with the king and thus ended their feud for the time being.

Home foolishly supported Bothwell's terrorising of James VI during early 1591, yet by July 1591 the lure of Bothwell's escheat and the advice of kinsmen made it politically expedient for him to make his peace with the king. James also insisted that Home sign a bond of friendship with Maitland, to prevent further trouble in the Borders. Home's kinsmen of Huttonhall, Broxmouth, North Berwick and Wedderburn did not want him to suffer the same fate as his father. They probably instigated Home's self-imposed exile during 1591–92 that avoided further embarrassment. It also kept him far from Bothwell's influence and Maitland's meddling. James welcomed Home upon his return and bestowed lands and honours on him for forsaking Bothwell's allegiance. These included Coldingham Priory and the offices of grand master stabler, gentleman of the bedchamber and captain of the king's guard.[96] Lord Home evidently delighted in Bothwell's downfall, as he kept a copy of his attainder in his charter chest. Bothwell was incensed but could not avenge this as Home now held a commanding position at court.

v. 1590–1603

The 1590s and early 1600s witnessed native Borderers becoming influential courtiers in their own right, rather than having to seek patronage from other courtiers as they had done in previous decades. Lord Home, Sir Robert Ker of Cessford and Sir George Home of Spott were typical of the new Border lobby at court. They maintained a strong link with the Borders and their kinsmen, as Home used his ascendancy to settle disagreements with Maitland such as Maitland's shabby treatment of his close kinsman Sir James Home of Cowdenknowes. Maitland had led an impatient scramble for Cowdenknowes' captaincy of Edinburgh Castle, just because he was ill. Home also blamed Maitland for fabricating his feud with Bothwell and unnecessarily prolonging his 1591–2 exile.[97] There was also the local matter of the Lauder teinds which Home had been forced to sell to Maitland through financial embarrassment.

Home was still antagonistic to Maitland in June 1593, but the unexpected return of Bothwell united them against him.[98] Bothwell naturally wanted his enemies the Homes, Maitland and Glamis expelled from court. He found support from his old allies in the Merse, such as Thomas Cranston of Morriston, his tenant lairds Home of Prenderguest and Craw of East Reston and frustrated younger sons, Alexander French of Thornydykes and Alexander Home of Blackadder. Further west the town of Kelso, the Kers of Ferniehirst and the Rutherfords of Hunthill and Hundalee all joined him though they were probably just using Bothwell as a means of getting at Cessford. Bothwell boasted that he 'had done, would doe, and could doe als muche in the king's service as anie Hume in the Merce', yet his coup collapsed in September 1593. Lord Home then 'entered into very boasting terms against Bothwell, saying that 'the Earl, all the Stewarts and their partakers durst not tak one silly bee out of the moss of his bounds against his will'.[99] Even Maitland was forced into a bond of friendship with Home that agreed to non-interference in each other's feuds. These included Home with Maitland's kinsman Cessford and Maitland with Home's kinsman Glamis. Local tensions remained though until Maitland's death in 1595. As a final gesture Maitland asked his former protagonists Cessford, Buccleuch and Home to protect his wife and children.[100] This made Home triumphant within the Merse and Lauderdale, but he now had a significant weakness in his adherence to Catholicism. This was overlooked by the King who tried hard to prevent the Kirk from excommunicating him, but it would return to haunt him.

James VI had acknowledged the loyalty of the Border lairds by giving them important roles during the baptism of Prince Henry in 1594. Lord Home carried a diamond crown in the ceremony and the tournament that followed this was won by the team of Lennox, Home and Cessford dressed as Turks. Buccleuch was in another team dressed as Amazons 'in wemens array', which would certainly have been an amusing sight.[101] Sir Robert Ker of Cessford was rising at court in 1594, having overcome earlier difficulties and he would eventually outshine the achievements of Lord Home. Cessford's murder of his rival William Ker of Ancrum in 1590 had delayed his ascendancy, yet Ancrum's support for Bothwell meant that young Cessford was never out of favour whilst officially remaining a rebel for two years. He even gained the support of English Border officials as Ancrum had been one of the suspected murderers of Lord Russell in 1585. Ancrum had denied this on his deathbed, much to the aggravation of English ambassador Robert Bowes who thought the minister had not dealt 'thoroughly with him'. Bowes was probably trying to find an excuse for Ancrum's denial, yet as he had taken twenty-two painful hours to die there should have been plenty of time for a confession. Bowes successfully lobbied James VI for Cessford's pardon in 1591, little knowing that this youthful and impetuous laird would become one of the major headaches of Border administration in the mid 1590s.[102]

Cessford accepted the King's gratitude for ousting Bothwell, but he was jealous of others who shared in Bothwell's forfeiture. His father was still alive, yet as fiar of Cessford he had access to much of the family's wealth. This was clearly insufficient for his pride and he looked elsewhere for profit. This is probably what led him to wreak havoc in the English Borders with his henchmen blackmailing the residents and stealing goods and animals in the manner of a twenty-first-century urban gang. During this time Cessford was still well received at court much to the chagrin of English Border officials. In August 1596 a report summed up Cessford as 'wyse, quicke spirited, perfecte in Border causes, ambisious, desyorus to be greate, poore, not able to mayntenye his estate to his greate mynd: attended by beggars and lowse persons whose mayntenance is by thefte supported by his countenance'.[103] Cessford's reiving was curbed when James VI, mindful of the succession, yielded to English pressure and insisted that he go into English custody in 1597. Lord Home handed his cousin Cessford over in February 1598 'with great entreatie of letting passe formal unkyndness', as Cessford was finally growing up and had the potential to be a responsible laird. Bowes expressed a vague desire to see him hang, but this would have offended the king. Instead Cessford received comfortable imprisonment and even befriended his former adversary Sir Robert Carey, warden of the English East March, who 'took him abroad with me at least thrice a week, a-hunting'.[104] Carey's brother John also noted Cessford's transformation into 'a fare altered man that ever I saw from so bade to so good', who for once gave 'good justice' to his opposite warden.[105]

Cessford returned from England and continued to advance at court as if nothing had happened. This undeserved rise contrasted with the peaceable Lord Home's slow decline at court, caused by his 1598 excommunication for continued adherence to Catholicism. Court gossip about Home was unkind such as 'the Lord Home is verie sicke, some doe suspecte the French disease' or the report that his house 'be infected with the plague'. Some resorted to wishful thinking saying that Home had left the country when he had not.[106] James VI still showed Home some favour by staying and hunting with him on several occasions for he respected his good work on the Borders. Home sensed, however, that Sir George Home of Spott and Cessford were more highly favoured so he went abroad as an ambassador in April 1599. James went too far in September 1599 when he granted Cessford rule over the Merse during Home's absence. Sir Alexander Home of Manderston objected to this as he had been left in charge of the East March as temporary warden. That Manderston's brother Spott was Cessford's main court rival no doubt intensified his annoyance. Manderston therefore summoned the barons of the Merse to an alternative meeting to one planned by Cessford. The trouble only subsided when James intervened and sensibly revoked his agreement with Cessford, leaving the Merse lairds to follow their warden and thus kept his safety net of lairds intact.[107] During Home's absence Spott and Cessford even had a 'champion of the chamber' contest, which Spott won. This was akin to being declared the King's chivalric champion, but it had more to do with political strength than muscle in 1600. It appeared that the Homes still had the upper hand.

Home was welcomed abroad and presented gifts to King Henri IV of France on James's behalf.[108] He was well received in England because of his exemplary Border service, but Elizabeth I remained sceptical about Cessford. She reprimanded James for favouring him, but he defended his actions in a personal letter. 'Think not therefore I pray you that my gracing of him is any ways in contempt of you . . . I protest my gracing of him does only proceed upon his resolution to quit all his wild Border fashions'.[109] Elizabeth remained unconvinced and Cessford was so preoccupied with his ascendancy at court that he forgot all about his kinsmen languishing in English gaols for not paying compensation to wronged English Borderers. James VI had definitely risked upsetting his safety net of lairds by favouring Cessford too much. He needed to keep these lairds happy at a time when Lord Home was rumoured to be intriguing with powerful Catholic interests in Scotland. Lairds such as the Homes of Wedderburn and Polwarth had benefited from this network, gaining many court offices and having Eyemouth and Redbraes made into privileged free baronies for them. The Homes were once again in control of royal hunting with Mr Patrick Home of Ayton as master hunter, an important office long held by the late John Home of Tinnis. William Home of Whitelaw was master stabler, an office once held by his elder brother Sir George Home of Spott. Lord Home was not offended by James' favouritism towards these lairds as he was in receipt of substantial patronage himself and his kin loyalty had experienced a renaissance.[110] When Home returned from his travels in May 1600 he found Cessford still entrenched as a court favourite. Nevertheless, he was still welcomed back with a banquet given by the king, after which Home gave James valuable intelligence reports from France.

In February 1600 James VI visited Cessford's houses at Holydean and Friars in Roxburghshire. He was there to attend the funeral of Cessford's father, but went hunting south of Kelso as well.[111] Cessford's favouritism at court was such that when he sought a licence to travel abroad, James VI offered him the title of Lord Roxburgh to dissuade him from going. He probably wanted to travel to be as fashionable as his fellow Borderers, Lord Home and Scott of Buccleuch, who had both been to France several times. The lure of a title was enough to keep him in Scotland and he tried to have the king and queen present at his sister's Border wedding to reaffirm his status.[112] Cessford argued with his cousin Lord Home after his return from France, but they fortunately decided to settle their rivalry with a horse race, rather than combat. James VI was conscious of their enmity and its possible destabilising effect on the Borders. He therefore offered Home the title of earl of March when ennobling Cessford in deference to Home's more ancient title. Home refused as he either did not want to be ennobled alongside his upstart cousin Cessford, or he might have felt too impoverished to merit the honour (though the title would have increased his revenue). His father was rumoured to have been offered the title in 1565, but his refusal of its too hints at some family disdain for it.[113]

James VI did not take offence at Home's rejection as he put him on his left hand when riding to Parliament, with Cessford and Spott leading. The king's even-handed and public favouritism towards the Border lairds continued in December 1600 when he asked Cessford's rival, Sir Andrew Ker of Ferniehirst and his children, to the baptism of Prince Charles. A recent pacification between the earl of Angus and Ferniehirst may also have been James's work for a marriage was arranged between them. This appeasement may have been the result of a new generation of Kers and Douglases deciding to forgive ancient animosity, just as Lord Home forgave his Manderston kin in the 1590s.[114] However the difficulties between Cessford and Ferniehirst proved far more troublesome to solve as the new generation was far from conciliatory. James VI intervened in July 1602 when the Border was likely to be destabilised by their feud and demanded that Ferniehirst immediately sign a bond of assurance to keep the peace. He must have had second thoughts about the harsh tone for in a postscript in his own hand he pushed back a deadline imposed on Ferniehirst 'because of my lords of roxburches going out of the cuntrey'.[115] There is no evidence that this feud ended before the Union of the Crowns in 1603 because it was a deep-rooted rivalry akin to the unwavering Ker and Scott bloodfeud.

Cessford (Roxburgh) did travel to France for a second time in the summer of 1602. As he was prone to seasickness he had to travel through England to reach France. This route served as a reminder that some of his erstwhile henchmen were still pledges in English custody. Four of them were in the notorious Haddocks Hole prison at Berwick where 'two of them [were] very sick and like to die' in February 1602. Although the two in question were later released, others remained complaining that 'we were brought out of a myre (York prison) to be thrown into a peat-pot'.[116] Cessford was not legally responsible for them, but as they were his kinsmen they looked to him for help. Cessford was granted an audience with Elizabeth I who promised to consider his kinsmen still in custody and marvelled at his changed character.[117] Lord Home met the queen a few days after Cessford's audience as he was journeying home from a second tour as ambassador to Henri IV. It is unclear if Cessford and Home met as they were not on the best of terms and Cessford probably would have resented Home's ambassadorship.

Lord Home may well have procured the appointment as ambassador with the connivance of his kinsman Sir George Home, then treasurer of Scotland and combatant of Cessford. There were scurrilous remarks about Home's absence, but he genuinely went abroad as a knowledgeable ambassador for James VI and not because he was 'sore grieved with the French pokis and being every year occasioned to go beyond sea for his health'! Home's travels were not annual, though he did travel to France and beyond on four occasions between 1591 and 1602. Another report that Home was going at his own expense is suspect for Home was not a wealthy nobleman and could not have accepted the office without crown resources. The impoverishment of the Scottish crown curtailed Home's 1602 embassy to a mere three months, but it was useful to the 'auld alliance' between Scotland and France. Home travelled in style with five gentlemen accompanying him, unlike his previous journey when he could only afford two companions. His embassy expenses amounted to £12,095–13s-6d Scots. He probably brought a fine horse back with him, which he sold to the king for £900 in January 1603.[118] Cessford must have returned to Scotland early in 1603 for both he and Home accompanied James VI on his journey to London to accept the English crown.

Scottish Border politics were fairly subdued during 1600–03 both in anticipation of the Union of the Crowns and because the political activities of local lairds were now centred on the court rather than in the Borders. A new generation of patronage was beginning to emerge from the household of young Prince Henry, where the 'young laird of mellerstanis . . .' was a page of honour in 1603.[119] Opportunities for the advancement of Borderers at court would continue for some time after the union, though the distance they had to travel to seek this became much greater and there would eventually be an English backlash against favouritism towards the Scots.

The political boundary between country and court in the Eastern Borders had clearly blurred with the rise of these lairds. They had seen off interference by non-resident nobility such as the earls of Angus, Morton, Bothwell and Maitland of Thirlestane. With Border lairds at court and in high offices of state, any courtier influence on the locality would now be their own. The nobility were equally triumphant as Lord Home had enjoyed a renaissance denied to other noblemen, such as the earl of Gowrie in 1584 and 1601 and the earls of Angus in the 1580s. Lord Roxburgh had also used his friendship with James VI to overcome opposition. This contrasted with the continual interference of non-native, London-based courtiers in north Northumberland at this time.[120]

There was no real sense of an impending British state in 1603 as Scotland would lose only her resident monarchy, not her parliament, privy council, laws, customs or currency. James VI and I reneged on his promise to visit Scotland often, but the policies he had begun setting in place during the 1580s would pay off. The Eastern Borders continued to be a relatively peaceful area with lairds milking crown patronage to increase their own power base. No outsider had ever been allowed to dominate this area for long. Therefore overall control of this area had arguably remained with the lairds throughout 1540–1603.

Notes

1 NAS GD150/1411. *ADCP*, 502–03. *APS*, ii, 43. Rae, *Scottish Frontier*, 12–14. Wormald, *Community*, 162.
2 *CSP Scot*, ix, 539. HMC, Home, 69; Salisbury, vi, 9. Pitcairn, *Trials*, i, pt 1, 451, 467–8.
3 NRAS 859/11/2. *ER*, xxi, 441. *RMS*, iv, 2152; v, 218 (which erroneously states that Bothwell was sheriff of Berwickshire in the 1580s), 1172, 2179. *RPC*, vi, 57–8. *Retours*, i, Berwick, 9.
4 NAS GD158/183, GD158/616. RH15/19/3/1. SC62/2/1, SC62/2/2, SC62/2/4, SC62/2/5. HMC, Home, 69.
5 *RPC*, vi, 57–8. See ch. iii.
6 NAS SC62/2/1. *Retours*, i, Berwick, 21; ii, 516.
7 NAS GD12/147. SC62/2/1. HMC, Marchmont, 61. For a full citation of lairds as jurors see Meikle, 'Thesis', ch i. app.

8 NAS GD40/3/232, GD53/4.

9 M. D. Young, ed. *The Parliaments of Scotland. Burgh and Shire Commissioners* (2 vols, Edinburgh, 1992), vol i, xviii.

10 Although this was seemingly based on the English franchise, the Scottish forty shillings of old extent was worth far more as inflation had far outstripped this medieval tax valuation.

11 M. Lee, *John Maitland of Thirlestane* (Princeton, 1959), 145–50. W. Croft Dickinson, 'Freehold in Scots Law', *Juridical Review* (1945), 135–51. J. Goodare, 'Parliament and Society in Scotland, 1560–1603', unpubl. PhD diss. Edinburgh 1989, 59–63, 'Parliamentary Taxation in Scotland, 1560–1625', *SHR*, lxviii (1989), 23–52. Wormald, *Community*, 157–8.

12 *Cf.* Sir George Home of Spott, Sir George Home of Wedderburn, William Ker of Cessford, Sir Andrew Ker of Ferniehirst and Thomas MacDougal of Makerstoun, in Young, ed. *The Parliaments of Scotland*. They were not listed by shire until 1600.

13 *CSP Scot*, ix, 365. *RMS*, iv, 1519.

14 *CSP Scot*, i, 879; xi, 94, 270.

15 NAS CH6/6/1 fos 76–8, 113–14. *cf.* Rae, *Scottish Frontier*, 15–18. Sanderson, *Rural Society*, 6–7, 11,

16 There is a good list in T. I. Rae, 'The Administration of the Borders in the sixteenth century', unpubl PhD. thesis. St Andrews 1961, app. ii. Eyemouth is an addition to this, *RMS*, vi, 668.

17 WMT/Wedderop 10, Various 120. *RMS*, iv, 1709. *cf.* P. J. Murray, 'The Lay Administrators of Church Lands in the Fifteenth and Sixteenth Centuries', *SHR*, lxxiv (1995), 26–44. See Meikle, 'Thesis', ch. i. app. for other examples.

18 NRAS 1100/717. *HMC*, Roxburghe, 95.

19 NAS CH6/6/1 fo. 42. GD40/3/241, GD40/3/6, GD40/5/3/1, GD40/13/9, GD40/ 13/32. *RPC*, iv, 70. Moysie, *Memoirs*, 67.

20 NAS GD267/27/76, GD267/27/78, GD267/27/84. Coldingham records are for 1568, 1583 and 1598 only.

21 *Cf.* Wormald, *Community*, 138. The following Kirk Session Registers were consulted NAS CH2/72/1 (Polwarth), CH2/113/1 (Duns), CH2/466/1 (Hutton), CH2/534/1 (Lauder), CH2/52/1 (Jedburgh), CH2/841/1 (Ednam), CH2/1173/1 (Kelso). J. Anderson & W. Angus, eds. *Protocol Book of Sir William Corbet 1529–1555* (Scottish Record Society, vol xxxix, 1911), no. 39.

22 NAS CS6/26 fo. 129. GD40/2/9/7, GD40/2/9/63. JEDJM508. *CSPScot*, iii, 865. *RPC*, i, 23, 155–56, 406–07, 653; iii, 600; v, 13. Even in 1672 there is reference to a 'Provost Rutherford' at Jedburgh. CH2/552/1.

23 NAS GD40/2/9/62, GD40/2/10/36, GD40/2/10/42. *RSS*, v, 728, 2812. Godscroft, *History*, 323. M. Lynch, 'The Crown and the Burghs 1500–1625', in M. Lynch ed. *The Early Modern Town in Scotland* (London, 1987), 55–80.

24 NAS GD40/2/9/82, GD40/2/11/55. Spottiswoode, *History*, ii, 411. *cf.* Lee, *Thirlestane*, 218 and K. M. Brown, 'Burghs, Lords and Feuds in Jacobean Scotland', in M. Lynch, ed. *The Early Modern Town*, 108–09 who both used *CSP Scot*, x, 602 and *CBP*, i, 395, that incorrectly note Cessford as previously holding the office.

25 *CSP Scot*, viii, 420; x, 496, 517; xi, 157. *RPC*, iv, 530, 544; v, 13; vi, 541. Moysie, *Memoirs*, 98.

26 *RMS*, vi, 365. J. H. Stevenson, 'The Usher of the White Rod', *Scot Antiq*, x (1897), 158–161.

27 *CSP Scot,* xiii, pt 1, 112, 343, 363, 364. *ER,* xxiii, xliii-xlvi. *RPC,* v, 490, 525–6, 530–1, 553–4; vi, 32, 39–41, 114, 598. *RMS,* vi, 868. *HMC,* Milne-Home, 142, 144, 150.
28 Rae, *Scottish Frontier,* 237–45. NRAS 859/134/4. *CBP,* ii, 323.
29 NAS GD40/2/10/51. CBP, i, 242, 258, 265, 270. *RPC,* i, 283. *cf.* Rae, *Scottish Frontier,* 239–40.
30 NAS GD40/2/11/56. *CBP,* i, 808, 1266. *CSP Scot,* ii, 574; iv appendix 65; v, 284; xii, 73. Fraser, *Douglas,* iv, 194. R. P. Hardie, *The Roads of Medieval Lauderdale* (Edinburgh, 1942), 23–52.
31 *CSP Scot,* xiii, pt 1, 375. *RPC,* v, 464.
32 NRAS 1100/633. *HMC,* Home, 313/3.
33 Rae, *Scottish Frontier,* 257–9.
34 *CBP,* ii, 442, 490.
35 *CSPDom Add,* 1547–65, 404–05. *CSP Scot,* i, 73.
36 *L & P. Hen VIII,* xvi, 1263. Border lairds who did or did not assure are mentioned in Meikle, 'Thesis', ch. i. app. For fuller accounts of the troubled 1540s see E. Bonner, *The French Reactions to the Rough Wooings of Mary, Queen of Scots,* (Journal of the Sydney Society for Scottish History, vi, 1998). M. H. Merriman, *The Rough Wooings of Mary Queen of Scots, 1542–1551* (East Linton, 2000), 'The assured Scots', *SHR,* xlvii (1968), 10–34 and 'War and Propaganda during the Rough Wooing', *Scottish Tradition* (1979–80), ix, 20–30. G. Phillips, *The Anglo-Scots Wars 1513–1550* (Woodbridge, 1999), 148–255 and 'Strategy and its limitations: the Anglo-Scots Wars 1480–1550', *War in History,* vi (1999), 396–416.
37 *L & P. Hen VIII,* xvi, 1263.
38 *Ibid,* xviii, pt 1, 529.
39 *Ibid,* 868, 910, 945, 978; pt 2, 74. *Sadler Papers,* i, 233.
40 LAMB MS 3192 fo. 363. *L & P. Hen VIII,* xix, pt 1, 301, 684, 692, 945; pt 2, 468, 503, 684, 760; xx, pt 1, 244, 355. I. MacIvor, 'Artillery and Major Places of Strength in the Lothians and East Border, 1513–1542', in D. H. Caldwell, ed. *Scottish Weapons and Fortification 1100–1800* (Edinburgh, 1981), 94–152.
41 *APS,* ii, 461–2. *L & P. Hen VIII,* xx, pt 2, 400, 534.
42 *CSP Scot,* i, 299. *RSS,* iv, 464, 1109. *Hamilton Papers,* ii, 624.
43 *CSP Scot,* i, 143, 236, 245, 247.
44 *L & P. Hen VIII,* xvii, 638, 644; xviii, pt 1, 23; pt 2, 146, 297, 298, 309; xix, pt 1, 49, 50, 293; xx, pt 1 1091; pt 2, 347, 400, 414, 456, 533, 534; xxi, pt 1, 1279. *ADCP,* 569. *Hamilton Papers,* ii, 65, 118–19, 287–8, 405, 465, 581, 619. Pitscottie, *Historie,* 28–9, 105. Merriman, *The Rough Wooings,* 259.
45 BL MS Add. Chrs 1252. *CSPDom Add,* 1547–65, 386. *CSP Scot,* i, 75, 86. *L & P. Hen VIII,* xvii, 1143. *CPR,* 1547–8, 247. *RSS,* iv, 221, 507. *HMC,* Home, 314. *Mary of Lorraine. Corresp,* 346. 'Patten's expedition to Scotland, 1547', in A.F. Pollard, ed. *Tudor Tracts* (London, 1903), 142–45. Merriman, *The Rough Wooings,* 249, 313, 322, 338–39, 351–2. See also M. H. Merriman, 'The Forts of Eyemouth: Anvils of British Union', *SHR,* lxvii (1998), 142–155. I am grateful to Dr. Elizabeth Bonner for the first reference.
46 *L & P. Hen VIII,* xvii, 1143; xix, pt 2, 736, 754; xx, pt 2, 137, 912. *CSPDom Add,* 1547–65, 326. *CSP Scot,* i, 63, 211, 330. W. Forbes-Leith, *The Scots Men at Arms and Life Guards in France 1418–1830* (Edinburgh, 1882), ii, 138–46.
47 NAS GD224/529/1/108. *APS,* ii, 462. *RSS,* iv, 464, 650, 724, 1513, 1880.

48 NAS GD224/529/1/126. *APC*, iii, 492. *RMS*, iv, 819. *RPC*, i, 133, 140–1. *RSS*, iii, 876. E. Bonner, *The Politique of Henri II: De Facto French Rule in Scotland, 1550–1554* (Journal of the Sydney Society for Scottish History, vii, 1999).

49 *CSP For*, 1558–9, 1096; 1559–60, 902. *CSP Scot*, i, 630. *HMC*, Home, 21, 313/3, 314.

50 *CSP For*, 1559–60, 681, 755, 902, 910, 1049, 1092; 1560–1, 42, 435, 458, 619, 661, 880. *CSP Scot*, i, 736, 751, 977. *HMC*, Home, 314; Salisbury, i, 176.

51 NAS *CSP For*, 1560–1, 792; 1561–2, 125, 211, 420.

52 NAS CC8/8/4 fos 30–1. *CSP For*, 1564–5, 1289, 1321, 1533; 1561–2, 968. *CSP Scot*, ii, 181.

53 NAS RD1/4 fo. 93. RD1/7 fo. 400. *CSP For*, 1566–8, 205, 575, 578, 604, 618, 677. *CSP Scot*, ii, 363, 458. *RSS*, v, 3171

54 *CSPScot*. ii, 502, 522, 632, 653, 766. *RSS*, vi, 354. *Bannatyne Misc*, i, 29. Calderwood, *History*, ii, 359, 361–3, 365, 414–16. M. Anderson, ed. *The James Carmichael Collection of Proverbs in Scots* (Edinburgh, 1957), 79.

55 *CSP For*, 1566–8, 2405, 2411, 2606. *CSP Scot*, ii, 650, 653, 654, 810, 836. *RMS*, iv, 1834.

56 BL MS Add 32,091. NRAS 2177/2690 fo. 169. *CSP Scot*, ii, 1199; iii, 33. *RSS*, vi, 481. *HMC*, Pepys, 145. Melville, *Memoirs*, 201.

57 NAS GD40/2/19/1/1A. NLS MS 7103 fo. 1.

58 See Home genealogy. BL MS Cotton Caligula C. iv. fo. 271. *CSPDom Add*, 1566–71, 160, 164. *CSP For*, 1569–71, 555, 556. *CSP Scot*, iii, 59, 78, 84, 176–7, 897. Pitscottie, *Historie*, 259.

59 *CSP For*, 1569–71, 735, 858, 872. *CSP Scot*, iii, 168, 177, 197, 250, 382, 783, 895. *Warrender Papers*, i, 56.

60 *CSP For*, 1572–4, 286, 300, 531. *CSP Scot*, iii, 405, 523; iv, 165, 310, 320, 420.

61 *CSP For*, 1572–4, 381, 402. *CSP Scot*, iv, 273, 316, 319, 322, 333. Fast Castle belonged to Lord Home's second wife in jointure. She was widow and mother of the owners, the Logans of Restalrig.

62 *CSP Scot*, iv, 702, 734. *RMS*, iv, 2177, 2178. *RSS*, vi, 1625, 2318, 2320, 2381. Godscroft, *De Familia*, 45–9, 52–3.

63 *CSP Scot*, ii, 204; iv, 645, 665, 666. Melville, *Memoirs*, 256. Melville wrongly states that Home died shortly after his capture in 1573. He died a prisoner of Morton in 1575.

64 NAS CS7/4 fo. 449. RD1/17 fo. 183. RH15/19/1. NRAS 859/8/9. *CSP For*, 1144. *CSP Scot*, iii, 415, 527, 636; iv, app. 53. *HMC*, Milne-Home, 540.

65 See ch. i.

66 *CSP Scot*, iv, 314, 319. *RMS*, iv, 1535. *HMC*, Salisbury, ii, 303 (the date of which should be 1573 not 1579 as printed). Godscroft, *History*, 336. Moysie, *Memoirs*, 2.

67 See ch. iii.

68 *CSP For*, 1572–4, 719, 791, 819, 1223, 1564. *CSP Scot*, iv, 527, 567, 595, 708, 731, 750, 762.

69 NAS RD1/14 fo. 11. *CSP For*, 1569–71, 841. *CSP Scot*, iii, 865; iv, 472. *APC*, viii, 158, 265. *RMS*, iv, 2347, 2369. *TA*, xiii, 148.

70 *CSP Scot*, v, 191. *TA*, xiii, 348–81. *SS*, xiv, (1842), 268.

71 PRO SP52/25/35 I. *CSP For*, 1569–71, 1078. *CSP Scot*, iii, 363, 897; iv, 477, 479, 625. *RPC*, ii, 385.

72 *CSP Scot*, v, 383, 284. *RPC*, ii, 535. *RSS*, vii, 1635. Godscroft, *De Familia*,

72–3. Moysie, *Memoirs*, 17, 19. G. R. Hewitt, *Scotland Under Morton* (Edinburgh, 1982), 120–2, 127–9.

73 NRAS 2177/2690 fo. 228. Godscroft, *History*, 336–40; *De Familia*, 74–5. Morton also meddled in the Scottish West March, depriving Lord Maxwell of the wardenship. K. M. Brown, 'The Making of a Politique', *SHR*, lxvi (1987), 153–4.

74 BL MS Cotton Caligula C, v/i. fo. 161. *APS*, iii, 108–09. *CSP Scot*, v, 285, 433. Godscroft, *De Familia*, 72–3. Donaldson, *All The Queen's Men*, 130.

75 *CSP Scot*, v, 434. *RSS*, vii, 2231; viii, 380. Fraser, *Annandale*, i, 45, 46.

76 *CSP Scot*, v, 476, 479, 512, 584, 591, 592, 615, 737; vi, 113, 182. *CSP Spain*, 1580–6, 163. *RPC*, iii, 368. Calderwood, *History*, iii, 575–6. Teulet, *Relations politiques de la France et de l'Espagne avec l'Ecosse a XVIe siècle* (Paris, 1862), iii, 141.

77 *CBP*, i, 111. *CSP Scot*, v, 781; vi, 86, 154, 164. *RPC*, iii, 422, 425, 427.

78 NAS RH15/1/98. NRAS 859/2/7. *RSS*, vi, 2816. *Bannatyne Misc*, i, 68.

79 *CBP*, i, 145. *CSP Scot*, vi, 330, 348, 361. Calderwood, *History*, iii, 637–9.

80 NAS GD40/2/9/75. BL MS Cotton Caligula C.vii. fo. 338. *CBP*, i, 228, 258, 265. *CSP Scot*, vi, 298; vii, 40, 77, 101, 109, 118–20, 180, 411. *HMC, Salisbury*, iii, 73.

81 PRO SP52/25/94. *CBP*, i, 278, 331. *CSP Scot*, viii, 32, 41, 45, 57, 60. Godscroft, *History*, 402.

82 *CBP*, i, 330.

83 PRO SP59/23 fos 231–2. SP52/24 fos 7–8. *CBP*, i, 331, 335, 336, 341, 346, 358. *CSP Scot*, viii, 60, 65. *CSP Spain*, 1580–6, 406. *Hamilton Papers*, ii, 690–2. Melville, *Memoirs*, 344. Moysie, *Memoirs*, 53.

84 PRO IND1/6887. *CBP*, i, 341, 359, 368. *CSP Scot*, viii, 58, 69, 75, 80, 85, 174, 187, 420, 656, 681, 701.

85 NRAS 2177/2690 fo. 242. BL MS Cotton Caligula C. vi. fo. 94. *CBP*, i, 215, 376. *CSP Scot*, vii. 138; 180; viii, 177, 209, 291, 305, 337, 343, 656, 681. *RMS*, v, 286. *RSS*, viii, 338, 355, 661, 1449. *Bannatyne Club*, 26 (1828). G. Donaldson, *James V to James VII* (Edinburgh 1978), 182–3. The marriage between Bothwell's sister and Cowdenknowes was not part of a pacification in the Bothwell and Manderston feud as suggested by K. M. Brown, *Bloodfeud in Scotland* (Edinburgh, 1986), 128 (NAS RD1/36 fo. 271). They were still rivals in the 1580s.

86 NAS RD1/26 fo. 306. *APS*, iii, 291, 387. *CSP Scot*, vi, 696; vii, 113, 304, 308, x, 191, 195, 386, 393, 409, 492–3, 755. *RMS*, v, 286. *RSS*, viii, 451, 611. *IR*, xxiii, (1972), 128–9.

87 NAS RD1/26 fo. 306. *APS*, iii, 454. *HMC*, Seventh R, 430.

88 BL MS Cotton Caligula, D. i. fos 336–7. *CSP Scot*, ix, 455. Moysie, *Memoirs*, 67.

89 NAS RD1/13 fo. 359. RD1/20/2 fo. 370. RD1/ 33 fo. 33. RD1/40 fos 143–8. RD1/37 fo. 405. RD1/45 fo. 142. RH15/19/3/1. RH15/19/8. (*RPC*, iv, 42 – twenty-three Fife lairds were drafted into the Privy Council.)

90 NAS RD1/22 fo. 369, RD1/26 fo. 437, RD1/27 fos 206, 243, RD1/44/2 fos 356–7. *CBP*, i, 523. *CSP Scot*, ix, 367; x, 743. *RMS*, v, 1172. *RSS*, vi, 2315.

91 NRAS 859/11/2. *CSP Scot*, v, 608; vii, 113; ix, 578.

92 NAS RH15/16/3. *RMS*, v, 218. *RPC*, iv, 423.

93 NAS RD1/14 fo. 11. *CBP*, i, 499, 671. NRAS 832/78. *CSP Scot*, vii, 138; viii, 488; x, 191, 386, 389, 590, 592, 598, 730, 749, 755; xi, 123, 130. *RPC*, iv, 13–14, 612–14, 633, 648, 662. *HMC*, Salisbury, iii, 268, 404, 434, 442; iv, 504. Calderwood, *History*, ii, 359; iii, 759. Godscroft, *History*, 296–7. Donaldson, *James V*, 190–2.

94 NRAS 859/134/3. *CBP*, i, 448. *CSP Scot*, x, 28, 37, 71, 81, 84, 103, 204. *HMC*, Salisbury, iii, 404, 434.

95 *CSP Scot*, x, 191, 195.

96 NAS GD206/1/7. NRAS 859/4/1, 859/78. NLS. ADV MS 33.1.1/vi/26. *CBP*, i, 723. *CSP Scot*, x, 559, 586, 590, 592, 594, 598, 600, 625. *RMS*, v, 2114. *HMC*, Home, 316; Salisbury, iv, 233.

97 *CBP*, i, 767. *CSP Scot*, x, 464, 520, 629, 652, 693, 680, 743.

98 *CBP*, i, 824, 852, 865, 881, 889. *CSP Scot*, xi, 78, 86, 116, 126, 127, 133. Calderwood, *History*, v, 141–2. For a fuller account of Bothwell's activities see R. Macpherson, 'Francis Stewart, Fifth Earl Bothwell, and James VI: Perception Politics', in T. Brotherstone & D. Ditchburn, eds. *Freedom and Authority. Scotland c. 1050–c. 1650* (East Linton, 2000), 155–64.

99 NAS GD267/26/5. *APS*, iii, 528. *CBP*, i, 709, 768. *CSP Scot*, x, 598 (some of the signatories of this bond against Bothwell are suspicious as they were pro-Bothwell), 691, 749, 752, 756; xi, 130, 152. *RMS*, iv, 1966. *RPC*, v, 26–7, 80. Calderwood, *History*, v, 257. J. G. Dalyell, ed. *Fragments of Scottish History* (Edinburgh, 1798), ii, 30.

100 NAS CC8/8/33. *CSP Scot*, xi, 134, 137, 157, 174, 206. See ch. vi.

101 PRO SP52/54/23. *CSP Scot*, xi, 326. *Warrender Papers*, ii, 84.

102 *CSP Scot*, x, 505, 507, 517, 598, 602, 606, 627, 639, 655; xiii, pt 1, 6. *RMS*, v, 2018. *HMC*, Salisbury, iv, 175.

103 *CBP*, ii, 232, 236, 343, 431, 449. *CSP Scot*, x, 730, 749; xii, 80, 507. *RMS*, iv, 2214. Moysie, *Memoirs*, 96.

104 *CBP*, ii, 347. *CSP Scot*, xii, 212, 224, 256, 341, 400, 438, *etc.*, 797, 831, 90; xiii, pt 1 82, 124. F. H. Mares, ed., *The Memoirs of Robert Carey* (Oxford, 1972), 33, 35, 40–1.

105 *CBP*, ii, 1116, 1122. *HMC*, Salisbury, viii, 315.

106 PRO SP59/37 fos 98–101. *APC*, xxviii, 405. *CBP*, ii, 546, 831, 946. *HMC*, Salisbury, ix, 137–8, 151.

107 *CBP*, ii, 403, 445, 471. *HMC*, Salisbury, ix, 17–18, 28–9, 104.

108 *CBP*, ii, 1059, 1060. *CSP Scot*, xi, 460; xii, 137; xiii, pt 1, 329, 356, 359, 380. *HMC*, Salisbury, ix, 382.

109 *CSP Scot*, xiii, pt 1, 362, 378, 382.

110 NAS E21/76 fo. 179r. *RMS*, vi, 80, 668.

111 *CBP*, ii, 1148. *CSP Scot*, xiii, pt 2, 497, 509. *HMC*, Sixth R, 666.

112 NAS GD40/2/11/64, GD224/529/2/196. *CBP*, ii, 1291. *CSP Scot*, xiii, pt 2, 559, 566, 571, 576, 579–80, 650.

113 *CSP Scot*, ii, 192.

114 NAS RH6/3742. NLS MS 7103 fo. 2. *CSP Scot*, xiii, pt 2, 579, 580, 583, 585, 586, 668. *RPC*, iv, 70. Moysie, *Memoirs*, 67.

115 NAS GD40/2/12/4, GD40/9/3. *CSP Scot*, xiii, pt 2, 529.

116 *CBP*, i, 916; ii, 1445, 1463. *CSP Scot*, xiii, pt 2, 768, 773, 797, 821, 841, 846. *HMC*, Salisbury, xii, 94, 128, 135–6. See ch. v.

117 *CSP Scot*, xiii, pt 2, 849.

118 NAS E21/76 fos 165r, 224r, 236v. *CSP Scot*, xiii, pt 2, 826, 832, 833, 837, 854, 866, 878. Teulet, *Relations*, iv, 263.

119 NAS E21/76 fos 287v-288r.

120 M. M. Meikle, 'Northumberland Divided: Anatomy of a Sixteenth-Century Bloodfeud', *AA*, 5th ser, xx (1992), 80–4. See ch. iii.

3

The Rise of the Eastern Border Gentry

I. The Gentry Community and the Demise of the Percies

The gentry who lived to the north of the Coquet should never be classified with the notorious thieves of impoverished upland Redesdale and Tynedale who lived according to different standards. The north Northumberland and North Durham gentry survived on their more productive agricultural land and therefore had no necessity to steal. There was unproductive ground in both the East and Middle Marches, yet the majority of these gentry families were happy to graze their livestock without raiding their English or Scottish neighbours.[1] This more peaceable mentality is at the heart of the divide between Eastern and Western English Borders, but the men of the East were not above violence. It is undeniable that they feuded amongst themselves with the ferocity known throughout all English gentry communities if tempers flared and weapons were to hand.[2]

The political structure of the gentry community is more complex than that of the lairds. In 1569 Lord Hunsdon, then warden of the English East March, reported that Northumberland knew 'no other prince but a Percy'. This was an exaggeration as the county had been without aristocratic leadership since the 1530s.[3] The Percy earls of Northumberland had a traditional power base in the barony of Alnwick, but mistrust of overmighty magnates led to a rather inconsistent crown policy to diminish the feudal power bases of northern magnates.[4] The Tudors wanted to get rid of the northern liberties that hindered royal justice, so in 1504 Tynedale's liberty was abolished, followed by Norham and Islandshire in 1536.[5] Henry VIII also bought the manors of Redesdale and Coquetdale in 1546 and exchanged land with the earl of Rutland in 1547 to gain the Etal estates which included lands in Glendale. These purchases were designed to extend royal influence near the frontier. Henry was therefore delighted when the sixth earl of Northumberland offered his estates to the crown.[6] The earl was pensioned in 1535 and when he died in June 1537 Henry VIII took full command of the vast Percy estates. George Bernard's assertion that Henry would have handed these to the earl's brother, had he not been charged with treason, is incredible. Sir Ingram Percy blamed the newly risen Sir Reynold Carnaby of Capheaton for 'the destruction of all our blood, for by his means the King shall be my lord's heir'. The Percy estates remained in crown control until the short-lived restoration of Thomas Percy, nephew of the sixth earl, in 1557. By the 1530s the crown and the Percies were anything but 'natural and trusted partners in government' as Bernard and Richard Hoyle would suggest. The crown sought direct loyalty by building upon anti-Percy sentiment amongst the gentry. Some even see the funeral of the sixth earl as 'the triumph of the Tudors over the Percies'.[7]

The twenty-year interregnum from Percy control in the barony of Alnwick (1537–57) had a devastating effect on their loyal gentlemen tenants. The process of wooing Percy squires away from their feudal superior had, however, begun much earlier. Lords Dacre, Eure and Wharton demonstrate the success of newly risen men resulting from Tudor dabbling in northern politics.[8] There were significant achievers amongst the gentry as well, such as Thomas Forster of Adderstone, who married Lord Wharton's sister Florence. Forster's younger brother John would rise to become the political leader of Northumberland by the 1570s.[9] Even the well-established Radcliffes of Cartington and the Grays of Horton and Chillingham were quick to respond to crown enticements of lands available after the dissolution of the monasteries. Then there were pensions or new offices such as the commissioners for the dissolution taken up by Sir Lionel Gray of Berwick, John Selby of Branxton and Robert Collingwood of Eslington.[10] If the crown's efforts to subvert magnatial power were sometimes inconsistent, this was not the case in the 1530s.

Without a resident magnate, direct crown and court influence expanded in the region and there was an undeniable rise of the gentry. This was not exceptional by English, or Welsh, standards as other counties experienced what Simon Adams has termed a 'gentry republic'.[11] Warwickshire and Staffordshire are good examples, but Kent, Norfolk and Suffolk also witnessed gentry power struggles when traditional aristocratic leadership was challenged.[12] However, as early as 1536 the rising known as the Pilgrimage of Grace tested the loyalty of these newly risen men.[13] The local gentry mobilised into two distinct groups. One consisted of Percy loyalists that included the Lisles of Felton, Swinhoes and Roddams of Roddam. The other group contained new crown supporters such as Sir Robert Ellerker, Robert Collingwood, Lionel Gray of Berwick, Sir Roger and Thomas Gray of Horton and Thomas Forster of Adderstone. Men from Tynedale and Redesdale, who were still loyal to the Percies, raided the Grays' properties in retaliation for their disloyalty. Therefore in Northumberland the Pilgrimage could be interpreted as a pro- or anti-Percy rebellion.[14] Henry VIII duly rewarded those pledging loyalty to him with direct patronage. Percy tenants John Carr of Hetton, Robert Collingwood, Richard Fowberry of Fowberry, Thomas Hepburn of Hepburn, and Ralph Ilderton of Ilderton all received life pensions of £13–6s–8d a year. Pensioners who were not Percy tenants included Thomas Carr of Newlands, Lionel Gray, Thomas Holburn of Holburn, Edward Muschamp of Barmoor, John Selby and William Strother of Kirknewton. As greater gentry Sir Robert Ellerker, Thomas Forster of

Adderstone, Sir Roger and Thomas Gray of Horton and Cuthbert Radcliffe received £20 a year. Robert Collingwood even received the court office of royal crowkeeper, which was unusual for a Northumbrian to achieve. It was ironic that many of these gentlemen had received fees for being in the Council in Household of the earl of Northumberland as warden of the East and Middle Marches in 1528. Perhaps they were displaying loyalty to the earl as a crown official rather than a territorial magnate. These pensions were only temporary as they dried up in 1547 when Edward VI came to the throne. They had secured immediate loyalty, but paying the gentry for services normally rendered freely would be highly damaging for Border defence in the long run.[15]

In 1540 a significant change was at work in north Northumberland and North Durham society. This community had been led by greater gentlemen, with the Forsters and Selbies being regarded as minor gentry, yet by 1557 the Forsters held a commanding lead over the other local gentry families.[16] The Forsters had received advantageous leases of monastic and Percy lands from the crown. These made their rise spectacular and put them at the head of the faction opposed to the Percies. In 1557 the restored seventh earl of North-umberland resented this loss of gentry support, but could do little to reverse the situation. His local patronage was impaired and he was dependent upon Queen Mary for his own patronage. He could not blame the crown for his family's misfortune, so he turned his vengeance on the Forsters. This action had the opposite effect to the one he intended, as it gained him more enemies than friends in the locality. The earl's unpopularity increased with his over zealous investigation of the Heron and Carr feud and his support for the villainous Thomas Clavering, captain of Norham.[17]

The Forsters, Collingwoods, Grays and Radcliffes, as new leaders of local gentry society, were alarmed at the restoration of the Percies in 1557. Yet it was only the Collingwoods of Eslington who defected back to Percy adherence to oppose their rivals, the Forsters, and gain the office of constable of Alnwick. P. G. Boscher and R. R. Reid argue that the restored Percies built up an impressive power structure on the Border in a short space of time. It was true that the earl was appointed warden of both East and Middle Marches, but he discovered that wardenships alone did not command the respect of the local gentry. The damage of the Percy interregnum to his tradition following would prove irreparable.[18] Even Sir Henry Percy, the earl's brother, who gained the captaincies of Tynemouth and Norham found ready opposition in the Selby family who were entrenched in Norhamshire and Berwick-on-Tweed.

When the privy council recommended Sir John Forster to the earl in 1558 he declined their advice and dismissed him as deputy warden of the Middle March. This small Percy triumph against a rival was short-lived. The death of Queen Mary in 1558 cut off the earl's court patronage. Subsequent courtier rivalry led to Forster being appointed as warden of the same March in 1560. The disillusioned earl then retreated from the Alnwick area to reside at his Yorkshire estates. He reluctantly accepted that Sir John Forster now had more local power. 'By 1570 the crown had broken the influence of the Percies' though Sir Henry Percy remained in Border service. He made little impact with the local gentry and was the subject of a damning investigation by the privy council in 1571.[19]

Forster's ascendancy was not without some obstacles as he had enemies in the locality, particularly amongst Percy servants like George Clarkson, keeper of Hulne Park near Alnwick. Clarkson surveyed the barony for the earl in 1567 and took every opportunity he could to snipe at the Forsters. He regretted the loss of the 'old order' in the barony and was imprisoned by Lord Grey, warden of the East March, for his pro-Percy stance. Nevertheless, the poor response from the barony to the 1569 rebellion by the earls of Northumberland and Westmorland would indicate how far Percy defection had reached. The earl of Westmorland had a good response from his tenants in County Durham, but at Alnwick only a few local gentlemen joined the earls. A small party held the castle, but it capitulated with suspicious rapidity and Forster then installed his son Nicholas as constable.[20] The small Percy following in the locality was shattered by the subsequent collapse of the rebellion. In 1572 Lord Hunsdon, warden of the East March, and Forster publicly feared that loyal Percy tenants would try to prevent the earl being escorted through Northumberland to his execution at York. This was probably just Elizabethan bravado to ensure that money came north to pay the Berwick garrison, for the task was not unduly perilous considering the earl's loss of his local following.[21]

The earl's execution symbolised a final victory for Forster. Sir Henry Percy was created eighth earl of Northumberland for his loyalty to the crown during the rebellion, yet he was not trusted to live in the north and spent the rest of his life in the south of England. His son, the ninth earl, was too preoccupied with science to bother with the north. The only interest the earls maintained in the north was the collection of their rents. The ninth earl would appoint a kinsman, Thomas Percy, as constable of Alnwick, but he also proved unpopular with the local gentry.[22]

With the eclipse of Percy power north of the Coquet local gentry responded to court patronage instead, but they could deviously switch allegiance or be clients of several courtiers at the same time. They were as shrewd as the Border lairds in this activity, for in local rivalries the gentry rarely maintained steady alliances to courtiers. Religious differences, personal jealousies, or even old loyalty to the absent Percies often came into play. They were normally loyal to the crown with the one exception of Border service, where they often tried to avoid the expense this duty involved. This decision was created by financial difficulties, rather than disloyalty, and makes them appear as typically canny Borderers.[23]

By 1600 the Forsters, Collingwoods, Grays and Selbies were still influential, but unlike the lairds, they still faced challenges from non-local office holders. Lord Hunsdon's sons Sir Robert and John Carey, Lord Eure and Lord Willoughby d'Eresby all appeared in Middle and East March offices in the 1590s. Sir John Forster had been dismissed from the Middle March, the Collingwoods' recusancy caught up with them and the Selbies had to fight to maintain their strength in Berwick. Ralph Gray also had a problem with his recusant family, but personal wealth and following kept him at the forefront of local society.[24] The sense of community amongst the north Northumberland and North Durham gentry was still strong and this enabled them to subdue personal quarrels to mount opposition to the newcomers. None of these men had sufficient local patronage to topple the local gentry community, yet their power at court and Elizabethan sense of arrogance had deemed them a threat to the gentry.

II. The Administration

i. Domestic Office

In the Eastern English Borders office holders were typically from the ranks of greater and middle gentry. The highest domestic officer was the high sheriff of Northumberland whose duties declined in the sixteenth century with the rise of receivers and feodaries. His writ did not extend into Norham and Islandshire nor the bounds of Berwick, but as there were no separate sheriffs in these areas justice was probably administered by J.Ps, town councillors, the captain of Norham Castle and the governor of the Berwick garrison. At Berwick the sheriff's authority stopped half way across the Tweed bridge.[25] From 1540 to 1603 twenty-eight sheriffs were substantial landowners north of the Coquet, but instead of welcoming its prestige most fought to avoid the office as it was an unwelcome financial burden. Sir George Radcliffe of Cartington, for example, avoided the office during 1547–52 but was appointed in 1558.[26] When Sir John Forster was appointed warden of the Middle March in 1560 he also became *Custos Rotulorum* with power to issue writs and search warrants. His kinsmen Sir Ralph Gray (1565), Thomas Forster (1572) and Ralph Gray (1582) were appointed sheriff and this may have disrupted the legal system as enemies of Sir John would not necessarily have co-operated with his kin. In 1596 Lord Eure despaired of bias and asked that a discreet sheriff be appointed 'not disposed to factions or to favour theft'.[27]

Sheriffs were required to go to London to accept office and give financial assurances. For example, Sir Cuthbert Radcliffe had sureties of 200 marks to account to the Exchequer for all the fines levied during his term of office.[28] Nevertheless, Northumbrian sheriffs were generally lazy about final accounting and were full of excuses for their lapses. In 1536 the demands of Border service were cited, yet in 1548 the situation had not improved as an Act of Parliament was passed 'for the Shirieff of Northumberlande to be accomptable for his office as other Shirieffs bee' including a penalty of £100.[29] This Act was not enforced so a commission was ordered to investigate in 1562, but this had a limited effect for the sheriff was still not accounting in 1563.[30] Exasperated Exchequer officials then recommended that past sheriffs be excused accounting and that lawsuits against them for not paying be dropped as 'an encouragement for them to doe better execution hereafter'. This optimism was unfulfilled as sheriffs remained indolent throughout Elizabeth's reign.[31]

Thomas Bradford of Bradford was sheriff during 1594–95 and he, exceptionally, remained in office for 1595–96 as the chosen candidate, Robert Widdrington, refused to take up the office.[32] Recusancy legislation prevented many sons of greater gentry families from becoming sheriff in the 1590s. This void was filled by middling gentry who were less skilled in the office and had fewer financial resources. These newer sheriffs were also slow to account to the Exchequer, but the reason for this remains unclear. They perhaps pocketed the money as a supplement to their meagre salary, or they may have been unable to levy fines from elusive Northumbrians. Both reasons are plausible as Northumbrian sheriffs sometimes rendered their accounts years after their shrievalty. Problems continued after 1603 as Sir William Selby begged not to receive the office in 1604 as he was then resident in Kent.[33]

Members of the commission of the peace, better known as justices of the peace (J.P.s), are difficult to trace in earlier years though they usually were drawn from the greater or middle gentry. However, in the 1540s and 1590s lesser gentry like John Carr of Hetton and Thomas Carr of Newlands were included. The *Libri Pacis* of 1547 and 1554 include leading gentlemen such as Sir Robert Ellerker of Hulne, Sir Thomas Gray of Horton, Sir George Radcliffe, Robert Collingwood of Eslington, Cuthbert Horsley of Screnwood and John Beadnell.[34] By 1562 the composition of the commission had changed little with the exception of risen gentry like Sir John Forster, who was listed for the first time. Sir John Selby was a noticeable addition in 1588, when Forster took precedence over all other gentlemen in the lists.[35] As with the shrievalty, many recusants were later excluded so there were no Grays, Collingwoods or Radcliffes in 1594. Appearing for the first time were Protestant gentry, such as William Selby of Shoreswood, George Muschamp of Barmoor and the Puritan Sir William Reed. There were also gentlemen from outside Northumberland in this commission to make up for the lack of suitable Protestants in the county. William Selby of Twizel was the only 'new' man in the commission from north of the Coquet in 1600. A few Catholics still managed to appear regularly in the list for Robert Clavering of Callaly remained a J.P. until he died in 1600 and both Thomas Bradford of Bradford and Edward Gray of Howick, as former sheriffs, prevailed in the commission in the early-seventeenth century.[36]

Justices of the peace had to hold land worth £20 a year and were paid the inadequate sum of four shillings a day for attending quarter sessions; their principal gathering. These sessions were held at various locations such as Morpeth in April 1557.[37] Their duties increased considerably throughout the century, so in spite of being regarded as leading figures in county administration they had to work hard. Special commissions from the Exchequer or London courts, such as the King's Bench or Common Pleas added to their workload.[38] Justices were supposed to license inns and taverns, yet as there were seventy four in Berwick, 137 in the East March and 123 in the Middle March even the most efficient justices would have felt overworked checking every hostelry.[39] As with the sheriffs, there were complaints about negligent justices. They were accused of not attending quarter sessions or carrying out inspections and their bail was reported to be 'as good as the Quenes pardon'. Sir John Carey, marshall of Berwick and William Selby, senior (of Shoreswood) both complained about local J.P.s in 1602, despite being J.Ps themselves. According to their exaggerated reports none of the justices were fit for service, with the exception of themselves. Sir William Reed of Holy Island was noted as being old and blind (though he had been an active J.P. only months before), Thomas Bradford of Bradford was in a dead palsy (yet he lived until 1612) and George Muschamp of Barmoor dared not be seen in public because of a feud (in which Selby opposed him).[40] It was only Muschamp who could not serve in 1602 and when William Selby needed a J.P. he hypocritically refused to call on Sir John Carey's help as they were rivals in the Berwick garrison. Local J.P.s were occasionally involved with faction fighting to the detriment of their duties, but they must have been reasonably efficient overall as the surviving *vetera indictamenta* records formal trial indictments against criminals from both north Northumberland and North Durham.[41]

Neither north Northumberland nor North Durham had a lord lieutenant or deputy lieutenants. The burden of Border service excluded the area from subsidy taxation, making a deputy lieutenant (in his tax collecting capacity) unnecessary until the Union of the Crowns in 1603. Military matters were dealt with by the wardens of the Marches, which again made lieutenants non-essential. The area still had administrative wards, but these were mostly for musters and crown rent collections rather than taxation. The Northumberland wards were Bamburghshire, Castle, Coquetdale, Glendale, Morpeth and Tynedale, with Norham and Islandshire as a separate North Durham unit.[42]

The assizes, like quarter sessions, involved important judicial congregations of J.P.s and local gentlemen before the circuit judges of the north. In Northumberland they were frequently held in Newcastle before the various assize commissioners such as oyer and terminer and gaol delivery. Sir John Forster was, for example, a commissioner for oyer and terminer in 1565. In 1596 the commissioners were Sir William Reed, Robert Clavering and William Selby senior.[43] Assize week, by its length alone, assured a large social gathering of gentlemen. Sir John Forster and Thomas Ilderton of Ilderton had houses in Newcastle and Sir Cuthbert Collingwood probably stayed with merchant kinsmen. This was similar to assize weeks in other counties, such as Yorkshire where the gentry congregated in York.[44]

The offices of escheator, coroner and feodary of Northumberland were held by local gentlemen. An escheator informed the crown of lands forfeited by felony, or through a lack of heirs and was present at all *Inquisitions Post Mortem*, but his powers were dwindling in the sixteenth century. Robert Roddam of Roddam was the escheator in 1588–89 and he had also been county coroner in 1582, a post that involved maintaining crown property in the shire. The county feodary worked solely for the Court of Wards established in 1540 and he received the rents and fines of lands subject to wardship.[45] John Beadnell of Lemmington held this post during 1559–60. As with other financial payments to the crown the guardians of minors were often slow to settle their dues with the feodary, or perhaps the feodary withheld the rentals for his own benefit.

Inquisitions Post Mortem gave lesser gentlemen a rare opportunity to serve on a jury assessing the estate of a deceased gentleman. They often succeeded in misleading the feodary as to the real value of the estate. This duty was unsalaried, but it was a way of showing mutual support for other gentry against the loathsome system of wardship. Being a juror may have been the only public duty carried out by lesser gentlemen, who were usually confined to their community by financial restraints. Nevertheless, it was their local knowledge that was valuable when an estate had to be evaluated. The Court of Wards once made a mistake by ordering an Inquisition concerning Thomas Ilderton of Ilderton from gentry who lived south of the Coquet. Realising their geographical error they re-commissioned it from more local gentlemen.[46] The commissioners for an *Inquisition Post Mortem* were normally directed to hold the inquiry by special commission of the Exchequer, acting upon information from the Court of Wards. The commissioners would have included the feodary and they ordered the sheriff to convene a local jury to hear depositions about the deceased's lands. The Escheator presided over the proceedings, but it was the commissioners who reported back to the Exchequer and the feodary to the Court of Wards. Commissioners were typically chosen from the greater or middle gentry, not just for *Inquisitions Post Mortem*, but for all sorts of special commissions into local matters including crown lands, tithes, fishing rights, surveys of lands and castles near the Border, enclosures, fords, harbours and piracy. Latterly there were additional commissions to examine recusants and report on the decline of Border service, which kept the gentry very busy.[47]

Commissioners of array were placed in charge of local musters and they worked closely with local gentry and the wardens of the Marches. The defence of the sixteenth-century English Borders relied on a unique tenure

system where tenants were given land in return for pledges to arm themselves against attack and give assistance to the March wardens.[48] Arms
would have included a steel helmet, a breast plate of armour and a long bow
with the addition of a horse if they were larger tenants. Musters were held by
administrative ward and the gentry were responsible for their tenants'
appearance. They seem to have been a social gathering for all concerned
for in 1558 'on the muster day there is never a plough going in Norhamshire
nor Bamburghshire that day; it is their principal feast'.[49] In 1583 the gentry
refused to appear because plague was rampaging through the county, but
turnouts had generally deteriorated by this time. Sir John Forster falsified
muster returns in the 1590s to try and cover up the serious decline in Border
defence. This was caused by several factors including the large numbers of
Scots living in the area, Scottish raiding, enclosing and engrossing of land,
and poor harvests that greatly impoverished English tenants.[50]

Other crown offices available to the gentry were the receivers, stewards
(seneschals), bailiffs, foresters, agisters, keepers of parks and constables of
castles. This gave the gentry a variety of positions such as the duchy of
Lancaster's lands at Dunstanburgh and Embleton which had Sir Thomas
Gray of Horton as receiver and Bamburgh Castle where John Horsley of
Outchester and Sir John Forster were captain (constable) and seneschal.
Henry Haggerston was receiver for the lands of the former Alnwick Abbey
during 1577–95 and was receiver of Glendale from 1587 to 1595, after
which his recusancy barred him from office. Henry Collingwood of Etal was
a hereditary constable of Etal Castle and he took over the receivership of
Glendale in 1600. At the same time Nicholas Forster of Alnwick Abbey was
receiver of Norham and Islandshire. On a lesser scale Robert Collingwood
of Bewick was bailiff of Bewick.[51]

Non-royal offices available to the gentry included the Percy estates
centred around the barony of Alnwick and the Grays' barony of Wark-
on-Tweed. The highest Percy office holder was the constable of Alnwick
Castle. This post was normally held by a Percy ally, with the exception of the
1537–57 interregnum and the 1569 rebellion. Sir Cuthbert Radcliffe held
office during 1540–45 and Sir Cuthbert Collingwood in 1569 and 1580–85.
Less important, although still salaried, were George Harbottle of Cawledge
as agister of Cawledge Park and Odnel Selby of Hulne, a keeper of Hulne
Park. Tristram Fenwick was steward and forester of Rothbury.[52] Lastly
there were numerous local manor courts that sometimes had gentlemen
present, but mostly concerned tenants below the rank of gentlemen, just like
the baron courts in Scotland.[53] The barony at Alnwick was more of a gentry
preserve, but it fell into abeyance during the Percies' prolonged absence. It
was revived by Thomas Percy, a distant relative of the ninth earl, when he
became constable of Alnwick Castle in 1586. He proved to be corrupt and
greedy, and in attempting to bolster the long-lost Percy influence in the area
he facilitated gentry opposition to himself. It was significant that only one

Forster (Cuthbert of Brunton) and none of the Grays attended this farce of a barony court.[54]

Borough patronage was another source of office for the gentry. The Berwick guild included at least four burgess gentleman, who were also accepted in the community outwith the town. Odnel Selby of Tweedmouth and John Ord of Longridge were both mayors of Berwick and William Selby was elected a burgess of Berwick to represent the borough in Parliament. Thomas Heron of Crawley was both a merchant of Newcastle and a local gentleman.[55]

The local gentry therefore had plenty of opportunity to gain offices whether they were crown or more localised appointments. If they were middle or greater gentry their chances of obtaining office were much greater than those of the lesser gentry. Overall, the gentry were the backbone of local administration – just as in the Eastern Scottish Borders. However, changes began in the 1590s when recusancy evicted many established gentlemen from crown offices, though a few clever church papists avoided recognition. With strong kinship there was no great divide between Catholic and Protestant gentry in this community so there was a limited return of Catholics to office in the early-seventeenth century. Placing unskilled middle gentlemen in office alongside ignorant outsiders had failed to fill the void left by recusants. Confrontational outsiders such as Robert and John Carey never surmounted local gentry opposition or the inherent local strength of men like Ralph Gray of Chillingham.[56]

Parliamentary representatives were not specifically local, nor connected to Border administration yet should still be noted. North Durham had no parliamentary representation as it was part of the principality of the bishop of Durham. However two members were sent from the shire of Northumberland, and towns of Morpeth, Berwick and Newcastle. There were only a few shire representatives from north of the Coquet; John Beadnell of Lemmington (1547), Sir Thomas Gray of Horton (1553), Sir Thomas Gray of Chillingham (1586) and William Selby junior (1601). By contrast the Selbies were well represented at Berwick with Odnel Selby of Tweedmouth (1554) and William Selby senior (1586, 1588, 1593, 1597, 1601), which reflected their strength within the town.[57] Parliamentary office allowed the gentry an expenses-paid trip to London, but there were only a few statutes concerning the area. These were not instigated by local members as they were mostly criticisms of Northumberland's sheriffs or poor defences. Perhaps the gentry were not interested in national politics and as this office gave little local power, it was probably seen as more of a sinecure than a purposeful office. This lack of political consciousness, whether English or British, is best exemplified by Berwick M.P. Martin Garnett. He was a burgess there and charged the guild £23 for his parliamentary expenses, but was more concerned about £3–15s owed to him for having a town bell cast at London.[58]

Overall control of north Northumberland and North Durham is difficult to determine as Westminster did not directly govern the area. Other areas such as the Welsh Marches, Ireland, Yorkshire and Lancashire were not directly controlled either. The Eastern English Borders were governed by a mixture of parliament, Star Chamber, the Council of the North, the privy council, the town guild of Berwick (which was inseparable from the garrison at this time) and J.P.s. Attempts to seek a British polity amongst this complicated system of government are inappropriate as there was little co-ordination. Parliament merely passed a few statutes and the privy council governed Border administration, so this left domestic administration to the Council of the North and the justices. The Council of the North did not have a great impact in the area and was therefore an ineffectual voice of local government. Only Sir Thomas Gray of Horton and Sir John Forster were members, although Sir Cuthbert Collingwood and Thomas Forster were recommended for membership. The Council was, none the less, a convenient source of justice for the local gentry. It was nearer to the community than the London Courts and legal fees were charged at a fixed rate.[59] However, it is questionable how much influence the Council had in Yorkshire, its home base, as it was always subordinate to the Court of Star Chamber. The Lord president of the Council could summon the local gentry to meet him in Newcastle, as the earl of Huntingdon did in 1586, 1593, and 1596, but this was in connection with special investigations into Border decay, recusancy and the activities of Sir John Forster. Such summonses were not a prerogative of the Council and it had no power in the Marches, with the exception of domestic justice in Berwick. Lord Willoughby unsuccessfully challenged this Berwick jurisdiction in 1600 as he arrested a man for a domestic crime and then had to release him. Just as the Council could not interfere in international Border law, Willoughby, as warden of the East March, had no power to meddle in domestic laws regarding Berwick. The only jurisdiction he had was over the captaincy of Holy Island, not the town of Berwick.[60]

Who really governed north Northumberland and North Durham? The answer perhaps lies with the gentry themselves, as they lived permanently in the area, held offices, fought the local political battles and dallied with courtier politics without holding court offices themselves. It was the justices who coped with the everyday administration of the area. Those who held high office were frequently in a commanding position if they had court patronage and had the backing of a good kinship network. However the area had another source of office that was unique to the Borders. This was the administration of Border law that gave some local gentlemen extra power in the community. It would advance the career of Sir John Forster to a level of authority previously thought unobtainable by a local gentleman on the English frontier.

ii. Border Office

The administration of the Anglo-Scottish frontier was based on a complex system of international law. Border officers had no jurisdiction over domestic incidents, which were dealt with by the sheriff and justices of Northumberland. Nevertheless, a warden of a March had the power to summon domestic law enforcers and the local gentry to assist him in Border duties. These tasks included days of truce between wardens of both nations and 'hot trod' recovery expeditions against Scottish raiders. Wardens were answerable directly to the privy council, rather than the Council of the North, which was probably not the best route as it slowed communications even further. Henry VIII did establish a Council of the Marches in 1537 in response to the rising of 1536, but it was short-lived and control of the Marches returned to the wardens and the privy council.[61] Before 1540 Border wardens were not usually chosen from the ranks of local gentlemen. Gentlemen pensioners appointed in 1537 were an exception to this rule, but their contribution to Border defence was erratic. They swung between savage attacks on Teviotdale to virtual sinecurism and were thus abolished when Henry VIII died in 1547. By contrast, Elizabethan pensioners were practical garrison men stationed in Berwick.[62]

A warden normally appointed two gentry deputies such as Sir Cuthbert Radcliffe of Cartington, a deputy warden for the Middle March from 1540–3. He was followed by Thomas Gray in 1552 and Sir Ralph Gray of Chillingham as a deputy in the East March in 1552–57 and 1559–60. Radcliffe was thought to be inadequate, but Gray was of 'good courage and much esteemed'.[63] The appointment of local gentlemen as deputies continued with Rowland Forster of Lucker (East March 1566), Sir John Selby of Twizel (East March 1568–95), Sir Cuthbert Collingwood of Eslington (Middle March 1595–6), Ralph Carr, younger, of Ford 'a very suffitient deputy' (Middle March 1597), Edward Gray of Howick (Middle March 1596–8) and Robert Clavering of Callaly (Middle March 1597). These were typical appointments, so the appointment of Sir John Forster as warden of a March was remarkable. He was the only local gentleman ever to be appointed to this top position in the sixteenth century.

Forster was first recommended for the wardenship of the Middle March in 1559, after a brief spell as deputy warden during 1557–58. The difficulties endemic to Border administration led to the view that a warden should now be 'one as is naturallie planted in the countrie'.[64] Forster was therefore an ideal choice and he remained in office until 1595, with a short interlude during 1587–88.[65] Warden appointments made in the reigns of Henry VIII, Edward VI and Mary were of relatively short duration and often linked to international crises. In the less internationally belligerent Elizabethan decades, wardens held office for many years as Lord Hunsdon was warden of the East March from 1568 to 1596 and Henry, Lord Scrope held the West March from 1563 to 1592. A reversion of Forster's office of captain of

Bamburgh was granted to Sir George Carey, eldest son of Lord Hunsdon, in 1574 to take effect on Forster's decease. Carey had the good sense to abandon the grant in 1582 as the indomitable Forster would live on until 1602 with George himself dying in 1603.[66] Forster's unrivalled local patronage and kinship network made him an effective Border officer until corruption overtook his administration. This led to his eventual dismissal from office in 1595. By contemporary standards he was then a very old man, yet he was not ninety four as Sir Robert Carey suggested. Forster would have been around eighty years of age, having been born *circa* 1515. If he had been over ninety his mother would have been a miracle worker who gave birth over a forty-year period![67]

Local gentry could be employed in other Border offices such as Border commissions or the Berwick garrison. Border commissioners were chosen by the monarchs of both realms to either prove foul (file) or refute the individually listed wrongs known as Border bills. If proved the commissioners then agreed upon compensation. There were normally several privy councillors in the commission as well as a bishop, but local knowledge was paramount to their enquiries. Therefore in 1581 Sir John Forster, Sir John Selby and Sir Thomas Gray of Chillingham joined the commissioners and in 1599 Nicholas Forster of Bamburgh and Thomas Bradford of Bradford were present.[68] Whenever the commissioners met many local gentlemen attended upon them in hope of their own bills being heard or to give evidence, or simply to socialise. At the Berwick meeting of 1585 the gentry stayed for a week, but commissions were not regular occurrences. They could only take place when Anglo-Scottish relations were favourable. The gentry's local knowledge was also useful during frequent English embassies to Scotland. Sir John Forster (1571), Sir John Selby (1595), Ralph Gray of Chillingham and William Selby senior (1598) all accompanied ambassadors to Scotland.[69]

The Berwick garrison offered more permanent offices with captaincies of garrison companies. Posts like gentleman porter or treasurer were also available to local gentlemen and their sons and as the size of the garrison grew, so did the opportunities for preferment. In 1554 Sir Thomas Gray, Ralph Swinhoe of Cornhill, John Selby of Branxton and Henry Haggerston of Haggerston all held positions in the garrison. Sir John Selby first made his mark as a captain in 1558 and went on to become gentleman porter during a lifetime's service in the garrison.[70] The gentleman porter was thought to be the equivalent of a sergeant major. It was a prestigious post with no great work attached to it for yeoman porters carried out the actual work of operating the gates of Berwick. The town was very much a 'garrison' borough run along military lines with the governor of the garrison, rather than the town council having overall control. The Selbies were predominant here as they made the post of gentleman porter seem hereditary and chose to live in the town rather than at their nearby estates. John Selby held the post from 1551–65, his son Sir John 1573–95, and grandson William junior from 1598–1603, though he was really an assistant to his uncle William senior, the porter during 1595–1603.[71] All their children were baptised in the borough church.[72] Ralph and John Selby, younger sons of Sir John Selby, were a constable and great gunner respectively in the garrison, continuing the Selby tradition. By the time of the 1598 garrison muster, John Selby had become a captain with fifty-two men in his company. Sir William Reed of Holy Island had 108 men in his company and was also captain of Holy Island and the Farne Islands, a post subservient only to the governor of Berwick. Other gentlemen in this muster included Clement Armorer, younger son of Roger Armorer of Belford, Ralph Carr, younger son of Ford and James Swinhoe of Berrington 'an honest and sufficient gentleman.' William Selby senior had been a captain and a gentleman pensioner, but had resigned these in 1596 to become comptroller of the office of ordnance in the north parts.[73]

Ralph Gray of Chillingham resented the Selbies' domination of Berwick, particularly when he was unsuccessful in attempting to become Berwick treasurer in 1596. As their families were feuding at this time the anger was very public. It was said that the Selbies were 'so allyed with most of the townesmen of Barwick by maryage and other allyance and of such authority and office within the same that it is impossible to have any indifferent tryall there'. William Selby senior, describing his part in their feud, pompously retorted that 'I thought that my place in this towne beinge Gentleman Porter and a Counsellor and my age had privyledged me from receiving violence of any man.'[74] John Carey also resented the Selbies' superior local power in Berwick when he was marshal there from 1598 to 1603, but his attempts to discredit them made him many local enemies. Captain John Selby's company for example had Selbies, Swinhoes and Forsters within it.

Native Northumbrians were supposedly banned from holding positions in the garrison below officer status, but they were tempted by payment for Border service. This should have been given at their own expense as part of Border tenure.[75] Attempts to expel these men were fruitless and by the time of the 1598 muster the garrison depended on the local men and others from the northern counties to keep up their number of 900.[76] Horsemen had, however, always come from Northumberland because of their renowned skills. Men from other northern counties could join as well, if they had served in Ireland or France. Traditional Border defence had been declining since the 1530s, but by the 1590s it was near ruinous with so many local men in the garrison. Instead of assisting the garrison the local people were now dependent upon the garrison for defence against Scottish raiders. Small parties were sent out from Berwick to the East and Middle Marches, but the gentry were still supposed to defend their lands. Ralph Gray of Chillingham and William Carr of Ford were criticised by Lord Hunsdon for not assisting the defence of the East March.[77]

The decline in Border defence can be linked to the 1530s' pensioning of the gentry. They had willingly participated in Border defence, when being paid for this, and many made their mark in the wake of the Percy interregnum, such as Robert Collingwood of Eslington, John Carr of Hetton, Sir John Forster, John Horsley of Screnwood and Gilbert Swinhoe of Cornhill. Indeed their service was so valued by Henry VIII that he excused all the Northumberland gentry from the Benevolence, a tax levied by the crown outwith parliament unconnected to the subsidy from which the gentry were already exempted. Henry also gave personal gifts to Robert Collingwood, John Carr and Gerard Selby of Pawston in the form of leases for monastic lands.[78] The problem was that many posts given to the gentry were salaried, for example John Carr's captaincy of Wark. The crown only intended to give these pensions and salaries for the duration of the 1540s wars. They could be interpreted as short-term patronage to lure the gentry away from the Percies, but a dangerous precedent had been set and the gentry thenceforth expected to be paid for Border service. By 1552 the gentry had to be ordered to obey the wardens, a duty they should have performed without a reminder, yet Thomas Ilderton was censured for going to London without permission in 1553.[79] Border service was not helped by corruption amongst gentry officers. Rowland Forster of Lucker, captain of Wark during 1556–62 and 1565–70 did not control the troops under his command for they forged coins as a profitable pastime. He sheltered outlaws, sold grain to the Scots, went absent without leave, supported thieves and generally caused trouble. Rowland was warded for these misdemeanours but owing to the influence of his elder, and not yet so corrupt, brother Sir John he was reinstated.[80] Rowland's adventurous career ended when he died of plague in 1570, but his terms of office cannot have helped Border defence.

The bad state of Border defence made some of the gentry move away from their houses near the frontier to safer areas or even to London, but this made defence problems even more acute. There were many complaints about this predicament from the 1560s until 1603.[81] Sir Thomas Gray of Horton went to live in London with licence to leave the Middle March probably being granted by his warden stepson, Sir John Forster. As problems of Border defence increased the back up of the Berwick garrison failed to compensate for absent gentlemen and the decline in Border tenure. Typical Elizabethan stinginess meant that the soldiers' salaries were continually in arrears and this led to low morale in the garrison. When the swashbuckling Lord Willoughby first came to Berwick in 1598 he could only describe their muster as a 'Bare vieu'.[82]

This came at a bad time as raiding by both Scots and English thieves had intensified to a previously unknown level in the 1580s and 1590s. Local political frictions compounded this problem as gentry officers were overworked and sometimes the victims of violence. As their offices were no longer deemed prestigious, some asked to be released from duty. By way of illustration Edward Gray of Howick, deputy warden in the Middle March in 1597, was attacked by opposing gentry for lawfully arresting some of their allies. He asked to be allowed to resign, making his excuse the fact that he was to be sheriff of Northumberland that year and could not justifiably fulfil both offices.[83] Even domestic office holders were subject to attack, for when J.P. Robert Clavering of Callaly 'one of the sufficientest men on the whole border', was called upon to help the warden of the Middle March he was 'left for dead' by some Scots.[84] Clavering survived the incident, but would probably have been less inclined to help the warden in future. These gentlemen would probably not have been interested in any 'British' state in the troubled 1590s when Scottish reivers from the Western Borders plagued this landed community. They would not have wanted to be associated with these rogues. However, the dynastic union would have been a less daunting prospect owing to their cross-border friendships with the Eastern Border lairds. In upholding justice they knew the difference between good and bad Scots, or Englishmen for that matter.

III. The Political Scene

As happened amongst the lairds, the political alliances of the north Northumberland and North Durham gentry were rarely consistent during 1540–1603. With no resident magnate in the area, courtiers vied with each other to build up a clientage amongst the local gentry. Therefore a small local feud between local gentlemen could prove to have far-reaching political undertones as various court factions battled for supremacy in the locality. For their part the gentry welcomed courtier patronage to bolster their local standing and in return they sent their patrons spy reports about Scotland, or their adversaries. Just as in Scotland, courtier rivalries varied with every decade so attempts to decipher individual gentlemen's allegiances are extremely complicated. Major interaction occurred with the Cecils, the earls of Bedford, Lord Hunsdon, Sir Francis Walsingham and the earl of Huntingdon, with the earls of Leicester and Essex in lesser roles. Courtier politics were not the only cause of political tensions in the area as religious differences, bonds of kinship, feuds, personal jealousies and the recurrent theme of whether any gentlemen still adhered to the Percies were all important factors.

i. Mid-century divisions

The complexities of regional politics cannot be underestimated. S. J. Watts devotes an entire chapter of his book on Northumberland to the wheeling and dealing behind Border appointments from only 1595 to 1603.[85] When researching politics during 1540–1603 the difficulties multiply considerably. In the 1540s the crown gained ground against traditional Percy adherents as a result of direct crown patronage in earlier decades. This basic opposition

persisted into the 1550s when they were manifest in the Heron versus Carr
of Ford inheritance feud, though opposition to the Percies would continue
throughout the century. Most of the Northumberland Carrs were Percy
allies and the Carrs of Ford were kin to the Carrs of Hetton. The Collingwoods of Eslington, Etal and Kimmerston, who leased land from the Carrs
of Ford, as well as the Horsleys of Screnwood were also allied to the Percies.
Overwhelming gentry opposition to the Carrs of Ford made their alliance to
the Percy camp a necessity, rather than an option, for they were not Percy
tenants.[86] In 1557 the newly restored seventh earl of Northumberland was
glad to have their support in this hostile gentry community. The group
opposing the Carrs of Ford consisted of many powerful gentry families who
had been lured away from the Percies. They were kinsmen and allies of the
Herons and included the Grays of Horton and Chillingham and the Forsters
of Adderstone.[87] In feuding with the Carrs these men put loyalty to friends
and kinsmen before the merits of the case, for the Herons were blatant
aggressors with no legal right or title to the lucrative Ford estates. The
Herons were in financial difficulties and they went to the extraordinary
length of forging documents to pursue their case, yet lost in the end. There
was so much local turmoil that the privy council intervened and the
Inquisition Post Mortem of Elizabeth Carr, heiress of Ford and wife of
Thomas Carr had to be ordered on three separate occasions.[88] Ill feeling
about the feud continued for several decades and the Carrs of Ford always
felt vulnerable with only a minority of local gentlemen supporting them.
This feud was the most intense battle amongst the Northumbrian gentry in
the sixteenth century, but its significance lies in the mobilisation of the
gentry into rival pro- or anti-Percy groups. In the absence of a resident
magnate instability would persist in the region, to the extent that some
gentry were more interested in feuding with each other than fighting the
Scots. Their rivalries were never consistent from each generation to the next
as the Grays of Chillingham fought the Carrs of Ford and their kin in the
1550s, yet were friends by the 1580s.[89]

ii. The rise of Sir John Forster
The 1550s witnessed the slow beginnings of courtier, rather than crown
interference in the locality. Lord Conyers, warden of the East March in
1553, tried to gain the local alliance of the Grays of Horton and Chillingham
and the Selbies of Twizel against his rival Lord Wharton, a kinsman of the
Forsters. Sir Ralph Gray of Chillingham called the duke of Norfolk 'my
master' in 1564, so he was probably a client of his.[90] Rowland Forster was
probably in the household of John Dudley, duke of Northumberland in
1553, which reinforces the Forsters' alienation from the Percies.[91] The earl
of Northumberland cynically praised Sir John Forster for a raid into Scotland in 1558, but in reality he was trying to oust Forster in support of his
own officers like Thomas Carr of Ford, the marshal of Berwick (1555–8).[92]

The earl's enemies were quick to follow him into local politics, as Sir Ralph Sadler hinted that he should be dismissed from the wardenship of the East and Middle Marches. Sadler also recommended that Sir John Forster should be appointed to the Middle March, whilst another enemy of Northumberland's, Lord Grey of Wilton was given the East March.[93] Apart from trouncing the earl this courtier politicking gave Forster a huge lift and greatly increased his local power and influence. Forster never missed a chance to denigrate Percy tenants and built up a successful local patronage network that was envied by his rivals. Forster's rise inevitably led him into corrupt practices such as ignoring smugglers' activities beneath Bamburgh Castle, where he was captain. Although his local strength prevented him from losing office, courtiers would later argue about whether Forster was corrupt or not.[94]

The early 1560s were Forster's most law-abiding years as Middle March warden. He even managed to subvert his personal hatred of Percy allies to praise John Carr of Hetton and the Collingwoods of Etal for their Border service. Forster was probably sincere about Border defence at this stage as it was his principal duty as warden. He also received better justice from the Scots than his counterpart in the East March, the second earl of Bedford, proving that local power was useful in Anglo-Scottish Border negotiations.[95] Forster respected Bedford and accepted his friendship and patronage, but this was mutually convenient as Bedford needed local support. Forster probably became a Puritan through his friendship with this earl and kept in contact with him once he had left the Borders. Forster's eldest daughter Juliana married Sir Francis Russell, third son of the earl in 1571. Russell remained in the Borders under Sir John's guidance but was tragically killed at a day of truce in 1585. Forster cared for his surviving grandson, who shortly afterwards became the third earl of Bedford. He asked the queen to be 'a mother unto him' and gave him an Alnwick lease. They remained close as the earl visited his grandfather with his countess in 1600.[96]

The arrival of the queen's cousin Henry, Lord Hunsdon, as warden of the East March in 1568, brought another major courtier into direct contact with the local gentry. Other London-based courtiers still kept up their campaigns for Sir Thomas Gray of Horton left his best gown and coat to Mr Secretary, Sir William Cecil, and his chosen heir Ralph Gray was drawn into the Cecil clientage from an early age. Sir Thomas had also been allied to the Darcies for he asked to be buried near his uncle Sir Arthur Darcy in St Botolphs, Aldgate, London.[97]

The events of 1569 divided the gentry again, but only in a small way as few gentlemen supported the earls' rebellion. Hunsdon and Forster successfully quashed the two 1569–70 risings, further boosting Forster's already ascendant career, but resentment of Forster's achievements was fermenting. Sir Cuthbert Collingwood of Eslington, a Percy ally, had held Alnwick Castle for the rebels, yet his true reasons for supporting the earls may have been rooted in his jealousy of Forster. Collingwood may well have felt excluded from local leadership as his uncle Robert Collingwood, who had once been one of the successful new men of the Percy interregnum, had tactically returned to Percy adherence in the 1550s. The earl of Sussex, who was sent north to crush the rebellion, believed Collingwood to be loyal to the crown rather than the Percies and may have knighted him after staying at Eslington. Collingwood, like his uncle, had tried to please both the Percies and the crown, but the eighth earl barely trusted him as constable of Alnwick and the ninth earl replaced him with a Percy kinsman. Collingwood grumbled that the Percies 'so little esteemed his thirty years service', but he now focused his resentment on Forster and feuded against him with the support of the earl of Huntingdon.[98]

After the rebellion there were complaints that Forster was 'possessing all in Northumberland', which was a slight exaggeration yet reflected Forster's greed. The sixth earl of Northumberland had sold some of his houses for building materials in the 1530s, but this was mild in comparison to Forster's appetite for rebuilding with Percy property. Even Lord Hunsdon was forced to report Forster's ransacking of the Percy castles at Alnwick and Warkworth. Forster's local power meant that 'no man howsoever oppressed dares complain.'[99] The booty from Alnwick castle was taken to embellish Abbey house, a nearby property belonging to Sir John. Articles transported there included 600 pairs of hewn stone, 160 joists, 180 panels and at least two cupboards later given to Sir Francis Russell as a wedding present.[100] Forster made good use of these items using the joists to make a portal for the Abbey's gallery and some beds, whilst panels were used for decoration and to make doors for Forster's slaughterhouse. Wainscot made a garret for the Abbey and two laundry doors were made into a dog kennel. Forster also received lucrative land grants from the crown 'in consideration of dyveris his services doone in the late Rebellione'. His son Nicholas received lands, but perhaps the most pleasurable bonus for the Forsters was the order to investigate Sir Henry Percy, the rebel earl's brother.

Forster seemingly could do no wrong in the eyes of government, but his great power in Northumberland was noted by the privy council who asked Lord Hunsdon to report on the local gentry 'and how neere they are allyed to Sir John Forster.'[101] Hunsdon's answer proved how widespread Forster's kinship was through cousinage and marriage. Although his eldest daughter was contracted in marriage to Sir Francis Russell, there was now a scramble by ambitious young men for his younger daughter Grace. In May 1571 Thomas Sutton asked his patron, the earl of Leicester, to intercede for 'one word of your lordship in my favour would give a great countenance to the matter'. Forster revelled in his powerful position and even went to court to receive the personal thanks of the queen.[102]

If Forster had not distinguished himself in the Northern Rebellion, complaints against him in 1568 would have been investigated. He was accused of not redressing Middle March grievances against the Scots while falsely claiming his March was quiet. However, he was contrarily blamed for hanging Scots thieves at the same time.[103] Forster must have been doing something about Scottish raids, but he chose not to exaggerate Border conditions, unlike his fellow wardens who were anxious to receive their salaries on time. The rebellion changed Forster's attitude to the Middle March as he was now the most powerful man in Northumberland, but great power can disguise corruption. His loyalty to the crown was unquestionable, but the decline in the Middle March was partly due to his conceit.[104]

iii. Collingwood vs. Forster

Henry Hastings, third Lord Huntingdon and president of the Council of the North 1572–95, along with Sir Francis Walsingham the spymaster of Elizabeth's regime entered local politics in the 1570s. Huntingdon looked for control of the north and therefore took an instant dislike to Sir John Forster and Lord Hunsdon. Fortunately for them he had no jurisdiction in the Marches and could only snipe at their fallacies and mistakes from York whilst canvassing the support of their enemies. Forster's main opposition came from Sir Cuthbert Collingwood of Eslington who switched from the Percies to Huntingdon in the 1580s. This alliance typifies the complexity of local politics as Collingwood was a Catholic and Huntingdon a Puritan, though faith was arguably a personal matter for the gentry. Walsingham began to work on the Forsters and Selbies, whilst the Grays stayed loyal to the Cecil camp. William Reed of Holy Island turned to Sir William Cecil, now Lord Burghley, for patronage in 1573. Reed wanted his previous grant of the captaincy of Holy Island renewed for life and needed favour after his disgrace during the 1569 rebellion. Reed was successful after visiting London with gift of a goshawk for Burghley, who welcomed a new client from a region where he wanted to expand his patronage network. Burghley's quest for local knowledge of the English localities was insatiable and from the 1570s onwards he used Christopher Saxton's new cartography of the English counties to locate his clientele; new and old. He took a particular interest in Northumberland by annotating his own copy of Saxton's *Atlas* with observations about local landed families.[105]

By 1580 Forster was still the supreme agent of the crown amongst the local gentry and it was this pervading loyalty that allowed him to remain in office despite serious problems in his March. Huntingdon repeatedly called for Forster's resignation, exploiting every tale of wrongdoing to favour his candidate Sir Cuthbert Collingwood.[106] The battle between Forster and Collingwood lasted until the mid 1590s, but it was at its height during the 1580s. The two men had different backgrounds that made their feud more than a courtier battle. Unusually for this area, they were not directly allied by kinship and they had opposing religions; Forster being Puritan and Collingwood a church papist. Sir Cuthbert Collingwood's son Thomas had married Forster's kinswoman Anne Gray of Chillingham, yet this marriage never entered their feud as the Grays were more powerful than the Collingwoods. The marriage did, however, prevent Forster persecuting the Collingwoods for being Catholic as this would have incriminated his Gray kinsmen. Forster's kin consciousness therefore lost him a valuable weapon against the Collingwoods.[107]

Collingwood was jealous of Forster's success and being a former Percy supporter he naturally invited the wrath of Forster. In terms of personal wealth and patronage Forster was superior, but Collingwood had substantial lands and a broad kin network. Court politics surfaced when Lord Hunsdon deliberately backed Forster in the feud purely to get at his rival, Huntingdon. Forster kept his options open by dabbling with Walsingham's support. He sent Walsingham a 'caste' of gyr-falcons in 1586 as a thank you for 'goodnes shewed unto me frome tyme to tyme'.[108] Huntingdon's loathing for Hunsdon was as intense as his campaign against Forster, with seditious letters about conditions in Hunsdon's East March and Berwick going south in an attempt to discredit him. Conditions were far from perfect in Berwick, but this was due to slow salary payments and poor victualling rather than Hunsdon's neglect. A report of 1587 by Robert Ardern, a gentleman pensioner of the garrison, was probably sponsored by Huntingdon and is therefore full of accusations against Hunsdon. It has little credibility as Ardern was seldom in Berwick during 1587.[109]

Propaganda against Forster by both Collingwood and Huntingdon increased towards 1587, but there had been a steady trickle of reports before this to the privy council, Burghley, Walsingham and the Queen.[110] In July 1587 Sir Cuthbert Collingwood mischievously sent a list of Scottish spoils in the Middle March to London, which was full of his usual attacks on Forster.[111] Forster was ultimately forced to admit that his March was weak and was asked to stand aside to allow Lord Hunsdon to investigate.[112] Now, just as Collingwood and Huntingdon thought they were winning their battle against Forster, Hunsdon decided to scupper their plans. To annoy Huntingdon, Hunsdon now looked favourably upon Forster's misdemeanours. Hunsdon assembled all the Middle March gentry including the Collingwoods in October 1587 to hear Forster's replies to the various allegations of misconduct. No one countered Forster's defence in public so Hunsdon duly reported back to Burghley

> I finde that meer mallis prosecuted by Sir Cuthbert Collingwood of longe tyme, and furthered and maynteyned by my lorde of Huntingdon. Their is no man (Forster) so perfitt and having so many great matters to doe in so great a wardenry, and having to deale with so many pervers and mallicious people as in this countrie'.[113]

Hunsdon got rather carried away in his report and managed to include a character assassination of Collingwood, whom he called a papist Percy supporter. He advised that Collingwood was not fit to continue as constable of Harbottle Castle.

A *via media* should be adopted here as both Forster and Collingwood had faults. It was true that Forster had gained little redress for Scottish raids and had rather too many Scottish friends, but Collingwood was guilty of March treason by selling horses to the Scots and inciting Scottish reivers with open challenges.[114] To make matters worse Collingwood began a skirmish with the same Scots after a raid in December 1587 and failed to inform the warden, Lord Hunsdon.[115] During Forster's absence from office Collingwood had single-handedly ruined the slim framework of good relations between the English and Scottish Middle Marches. Forster had been far more diplomatic, having the good sense to befriend some of the more troublesome Scots to prevent outright warfare between these Marches. This was an unconventional, illegal and frankly corrupt way of dealing with Border problems, but it was based on Forster's vast experience of wardenship and his pragmatism. By comparison, Collingwood's attempts at Border government look immature, foolish, irrational and power-crazed.

Forster was reinstated in 1588 following Hunsdon's recommendation that he was 'the fitteste man for the tyme', much to Collingwood and Huntingdon's annoyance.[116] Hunsdon was glad to relinquish the Middle March wardenship back to Forster as the size and problems of the area daunted him. Collingwood and Huntingdon refused to admit defeat so their campaigning began afresh. In 1593 Collingwood wrote directly to the privy council to complain and Huntingdon asked local gentry to report to him on Scottish raids. Neither of them had any authority to do this, but they were determined to make Forster look ineffective as warden. He was now forced to retaliate against Collingwood's most obvious weakness, his recusancy. He searched Collingwood's house at Eslington on several occasions looking for seminary priests, but was unsuccessful. Unfortunately, he also had to search the house of his kinsman Ralph Gray of Chillingham, which incurred Gray's wrath and was probably why he had long deferred this action.[117]

No warden, whether local or not, could cope with the constant pressure of Scottish incursions and the lack of redress being offered by the Scots during the troubled 1590s. Forster's slackness in gaining justice helped Huntingdon's campaign against him, but knowledge that Forster had been openly colluding with the Scots finally led to his dismissal in August 1595.[118] Collingwood did not have long to savour this victory as recusancy soon forced him into temporary exile at his Durham estates. Huntingdon began a thorough investigation into the Middle March at Newcastle on 3 December 1595, but found Forster unco-operative. Huntingdon did not complete this task as his health deteriorated and he died shortly afterwards.[119]

Forster found himself far from crown favour as the Queen indirectly blamed him for the death of Huntingdon. In a letter to the bishop of

Durham, she referred to the investigation of the Middle March 'his grief at the state of affairs, and death in consequence.' Forster denied contributing to Huntingdon's death, yet the death of his antagonist did not stop the investigation. It moved to the direction of the bishop of Durham, who kept Forster under house arrest for over a year.[120] Ralph, third Lord Eure, who replaced Forster in the Middle March found support from the Collingwood faction and naturally carried on the vendetta against Forster. Eure stated that 'Sir John has ruined the country', but he also observed that 'there is no gentleman of worth in Northumberland not near of kin or allied to Sir John Forster'.[121] Eure would soon discover that having no great landholding or kinsmen in the region gave him little local support in his March and the flighty Scots ran circles around him. By 25 February 1596 his wardenship was in so much trouble that he hypocritically asked the Queen to reward Forster for 'his former deutifull service to your heignes with gratious pardon of his defectes or negligence, whose oulde age shall with joye creep to his longe home and lengthen what maie be his decrepett age with comforthe.' Henry Anderson of Newcastle had even asked Huntingdon to thank Forster for his service, prior to his death. No such thanks were forthcoming, but Forster was probably glad to relinquish the responsibility of the Middle March as he admitted to 'having one foote alreadie in the grave' in 1597.[122]

Eure's attempt to appease Forster's kinsmen failed and his overall wardenship was little short of disastrous. Even the Forster-hating Sir Cuthbert Collingwood deserted Eure by resigning as deputy warden and returning to his Durham estates. Eure had been desperate for local support so, in spite of being a Puritan, he even tried to court the favour of the Catholic Grays of Chillingham. Swayed by promises, the Grays did leave their old alliance with Sir John Forster for a while. They were probably angry at his searching Chillingham for priests and they had ongoing tithe disputes as well. Ralph Gray, however, failed to become treasurer of Berwick on Eure's recommendation. Edward Gray of Howick became his deputy warden, though he subsequently asked to relinquish his post when the Widdringtons of Widdrington attacked him in 1597.[123] Eure blamed 'the ould faction of Sir John Forster' for his lack of popularity in the Middle March, but this was not true. Forster realised that he would never return to the office of warden and therefore ceased to annoy his rivals. The attack on Gray had nothing to do with Forster. Instead it was premeditated by Sir Robert Carey, youngest and most ambitious son of Lord Hunsdon, whose kinsmen by marriage included the Widdringtons of Widdrington. Carey had wanted the wardenship of the Middle March since 1594, when he moved to his absent father's East March after being a deputy warden in the West March.[124] Eure had to endure the embarrassment of an investigation into his wardenship in 1597, just like the inquiry into Forster in 1595–96. This time it was Carey's propaganda that succeeded in ousting the warden, rather than Huntingdon's, and Carey became warden in 1598.[125]

iv. Other struggles, 1580–1603

The long power struggle between Forster and Collingwood was not the only battle going on within the later-sixteenth century gentry community. Sir Cuthbert Collingwood also feuded with the Selbies of Twizel in the 1580s. This was a violent feud, rather than a war of words, yet the causes were the same with political rivalry, differences in religion and personal jealousy involved.[126] Courtier politics were evident again as Huntingdon backed Collingwood and Hunsdon supported the Selbies. Sir John Selby was one of Hunsdon's deputy wardens throughout his tenure in the East March. The Selbies were also clients of Walsingham, though this did not surface in this particular feud. Just as Collingwood had envied Forster's power in the Middle March he was jealous of the Selbies' predominance in Berwick and the East March. The Selbies had received undisclosed patronage from the spymaster Sir Francis Walsingham in 1584. In return they promised service, which usually entailed sending spy reports to him at court. Walsingham also communicated with Sir John Forster at this time, but not with Collingwood.[127] In 1589 Sir John Selby and his son William Selby junior were again grateful to Walsingham, firstly for gaining a pardon for William's involvement in their feud with the Collingwoods and secondly for arranging a propitious marriage for William. This explains why a North Durham gentleman married a Kentish lady.[128] The Selbies sometimes went to London and would probably have visited Walsingham whilst there. This may account for the advantageous mortgage William Selby senior acquired for Ightham Mote in Kent, which he fully owned by 1592. Lord Hunsdon similarly rewarded them with the marriage of his ward, Thomas Carr of Ford, who took Isabel Selby of Twizel as his wife.[129]

The feud between the Collingwoods and Selbies inevitably drew in their kinsmen. At one violent encounter in 1582 the Collingwoods' support included Robert Clavering, sheriff of Northumberland, whose son Robert had married Mary Collingwood, and William Clavering, a younger son of Robert's, who was killed in the fracas. The Selbies were joined by the Strothers of Kirknewton as William Strother had married Jane Selby. The violence was far from one-sided as Clement Strother had been left 'lame as long as he lives' after a previous encounter.[130] Episodes such as these somewhat diminish the relative peacefulness of the gentry, but this really only applies in a cross-border context. Local politics were powerful weapons to be exploited in any gentry community and they are never easily unravelled. Elite violence was also far from uncommon in England and demonstrating just how complex political rivalries could be, Sir John Forster took the Collingwoods' side in this feud because the murdered Gavin Clavering had been his stepsister's son.[131] Forster also opposed the Selbies as they were involved in a tithe wrangle. William Selby senior retaliated against Forster's bullying tactics by getting the Court of Star Chamber to issue a writ against Forster for a mere 13s 4d. Forster was therefore forced into the much greater expense of answering the writ at York. William was himself on the receiving end of this sort of tactic in 1596, when he had to travel from Kent to Durham to answer a writ at a cost of £40.

The gentry were thus capable of putting basic kinship considerations before the interests of their courtier patrons. The dabblings of courtiers must therefore be seen in the context of local kinship and rivalries that occurred naturally in the community.[132] Other courtiers were active in the area during the 1580s as William Reed of Holy Island and William Selby senior both served with the Puritan earl of Leicester in Holland and were knighted by him. This may just have been in their capacity as professional soldiers, but their shared Puritanism cannot be coincidental. Robert Lisle of Felton won a suit in Chancery with the assistance of Huntingdon, and William Carr of Ford also sent spy reports to Walsingham.[133] The Cecils presumably kept the Grays of Chillingham in their allegiance, but they were inactive during the 1580s. Ralph Gray appears not to have sent any reports to Burghley in the 1580s, but began to communicate with him from 1592 onwards and was known as 'my Lord Treasurer's defender'. Burghley kept a close watch on Ralph's family, even to the extent of enforcing a Protestant baptism on Ralph's son and heir, William, in an attempt to curb the family's recusancy.[134] In 1594 Robert Carey noticed how favoured Ralph Gray had become. Fearing that Gray might be appointed to the wardenship of the Middle March instead of him, Carey launched a crusade against him. Ralph was an influential local gentleman, noted for being 'honest and wise', unlike his kinsman Sir John Forster. Carey therefore chose to emphasise his recusant family and the risk this would create if he were made warden. Burghley had prior knowledge of this and decided to snub Carey by appointing Lord Eure as warden. The impetuous Carey would now have to wait another four years before becoming warden of the Middle March.

The Grays' lack of top office did not sway them from allegiance to Burghley. When a violent incident occurred in Berwick in 1597, as a result of a feud between them and the Selbies, it was the Selbies who had to grovel before Burghley. William Selby senior 'much wished to live in kinde sort with such as you seme to favour, as with any other gentlemen of my countrey . . .'[135] The Selbies were now trying to gain Burghley's patronage as their previous patrons, Walsingham and Hunsdon, were dead. Burghley had taken an interest in the Selbies in 1596 along with the feuding Collingwoods and Forsters. He was obviously considering them as clients, but first he made sketches of their genealogies to try and unravel their complex kinship networks.[136] The Selbies duly became clients of Burghley and his second son Sir Robert Cecil. They stayed in this allegiance with the exception of their John, who joined the earl of Essex's trip to the Azores in 1597. In true Northumbrian fashion this did not stop the Selbies from feuding with the other Burghley clients such as the Grays. The Cecils remained nonplussed as they were only too glad to have new clients in their struggle for predominance of the north with the earl of Essex. This struggle had arisen after the death of Huntingdon in 1595, but Essex made very little impact north of the Coquet where intensified raiding was then of more concern to the gentry than a new patron.

Remaining gentry rivalries were centred on Berwick, where Sir John Carey and Lord Willoughby made themselves unpopular with the Selbies by overtly seeking some of their power. John Carey antagonised William Selby senior in 1597 by helping his enemies, the Grays of Chillingham, in their feud. Selby therefore retaliated with an attempt to discredit Carey in his office of deputy governor of Berwick, but Burghley supported Carey, much to Selby's disgust. Carey also tried to gain the captaincy of Holy Island from Sir William Reed by foul and persistent slandering during 1601–02. Lord Hunsdon had tried a similar tactic, but both failed as both Reed and his son had a liferent of the office.[137] Willoughby, as governor of Berwick and warden of the East March, tried to test his leadership against William Selby junior by not allowing him to choose his own lieutenant. This time Sir Robert Cecil contrarily chose to support Selby as his family was still powerful in the locality. Cecil was probably now looking ahead to the Union of 1603, when loyal Borderers would be useful to him.[138] The Selbies, however, were more concerned with their local prestige than with dynastic union.

The politics of the north Northumberland and North Durham gentry throughout 1540–1603 were intricate and rooted in many different causes. The intensity of some of the family feuds does diminish the image of relative peace in this area, but these were domestic feuds – not cross-border raids. Every English town and county had feuding families in the sixteenth century, who resorted to interpersonal violence in moments of irrationality. This disorder was intermittent, though serious whilst it lasted, but it often underpinned changes in the local political scene. This political landscape had changed dramatically with new men triumphing over the traditional leadership of the Percy earls of Northumberland. Then from the 1550s onwards courtier politics were apparent, though they should not be treated in isolation. This intrusion of court politics made rivalries amongst the new leaders more acute, yet kinship, religion, jealousy and loyalty to the Percies all played their part in the numerous power struggles of the region. There was never an outright victory for any courtier's clientage as the gentry switched their allegiance and were rarely consistent feuding partners. Outsiders like Lord Eure, the Careys and Lord Willoughby sought power but had to concur with the strength of the local gentry's opposition, even if this opposition was not unified and came from different power groups within the gentry community such as the Forsters, Collingwoods or Selbies.

The outstanding gentleman of this era was undoubtedly Sir John Forster, but many other gentlemen advanced as well in the wake of the Percy interregnum. Forster's long wardenship may have been corrupt, but he was the most sensible incumbent in the post with his local support and

knowledge of Border conditions. His power was unsurpassed in the Middle
March, but the Grays of Chillingham were wealthier and the Selbies
dominated Berwick and Norhamshire. Overall, the Percies' downfall was
probably the most important political event of the sixteenth century as it
overshadowed even the Reformation in its effect upon the gentry. They had
changed from being a fairly subservient squirearchy into a courtier-influ-
enced, though still independent gentry community.

Notes

1 Camden referred to 'the better sort' in his *Britannia* (London, 1610), 799. B.
   W. Beckingsale refers to Borderers with no distinction in 'The Characteristics of
   the Tudor North', *NH*, iv (1969), 79–81, and A. L. Rowse identifies 'settled
   folk' in *The Expansion of Elizabethan England* (London, 1955), 7.
2 See ch. vii.
3 *CSP For,* 1569–71, 568.
4 W. Palmer, 'High Officeholding, Foreign Policy, and the British Dimension in
   the Tudor Far North, 1525–1563', *Albion*, 29 (1998), 581. For a more detailed
   history of the Percies see R. Lomas, *A Power in the land: the Percies* (East
   Linton, 1999).
5 Elton, *England Under The Tudors* (London, 1974), 175–6. F. Heal and C.
   Holmes, *The Gentry in England and Wales 1500–1700* (Basingstoke, 1994),
   195–7.
6 PRO E305/10/82. E305/F/23.
7 *L&P.Hen VIII,* xii, pt 1, 1090. G. W. Bernard, ed. *The Tudor Nobility*
   (Manchester, 1992), 13–14, 39. R. W. Hoyle, 'Henry Percy, sixth earl of
   Northumberland, and the fall of the House of Percy', *cf.* Bernard, *Tudor
   Nobility*, 180–211. G. Broce & R. M. Wunderli, 'The Funeral of Henry Percy,
   sixth earl of Northumberland', *Albion*, xx (1990), 215.
8 S. Ellis, 'A Border Baron and the Tudor State: The rise and fall of Lord Dacre
   of the North', *Historical Journal*, 35 (1992), 253–77. Hoyle, 'Henry Percy',
   186–7. M. E. James, 'Change and Continuity in the Tudor North', *Borthwick
   Papers*, 27 (1965). Palmer 'High Officeholding', 579–595. Pollard, *Wars of the
   Roses,* 402–04.
9 M. M. Meikle, 'A Godly Rogue: The career of Sir John Forster, an Elizabethan
   Border Warden', *NH*, xxviii (1992), 126–163.
10 *L&P.Hen VIII,* viii, 149 (73); x, 1260; xi, 504; xii, pt 1, 1090.
11 S. Adams, ' "Because I am of that countrye & mynde to plant myself there":
   Robert Dudley, earl of Leicester and the West Midlands', *Midland History*, 20
   (1995), 38. J. G. Jones, *The Welsh Gentry 1536–1640. Images of Status,
   Honour and Authority* (Cardiff, 1998).
12 *Cf.* Adams, 'Leicester', 52. A. Everitt, *The Community of Kent and The Great
   Rebellion, 1640–60* (Leicester, 1966). A. Hassell Smith, *County and Court,
   Government and Politics in Norfolk 1558–1603* (Oxford, 1974). D.
   MacCulloch, *Suffolk and the Tudors* (Oxford, 1986).
13 *Cf.* M. H. & R. Dodds, *The Pilgrimage of Grace 1536–7 and the Exeter
   Conspiracy 1538* (Cambridge, 1915). M. Bush, *The Pilgrimage of Grace*
   (Manchester, 1996), chs iv & v. M. Bush & D. Bownes, *The Defeat of the
   Pilgrimage of Grace* (Hull, 1999), ch v. M. Bush, 'The Pilgrimage of Grace:

Reactions, Responses and Revisions', *The Historian*, lx (1998), 16–20. R. Hoyle, *The Pilgrimage of Grace and the Politics of the 1530s* (Oxford, 2001).

14 *L&P.Hen VIII*, xi, 1293, 1294; xii, pt 1, 1090; xviii, pt 1, 198, 237, 567. *cf.* Hoyle, 'Henry Percy', 197–9

15 *L&P.Hen VIII*, iv, pt 2, 5085; xii, pt 2, 249–250; xix, pt 1, 278 (39); *addenda* i, pt 1, 618, 828. *APC*, ii, 168, 477.

16 BL MS Cotton, Caligula, B vi, 2, fos 518–19.

17 *Cf.* Beckingsale, 'Tudor North', *NH*, iv (1969), 67–83. R. W. Hoyle, 'Faction, Feud and Reconciliation amongst the Northern English Nobility, 1525–1569', *History*, lxxxiv (1999), 590–613. *APC*, vi, 270–1.

18 *CSP For*, 1558–9, 1128. *cf.* Boscher, 'Anglo-Scottish Border', 290, 294, 438. R. R. Reid, 'The Rebellion of the Earls, 1569,' *TRHS*, 2nd series, xx (1906), 176.

19 *APC*, viii, 51. G. R. Batho, 'The Percies and Alnwick Castle, 1557–1632', *AA*, 4th ser, xxxv (1957), 49–50. S. Ellis, 'Civilizing Northumberland: Representations of Englishness in the Tudor State', *Journal of Historical Sociology*, 12/2 (1999), p. 107.

20 ALN MS Al/I/a – q. E164/37 fo. 111. M. E. James, 'The Concept of Order and The Northern Rising, 1569', *P&P*, lx (1973), 49–83 and Family, Lineage and Civil Society (Oxford, 1974), 32–3, 42, 67–8.

21 *CSPDom Add*, 1566–79, 117–18, 195, 417.

22 ALN MS CIV/10/1. Watts, *Border to Middle Shire*, 58.

23 See ch. iv.

24 *CSP Scot*, xiii, pt 2, 908.

25 BRO B1/2 fo. 55. *CBP*, i, 838; ii, 31, 1271. *CSP For*, 1564–5, 196. The sheriff's writ did not extend to Hexham or Newcastle either.

26 *L&I*, ix, 99. J. T. Cliffe, *The Yorkshire Gentry* (London, 1969), 235.

27 *CBP*, ii, 422. *CSP Dom Add*, 1580–1625, 342–3.

28 *L&P. Hen VIII*, xv, 144 (11).

29 *L&P. Hen VIII*, x, 1260. Stat, 2 & 3 EDW VI c. 34.

30 *CSP For*, 1562, 1393; *ibid*, 1563, 1273.

31 PRO E199/33/59. E370/14/46. WARD9/442. STAC5 A36/7, B90/2, K6/40. *APC*, xxvi, 426. *HMC*, Salisbury, xiv, 67. Accounts survive only from 1608–10.

32 *CBP*, ii, 466. Watts, *Border to Middle Shire*, 64–5.

33 J. P. Collier, ed. *The Egerton Papers*, Camden Society, 12 (1840), 389–90.

34 *CPR*, 1547–8, 87; 1553–4, 22. For more details on Collingwood see J. Sanders, ' "A true man minded to justice" Robert Collingwood (*c.* 1490–1556) of Eslington, Northumberland', *AA*, 5th ser, xxvi (1998), 87–104.

35 PRO C66/1421 m. 11 d. C66/1468 m. 26d. E163/14/8. *CPR*, 1560–3, 441.

36 PRO C66/1421 m. 2 d. C66/1523 m. 22 d. 5P13/F/11. *APC*, xxiii, p. 259. See ch. vi.

37 LAMB MS 3195, fo. 5.

38 J. H. Gleason, *The Justice of the Peace in England, 1558–1640* (Oxford, 1969), 3, 48, 58, 67–72, 99, 225.

39 *CBP*, i, 21. *Stat*, 7 Edw VI, c. 5 iii.

40 PRO C66/1594 m. 27 d. *CBP*, ii, 746, 881.

41 PRO STAC5 S81/2. Morpeth Records Centre QS1/1 (surviving records are from 1595 only). *CBP*, ii, 1434, 1470. *CSP Dom*, 1601–03, 213. *CSP For*, 1572–74, 603. Watts, *Border to Middle Shire*, 130–1. C. M. F. Ferguson, 'Law and Order on the Anglo-Scottish Border, 1603–1707', unpubl. PhD diss. St Andrews, 1981. J. A. Sharpe, *Crime in early modern England* (Harlow, 1990), 36–37.

42 Watts, *Border to Middle Shire*, 289 and Williams, 'Northern Borderland', 126–7.
43 *CPR, 1563–6*, 254. *CBP*, ii, 271.
44 DPRW, v, fo. 68. *SS*, xxxviii, (1860), 173n. *cf.* Cliffe, *Yorkshire Gentry*, 20.
45 PRO C66/1227 m. 5. C142/75/13. C142/108/80. C142/227/195. WARD7/23/38.
46 *CPR, 1575–8*, 448, 450; 1578–80, 1074, 1096.
47 Typical commissions and commissioners are found in E134 (Exchequer K.R. Depositions) and E178 (Exchequer K.R. special commissions). *APC*, vi, 284. H. E. Bell, *An Introduction to the History and Records of the Court of Wards and Liveries* (Cambridge, 1953), 40–2.
48 M. Bush, 'Tenant Right under the Tudors: a revision revised', *Bulletin of the John Rylands Library*, 77 (1995), 161–188.
49 *CSP For*, 1558–9, 139, 365.
50 PRO SP59/31 fos 35–7. *CBP*, i, 47, 50, 181, 253, 259; ii, 211, 271. *CSPDom*, 1595–7, 143–4. See ch. iv.
51 PRO DL29/360/5956. SC6 Eliz I 1693 & 1698. SC6 Hen VIII 7357. *APC*, v, 313. *CPR*, 1572–5, 316.
52 *L&P. Hen VIII*, xx, pt 1, 1042. *cf.* Batho, 'Percies', 56–7.
53 NRO ZCR2 (Bamburgh manor court). ALN MSS CIV/10/1 (Lesbury).
54 Thomas Percy was a great grandson of the fourth earl and later became embroiled in the 'Gunpowder Plot' of 1605. Alnwick Castle SYON MS AII/8 fo. 5. ALN MS DI/1. *cf.* Batho, 'Percies', 57–9. Stone, *Open Elite?*, 296.
55 BRO B1/1 fo. 13, B1/3 fo. 81, B1/5 fo. 27, B1/6 fo. 66. *NCH*, xiv, 412. *SS*, xxxviii (1860), 55–6.
56 *Cf.* Watts, *Border to Middle Shire*, 64–5, 130, 133–58.
57 PRO C193/32. The members are listed by C. H. Hunter Blair in *AA*, 4th ser, xii, xiv, xxiii, xxiv (1935, 1937, 1945, 1946).
58 BRO B1/3 fos 36–7.
59 PRO SP15/21/86 (I). *HMC*, Talbot, 44. S. Ellis, 'Crown, Community and Government in the English Territories, 1450–1575', *History*, lxxi (1986), 187–206. F. W. Brooks, *The Council of the North* (London, 1953), 17–18. R. R. Reid, *The King's Council of the North* (London, 1921), 494. P. Williams, *The Council in the Marches of Wales* (Cardiff, 1958).
60 BRO B1/2 fo. 55 B1/3 fo. 72. *CBP*, i, 267; ii, 1269, 1429. *CSPDom Add*, 1580–1625, 213, 353. *HMC*, Salisbury, iii, 74. *cf.* Brooks, *Council of the North*; Reid, *King's Council*, 349; Watts, *Border to Middle Shire*, 130.
61 *L&P. Hen VIII*, xii, pt 2, 422.
62 *L&P. Hen VIII*, xvii, 1084; xviii, pt 1, 1543.
63 *ibid*, xvi, 100. *CSPDom*, 1547–53, 771. *CSPDom Add*, 1547–65, 417.
64 PRO SP59/1 fo. 50. A warden's duties are specified in *Sadler Papers*, ii, 12.
65 *CBP*, i, 534, 596, 627.
66 *CPR*, 1572–5, 316; 1580–2, 1505. Tough, *Last Years*, 279–81.
67 See Forster of Adderstone genealogy. *CBP*, ii, 111, 129.
68 *CBP*, i, 83; ii, 1042. *CSP Scot*, viii, 490.
69 *CSP Scot*, xii, 890. *CBP*, i, 368. G. M. Bell, *A Handlist of British Diplomatic Representatives 1509–1688* (London, 1990).
70 *APC*, v, 96. *CSP For*, 1558–9, 450. The careers of younger sons the gentry are discussed in ch. v.
71 BRO B6/11 fo. 2. *APC*, vi, 249; xxx, 241. *L&P. Hen VIII*, xviii, pt 2, 214, 237, 277. *CBP*, ii, 165–7.
72 NRO 647 EP38/1.

73 PRO SP59/37 fos 107–25. NRO 1D/1/117. BRO B6/1 fos 148–9. *CBP* i, 545; ii, 470. *APC,* xxvi, 184–5. *CSP Scot,* vii, 313, 363. *SS,* xxxviii (1860), 256n.
74 PRO SP59/33 fos 78–81. STAC8/261/20. BL MS Harl 851 fo. 23. *CBP,* ii, 370.
75 *Cf.* Bush, 'Tenant Right'.
76 *CBP,* ii, 1035, 1138. *CSP For,* 1560–1, 466. *L&P. Hen VIII* x, 1260.
77 *CBP,* i, 499, 571; ii, 1280.
78 PRO SC6 Edw VI 356. E318/7/246. *L&P. Hen VIII,* xvii, 808, 1180; xix, pt 1, 278(39), 342; xx, pt 1, 162, 339, & pt 2, 4; xxi, pt 1, 970(47). *HMC,* Talbot, 12. *CSP Scot,* i, 258.
79 *APC,* iii, 473. *CSPDom,* 1547–53, 826.
80 PRO SP59/6 fos 87–8. *CSP For* 1562, 250, 275, 289, 299; 1564–5, 984; 1566–8, 1362; 1569–71, 1230. *CSPDom Add,* 1547–65, 463, 454; *ibid* 1566–79, 182. *HMC,* Rutland i, 80–1.
81 *HMC,* Salisbury, i, 397. *CSP For,* 1560–1, 761. See chs. iii and viii.
82 *CBP,* ii, 936.
83 *CBP,* ii, 894. *HMC,* Salisbury, viii, 73–4.
84 *CBP,* ii, 351, 366, 860.
85 *Cf.* Watts, *Border to Middle Shire,*113–131.
86 ALN MS AI/1/m fo. 22. SYON MS AII/8 fo. 5, MII/11/9. *CPR,* 158–60, p. 245. M. M. Meikle, 'Northumberland Divided: Anatomy of a Sixteenth-Century Bloodfeud', *AA,* 5th ser, xx (1992), 79–89. See ch. vii.
87 LAMB MS 3195 fo. 8. *CSP For,* 1558–9, 168.
88 PRO CP25/2/192/ 5 Eliz/HIL. C78/54/4. C142/131/159. *CPR,* 1557–8, 112, 250, 365–6; 1558–60, 270.
89 PRO SP59/20/80. DPRW 1588 (1) John Carr of Lesbury.
90 PRO C142/141/31. Lambeth Palace LAMB MS 3194 fos 27, 111, 113, 241.
91 PRO LR 2/118. I am grateful to Simon Adams for this reference.
92 PRO SP15/8/66. *HMC,* Talbot, 78. *APC,* v, 206 (Carye = Carr).
93 *CPR,* 1558–60, 348, 411–12. *CSP For,* 1559–60, 187; 1562, 55. *Sadler Papers,* i, 471–3, 615–17.
94 *CSP For,* 1575–7, 438.
95 *CSP Scot,* ii, 97. *CSPDom Add,* 1547–65, 562–3.
96 *CBP,* ii, 1221. *CSPDom Add,* 1580–1625, 160–1. *CSP Dom,* 1595–7, 176. *cf.* Meikle, 'Godly Rogue', 160–1.
97 PRO C142/158/19, C142/141/3. SP15/19/15. *CSPDom Add,* 1566–79, 321. *SS* cxxi (1912), 61.
98 PRO E134/12 Eliz/Trin3. IND1/6887. *CSPDom Add,* 1566–79, 114, 173. *CSP For,* 1569–71, 1137.
99 *CSP Dom Add,* 1566–79, 325, 393–4. *cf.* Hoyle, 'Henry Percy', 199–200.
100 SYON MS NII/6/l, m, p.
101 See Forster of Adderstone genealogy. PRO E318/43/2346. BL Cotton MS, Caligula, C iii, fos 118–120. *CPR, 1566–9,* 398.
102 Longleat, Dudley MS 1, fo. 228. (HMC, *Bath,* v, 173.) Thanks are due to Simon Adams for a transcript of this reference. Grace married William Fenwick of Wallington.
103 *CSP For,* 1566–8, nos 2496, 2497, 2498, 2560. *CSP Scot,* ii, no 821.
104 BL MS Cotton, Caligula, C iii, fos. 111–18. *CSP Scot,* iv, 32. Meikle, 'Godly Rogue'.
105 PRO SP59/33 fos 78–83. *CSP For,* 1572–4, 1211. *CSP Dom,* 1591–4, 489. *CPR,* 1578–80, 1301. V. Morgan, 'The Cartographic image of "the country" in

early modern England', *TRHS*, xxix (1979), 129–54. See ch. vii.

106 *HMC*, Hastings, ii, 18. Fraser, *Douglas*, iv, 179.

107 DPRW 1602 (Forster). DPRW Reg vii, fo. 254 (Collingwood). *SS*, xxxviii (1860), 267–72.

108 *CBP*, i, 201–07, 445.

109 *CBP*, i, 545. M. C. Cross, 'Berwick upon Tweed and the neighbouring parts of Northumberland on the Eve of the Armada', *AA*, 4th ser, xli (1963), 123–4.

110 PRO SP15/28/80. *CBP*, i, 181, 451–6. *CSPDom Add*, 1580–1625, 168. *CSP Scot*, viii, 351.

111 *CBP*, i, 493, 494, 515, 522. *CSPDom Add*, 1580–1625, 205. *CSP Scot*, viii, 193, 197–8.

112 *CBP*, i, 485, 532, 546, 551, 554.

113 *ibid*, 556

114 *ibid*, 601, 646; ii, 111. *CSP Scot*, viii, 452, 459–61, 512. HMC, *Salisbury*, iii, 290–1; v, 477.

115 *APC*, xxiv, 53–4. *CBP*, i, 570–1, 574–6, 646. *CSPScot*, viii, 452, 459–61, 465, 512; ix, 476. *RPC*, iv, 81. HMC, *Salisbury*, xiii, 353–7.

116 *CBP*, i, 596.

117 *ibid*, 901, 907. *APC*, xxiv, 53–4. *CSPDom Add*, 1580–1625, 344, 367–8. See ch. v.

118 *CBP*, ii, 111, 129. *CSP Scot*, xi, 259.

119 *CBP*, ii, 174, 217, 292, 492. *CSP Scot*, xii, 73. HMC, Salisbury, v, 458–9, 476–7; vi, 38–9, 149.

120 *CBP*, ii, 197, 206, 233.

121 *ibid*, 209.

122 *ibid*, 219, 492. HMC, Salisbury, iv, 209.

123 PRO C66/1238 m. 6–7. Chillingham Castle Docs, 5. *CBP*, ii, 370, 381, 499. *APC*, viii, 73–4. *CSPDom*, 1580–1625, 367–8. HMC, Salisbury, vi, 430. *CSP Scot*, xii, 338. *cf*. Watts, *Border to Middle Shire*, 116.

124   *CBP*, ii, 441, 547, 861.

125 *ibid*, 756, 763, 862, 881, 894. *CSPDom Add*, 1580–1625, 365–6.

126 PRO SP15/29/317. *CBP*, i, 521,601. *CSPDom Add*, 1580–1625, 193–7, 213–4, 249. HMC, *Salisbury*, iii, 198–9, 444.

127 *CBP*, i, 201–08, 209, 408.

128 *ibid*, 617, 618.

129 PRO C142/227/195. KAO U947/T2/1. *CBP*, ii, 728.

130 *CSPDom Add*, 1580–1625, 193–7.

131 PRO STAC5 56/5. *CBP*, i, 678.

132 *CSPDom Add*, 1580–1625, 376.

133 PRO C3/244/42. *CBP*, i, 540, 545, 678. *CSP For*, 1575–7, 1435. Sharp, *Memorials*, 16n.

134 *CBP*, i, 776,877. *CSP Scot*, x, 732. HMC, Salisbury, xii, 35, 127, 301; x, 369.

135 PRO SP59/33 fos 232–4. *CBP*, 555, 573.

136 See Forster of Adderstone genealogy. PRO SP52/51/81. SP59/32 fos 238–9. *CBP*, ii, 697.

137 PRO C66/1409 m. 18. *CBP*, ii, 498–501, 690, 697, 706, 727, 1171, 1429, 1433, 1438, 1460–1. *CSP Scot*, vii, 363, 480.

138 *CBP*, ii, 1255–6. *APC*, x, 172. *cf*. Watts, *Border to Middle Shire*, 124–5. Cecil had been secretly corresponding with James VI for several years before 1603.

4

The Wealth of the Lairds and Gentlemen

The Eastern Borders contain some of the most fertile soils in Britain, yet this area was regarded as being impoverished in the sixteenth century owing to relatively low levels of agricultural income and trade. Northumberland's level of poverty was apparently only surpassed by that of Cumberland,[1] whilst Scotland's economy was regarded as primitive.[2] Scotland and England both suffered from debasement of their coinage and inflation during 1540–1603, but there was relative stability in the English economy after 1560. Scotland's economy remained stifled by the crown's failure to adopt a sound monetary policy, yet the lairds and gentlemen generally prospered from agricultural price rises and increased rentals.[3] So was this area really as impecunious as observers thought? The sixteenth-century land market was advantageous to those lairds and gentlemen who capitalised on the availability of monastic and crown lands.[4] Many lairds used their land to raise credit by wadset and there were a few gentry mortgages as well. The income gained by landed men from agriculture was dependent upon good harvests and adaptable leasing. The gentry circumvented the restraints of Border tenure to increase their revenue by evicting, enclosing, engrossing and converting arable land to pasture. Lairds were not as brutal in their land management owing to the nature of Scottish kinship and their paternalism towards tenants. Lairds and gentlemen had alternative sources of income in office-holding, fishing and coal mining, but these were supplementary to agriculture revenue. Comparing the relative wealth levels of the lairds and gentlemen is complicated by the ever-changing exchange rate of the pound sterling to the pound Scots, but analysis is still possible. Wealth levels were usually linked to status and it is possible to gauge the standard of living of the lairds and gentlemen from inventories and other sources.

I. The Land Market

i. England
The initial impetus for gentry acquiring more land began with the Reformation in the 1530s. This precipitated the dissolution of the monasteries and subsequent sales of monastic leases through the Court of Augmentations.[5] Some monasteries had granted generous leases to local gentlemen in antici-

pation of dissolution, but they led to friction as new leases invariably contradicted them.[6] There was a limited supply of monastic land in the Eastern English Borderland. Alnwick abbey and the priories at Brinkburn, Holy Island and Hulne were quickly sold, leaving only small pockets of land belonging to distant houses such as Nostell and Kirkham in Yorkshire. However, this shortage would be alleviated by sales of crown land to the gentry.

The greater gentry of north Northumberland and North Durham gained most from the dissolution as they had more influence and income to acquire leases.[7] Sir John Forster began his rise to prominence with the purchase of Nostell Priory's cell at Bamburgh in 1541.[8] He gradually acquired more monastic property and renewed his leases until he dominated the monastic houses of Alnwick, Bamburgh, Hulne and Hexham.[9] The discovery of concealed lands in Northumberland also benefited Forster and his son Nicholas.[10] Forster's local power ensured success for his kinsmen's applications for monastic property, including that of his brother Rowland of Lucker and his cousin Ralph Gray of Chillingham.[11]

Monastic leases were for twenty-one years or several lifetimes. In an era of inflation this favoured the leaseholding gentry rather than the grantor. Rentals were relatively low after purchasing the lease and fines payable upon renewal were between one and four times the annual rent.[12] Those most in political favour, such as the Forsters, had the lowest fines to pay, but by the end of the century most fines were kept to a low level as land near the frontier had deteriorated in value.[13] Tithe leases were renewed in line with the general rise in prices for they were paid in kind and were thus more profitable.[14]

Opportunities for leasing crown land in the Eastern English Borders were enhanced when Henry VIII acquired the Percy estates in 1537 and then exchanged land with the earl of Rutland for lands at Etal and Glendale in 1547. This policy continued in 1560 when Elizabeth obtained North Durham from the Dean and Chapter of Durham, making the crown one of the largest landowners in the Borders.[15] Sir John Forster's longevity helped him become the greatest accumulator of land in sixteenth-century Northumberland, but others faired quite well, as the Swinhoes were granted crown leases at Goswick[16] and William Selby capitalised on military service in Ireland to secure a lease of Shoreswood.[17]

The gentry sold, mortgaged and deviously conveyed lands to their friends to avoid paying relief upon the entry of an heir to land held by feudal tenure. The Feet of Fines for Northumberland[18] record conveyancing of land held by knight service or socage (freehold) tenure. This was designed to prevent multiple conveyancing and tax evasion, but mortgages could disguise such transfers and the Strothers of Kirknewton certainly used this tactic in 1535.[19] There was some relief for the gentry in the Statute of Wills of 1540 which allowed two-thirds of land held by knight service to be disposed of by will, leaving only one third liable to duty. Despite this the gentry still tried to avoid paying duty on the remaining third[20] as Sir George Radcliffe of Cartington (1577), William Strother of Kirknewton (1579) and Ralph Gray of Chillingham (1593) all made suspicious conveyances.[21]

There were some genuine sales of land and mortgages like the purchases of Eslington by Robert Collingwood in 1542 and Fallodon by Robert Lawson of Rock in 1561.[22] Mortgages were readily accepted by Sir John Forster, who helped Roger Widdrington of the Friars (1568), John Burrell of Howtel (1576), Roger Armorer of Belford (1582) and his elder brother Thomas Forster of Adderstone (1588).[23] Other gentlemen mortgaged their land to merchants (Edmund Craster of Craster, 1573) or to non-local gentlemen stationed at the Berwick garrison (John Carr of Hetton, 1574).[24] Forster bought Middleton Hall (1574) and two-thirds of Belford (1582–4) outright to add to his already lucrative crown and monastic estates. He also made purchases at Elwick, East Duddo and Spindelston (1594–5) through his former mistress and second wife Isabel Sheppard.[25] Forster's fortune was built up through these acquisitions and the shrewd financial practice of delaying payments. For example, he withheld the rental of his concealed lands from 1573 until 1590 when £480 were due to the crown.[26]

At the other end of the financial spectrum were lesser gentlemen struggling to keep their land such as John Horsley of Outchester and Roger Fowberry of Fowberry, who both held mortgages. Horsley was forced to sell his land to the Grays of Chillingham after many years of mortgaging to Thomas Jackson, a burgess of Berwick (who later sold his interest to Valentine Brown the treasurer of Berwick).[27] Roger Fowberry consistently under-valued his small estate and stupidly gave long leases to friends. He also gave a ridiculously cheap six-year lease of Fowberry to his erstwhile friends the Strothers of Kirknewton for a total sum of £120. His estate was worth £50 a year, so he was inevitably impoverished and defaulted on repayment to the profiteering Strothers. He lost his entire 1,210 acre estate to the Strothers under the terms of common law.[28]

Total landholding is an indicator of wealth, but it is difficult to estimate exactly how much land the Northumbrian gentry families held as acreages given in *Inquisitions Post Mortem* are estimated. There is little differentiation between fertile and less productive land and messuages, cot lands, orchards and common pasture are not specified in acres. The following acreages are therefore approximate.

TABLE 4.I. THE ESTATE ACREAGES
OF THE GENTRY

Name and status	Date[29]	Minimum acreage	Reference (PRO)
Robert Lawson of Rock, esq.	1565	4600	C142/143/71
Roger Widdrington of the Friars, gent.	1568	340	CP25/2/192/10 Eliz/HIL
Edmund Craster of Craster, esq.	1573	2400	CP25/2/192/15 & 16 Eliz MICH
John Carr of Hetton, gent.	1574	2065	CP25/2/192 16 & 17 Eliz MICH
Vincent Rutherford of Middleton Hall, gent.	1574	3220	*ibid.*
John Burrell of Howtel, gent.	1576	430	CP25/2/192/18 & 19 Eliz MICH
Roger Armorer of Belford, gent.	1582	536	CP25/2/192/24 Eliz/HIL
Robert Beadnell of Lemmington, esq.	1583	2070	C142/201/96
Thomas Forster of Adderstone, esq.	1588	4300	CP25/2/192/30 Eliz/HIL
Ralph Gray of Chillingham.	1593	427500	CP25/2/192/35 Eliz/HIL NRO 2088
John Horsley of Outchester, gent.	1595	1000	CP25/2/192/43 Eliz/TRIN
Sir John Selby of Twizel.	1597	4850	C142/245/62
William Haggerston of Haggerston, esq.	1608	1940	C142/344/82
Sir Cuthbert Collingwood	1612	8600	C142/432/134

These acreages only refer to the Northumberland and North Durham lands of these gentlemen, yet a pattern of size in relation to status still emerges. Gentlemen held between 340 and 3,220 acres; esquires 1,940 – 4,600 acres and knights (including Ralph Gray of Chillingham) 4,850– 427,500 acres.[30] These statistics are slightly misleading as 340 acres of land with arable potential were worth more than 3,220 acres of upland pasture. Much of Ralph Gray's huge and probably overestimated acreage was near the Border and was perhaps difficult to lease, or may have been used only as summer pasture. Nevertheless these proportions of landholding are notable for their correlation of income and status, which will be discussed later.

Those gentlemen who held land outwith the Eastern Borders included Edmund Craster of Craster in Richmondshire (Yorkshire) and Sir Cuthbert Collingwood at Eppleton (Durham) and Benton (Yorkshire). William Selby of Shoreswood had the most distant property at Ightham Mote in Kent, owing to courtier patronage.[31] Several gentry families also held land in local boroughs, such as the Grays of Horton, Ords of Longridge, Reeds of Fenham, Selbies of Twizel and Strothers of Kirknewton in Berwick.[32] The Alders of Prendwick, Claverings of Callaly, Forsters of Bamburgh and Ogles of Eglingham held land in Alnwick.[33] These borough properties were probably just tenanted investments, with the exception of the Selbies and Ords, who held land in Berwick through holding offices within the town and garrison.

ii. Scotland

Lairds also held land in local burghs, for the Homes of Ayton and Wedderburn and the Edingtons of that Ilk held lands in Duns.[34] The Kers of Cavers and Cessford had property in Kelso.[35] The Pringles of Smailholm held various parcels of Lauder, whilst the Kers of Shaws, Greenhead, Gateshaw, Yair and Primsideloch held many burgages in Selkirk.[36] The dominant laird of the Eastern Border burghs was probably Sir Thomas Ker of Ferniehirst, who held fourteen burgages in Jedburgh.[37] Lairds also held diverse lands outside their locality, such as the Homes at Dunglass, Spott, Dunbar, Gullane and Broxmouth (East Lothian). The Homes of Manderston and Cockburns of that Ilk held land at Stracathro and Inverarity in Forfarshire (Angus) and the Lumsdens of Blanerne owned some Edinburgh property.[38]

Properties held at a distance were sometimes linked to former monasteries, as the Homes' dominance over Jedburgh Abbey allowed them access to its daughter house at Restenneth (Forfarshire), whilst George Cranston of Corsbie held Southside in Midlothian from Newbattle Abbey.[39] Unlike Northumberland, there was a wealth of monastic land in the Scottish Borders and no abrupt 'dissolution'. A gradual secularisation of monastic land had begun well before the Scottish Reformation and continued throughout the sixteenth century. Monastic feu charters were first granted by abbots, priors and prioresses to meet large tax demands from King James V.[40] The feuars were often the existing tacksmen of these lands like the Linlithgows of Drygrange who feued from Melrose Abbey in 1540.[41] Other laird feuars included the Stewarts of Eildon (Melrose), the Kers of Newhall (Kelso Abbey) and the Bennets of Chesters (archbishop of Glasgow).[42] These grants benefited the lairds in the long-term as price rises favoured those with heritable leases, which did not have to be renewed as frequently as short tacks. Therefore Scottish feu charters of monastic origin were a better prospect for landed men than the non-heritable leases of the English Court of Augmentations.

Apart from feu charters, lay control of local Scottish monastic foundations were much sought after by landed families. This system of appointing lay commendators in place of the religious heads of houses guaranteed great riches to those in royal favour. Outwith the Borders Mark Ker, a younger son of the Kers of Cessford, amassed a fortune through gaining the commendatorship of Newbattle Abbey near Dalkeith in 1549.[43] Within the Eastern Borders local lairds gained Coldingham, Eccles, Jedburgh and Kelso after the Reformation. Coldingham was contested between the Homes of Manderston, Maitlands of Thirlestane, the Lords Home and the earls of Bothwell, who were all commendators there after 1560.[44] Eccles was granted to the Homes of Cowdenknowes, whilst Jedburgh was held by the Lords Home through their younger son and nominee commendator, Andrew Home.[45] Kelso eventually went to the Kers of Cessford in 1592,

though they had sought it since the 1560s.[46] Some lairds had their sons
appointed commendators whilst they were still minors to manipulate the
monasteries' lands for their own purposes. Even if the lands had all been
feued there were still teinds to exploit. Female relations were similarly taken
advantage of at the nunneries of Abbey St Bathans, Coldstream and North
Berwick. In 1565 the fifth Lord Home recommended his niece, Elizabeth
Home daughter of the commendator of Jedburgh, as prioress of St Bathans.
He then secured most of the abbey's lands in a feu charter and had the
remaining lands and teinds granted to his kinsman, Alexander Home of
Huttonhall.[47] The Pringles of that Ilk had three successive female kins-
women as prioresses of Coldstream, yet they did not command all the
nunnery's lands by this tactic. As they had no power base in the Merse they
leased the land to local lairds such as the Homes of Huttonhall and
Manderston and the Kers of Hirsel. The commendatorship was eventually
granted to the Kers after all the nuns had died.[48] The Homes of Polwarth
had many kinsmen in the locality of North Berwick in East Lothian so their
acquisition of this priory, through a succession of prioress daughters, was
more secure. The earl of Bothwell provocatively stole the convent seal in the
1560s, but the Homes conceded little as a result, in contrast to the Pringles at
Coldstream.[49] Interestingly the Homes of Polwarth were ardent supporters
of the reformed church, but they must have had some pangs of guilt about
their monastic wealth as a nun's portion was granted to a disabled girl in
1565.[50]

   In addition to monastic lands, parish kirklands and teinds were feued to
local lairds by both pre-Reformation priests and post-Reformation ministers. For instance, Swinton went to John Swinton of that Ilk in 1543 and
Langton was leased to William Cockburn of Choicelee in 1585.[51] Kirklands
could belong to several different lairds throughout the century as the
kirkland of Morebattle was leased to the Kers of Cessford and Corbethouse
and the parsonage of Duns was contested amongst several Home lairds.[52]
Lairds often received teind leases from other lairds as superiors, such as the
Erskines at Dryburgh who granted the teinds of Lauder to Andrew Home in
1541.[53] Teind leases could be generous as the 1561 tack granted to Thomas
MacDougal of Makerstoun by Kelso was for nineteen years. This specified
that a rental of eight chalders of victual *per annum* was required only for the
first five years of the lease after an initial payment of 800 merks. Thomas
had previously held these Makerstoun teinds at 200 merks *per annum*.[54]
George Pringle of Blindlee was not so favoured when he renewed his tack of
the kirklands of Stichill in 1576 as he previously paid forty shillings a year
and now had to find £10 Scots.[55] These leases were, none the less, still
profitable during such inflationary times.

   Feuing was not confined to ecclesiastical lands in Scotland for crown lands
were also granted to lairds in perpetuity. As there has been little research on
crown lands the importance of church land has perhaps been overemphasised.

The significance of crown lands should therefore not be underestimated in the sixteenth century. In the Eastern Borders the main source of crown land was Ettrick Forest, and the Kers of Linton, Primsideloch and Yair as well as the Lords Home and the Pringles of Galashiels, Torwoodlee and Trinlyknowe all held land there in feu.[56] As with monastic feu charters, the advantage was mostly with the feuar rather than the grantor. For instance, George Pringle of Torwoodlee paid £33–6s–8d a year for Torwoodlee in 1555 and was still paying the same amount to the Exchequer in 1587. He feued Caddonlee for only £26–13s–4d *per annum* yet was owed £272 rent by his tenants in 1599.[57] The Kers of Linton held Fairnilee at £50 Scots *per annum* with a mere six shillings and eight pence augmentation in 1595. They had wadsetted the property at a more realistic yearly value of 313 merks in 1565.[58] Feuing was therefore undeniably profitable to the lairds and this probably accounts for their greater housebuilding in comparison to the Eastern Border gentry, which will be discussed later.

The Brounfields of Hassington Mains were typical of lairds who held land from other lairds. In 1555 they renewed their charter of the £4 land of Hassington from Lord Home for 200 merks. With inflation and currency devaluation the same procedure cost them 1,200 merks in 1588.[59] A £4 land, measured by the medieval tax assessment of old extent would have been a substantial acreage in the sixteenth century worth far more than £4 Scots, but 1,200 merks (£800 Scots) would still have been cheaper than buying land afresh. The value of land had soared along with the inflation of prices so a mere two acres in Coldingham were redeemed for £200 Scots in 1592.[60] Overall this benefited the lairds, but extravagance led a few to sell land to cover their debts rather than wadset on an extended basis. The sixth Lord Home initially wadset the barony of Broxfield in 1583 to the Mac-Dougals of Makerstoun for 12,600 merks, but lost it by not repaying the loan by 1592.[61] His long-term financial mismanagement continued for in 1591 he sold Ladykirk to his kinsman Alexander Home of Huttonhall for 6,000 merks and then the barony of Greenlaw to Sir George Home of Spott in 1596. Meanwhile he continued to wadset lands in East Lothian to Alexander Home of North Berwick.[62] His father, the fifth Lord Home, had experienced similar problems during 1550–51 when he sold Easter Muirdean to Thomas MacDougal of Makerstoun. Whilst absent in France Lord Home's factrix, his wife Margaret Ker, Lady Home, had to borrow £80 Scots from Sir John Home of Cowdenknowes.[63] Neither lord considered wadsetting land to Edinburgh advocates or merchants, yet many Border lairds overlooked their kinsmen in favour of borrowing without embarrassment from affluent strangers.

Advocates were patronised more than merchants for loans before 1603.[64] Mr Thomas Weston seemed to oblige many Eastern Border lairds with wadsets from 1567 to 1585. He often helped the Pringles of Galashiels, as well as the Kers of Primsideloch and Hirsel and Nicol Cairncross of Calfhill.[65] The Pringles seem to have repaid a loan only to take out another wadset almost immediately, thus remaining in constant debt to Weston and others including William Pringle, a litster burgess of Edinburgh. Other lending advocates included Mr Edward Hay, Mr Oliver Colt, Mr George Crichton and Mr John Moscrop.[66] Wadsets were only beneficial as short-term loans for interest rates were generally high. Where interest was taken as an annual money rent of the lands wadsetted, the rate can be calculated as table 4.2 demonstrates.

TABLE 4.2. INTEREST RATES PAID BY LAIRDS, 1556–1594

Date	Borrowing Laird/Lender	%	Reference (NAS)
1556	MacDougal of Makerstoun/Alex Cockburn	4	RD1/1 fo. 336
1563	Ker of Primsideloch/John Weston	12	RD1/6 fo. 369
1567	Ker of Primsideloch/Thomas Weston	12	RD1/9 fo. 65
1570	Home of North Berwick/Home of Heugh	8.5	RD1/9 fo. 286
1574	Andrew, commendator of Jedburgh/John Stewart	15	RD1/13 fo. 230
1575	Cairncross of Calfhill/Thomas Weston	12	RD1/14 fos 197–9
1575	Pringle of Galashiels/Thomas Weston	10	RD1/14 fo. 196
1579	Ker of Hirsel/Henry Lumsden	10	RD1/17 fo. 131
1582	Cockburn of that Ilk/Archibald Boyman	10	RD1/20/2 fo. 93
1583	Home of Ninewells/John Moscrop	12	RD1/21 fo. 86
1584	Andrew, c. of Jedburgh/Margaret Home	12	RD1/24 fo. 48
1587	Ker of Cessford/Cairncross of Calfhill	12	RD1/24/1 fo. 304
1587	Lauder of Whitslaid/John Moscrop	10	RD1/25 fo. 214
1588	Lauder of that Ilk/William Pringle	10	RD1/28 fo. 163
1589	Haitlie of Mellerstain/William Napier	10	RD1/30 fo. 238
1591	Spottiswoode of that Ilk/Home of Carolside	13	RD1/38 fo. 197
1592	Home of Blackadder/John Moscrop	12	RD1/41 fo. 179
1592	MacDougal of Makerstoun/John Ferguson	12	RD1/43 fo. 373
1593	Home of Manderston/Richard Cass	10	RD1/46 fo. 128
1594	Home of Wedderburn/John Nicholson	10	RD1/50 fo. 131

Charging interest for loans was technically illegal before the Reformation, but the situation remained unclear until a 1587 Act of the Scottish Parliament settled the amount at no more than ten per cent, the accustomed rate.[67] Several of the lenders in table 4.2 were clearly breaking the law, yet were not apprehended. Although advocates dominated the lenders, there was no overall pattern of wadsetting as lairds borrowed from each other. Cairncross of Calfhill, for instance, appears as both borrower and lender. Financial embarrassment could occur at any time for the lairds, but family marriage contracts were a probable source of some loans. Even the wealthy Maitland of Thirlestane was forced to raise money by this method in 1593.[68] When a laird repeatedly mortgaged his land it was a sure sign of financial difficulties. The Haitlies of Mellerstain were lucky not to lose their estates during the second half of the century as they deviously wadsetted the same land to several people at once. This was only uncovered when the family of Henry

Haitlie's wife were trying to settle her jointure in 1573.[69] Henry died heavily in debt, but his successor John managed to salvage the estates and he died in 1603 with an inventory worth over £9,000 Scots.

The Haitlies were also disadvantaged by the fiar system, by which a laird granted his estate to his heir in fee-simple during his lifetime. This was normally transacted in return for a liferent of the estate and security of the third for his widow. This typically took place when a marriage was arranged for the heir, but it caused all sorts of trouble if the heir then predeceased his father after being infeft of the land. The Haitlies discovered that this process could not be legally reversed when two heirs died prematurely. There are many examples of fiars amongst the Border lairds, yet this procedure was not designed as a measure to avoid paying feudal relief like suspicious conveyances in England. It was merely a means of securing property and examples include John Ker, fiar of Corbet, Philip Nisbet, fiar of the Ilk and William Douglas, fiar of Bonjedward.[70]

II. Land Management and Agriculture

The majority of landed men in this region seem to have prospered against a background of rising prices and rentals, though there were some Anglo-Scottish variations to this.[71] Husbandry in the Eastern Borders was similar on either side of the frontier, but land management as it was practised by the lairds and gentlemen differed sharply. The same crops and livestock were raised amidst corresponding topography and climatic conditions, but the gentry proved to be the profiteers of new land management. They perpetrated evictions, enclosure and engrossment with little regard to the restraints of Border tenure to increase profits from tenanted land. By contrast, the lairds' lands remained relatively unchanged.

Lairds and gentlemen gained income from land in two ways: firstly by leasing their land to tenants for an annual rent in kind or money, with entry fines or gressum payable upon the entry of an heir or when the lease was renewed; and secondly by farming their own demesne and lands nearby. The first source would have made up the majority of their landed income, but demesne farming was profitable as well if a surplus was produced for sale when prices were increasing.[72] The lairds could augment their rents and reversions in line with inflation, but the gentry were supposed to remain within the limitations of Border tenure. This tenure was a unique form of tenant-right leasing found only in the north of England. Basically it gave the tenant security of tenure if he was armed on horse or on foot for Border defence, though the nature of these leases are debated by historians. The expense involved in this exempted him from normal taxation, but he still had to pay a nominal rent.

Border tenure was principally for non-gentry tenants as the gentry had obligations to defend the realm through holding their land by socage (freehold) or military (knight) service, but they too were excluded from taxation.[73] In Scotland men between sixteen and sixty were supposed to be armed and appear at wappinshaws, but this was not linked to tenure and they received no tax concessions. North Northumberland and North Durham were apparently well armed and plenished (cultivated), according to the muster roll of 1539. Decay set in soon after this as later musters in 1586, 1593 and 1595–96 show a very serious decline in numbers ready for Border defence. With the garrisons at Berwick and Carlisle in decline at this time, the situation for the government was critical. For instance North Durham had 320 horse in 1540, yet by 1593 there were only 130 – not nearly enough to defend this area's frontier adequately.[74] The reasons for this decline in Border tenure can be attributed to a number of factors such as crown policy during the 1530s and 1540s (when the gentry received remuneration for Border service), Scottish settlement, poverty caused by both the crown and gentry's actions to increase their income from tenants and persistent raiding.[75] Historians disagree about the effectiveness of Border tenure as: R. A. Butlin, P. J. Dixon, A. Knowles and R. Newton believe that it restricted rent increases and land improvement, whilst J. Thirsk, E. Kerridge and R. W. Hoyle think that it was undermined by rent and entry fine increases. M. L. Bush questions its decline because of parliamentary statutes, but these were only ever as good as their local enforcement. However, he does note that even if tenants had lost their tenant right through conversion to leasehold, they were still customarily obliged to give Border service. Only S. J. Watts correctly attributes some of the decay to the incidence of Scottish tenants in the area.[76] In truth, Border tenure was frequently circumvented by the Eastern Border gentry by various means.

The gentry were conscious of their area's impoverishment in comparison to the south of England. They therefore copied the agricultural innovations known in the south by raising rents and entry fines. They also exploited their proximity to the frontier by encouraging illegal Scottish tenants to settle in the area. These Scots, as aliens, were not bound by Border tenure and could offer a higher rent as they were less likely to be raided by fellow Scots. There were far more Scots living here during 1540–1603 than has previously been acknowledged. A survey of the Gray lands in the late-sixteenth century records both Scottish and English surnames. A number of Scots had lived in England for decades, but these names were more recent.[77] They could only have replaced evicted English tenants. These evictions were occasionally reported to Border officers as they were carried out by a well-organised gang of Scottish thugs, such as those at Branxton in 1580 and Ilderton in 1586. It appears that the gentry kept a conspiracy of silence about their Scots tenants. Muster rolls frequently recorded 'no cause' for Border decay, probably to disguise evidence that these lands had been leased to Scots.[78]

Agricultural changes adopted by the gentry included the conversion of arable land to pasture, engrossment and enclosure. Pasture was preferable to arable in the middle decades of the sixteenth century when wool prices were high. Changes could be accomplished only by evictions, though these were supposedly outlawed in 1555 by a government fearing depopulation in a sensitive frontier area.[79] When wool prices fell the gentry probably switched over to cattle, rather than re-convert to arable. There were thirty-nine townships in the Eastern Borders affected by this type of convertible husbandry including Howtel, Hetton, Outchester, Ross, Newland, Crooklaw, Warenton and East Bradford.[80]

Engrossment involved the amalgamation of several holdings into larger units, with the inevitable eviction of some or all of the tenants. Depopulation was created by gentry action for Sir Thomas Gray of Chillingham evicted 340 people from Newham in a single day in the 1580s and the Selbies of Biddlestone made twenty-two holdings into thirteen at Biddlestone in 1584. There was an irony to this situation because engrossment was against Border law, yet the government wanted tenants to have larger holdings to prevent partible inheritance depleting the strength of Border defence. The gentry were therefore presented with an excuse for engrossing their lands for their own profit. Engrossment also led to the creation of some additional townships such as New Etal, Chillingham Newton and New Bewick.[81]

The taking of excessive entry fines and increasing of rentals was yet another source of gentry income that encouraged the decline of Border defence. This practice was officially discouraged from 1543 onwards but the gentry, eager for more revenue, disregarded this advice. They were classed as notorious oppressors of their tenants as early as 1552.[82] Accusations about this type of oppression were numerous in the 1580s and 1590s when both local and non-local gentlemen were cited, but this must have been happening in the 1560s and 1570s as well. Henry Haggerston of Haggerston was reported for taking excessive fines from tenants at Old Etal, Doddington, Berrington, Cheswick and Haggerston. Arthur Cresswell, a Londoner, also overcharged his former Percy tenants at Ellingham and Swinhoe. A crown directive that fines should be kept to no more than one year's rent had obviously been ignored.[83] There were many murmurings about gentlemen 'enhancing' rents, such as Ilderton of Ilderton at Ilderton and Roseden, Robert Clavering of Callaly at Yetlington, Sir John Forster at Shoston and Sir William Reed at Scremerston.[84] The most vicious example of this behaviour occurred in 1600 when the violent Henry Collingwood of Etal imprisoned Peter Lawe, a tenant of Etal, in a 'deepe dungeon'. Collingwood was also reported to generally 'wounde, beate and oppress' the other tenants because they refused to leave. Unlike previous evictees, Lawe went before the Court of the Star Chamber to complain and Collingwood was later gaoled. This court had been interested in punishing oppressive Border landlords like Collingwood since 1597, but they had to await a brave tenant prepared to tackle the local gentry's cartel.[85] Paradoxically, when Thomas Clavering was reported to the privy council for evicting an old soldier from Buckton in 1589, no action had been taken.[86]

The gentry were guilty of enclosing some of the best land and common grazing for their own use.[87] Local tenants could not keep horses for Border defence on common land if the gentry put their cattle there instead. In 1567 the tenants of Ellingham and Chatton complained that they were 'over rune with gentlemen planted nowe amongst them'.[88] Sometimes the gentry enlarged their own demesne, or to re-let the land 'at suche a rackede rent, as the tenants are not hable to mainteine the service . . .'[89] The lands of Little Houghton were made into demesne in 1584 and part of the common of Houghton and Alnmouth was enclosed in 1567 for John Carr of Boulmer. By 1601 most common fields in Northumberland had been enclosed or divided. This was regretted by the ninth earl of Northumberland who realised that the gentry were exploiting the commons against the interests of his tenants.[90] He ordered his bailiffs to pull down the enclosures at Thirston, Shilbottle and Chatton in 1602 and ordered that cattle belonging to the gentry should be impounded from Lucker, Houghton and Rennington commons. This action had come much too late though to reverse localised depopulation and its part in the decline of Border defence.[91]

There was little relief from government as a 1597 Act against enclosure included Northumberland, yet exempted this county from a similar measure in 1601.[92] It was ironic that enclosure had been encouraged in the English Eastern Border in 1555 as a defence mechanism against Scottish reivers. Ditches would have hindered the path of these thieves, but as the expense of enclosure was to be met by the tenant the scheme failed. That the gentry adopted the practice well away from the Border for their own profit, rather than for Border defence, made a mockery of the government's good intentions.[93] Futile attempts were made to persuade the gentry to grant leases of twenty-one or even forty years' duration to benefit Border defence by letting tenants avoid many entry fines.[94] Many signed a 1561 agreement to this effect, then disregarded it in their usual avaricious fashion.[95]

The tenants did not take all these changes without some resistance for in Northumberland there were recorded incidents of tenants abusing their gentry landlord's rights. In 1554 Edward Bradford complained that the tenants of Embleton did not grind their corn at his mill and hunted without his licence.[96] This type of evasion was also a problem for the lairds. William Home of Prenderguest and William Home had trouble at Eyemouth and Coldingham in 1568 and 1598.[97] The distance between a laird's mill and his tenant's lands could, however, be cumbersome. Home of Wedderburn's tenants at Darnchester and Ladykirk were bound by their tenure to travel five miles to the east mill at Kimmerghame.[98] Distance may not have been the problem at Embleton, Eyemouth and Coldingham as millers there were perhaps overcharging for their services.

Oppression of tenants was not unknown in Scotland, but it was on a much smaller scale than in Northumberland and North Durham. Here the reformed church wished lairds to be content with their rents. There was also no equivalent of Border tenure in Scotland, so lairds were not under the same pressure to override an outdated land system. Nevertheless there were cases of individual evictions at Longnewton (1561 and 1574) and Edington (1589).[99] The reasons for these ejections are unknown, but the Longnewton cases involved the ejection of a tenant's wife and a widow. Andrew Pringle of Galashiels even tried to evict a fellow laird, John Pringle of Wrangholm, from Smailholm Tower in 1578 and Lady Home of Wedderburn was attacked by her tenants at Kimmerghame in 1584, for an unrecorded reason.[100] However, none of these Scottish evictions are comparable with the numbers forcibly expelled from their lands on the other side of the frontier.

Levels of oppression therefore differed, yet as farmers these landed families used practically the same crop and animal husbandry on both sides of the Border. The area's topography of upland pasture suited to livestock and lowland river valleys geared to grain production gave them relative prosperity, though there were bad harvests in 1555–56, 1565, 1577, 1585–87 and 1594–98.[101] The 'Little Ice Age' that began in 1550 badly affected agricultural production because of its long and severe winters.[102] Wet summers hindered grain production and made imports into Scotland a necessity for much of the sixteenth century.[103] The Merse and Northumbrian coastal plain were none the less fertile and well suited to cereal production, including wheat. This amazed some commentators who thought this part of England and Scotland too cold for growing wheat.[104] Watts' suggestion that North Durham's husbandry was affected by raiding cannot be substantiated. Reivers favoured the theft of livestock rather than immobile sacks of corn and it appears that this grain-growing region still prospered when weather conditions were favourable.[105]

The basic field system in Scotland was infield and outfield, but Northumberland did not conform to any set system as it had wide variations in cultivation.[106] Inventories are an excellent source for identifying which crops grew in the Eastern Borders, though only the Scottish inventories estimate the yields of these crops. In 1568, during a poor harvest, oats were expected to yield a ratio of 1:2.5, wheat and bear 1:3 and peas 1:2 at Holydean near Melrose.[107] However, in better years wheat usually yielded 1:4 or 1: 4.5, oats 1:3, bear 1:4 and peas 1:4 or 1:5. Rye, where it was grown returned 1:4.[108] The yields in the Eastern English Borders are stated as oats 1:5 and barley (bear) 1:3, by Watts, but as English inventories do not give any information on yields it is more probable that their correct ratios were nearer those of Scotland as the growing conditions were very similar.[109] Peas and beans were grown less in Northumberland than in Scotland, but they were not 'rare' as Watts claims.[110]

The highest areas of the Eastern Borders were used for transhumance. These shielings were mainly for cattle driven up there in May or June to fatten. They returned to lower ground in late August. This practice was generally beneficial as it allowed hay to be made on some of the lowland pastures and helped prevent cattle disease.[111] The level between the shielings and the river valleys was probably used all year round for breeding sheep and cattle, whilst the river valleys and the coastal plain of Northumberland were predominantly arable with intermittent pastures. Lairds and gentlemen who lived in the arable zone seem to have bought cattle and sheep from landed men living in the intermediate area to fatten for market. George Nisbet of that Ilk, for instance, owed £42 Scots to William Pringle of Torwoodlee in 1577, for lambs.[112] Wealthier gentlemen who owned numerous properties, could breed their own cattle and sheep on higher ground before taking them to coastal pastures for fattening.[113]

There was a ready market for cattle and sheep as flesh was in demand locally and their skins, wool and fells were profitable export commodities.[114] Exports were at a high level in the 1530s, but declined in the 1540s and did not peak again until the 1590s. The landed men's interest in livestock never faltered throughout the sixteenth century, despite downturns in the economy and occasional losses in raids. The lairds were even known to lend oxen for ploughing amongst themselves, rather like a modern-day farming co-operative.[115] Other livestock recorded in inventories included pigs and bees, but they would have been for domestic consumption rather than the production of surplus goods for sale.[116] The marketing of the lairds' foodstuffs was principally through local market centres such as Melrose, Kelso, Jedburgh, Duns and Eyemouth, but there was also the option of trading across the frontier in Berwick.[117] Lairds who lived more than twelve miles from Edinburgh were not constrained as to how they could market their grain, unless it was for export. In 1586 David Home of Ninewells and James Home of the Style chose to deliver their cereals to Eyemouth harbour to be uplifted by John Fortune, a merchant of Edinburgh.[118] Coldingham may also have been used as Robert Home of the Fleurs has an obligation with John Burn, maltman in Leith for bear.[119] The gentry would normally have used Berwick or Alnwick as a market centre, but there was a lively trade in smuggled goods for all landed men in the Eastern Borders.[120]

III. Alternative Sources of Income

Non-agricultural income for landed families came from many sources including domestic and Border offices, pensions, forfeitures, wardships, coalmines and fisheries. The actual salaries paid to landed men holding domestic offices are mostly unrecorded, but an under-sheriff in England received £10 *per annum* and Sir Cuthbert Radcliffe complained that he was underpaid as constable of Alnwick in 1539.[121] In Scotland Sir James Home of Cowdenknowes bemoaned the 'great charges' not repaid to him as captain of Edinburgh Castle, but conversely the Cockburns of Langton were accused of exacting high fees as ushers of the White Rod.[122]

On the Scottish side of the frontier payments to the wardens of the East and Middle Marches were sporadic in the second half of the century, but they would have been around £100 Scots *per annum* with £50 Scots for the deputy wardens.[123] The wardens had their salaries augmented by pensions to compensate for inflation, but this supplement was inconsistent. Lord Home received £400 Scots pension in 1564,[124] whilst Sir Thomas Ker of Ferniehirst had £1,000 Scots *per annum* in 1585.[125] There were some additional payments to the Scottish wardens, as Lord Home obtained £20 Scots for searching out individuals summoned before the privy council in his March.[126] In the English Marches basic Border salaries were also static throughout the sixteenth century, but unlike Scotland there were fewer opportunities for augmenting salaries against inflation. This led to numerous pleas of impoverishment by those in office as salaries could be in arrears by up to two years.[127] The warden of the East March (who was normally governor of Berwick as well) received £466–13s–4d *per annum* whilst the warden of the Middle March had £333–6s–8d (or 500 marks) *per annum*. The deputies typically earned £10 *per annum*, but in 1552 Ralph Gray of Chillingham received £333s–6–8d as deputy of the East March whilst standing in for the warden and in 1540 a deputy earned £133–6s–8d. During wartime deputies were paid more as Sir Ralph Gray had ten shillings a day and Sir John Forster had thirteen shillings in the Middle March, but these were exceptional payments.[128] The slowness of payment led a frustrated Sir John Forster to detain crown rentals to the equivalent of his Middle March warden salary in 1590, but he was also owed £26–13s–4d by the crown as keeper of Tynedale and Redesdale and £6–7s–0d as bailiff of Bywell.[129]

Salaries due to the officers of the Berwick garrison were not increasing during the sixteenth century and to make matters worse, they were rarely paid on time. As gentleman porter in 1551, John Selby of Twizel was paid £20 *per annum* with normal profits (that is grazing and haymaking rights in the bounds of Berwick). In 1573 his son, Sir John Selby, was still receiving £20.[130] Even when two William Selbies shared this office the salary remained at £20, but an entry in the 1576 guild register notes that the gentleman porter was paid £184–23s–4d *per annum*, which is perhaps the real value of the office with the additional payments in kind.[131] The chamberlain and treasurer were consistently paid £20 and the captains of each garrison company, such as William Selby senior and Sir William Reed, received £105–18s–8d *per annum*. The gentry received additional payments for duties such as riding into Scotland with letters, for which John Selby was paid £14, but Sir John Forster gained the largest reward of £154–11s–4d for escorting the seventh earl of Northumberland from Alnwick to York for execution. Forster would probably have undertaken this task for nothing, considering the animosity between himself and the earl, but he never refused payment.[132] Finally there were the gentlemen pensioners of Berwick who were paid three shillings (36d) per day in 1589, but they succumbed to government stinginess as they only received twenty pence a day in 1593 and 1601.[133]

William Selby senior of Shoreswood seems to have treated his offices at Berwick as a sinecure. There were complaints that he had three concurrent salaries there in 1593, yet had been absent for two years. Selby had been favoured for his military service in Ireland for which he had been paid £100 in 1575. Other pensioners received three shillings a day, yet Selby was paid five shillings.[134] Sir William Reed similarly combined offices in the garrison as he had his own company and the office of captain and keeper of Holy Island and the Farnes. Reed was only paid £36–10s–0d *per annum* for the Holy Island office in 1555, but as a means of compensation he was granted a lucrative lease of the tithes of Holy Island parish to be held in conjunction with this office. By 1600 his annual salary was a respectable £909–10s–10d *per annum* of which £362–17s–4d was for Holy Island and £366–13s–4d was from tithes. This salary was no doubt envied by other garrison officers who failed to gain tithe leases. The tithes of North Durham were supposed to be granted to the garrison officers to help augment their salaries, but few were successful with the local gentry also competing for them.[135]

Pensions granted to the lairds and gentlemen varied from small amounts, like twenty shillings to John Ord as mayor of Berwick in 1576, to much larger amounts granted to lairds as political favours. Lord Home received 10,000 francs in 1560, whilst the Homes of Cowdenknowes and Ayton and the Kers of Ferniehirst gained pensions of 500 or 650 merks from the revenues of Border abbeys.[136] Because of its overseas origin, Lord Home's pension was not paid regularly and later pensions due to the Kers of Ferniehirst from the king of Spain were also intermittent. Other lairds were paid annual pensions by the commendator of Kelso.[137] These pensions were particularly beneficial to younger sons, such as William Home of Bassendean.

Forfeitures and ransoms could also be lucrative for lairds and gentlemen. Forfeiture, in the form of horning and poinding, was commonplace in the Scottish Borders. It was a convenient mechanism for collecting debts or enforcing an appearance at a law court, or before the privy council.[138] They were usually short-term, but they would have inflicted some financial loss on the recipient if his goods were poinded. A laird's public image would also have been tarnished, for horning, as the name suggests, was announced by a messenger blasting a horn at local market crosses. In the English Borders forfeiture was normally for the serious crime of treason and not for trivial matters like debt. Therefore it only affected those gentry involved in rebellions such as that of 1569–70.[139]

Innumerable examples of lairds being forfeited for petty offences include Adam and John Grahamslaw of Newton (1540 & 1566),[140] Adam Ker of Dalcove (1552), Steven Brounfield of Greenlawdean (1555) and John Brounfield of Tenandry (1584).[141] Forfeitures for treason benefited those lairds fortunate enough to be granted part of the escheat. Wealthy forfeitees included the fifth Lord Home, William Maitland of Lethington, the fifth earl of Bothwell and the earls of Angus. David Home of Fishwick, a younger son of the Homes of Blackadder, gained the East Lothian lands of Maitland of Lethington for much of the 1570s and made a great fortune.[142] Lord Home's estates were granted to his former kinsmen the Homes of Manderston and Cowdenknowes, who fully exploited them before handing them back to the sixth Lord.[143] The lands forfeited by Bothwell were never returned to him so the sixth Lord Home, William Ker of Cessford and Sir Walter Scott of Buccleuch gained significantly from his Border estates.[144] Patrick Home of Polwarth also received part of the Bothwell escheat, but his temporary possession of some of the earl of Angus's lands was probably more lucrative.[145] The ascendancy of George Home of Spott was no doubt assisted by the gain of 3,500 merks from an Edinburgh burgess charged with treason.[146] Forfeiture was not necessarily disastrous as lesser lairds Ferdinando Home of Broomhouse and Robert Pringle of Blindlee had their estates forfeited to Alexander Home of Manderston in 1568 and James Pringle of Buckholm in 1548, respectively.[147] Both were restored within a short period and as their escheats were given to loyal kinsmen, they may not have lost much revenue.

Alexander Home of Huttonhall established himself on an upwardly mobile path when he was allowed to keep a ransom of £300 sterling from Englishman, John Dudley, in 1568.[148] Huttonhall was not alone in this alternative source of wealth, as ransoming was commonplace during warfare. The amounts paid are rarely recorded though the gentry were adept at gaining from the misfortune of others. Sometimes they were entitled to collect 'felon's dues' and the recipient was usually the immediate feudal superior of the convicted felon. In 1591 Thomas Swinhoe, bailiff of Chatton, collected £13–10s–0d from a local felon and Sir John Forster received £4–6s–8d from a South Middleton delinquent.[149] Even though the Borders were the original place for blackmail, very few of the Eastern Border landed families were directly involved with this nefarious practice. Sir Robert Ker of Cessford's youthful activities did resemble this, but he later repented the error of his ways.[150]

The gentry used the cruel system of wardship as another source of income, but these were not easily obtainable. Sir Cuthbert Collingwood had to pay £70 for that of John Swinburne of Edlingham in 1575 and Ralph Gray paid £120 for Robert Collingwood of Eslington's ward in 1598.[151] These two examples were founded in kinship rather than profiteering, but Robert Roddam of Roddam's guardianship of Thomas Weetwood of Weetwood was profitable. Roddam paid only £3–6s–8d for Weetwood's lands in 1571 when they were really worth at least £10 *per annum*.[152] If they did not succeed in gaining local wardships, gentlemen were often leaseholders of ward's lands. For example the Collingwoods of Eslington held the Collingwood of Etal lands, the Grays leased the Proctor of Shawdon lands and Sir

John Forster, Sir John Selby and the Wallises of Coupland held the Gray of
Chillingham lands.[153] Lairds were also guardians of wards and could be as
exploitative if they wanted. The Kers of Mersington and Primsideloch both
demanded compensation from female wards after they married without
their permission.[154]

Apart from agricultural revenue there were mineral resources for the
gentry to exploit. Typically these were coal mines leased from the crown. A
1584 lease to William Selby of Shoreswood specified that he could have 'all
maner of mynes of coole, leade, iron and other metal' at Shoreswood, but it
was probably only coal that was mined in the Eastern Borders.[155] There
were small, unsophisticated, mines in north Northumberland and North
Durham at Etal, Ford, Bilton, Dunstanburgh, Shilbottle, Norham, Duddo,
Thornton, Murton, Unthank and Kyloe. They produced less than 5,000 tons
a year before 1603. J. U. Nef has underestimated the number of working
coalmines in the Eastern Borders before 1603 as there were also mines at
Gatherwick, Fenham and Bamburgh. There may also have been some
mining near Ayton in the Merse, but this was dwarfed in comparison to
the rich coal seams of Tyneside and Durham.[156] Rentals were correspond-
ingly low in comparison, such as 13s 4d paid by George Muschamp of
Barmoor for Etal and £2–6s–8d by Sir John Forster for Bamburgh.[157] Coal
produced in the Merse was perhaps used by the greater lairds as Lord Home
had three coal fires burning at Old Cambus in 1597 at a cost of £18 Scots.
The majority of the population would still have used peat as this was
cheaper and more easily extracted.[158] English Border coal was probably
exported from Berwick, as there were complaints about coal being spilled on
the highway there in 1599.[159]

The remaining source of alternative wealth came from river and sea
fishings, or the occasional shipwreck.[160] Tweed fisheries were profitable
ventures for both local merchants and gentlemen, who often held joint
leases. They were typically reluctant to pay their rental to the crown as £374
was outstanding in 1574 for three years rent of the 'Newatter'.[161] The other
fishing grounds were all carefully named in leases such as Crale, Elstell,
Outwaterstell and Stark Olstell, all of which were all leased by Sir John Selby
of Twizel.[162] On the Scottish side of the Tweed many of the salmon rights
originally belonged to religious houses and were subsequently leased to local
lairds, such as Sir John Ker of Hirsel at Lessuden (Dryburgh Abbey) and
Alexander Home of Manderston at Tillmouthhauch (Coldstream Priory).[163]

The non-agricultural wealth of the lairds and gentlemen therefore came
from many different sources. Exactly how much of their annual income was
made up from alternative sources is difficult to gauge. The men with the
most power and influence in the area would have earned more from their
office-holding than many lesser landed men earned in total from their lands.
These sources were only intended as a supplement to existing landed
income, though forfeitures and pensions could be substantial.

IV. Comparative Levels of Wealth

Comparing wealth levels of lairds and gentlemen is problematical, but inventories are a reasonable, if controversial, indicator of prosperity.[164] Many inventories have survived from the Eastern Borders in the Durham Probate Registry (Durham University Library: Archives and Special Collections) and the National Archives of Scotland (formerly the Scottish Record Office). They have certain disadvantages, for English and Scottish inventories concern only moveable goods of the deceased and generally make no mention of their lands, with the exception of the crops growing or harvested there. The inventories do not give a reliable guide to the total wealth of an individual either. Totalling was often inaccurate as goods could have been omitted or distributed before appraisal to the widow and heir. Goods were also priced at their second-hand value, which would probably have been less than the laird or gentleman paid for them.[165] A persistent difficulty exists with the ever-changing exchange rate of pound sterling to pound Scots. In 1560 there were £4 Scots to £1 sterling, but this had deteriorated to £6: £1 in 1576 and continued to slide to £7–6s–8d: £1 in 1582, £10: £1 in 1594 and £12: £1 in 1603.[166] These changes have to be remembered when making cross-border comparisons from the following tables. However, inventories as an indicator of wealth can be supplemented by land rentals, dowries, mercantile debt records, household accounts and the evidence of housebuilding to gauge the landed families' standard of living.

TABLE 4.3. THE PERSONAL ESTATES OF THE GENTRY[167]

	Moveable Goods	Debtors	Creditors	Total Estate
KNIGHTS & ESQUIRES				
Thomas Haggerston of Haggerston 1545	135	–	–	135
Thomas Swinburne of Edlingham 1572	223	–	–	193
Isabel Gray of Chillingham 1581	701	871	179	1393
Robert Clavering of Callaly 1583	377	–	40	337
Thomas Forster of Adderstone, younger 1587	145	64	14	195
Sir John Selby of Twizel 1595	292	82	177	197
Sir Cuthbert Collingwood of Eslington 1597	533	546	241	838
Thomas Collingwood of Eslington 1597	350	–	–	350
Sir John Forster of Bamburgh 1602	1020	–	–	1020
Sir William Reed of Fenham 1604	448	–	–	448
William Haggerston of Haggerston 1606	218	33	118	133
Nicholas Forster of Bamburgh 1608	824	–	–	824
GENTLEMEN				
Gerard Selby of Pawston 1549	84	138	–	222
John Carr of Hetton 1551	87	16	105	-2

Table 4.3—contd

Gentlemen—contd	Moveable Goods	Debtors	Creditors	Total Estate
Odnel Selby of Tweedmouth 1555	34	20	77	-23
Ranold Forster of Capheaton 1565	99	77	139	37
John Selby of Twizel 1565	240	–	–	240
William Selby of Grindonrig 1570	30	–	27	3
Ralph Collingwood of Titlington 1570	81	10	12	79
Roger Widdrington of the Friars 1572	480	165	10	635
John Carr of Lesbury 1574	327	–	104	223
George Harbottle of Cawledge 1577	25	?	?	38
Richard Middleham of Alnmouth 1577	3	–	–	3
Mark Horsley of Screnwood 1581	42	–	4	38
John Gallon of Cawledge Park 1583	25	–	–	25
Michael Harbottle of Tughall 1585	40	86	46	80
Odnel Selby of Hulne Park 1586	65	–	–	65
George Carr of Lesbury 1587	50	–	–	50
John Carr of Lesbury 1587	327	–	104	223
William Clavering of Duddo 1587	127	52	35	144
George Middleham of Alnmouth 1587	57	20	44	33
Robert Muschamp of Gatherwick 1587	58	–	–	58
Thomas Weetwood of Weetwood 1587	45	14	33	26
Ralph Selby of Berwick 1588	28	–	–	28
John Carr of Hetton 1589	63	–	77	-14
Richard Ord of Horncliffe 1589	43	41	38	46
James Wallis of Coupland 1589	38	1	2	37
William Wallis of Akeld 1589	125	13	57	81
William Collingwood of Barton 1590	64	–	11	53
Henry Gray of Newminster 1597	730	172	124	778
Ingram Salkeld of Alnwick West Park 1598	52	–	–	52
William Collingwood of Kimmerston 1603	28	–	21	16
James Swinhoe of Berrington 1603	224	–	–	224
Luke Ogle of Eglingham 1604	97			97
John Collingwood of Abberwick 1605	96	–	139	-43

TABLE 4.4. THE PERSONAL ESTATES OF THE LAIRDS[168]

GREATER LAIRDS	Moveable Goods	Debtors	Creditors	Total Estate
John Swinton of that Ilk 1564	22	133	65	90
*[169] Alexander, 5th Lord Home 1568	3504	–	1653	1851
Sir Andrew Ker of Hirsel 1573	5544	1219	56	6707
William Cockburn of Choicelee 1574	287	–	129	158
Robert Cairncross of Colmslie 1575	1870	1262	154	2978
Thomas MacDougal of Makerstoun 1576	1980	315	318	1977
Sir James Cockburn of Langton 1578	1984	30	579	1435
John Swinton of that Ilk 1579	3971	169	1175	2965
William Chirnside of East Nisbet 1581	2661	368	262	2767
Alexander Cockburn of that Ilk 1583	2289	160	136	2313
Sir Walter Ker of Cessford 1586	5901	–	1036	4865

Table 4.3—contd

	Moveable Goods	Debtors	Creditors	Total Estate
Greater Lairds—contd				
Andrew Pringle of Galashiels 1587	1817	170	–	1987
James Cockburn of Choicelee 1587	992	–	161	831
John Renton of Billie 1588	4858	280	313	4825
Thomas Cranston, fiar of Corsbie 1589	744	160	32	902
William Cockburn of Langton 1590	2842	–	452	2390
George Home of Ayton 1590	5479	1068	396	6150
*Sir David Home of Wedderburn 1591	1034	206	148	1092
George Cranston of Corsbie 1592	2265	207	1852	620
Cuthbert Cranston of Thirlestane Mains 1592	1726	–	637	1089
Alexander Home of Huttonhall 1594	4651	5361	4501	5511
*Patrick Home, fiar of Ayton 1595	570	667	3015	-1778
Sir James Home of Cowdenknowes 1598	7545	712	11814	-3587
John Cranston of Morriston 1599	1468	843	4568	-2257
Andrew Ker of Faldonside 1599	2967	1345	306	4006
Robert Lauder of that Ilk 1599	868	5	36	837
John Maitland of Thirlestane 1599	6005	9094	235	14864
Patrick Home of Polwarth 1600	4531	–	774	3757
*Alexander 6th Lord Home 1608	11049	1980	9515	3514
LESSER LAIRDS				
Mr Andrew Home of Lauder 1568	103	747	207	643
William Craw of Flemington-Fluris 1571	1882	228	245	1865
George Home of Edrom 1573	698	1678	129	2247
William Linlithgow of Drygrange 1574	355	39	–	394
David Spottiswoode of that Ilk 1575	1919	486	40	2365
George Pringle of Torwoodlee 1576	1292	540	71	1761
*Robert Dickson of Hassington 1576	507	10	53	464
James Brounfield of Nether Mains 1576	363	–	30	333
Robert Haig of Bemersyde 1576	75	–	–	75
Henry Haitlie of Mellerstain 1576	470	112	641	-59
Alexander MacDougal of Stodrig 1576	1126	–	768	358
*George Pringle of Blindlee 1576	946	47	177	816
Andrew Brounfield of Pittlesheugh 1577	312	–	24	288
Alexander Home of Carolside 1577	1667	–	–	1667
Richard Ker of Gateshaw 1577	162	617	629	150
George Pringle of Wrangholm 1577	696	16	107	605
*David Ellem of Renton 1578	667	–	449	218
Adam French of Thornydykes 1579	809	–	–	809
William Pringle of Torwoodlee 1579	1976	375	132	2219
*Robert Home of Reidheuch 1579	1192	601	1517	276
Patrick Sleigh of Cumledge 1579	1123	533	–	1656
*Archibald Auchinleck of Cumledge 1580	671	8	563	116
John Pringle of Wrangholm 1580	1091	506	800	797
Mark Haliburton of Mertoun 1581	1801	–	–	1801
David Home of Fishwick 1581	3968	–	–	3968
Andrew Redpath of Rowchester 1581	300	478	666	112
William Ker of the Yair 1582	513	–	104	409
Andrew Ker of Linton 1582	380	32	26	386
James Spottiswoode of Whinrig 1582	284	–	12	272
Thomas Trotter of Fogorig 1582	266	–	156	110

Table 4.3—contd

Lesser Lairds—contd	Moveable Goods	Debtors	Creditors	Total Estate
Oliver Edgar of the Flass 1586	627	38	417	248
*David Lumsden of Blanerne 1586	618	160	361	417
James Hamilton of St John's Chapel 1586	529	–	433	96
*Alexander Pringle of Slegden 1586	1258	–	–	1258
John Hamilton of St John's Chapel 1588	1166	505	37	1634
William Spottiswoode of Quhitlie 1588	665	–	95	570
David Home of Cranshaws 1590	8324	205	48	8481
George Craw of Flemington-Fluris 1591	3668	1240	1400	3508
John Dickson of Belchester 1591	842	44	147	739
*David Edington of that Ilk 1591	2138	349	653	1834
*Thomas Ker of Maisondieu 1591	765	135	446	454
Lancelot Ker of Little Newton 1593	400	32	343	89
James Pringle of Whytbank 1593	1244	–	400	844
Richard Spence of Chirnside Mains 1592	1202	–	491	711
James Craw of Gunsgreen 1595	1345	–	240	1105
Thomas Ker of Mersington 1595	1711	11	389	1333
James Ker of Middlemist Walls 1596	1224	2837	–	4061
David Home of the Law of Coldingham 1597	1833	1126	172	2787
*Mr John Shoreswood of Bedshiel 1598	1094	36	882	248
*Charles Cairncross of Allanshaws 1599	1372	–	45	1327
Alexander Cockburn of Caldra 1599	511	–	42	469
Alexander Cockburn of Stobswood 1599	741	248	125	864
Alexander Haitlie of Lambden 1599	1264	2035	189	3110
*John Home of West Reston 1599	2193	–	1436	757
John Lumsden of Blanerne 1599	2062	–	2009	53
Thomas Pringle of Wrangholm 1599	1612	808	–	2420
*Alexander Trotter of Chesters 1599	991	–	152	839
Alexander Home of Carolside 1600	787	–	–	787
William Spottiswoode of that Ilk 1600	1082	20	48	1054
*George Cranston of Kirkhill 1601	825	80	209	696
Henry Haliburton of Mertoun 1601	4059	549	1444	3164
Patrick Cockburn of East Borthwick 1601	4862	484	6378	-1032
*John Ellem of Butterdean 1602	1484	400	1090	794
Robert Dickson of Buchtrig 1603	1783	–	935	848
David Edington of Harcarse 1603	2762	689	927	2524
John Ellem of Bassendean 1603	779	–	–	779
John Haitlie of Mellerstain 1603	4199	5167	239	9127
Robert French of Thornydykes 1605	2491	128	153	2466
*David Home of Ninewells 1605	1623	62	1041	644
John Edgar of Wedderlie 1606	2541	146	1030	1657
Ralph Erskine of Shielfield 1606	1151	120	1640	-369
Simon Redpath of Angelrow 1606	884	38	537	385

The personal wealth of the greater lairds and the knights and esquires could be similar, despite the aforementioned difficulties of comparison. For example the 1583 estates of Robert Clavering of Callaly at £387 and Alexander Cockburn of that Ilk at £2313 Scots (£317). In 1597 Thomas Collingwood's £350 was close to Andrew Ker of Faldonside's £4,006 Scots (£364). Amongst the strata of lesser lairds and gentlemen there were wide variations across the Border, but occasional parity is possible with Mark Horsley of Screnwood's £38 and John Gallon of Cawledge Park's £25 in the early 1580s, compared to James Spottiswoode of Whinrig's £272 Scots (£37) and Andrew Redpath of Rowchester's £112 Scots (£15). At the Union of the Crowns James Swinhoe of Berrington's £224 was approximately the same as David Edington of Harcarse's £2,524 Scots (£210). Some of the landed men in the Eastern Borders appear to have had a similar standard of living, yet they had the same problems of debt as well.

On the English side of the frontier at least four gentlemen died in debt, including two generations of the Carrs of Hetton who lost their estates by mortgaging and bad management. John Collingwood of Abberwick's debt was probably caused by his recusancy fines.[170] On the Scottish side of the Border, there were at least six lairds who were registered as '*debita*' at the commissary court that proved testaments and inventories. This could be deceptive; the inventory of the wife of Patrick Home of Ayton was deliberately registered in debt to avoid having to pay the commissaries their '*quotta*' (percentage fee). Other debtor lairds were either over-indulgent, or in trouble with their wadsets. John Cranston of Morriston and Sir James Home of Cowdenknowes belong to the first category as they left large bills unpaid to Edinburgh merchants.[171] The Haitlies of Mellerstain belong to the second category of debtors, but there were other small lairds, such as Robert Haig of Bemersyde who were not in debt yet still left small inventories. In this case Haig had infefted his son and heir in his lands, leaving him with very little income.[172]

At the other end of the wealth structure there were a few successful lairds and gentlemen whose inventories were far above the average. In England the traditional wealth of the Grays of Chillingham was rivalled by the newer Collingwoods of Eslington and Forsters of Bamburgh who made their fortunes out of advantageous marriages, monastic land grants and offices. In Scotland the established laird families such as the Lords Home, the Homes of Ayton and the Kers of Cessford were also equalled in wealth by newer families like the Kers of Hirsel and Middlemist Walls, the Homes of Fishwick and Huttonhall and Maitland of Thirlestane, again through offices and monastic land.[173]

The average wealth of the greater lairds in table 4.3 was £2,512 Scots in a range from £90 to £14,864 and the average for the lesser lairds was £1,263 Scots in a range from £53 to £9,127.[174] Nationally the greater lairds were impoverished when compared to the Earl Marischal's £44,153 Scots inventory of 1600, yet some were certainly wealthier than Lord Somerville's £1,284 Scots in 1576.[175] At a local level there were several men below the rank of lairds whose inventories were nevertheless higher in value than some of the lesser lairds. They included prosperous tenant farmers like Robert Anderson in Kelloe (£878 Scots in 1597), John Home in Chirnside (£358 Scots in 1588), William Pringle in Mersington (£1,259 Scots in 1587) and Robert Hopper in Nether Stichill (£875 in 1598).[176] Greater lairds worried about their estates, even on the point of death, for in 1551 Mark Ker of

Littledean told his son and heir Sir Andrew Ker of Hirsel that he had 'gewyn mair awaye than I haiff . . .' Ker made a new will on his deathbed and instructed Ker to satisfy all parties.[177]

The average wealth of the gentry was £787 for the knights, ranging from £197 to £1,020; £310 for the esquires, ranging from £135 to £824 and £107 for the gentlemen, who ranged from £53 to £778.[178] In comparison with the merchants of Newcastle these averages are low. However merchants may not have invested in land to the extent of the gentry, as their moveable wealth was concentrated on household goods and coinage.[179] When the gentry's inventories are compared to the local yeomanry clear discrepancies appear between the lesser gentry and some prosperous yeomen. For instance yeoman Richard Strother of Coldmartin had £71 in 1586, Thomas Grame of Coupland £93 in 1603, Thomas Younghusband of Budle £28 in 1587 and Cuthbert Watson of Bamburgh £44 in 1598.[180]

Inventories can ultimately be only a partial guide to the wealth of the lairds and gentlemen as they do not give any indication of annual income. Sources for the landed income of the lairds are scarce yet there is reasonable, if inaccurate, information about the gentry. *Inquisitions post mortem* and recusancy rolls, for example, often undervalued the gentry's income for deliberate avoidance of wardship dues and fines, but they are still useful.[181]

TABLE 4.5. THE APPROXIMATE LANDED INCOME OF THE GENTRY

Name and Date	Annual income	Reference (PRO)
John Roddam of Roddam 1556	£28	C142/108/80
Robert Lisle of Felton 1558	£80	C142/112/121
Elizabeth Carr of Ford 1560	£76	C142/131/159
Robert Collingwood of Eslington 1561	£81 (£100)	WARD7/88 (WARD9/438 fo. 34)
Sir Ralph Gray of Chillingham 1565	£301	C142/141/71
Robert Lawson of Rock 1565	£21	C142/143/31
William Carr of Ford 1570	£64	WARD9/438 fo. 50
Thomas Ilderton of Ilderton 1579	£27	C142/186/47
Robert Beadnell of Lemmington 1583	£11	C142/201/96
Edward Gray of Howick 1584	£200	*CSP Dom Add*, 1580–1625, 118
Sir Thomas Gray of Chillingham 1591	£303	C142/231/82
John Radcliffe of Thropton 1591	£7	E377/1
Michael Hepburn of Hepburn 1591	£20	E377/1
Francis Radcliffe of Dilston 1591	£300	E377/1
John Swinburne of Edlingham 1591	£100	E377/1
William Selby of Twizel 1591	£200	NRO ZHG1/14
Ralph Gray of Chillingham 1597	£380	*CBP*, ii, 762

These figures are mostly based on land held in chief (knight service) or by socage tenure (freehold) and are not a true reflection of their sixteenth-century value. For instance Sir Thomas Gray of Horton only paid £8 a year for Newstead and two shillings for Doddington, whilst Robert Roddam paid

14s-8d for Little Houghton.[182] The inaccuracy of these figures is reflected in the report that Sir Ralph Gray of Chillingham could spend 600–700 marks a year in 1552 and his son Ralph made at least £1,000 a year from his land rentals in 1591.[183] A more realistic estimate was made by Thomas Wilson in 1601 that 'northward and farr off a gentleman of good reputation may be content with (£)300 and 400 yerly . . .' compared to the £666–£1,000 he appraised for the south of England.[184] Earlier estimates of how much the gentry's lands were worth in 1535 and 1540 included the number of horse, they had available for Border service at musters. These are more accurate than later records which show a sharp decline in the numbers of horses available for Border service.[185]

TABLE 4.6. ESTIMATED ANNUAL INCOME OF THE GENTRY, 1535–40

Name and Date	Income	Horse
Gilbert Swinhoe of Cornhill 1535	20 marks	20
Henry Collingwood of Etal 1535	20 marks	30
Robert Collingwood of Bewick 1535	£ 5	20
Gerard Selby of Pawston 1535	£ 10	20
Thomas Collingwood of Ryle 1535	10 marks	16
Percival Selby of Biddlestone 1535	50 marks	30
Edward Gallon of Trewhitt 1535	£ 20	24
Sir Cuthbert Radcliffe of Cartington 1540	£200	110
Sir Roger Gray of Horton 1540	100 marks	40
Sir Robert Ellerker 1540	100 marks	–
Thomas Gray of Kyloe 1540	20 marks	–
Thomas Forster of Adderstone 1540	£ 20	12
Robert Collingwood of Eslington 1540	£ 40	30
John Carr of Hetton 1540	£ 20	12
Thomas Carr of Newlands 1540	£ 8	4
William Strother of Kirknewton 1540	£ 20	12
Thomas Holburn of Holburn 1540	20 marks	6
Thomas Hepburn of Hepburn 1540	£ 20	8
Richard Fowberry of Fowberry 1540	20 marks	6
Edward Muschamp of Barmoor 1540	5 marks	–
Ralph Ilderton of Ilderton 1540	£ 20	20

The gentry were probably not as impoverished as they appeared. Their profit-based land management would have boosted their income, but as this was illegal there are no records of exactly how much income they obtained from their circumvention of Border tenure. Officially it was better for the gentry to collectively plead poverty to lower gressums on crown leases and avoid taxation.

The wealth of the lairds is difficult to judge beyond inventory evidence as there are few accurate details of how much they made from their lands annually. There are occasional references to their standard of living as Godscroft noted that 'the gentlemen of the Borders abounded with men, those in Lothian rather abound in wealth and riches'.[186] Godscroft's comment is an ambiguous generalisation, because having men must have denoted some wealth and status in the Eastern Borders. It is also unclear if he considered his own family to be wealthy or poor as their lands straddled both Berwickshire and East Lothian. In 1566 Godscroft's father was noted as a Home 'of good living'. References to 'good' living lairds do not give any indication of their financial state, but it presumably denoted a comfortable lifestyle in comparison to lairds of 'some' living like Robert Frisell in 1599. Sir John Ker of Hirsel was probably very comfortable as 'a man of great living' in 1589.[187] Lairds were generous when they married their daughters, so tochers are a perhaps a better indication of the income they considered disposable. Tochers were irrevocably linked to power and prestige, but they still help to indicate the wealth levels of the lairds, regardless of those few lairds who came near to financial ruin by being too generous.

TABLE 4.7. THE TOCHERS OF LAIRDS' DAUGHTERS[188]

Name and Date	Amount (£ Scots)	Reference (NAS, except WMT & Corbet)
Margaret MacDougal of Makerstoun 1529	200 merks	WMT/various 156.
Isabella Robson of Gledswood 1545	80 merks	*Corbet Protocol Book*, 25
Barbara Haliburton of Mertoun 1546	160 merks	*Corbet Protocol Book*, 27
Barbara Home of Cowdenknowes 1557	£1000	RD1/2 fo. 87
Margaret Ker of Ferniehirst 1559	5000 merks	RD1/3/2 fo. 272
Euphamie MacDougal of Makerstoun 1561	800 "	RD1/4 fo.147
Marion Lauder of Whitslaid 1561	240 "	RD1/4 fo. 432
Marion Pringle of Whytbank 1561	800 "	RD1/4 fo. 265
Katherine Home of Blackadder 1562	£1000	RD1/7 fo. 192
Margaret Pringle of Galashiels 1563	1200 merks	RD1/4 fo. 144
Christine Pringle of Blindlee 1563	£1000 "	RD1/5 fo. 411
Helen Edmondston of that Ilk 1566	600 merks	RD1/8 fo. 393
Margaret Sinclair of Blainslie 1570	1000 "	RD1/11 fo. 306
Janet Home of Manderston 1574	1000 "	RD1/13 fo. 254
Isobel Home of Wedderburn 1575	3000 "	RD1/14 fo. 7
Isobel Home of Polwarth 1576	1000 "	RD1/16 fo. 92
Jonet Ellem of Renton 1576	400 "	CC8/8/6 fo. 136
Margaret Ramsay of Wyliecleuch 1579	800 "	RD1/17 fo. 8
Margaret, dau. of the 5th Lord Home 1581	8000 "	RD1/19 fo. 180
Margaret Cairncross of Colmslie 1579	600 "	RD1/20/2 fo. 446
Elspeth Ker of Kippilaw 1587	800 "	RD1/24/1 fo. 259
Margaret Ker of Cessford 1586	10000 "	RD1/26 fo. 34
Agnes Lauder of Whitslaid 1587	£1000 "	RD1/28 fo. 237
Katherine Home of Fans 1589	800 merks	RD1/30 fo. 237
Isobel Pringle of Galashiels 1591	2000 "	RD1/43 fo. 230

Lairds were conscious of both the prospective husband's wealth and status and the seniority of their daughter when agreeing a tocher. Greater lairds such as the Kers of Ferniehirst and Cessford were clearly emulating the nobility in their gifts. Lesser lairds like the Pringles of Blindlee and the Homes of Blackadder were equally magnanimous with their £1,000 Scots provision in the 1560s considering that the Lauders of Whitslaid could afford this amount only in the 1580s. The actual payment of tochers is quite revealing of the lairds' liquidity, as John Edmonston of that Ilk paid 600 merks to Henry Haitlie of Mellerstain within a month during 1566, yet Sir John Home of Cowdenknowes did not pay Robert Cairncross of Colmslie £1,000 Scots until nine years after his daughter Barbara's wedding in 1557.[189] A lapse in payment could, of course, signify a long time between the marriage contract and the wedding, but John Home of Cowdenknowes had cash of 800 merks in 1548. His son was clearly less affluent when arranging Barbara's tocher. Other lairds who had good sums of cash in hand included Gilbert Home, tutor of West Reston (£336 Scots) and Thomas MacDougal of Makerstoun (£529 Scots), but these amounts were perhaps only temporary and not necessarily available when a tocher was agreed.[190] There is less information about gentry dowries, though Dorothy Gray of Chillingham had 800 marks and Anne Collingwood of Eslington had £1000 in 1572. The Strothers of Kirknewton received 1,000 marks from the Conyers of Sockburn in Durham, but Ann Ord of Longridge's £100 dowry was never paid as her contract was broken by an unfaithful fiancé in 1590.[191]

Alongside tochers, bairns' portions and thirds were an additional drain on Scottish income. Bairns' parts were given from the residue of a deceased lairds' goods. They were divided equally amongst sons and daughters, after the heir and the widow had claimed their share. These portions were set by the commissary court and were supposed to be strictly adhered to. The five children of George Pringle of Torwoodlee (1568) were to be given £352 Scots each by their brother William, but he had not honoured the bairn's part due to Agnes before she died in 1576.[192] The slowness of payments was predictable as a laird's heir could not be expected to immediately sell his father's goods or lands, yet if he took too long friction could arise between the siblings.[193] The payment of the widow's third was equally difficult for the heir and if a grandmother was still alive this led to further complications. For instance Margaret Ker of Cessford, who married Sir John Home of Cowdenknowes in 1524, was still living in 1595. The Homes of Wedderburn had similar problems with female longevity in 1581.[194] Some arrangements were more harmonious as Alexander Home of Manderston peaceably accepted a wadset of his mother's third of £80 Scots *per annum* in 1555 and promised to pay the bairns' portions due to his brothers and sisters.[195]

If there were no widows or children to be satisfied an inventory should have been straightforward, but Alexander Pringle of Slegden was less than honest when he registered his wife's will in 1586. Pringle was the principal beneficiary of his wife, Isobel Home of Polwarth, so he undervalued her estate either to keep the *quotta* low or deceive her relations. Isobel's brother,

Alexander Home of North Berwick, uncovered the deception and re-registered the inventory at £1,258 Scots, nearly twice its original value.[196] Pringle may well have resented the Homes, as his father had been forced to sell Slegden to the Homes of Manderston in 1556 and he was now just a tenant there. He was finally evicted by the Homes in 1591.[197]

Lairds' inventories do not take account of any debts unconnected to wadsets that were incurred and settled during the laird's lifetime. For example, Sir Thomas Ker of Ferniehirst amassed domestic and foreign debts during his exiled years in France. During the 1570s and 1580s he borrowed from many people, often without repayment. For example, 200 merks, £200 Scots, 100 merks and another £200 Scots were borrowed from his aunt Isobel Ker of Cessford.[198] A further 1093.3 French crowns (£2,733 Scots), 1,500, 500, 300 and 500 French francs were loaned to him in Paris.[199] In 1581 Ferniehirst wadsetted lands recently restored to him as a last resort, but as his inventory does not survive it is unclear how many of debts were settled, or how many more existed.[200] It was not surprising that Ferniehirst was thought to be a 'poor' laird by his contemporaries.[201]

There were a number of lairds who were affluent enough to lend money to other lairds such as Alexander Cockburn of that Ilk, Robin Ker of Ancrum and John Lumsden of Blanerne; but the most active moneylender amongst the lairds was Alexander Home of Huttonhall.[202] Huttonhall gave loans to James Home of the Style, David Home of Godscroft, William Ker of Ancrum, Lady Home, Alexander Home of Manderston and George Auchinleck of Cumledge. Affluence could also be disadvantageous for the lairds as it made them more liable to be named as sureties for offenders. Robin Ker of Ancrum, for example, was penalised 500 merks for not entering some malevolent Elliots he was cautioner for in 1583.[203]

The gentry were similarly afflicted with debts and debtors. Sir John Forster was forced to mortgage a tithe lease, after the loss of his wardenship, which had clearly diminished his influence and income.[204] Forster did not pay his debts quickly, yet he now expected his creditors to pay him promptly and took a deceased kinsman's executors to court in 1598 to force payment of £150 rent.[205] Forster's kinsman Ralph Gray of Chillingham was equally impatient with slow payment during 1588 and 1602–1603 by his kinsmen by marriage the Delavals of Seaton Delaval. An interesting correspondence ensued between the two brothers-in-law in 1602 until Ralph finally sent John Horsley of Screnwood to collect the £200 owed or goods to that amount.[206] This provocation severed their friendship, but Ralph had warned that he would use 'circumstance to presse' Delaval. Gray had a dowry to find for his eldest daughter as well as legal expenses at the Court of Wards in London, yet he was perhaps being a little over zealous as he was 'of great account, living and wealth' in 1598.[207] In a probable act of solidarity with his brother, Arthur Gray was slow to pay his rent to the Delavals in 1600.[208]

The sixth Lord Home's estate was impoverished in comparison to the Grays. The English ransacking of Hume Castle and Dunglass in the early 1570s had led to most of the household furnishing, including a charter chest, being destroyed or stolen. The crops at Hume had also been harvested by the occupying garrison.[209] Lord Home did not help his financial situation by indulging in luxuries from an early age. When he was at St Andrews University in 1580 he spent £500 Scots within a few months. In 1582, when he was still only sixteen, he was noted for his great living and many friends.[210] His opulence embarrassed his mother during a visit to Glamis Castle in 1583. As she was 'nocht weill provydit in sylwer work' Lady Home had to borrow silverware from a neighbouring laird, Sir James Ogilvy of Inverquharity.[211] When Home reached his majority in 1586 he was no longer constrained by curators, or even by his older kinsmen, and thus began to overspend uncontrollably leading to his forced land sales in the 1590s.[212] His marriage in 1586 did not enhance his finances as his wife, Christian Douglas, was a widow with no tocher, except for her third of the Oliphant estates. She proved to be as spendthrift as her husband, owing an Edinburgh draper £320 Scots for her silks, taffeta, satins, tweeds and gowns during 1589–90. This bill did not include household linens, so these items were presumably for her own use.[213] In contrast to this, the wife of John Renton of Billie owed a mere £20 Scots for tailoring and £12 for cloth in 1582.[214] Lord Home's lifestyle continued to be extravagant for when he went to France in 1599 he allegedly took eleven horses and some dogs as a gift for the king, yet pleaded poverty upon arrival at London as an excuse not to meet Elizabeth I. His greater laird kinsman, John Home of Cowdenknowes, had only taken six horses to France in 1547.[215]

Lord Home's expenditure at Coldingham Priory in 1592 and at Old Cambus in 1596–97 are rare survivals of Border household accounts from the sixteenth century.[216] The sumptuary laws of Scotland allowed a baron to have four meat dishes at his table and Lord Home seems to have conformed to this as he bought beef, mutton, capons and wildfowl for Old Cambus in 1596.[217] He supplemented this with herrings that were presumably salted as he bought 10,000 on one occasion for £45 Scots. Home though was not financially overstretched at Old Cambus as his chamberlain, William Craw, satisfied all the bills from local teinds. At Coldingham Home's expenditure was greater as he had just acquired the Priory from the forfeited earl of Bothwell and was eager to show off his new possession to his friends and kinsmen.[218] The Coldingham account records that he sent workmen to renovate and set up furniture in the priory soon after he took possession in August 1592. The bills included £6–8s–7d Scots for mending the chimney, £4–6s–8d Scots for setting up four beds, £1–12s–6d Scots for bedding and £6 Scots for cleaning the abbey. By 25 October Lord Home had taken up residence and stayed for a month. Wine and 'aquavytie' were bought before he arrived and meat, fish and beer were regularly purchased thereafter. A typical succession of the accounts (all in £ Scots) read[219]

25 October	Meal £4–10s, pepper 5s-4d, butter 3s-4d, onions 2s, 200 herring £1–12s, 200 oysters 13s-4d.
26 October	a beef £6, mutton £1–16s.
27 October	two muttons £3–6s.
28 October	two muttons £1–16s, two nolt 11s-4d, fish 10s, eggs 2s-4d, 5lb plewindaimes (prunes) 16s-8d, saffron 12s, 4oz ginger 8s, pepper 10s-8d, cinnamon 6s-8d, vinegar 6s-8d, 200 oysters 13s-4d.

Other greater lairds probably had a similar standard of living to Lord Home as Sir James Home of Cowdenknowes had £2,000 Scots worth of household goods. Sir James Cockburn of Langton had five carcasses of beef, three stones of butter, a barrel of salt salmon, 3,000 herring and fifty-two capons in his cellar in 1584.[220] Robin Ker of Ancrum lost many household goods in 1573 during a feud with the Turnbulls including £56–13s–4d Scots worth of claret and white wine, fifty stones of cheese, silverware, flanders-ware, forty feather beds and 500 merks in 'white' money.[221] Thomas MacDougal of Makerstoun also lost goods during a Border raid in 1601 including pistols, a sword, and luxuries like handkerchiefs and silk garters. Lesser lairds also enjoyed expensive clothes and foods, as Andrew Home of Lauder's inventory specified his finery. David Home of Ninewells patronised local merchants in a manner similar to Lord Home, as he owed money for flesh, fish, wine, butter, spices and aquavitae in 1600.[222] The significant costs of a lairdly household were recognised in 1587, when a marriage contract noted that John Home of Cowdenknowes was to have 500 merks a year to keep a separate household from his father.[223] This amount seems low compared to the standard of living enjoyed by Sir Walter Scott of Buccleuch. He was in custody of William Selby of Twizel for twenty-five weeks during 1598–99 and cost £10 sterling a week to entertain compared to other Scottish pledges who only needed 10s-4d per week.[224]

The standard of living amongst the gentry would have been similar to the lairds, but with no household accounts surviving, comparisons are confined to inventories.[225] The gentry had featherbeds, linen, carpets, silver, flanders-ware and other furniture similar to the Scottish records.[226] The greater gentry also enjoyed wine as Sir John Forster regretted that bad weather would not allow carriages of wine through to Hexham in 1555. He had to inform his guest that he 'muste be content to drenke beare'.[227] Lesser gentry perhaps had simpler tastes as John Reveley of Berrington had no wine in his house during 1563.[228]

Landed families probably had similar numbers of household servants, with the greater men employing most people. The fifth Lord Home maintained his household even when he was besieged in Edinburgh Castle in 1573. In his entourage he had a brewer, a cook, two boys, a washer, tailor and a shoemaker.[229] Beyond the expected bailies, stewards, grieves and household servants a few lairds, such as John Swinton of that Ilk had gardeners.[230] Sir Cuthbert Radcliffe had at least eighteen household men, whilst Luke Ogle had eight in 1539, but this does not give any indication of how many additional women and children were employed.[231] When Thomas Carr of Ford's servants were forced to flee from his house during the Heron and Carr feud, there were five men and three women.[232]

Another possible comparison of the wealth and status of lairds and gentlemen is the cost and manner of their funerals. The costs of lesser gentlemen were usually lower than those of the greater gentry as Roger Widdrington of the Friars (1572) was buried for £20, John Carr of Lesbury (1574) for £3–6s–8d and Luke Ogle of Eglingham (1604) for £20. Lady Dorothy Gray of Chillingham (1581) had a far more ostentatious funeral costing £100 and Sir John Selby of Twizel (1595) was slightly more expensive at £163. Sir John Forster's heraldic funeral cost the most at £455, but any involvement of heralds was inevitably expensive.[233] The gentry were usually buried within a church and the Gray of Chillingham tomb had by far the most elaborate sculpture in north Northumberland dating from the fifteenth century.[234] The lairds were also buried within their local parish churches for Thomas MacDougal of Makerstoun requested to lie 'in the quier (choir) of macarston' and Alexander MacDougal of Stodrig asked to be 'in the Ile (aisle)' of the same church. Andrew Pringle of Galashiels was to go 'in the abbay of Melros in his tomb maid there to himself to that effect' and Cuthbert Cranston of Thirlestane 'in the common sepulchrie of his foirbearis within the paroche kirk of Legerwood'.[235] The Pringles of Whytbank and Galashiels were buried in Melrose Abbey. They perhaps thought the Abbey more prestigious than their local parish kirks, but they would have paid for the privilege as the commendator of Melrose received an unexplained 300 merk loan from Whytbank in 1564.[236] The actual cost of lairds' funerals is seldom recorded, though Alexander Home of Manderston's was £12 Scots in 1555.[237] Lairds do not seem to have indulged in lavish funerals akin to the greater gentry owing to the spread of the Reformation in the Eastern Scottish Borders. Burials within churches were discouraged by the kirk, so Alexander Home of North Berwick, specified that he should be buried 'without vane pompe or ceremonie' in 1597. Robert Lauder of that Ilk merely wished to be buried in the earth and did not even specify a kirkyard in 1598.[238]

The lairds' relative modesty in death was not reflected in their house-building which was a monument to conspicuous consumption in Scotland during the second half of the sixteenth century. The lairds looked beyond the necessity of building strongholds in a frontier zone to use housebuilding as a sign of their new affluence. The gentry did not build on the same scale as the lairds, though they did make some improvements that have been ignored by historians. They may have been intimidated by Scottish raiding, but the English incursions into Scotland did not hinder the lairds.[239] Claims of impoverishment do not explain this phenomenon either, as the lairds had to pay taxes, whereas the gentry were exempted from taxation by Border tenure.[240]

The lairds' tax burden came from a number of sources such as irregular parliamentary demands based on old extent, taxation of feuars' lands after 1581 (also based on old extent), ecclesiastical taxation of their monastic lands (the thirds of benefices) and taxes on their teind leases. Taxation based on medieval land assessments was not burdensome, but it could mount up if a laird held land in chief and in feu, so there was some evasion of this by lairds.[241] Lord Roxburgh was summonsed in 1604 for concealing land at Sprouston that should have yielded £24–6s–8d Scots for the King's wedding in 1589 and the same amount for Prince Henry's baptism in 1594.[242] Thomas MacDougal of Makerstoun was summoned in 1586 for not paying £20 Scots and John Rutherford was similarly chastised in 1599.[243] The tax due from monastic land was a new impost that was more realistic to sixteenth-century values than the older taxes. It was designed to help fund the reformed church and was collected by commendators. As a continuing Catholic Andrew Home, commendator of Jedburgh, proved reluctant to pay his abbey's third of £335 Scots between 1569 and 1572.[244] Lesser amounts were also begrudged as George Home of Wedderburn owed the commendator of Coldstream £14 Scots for his teinds of Darnchester in 1594.[245]

Scottish taxes, although not heavy, would have influenced the wealth of the lairds to some extent, yet it was these lairds who were the progenitors of new housing in the Eastern Borders. They may have been following the fashionable wave of country-house building that took place across Renaissance Scotland. This was characterised by a declining emphasis on fortification and a new awareness of aesthetics and domestic comfort.[246] New building and rebuilding in the Borders was also influenced by profits from the feuing movement.[247] There were parliamentary incentives as well for an Act of 1535 had ordered all 'landit men' living in the Borders to build a defensive barmkin or 'big pelis and gret strenthis'.[248] Defence was undeniably important near the Border, but the lairds' new buildings did not necessarily have barmkins and they were not all towers or in a tower-house style. Alexander Home of Huttonhall built an imposing L-shape house at Huttonhall in 1573 that was only five miles from the Border and Sir Andrew Ker of Ferniehirst rebuilt Ferniehirst as a large fortified house in 1598. They were arguably both like the new 'Scottish Chateau' identified by Charles McKean in early modern Scotland.[249] Those lairds who did not rebuild seem to have improved their existing dwellings, as various Rutherfords owed a glazing wright £43 Scots in 1587 [250] and the Homes of Polwarth and Cowdenknowes made 'new work' from existing monastic buildings at

North Berwick and Eccles.[251] The following table of new buildings ranges from basic towers (Corbet), to fortified tower houses (Greenknowe) and fortified houses (Holydean).

TABLE 4.8. NEW HOUSES IN THE EASTERN SCOTTISH BORDERS

Name and County	*Laird and date of completion*	*Reference*
BERWICKSHIRE		
Huttonhall	Home of Huttonhall 1573	*Architecture,* [252] iv, 193–9.
Cowdenknowes	Home of Cowdenknowes 1574	*RCAHM,* Berwick, 71–2.
Greenknowe	Seton of Touch 1581	Tranter,[253] i, 17.
Thirlestane	Maitland of Thirlestane 1595	Tranter, i, 24.
ROXBURGHSHIRE		
Ancrum	Ker of Ancrum 1558	*Bannatyne Club,* 122, i, 62–4.
Littledean	Ker of Littledean 1540	*Architecture,* iii, 351–3.
Riddell	Riddall of that Ilk 1567	*RCAHM,* Roxburgh, 256.
Corbet	Ker of Corbethouse 1572	*Architecture,* iii, 423–5.
Holydean	Ker of Cessford 1580	*RCAHM,* Roxburgh, 68.
Buckholm	Pringle of Buckholm 1582	Tranter, i, 130.
Hillslap	Cairncross of Calfhill 1585	Tranter. i, 144–5.
Newton	Grahamslaw of Newton 1586	*RMS,* v, 1058.
Colmslie	Cairncross of Colmslie 1596	*RCAHM,* Roxburgh, 292–3.
Ferniehirst	Ker of Ferniehirst 1598	*Architecture,* i, 156–62.
SELKIRKSHIRE		
Gala	Pringle of Galashiels 1583	*Architecture,* v, 279.
Torwoodlee	Pringle of Torwoodlee 1601	*Architecture,* iv, 209–10.

Other new building may have taken place during 1540–1603, but no architectural evidence survives. The buildings usually conformed to the status of the laird, but tower houses can be deceptive. Greenknowe Tower, for instance, has a plain exterior yet has ten fireplaces within its walls.[254] Huttonhall was the epitome of a greater laird's house as it had a panelled dining room with an elaborate plaster ceiling used for entertaining Border commissioners on several occasions.[255] Other greater laird's houses at Blackadder, Wedderburn, Manderston, Duns, Langton and Spylaw were also thought to be suitable for the Border commissioners.[256] These would have been substantial houses, though sadly little of their sixteenth-century architecture has survived.

The apparent contrast between the building activities of the lairds and gentlemen is highlighted by the lack of new building before 1603 in north Northumberland and North Durham, but Jacobean affluence has sometimes obscured research into Elizabethan improvements. A shortage of surviving Elizabethan buildings in the English Eastern Borders has not helped this situation. The local gentry were probably reticent about building expensive new houses in the style of the elegant and magnificent houses being built further south in England.[257] They may have feared that open affluence would make them liable to taxes they were normally exempted from for living near the frontier. However, they were not so impoverished as to be unable to improve their houses as there were a few fortified manor houses in Northumberland before 1603 that were mostly alterations of older castles or monasteries, such as Alnwick Abbey, Clennell, Chillingham, Fenham and Ford. Some strongholds like Coupland Castle were still being built, but they were not the preoccupation of the greater gentry.[258]

Alnwick Abbey was replenished to a high standard by Sir John Forster after he had plundered lead, glass, panelling and iron from Alnwick and Warkworth in the wake of the Northern Rebellion.[259] Forster's son Nicholas improved Bamburgh Castle around 1601, as a deceased local glazier left him eight sheets of glass 'for glasoning about his hous . . .' and Matthew Forster of Fleetham owed the same glazier twenty shillings, possibly for alterations to his house.[260] Clennell Tower was extended in 1568 with a new wing and elaborate plaster work and similar improvements took place at Chillingham, where a modest (by southern standards) Elizabethan long gallery was constructed.[261] Fenham had once belonged to Holy Island Priory, but Sir William Reed made it into a substantial gentleman's residence and was reported to want to spend £400 on building alterations there in 1575. Nothing remains of this house, but Reed's inventory was lavish by local standards and listed many rooms including the bedchamber, governor chamber, great and little chambers, gallery, gallery chamber, hall, nursery, parlour, still house, brewhouse, wine cellar, servants' chamber, milkhouse, ox and cow house, butterie, larder, pasterie, scullery, various lofts, a long stable and a barn. It was even suitable for a royal visit in 1603 when James VI & I was going south.[262] Ford Castle's improvements have also been overlooked because of subsequent structural changes, yet there was a new E-shaped structure built there between 1584 and 1589.[263]

The Elizabethan improvements at Ford are remarkable considering that the Carrs of Ford were still embroiled in a feud with the Herons at this time and needed thick walls more than an Elizabethan facade.[264] Ford is therefore a clear example that the Northumbrian gentry were not architecturally backward. The lack of large new houses cannot be fully explained, though they did build smaller manor houses, such as Rowland Forster's at Lucker and the Lawsons' of Rock at Rock.[265] Their improvements to existing buildings were financially prudent compared to the cost of building completely new structures, so the gentry were perhaps saving money as well as hiding their true affluence from the authorities. It is no longer acceptable to suggest that the gentry did not build grand houses before 1603 because of Scottish reivers and poverty. The lairds were in a similar defensive situation and possibly a worse financial state, owing to the taxes they paid, yet still managed to build new houses on a wide scale.

The true levels of wealth amongst the lairds and gentlemen will have to remain an enigma, despite all the evidence presented. Wealth and status generally intermingled, but it is difficult to determine exactly how rich or poor they really were in national terms. The English land market favoured the gentlemen who managed to secure leases of monastic and crown land. The overall wealth of the gentry increased during the sixteenth century, but there were a few losers as well. In Scotland the wealth of many lairds was equally enhanced by the availability of similar monastic and crown land, although the processes by which they were obtained were different. There was also a broader cross-section of landed men holding these lands by 1603 than there was in England. The lairds had financial problems as well, though the greater availability of credit through wadsetting helped many of them survive troubled times. The rising price of agricultural products certainly benefited both lairds and gentlemen as their principal source of wealth was land, but it was the gentry who gained most from rentals with their harsh land management and avoidance of Border tenure. Overall, the majority of lairds and gentlemen must have quietly prospered from their lands and agriculture, although those lucky enough to have an alternative source of income could further enhance their resources. The actual wealth of these families can only be surmised, but it is clear that many did enhance their wealth relative to their status on both sides of the Border during 1540–1603.

Notes

1 Watts, *Border to Middle Shire*, 39.

2 S. G. E. Lythe, *The Economy of Scotland, 1550–1625* (Edinburgh, 1960), 1–15; 'The Economy of Scotland under James VI and I,' in A.G.R. Smith, ed. *The Reign of James VI and VI* (London, 1973), 57–73.

3 T. M. Devine and S. Lythe, 'The economy of Scotland under James VI – A revision article', *SHR*, l (1971), 91–106. Palliser, *Age of Elizabeth*, 135–9.

4 It is not possible to include all the land transactions of lairds and gentlemen in this chapter as a prodigious amount of material has survived from 1540–1603. Select examples will therefore be used throughout.

5 C. Kitching, 'The Disposal of Monastic and Chantry Lands,' in F. Heal and R. O'Day, eds. *Church and Society in England: Henry VIII to James I* (London, 1977), 119–136. W. C. Richardson, *History of the Court of Augmentations 1536–54* (Baton Rouge, 1961), 1–13.

6 George Muschamp of Barmoor fought Henry Haggerston of Haggerston over the tithes of Fenham parish (Dean and Chapter of Durham). PRO E134/15 Eliz EAST 2. DDR iii, 2 fos 11, 26, 53, 55, 57, 61, 72, 80, 83, 173, 176, 294, 318, 322; v, 2 fos 39–40. Another dispute between Sir William Reed of Holy Island and Nicholas Holburn of Holburn concerned Holburn tithes (Holy Island Priory). PRO E134/26 & 27 Eliz MICH 20, SC6/Ph & M/ 222. BL MS Add 24,815 fos 216–17.

7 D. Hay, 'The Dissolution of the Monasteries in the diocese of Durham', *AA*, 4th ser, xv (1938) 69–114. Cliffe, *Yorkshire Gentry*, 93–100. *cf.* H. A. Lloyd, *The Gentry of South-West Wales, 1540–1640* (Cardiff, 1968), ch. i. Leases were granted to lesser and middle gentry, as well as yeomen, but they tended to be smaller than those of the greater gentry.

8 PRO E318/10/450, E371/336/lxxvi, SC6/Hen VIII/4579 m. 8. Lands and tithes were included.

9 PRO C66/1238 m. 6–7, E310/21/107, E310/21/109, E367/978. *CPR, 1566–9*, 250–2. M. M. Meikle, 'A Godly Rogue: The Career of Sir John Forster, an Elizabethan Border Warden', *NH* xxviii (1992), 128–9, 142.

10 PRO E310/21/111. E318/43/2346. Concealed monastic lands were a widespread problem for the crown. They stemmed from administrative oversights in the Court of Augmentations.

11 PRO C66/1374 m. 21–2, C66/1389 m. 9–11, C66/1585 m. 22–3, E310/21/109, E310/21/110, E310/21/111. *CPR, 1563–6*, 397; *1566–9*, 126–7, 141; *1572–5*, 200–01.

12 In 1563 some of the Northumberland rentals had been static for twenty years. PRO SC6/Eliz/1663.

13 For instance in 1566 Rowland Forster – no fine at all; 1583 Sir John Forster – one year's rent; 1590 Ralph Gray of Chillingham – 1.3 years rent and 1599 the Swinhoes of Cornhill 0.25 year's rent. PRO E310/21/107 fos 55, 74, E310/21/109 fos 1–3, 50.

14 The gentry were mostly interested in the great tithes (i.e. grain tithes) as the small tithes (i.e. animal tithes) usually went to the vicar. J. S. Purvis, *An Introduction to Ecclesiastical Record* (London, 1953), 55–6. The privy council wanted all the tithes near the Border to be granted to members of the Berwick garrison, but the local gentry monopolised them. *APC*, iii, 442.

15 PRO E305/F23, SC6/Edw VI/355, SC11/959. *CPR, 1560–3*, 120. *Stat* 1 Eliz. c. 19. R. Hoyle, *The Estates of the English Crown* (Cambridge, 1992), 197.

16 PRO E310/21/107. NRO 683/19/1. Raine, *ND*, 185.

17 D & Ch Reg, 2a, fo. 216; 4d, fo. 18; 6f, fo. 126. Selby also received many tithe leases in Norham and Islandshire such as Berrington and Kyloe.

18 PRO CP25/2.

19 *Laing Chrs*, 401.

20 A. A. Dibben, *Title Deeds* (London, 1968), 4–9, 27. J. Hurstfield, *The Queen's Wards* (London, 1958), 12–14.

21 PRO CP25/2/192/19 Eliz/EAST, CP25/2/192/21 & 22 Eliz/MICH, CP25/2/192/35 Eliz/HIL. The Gray conveyance was possibly linked to his wife's recusancy.

22 PRO CP25/2/32/219/EAST 1542, CP25/2/192/3 & 4 Eliz/MICH.

23 PRO CP25/2/192/10 Eliz/HIL, CP25/2/192/18 & 19 Eliz/MICH, CP25/2/192/24 Eliz/HIL, CP25/2/192/30 Eliz/HIL.

24 PRO CP25/2/192/15 & 16 Eliz/MICH. CP25/2/192/16 & 17 Eliz/MICH.

25 PRO CP25/2/192/26& 27 Eliz/MICH, CP25/2/192/35 & 36 Eliz/MICH, CP25/2/192/36 & 37 Eliz/MICH.

26 PRO SC6/Eliz 1/1672–1699, SC6/Jas 1/763. Forster let these debts amass again until they reached £300. Arrears for monastic land were known in Northumberland as early as 1539. PRO SC6/Hen VII 1/7374.

27 PRO ADM75/101, CP25/2/76/646 MICH 1558, CP25/2/192/37 Eliz/HIL, CP25/2/192/43 Eliz/TRIN.

28 PRO CP25/2/33 & 34 Eliz/MICH, REQ2/64/70, REQ2/270/67, SP15/28/95 v. Laing Chrs, 1050, 1051. Cliffe, *Yorkshire Gentry*, 147.

29 The date refers to that of the source of information.

30 This compares with the Yorkshire gentry who held 50–1000, 1000–5000 and over 5000 acres respectively. Cliffe, *Yorkshire Gentry*, 29–32. See also J. E. Hollinshead, 'The gentry of south-west Lancashire in the later sixteenth

century', *NH* xxvi (1990), 90.
31 PRO C142/112/121, C142/263/27, C142/432/134. DPRW Reg vi, fos 219–20. KAO U947/T2/1. See ch. iii.
32 PRO C142/158/19. BRO 36/1 fos 43–114. NRO 452/D1/22. Laing Chrs, 1213.
33 PRO C142/103/55, C142/267/69, CP25/2/192/42 & 43 Eliz/MICH, E310/21/109, E310/21/111.
34 NAS GD267/27/67. *RMS*, iii, 279; iv, 49; vi, 618.
35 NLS CH5157. *RMS,* vi, 1462, 3142.
36 *Selkirk Protocol Books,* 53–6, 58–9, 63–64, 98, 103, 108, 112, 140.
37 This probably explains why Ferniehirst battled to be provost of Jedburgh in the later-sixteenth century. NAS GD1/33/31. NRAS 859/130/2.
38 *RMS*, iii, 447; iv, 2228, 2169.
39 NAS CC8/8/23 fos 284–6, CH6/6/1 fos 71–2, GD40/3/448.
40 D. E. Easson, 'The Reformation and the monasteries in Scotland and England: Some Comparisons', *Transactions of The Scottish Ecclesiological Society,* xv (1957), 7–23. J. F. S. Gordon, *Monasticon* (Glasgow 1868), 341–44, 395–98, 485–6. W. Stanford Reid, 'Clerical Taxation: The Scottish Alternative to Dissolution of the Monasteries, 1530–60', *Catholic Historical Review,* xxxv (1948), 129–153.
41 PRO SC62/2/1. *RMS*, iii, 2081. G. Neilson, 'The Feuing of Drygrange from the Monastery of Melrose', *SHR*, vii (1910), 355–63.
42 NAS SC62/2/1. NLS CH 9054. *RMS*, iv, 1624.
43 NAS CC8/8/16 fos 79–83, GD40/14/4. His inventory (1586) amounted to £16046 but this may be incorrect as the commissaries did not approve it. M. Dilworth, 'The Border Abbeys in the Sixteenth Century', *RSCHS*, xxi (1981–3), 233–245.
44 *CSP Scot*, v, 592. *RMS*, iv, 2178; v, 109, 1880. *RSS*, v, 2182; vi, 927. *HMC*, Home, 316; Milne-Home, 89. M. Dilworth, 'The Commendator System in Scotland', *IR*, xxxvii (1986), 51–72.
45 *RMS*, iv, 1737. *RSS*, vi, 2186. *HMC*, Home, 316.
46 *APS*, iii, 454. *CSP Scot,* ii, 99. *RMS*, iv, 1905. *RSS*, v, 3212, 3245. *HMC*, Home, 176.
47 NAS GD158/454, GD242/45. NRAS 859/10/6. *RMS*, iv, 1716. *RSS*, v, 3412.
48 NAS RD1/19 fos 417–24. *RMS*, iii, 666; iv, 1709, 2565, 2928; v, 450, 533, 1538.
49 NAS GD110/547. BL MS Royal 18.B.VI. fo. 166b. *L & P. Hen VIII*, xix, pt 1, 49. *RMS*, iv, 1824. *HMC*, Marchmont, 24. *Carte Monialium de Northberwic* (Edinburgh, 1847). A. Spratt, 'The Cistercian Nunnery of North Berwick and the Hume Family', *East Lothian Life*, xxxv (Spring 2001), 28–9.
50 *RSS*, v, 2268.
51 NAS GD12/117, GD242/46. M. H. B. Sanderson, 'Manse and Glebe in the Sixteenth Century', *RSCHS*, xix (1975–7), 81–92.
52 NAS E48/1/1/fo. 213, RD1/1 fo. 79. *RPC*, ii, 723; iii, 710, 723, 737; iv, 2, 77–8, 779. *RSS*, v, 2511; vii, 2465; viii, 66.
53 Mr Andrew Home, a younger son of Wedderburn, was ostensibly a priest who made a fortune out of the teinds of Lauder. NAS CC8/8/1 fo. 117, CC8/8/14 fos 234–7. WMT, *Protocol Book of Robert Wedderop,* nos 11, 33, 38. *RMS*, iv, 1645. *RSS*, vii, 1108. A. A. Cormack, *Teinds and Agriculture* (Oxford, 1930), 79–108. Sanderson, *Rural Society,* 33–4.
54 NAS CS7/10 fo. 168, RD1/2 fo. 102.
55 NAS CC8/8/4 fo. 67. *RMS*, iv, 1229.

56 NAS CC8/8/10 fos 86–7, CS7/5 fo. 138, RD1/3 fo. 213. NRAS 482 Add 31/5. *RMS,* iii, 852, 3133; v, 1390; vi, 329. *RSS,* iv, 2954. *RPC,* ii, p. 492. *HMC,* Home, 149.

57 NAS CC8/8/45 fos 262r-63r. NRAS 482 Add 31/2. *ER,* xviii, 371. *RMS,* v, 1390.

58 NAS RD1/6 fo. 36. *RMS,* vi, 329.

59 NAS RD1/28 fo. 405. *HMC,* Home, 194.

60 NAS RD1/40 fo. 436. For a description of 'old extent' see J. Goodare, 'Parliamentary Taxation in Scotland, 1560–1603', *SHR,* lxviii (1989) 23–26.

61 NAS RD1/28 fo. 230, RD1/45 fo. 414. NRAS 859/14/8. *RMS,* v, 1995. *RSS,* viii, 1254.

62 NRAS 859/9/3. *RMS,* v, 1963; vi, 500, 741. *HMC,* Home, 286.

63 J. Anderson & W. Angus, eds. *Protocol Book of Sir William Corbet 1529–1555* (Scottish Record Society, vol xxxix, 1911), nos 52, 53, 70–73. Easter Muirdean may have been bought back as Lord Home leased it to a kinsman, Alexander Home of Huttonhall, in 1557. NRAS 859/13/7.

64 Mercantile credit at interest from Edinburgh was more evident in the Borders after 1603. J. J. Brown, 'The economic, political and social influences of the Edinburgh merchant community, 1600–38', unpubl. Ph.D diss. Edinburgh 1985.

65 NAS GD237/11/1/3, GD237/11/1/7, RD1/9 fos 65, 279, 310, RD1/13 fo. 136, RD1/14 fos 125, 196–9, RD1/16 fo. 291, RD1/20/1/2 fo. 322, RD1/26 fo. 430.

66 NAS CS7/39 fo. 36, GD157/9, RD1/6 fo. 267, RD1/9 fos 338, 394, RD1/15 fo. 302, RD1/41 fo. 179.

67 *APS* iii, 451, ch. 35. R. H. Tawney, *Religion and the Rise of Capitalism* (Harmondsworth, 1980), 134–5. I am grateful to Julian Goodare for this reference.

68 NAS GD158/302.

69 There were a succession of Haitlie wadsets from 1552–1589 ranging in value from 400–8000 merks. NAS CS6/27 fo. 110, CS7/7 fos 16, 25, CS7/8 fo. 605, CS7/15 fo. 255, CC8/8/4 fos 267–8, GD158/108, RD1/1 fo. 311, RD1/5 fos 168, 170, RD1/6/2 fo. 26, RD1/9 fo. 312, RD1/10 fo. 81, RD1/12 fo. 350, RD1/31 fo. 61.

70 NAS RD1/20/2/2 fo. 80. *RMS,* iii, 2867. *RSS,* vii, 710, 714; viii, 1759. *RPC,* iii, 299–300, 547–8, 552. *RPC,* iv, 756; v, 395; vi, 829.

71 Cliffe, *Yorkshire Gentry,* 161. A. Simpson, *The Wealth of the Gentry* (Cambridge, 1961), 179–216.

72 P. J. Bowden, 'Agricultural Prices, Wages, Farm Profits and Rents', in Thirsk, *Agrarian History,* v, pt 2, 1, 15. *ibid.* iv, 594–609. Palliser, *Age of Elizabeth,* 336–7.

73 M. L. Bush, 'Tenant Right under the Tudors: a revision revised,' *Bulletin of the John Rylands Library,* 77 (1995), 161–188. R. W. Hoyle, 'An Ancient and Laudable Custom: The Definition and Development of Tenant Right in north-western England in the sixteenth century', *P&P,* cxvi (1987), 22–55 and 'Lords, Tenants, and Tenant Right in the Sixteenth Century: Four Studies', NH, xx (1984), 38–63. E. Kerridge, *Agrarian Problems in the Sixteenth Century and After* (London, 1969), 58–59. R. T Spence, 'The Backward North Modernized? The Cliffords, Earls of Cumberland and the Socage Manor of Carlisle', *NH,* xx (1984), 64–87. Thirsk, *Agrarian History,* iv, 292–3. S. J. Watts, 'Tenant-Right in early Seventeenth Century Northumberland', *NH,* vi (1971), 64–87. A. Knowles, 'Customary tenure on the northern estates of the Percy earls of Northumberland in the sixteenth century', unpubl. MA diss. Manchester 1983.

Border tenure effectively ended with the Union of the Crowns in 1603, but there was much confusion about this.

74 NRAS1100/717. PRO E36/40, SP15/28/95, SP15/32/76. *CBP*, i, 47. *HMC, Roxburghe*, 94. C. J. Bates, *The Border Holds of Northumberland* (Newcastle, 1891), 28–44. Bush, 'Tenant Right', 184.

75 *L&P. Hen VIII*, iv, pt 2, 5085; xii, pt 2, 249–50; Add i, pt 1, 618.

76 R. A. Butlin, 'Enclosure and improvement in Northumberland in the sixteenth century', *AA*, 4th ser, xlv (1967), 149–160. P. J. Dixon, 'The Deserted Medieval Villages of North Northumberland: A Settlement History From The Twelfth to the Nineteenth Century', unpubl. PhD diss. University of Wales 1984. *Cf.* Kerridge, *Agrarian Problems*, 59 and Knowles, 'Customary tenure', 83. Hoyle, 'Ancient and Laudable', 51–2. Bush, 'Tenant Right', 163, 187. R. Newton, 'The Decay of the Borders: Tudor Northumberland in transition', in Chalkin and Havinden, eds. *Rural Change and Urban Growth, 1500–1800* (London, 1974), 3. Thirsk, *Agrarian History*, iv, 292–3. Watts, *Border to Middle Shire*, 39–40.

77 NRO 2088. See ch. viii.

78 PRO SP1/179 fos. 157–60. *CBP*, i, 47, 435; ii, 762, 796, 881. *CSP Dom Add, 1580–1625*, 93–5, 359. *CSP Scot*, viii, 351 (p. 321). *Hamilton Papers*, i, 120–1. Scottish settlement in England will be discussed further in ch. viii.

79 *Stat*, 2 & 3 Ph. and M. c. 2. xxv. D. C. Coleman, *The Economy of England, 1450–1750* (Oxford, 1977), ch. iii. S. Pollard and D. W. Crossley, *The Wealth of Britain, 1085–1966* (London, 1968), 83–124. L. A. Clarkson, *The Pre-Industrial Economy in England* (London, 1971), ch. iii. Hoyle, *Estates*, 196–7.

80 PRO SP15/28/80, SP15/28/95, SP15/32/76. *CBP*, i, 47. There were 165 deserted medieval villages in Northumberland, but there were new townships as well. R. Newton, *The Northumberland Landscape*, 109–111. There was only one example of pasture being turned into arable by Robert Ellerker of Hulne in 1567. ALN MS AI/1/b fo. 17.

81 PRO SP15/28/95. Durham, Chapter Library, MS C.III. 20/3 fo. 20. *cf.* Dixon, 'Deserted Villages', 80 and Newton, 'Decay', 2–31.

82 *CSP Dom Add, 1547–65*, 419. *Cf.* Kerridge, *Agrarian Problems*, 58–9.

83 PRO E310/21/109 fo. 7, E310/21/110 fo. 26, SP59/20/80. *CBP*, i, 47. *CSP Dom Add, 1547–65*, 568; *1580–1625*, 231.

84 PRO SP15/28/95, iii – v.

85 PRO STAC5/L8/40, STAC5/L49/23. *CBP*, ii, 746.

86 *APC*, xviii, 217.

87 Enclosure did not necessarily signify agricultural improvement. It merely indicated that a ditch or hedge had been used to encircle the land.

88 ALN MS AI/1/f fo. 34, AI/1/g fo. 13.

89 PRO SP15/28/80 fo. 238. *CBP*, i, 75, 181.

90 ALN MS AI/1/e fo. 16. *cf.* Butlin, 'Enclosure', 159–60. Thirsk, *Agrarian History*, iv, 27–8.

91 ALN MS DI/1 fo. 14. SYON MS Al 1/8 fo. 248. M. E. James, Estate Accounts of the Earls of Northumberland, 1562–1637, *SS*, clxiii (1948).

92 J. E. Neale, *Elizabeth I and her Parliaments* (London, 1953), i, 339, 344–5. Watts, *Border to Middle Shire*, 48–50.

93 BL MS Cotton, Caligula B, v, fos 53–5. *Stat* 2 & 3 Ph & M. c.1; 23 Eliz c.4. The Act was revived in 1561 and 1581, without success. *CSPFor, 1561–2*, 360, 370, 439, 503, 680.

94 *CPR, 1563–6*, 182–3, 213–14. *CSP For, 1561–2*, 440.

95 PRO SP59/5 fos 3–4, SP59/17 fos 144–5.
96 PRO DL1/33/B15, DL14/6/69.
97 NAS GD267/27/78. *HMC*, Milne-Home, 450, 452, 460.
98 NAS GD267/31/16.
99 NAS GD150/1147, GD150/1425. *Laing Chrs*, 1186.
100 NAS CS7/71 fo. 351. *HMC*, Milne-Home, 588.
101 Lythe, *Economy of Scotland*, 15–23. P. C. Waite, *The Land of Britain*, xiv –
    Berwickshire (London, 1941), 1–19. Newton, *Northumberland Landscape*, ch.
    i. R. A. Butlin, 'Field Systems of Northumberland and Durham', in Baker and
    Butlin, eds. *Studies of Field Systems in the British Isles* (Oxford, 1973), 93–144.
102 H. H. Lamb, *The Changing Climate* (London, 1966), 10–11. T. B. Franklin, *A
    History of Scottish Farming* (Edinburgh, 1952), 102–03. This cold cycle may
    also have lowered cultivation levels in south-east Scotland. M. L. Parry,
    'Changes in the Upper Limit of Cultivation in South East Scotland, 1600–1900',
    unpubl. Ph.D diss. Edinburgh 1973, 192.
103 *L & P. Hen VIII*, xviii, 682. *cf.* Devine and Lythe, 101.
104 *CSP Spain*, 1580–6, 470. *L & P Hen VIII*, xx, pt 2, 458. J. Speed, *The Theatre
    of the Empire of Great Britaine* (London, 1611), 89. P. Hume-Brown, *Early
    Travellers in Scotland* (Edinburgh, 1978), 60. Lesley, *History*, i, 98.
105 Watts, *Border to Middle Shire*, 41–3.
106 *Cf.* Lythe, *Economy*, 9–10 and Watts, *Border to Middle Shire*, 44. R. A.
    Dodgshon, *Land and Society in Early Scotland* (Oxford, 1981), chs. v–vi. *Cf.*
    Butlin, 'Field Systems'. I. D. Whyte and G. Whittington, *An Historical
    Geography of Scotland* (London, 1983), ch. vi. G. Whittington, 'Field Systems
    of Scotland', in Baker and Butlin, eds. *Studies of Field Systems*, 530–579.
107 NAS CC8/8/1 fo. 144.
108 These ratios are found in inventories for 1586 (Roxburgh), 1587 (Billie), 1589
    (Cranshaws and Little Swinton), 1590 (Ayton) and 1598 (Cowdenknowes).
    NAS CC8/8/16 fo. 96, CC8/8/18 fos 143–4, CC8/8/21 fo. 71, CC8/8/22 fo.
    120, CC8/8/31 fo. 38. The yields seem poor when compared to 1980s ratios of
    approximately 1:48 for wheat, 1:33 for barley (bear), 1:20 for oats and 1:10
    for peas, but conditions were very different in the sixteenth century. See also M.
    Overton, 'Estimating crop yields from probate inventories: an example from
    East Anglia 1585–1735', *Journal Of Economic History*, (cited hereinafter as
    Econ H R), 39 (1979), 363–78.
109 The inventories of Roger Widdrington of the Friars and Sir William Reed of Fenham
    list field crops and their total value, but there is no indication of the amount of grain
    actually sown. DPRW 1572, 1604. Watts, *Border to Middle Shire*, 45.
110 DPRW 1572, 1587 (3), 1588 (1).
111 *Cf.* Franklin, *Scottish Farming*, 65. Thirsk, *Agrarian History*, iv, 22. Cattle
    disease occurred at Chatton in 1580. *CBP*, i, 47. See map two.
112 NAS CC8/8/6 fo. 392.
113 Thirsk, *Agrarian History*, iv, 26–7.
114 I. Guy, 'The Scottish Export Trade, 1460–1599', in T. C. Smout, ed. *Scotland and
    Europe* (Edinburgh, 1986), 62–82. C. Wilson and G. Parker, *An Introduction to
    the Sources of European Economic History*, (Cornell, 1977), 47–8.
115 *RPC*, i, 493.
116 *SS*, ii (1835), 366.
117 I. D. Whyte, *Agriculture and Society in Seventeenth-Century Scotland*
    (Edinburgh, 1979), 182, 225. See ch viii.

118 NAS RD1/35 fo. 176, RD1/47 fo. 407. *RPC*, iii, 464–5.
119 NAS RD1/45 fo. 174b.
120 See ch. viii.
121 *L & P. Hen VIII*, xiv, pt 1, 151. *CSP For*, 1562, 1393. The English sheriff's job was not lucrative either.
122 *CSP Scot*, x, 595. J. H. Stevenson, 'The Usher of the White Rod', *Scottish Antiquary*, x (1897), 161.
123 Rae, *Scottish Frontier*, 29–32, 250–2.
124 *TA*, vii, 479; x, 244, 304, 331, 393; xi, 54, 88, 167, 512–5. *HMC*, Salisbury, ii, 284. *RPC*, i, 278.
125 *RPC*, iii, 700.
126 NRAS 859/134/4.
127 *CBP*, i, 719; ii, 395, 925. *HMC*, Salisbury, i, 372; vi, 23–4. *CSP For*, 1562, 268, 914, 996, 1012.
128 CPR, 1549–51, 162–3, 404; 1550–3, 258; 1558–9, 411. *L & P. Hen VIII*, xv, 465; add. i, pt 1, 828. *CSP For*, 1559–60, 349. *Sadler Papers*, ii, 21.
129 *CBP*, ii, 122. *CSP Dom Add*, 1580–1625, 311.
130 CPR, 1550–3, 53; 1572–5, 53.
131 BRO B6/11 fos 26, 28. *CSP Dom*, 1598–1601, 306.
132 *CBP*, i, 19, 817. CPR, 1572–5, 465. *CSP Dom Add*, 1566–79, 424. *Sadler Papers*, ii, 9.
133 PRO C66/1301 m. 16. *CBP*, i, 830; ii, 1321.
134 PRO C66/1301 m. 16. *APC*, viii, 361. *CBP*, i, 830.
135 *CBP*, ii, 1308. CPR, 1554–5, 119–20; 1560–3, 251, 530; 1563–6, 200–01. See note 17 above.
136 BRO 36/11 fo. 28. *CSP For*, 1559–60, 619, 623, 902. *RSS*, v, 336, 889, 890, 906, 962, 1003; vi, 945; vii, 56. *HMC*, Roxburghe, 94.
137 PRO E48/1/1 fos 228–9. BL MS Cotton Caligula, C vii, fo. 341. *TA*, xii, 74.
138 P. Gouldesbrough, ed. *Formulary of Old Scots Legal Documents* (Stair Society, 1985), 21–8.
139 *Stat*, 13 Eliz c. 16, i – ix. Most of these rebels were later restored. See ch. vii.
140 *RSS*, ii, 3611; v, 2706. *TA*, vii, 375–6.
141 NAS RD1/6 fo. 222. *RSS*, viii, 1974; iv, 3165. *TA*, x, 10.
142 *APS*, iii, 111, 162–3. *RSS*, vi, 1183.
143 *RSS*, vi, 2007.
144 NRAS 859/5/10. *RMS*, v, 218, 2125. *HMC*, Home, 316.
145 *RMS*, v, 1974. *HMC*, Marchmont, 81.
146 Pitcairn, *Trials*, ii, pt 1, 33–34.
147 *RSS*, vi, 354; iii, 2676.
148 *RPC*, i, 606.
149 SYON MS CIV/3.
150 See chs. ii & viii.
151 NRO ZSW6/18. Hatfield MS, C. P. Petitions 991.
152 CPR, 1569–72, 239.
153 PRO WARD9/438 fos 32, 48, WARD9/641 fos 9, 11.
154 *Selkirk Protocol Books*, 22, 97, 118–19, 164–5, 195. *RMS*, iii, 1518. See ch. i.
155 D & Ch. Reg, 5, e, fos 40–1.
156 PRO C142/172/108, E310/21/109 fo. 11, E310/21/112 fo. 40. J. U. Nef, *The Rise of the British Coal Industry* (London, 1932), i, 19, 25, 40–4, 52. M. E. James, *Family, Lineage and Civil Society* (Oxford, 1974), 69–71, 86–96.

157 PRO E310/21/112 fos 11, 12, 25, 40. R. P. Sanderson, *Survey of the Debateable and Borderlands, 1604* (Alnwick, 1891), 128–33.

158 PRO STAC5 581/2. NRAS 859/6/2.

159 BRO C1/3.

160 For shipwrecks see ch. viii.

161 PRO E178/1723. Tweed fishing rights had mostly belonged to the Dean and Chapter of Durham before they were ceded to the crown in 1560.

162 PRO C66/1326 m. 30. NRO 452/D1/14.

163 *RMS*, iv, 2140; v, 450. For disputed fishings see ch. viii.

164 The helpfulness of inventories is recognised by Hollinshead, 'Gentry of South-West Lancashire', 87. However, their limitations are clearly cited in J. Thirsk, 'The limitations of the probate inventory', in J. Chartes and D. Hey, eds. *English Rural Society, 1500–1800* (Cambridge, 1990), 139–74.

165 N. & J. Cox, 'Probate Inventories: the legal background', *The Local Historian*, xvi (1984), 133–45, 217–27. J. L. Drury, 'Inventories in the Probate Records of the Diocese of Durham', *AA*, 5th ser. xxviii (2000), 177–91. J. S. Moore, 'Probate Inventories: Problems and Prospects', in P. J. Riden, ed. *Probate Records and the Local Community* (Gloucester, 1985), 11–28. Sanderson, *Rural Society*, 172–8. Yorkshire inventories were similar to Northumberland, P. C. D. Brears, 'Yorkshire Probate Inventories, 1542–1689', *Yorkshire Archaeological Society*, record ser, cxxxiv (1972). The inaccuracy of some of the Scottish inventories was recognised by contemporaries as wills were sometimes re-registered e.g. Sir James Cockburn of Langton NAS CC8/8/6 & CC8/8/13 and George Pringle of Wrangholm NAS CC8/8/4 & CC8/8/5.

166 *cf.* Lythe, *Economy*, 101–02. J. Gilbert, 'The usual money of Scotland and exchange rates against foreign coin', in D. M. Metcalf, ed. Coinage in Medieval Scotland, *British Archaeological Reports*, 45 (1977).

167 All the figures have been based solely on inventories and have been rounded off to the nearest pound sterling. The dates indicated are that of the appraising of the inventory rather than the time of death. The goods include all listed household stuffs, crops and farm implements. The debtors are all those listed as owing money to the deceased given as a total and the creditors are all those known to be owed money by the testator, again given as a total. The total estate figure is derived by adding the goods to the debtors and subtracting the creditors. The sources used are DPRW and *SS*, ii, xxxviii, cxii, cxvi, cxxi, cxlii, (1835, 1860, 1906, 1908, 1912, 1929).

168 Based on the same formulation as table 4.3. Dates refer to the time of registration of the inventory at the commissary court, rather than the death of the testator. The figures are in pound Scots rounded off to the nearest pound. Based on the testaments NAS CC8/8 and CC15/5, none of which are published, or predate 1564. For full citation of references see Meikle, 'Thesis', app. ch. i.

169 * Denotes the inventory of a laird's wife (whose goods were listed in conjunction with those of her surviving husband) or that of a laird's widow (which was probably only her third of the deceased laird's goods).

170 PRO CP25/2/192/16 & 17 Eliz/MICH, E377/1, E377/10. *CPR*, 1569–72, p. 352.

171 Cowdenknowes owed £1440 Scots to James Purves, flesher, either from his incumbency as captain of Edinburgh Castle or through sheer indulgence. Morriston owed £53 Scots to an Edinburgh baxter for bread. NAS CC8/8/32 fos 381–2, CC8/8/33. *CSP Scot*, x, 595.

172 NAS CC8/8/4 fo. 84.

173 Meikle, 'Thesis', apps. chs. i, ii.
174 Negative balances are included in the average, but they are excluded from the range cited.
175 NAS CC8/8/35, CC8/8/4 fo. 47. The nobility had approximately 16–20 chalders of victual p.a., (256–320 bolls). *CSP Scot*, xiii, pt 2, 906. For a comparison to merchants see M. H. B. Sanderson, 'The Edinburgh Merchants in Society, 1570–1603; the Evidence of Testaments', in Cowan & Shaw, eds. *The Renaissance and Reformation in Scotland* (Edinburgh, 1983), 182–199.
176 NAS CC8/8/29 fos 468–9, CC8/8/19 fos 146–7, CC8/8/17 fo. 225, CC8/8/31 fos 337–8.
177 *Protocol Book of Sir William Corbet 1529–1555*, nos 63 & 64.
178 The Yorkshire gentry ranged from £248 to £3000. Cliffe, *Yorkshire Gentry*, 380–1. Figures are not available for sixteenth-century Lancashire, *cf.* Hollinshead, 'Gentry', 87, 90, but incomes are estimated in 1642, B. G. Blackwood, *The Lancashire Gentry and the Great Rebellion*, Chetham Society, third ser, xxv (1978), 11–16.
179 William Jenison had an inventory of £4059 in 1587. DPRW 1587 (1).
180 DPRW 1586 (2). DDR, ii, 5, f, fo. 55. DPR Bond 1587/432. DPRW 1598 (2).
181 It should be remembered that their lands were mostly sublet at higher rentals.
182 PRO E164/37 fos 134, 105.
183 *CSP Dom Add, 1547–65*, 417. CRS, liii, (1969), 57. A mark was worth 13s-4d.
184 Sir Thomas Wilson, 'The State of England', in *Camden Miscellany*, xvi (1936), 23–4. Wilson probably overestimates for the rest of England. Palliser, *Age of Elizabeth*, 96. Mingay, *Gentry*, 11–14.
185 BL MS Cotton, Caligula, B vi, fos 518–19. *L & P. Hen VIII*, ix, 1078.
186 NAS GD267/2/4 fo. 44.
187 *CSP Scot*, x, 53. HMC, Salisbury, i, 335; ix, 17.
188 The dates refer to the signing of the contract. Corbet references are to numbers, see the *Protocol Book of Sir William Corbet*.
189 NAS RD1/8/fos 383, 395. RD1/2 fo. 87. RD1/7 fos 379.
190 NAS CC8/8/10 fos 131–3, CC8/8/4 fo. 46. *RSS*, iv, 2255.
191 PRO REQ2/164/119. NRO 1DE/1/162, 1DE/4/11, ZSW1/194. *Laing Chrs*, 1195, 1214. See also A. L. Erickson, 'Common law versus common practice: the use of marriage settlements in early modern England', *Econ H R*, 2nd ser, xliii (1990), 21–39.
192 NAS CC8/8/3 fos 475–6, CC8/8/10 fos 21–2, CC8/8/13 fos 31–3.
193 NAS CC8/8/13 fos 366–8, CC8/8/27 fos 120–1, GD267/27/18, GD267/27/77, RD1/28 fos 175, 392, RD1/33 fo. 82, RD1/44/2 fo. 280. HMC, Milne-Home, 396.
194 NAS CC8/8/33, GD1/33/31, GD40/3/403, RD1/11 fo. 75. HMC, Milne-Home, 93. RPC, ii, 320–1; iii, 290–1, 373, 375. Godscroft, *De Familia*, 56, 63. A tocher was supposed to compensate for the provision of a widow's third, but if the lady in question lived to a great age inflation would have far outstripped this arrangement.
195 NAS GD267/27/76.
196 NAS CC8/8/15 fos 331–4, CC8/8/16 fos 279–81.
197 NAS RD1/39 fo. 38. NRAS 1351/22. *RMS*, iv, 1057.
198 NAS CC8/8/16 fo. 97. For money borrowed from Sir John Forster see ch. viii.
199 NAS GD40/5/3/18, GD40/6/1/6.
200 NAS GD40/1/312, GD40/3/415/1, RD1/20/1/1 fos 78, 81.
201 *CSP Scot*, iii, 84. His son Andrew had a better grasp of the family's finances, but he was never forced into exile.

202 NAS CC8/8/26 fos 180–1, RD1/20/2 fo. 95, RD1/34 fo. 398. *RMS*, iv, 3015.

203 *RPC,* iii, 53. For similar examples see *RPC,* iv, 408, 531, 554.

204 PRO E134/3 Jas I/EAST 13.

205 BRO C3/2. (Richard Forster of Tughall). See note 26 above.

206 NRO 1DE/5/4 a-c, 1DE/1/123, 650/B/1602. The only surviving Scottish correspondence equivalent to the Gray-Delaval sequence was between Robert Swinton of that Ilk and Thomas Wolf of Weatherly (East Lothian) in 1600. NAS GD158/2788.

207 Chillingham Castle, Documents 21. *CSP Scot*, xiii, pt 2, 908.

208 *Newcastle-upon-Tyne Records Committee Series,* ix (1929), 152, 156, 159.

209 NRAS 859/16/3. *CSP For,* 1572–4, 531.

210 NAS RD1/18/1/fo. 2, RD1/19/fo. 90. *Bannatyne Misc.,* i, (1827), 68.

211 NAS GD205/1/32.

212 NAS CC8/8/27 fos 123–4, RD1/34 fo. 369, RD1/49 fo. 594, RD1/50 fo. 336. NRAS 859/16/2. See note 62 above.

213 NAS NRAS 859/5/7. *HMC*, Home, 43. The royal marriage of 1589 may have increased her expenses.

214 NAS CC8/8/10 fo. 229.

215 *CSP Scot*, xiii, pt 1, 370. *HMC*, Salisbury, ix, p. 382. *CPR,*1547–8, 247.

216 NRAS 859/6/2. *HMC*, Home, 58.

217 *APS*, ii, 488.

218 NRAS 859/6/2. *HMC*, Home, 95.

219 NRAS 859/6/2.

220 NAS CC8/8/13 fo. 306, CC8/8/31 fos 381–2.

221 *RPC,* ii, 117, 266–71. Godscroft, *History,* 338; *De Familia,* 47.

222 NAS CC8/8/1 fo. 118, CC8/8/40 fos 42–4.

223 NAS RD1/36 fo. 271.

224 *CBP*, ii, 924.

225 There are fragments of accounts for the Grays of Chillingham, but they mostly list luxury items bought at London and servants expenses in travelling there, rather than everyday domestic purchases. Chillingham Castle, Documents 21.

226 See John Selby of Twizel (1565), Roger Widdrington of the Friars (1572) and Sir William Reed (1604). DPRW 1560–9, 1572, 1604.

227 *Sadler Papers*, i, 590.

228 *CSP For*, 1563, 112.

229 PRO SP52/25/35 I.

230 NAS CC8/8/21 fos 72, 295, CC8/8/7 fo. 13.

231 *L & P. Hen VIII*, xiv, pt 1, 652.

232 LAMB MS 696 fos 83–4, MS 3195 fos 3–10.

233 DPRW 1572, 1574, 1582, 1597, 1602, 1604. J. Woodward, *The Theatre of Death* (Woodbridge, 1997), 15–36.

234 *NCH*, xiv, 313. D. Heslop & B. Harbottle, 'Chillingham Church, Northumberland: the South Chapel and the Grey Tomb', *AA*, 5th ser., xxvii (1999), 123–34.

235 NAS CC8/8/4 fos 30, 47, CC8/8/16 fo. 346, CC8/8/24 fo. 92.

236 NAS RD1/7 fo. 92. Both Pringle tombs are still extant in aisle chapels at Melrose.

237 NAS GD267/27/76.

238 NAS CC8/8/32 fo. 75, CC8/8/33.

239 P. Dixon, 'Towerhouses, Pelehouses and Border Society', *Archaeological*

Journal, 136 (1979), 240–52. A. M. T. Maxwell-Irving, 'Early Firearms and their influence on the military and domestic architecture of the Borders', *Proceedings of the Society of Antiquaries of Scotland*, ciii (1970–71), 194–224.

240 *Stat*, 34 & 35 Hen VIII c. 27.

241 *Cf*. Goodare, 'Parliamentary Taxation', 23–52.

242 *RPC*, vi, 812–13.

243 *ibid*. iv, 132; vi, 57.

244 NAS E48/1/1/fos 216–20. *RSS*, vi, 2118. *STS*, 3rd ser, xliii, (1949), x-xiii.

245 *RPC*, v, 625.

246 *Cf*. Devine and Lythe, 'Economy of Scotland', 105.

247 M. M. Meikle, 'The sixteenth-century Border Lairds: a study of the links between wealth and house building', *HBNC*, xlvi (1993), 9–36.

248 *APS*, ii, 346, ch. 22. G. Neilson, *Peel: its meaning and derivation* (Edinburgh, 1894), 20–1.

249 MacGibbon & Ross, *Architecture*, ii, 156–62; iv, 193–9. *APS*, ii, 346, ch. 22. H. Fenwick, *Scottish Baronial Houses* (London, 1986), 67–8. C. McKean, ' "Castle-wise" country houses', in D. Howard, ed. *The Architecture of the Scottish Renaissance* (Edinburgh, 1990), 17–18. C. McKean, *The Scottish Chateau. The Country House of Renaissance Scotland* (Stroud, 2001).

250 NAS RD1/30 fo. 162.

251 NAS RH15/19/118. MacGibbon & Ross, *Architecture*, iv, 330–34.

252 MacGibbon and Ross, *Architecture*.

253 Tranter, *Fortified House*.

254 P. W. Dixon, 'Fortified Houses on the Anglo-Scottish Border. A Study of the Domestic Architecture of the Upland area in its Social and Economic Context'. Oxford D.Phil. 1977, 203. M. M. Meikle, 'The Homes and the East March', in R. Oram & G. Stell, eds. *Family Fortunes: Architecture and Patronage in Scotland from the twelfth to the seventeenth centuries*, forthcoming.

255 R. Marks, *Burrell*, (Glasgow 1983), 109–10. See ch. viii.

256 *CBP*, ii, 1045. For comparisons with the West March see A. M. T. Maxwell-Irving, *The Border Towers of Scotland: Their History and Architecture. The West March* (Blairlogie, 2000).

257 Palliser, *Age of Elizabeth*, 110–14. N. Cooper, *Houses of the Gentry 1480–1680* (New Haven 1999). M. Girouard, *Life in the English Country House* (London, 1980), ch. iv.

258 Elizabethan improvements are ignored by P. Williams, 'The Northern Borderland Under The Early Stuarts', in Bell and Ollard eds. *Essays Presented to David Ogg* (London, 1963), 16–17, *cf*. R. Newton, *Northumberland Landscape*, 97–101 and P. W. Dixon, 'Fortified Houses', 249.

259 *CSP Dom Add*, 1566–79, 393–4.

260 DPRW 1601 (Thomas Collingwood).

261 *NCH*, xiv, 337–9; xv, 434. N. Pevsner, *The Buildings of England – Northumberland* (London, 1957), 124. See ch. viii.

262 DPRW 1604. *CSP Dom Add*, 1566–79, 495.

263 The castle needed £300 worth of repairs in 1584 and this may have been the result. *Cf*. Pevsner, *Northumberland*, 154–5 and Bates, 'Border Holds', 307.

264 M. M. Meikle, 'Northumberland Divided: Anatomy of a sixteenth-century Bloodfeud', *AA*, 5th ser, xx (1992), 79–89.

265 ALN MS AI/I fo. 9. Bodleian Library, Northumberland Rolls 2.

5

A Civilised Society? Education, Culture and Pastimes in the Eastern Borders

According to contemporaries, the inhabitants of north Northumberland and North Durham were 'backward and warlike', unlike the more civilised south of England. In 1583 Sir John Forster informed Sir Francis Walsingham that 'we that inhabite Northumberland are not acquaynted with any lerned and rare frazes . . .'[1] Forster was old and had probably been educated in the 1530s before the increase of gentry participation in higher education. What he did not tell Walsingham was that many of his younger kinsmen were now well educated and civilised. Forster was guilty of perpetuating the myth that local men were backward and untaught, perhaps to make his wardenship of the Middle March appear even more burdensome than it really was. In truth, the lairds and gentlemen in the Eastern Borders had a higher level of education and cultural appreciation than they have been given credit for, but the stigma of backwardness has persisted until recent times. The Victorian historian Macaulay further insulted northerners by referring to continuing barbarism in 'a large part of the country beyond (the) Trent' that lasted well into the eighteenth century. He described nineteenth-century upland North-umbrians, near Kielder, as 'a race scarcely less savage than the Indians of California . . . half naked women chanting a wild measure, while the men with brandished dirks danced a war dance'.[2] M. H. Dodds still referred to a backward Tudor north in 1915, W. R. Prest continued this perception in 1972 and it still appears in the recent work of S. Ellis.[3] Fortunately their opinions have been convincingly challenged by D. L. W. Tough, B. W. Beckingsale, A. E. Goodman and A. J. Pollard.[4] The English Borders may not have been at the forefront of Renaissance knowledge or culture, but their reputation for violence coupled with ignorance needs significant revision. They were certainly on the edge of a civilised society, if not within one. It just depends how civility in past societies is classified and this is currently an area of debate amongst historians.[5]

On the Scottish side of the frontier the accomplishments of David Home of Godscroft and the poets Patrick and Alexander Home of Polwarth are recognised, yet are rarely connected to their native Borders.[6] They symbolise the more peaceable culture that the Eastern Borderers were capable of producing. Northumberland also had a talented family of poets in the Ildertons of Ilderton. They were all products of the general improvement in landed families' education in the later-sixteenth century. Younger sons who had no lands of their own gained most from this upsurge in education, though the completion of their education was still deemed to be the acquisition of hunting and hawking expertise – the sports of civilised sixteenth-century gentlemen.

I. Education

Sources for the education of Eastern Border lairds and gentlemen are not plentiful, yet there is enough evidence to suggest that schooling was increasingly important to them. The expansion of educational facilities in sixteenth-century England and Scotland owed much to the influences of humanism and Protestantism.[7] By the mid-sixteenth century many landed men educated their sons within their own household or at a grammar or high school, rather than sending them to a noble house. In England formal education began at about seven and boys would have gone on to grammar school or Latin instruction with a tutor between nine and twelve years. In 1588, for instance, John Carr of Lesbury asked his wife to bring up their children 'in learning and vertuous exercises' and send their younger sons James, Lancelot and Thomas to 'gramer schoole'. Robert Muschamp of Gatherwick also asked the supervisors of his will to keep his eldest sons John and Edward 'at schole'. The wills of Humphrey Lisle of Dunstanburgh, James Swinhoe of Berrington and Thomas Swinburne of Edlingham similarly specify schooling for their children. Edmund Craster of Craster even remembered 'my scholmaster Sir Thomas' in his will, by leaving him ten shillings.[8]

The large number of recusant gentry families in Northumberland favoured household tutors for their children. The Bradfords of Bradford and Forsters of Fleetham were, for example, censured by the diocese of Durham for having unlicensed teachers in their houses. These private tutors were certainly suspect Catholics, but they were a post-Reformation phenomenon. The Grays of Chillingham had sent their sons to 'scole' until the Reformation took hold of education in the region and forced them to employ a tutor. The lack of public school teachers between Alnwick and Berwick, as well as the high incidence of recusancy in this area, would have led to a proliferation of private tutors in gentry households.[9] This may also have given the wrong impression to visitors about the level of gentry education here, as this schooling was very much in the private, rather the public sphere.

The grammar school referred to by John Carr was undoubtedly at Alnwick. This school had been run by a chantry priest until it was subsequently refounded after the 1547 Act abolishing chantries. It was funded by an annual payment of £4–1s–6d by the Court of Augmentations (from the former chantry's endowment). Thomas Thompson, a former priest, was appointed as 'scholemaster' so there was relatively little disruption to education in 1547. Alnwick did have two schools before this 'thone for gramer and thother for synge', but the song school's closure was hardly the disaster that M. B. Joyce claims.[10] Alnwick continued to attract pupils from a wide area, but in 1578 there were three teachers in Berwick as well. Only one teacher, Aristotle Knowsley, was thought to be competent and fortunately he was still there in 1604. There were also grammar schools at Morpeth, Newcastle and latterly at Hexham that may have attracted gentlemen's sons from north of the Coquet.[11] Northumberland and North Durham therefore had elementary educational facilities that were comparable to other northern counties,[12] yet Elizabethan propagandists were determined to enforce the impression of backwardness in the area to prove a need for 'godliness'. An anonymous, yet typically erroneous, report of 1597 maintained that 'in theire yonger yeares they (the children) shall not fynde so mutche as a gramer schoole in all Northumberland'. Hexham grammar school was refounded in 1597, but the others at Alnwick, Morpeth and Newcastle were certainly functioning before this.[13]

Some of the local gentry sent their sons out of the county for education. For example, Thomas Ilderton of Ilderton went to Eton College in 1552 and in 1602 Thomas Haggerston of Haggerston was sent to his grandfather's recusant household in Lancashire. A son of Richard Forster of Tughall even crossed the Border to attend the High School at Edinburgh in 1595.[14] Forster may have sent his son there because of a cross-border friendship between his kinsmen and the Homes of the Merse, or perhaps through the personal recommendation of an Edinburgh merchant they traded with. This alliance certainly proved beneficial as young Forster became involved with the infamous High School riot of September 1595 and had to be rescued by Lord Home. The High School riot provides a rare opportunity to notice other pupils there at the time. They included some Scottish Borderers noted as being gentlemen's sons, such as Robert Pringle, a younger son of Whytbank, Raguel Bennet of Chesters and a Kirkton. They were all subsequently pardoned for their participation in the riot during which John Macmorran, a prominent Edinburgh bailie, was killed by a newly-fashionable pistol.[15]

In Scotland, an Act of parliament of 1496 had ordered all barons and substantial freeholders to send their eldest sons to grammar school from the age of eight. They were to remain there until they were conversant with Latin. It is unclear if all barons complied with this statute, but the Scots' zeal for education was such that by the second half of the sixteenth century many lairds were also educating their younger sons and daughters. There were increasing numbers of local parish schools and schoolteachers, but they were not seen as centres of academic excellence. Greater lairds' sons were therefore sent to better urban schools outwith the Borders.[16] Walter Ker of Littledean had specifically to promise to send his ward Henry Haitlie of Mellerstain to 'the scoles outwith Tewedaill and the Mers'.[17] Distance was never an obstacle to the Scot requiring a good education, so lairds sent their sons to the prestigious schools at Edinburgh and Dunbar. Owing to its outstanding teacher, Andrew Simpson, Dunbar grammar was the most fashionable school in the 1570s. The Homes of Wedderburn and Polwarth and the Spottiswoodes of that Ilk all sent their sons to Dunbar, yet by the 1590s Edinburgh High School had supplanted Dunbar because of Mr Alexander Home's renowned Latin teaching there. Boarding was essential so David Spottiswoode's inventory has debts 'To robert suthre in dumbar for half ane yeir burding of Johne Spottiswood his sone ten punds. To Janet Murray for the burds of uther twa his sons twentie punds'.[18] No records survive of the Homes' boarding expenses, but when James Pringle of Galashiels was eight his tutors' testamentars insisted that he be 'placed in burding in the hous of david hoppringle hypothecar in edinburgh and to be put to the scolis of education . . .' Some lesser lairds could not afford to send their sons to fashionable schools; Alexander Trotter of Chesters owed 'William Currie in Dunce' £10–13s–4d Scots for 'buirding of his bairns'.[19]

The lairds normally employed household tutors for the pre-school education of sons and daughters. Tutors sometimes stayed on with the family instead of sending the children to board near schools, though in Scotland this would have been for economic, rather than religious reasons. The Redpaths of Angelrow, for example, had their own schoolmaster in 1600 and the young William Ker of Cessford had a 'pedagog' in 1602. The Homes of Wedderburn received pre-school tutoring in Latin at their grandfather's house at Elphinstone in East Lothian, alongside their step-cousin George Ker of Linton.[20]

Lairds and gentlemen may have been influenced by Vives's *The Instruction of a Christian Woman* (1529) and Elyot's *The Governour* (1531), that advocated elementary education for both sexes. However there is little local evidence for daughters being educated before 1550, when the golden age of elite female education was flourishing at the Tudor court. Where there is mention of female education, few details are given about their syllabi. This may have been basic and primarily religious, but teaching gentlewomen some technical abilities for use within the household was far more useful than has previously been recognised. For instance, gentlewomen were the frequently the medicinal herbalists and supervisors of brewing for the household and beyond.[21] In England Jane Alder was being tutored in 1587, whilst Jane Widdrington of the Friars could sign her own name in 1572 and Rebecca Collingwood of Eslington was staying at a recusant household in Durham for education in 1595.[22] The pious and progressive Homes of Polwarth and Wedderburn also believed in educating their daughters and oversaw the education of their Cranston of Corsbie grandchildren as well.[23] Other evidence of lairds educating their daughters can probably be ascertained from their signatures on documents; for example those of the fifth Lord Home's daughters, Margaret and Isobel, (1555 and 1596), Barbara Home of Cowdenknowes (1565), Isobel and Margaret

Home of Wedderburn (1579 and 1575) and Margaret Home, granddaughter of Patrick Home of Polwarth.[24] It is difficult to determine whether signatures denote an elementary education or rigorous classical instruction, but they signify a degree of literacy amongst landed women. The writing skills of women were usually lower than men's but they may have been more evenly balanced in their reading skills.[25]

It is probable that the majority of landed children went to school or received education at home by 1600.[26] However there was a marked difference between lairds and gentlemen in higher education. Few Northumbrian gentlemen went to university or the Inns of Court in London, yet many lairds' sons went to university in Scotland or Europe, probably because of differing academic cultures in Scotland and England. Relative impoverishment, the requirement of military service from Border residents and recusancy could all have contributed to there being a small number of matriculated students. There was a noticeable increase in the numbers of gentry attending university after the Union of the Crowns in 1603, so the Border problem may have been of greatest significance. In other remote areas that were no longer near a frontier, such as south-west Wales, more gentlemen's sons went to university in the sixteenth century.[27]

Published lists of matriculations and graduations at the English and Scottish universities in the sixteenth century are imperfect, yet they provide more information than is available for earlier schooling. John and Cuthbert Clavering, younger sons of Callaly and John Craster of Craster graduated with a Master of Arts from Oxford University in the later-sixteenth century. William Selby of Twizel, a kinsman called William Selby and Thomas Ilderton of Ilderton all attended Cambridge University, but only the latter two graduated with an MA. William Selby of Twizel followed the fashionable gentry routine of matriculating without graduating. Walsingham praised Selby's skill 'in the French tongue' and asked him to meet the French ambassador in 1582.[28]

London's Inns of Court were almost a 'third' university in England, but they were sometimes more like a finishing school than a place of serious legal learning. They attracted some young northern gentlemen, but published lists of registered students are not geographically detailed and may omit some gentlemen who attended the Inns.[29] For instance Robert Roddam of Roddam a 'broker in the lawe' and William Ilderton of Ilderton a 'commen wryter of supplications aboute the Courte and Westmenster Hall' in 1586 must have attended to one of the Inns as this was the only way to obtain legal training in sixteenth-century England; their names, however are not listed. Names that have been officially listed or noted elsewhere are all for Gray's Inn, for example Philip Gray of Howick (1598), Cuthbert Forster an unidentified kinsman of the Forsters of Adderstone (1574), Richard Ord a younger son of Horncliffe (1591) and William Lawson of Rock (1571).[30] Forster and Ord may have been career lawyers attracted to the pre-eminent profession of the times, but Gray and Lawson were only there to acquire legal knowledge as an accoutrement of gentility.[31]

Ilderton and Forster returned to their native Northumberland 'out of terme' to hunt with their local gentry friends. If Northumberland was as backward as reports suggest then these well-educated gentlemen would probably have been isolated from the mainstream of local gentry. That they were not treated as being unusual may indicate the true extent of education amongst the local gentry. Recusant families do not appear to have secretly sent any of their sons or daughters to Catholic schools abroad, yet contrary to Watts' assumptions one Northumbrian did attend a Scottish university.[32] Edward Muschamp of Barmoor graduated MA from Edinburgh University in 1593. Edinburgh was nearer than Oxford or Cambridge and a Scottish MA was obtainable in four years, rather than seven years in England. The Claverings of Callaly both matriculated at Queen's College Oxford aged twenty and William Lawson was eighteen when he entered Gray's Inn, but Scottish lairds' sons went to university at about fifteen years.[33] Lairds' sons who graduated with an MA are easily recognised as they qualified for the distinct title 'Mr' (*Magister*) and used this designation in documentation. In England the use of 'Mr' (Master) was a mark of respect for a gentleman and should not be confused with the distinctive Scottish terminology.

Scottish university lists are as misleading as their English counterparts for they only mention student names and not geographical origins. Many Border surnames appear so it is likely that far more lairds than gentlemen sent their sons to university in the second half of the sixteenth century. Universities were becoming increasingly popular in both nations, though there were more universities to choose from in Scotland.[34] There are many lairds' sons entitled 'Mr' who cannot be accounted for in university lists, either through omission or by their going abroad for higher education. The majority were younger sons, though lairds' heirs also went to university. William Home of Ayton was not designated 'Mr' but he was regarded as being learned and may have been a non-graduating student.

TABLE 5.1. UNLISTED 'MR' YOUNGER SONS BEFORE 1603[35]

Mr Patrick Cockburn of Choicelee.
Mr Alexander Dickson of Overmains.
Mr Adam Galbraith of East Windshiel.
Mr David Home of Crossrig.
Mr Alexander and Mr Samuel Home of Huttonhall.
Mr Patrick, Mr Andrew, Mr John and Mr James Home of Wedderburn.
Mr Alexander and Mr James Home of Cowdenknowes.
Mr John and Mr Alexander Home illegitimate sons of the abbot of Jedburgh.
Mr George Ker of Cavers.
Mr Mark, Mr Robert and Mr Thomas Ker of Littledean.
Mr James Ker of Ferniehirst.

Table 5.1—contd
  Mr William and Mr George Ker of Primsideloch.
  Mr William Linlithgow.
  Mr William MacDougal of Stodrig.
  Mr Robert Pringle of Whytbank.
  Mr Robert Ramsay of Wyliecleuch.
  Mr George Redpath of that Ilk.
  Mr Nicol Rutherford of Hundalee.
  Mr John Rutherford of Hunthill.
  Mr Richard and Mr John Shoreswood of Bedshiel.
  Mr David Swinton of Swinton.

The majority of Border lairds' sons went to St Andrews, but many were non-graduating if they had no future need for an MA degree. In the 1550s Adam Home, a younger son of Polwarth, graduated from St Andrews with an MA, but Hugh and William Douglas of Bonjedward and Ninian Spottiswoode of that Ilk only matriculated. There were no identifiable Borderers there in the 1560s, yet in the 1570s there were Alexander Home a younger son of Polwarth (BA), Alexander sixth Lord Home (non-graduating) and Thomas and William Cranston of Morriston (MAs). Four sons of Home of Manderston were also there – Alexander and George (non-graduating), John and William (MAs).[36] There were many other Homes and Kers in the 1570s who cannot be positively identified as Borderers or who belonged to families resident elsewhere. Apart from John Spottiswoode, a noted Reformer and younger son of that Ilk, there were no traceable Borderers at Glasgow and there were none at Aberdeen. Edinburgh, although it was nearer to the Borders was not officially founded until 1583. Patrick Home, younger, of Polwarth may have been attending there by 1587.[37] Finally there were no equivalent Inns of Court in Scotland. If a younger son wished to study law he had to go to Paris or a provincial French university as both Scottish and French legal systems were based on Roman law.[38]

The high standard of education amongst Eastern Border lairds is demonstrated by three younger sons of David Home of Wedderburn – David, James and John who were all MAs by the 1590s. David became one of the most outstanding intellectuals of early modern Europe, and was subsequently known as Home of 'Godscroft'. His university education is unknown except for a possible visit to Paris university and a short stay at Geneva's Academy. He registered for civil law at Geneva along with his future brother-in-law, Haldane of Gleneagles, who elected languages and theology. It is surprising that Godscroft did not take theology considering the Academy's emphasis on this subject and his later sympathy for Andrew Melville and Presbyterianism.[39] The education of the Homes of Wedderburn is detailed in Godscroft's history *De Familia de Humia Wedderburnensi*. David Home of Wedderburn, who died in 1574, was conversant in Latin and logic. His heir George went to Dunbar grammar and then joined the earl of Morton's household. George gained a truly universal knowledge by studying logic, French, history, geography, geometry, physic (medicine), scripture, philosophy, agriculture, economics and politics. Godscroft mentioned that Alexander Home of Manderston was skilled in law, so he may well have been to a French university.[40]

The 'auld alliance' between Scotland and France contained many commercial privileges, but it also encouraged many young men to travel to the 'schooles in France' or beyond for education.[41] Unlike later-Elizabethan England, there were no government restrictions upon young Scots travelling abroad. Unfortunately the records of these students are poor as there was no compulsion to matriculate at some French universities. None the less Mark Ker of Newbattle and Andrew Ker of Ferniehirst are on record as attending Paris.[42] Alexander Home, a younger son of Polwarth, wrote an autobiographical poem that included mention of his spending four years studying law at the Sorbonne during the 1570s.[43] Alexander would be the last of the Homes of Polwarth to go abroad as his Protestant family rigorously adhered to the interdict of the 1579 General Assembly of the Church forbidding youths from travelling overseas. The kirk did not want them to be 'corrupted be pestilent poprie' and the persecution of the Protestant Huguenots in France gave additional cause for concern. Alexander's younger brother George was therefore left 500 merks by his father providing 'he remane within the realm'.[44] Less zealous lairds continued to send their sons abroad as the sixteen-year-old Robert Ker of Cessford was in France in 1586 probably for service in the Scots Guard. Cessford always denied any higher education preferring to be seen as an artless and ambitious Borderer, rather than a polished graduate. His only acknowledged studies were 'to mayntayn his owne greatnes and ambision' and he was remembered thus;–

> Roxbrough's no scollar: yet he's neer a kin
> To learning, for his verie natural pairts
> Exceed all other sciences and airts. [45]

Cessford may have found academic study too tedious for his worldly and violent views that were particularly noticeable in the 1590s. Violence and education were not incompatible in the sixteenth century for even the academically gifted Godscroft used violence to defend his sister Julia's honour during a feud.[46] As a son and heir, Cessford's lack of university education never hindered his social ascendancy and may well have saved his father some considerable expenditure.

The cost of educating a son at a domestic university was at least £40 in England and at a foreign university a Scot would have spent a minimum of 500 merks. These amounts would have increased with inflation and the debasement of the Scottish coinage, especially during the 1570s and 1590s. The sixth Lord Home did not go abroad, yet his expenditure at St Andrews was a headache for his tutor (and uncle) Andrew Home, commendator of

Jedburgh. Home only stayed at St Leonard's college during 1578–9 and amassed a bill of £488–13s–9d Scots for his furnishing from Alexander Carstairs, a local merchant. The fifteen-year-old Lord enjoyed good, if expensive, company during his studies. Home ironically associated with influential Catholic sympathisers that the Kirk had been so anxious for youths to avoid overseas.[47] There were few traceable post-Reformation Eastern Borderers attending any of the new European Catholic seminaries before 1603, but if domestic universities had retained Catholic interests this may have been unnecessary. Only those wishing to join a religious order or be ordained went overseas in secret.[48]

II. Literacy

Watts' observation that 'we can no longer accept assertions that Elizabethan and Jacobean Northumbrians were unlearned' is certainly correct, but general standards of literacy also reached a higher level than has previously been recognised.[49] Signatures are sometimes the only literary source available for the Eastern Borders, so they form the basis of the following appraisal of gentry literacy. They were, after all, the most easily recognisable form of writing literacy in the sixteenth century though there are limitations to their usefulness. Without secondary evidence it is impossible to determine whether a signature denoted a crude ability to write, or genuine fluency in both reading and writing techniques. Reading and writing literacy were taught separately in the 1500s, so an ability to read did not necessarily mean that one could write as well and *vice versa*. Reading literacy is very difficult to determine, so regrettably it will not be discussed here through lack of surviving evidence.

David Cressy's statistics from signatures in the deposition books of the ecclesiastical court at Durham suggest fifty-nine per cent literacy amongst the gentry in the 1560s, whom he unkindly refers to as 'amazingly illiterate'.[50] He is nearer the truth than others who have based their judgement on an indenture signed by the gentry of the East and Middle Marches in 1561.[51] James Raine and Paul Boscher both quote this as an example of illiteracy and backwardness in Northumberland. Close examination reveals that twenty-four men from north of the Coquet signed and twenty put their mark to the document. However, at least three of the gentlemen who marked as if they could not sign are suspect, for Edmund Craster of Craster, Thomas Ilderton of Ilderton and Cuthbert Collingwood of Eslington were all known to be well educated in 1561. It was not unknown for literate people to make a mark instead of a signature, or they may simply have left the meeting before the document was actually signed.[52] The correct ratio should be at least twenty-seven to seventeen, suggesting a signature literacy rate of sixty-one per cent for these gentry.

Considering the ages of writing literate gentry in 1561, the standard of their education in the 1520s and 1530s must have been higher than has been presumed. Many gentry who grew up before the 1520s were illiterate, such as Lionel Gray, gentleman porter of Berwick, and Cuthbert Ogle of Eglingham, but their successors were literate by 1561.[53] Literacy of sixty-one per cent in the 1560s may seem low when compared to the south of England, but this comparison is unfair for the wealthier south had more teachers. The figure of thirty per cent literacy ascribed by Raine, Tomlinson, Wilson and Stone would have certainly designated the gentry as backward, but sixty-one per cent in 1561 was substantial enough to repudiate the 'backward' jibe of southerners.[54] From the evidence of wills and signed lists the standard of gentry signature literacy north of the Coquet appears much nearer 100 per cent by the 1590s, which conflicts with Cressy's sixty-four per cent. Cressy believes that the parish gentry of the North East were still widely illiterate in the 1590s and remote from mainstream culture. This was certainly not true of the area north of the Coquet where, for instance, lesser gentry William Wallis of Akeld, Thomas Ogle of Holy Island and Thomas Manners of Cheswick were fully writing literate in the 1590s.[55] Owing to good local schools there were reasonably literate yeomanry near Alnwick and the burgesses of Berwick were near to 100 per cent writing literate by 1600.[56]

The evaluation of literacy amongst the lairds is also based on signatures. The higher number of graduates in the Eastern Scottish Borders did not necessarily lead to a higher ratio of literacy by 1603, though there was increasing literacy amongst landed men. Anomalies occur with the Rutherfords of Edgerston, Hundalee and Hunthill and Douglas of Bonjedward who did not sign their names in 1581.[57] This may have been a clerical error as these lairds had graduates in their families and were literate in 1585. By 1602 only two lairds, Rutherford of Fairnington and Ker of Shaw, were illiterate out of seventeen signatories and only William Tait of Cherrytrees could not sign in 1600.[58] The rate of writing literacy amongst the Eastern Border lairds averaged about ninety per cent by 1603, which was less than the gentry, but the more sophisticated Merse had nearly 100 per cent literacy. Many Merse lairds could, in fact, sign their names from the mid-sixteenth century onwards with the Homes being most literate.[59] Remote lairds, such as the Redpaths of that Ilk and the Riddalls of that Ilk proved to be writing literate in 1563 and 1581 respectively, but progress was slow with the Kers of Primsideloch. Their eldest son could sign in 1579 whilst a younger son's signature was led, either through illiteracy or youth, by a notary.[60] The Haitlies of Mellerstain had an illiterate father with a literate son in the 1550s, as did the Rutherfords of Hunthill in 1574. Patriarchal illiteracy would have been quite common amongst Border lairds before the establishment of the Reformation with its strong emphasis on education and schooling.[61] The new Protestant Church advocated that every parish should have a school, although this remained an impractical ideal for decades. Where schools were established they helped lairds and non-lairds alike. For instance, when the parishioners of Eccles in Berwickshire petitioned their synod in 1602 there were seventeen signatures appended from local lesser lairds and husbandmen.[62]

III. Careers for Younger Sons

A good education was valued by landed families for Bible or general reading and better management of their own affairs. It was particularly helpful to younger sons, as they often held no lands in perpetuity and were forced to find an alternative career to avoid downward social mobility.[63] Younger sons followed various careers including farming, service in an aristocratic household, court appointments, the law, apprenticeship to merchants or craftsmen, and military service overseas. With the exception of court offices, which were too distant from Northumberland to be of use to younger sons of the gentry, there were similarities between the sons of landed men. There is more evidence of careers on the Scottish side of the Border, but there were direct comparisons in land allocations, apprenticeships and military service. Land was the primary source available to lairds and gentlemen for endowing their younger sons, yet very few of them could give land in perpetuity. There were a few perpetual gifts in Scotland and none in Northumberland. The majority were granted a liferent, as the widow and heir had priority in the settlement of an estate, with youngest sons receiving least.[64] In Northumberland the Gray of Chillingham sons were well endowed with liferents as they were one of the wealthiest families. Their sons added some permanency to these grants by gaining former monastic properties and crown lands on a secure lease. Ralph, as second son of Sir Ralph Gray (who died in 1564), had the largest liferent of local lands and later gained the Horton estate in perpetuity.[65] Edward, the third son, was left the office of constable of Wark with its £30 annuity, but he later leased land from the earl of Northumberland at Rothbury and bought the estate of Howick in the 1590s.[66] Henry, the fourth son, only received a liferent of Wooler Mill worth £6–6s–8d *per annum,* but later acquired Newminster Abbey near Morpeth.[67] Roger, the fifth son, was made bailiff of Akeld and Ewart manors and received a £7 annuity from Howick. He eventually acquired the lands of Outchester near Bamburgh with his younger brother Arthur. As the youngest son, Arthur was left two tenements in Howtel and a £6–13s–4d annuity, though he managed to buy the manor of Spindelston in 1602. The Forsters of Adderstone also helped their younger sons to success and formed branches at Bamburgh, Capheaton and Lucker.[68]

Younger sons of the middle gentry, such as the Beadnells of Lemmington, had to be content with a lease of the grain tithes of Wooden, Sheilupdykes and Hazon. The Carrs of Ford gave a short-term lease to their younger son Ralph at £30 *per annum,* but he later acquired Holburn and Downham through good fortune.[69] Robert Carr, a rebellious younger son of Hetton, only received a small grain tithe lease at Pressen and some Tweed fisheries worth £10 *per annum*.[70] The middle gentry provision for their sons was therefore barely adequate, whilst the younger sons of the lesser gentry were mostly forced away from the land if they wished to prosper. Some chose to stay and accept inevitable downward social mobility, such as the sons of James Swinhoe of Berrington, a younger son of Cornhill himself, who could only secure a lease of Berrington to be shared by his sons and a nephew in 1599. William Manners of Ord left his second son Thomas a cot house and croft with limited fishing rights for his lifetime only and John Carr of Lesbury gave his second son a small lease in Lesbury.[71] Some younger sons did not even get a liferent as Robert Weetwood of Weetwood received a twenty-one year lease and Robert Lawson of Rock gave his brothers the same. Sometimes younger sons were only left a portion of their father's goods, leaving them landless, like Richard Ord of Horncliffe who went to Gray's Inn.[72] What became of most of the younger sons of the gentry is unknown. It is assumed that they fell below the rank of gentleman, unless they took up a profession, leased land or moved away. Ralph and James Swinhoe of Cornhill, for example went to Durham and George Fowberry of Fowberry established himself in Yorkshire.[73]

Younger sons of the lairds had similar opportunities to gentlemen's sons in the sixteenth century, but their proximity to the Scottish court gave them greater access to pensions and land grants. Pensioners of Kelso Abbey, for instance, included the following younger sons – William Ker of Ferniehirst (500 merks), Thomas Ker of Cessford (650 merks), Alexander Home of Ayton (300 merks) and William Home of Cowdenknowes, later of Bassendean (£200 Scots). William and Alexander made good use of their pensions and held land in their own right.[74] As in England, the wealthiest gave their sons most and whilst there were some grants of land in perpetuity, the majority were in liferent. These gifts were often supplemented by monastic grants in a manner similar to the Grays of Chillingham in Northumberland.

The most successful younger sons came from branches of the Home family, of whom there are too many to mention individually. Mr Adam Home, for example, was parson of Polwarth and a younger son of that branch. He was not a minister, but held the kirklands of Polwarth, a £200 Scots pension from North Berwick Priory which his family dominated and other lands in East Lothian.[75] His brother, Alexander Home of North Berwick, was a valued diplomat and provost of Edinburgh in the 1590s. He amassed a fortune in land after acquiring North Berwick Priory. His lands there were exempted from the 1587 Act of Annexation to the crown as a mark of royal favour and they helped endow some of his Polwarth nephews.[76] The Homes of Manderston also had several successful cadet branches including Cranshaws, Slegden and Tinnis, though none could equal the rise of George. He was known consecutively as Sir George Home of Spott, Primroseknow, Greenlaw, Berwick and finally earl of Dunbar in 1605. During his rise to power he accumulated many properties in Berwickshire, East Lothian and England (after 1603).[77] Another Home younger son associated with the lands of Spott in East Lothian was Alexander of Cowdenknowes, known as parson of Spott or of Gartsherry in Lanarkshire.[78] He was helped by generous land grants from his uncle Mark Ker, commendator of Newbattle. Ker was himself a younger son of the Kers of Cessford, whose gift of Newbattle made him into a wealthy independent laird.[79] Two other successful sons of the Homes of Cowdenknowes were James, commendator of Eccles Priory, and William Home of Bassendean.

The Homes of Wedderburn managed to establish eight cadet branches and the Kers of Ferniehirst had two younger sons gain success outwith the Borders. William Ker inherited his mother's lands and title of Kirkcaldy of Grange near Edinburgh, despite opposition from the Kirkcaldies, and Andrew Ker probably borrowed money from his father to buy Nether Gogar in West Lothian.[80] Thomas and Richard MacDougal of Makerstoun were amongst fortunate younger sons granted land in perpetuity. Instead of being given the liferent of two husbandlands, they held them under reversion of 700 merks. The Kers of Primsideloch also used this system, but the majority of their sons were endowed with liferents. Alexander and George Swinton of that Ilk were each given eight husbandlands, which assured them a lesser laird status, and John Cranston of Corsbie held a fourteen merkland. Liferents were generally more acceptable to lairds' heirs as grants in perpetuity caused resentment in the Grahamslaw of Newton and Ker of Ferniehirst families.[81]

Lesser lairds' sons also used monastic leases, crown land grants and heiresses as a means to advancement. Robert Mow, a younger son of that Ilk had the lease of a four merkland of Kelso Abbey and James Lumsden of Blanerne rose up the social scale by marrying a distant kinsman's daughter and heiress of the lands of Airdrie in Fife.[82] George Home, portioner of Gullane in East Lothian, was a younger son of Home of the Law, but the reasons for his prosperity remain elusive. He was affluent enough to oblige his kinsman Lord Home with a loan of over £500 Scots in 1590 and may even have been a professional moneylender. Some younger sons were prepared to travel great distances to establish themselves, such as David Pringle of Galashiels who went to Bondarroch in Kirkcudbrightshire. In 1574 the nephews of James Brounfield of Whitehouse were 'absent from the Merse', so they were presumably pursuing careers elsewhere at the time.[83] At the other end of the spectrum were the younger sons who received very little. James Brounfield of Nether Mains received his bairn's portion of £200 Scots, but no land whatsoever. Patrick Cockburn of Choicelee had an unpromising lease of land at Simprim and Walter Ker of Faldonside was left a barnyard in Jedburgh worth a miserly 13s 4d *per annum*.[84]

One solution to the problem of providing for younger sons was to carry on the medieval tradition of placing sons in an aristocratic household in hope that the nobleman concerned would offer them lasting employment. As this practice was in sharp decline during the sixteenth century there are only a few examples in the Eastern Borders. Roger Swinburne of Edlingham was in the service of the earl of Rutland in 1553 and Robert Lisle of Felton was in the earl of Sussex's household in 1573. Lisle as an heir, was probably working for Sussex as Lord President of the Council of the North.[85] David Home of Godscroft was a servitor of the earl of Angus in the 1580s, but this was in deference to kinship rather than a career. The master of Glamis employed John Ker of Primsideloch as a servitor in 1586, but it is again unclear if this was a career or an educational pursuit.[86]

There were more younger sons serving other lairds than the aristocracy and they seem to have been career servitors. Mr George Home of Carolside served Mr William Hart, an advocate, Ninian Edgar of Wedderlie was servitor to Sir James Home of Cowdenknowes, Adam Pringle of Blindlee took care of Seton of Touch's legal affairs and Thomas Trotter of Ryslaw was in the service of Lord Borthwick. John Home, an illegitimate son of Cowdenknowes may have been in the employ of the Kers of Ferniehirst as he was their procurator in 1586, whilst Henry French of Thornydykes was possibly in the household of Robert Stewart, commendator of Holyrood. Adam Brounfield of Tenandry started his career in Lord Home's service but he was later seconded to the laird of Powrie Ogilvy, a Catholic friend of Lord Home.[87] Alexander Home of North Berwick employed fellow Borderers Andrew Home of Prenderguest, Andrew Dickson of the Peel and Robert Pringle of Blindlee as bailiffs of his priory lands, but it is unclear if this involved full-time employment.[88] The duration and remuneration of these posts cannot be ascertained. Court offices were undoubtedly more lucrative and thus more sought after by younger sons.

Success at court depended upon the sycophantic behaviour of the individual and the predominant politics of the time. Sir George Home enjoyed supreme success amongst all Border lairds' younger sons. He rose from being Master of the King's Stables in 1585 to Master of the Wardrobe and finally Treasurer of Scotland in 1600. After the Union of 1603 he was the most important Anglo-Scottish courtier. His achievements were resented by more established courtiers who even plotted to kill him, though without success.[89] Sir George's uncle John Home of Tinnis made his way up at court in the 1570s and 1580s through various salaried positions. Tinnis never reached beyond being King's Master Hunter, but this was a position of esteem that gave excellent access to a hunting obsessed monarch. Tinnis also received an annual salary of £100 Scots.[90] Robert Ker, a younger son of Ferniehirst, became a page of honour to James VI in 1600 and later encountered both fame and infamy in England as earl of Somerset.[91] Walter Ker of Littledean was an almoner in the 1550s before succeeding his father as laird. Amongst the lower level of court offices were younger sons like

Hew French of Thornydykes, a servitor and controller of his Majesties
Horse, who died leaving only £92 Scots and no land. In the 1550s William
Pringle of that Ilk was a servitor and in 1600 David Dickson of Buchtrig held
an accounting office as 'compter warden in his majestis cunziehous.'[92]

Court life did not suit all younger sons who tried to gain a foothold there.
During the early 1580s Alexander Home, a younger son of Polwarth, tried
to emulate his father's 1570s success as a court poet, yet found his path
blocked by a rival poet, Alexander Montgomerie. The only patronage he
received were two monks' portions of Dunfermline in 1584, which were
hardly lucrative. Home was suffering from a lung complaint at the time and
was also sickened by the

> fraud, treasone, lies, dread, guile, sedition,
> Great greediness and prodigality, lust sensual and partialitie . . .
> Of learning, wit and vertue all denude
> Maist blockith men, rash, riatous and rude:
> And flattering fallowis oft ar mair regarded:
> A lying slave will rather be rewarded.

Alexander had previously tried to become a lawyer, but he had been equally
disenchanted with procedures there after spending four years training for
this career in France.

> My breast was brusd with leaning on the bar
> My button brist, I partely spitted blood
> My gowne was trald and trampled where I stood[93]

Not all younger sons found the law so disagreeable for George Trotter of
Catchelraw became a Writer to the Signet. This was an acceptable profession to landed families for between 1594 and 1688, fifty-four per cent of
Writers were lairds' sons.[94] None the less, the expense involved in training a
son for the law, whether in France or London might have inhibited many
from taking up this career. Other opportunities open to them were in the
commercial world, military service or the church.[95]

Apprenticeships to merchants and burgesses were scorned by aristocratic
idealists, yet they were still attractive to younger sons in the second half of
the sixteenth century and did not necessarily take away their gentry status.[96]
The 1563 Statute of Artificers had standardised a minimum seven-year
apprenticeship throughout England and introduced a property qualification
for entrance to some crafts. This made apprenticeship more elitist than
before and thus attractive to younger sons of the gentry. In Northumberland
the majority of gentlemen sent their sons to prosperous Newcastle upon
Tyne, but a few went to Berwick or London. There was no guarantee of
success in the commercial world and some younger sons failed to complete

their apprenticeships. Nevertheless, that a few became very wealthy by trade justified the gentry's interest in this hitherto denigrated career for their younger sons.

James Clavering, a younger son of Callaly, chose not to go to university like his brothers. In 1578 he opted to become a Newcastle apprentice. He typically married his master's daughter for advancement and went on to become the mayor of Newcastle and founder of a wealthy gentry family based at Axwell in County Durham.[97] The Crasters of Craster apprenticed two of their younger sons in 1592 and 1594, so they seemed to be copying the Claverings' example of having graduates and apprentices within the same family. The Merchant Adventurers of Newcastle welcomed many gentlemen's sons into their guild from parts of Northumberland, Lancashire, Yorkshire, Westmorland and even Lincolnshire. They absolutely refused to take anyone from Tynedale and Redesdale owing to the deservedly wild reputation of these dales,[98] which were a different world to the more civilised areas north of the Coquet and along the Northumbrian coastal plain. Apprentices who enrolled for ten years at Newcastle were often from middle or lesser gentry families, though the majority of apprentices were from below the level of gentry. Greater gentry families could afford to endow their younger sons without resorting to apprenticeships. Therefore the Grays of Chillingham, Forsters of Adderstone and Selbies of Twizel had no mercantile sons, but the impoverished Odnel Selby of Hulne Park apprenticed four of his sons at Newcastle between 1581 and 1592.[99] Marmaduke Selby disliked his apprenticeship and was discharged in 1593, but what became of his brothers in unknown. He probably persuaded his friend Gavin Salkeld of Alnwick West Park to enrol at Newcastle as their indentures bear the same date (20 June 1589).[100] Gavin later became heir to his father, but at the time of his enrolment his elder brother George was still alive. Elder sons of the gentry did not normally become apprentices.

George Armorer of Belford was in 1567 the earliest recorded younger son to be enrolled from north of the Coquet, but there must have been others. Cuthbert Carr of Hetton (later of Benwell Tower), Thomas Hoppen of Hoppen and Bartharam Ord of Ord were all mid-century merchants of Newcastle.[101] Newcastle was not the sole recipient of younger sons as apprentices. William Fenwick of Brinkburn and Anthony Ilderton of Ilderton went to London, the latter becoming a stockfishmonger at Chigwell. Others preferred the nearest borough at Berwick upon Tweed.[102] George Ord, son of John Ord of Longridge was apprenticed at Berwick in 1582, but he switched masters in 1584 by payment of 'twoe Barrel's of Sault Salmon to the Chamber of the Towne' and was made a free burgess in 1588.[103]

In Scotland lairds' sons were also apprenticed in spite of social reservations about 'mean trades'. The well-educated Mr David Swinton, parson of Cranshaws, instructed his executors to put his son George to 'ane crauft' and 'wair the parte of heos [Helios] upon him to lerne him the craift'.[104]

Edinburgh was the most obvious location for lairds' younger sons to be apprenticed. It was by far the most prosperous burgh in sixteenth-century Scotland with thriving overseas trade and long-established trading links with the Eastern Borders. After 1585 there were substantial property qualifications of 1,000 merks of moveable goods for those younger sons who wished to be admitted to the merchant guild. A cheaper alternative was to marry the master's daughter.[105] Some therefore went to less prosperous places, such as Duns, Kelso, and Jedburgh to seek cheaper apprenticeships. There were proportionally more younger sons apprenticed in Scotland than in Northumberland, owing to the proximity of Edinburgh and the higher density of burghs in Eastern Scotland. There were several successful burgess families established by lairds' sons, but this did not tempt the Homes who with very few exceptions resolutely refused to apprentice their sons. The Pringles, Trotters and Brounfields were not so elitist in their attitude and apprenticed many of their sons.[106] Four younger sons of the Pringles became burgesses of Edinburgh, namely James of Blindlee, David of Torwoodlee, William of Whytbank (tailor) and David of Buckholm (apothecary).[107] The latter David kept up his connections with the Borders by supplying drugs and loans to Henry Haitlie of Mellerstain, Isabel Pringle of Slegden and Sir James Home of Cowdenknowes.[108]

John Trotter of Catchelraw was the most successful of the younger sons apprenticed from the families at Catchelraw, Chesters and Sisterpath. As a prosperous Edinburgh merchant he purchased Mortonhall near Edinburgh in the seventeenth century, whereas his trading uncle had only been a merchant in Duns. John Sinclair of Longformacus was just as successful as John Trotter for he bought Stevenson in East Lothian in 1624.[109] John Brounfield of Nether Mains sought his advancement by marrying his master's daughter, but he also kept up his Border connections.[110] Other younger sons apprenticed at Edinburgh include Robert Redpath of that Ilk, David Redpath of Greenlaw, Thomas Ker of Ancrum, Mark and John Ker of Cavers (Mark being the progenitor of the Kers of Duddingston), Robert Ker of Linton, John Dickson of Herdrig and George Home of Crumiecruke, one of the few Home apprentices. Younger sons who did not enrol at Edinburgh were found trading at various locations such as Kelso (William Lauder of Whitslaid), the Merse (Andrew Redpath of Crumrig), Inverkeithing (Mark and John Swinton of that Ilk), Dundee (Walter Haliburton of Mertoun), Haddington (Nicholas Swinton of that Ilk) and Jedburgh (sir James Ainslie of Thickside, a former priest of the altar of St Ninian in the burgh).[111] The Redpaths of that Ilk were like the Claverings and Crasters of Northumberland as they had both graduates and apprentices in their families. Landed families with many sons could not afford to discriminate between the relative values of academic prowess and purely commercial pursuits.[112]

Apprenticeship was seen as a worthwhile option for younger sons, yet this must have been an arduous and 'ungentle' career for those apprenticed in unglamorous trades such as the fleshers. For some there was an alternative in military service. This could be a career or a short-term occupation for sons of landed men. Amidst the bellicose environment of sixteenth-century Europe there were plenty of opportunities in this field. The Northumbrian gentry were fortunate to have a substantial garrison town nearby that could offer permanent military offices, but this could also lead to service overseas. John Carr of Hetton was forced to be a soldier by impoverishment and died whilst serving in Portugal in 1589, but William Selby of Shoreswood served in Ireland without mishap. William's nephews Ralph Selby of Weetwood and Captain John Selby of Berwick served in the Low Countries in 1603–04 and in the Azores in 1597 respectively.[113] William Selby did not have to fight for financial reasons, as he held substantial lands and was able to purchase Ightham Mote in Kent. His service was probably in deference to his family's tradition of serving the Berwick garrison.[114] Cuthbert 'Cuttie' Armorer of Belford as constable of the horse garrison was another younger son with a career in the garrison. He was, moreover, a respected Anglo-Scottish messenger between James VI and Lord Hunsdon, the governor of Berwick. In 1584 he was extraordinarily favoured when he was named as one of James VI's huntsmen, making him the only local gentleman's son to succeed to a Scottish Court office before 1603.[115]

Military options for lairds' sons were at court, in the Scots Guard of the King of France, or as a mercenary in the troubled Low Countries. The Scots Guard was a prestigious military unit offering little, if any payment, though it was probably viewed as a form of finishing education for lairds' sons, including their heirs. It was a popular destination for the Cockburns of Choicelee, who sent three of their sons to serve in the Guard between 1553 and 1578. Andrew Redpath of Rowchester resigned his place to his son William, but had to pay £200 Scots for this changeover so the Guard may well have been a financial liability.[116] It was certainly a burden for Walter Ker, a younger son of Primsideloch, whose grandfather arranged a wadset of his father's lands to provide him with 600 merks to 'mak his furnesing and to do his wyers lefull effors and buisnes in the partes of france wher he is now bound to serve in the king gaird thereof.'[117] The published lists of the Scots Guardsmen, like university registers, are unhelpful as they give no territorial designation. That the French registrars were poor spellers of Scottish surnames only compounds the problems of identification. It is highly likely that Eastern Border lairds' sons served in the Guard as there are many references to Homes, Cockburns and Swintons.[118] One of the listed Homes, Gavin, an archer in 1546, 1550 and 1554 was probably a younger son of Polwarth; his nephew Patrick may have served in 1554 as there is a reference to 'Patric Hume le jeune'.

Guard service proved useful to Gavin Home when he fought with the French forces in Scotland during the late 1540s. He was much respected by them and was rewarded with the captaincy of Tantallon Castle. This gave him a foothold in domestic military service as Tantallon was intermittently a royal possession during the sixteenth century, owing to the many forfeitures of the earls of Angus.[119] The military opportunities at the Scottish court were usually captaincies and lieutenancies of the King's or Queen's Guard. These offices were restricted to crown favourites and could only be competed for by exploiting patronage networks. William Home of Bassendean, for example, was a lieutenant of the Guard in 1586 as a highly favoured younger son of the Homes of Cowdenknowes. He was even pardoned for murdering three Border lairds because of his high rank.[120] Mr William Home of Whitelaw, a younger son of the Homes of Manderston, was a captain of Tantallon and later a lieutenant of the King's Guard as a reward for helping James VI against Francis Stewart, the rebel earl of Bothwell. Bothwell hated surrendering to William in 1589 and his treasonous brother, Hercules Stewart, was executed in 1595 after being captured by William. In 1584 Hercules had killed William's brother, Davy Home of Cranshaws, another Home younger son and a King's Master Stabler, so there was a sense of justice in William's actions.[121] He was not the most rewarded Home younger son in the military service, however, for Captain David Home of Fishwick gained more when Marian rebels surrendered Edinburgh Castle to him in 1573. He was rewarded with many of their escheats, though the peace after 1573 forced him to continue his military career as a mercenary overseas.[122]

Post-Reformation Scots mercenaries went to the Low Countries to fight for the Prince of Orange against occupying Spanish forces. Fishwick went there in 1573, as did Andrew Ormiston, a younger son of that Ilk. Ormiston was designated a Captain in 1573 and paid £50 *per annum*. He was promoted to a Colonel in 1574, but his mercenary career ended abruptly a year later when he was killed in a duel.[123] Others followed in their wake, no doubt lured by the financial rewards. John Ker of Primsideloch and William Home of Bassendean accompanied Lord Glamis's expedition in 1586 and in 1601 Captain John Ker, who was probably a Border laird's son, served there as well.[124] The only other mercenary connection with a laird's son was a Captain William Renton, possibly a younger son of Billie, who was to levy 150 men to serve the Hanseatic city of Danzig in 1577.[125]

IV. Culture

Young Scotsmen who travelled abroad for education or military experience would certainly have encountered different European cultures, but they came from distinct cultures themselves. The achievements of William Ilderton of Ilderton, David Home of Godscroft, Patrick Home of Polwarth and his son Alexander seem anachronistic in a region previously renowned for its endemic violence. The Eastern Borders were, of course, relatively less violent than the West and an appreciation of music, literature and poetry was always possible here. The increasing number of sons going to university and a higher level of general education alone must have led to greater cultural appreciation in this frontier region before 1603. Some of the greater lairds even indulged in travel for fashionable reasons, so labelling the whole Borders as a barbaric backwater is a gross distortion of reality.

The poet William Ilderton of Ilderton was really a distant descendant of the Ildertons. He had been resident in London for most of his life when, after a prolonged legal struggle, he inherited the Northumbrian estate. His cultural achievements were therefore not native to Northumberland and his predecessor, Ralph Ilderton, had even been described as 'a ryotous man gevyn to sensual pleasure'. William, however, was more virtuous as a sensitive poet, actor, lawyer and ballad writer. He acted before Edward VI and Elizabeth I and his poem *The Pangs of Love and Lovers Fits* (1560) was well known throughout England and Scotland, where it had a religious parody in the 'Gude and Godly' ballads of the 1560s.[126] William had a ribald manner of presenting his ballads and became the premier balladeer of London, yet he was also capable of writing serious poetry based on the work of classical philosophers. William Ilderton's poetry was limited in its success only because this was an outstanding era of English poetry and his poems were not of great quality. His ballad *Northumberland News*, published at the time of the 1569 Rising, demonstrated both his loyalty to the crown and remoteness from the beliefs of many of his Northumbrian friends. Many gentry were still Catholic and though they mostly refused to join the rebels, they would have disliked his anti-papal stance in this ballad.

> And Catholiques old that hold with the Pope
> And carie dead images uppe and downe
> To take better hold they shall have a Roope
> To teache them once to be trew to the Crowne[127]

The Scottish poetry of the Homes of Polwarth was heard with appreciation at court, but Patrick's work was not especially distinguished. His son Alexander, although he was a far superior poet, left court before fulfilling his true potential as a court poet. Patrick had been the favourite poet of the Scottish Court in 1579, when he composed the grovelling poem about the thirteen-year-old King James VI's first hunting expedition on 12 June 1579 called *The Promine concerning the maner, place and time of the maist illyster King James the sext his first passing to the feildes*.[128] Patrick's position as court poet was short-lived with the arrival of the gifted Alexander Montgomerie. He challenged Patrick to a 'flyting', an ancient form of court entertainment consisting of a libellous battle of poetic invective and counter-invective. Montgomerie easily won this rhythmic slandering contest and ousted Patrick from the court poet's chair in the 'chimney nuike' by describing Patrick as

> Polwarth, yee peip like a mouse amongst thornes
> Na cunning yee keipe: Polwarth, yee peip
> Ye look like a shiepe and yee had twa hornes . . .

Published as *The Flyting of Montgomerie and Polwart* this poetic combat was widely read for the next century.[129] More immediately Montgomerie's victory prejudiced the success of Patrick Home's second son, Alexander. His university education in France gave him an awareness of Renaissance ideas that were reflected in the precise cosmological details of his poetry. Sadly a disillusioned Alexander destroyed many early poems written when he was associated with the 'Castalian' poets at court. He had been part of the 1580s and 1590s zenith of Scottish court culture that would come to an end with the Union of 1603. Later poems such as *Hymnes and Sacred Songs* reflected his ultimate career in the church as minister of Logie in Stirlingshire and were for Christian, rather than courtier, appreciation. One early poem that did survive is one of the most beautiful works of sixteenth-century Scots poetry. Called *The Day Estivall,* it describes a fantasised summer's day in rural Berwickshire (and perhaps France as well) from dawn until dusk in fifty-one stanzas.

> Quhilk Sunne perceaves the little larks,
> The lapwing and the snyp,
> And tunes their sangs like natures clarks
> Ou'r midow, mure and stryp.[130]

There is no hint of any Border violence in this beautiful depiction of flora, fauna and the agricultural working day, which reminds the reader how different the Eastern Borderers could be from their Western neighbours. Patrick and Alexander Home wrote their poetry in Scots as this was the favoured medium of James VI before 1603, but David Home of Godscroft wrote almost exclusively in Latin. Godscroft wrote his first poem *Daphn Amaryllis* when only fourteen years old, but he did not publish any of his work until 1605.[131] This use of Latin probably reflected his great mind that was noted by European intelligentsia, but it denied his poetry a public following in Scotland.

Ballads were by far the most popular form of poetic entertainment in sixteenth-century England and Scotland, but they were not thought suitable for landed families' appreciation. A Border ballad was, ironically, the most popular song in sixteenth-century England; namely the *Chevy Chase* about the fifteenth-century exploits of Henry Percy and William Douglas. Most surviving Scottish Border ballads were probably meddled with by Sir Walter Scott when he transcribed them in the nineteenth century. However they were really the products of the West and Middle Marches rather than the East, with the exception of '*The Broom of the Cowdenknowes*' and a few others.[132] The lairds of the Scottish East March were probably more sophisticated than

Western Border lairds and may well have read books and poetry in preference to participating in the popular oral tradition of the ballads. These lairds were, after all, renowned men of peace who abhorred the violence of the Western Border reivers. The last thing they wanted to do was glorify the actions of the reivers in song. However lesser men in the East March would still have enjoyed the ballad tradition though the only authentic ballad to come from this area concerns a small tenant farmer, George Ramsay in Foulden Bastle. Even here though, there are classical allusions that point towards the good education of a small farmer in Berwickshire.

> Fyfe fostring peace me bred
> From thence the Merse me cald
> The Merce to Marsis lavis led
> To byde his battelis bald
> Weried vith vares and sore opprest
>
> Death gave to Mars the foyl
> And nov I have more qvyet rest
> Than in my native soyl
> Fyfe Merce Mars Mort these fatal fovr
> Al hail my dayes hes dreven ovr[133]

Beyond poetry, there were also good supplies of printed books in Scotland. The substantial library of Alexander Home the poet was mentioned in his will of 1609 and other well-educated lairds, including Home of Godscroft, must have had collections. Some may have only owned the minimum of a household Bible and Psalm book as a 1579 Act of parliament ordered all gentlemen to have these books in their household. Evidence of book ownership is hard to find in the Eastern Borders.[134] The inventories of the Northumbrian gentry rarely list books, yet they must have had some volumes as popular books were relatively inexpensive in England. Books of a religious nature were prominent in Sir William Reed of Fenham's 1604 inventory. They included 'Mr Calvin's comentarie upon Job' and a large Bible 'standing upon a desk', but he also had Holinshed's Chronicle, Joannes Sleidanus's chronicle and a dictionary.[135] Thomas Forster, younger, of Adderstone had eighteen unspecified books and a Bible in his household, but his reading material would have been very different from that the of Puritanical Sir William as he was Catholic.[136] Reed's inventory included two maps of the World and the Low Countries that were probably connected to his military interests. They would not have been a local product as there were few, if any, cartographers in Northumberland.[137] Sir William was the only Eastern Borderer to have paintings listed, but it is inconceivable that the Grays, Forsters, Selbies, Homes, and Kers had none in their houses. Reed's paintings were religious with one depicting Abraham offering up Isaac and another showing the Holy Ghost descending on the Virgin Mary. The only cultural accoutrement missing from Reed's household was a musical instrument.

Landed families must have appreciated music to some extent and a few were probably accomplished musicians. Alexander Home the poet had a lute and the Homes of Wedderburn played the harp. In Northumberland Nicholas Forster had 'a paire of decayed virginalls' in his great chamber that had perhaps belonged to a female member of his household.[138] Nicholas may have preferred to watch other forms of gentry entertainment including singing, dancing or feasting. The Catholic gentry upheld feasting more than the Protestants as Thomas Carr of Ford and William Haggerston of Haggerston travelled to Lincolnshire and Lancashire respectively, just to celebrate Christmas with recusant kinsmen. In Scotland the Homes of Wedderburn gave lavish banquets, but only for their daughters' weddings as they were Protestants. Sir Cuthbert Collingwood of Eslington employed 'Carnir Bell a Scotishe fooleboy' in his household to liven his family's entertainment and Ralph Gray of Chillingham rewarded a 'Scottishe woman that singe' with two shillings in 1600. These Scottish entertainers may have been migrants who crossed the Border in search of work. Their talents would have been much sought after for the Merchant Adventurers of Newcastle also kept official fools with Scottish surnames in the sixteenth and early-seventeenth centuries.[139]

The remaining source of culture for the landed men was overseas travel. The gentry were not as fortunate as the lairds, for European anti-English alliances and the need for a licence from the privy council effectively barred many from travelling, particularly those with Catholic sympathies. Travel was a costly undertaking, yet this did not seem to inhibit the lairds who travelled to France for fashionable reasons, as well as educational or military pursuits. For instance the young laird of Broxmouth, an East Lothian Home, went to France in 1600 'to see the fashions of the country' and he probably visited his kinsman Lord Home, who was Scottish ambassador there at the time.[140] Lord Home visited Brussels in 1591 and may have been to Italy during his three journeys abroad before 1603. Sir Walter Scott had been abroad on two occasions by 1600, which made his brother-in-law Sir Robert Ker jealous and eager to catch him up on foreign travel.[141] Even lesser lairds like Patrick Home of Broomhouse and Patrick Lumsden of Blanerne were prepared to undertake the expense of a foreign visit. Mr Mark Ker, later of Newbattle, went to France in 1547, but Alexander MacDougal of Stodrig's visit in 1568 was not for mere fashion as he was seeking a remedy for an illness.[142]

V. Pastimes

Levels of cultural awareness may have differed across the Border, but lairds and gentlemen enjoyed similar sports and pastimes. There was no sharp division between academic achievement and sporting prowess in the six-teenth century as the Renaissance ideal of the 'complete man' prevailed. The Borderers were renowned horsemen and seem to have bred horses for regular races held at Stockstruther near Kelso, Haddington, Peebles and Berwick. Sir David Home of Wedderburn enjoyed attending race meetings at Haddington and Peebles that lasted three days. His Home kindred, such as John Home of Tinnis in 1576 were frequent winners of the Haddington silver bell. There were also races at Berwick as members of the garrison competed for the 'Scottish Bell' trophy and in Carlisle there were two silver bells as prizes.[143] Scottish race meetings usually went unnoticed unless trouble occurred which had to be reported to the privy council.[144]

Horse breeding was important throughout the Borders, so the theft of George Muschamp of Barmoor's black horse from Capheaton, a gentry residence south of the Coquet, upset his bloodstock arrangements.[145] Robert Pringle, tutor of Blindlee, must have bred racehorses before his death in 1587, as his inventory debtors include James Douglas, commen-dator of Melrose (£240 Scots for a gray), David Edmondston of Burnhouse (£120 Scots for a brown horse), Lord Borthwick (£66–13s–4d Scots for a gray) and James Hepburn of Craig (£50 Scots for a white horse).[146] As the normal price for a horse was about £20 Scots, these must have been highly prized animals. Good hunting dogs were also valued in the Borders as Thomas Forster, younger of Adderstone had two dogs 'Perrye and Revell' worth 20s each, and Thomas Ilderton of Ilderton appeared to value 'Waklet and Ruffler' more than his own wife in 1578! Hounds were used to hunt in packs for hares and other small game. They had a high value for they were 'deir boght and gyve a gret price', but they should not be confused with the specialised sleuth hounds used to follow goods stolen by reivers. There was also a mutual liking of dog racing as Anglo-Scots greyhound races were noticed between the Kers and Forsters.[147]

The popularity of pastimes was unquestionable as there was a complaint in the tense year of 1548 that the Northumbrian gentry 'lyeth at home hawking, hunting and going to weddinges', rather than fighting the Scots. Hawking was enjoyed by George Home of Wedderburn, who favoured merlins but later changed to falcons and tercels. He even built a hunting lodge at Handaxwood in the Lammermuirs to facilitate this obsession for hawking.[148] Alexander MacDougal of Stodrig also valued hawks and promised one to the earl of Rutland in 1550. Hawking was seen as an aristocratic pursuit, mostly followed by the greater lairds and gentry, but its companion sport of hunting was enjoyed by all levels of landed society.[149] James VI hunted in the Eastern Scottish Borders on several occasions, as there were good supplies of game.[150] The English East March was reported to be poorly provisioned with wild game in 1589, yet there was enough game to satisfy the East March gentlemen on other occasions. This reported dearth may only have transpired because the English ambassador requested that Sir John Selby provide game for James VI's wedding feast.[151]

Football was not thought to be a gentleman's pastime, but some lairds digressed. In 1601 the Cockburns of that Ilk were involved in a shooting incident while playing against some Teviotdale thieves. They may well have been trying to prove the Merse's superiority over Teviotdale.[152] Football was probably enjoyed more by non-landed men and seems to have been a convenient means of settling disagreements. Its violent reputation alarmed Border officials when any contest was to be across the Border,[153] but the same officers could be equally violent when their own 'Lord of May' games at Cornhill and Wark went awry in 1562.[154] Indoor activities were more peaceable occasions for lairds, gentlemen and commoners alike, though gambling was inevitably linked with these pastimes. During the evenings, or when the weather was bad, they gambled with ale, plaques, hard heads, silk points and money. Dice, draughts, chess and fencing were also noted as lairds' indoor activities and some of the lairds may have played golf if they had lands near the East Lothian coastline. The only other sport noticed was athletics, as the Homes of Wedderburn participated in both cross-country horse and foot races.[155]

Lairds and gentlemen had a variety of sports and pastimes available to them, but hunting was probably the most popular mutual pursuit. The Homes of Polwarth and Wedderburn would have certainly qualified as Renaissance men with their university education, poetic attributes and sporting prowess, but this should not detract from the overall evidence that lairds and gentlemen in the Eastern Borders enjoyed a higher level of education and culture than has hitherto been acknowledged. This was significant enough to reject the view that the area was backward, but it does not make the Eastern Borders the equivalent of Renaissance Florence or even the court of Elizabethan I. If a *via media* is adopted when interpreting their education, culture and pastimes a picture of relative sophistication emerges from this sixteenth-century frontier. It is now surely unacceptable to refer to this area as being uncivilised, though historians and novelists persist in misinterpreting the whole frontier.

Notes

1 *CBP*, i, 180. *CSP Scot*, ii, 668. W. Camden, *Britannia* (London, 1586), 799. J. Speed, *The Theatre of the Empire of Great Britaine* (London, 1611), 89.

2 T. B. Macaulay, *History of England* (London, 1849), i, 213–14.

3 M. H. & R. Dodds, *The Pilgrimage of Grace 1536–7 and the Exeter Conspiracy 1538* (Cambridge 1915), ii, 227. W. R. Prest, *The Inns of Court Under Elizabeth I and the Early Stuarts* (London 1972), 36. S. Ellis, 'Civilizing Northumberland: Representations of Englishness in the Tudor State', *Journal of Historical Sociology* 12/2 (1999), 103–27.

4 Tough, *Last Years*, xiii. B. W. Beckingsale, 'The Characteristics of the Tudor North', *NH*, iv (1969), 79–83. A. Goodman 'The Anglo-Scottish Marches in

the Fifteenth Century: A Frontier Society?' in R. A. Mason, ed., *Scotland and England 1286–1815* (Edinburgh, 1987), 18–33. A. J. Pollard, 'The Characteristics of the fifteenth-century North', in J. C. Appleby and P. Dalton, eds. *Government, Religion and Society in Northern England 1000–1700* (Stroud, 1997), 131–143.

5 P. Burke, B. Harrison & P. Slack, eds. *Civil Histories Essays presented to Sir Keith Thomas* (Oxford, 2000). P. Slack, *From Reformation to Improvement. Public Welfare in Early Modern England* (Oxford, 1999), ch. vii.

6 A. H. Williamson, 'A Patriot Nobility? Calvinism, Kin-Ties and Civic Humanism', *SHR*, lxxii (1993), 4–9 places Home as a Scot rather than a Borderer.

7 M. Dowling, *Humanism in the Age of Henry VIII* (London, 1986), ch. vi. R. A. Houlbrooke, *The English Family, 1450–1750* (London, 1984), 32–4. H. M. Jewell, ' "The bringing up of children in good learning and manners": a survey of secular educational provision in the north of England, *c.* 1350–1550', *NH,* xviii (1982), 1–25. O'Day, *Education*, ch. iii.

8 DPRW 1575, 1587 (1), 1588 (1), 1603 (2); Reg vi, fos 219–220. *NCH,* ii, 69–70. *SS,* ii, (1835), 371. N. Orme, *English Schools in the Middle Ages* (London, 1973), 116–117. Craster's teacher was probably Thomas Benyon, rector of nearby Embleton in 1565.

9 PRO C142/141/31. DDR, ii, 4, fo. 94. Recusancy will be discussed in ch. vi.

10 M. B. Joyce, 'Catholic Education in Sixteenth-Century Northumberland,' *Northern Catholic History*, ii, (1975), 9–15.

11 PRO E319/1/20. *CSP Dom*, 1598–1601, 214–15. *CSP For*, 1560–1, 683. *CPR*, 1550–3, 384. See also J. W. Fawcett, 'Early Schools in Northumberland', *Proceedings of The Society of Antiquities of Newcastle*, 3rd ser, ix (1921), 264–5. H. Pollard, 'Some aspects of the History of Education in the area of Northumberland, 635–1600'. unpubl. M.Ed. Durham (Newcastle) 1952. J. Simon, *Education and Society in Tudor England* (Cambridge, 1966), 244. R. F. Tuck, 'The Origins of the Royal Grammar School Newcastle Upon Tyne', *AA*, 4th ser, xlvi (1968), 229–271. B. N. Wilson, 'The Changes of the Reformation Period in Durham and Northumberland'. unpubl. PhD diss. Durham 1939, 641. There were medieval schools at Alnwick, Hexham and Norham. N. Orme, *English Schools*, 295, 305, 311 and chs ix-x.

12 Cliffe, *Yorkshire Gentry*, ch. iv. *cf.* Jewell, 'bringing up', 22–5.

13 *CBP*, ii, 746, 881. A. R. Laws, *Schola Novocastris* (Newcastle, 1925), i, 14 -15. This propaganda is misquoted in Stone, *Open Elite?*, 48.

14 *CBP*, ii, 1496, 1497. W. Sterry, *The Eton College Register, 1441–1698* (Windsor, 1943), 113 (*vide* Elderton).

15 PRO SP52/57/31. APC, xxv, 153. *CSP Scot*, xii, 17, 30. *RPC*, v, 236–8. *Extracts of the Records of the Burgh of Edinburgh,* (Scottish Burgh Records Society, Edinburgh, 1927), v, 138–9, 147–8. R. Chambers, *Domestic Annals of Scotland* (Edinburgh, 1861), 261–5. J. G. Dalyell, ed. *Fragments of Scottish History* (Edinburgh, 1798), ii, 35. Pitcairn, *Trials*, i, pt 2, 349, 362. G. Boothroyd, 'The Birth of the Scottish Pistol', in D. H. Caldwell, ed. *Scottish Weapons and Fotifications 1100–1800* (Edinburgh, 1981), 315–38.

16 G. G. Simpson, *Scottish Handwriting* (Aberdeen, 1983), 11–12. J. Durkan, 'Education in the Century of the Reformation', in D. M. Roberts, ed. *Essays on the Scottish Reformation, 1513–1625* (Glasgow, 1962), 145–168 and 'Education: the laying of fresh foundations', in J. MacQueen, ed. *Humanism in*

Renaissance Scotland (Edinburgh, 1990), 123–60. The references to local schoolmasters certainly increased towards the end of the century – 1582 Mr Patrick Hamilton schoolmaster in Duns, 1588 Mr John Home schoolmaster in Eyemouth, 1590 Mr Alexander Watson in Coldingham, 1593 Laurence Neilson in East Reston, 1595 George Sprott in Eyemouth (later of Gowrie conspiracy infamy), 1601 John Duncan at or near Dryburgh and 1602 John Oswald in Coldingham. NAS CC8/8/41 fo. 70, RD1/21 fo. 3, RD1/48 fo. 5, RD1/49 fo. 440. *HMC*, Milne-Home, 384, 425, 526. H. Scott, *Fasti Ecclesiae Scoticanae* (Edinburgh, 1915–61), ii, 36.

17 NAS RD1/20/2 fos 89–91. *APS*, ii, 238. Chambers, *Domestic Annals*, 94.
18 NAS CC8/8/3 fo. 332. T. McCrie, *The Life of Andrew Melville* (Edinburgh, 1819), ii, 298–9. The amounts are in £ Scots.
19 NAS CC8/8/33, CS7/116 fos 195–6, 198–9, 234. David Pringle was a prominent burgess.
20 NAS CC8/8/40 fo. 36. NRAS 859/5/10, 859/11/7. Godscroft, *De Familia*, 59–61.
21 Alice T. Friedman, 'The Influence of Humanism on the Education of Girls and Boys in Tudor England', *History of Education Quarterly* (1985), 57–70. Suzanne W. Hull, ed. *Chaste, Silent and Obedient: English Books for Women 1475–1640* (Pasadena, 1988). Gloria Kaufman, 'Juan Lius Vives on the education of women', *Signs*, 3 (1978), 891–96. Norma McMullen, 'The education of English Gentlewomen 1540–1640', *History of Education*, 6 (1977), 87–101. Rosemary O'Day, 'The education of girls and women in society 1500–1800', in O'Day, *Education*, 179–95. J. K. Sowards, 'Erasmus and the education of women', *The Sixteenth Century Journal*, xiii (1982), 77–89. Elizabeth Tebeaux, 'Women and Technical Writing, 1475–1700: Technology, Literacy and Development of a Genre', in Lynette Hunter & Sarah Hutton, eds. *Women, Science and Medicine 1500–1700* (1997), 29–62.
22 DPRW 1572, 1587 (1). *CRS*, liii (1970), 49. N. Orme, *From Childhood to Chivalry* (London, 1984), ch. vi. O'Day, *Education*, ch. x.
23 NAS GD16/37/8.
24 NAS RD1/1 fo. 48, RD1/8 fo. 76, RD1/14 fo. 209, RD1/19 fo. 47, RD1/39 fo. 188, RH15/19/3/1.
25 Margaret Spufford, *Small Books and Pleasant Histories: Popular Fiction and its Readership in the Seventeenth Century* (Cambridge, 1985), 19–44. *cf.* D. Cressy, *Education in Tudor and Stuart England, Literacy and the Social Order* (Cambridge, 1980).
26 Simon, *Education and Society*, ch. xiv. R. A. Houston, *Scottish Literacy and the Scottish identity: illiteracy and Society in Scotland and Northern England, 1600–1800* (Cambridge, 1985). O'Day, *Education*, chs iv-v.
27 H. A. Lloyd, *The Gentry of South-West Wales, 1540–1640* (Cardiff, 1968), 194–95.
28 *CSP Dom*, 1598–1601, 385. AA, 4th ser., xxx (1952), 136. SS, xiv (1842), 289–9. J. Foster, *Alumni Oxonienses 1500–1714* (Oxford 1891–92), i, 286, 346. J. & J. A. Venn, *Alumni Cantabrigienses* (Cambridge, 1922–27), ii, 100; iv, 41. O'Day, *Education*, ch. vi.
29 W. R. Prest, 'Legal Education of the Gentry at the Inns of Court, 1560–1640', *P&P*, xxxviii (1967), 23.
30 PRO C3/206/13, E310/21/111 fo. 19, STAC5 S6/5. *CBP*, i, no 435. SS, cxxi (1912), 216. J. Forster, *The Register of Admissions to Gray's Inn 1521–1889* (London, 1889), 47, 78, 95.

31 Prest, *Inns of Court*, 21–3 and *The Professions of Early Modern England* (Sydney, 1987), ch. iii. J. A. Sharpe, *Early Modern England. A Social History 1550–1750* (London, 1987), ch. x.

32 Watts, *Border To Middle Shire*, 91.

33 Sharpe, *Early Modern England*, 259. *A Catalogue of the Graduates in the Faculties of Arts, Divinity and Law of the University of Edinburgh*, ed. D. Laing (Bannatyne Club, 1858), 11. *Early Records of the University of St Andrews* (Scottish Record Society, 1902), xxiv, xxx.

34 England had only Oxford and Cambridge, whilst Scotland could offer degrees from St. Andrews, Aberdeen (Marishal and King's Colleges), Glasgow and Edinburgh (after 1583).

35 NAS CC8/8/28 fos 351–2. *CSP Scot*, xiii, pt 1, 122. *RPC*, vi, 57. Meikle, 'Thesis', ch. i. app. Some of these MAs may have been overlooked on university lists as positive identification is difficult.

36 *Early Records of the University of St Andrews*, ed. J. M. Anderson (Scottish History Society, 1926). *Acta Facultatis Artium Universitatis Sanctandree, 1413–1588*, ed. A. I. Dunlop, (Scottish History Society, 1964).

37 J. Spottiswoode, *History of the Church of Scotland* (Spottiswoode Society, 1847–51) ii, 335–7. *A Catalogue of Graduates*, ed. D. Laing (Bannatyne Club, 1858), 8. *Roll of Alumni of the University of Aberdeen*, ed. P. J. Anderson (Aberdeen, 1900). *Munimenta Alme Universitatis Glasguensis: Records of the University of Glasgow till 1827*, ed. C. Innes (Maitland Club, 1854), 4 vols.

38 A. Fleming, *The Medieval Scots Scholar in France* (Glasgow, 1952), 192.

39 *Le Livre du Recteur de L'Academie de Genève* (Geneva, 1959–66), i, 103. Godscroft, *De Familia*, 73. K. Maag, 'Education and training for the Calvinist ministry: the Academy of Geneva, 1559–1620', in A. Pettegree, ed. *The Reformation of the Parishes* (Manchester, 1993), 133–52. *cf.* Williamson, 'Patriotic Nobility', 1–21 and his *Scottish National Consciousness in the Age of James VI* (Edinburgh, 1979), 89–94. Godscroft married Mr John Haldane of Gleneagles's widowed second wife in 1594, who was also a first cousin (Barbara Johnstone of Elphinstone). Andrew Melville had been at Geneva until 1574.

40 Godscroft, *De Familia*, 43, 59–61.

41 BL MS Cotton Caligula C vii, fo. 338.

42 W.A.McNeill, 'Scottish Entries in the *Rectoria Universitatis Parisiensis* 1519–1633', *SHR*, xliii (1964), 66–86.

43 A. Home, 'An Epistle to Maister Gilbert Moncrieff mediciner to the Kings majestie, wherin is set down the experience of the Authors youth', *Hymnes and Sacred Songs* (Edinburgh, 1599), 48–9. D. Nobbs, *England and Scotland, 1560–1707* (London, 1952), 27.

44 NAS C8/8/34. *BUK*, ii, 437. J. Durkan, 'The French Connection in the Sixteenth and Early Seventeenth Centuries', in T. C. Smout, ed. *Scotland and Europe, 1200–1850* (Edinburgh, 1986), 14–44. Fleming, *Medieval Scots*, 134.

45 *CBP*, ii, 1481. *CSP Scot*, viii, 464. *Bannatyne Misc*, i, 194.

46 NAS GD267/31/6. NRAS859/6/3, 859/6/4. *RPC*, v, 589. Godscroft, *De Familia*, 78–80. See ch. vii.

47 NAS RD1/18/1 fo. 2, RD1/19 fo. 90. *Early Records of the University of St Andrews*, 286, 294. Thomas Tyrie, a known Catholic, matriculated at the same college as Home in 1576 and later joined Home's household.

48 See ch. vi.

49 Watts, *Border to Middle Shire*, 93.
50 Cressy, *Literacy and the Social Order* and 'Social Status and Literacy in North East England, 1560–1630', *Local Population Studies,* xxi (1978), 19–23. J. H. Moran, 'Literacy and Education in Northern England, 1350–1550: A Methodological Inquiry', *NH,* xvii (1981), 1–23. P. Laslett, *The World We Have Lost* (London, 1983), 229–231. *cf.* Summerson, *Medieval Carlisle,* ii, 688–91.
51 BL MS Cotton, Caligula B, v, fos 52–60. Raine, *North Durham,* xxxi–xxxiii, xlix. P. G. Boscher, 'Politics, Administration and Diplomacy', 13.
52 W. Ford, 'The problems of literacy in Early Modern England', *History,* lxxviii (1993), 22–37.
53 PRO ADM75/71. *L & P. Hen VIII,* xviii, pt 1, 237. Meikle, 'Thesis' ch. i. app. for full biographical details.
54 W. W. Tomlinson, *Life In Northumberland During The Sixteenth Century* (London, 1897), 163. Wilson, 'Changes', 664. L. Stone, *The Crisis of the Aristocracy, 1558–1641* (Oxford, 1965), 676.
55 PRO SP59/35 fo. 209. DPRW 1589 (2), 1591, 1593, 1594, 1595 *etc.* On the basis of these lists and wills, there was approximately 100% literacy by 1597. *cf.* Cressy, *Literacy and the Social Order,* 123.
56 PRO ADM75/71 William Gray, yeoman of Alnwick. NRO ZSW1/192 Hugh Palliser, yeoman of Shilbottle. BRO B1/6 fo. 35.
57 NAS GD40/2/9/72. *RPC,* iii, 368.
58 *CBP,* ii, 1164. *RPC,* vi, 828–9.
59 NAS CS6/27 fo. 130, RD1/19 fo. 287. *HMC,* Home, 20.
60 NAS CC8/8/9 fos 102–04, GD237/254/3, RD1/17 fo. 232.
61 NAS CS6/7 fo. 110, RD1/8 fo. 393. Fraser, *Douglas,* iii, 213.
62 NAS RH15/19/14. G. Donaldson, *James V to James VII* (Edinburgh, 1965), 265. J. Wormald, *Community,* 181–4.
63 L. Pollock, 'Younger Sons in Tudor and Stuart England', *History Today* (June 1989), 23–9.
64 Cliffe, *Yorkshire Gentry,* 83–6. Houlbrooke, *English Family,* 234–7. E. Spring, *Law, Land and Family* (Chapel Hill, 1993), ch. iii. T. Wilson, 'The State of England', *Camden Miscellany,* xvi (1936), 24.
65 PRO C142/141/31.
66 PRO CP25/2/192 MICH 43 & 44 ELIZ. ALN MS AI/1/9.
67 PRO E310/21/109, E401/1858.
68 PRO ADM75/95, ADM75/101, CP25/2/192 TRIN 43 ELIZ, HIL 37 ELIZ & HIL 42 ELIZ.
69 PRO CP25/2/192 44 & 45 ELIZ, C142/277/195, SC6 Hen VIII 7364.
70 PRO SC6 ELIZ I 1700. *CPR,* 1563–6, 338.
71 PRO E310/21/109. DPRW 1570, 1588 (1).
72 PRO C142/143/71. DPRW 1587(2), 1589 (2).
73 Stat. 13 ELIZ, c. 16.i. *SS,* cxxxiii (1920) 109.
74 NAS CC8/8/8 fos 119–120. *RSS,* v, 336, 889, 890, 962, 1003; vi, 945.
75 NAS RD1/12 fo. 76. NRAS 859/12/9. *RSS,* v, 2826. *Acta facultis artium Universatis Sanctandree,* 112.
76 BL MS Cotton Caligula. C vi fo. 108b. NAS CC8/8/32 fos 74–6. GD110, GD158/308, GD158/309. *APS,* iii, 436. *RMS,* iv, 1604, 1919, 1920; v, 1492, 1942, 1943. *Records of the Burgh of Edinburgh,* v, 97–8, 119, 139, 163.
77 *RMS,* v, 2096, 2097, 2098; vi, 433, 500, 1446.
78 NAS GD40/3/151/1, RD1/23/1 fo. 89, RD1/32 fo. 283. *RMS,* iv, 1351, 1354,

1377, 2677; vii, 964. *RPC,* i, 621. *RSS,* iii, 2410; v, 2189, 2190, 2193, 3052. *Registrum S. Marie de Neubotle* (Bannatyne Club, 1849), 338–40.

79 NAS CC8/8/16 fos 79–83, CC8/8/29 fos 280–2, CS6/23 fo. 49, GD40/14/4. *RMS,* v, 1307. Andrew Home, commendator of Jedburgh, was a mere figurehead in comparison to Mark Ker, as his monastery's lands were leased to his family. NAS CH6/6/1 fos 25–6. NRAS 859/4/1. *RMS,* iv, 1737.

80 NAS GD40/3/103, GD40/5/4/12, RD1/8 fo. 35, RD1/28 fo. 302. *RMS,* v, 39, 1500. *RPC,* v, 673. *RSS,* ii, 2843. Meikle, 'Thesis', ch. i. app.

81 NAS CC8/8/4 fo. 47, GD12/138, GD12/139, GD40/1/227–8, GD40/2/10/54, GD40/2/10/61, GD40/3/219, GD40/3/220, GD158/201, RD1/28 fo. 208, RD1/30 fos 121–4, RD1/49 fos 525, 527, SC62/2/2 (18 Jan 1541).

82 NAS CC8/8/15 fos 62–3, RD1/1 fo. 31, RD1/9 fo. 144, RD1/23/2 fo. 411. *RPC,* i, 484. *RSS,* v, 3148.

83 NAS CC8/8/27 fo. 123. *RPC,* ii, 322; iv, 600.

84 NAS CC8/8/7 fos 298–9, CCS/8/9 fo. 371, CH6/6/1 fo. 70.

85 NRO ZSW1/181. *NCH,* vii, 380.

86 NAS RD1/25 fo. 154. *HMC,* Milne-Home, 174.

87 NAS CC8/8/2 fos 96–7, CC8/8/15 fos 44–5, CC8/8/32 fos 295–6, CC8/8/35. CS7/73 fo. 342. *Selkirk Protocol Books,* 31, 34. *RPC,* iv, 66.

88 NAS GD172/1407. NRAS 3215/6/13. *RMS,* v, 146.

89 NAS GD16/37/42, RD1/28 fo. 208, RD1/37 fos 244–5. *CSP Scot,* x, 612; xi, 290, 360; xiii, pt 1, 571. *RSS,* viii, 2392. R. Zulager, 'A Study of the middle-rank administrators in the government of King James VI of Scotland, 1580–1603', unpubl. PhD diss. Aberdeen 1991, 109–11.

90 NAS E22/14 fo. 137v. *TA,* xiii, 124, 307.

91 NAS E21/73 fos 103v-104v. A. Somerset, *Unnatural Murder* (London, 1998).

92 NAS CC8/8/3 fo. 200, CC8/8/5 fo. 80. Edinburgh University Library, Laing MS: La. Add2 fo. 69. *Mary of Lorraine, Corresp,* 368.

93 *RSS,* viii, 2553. Home, *Hymnes and Sacred Songs,* 52, 55–7.

94 G. Donaldson, 'The Legal Profession in Scottish Society in the sixteenth and seventeenth centuries', *Juridical Review* (1976), 11. *A History of the Society of Writers to the Signet* (Edinburgh, 1890), 204.

95 Younger sons who entered the church will be discussed in ch. vi.

96 J. Ferne, *The Blazon of Gentrie* (London, 1586), 7. M. J. Sayer, *English Nobility* (Norwich, 1979), 10. Simon, *Education and Society,* 355.

97 T&WAS, 988/1 fo. 61. Durham County Record Office, D/CG7/15, D/CG7/16. He initially apprenticed with Henry Weldon, but changed to Roger Nicolson and married his daughter.

98 T&WAS 988/1 fo. 57. *SS,* xciii, (1895), 27–8.

99 T&WAS 988/1 fos 62, 64, 71, 75. Printed in *SS,* ci (1899).

100 T&WAS 988/1 fos 71, 72.

101 *ibid.* fos 74, 76. PRO REQ2/248/28. DPRW 1572. R. E. & C. E. Carr, *The History of the Family of Carr* (London, 1893–99), 176.

102 PRO REQ2/270/1, REQ2/272/18. *NCH,* vii, 473. *SS,* cxvi, (1908), 281.

103 BRO B1/3 fos 54, 77, B1/4 fo. 81.

104 NAS CC8/8/28 fo. 131. G. Mackenzie, *Works* (Edinburgh, 1716–22), ii, 584.

105 *HMC,* Salisbury, viii, 295. T. C. Smout, *A History of the Scottish People, 1560–1603* (London, 1969), 159–60.

106 The route into commerce for many lairds' sons is obscure for records of Edinburgh apprentices only begin in 1583.

107 NAS CC8/8/24 fo. 304, GD157/91. *HMC* Home, 40. *RMS*, v, 1229. M. Lynch, *Edinburgh and the Reformation* (Edinburgh, 1981), 289. Alexander Home, burgess of Edinburgh also supplied Homes at Ayton. NAS CC8/8/1 fo. 308.

108 NAS CC8/8/4 fo. 268, CC8/8/15 fos 331–4, CC8/8/31 fo. 382.

109 *RMS*, vi, 1797. *The Register of Apprentices of the City of Edinburgh, 1583–1666*, ed. F. J. Grant (Scottish Record Society, 1906), 186.

110 NAS CC8/8/16 fos 299–301.

111 NAS CH6/6/1 fos 32–3, RD1/14 fo. 380, RD1/21 fo. 262, RD1/28 fo. 303, RD1/31 fo. 247. *Selkirk Protocol Books*, 35. *RMS*, iv, 1882; vi, 737. *RPC*, iv, 156.

112 NAS RD1/6 fo. 369. NLS CH5155. *RPC*, vi, 779. *Edinburgh. Apprentices*, 50, 91, 105, 151.

113 *CSP For*, 1575–7, 437. *NCH*, xiv, 233. J. Ferguson, *Papers illustrating the history of the Scots Brigade in the Service of the United Netherlands*, (Scottish History Society, 1899), 65, 186.

114 PRO E310/21/112. D & Ch Reg, 2(A), fos 214, 216; 5(E), fos 40–1, 79, 101. KAO U947/T2/1, U947/T2/14. NRO 1DE/1/117.

115 BRO B6/1 fo. 163. *CBP*, i, no 536, 572. *CPR*, 1572–5, 203. *CSP Scot*, vii, 13, 56, 179, 661. *HMC*, Salisbury, iii, 417; vi, 342. Calderwood, *History*, iv, 171; vii, 275.

116 NAS CC8/8/8 fos 294–5. G. Donaldson, ed. 'Thirds of Benefices', (Scottish History Society, 1951), 283. G. Simpson, *The Scottish Soldier Abroad 1247–1967* (Edinburgh, 1991), ch. iii. W. Forbes-Leith, *The Scots Men-at Arms and Life-Guards in France, 1480–1830* (Edinburgh, 1882), ii, 152–83.

117 NAS RD1/33 fo. 12.

118 Forbes-Leith, *Scots Men-at-Arms*, i, 188–92; ii, 138–179.

119 NAS RD1/13 fo. 41. *L & P. Hen VIII*, xx, pt 1, 924, 1100; pt 2, 347, 432. *RSS*, iii, 1732; v, 2566; vi, 585.

120 NAS CC8/8/4 fos 93–4, RD1/36 fo. 433, RH15/19/17. NLS CH1554. *APS*, iii, 623–4. *CSP Scot*, viii, 396. *RMS*, iv, 2196; v, 123. *RSS*, v, 336. Pitcairn, *Trials*, i, pt 2, 2; ii, 336. William was pardoned for murdering Alexander and John Haitlie of Mellerstain and Mr Alexander Dickson of Hassington).

121 *CSP Scot*, x, 15, 81, 84; xi, 465, 472, 474, 475, 477. *RMS*, v, 2195. *RSS*, viii, 883. Calderwood, *History*, iv, 200.

122 NAS CC8/8/9 fos 162–3, CC8/8/10 fos 221–2. *CSP For* 1572–4, 1047. *RSS*, vi, 1183, 1739; vii, 330, 471. Calderwood, *History*, iii, 284. Melville, *Memoirs*, 254.

123 Ferguson, *Scots Brigade*, 6, 8, 26.

124 *ibid.* 31, 59, 60, 63–4, 182–3. *CSP Scot*, viii, 437.

125 *RPC*, ii, 621. There were no Border lairds recorded in Prussia or Germany by E. L. Fischer, *The Scots in Germany* (Edinburgh, 1902) and his *The Scots in Prussia* (Edinburgh, 1903).

126 PRO REQ2/226/3. BL MS Cotton Caligula B, vi, fo. 319. *NCH*, xiv, 272. H. E. Rollins, 'William Elderton: Elizabethan Actor and Ballad Writer', *Harvard University Studies and Notes in Philogy and Literature*, xviii (1920), 199–245.

127 BL MS 1471.d.7 (12).

128 There has been much confusion about the Homes of Polwarth. There were three Patricks in succession in the second half of the sixteenth century. Patrick, father of Patrick the poet died in 1579. Patrick the poet died in 1599 and he was the father of Alexander the poet and Patrick, younger of Polwarth, a courtier, who died in 1609.

129 P. Bawcutt, 'The Art of Flyting', *Scottish Literary Journal* x (1983), 5–24. H.
    M. Shire, *Song, Dance and Poetry of the Court of Scotland under King James
    VI* (Cambridge, 1969), 79–80.
130 *ibid.* 81, 203–04. A. Home, *Hymnes and Sacred Songs* (Bannatyne Club, 1832). A.
    Lawson, The Poems of Alexander Home, *Scottish Text Society*, xlviii (1902). W. S.
    Crockett, *Minstrelsy of the Merse* (Paisley, 1893), 39–40 thinks this poem was
    inspired by Logie, rather than Berwickshire. For the Castalians see R. D. S. Jack,
    The Italian Influence on Scottish Literature (Edinburgh, 1972), ch. iii and P.
    Bawcutt, 'James VI's Castalian Band: a modern myth', *SHR*, lxxx (2001), 251–59.
131 *CSP Scot,* vii, 267, the reference here to David Home's 'buik' (1584) relates not
    to Godscroft, but the minister of Coldingham of the same name. McCrie,
    Andrew Melville, ii, 324, 329 and Wormald, *Community,* 185–6. R. D. S. Jack,
    ed. *The History of Scottish Literature* (Aberdeen, 1988), i, 105–38.
132 Crockett, *Minstrelsy.* W. Scott, *Minstrelsy of the Scottish Border* (Edinburgh,
    1802), 305–08. A. Fox, *Oral and Literate Culture in England 1500–1700*
    (Oxford, 2000), 1–2. K. McAlpine, 'Proude Armstrongs and Border Rogues:
    History in Kinmont Willie, Jock o the Side and Archie o Cawfield', in E. J.
    Cowan, ed. *The Ballad in Scottish History* (East Linton, 2000), 73–94. The
    Border ballads have been extensively researched by J. Reed, *The Border Ballads*
    (London, 1973) and M. Brander *Scottish and Border Battles and Ballads* (New
    York, 1975), amongst others, and are therefore not discussed here.
133 NAS CC8/8/31 fo. 186. This ballad is inscribed on his tombstone in Foulden
    churchyard. He died on 4 January 1592.
134 *APS*, iii, 139. *HMC,* Marchmont, 91–2. *Bannatyne Club,* Miscellany, ii (1836),
    187–237.
135 DPRW 1604. L. B. Wright, *Middle Class Culture in Elizabethan England*
    (Chapel Hill, 1935), ch. viii. Palliser, *Age of Elizabeth,* ch. xii.
136 DPRW 1587 (1).
137 *L & P. Hen VIII,* xvi, 1399.
138 DPRW 1608. Godscroft, *De Familia,* 43, 61.
139 PRO SP15/29/160. Chillingham Castle, Document 28. *CBP,* ii, 1434, 1497. *SS,*
    ci (1899), xxi-xxii, 165, 168. Godscroft, *De Familia,* 68. J. Southworth, *Fools
    and Jesters at the English Court* (Stroud, 1998), 166. I am grateful to Dr Bill
    Lancaster for informing me about the Newcastle fools.
140 *HMC,* Salisbury, x, 82. See ch. ii.
141 NAS GD40/2/11/64. *CSPScot,* x, 629; xiii, pt 2, 559, 566, 841.
142 NAS CS6/23, GD214/112. *CSP For,* 1560–1, 435, 661, 880. *RPC,* i, 605.
143 *CBP,* 11, 1162. Godscroft, *De Familia,* 51–2. Summerson, *Medieval Carlisle,*
    ii, 677–78. E. Williamson, 'Horse-racing in Scotland in the sixteenth and earlier
    seventeenth centuries: Peebles and beyond', *Review of Scottish Culture,* 14
    (2001–02), 31–42. I would like to thank Eila for showing me an advanced copy
    of her manuscript.
144 *RPC*, vi, 259; viii, 81. Tough, *Last Years,* 53–5.
145 Morpeth Records Centre QS1/1 fo. 14.
146 NAS CC8/8/19 fos 159–161.
147 DPRW Reg, v, fo. 68. *SS*, xxxviii (1860) 303, 173. Raine, *North Durham,*
    308–09. Lesley, *History,* i, 20–1.
148 *Hamilton Papers*, ii, 454. Godscroft, *De Familia,* 61–2. *HMC*, Rutland, i, 56.
149 M. Vale, *The Gentleman's Recreations, 1560–1630* (Cambridge, 1977), 27–8,
    41–2.

150 *CBP*, ii, 1496. *CSP Scot*, xii, 137. J. M. Gilbert, *Hunting and Hunting Reserves in Medieval Scotland* (Edinburgh, 1979).

151 *CBP*, ii, 1085. *CSP Scot*, x, 235.

152 *RPC*, vi, 262. Vale, *Recreations,* 112. In 1632 Sir Robert Ker of Ancrum wanted 'all Gaven Turnbulls croft left for an utter green for football'. D. Laing, ed. *Correspondence of Sir Robert Kerr, first Earl of Ancram*, 2 vols (Bannatyne Club, 1875), i, 67.

153 *CSP Scot*, xiii, pt 1, 371. Carey, *Memoirs*, 38.

154 *CSP For*, 1562, 250, 275. Meikle, 'Godly Rogue', 134.

155 *CSP Scot*, iii, 84 (p. 50). *HMC*, Rutland, i, 40. Godscroft, *History*, 338, *De Familia*, 51–52. See also J. Burnett, *Riot, Revelry and Rout: Sport in Lowland Scotland Before 1860* (East Linton, 2000).

6

The Reformations in the Eastern Borders

The Reformation began earlier in England than in Scotland and its impact differed on either side of the frontier. The persistence of Catholicism was notable in north Northumberland and North Durham as Protestant ideas and practice made little impact on the gentry before 1578. This survival of Catholicism was made possible by a lack of reformed preachers, geographical isolation and ineffective legislation against recusancy. As few sheriffs or their deputies were unconnected to Catholic families, fines went unpaid and arrests were infrequent until the 1590s. In 1560 Scottish churchmen faced similar problems in establishing a Protestant ministry. However as the Scottish Borders were nearer their centre of government, the Protestant Church of Scotland established itself more quickly than the reformed church within the diocese of Durham. Scottish recusants were not legislated against with the same ferocity as in England, so beyond the elite lairds they are difficult to trace. Upland Teviotdale was probably similar to Northumberland with a strong survival of Catholicism, but this was a small area of the Eastern Borders and the Merse had effectively established Protestantism by 1603. Both sides of the Border had difficulty in maintaining church buildings and discipline amongst the lairds and gentlemen, regardless of whether they were Catholic or Protestant. Fighting in the churchyard, illegitimacy and greed for church land were all common problems.

I. England

i. A delayed Reformation

The debate about the spread of the English Reformation is still ongoing.[1] The example of the diocese of Durham will support those who argue for a slow spread of reformed religion. When the Elizabethan church settlement was enacted here in 1559, the Reformation had yet to be established. Geographical remoteness and the incumbency of the conservative Cuthbert Tunstall as bishop of Durham from 1530 to 1559 contributed most to this situation.[2] A few of the north Northumberland gentry had supported the quasi-religious uprising known as the Pilgrimage of Grace in 1536. However their participation was connected to local political feuds, rather than religious motives. This pattern would be repeated in the later Northern Rebellion.[3] After Tunstall was deprived in 1559 Catholicism endured within the diocese because of surviving priests and émigré Scottish priests. The first

Protestant bishop of Durham, James Pilkington, was more concerned with his revenues than with recusants. Therefore it was not until Richard Barnes became bishop of Durham in 1577 that action was taken to spread Protestantism amongst the parishes of north Northumberland and North Durham. Progress had been equally slow at first in Cumbria, a comparable northern diocese to Durham, though there had been more Scottish Protestant activity here in the 1540s. Carlisle Cathedral had been re-founded in 1545, four years after that of Durham, but Bishop Best of Carlisle began to take reforming action upon his appointment in 1562. He 'faced an uphill struggle against a conservative diocese' and was succeeded by the enthusiastic Richard Barnes in 1570. He made capital from Best's beginnings and clearly brought this reforming zeal with him upon his appointment to Durham in 1577.[4]

The religious persuasions of many landed families will never be known, yet where there is evidence in surviving wills, recusant rolls and kinship patterns, Catholicism or Protestantism can be conjectured as follows.

TABLE 6.1. PROBABLE RELIGIOUS ALLEGIANCE OF THE LANDED FAMILIES IN NORTH NORTHUMBERLAND AND NORTH DURHAM, 1544–1603[5]

Catholic Gentlemen and Gentlewomen

Thomas Manners of Cheswick, d. 1544.
Sir Roger Gray of Horton, d. 1545.
George Craster of Craster, d. 1546.
Gerard Selby of Pawston, d. 1549.
Janet Muschamp (of Barmoor?), d. 1549.
John Carr of Hetton, d. 1551.
Edward Muschamp of Barmoor, d. 1554.
Janet Carr of Hetton, d. 1554.
Odnel Selby of Tweedmouth, d. 1555.
Robert Fowberry of Fowberry, d. 1558.
Robert Collingwood of Eslington, d. 1558.
George Carr of Lesbury, d. 1560.
Sir Ralph Gray of Chillingham, d. 1564.
Sir Robert Ellerker of Hulne, d. 1566.
Sir Thomas Gray of Horton, d. 1570.
Ralph Collingwood of Titlington, d. 1570.
Thomas Swinburne of Edlingham, d. 1572.
Gavin Hoppen of Hoppen, d. 1572.
Roger Widdrington of the Friars, d. 1574.
Thomas Hepburn of Hepburn, d. 1574.
William Gallon of Trewhitt, 1574.
Francis Armorer of Belford, d. 1574.
Robert Beadnell of Lemmington, d. 1578.
Thomas Collingwood of Titlington, d. 1579.
Thomas Holburn of Holburn, d. 1581.
Gavin Clavering of Callaly, d. 1581.

John Gallon of Alnwick, d. 1582.
Dame Isabel Gray of Chillingham, d. 1582.
Robert Clavering of Callaly, d. 1583.
William Clavering of Duddo, d. 1586.
Michael Harbottle of Tughall, d. 1586.
Thomas Forster of Adderstone, d. 1587.
Thomas Weetwood of Weetwood, d. 1587.
John Carr of Lesbury, d. 1588.
William Carr of Ford, d. 1589.
William Collingwood of Barton, d. 1590.
Sir Thomas Gray of Chillingham, d. 1590.
Ursula Brandling of Newcastle, d. 1593.
Sir Cuthbert Collingwood of Eslington, d. 1597.
Thomas Collingwood of Eslington, d. 1597.
Cuthbert Collingwood of Ingram, d. 1599.
Robert Clavering of Callaly, d. 1600.
Cuthbert Armorer of Belford.
George Beadnell of Lemmington.
Thomas Bradford of Bradford.
Robert Carr of Hetton.
John Collingwood of Abberwick.
Robert Collingwood of Abberwick.
John Collingwood of Bewick.
Cuthbert Collingwood of Branton.
George Collingwood of Broome Park.
Cuthbert Collingwood of East Ditchburn.

Table 6.1—contd
Catholic Gentlemen and Gentlewomen—contd

John Collingwood of Fawdon.
Thomas Collingwood of Little Ryle.
Cuthbert Collingwood of Netherwitton.
Edward Collingwood of Shipley.
Anthony Collingwood of Shipley.
George Collingwood of Thrunton.
Alice Conyers of Lemmington.
Tristram Fenwick of Brinkburn.
Matthew Forster of Adderstone.
Matthew Forster of Fleetham.
John Forster of Tughall.
Hugh Gallon of Trewhitt.
Lady Katherine Gray of Chillingham.

Ralph Gray of Chillingham.
Edward Gray of Howick.
Henry Haggerston of Haggerston.
Michael Hepburn of Hepburn.
John Ilderton of Ilderton.
Elizabeth Muschamp of Middleton-by-the-Sea.
Jane Proctor of Shawdon.
Lady Katherine Radcliffe of Cartington.
Francis Radcliffe of Cartington.
John Radcliffe of Thropton.
Robert Roddam of Roddam.
John Swinburne of Edlingham.
Thomas Swinhoe of Goswick.

Protestant Gentry

John Selby of Twizel, d. 1565.
Robert Lawson of Rock, d. 1565.
William Manners of Ord, d. 1565.
William Selby of Grindonrig, d. 1570.
John Lisle of Hazon, d. 1571.
Thomas Gray of Elwick, d. 1571.
John Reveley of Chatton, d. 1573.
John Carr of Lesbury, d. 1574.
Humphrey Lisle of Dunstanburgh, d. 1575.
Nicholas Rutherford of North Middleton, d. 1576.
George Harbottle of Cawledge Park, d. 1577.
Thomas Ilderton of Ilderton, d. 1578.
Peter Gray of Doddington, d. 1578.
John Morton of Unthank, d. 1581.
George Strother of Abberwick, d. 1584.
George Alder of Prendwick, d. 1585.
Odnel Selby of Hulne Park, d. 1586.
Thomas Alder of Little Ryle, d. 1587.
George Midlam of Howick, d. 1587.

Robert Muschamp of Gatherwick, d. 1587.
Ralph Selby of Berwick, d. 1588.
John Carr of Hetton, d. 1589.
Thomas Lilburn of Middleton-by-the-Sea, d. 1589.
Richard Ord of Horncliffe, d. 1589.
William Wallis of Akeld, d. 1589.
Thomas Forster of Adderstone, d. 1589.
Thomas Ogle of Holy Island, d. 1590.
Ralph Collingwood of Bolton, d. 1591.
Thomas Manners of Cheswick, d. 1593.
Edmund Craster of Craster, d. 1595.
Sir John Selby of Twizel, d. 1596.
Luke Ogle of Eglingham, d. 1596.
Ingram Salkeld Alnwick West Park, d. 1599.
Sir John Forster of Bamburgh, d. 1602.
James Swinhoe of Berrington, d. 1603.
Sir William Reed of Fenham.
Henry Collingwood of Old Etal.

By 1603 the gentry were divided into distinct Catholic and Protestant communities, yet political faction, kinship and greed for local monastic leases dating from before the Reformation transcended this religious divide. The incidence of Catholic women is indicative of their strength within household religion, whereas no Protestant women can be individually identified.[6]

In October 1587 Lord Hunsdon reported that

the mydill and thys est marche, ar almost all becum papysts, for wher yn thys est marche at my goinge hens, I knew nott 3 papysts, I fynd nott now 3 protestants, for thohe sum of them wyll sum tyme cum to churche, and that nott past onse a quarter, theyr wyves ar notoryous recusants.[7]

Hunsdon exaggerated a little to stir action against local recusants who were increasing in number, yet they were not the recent phenomenon he claimed.

Recusancy had been building for decades as the government had been more concerned with political stability in the north after the risings of 1569 and 1570. There was no enforcement of recusancy legislation prevalent elsewhere, such as the fine of 12d for not attending church which had first been introduced during Edward VI's reign. An Act of 1581 introduced a much harsher fine of £20 a month and in 1586 the crown was sanctioned to seize two-thirds of a recusant's property, yet Northumberland Catholics were generally overlooked until the £20 a month fine was enforced in 1591.[8] Another 1587 report noted 'the greater part of the gentry are papist or addicted to papistry', but the government was still more concerned with dangerous Catholics in Norfolk, Suffolk and Kent.[9] Legislation was first introduced into Northumberland in 1585, but its immediate effect was minimal. When it was widely used from 1591 onwards recusant numbers continued to increase and by 1600 even the privy council warned the bishop of Durham about their growth.[10]

ii. Catholic survival

Why had the reformed church failed to penetrate the diocese of Durham and thus allowed the rise of such a strong recusant body? The people were certainly conformist in religion and the long incumbency of the conservative Bishop Tunstall from 1530 to 1559 ensured that new Protestant doctrines were not introduced, regardless of the preaching of Scots reformer John Knox within his diocese. Although the duke of Northumberland tried to engineer his deprivation in 1553, politics intervened and Tunstall delighted in the official return to Catholicism under Mary Tudor.[11] Tunstall was not an instrument of the counter-Reformation, but by simply refusing to allow changes in Durham he had effectively shut out the Reformation until the accession of Elizabeth. Even then he was not deprived of his bishopric until 1559.[12] At the same time John Knox lamented the lack of Protestant preachers in the North of England and particularly in Berwick where the vicar was more ignorant than the curate.[13] The majority of north Northumbrian clergy were probably unreformed in 1559 and they would be reinforced by Scottish Catholic exiles, who fled across the Border during the 1560s as Protestantism began to take hold there. These Scots were willing to serve in the many Northumbrian chapelries that were really too impoverished to support a resident curate. At the first full visitation of Bishop Barnes in 1578 Scottish priests were still at Rock (Andrew Hastings), West Lilburn (Andrew Wright) and Alwinton (George Livingston). There had been an earlier reverse flow of priests from England to Scotland because of the English Reformation, but this did not have much impact in the Eastern Borders.[14] Poorly endowed churches were really more of a problem as they led to pluralism and absentee preachers.[15]

Bishop Barnes made the first attempt to tackle surviving Catholicism north of the Coquet by insisting that the injunctions of Elizabeth I be obeyed.

These included not saying Mass for the dead, not observing holy days and not allowing anyone to grant penance. The statistics for this 1578 visitation were dismal in the forty-eight churches and chapels in the deaneries of Alnwick and Bamburgh.

TABLE 6.2. VISITATION OF THE DEANERIES OF ALNWICK AND BAMBURGH, 1578

Unlicensed incumbents	16
Refused to appear	3
Vacant	5
Charges held by Scots	5
Vicars of uncertain competence	20
Able to give a correct rendering of St Matthew	12

Vicars were only found in twenty charges, yet they and the unlicensed curates may have been Catholic sympathisers or unqualified to preach. Allowing for a few absentees this statement gives a poor view of the state of north Northumberland and North Durham's clergymen. However, the situation was never as bad as propagandists stated, such as the 1539 report that 'there is never one preacher betwixt Tyne and Tweed'.[16]

The total absence of clergymen in some upland areas was confined to parts of upper Coquetdale in the Eastern English Borders. The northerners described in 1568 as being 'mere ignorant of religion' were perhaps some Middle and West March reivers who 'if Jesus Christ were emongest them, they would deceave him, if he would heere, trust, and followe theire wicked councells'.[17] Bernard Gilpin, the prominent post-Reformation preacher, tried to reach these people in his annual preaching tours of Tynedale and Redesdale in the 1560s and 1570s. His action against religious sloth was an ineffectual 'stopgap solution' as few were brave enough to follow his example and a sermon could not match the influence of a resident clergyman. Even Gilpin had to put up with his horse being stolen and he only visited Rothbury to the north of the Coquet. Upland Borderers may have lacked preachers, but this did not mean that they were unchristian or ignorant of religion. Sir John Forster referred to notorious reivers in the West and Middle Marches as 'professed Christians' in 1586, when trying to pacify a cross-border blood-feud. Backwardness in religion may well have referred to Catholic adherence rather than ignorance, though the true extent of Christianity in the upland regions of the Borders remains unclear owing to sparse source material.[18]

iii. The rise of recusancy

Catholic gentry came to rely on itinerant seminary priests to serve their religious needs. They first appeared during the 1580s as the old Marian priests and Scots were dying out or being deprived of their charges. The shortage of Protestant preachers was beneficial to the Catholic gentry as their absence from Sunday service went unchecked. By 1600 there were still vacancies and inadequacies in north-eastern parishes.

TABLE 6.3. VISITATION OF THE DEANERIES OF ALNWICK AND BAMBURGH, 1600

Charges only served by curates	4
Charges held by Scots	0
Pluralists	1
Parishes with vicars	13

The vicar of Bamburgh died in 1590 and was replaced by a curate; Alnmouth, Ellingham and Lowick only had curates and Ingram was served by the vicar of Whittingham.[19] Berwick's preacher was appointed by the governor, but the original parish church had been demolished to make way for fortifications and the badly built replacement could only hold a third of the congregation.[20] Other churches were also in poor repair, whilst Rennington had the distraction of a 'tiplinge house', to which many resorted in service time. Only Alnham, Berwick, Branxton, Eglingham, Embleton, Ford, Kirknewton, Lesbury, Longhoughton, Norham, Rothbury, Shilbottle and Wooler had permanent vicars after 1577.[21] This total of thirteen in north Northumberland and North Durham is rather more than the 'three or fowre preachers in the whole shire' commonly exaggerated in 1587 and 1597 reports, but it was none the less inadequate to serve these churches and challenge recusancy. Chatton, for instance, 'had but one sermon these xii monethes' because their vicar was ill in 1598.[22]

There is no disputing the Northumbrian Catholic resolve, which would make them into defiant recusants by the 1590s. They were openly Catholic throughout the muddled decades of the English Reformation. For instance when Robert Collingwood of Eslington died in 1558 he 'devised the erection and contenewed for ever by my hayres of a chantrie preste to celebrait in the parishe churche of Whittingham at the altar of Saint Peter . . .'[23] He had delighted in the official reinstatement of state Catholicism under Philip and Mary, but it is unclear how long his chantry survived into Elizabeth's reign once she resolved upon a Protestant church settlement. This was, however, easily ignored by many of the local gentry who continued to invoke the saints in their wills or request Catholic burial, until Bishop Barnes was appointed in 1577.[24] Thomas Collingwood of Eslington's defiant attempt to invoke the saints as late as 1597 was crossed out by a clerk.[25]

When some of these gentry wills were published by the Surtees Society the editors regrettably omitted many dating clauses that contain Catholic invocations.[26] A number of wills after 1577 are superficially Protestant as they list only Catholic supervisors. They probably conformed to a standard Protestant formula only to allow probate to be granted. Others are more obviously Protestant as they exalt the merits of Christ's death to help secure the testator's salvation. The obviously Puritan evocation at the start of Sir John Forster's will of 1602 contrasts with other Protestants who probably 'paid scant attention to the wordings of their preambles . . .' Forster asked 'God to call me out of this perplexed state of lyffe unto Mounte Sion to the citie of the living God, the celestial Jerusalem, to the Assemblie and Congregation of the first borne.'[27] Forster had a full heraldic funeral at Bamburgh, which was unusual for Northumberland, and true to his Puritan ideology no monument marked his grave.[28]

The evidence of wills is controversial amongst historians, but they are still significant, particularly when they can be consolidated by studying kinship and marriages between known Catholic families or known Protestant families.[29] C. Litzenberger's definition of traditional, ambiguous and Protestant will preambles is useful for anyone studying the progress of the English Reformation. Nevertheless the clearest source for identifying recusant gentry in the Eastern English Borders are the recusant rolls initiated in the 1590s; there being no previous bishop's lists extant for Durham.[30] Even then Northumberland is absent from recusant rolls two to eight (1593–9), as fines were either paid to the Queen's Auditor on circuit, successfully evaded by recusants, or never collected through the negligence or connivance of the sheriff. The sheriffs Ralph Gray (1593–4), Thomas Bradford (1594–5), Cuthbert Collingwood (1596) and Edward Gray (1597–8), were all Catholics and they would have been reluctant to persecute their families, kinsmen or tenants in order to extract fines.[31] In 1600 the privy council, angered by the slackness of the sheriffs in pursuing recusants demanded that the bishop of Durham call 150 indicted recusants before him with the assistance of the wardens of the Marches, rather than the sheriff who 'dothe not accompt in the exchequer or before somme Auditor and consequentlie there is no execution for their landes and goodes upon conviction as in other places . . .'[32] Sir Robert Carey, warden of the Middle March, complained that the instruction to apprehend recusants was leaked and 'three of the greatest got knowledge and left the March'. Lesser recusants did turn up and 'yealded to cum to churche, th'others not very obstinat, but good hope of reformation . . .'[33] Only Henry Haggerston of Haggerston defied the ecclesiastical commissioners by refusing to pray for the Queen and was promptly imprisoned for a second time.[34] 1600 was the first time that the commissioners made any real impact on overall recusancy in Northumberland and North Durham. When they previously visited Newcastle in 1592 none of the indicted recusants had appeared.[35]

There are mistakes in the recusancy rolls concerning recusants' names and geographical location as the Catholics of North Durham are confusingly listed under both Durham and Northumberland. The fines levied are inconsistent as recusants cannot have been watched for twelve months of the year, but the cumulative burden on the gentry would have been great. Many families would not have been able to pay their fines, even if they wanted to. Some chose the path of superficial conformity as church papists, but William Carr of Ford sacrificed his Catholicism to protect his children from the avaricious Herons. Before he died he asked Lord Hunsdon to be guardian to his children though he realised this would mean that they had a Protestant upbringing.[36] Cuthbert Collingwood of Branton appeared as a J.P. in 1602, so he must have may have disguised his recusancy as a church papist. Margaret Hepburn conformed in 1592, but she reconverted and was listed again in 1601.[37] Her spouse Michael Hepburn chose to avoid prosecution by conveniently changing address from his bastle house at Hepburn to a house at Thirston.[38] This tactic was used by Sir Cuthbert Collingwood of Eslington who held lands in County Durham and Francis Radcliffe of Cartington and Dilston who held the lordship of Derwentwater, including a convenient island near Keswick.[39] This island did not prevent Radcliffe from being warded at Durham in 1594, or from being imprisoned at Sedbergh in 1599, but it did allow his large family to live there relatively undisturbed. None attended the local church and at least one child was baptised by a seminary priest. Radcliffe never conformed or paid his fines, even though he could have afforded them at first. In 1592 his Northumberland estates were the first to be subject to the penal two-thirds sequestration law for recusants. These lands were still sequestrated in 1602, though Radcliffe conveyed certain lands to Roger Widdrington on 18 November 1601 and Francis Featherstonehaugh to raise funds.[40] His courageous defiance of authority brought him close to financial ruin, yet even Tobie Matthew, bishop of Durham, respected him as he thought Radcliffe was 'not unlearned' in theology.[41]

Radcliffe was fortunate not to have been sequestrated before 1592 for Jesuits were thought to be at Cartington in 1586 and the house was searched in 1587. Sympathy for Catholicism amongst the county's administration gave him a respite; though the situation was different for Catholics further south.[42] Lady Katherine Gray, widow of Sir Thomas Gray of Chillingham was known to shelter priests in her second home, Greencroft, near Lanchester in Durham. Here there were 'many shifting contrivances', yet she eluded arrest until 1598.[43] Her brother-in-law, Ralph Gray of Chillingham was a church papist with a recusant wife and family.[44] Chillingham was another hideout for priests in the 1580s and 1590s, but surprise searches by Sir John Forster were fruitless. He was not prepared to wait and starve the priests out of his kinsman's house.[45] Ralph Gray would have been a strong contender for the office of warden of the Middle March in 1594 had he been Protestant. Sir Robert Carey, who wanted the post himself, sent a letter south emphasising Gray's recusant links.

Not a kinsman has he in the whole country but in heart are known to be papists. He is matched with a tribe known to be all recusants, and the worst subjects the Queen has, and some of them have proved traitors; his wife is Ardington's daughter of Yorkshire, Dave Ingelby is her uncle, and was kept in Northumberland by her means many a day unknown, and she has never come to church since he married her.[46]

Ralph was still allowed to be sheriff in 1594–5 as the letter did not reveal any unknown information to Lord Burghley, godfather to Gray's first son, William. In 1593 he directed Sir William Reed and John Carey to snatch the baby from his recusant nurse and give him a Protestant baptism. It was a blatant attempt to enforce conformity on the leading family of north Northumberland, yet as William's mother entertained priests it was unlikely that he would receive a Protestant education. The Catholic children of the deceased Robert Clavering of Callaly had a Protestant guardian as part of the same 1590s policy to try to Protestantize the gentry through their children.[47]

Seminary priests were seldom found during 1580s' searches despite the puritanical Sir John Forster heading the Northumbrian commission against Jesuits and seminarists.[48] He knew of Jesuits in his March in 1582 and was annoyed that a captive priest had escaped, but later apprehended a Jesuit.[49] Forster's Protestant zeal was rare amongst the local gentry, but he preferred to target priests rather than his Catholic kin. Sir William Reed of Fenham shared Forster's Puritanism and is the only local gentleman to have religious paintings and books recorded in his inventory, such as 'Mr Calvin's Commentary upon Job and Sleidan's Chronicles'.[50] Forster willingly gave shelter to exiled Scottish Presbyterian ministers and their followers at Alnwick in 1585. His zeal apparently impressed them for 'at the mides of dinner, (Forster) began bathe to glorifie God . . . we war estonished to heir the mouthe of a waldlie [worldly] civill man so opened to speak out the wounderfull warkes and prases of God . . .'[51] In 1587 Forster was described as being 'a great heretic' by Bernardino de Mendoza, the Spanish ambassador. Had he known this, Forster would have regarded it as an accolade.[52] Forster's Protestantism was politically beneficial, but it must have tested his loyalty towards Catholic kinsmen as his first wife was the aunt of Francis Radcliffe and his daughter, Grace, married William Fenwick of Wallington, a suspected Catholic.[53] By 1594 he had to be ordered to search the house of Ralph Gray, his step-sister's son. He knew that his 'nearest friend' would be angry, but he was now forced to carry out this task against kin and enemy alike. Forster's personal friendships could no longer ignore religion and he reluctantly searched Cartington (Francis Radcliffe) and Lemmington (George Beadnell), though he probably enjoyed tackling Eslington, the home of his enemy Sir Cuthbert Collingwood.[54]

True to the complex nature of these gentry, Sir Cuthbert Collingwood, Robert Carr of Hetton and Cuthbert Armorer of Belford were willing to betray priests hiding with their recusant kin for political advantage in the

1580s and 1590s.[55] However the priests were undeterred and kept coming as there were still Jesuits in the East March in 1597 and 1600 when they did 'lurk yet quietly and manage their affayres in disguised habittes'.[56] Collingwood must have been a church papist as he managed to belong to the commission to inquire into recusancy in Northumberland.[57] Measures against recusants thus made little progress in Northumberland, though Collingwood was not the only suspect office-holder. Robert Clavering of Callaly was either Protestant or church papist, but his wife's family were recusant. He must have appeared convincing in 1586 when the earl of Huntingdon referred to him as being 'well given to religion – a rare matter here' and Sir Robert Carey thought him 'one of the sufficientest men on the whole border' in 1596. Subsequent evidence suggests that he was bluffing as his descendants were Catholic for three centuries and his widow married the Protestant Henry Guevara only because he was guardian to her children.[58] Other Catholics holding office in the 1580s included Robert Roddam as county coroner, Henry Haggerston as commissioner for Exchequer depositions and Thomas Bradford as a recusancy commissioner in the 1590s.[59] The commission of the peace was purged in 1594, but church papists survived. Catholic office bearers were not unknown in less remote counties such as Sussex, so Northumberland was far from unique.[60] In Lancashire geographical isolation helped Catholicism linger, whilst Yorkshire had a strong recusant community with many others well disposed to Catholicism. Persecution was more severe in Yorkshire, yet recusancy flourished there and crypto-Catholic Yorkshire J.P.s also went undiscovered.[61]

Recusancy did not exist in Northumberland during most of the 1560s and 1570s because Catholics would have attended parish churches until Bishop Barnes expelled the 'massing priests' in 1578.[62] A few younger sons became priests such as William Carr, brother of Robert Carr of Hetton, who was a massing priest in the countess of Northumberland's household. He fled with her to Scotland when the 1569 Rising collapsed, though he was captured at Berwick in 1572 and put 'to the rack a little'.[63] If the Northern Rebellion was 'an avowedly Catholic revolt in an officially Protestant England', then the poor support for the rebellion from the predominantly Catholic Percy tenantry in north Northumberland was a consequence of local politics. It was not, as J. H. Hilton suggests, because they were Protestant.[64] The seventh earl of Northumberland had failed to recover the status held by his ancestors. The Percy tenants regarded their feudal superior as an absentee, rent-collecting landlord rather than a social chieftain. Neither could he have sheltered local Catholics from prosecution, as Hilton implies, for surviving Catholics were simply not prosecuted at this time by Catholic J.P.s or the bishops of Durham.[65]

The overall survival of Catholicism in Northumberland was possible because of old massing priests and the seminary priests who replaced them after training abroad. However this contradicts S. M. Keeling's theory that

Catholicism was not enforced in the Borders during the 1550s and 1560s.[66] Faced with a choice of going to hear mass by an impoverished curate or not going to church at all, the local gentry seem to have preferred the former. The few Protestant gentry probably heard infrequent sermons by visiting pastors rather than resident clergymen. By the time Protestantism took hold in the diocese under Barnes' direction, mass would no longer be said in local churches. The seminarists therefore moved Catholics to the safety of local gentry houses where they were blamed for having 'throughly poysoned and infected' many gentlemen and 'their wieves, brethren, systers, children and kyndred'.[67] It was probably Jesuit insistence that Catholics separate completely from the established church that led many gentry away from the token conformity of church papistry.

iv. Estimations of Catholic gentry numbers

Estimating how many gentry families were Catholic before 1574 is difficult as no accounts were compiled. Nevertheless in north Northumberland and North Durham the majority of the gentry were Catholic in 1574 and the seminarists kept many of them faithful. In 1603 thirty-two traceable gentry families were still Catholic and thirty were probably Protestant, so there appeared to be a clear division between Catholic and Protestant communities with no distinct majority. The population as a whole may have been Protestant in 1603, but not greatly so. R. G. Usher estimated that the number of open and secret Catholic laymen in Northumberland in 1603 was eighty-five per cent.[68] This figure is too high, yet Watts and Hilton are too quick to assume a Protestant majority.[69] In 1586 de Mendoza had described Northumbrians as 'all Catholic or schismatics . . .'[70] If one disregards Mendoza's political intentions, this report still leaves the impression that Northumberland looked Catholic in the 1580s. The concentrations of Catholic gentry had, after all, alarmed Hunsdon and others in the 1580s.

When they arrived in 1581, the Jesuits had specifically targeted gentry households as future Catholic communities.[71] This effectively cut off lesser Catholics, who may have conformed. Catholicism was therefore destined to be a gentry movement and by 1603 Northumberland was well on its way to becoming this. It was not a minority movement in 1603, but it would be by 1625. The role of women in sustaining household Catholicism should never be underestimated, nor should the Catholics' sense of community. This was apparent to the west and south-west of Alnwick, where the Beadnells, Collingwoods, Radcliffes and Swinburnes lived. They had marriage links with other Catholic communities in the region as Anne Beadnell of Lemmington near Alnwick married Henry Haggerston of Haggerston in North Durham. Alice Beadnell borrowed money from her trusted friend Ralph Gray of Chillingham.[72] The Collingwoods are a particularly good example of a Catholic community, for their kin group reportedly had 'not one good Protestant' in 1606.[73] A few were Protestant, but the majority of their kin were Catholic. Their tenants and servants may well have been Catholic as well for one recusant roll listed forty non-gentry people in Edlingham, the domain of the Swinburnes.[74] Marriages amongst Catholic gentry were commonplace, as in other counties, and are often proof of recusancy.[75] There were a few mixed marriages, such as William Reed of Fenham and Anne Collingwood of Eslington. This may have been arranged for reasons of property, rather than religion, for faith was normally a private matter amongst the elite that rarely interfered with friendships.[76]

v. Ministry, morality and church property

North Northumbrian Catholics do not appear to have sent any children to be educated at continental English seminaries. Younger sons of the greater gentry would have been missed at musters as they were being closely watched by government officials in the 1580s and 1590s. Protestant gentlemen could place sons or kinsmen in vacant benefices if they held the right of patronage. William Carr of Ford, for example, presented his kinsman Thomas Carr to the rectory of Ford in 1581. Carr was later suspected of Catholicism and as his uncle Robert Carr of Hetton had murdered a previous vicar in 1576 this presentation may not have been for Protestant purposes.[77] John Clavering, second son of the Catholic Robert Clavering of Callaly, adopted the reformed faith to progress in the church and became vicar of Gamlingay in Cambridgeshire in 1590. William Selby's presentation to both Berwick and Norham in 1597 was undoubtedly Protestant and would have been influenced by his Selby relations, though the earlier placement of Robert Selby in 1541 would have been Catholic.[78]

Protestant clergy were sometimes victims of violence in Northumberland because of their faith and general indiscipline in the parishes. Edward Colston, Protestant vicar of Chatton, had to go the consistory court at Durham in 1578 and 1580 to force Catholics Thomas Swinhoe of Goswick and Sir Cuthbert Collingwood of Eslington to pay him £51.[79] During bloodfeuds both Catholic and Protestant gentry could be disrespectful to the sanctity of the church.[80] Thomas Forster was equally disrespectful to the clergy in 1600 when he was presented at a Bamburgh visitation for 'strickinge the minister there [Tughall] upon the heade with his dagger'. The unfortunate vicar also had John Forster presented for 'rideninge into the churche on horseback in service time'. Things had not improved by 1603 when Cuthbert Horsley of Lucker was presented for fighting 'within the churchyard on the Sabbath day',[81] but at least the vicar was still trying to impose good order on his congregation.

The gentry's moral standards were similarly imperfect with a high incidence of illegitimacy akin to other sixteenth-century gentry communities. Cuthbert Ogle, parson of Ford and founder of the Ogles of Eglingham, bequeathed much to Isabel Musgrave his 'servant' as she was his longstanding mistress and mother of his four sons. Sir Ralph Ellerker of Hulne left 2s 6d in his will to 'the woman that company's with me' and Thomas Ilderton of Ilderton had 'two wenches of the Newcastell' who 'kepes my house' and probably provided sexual favours for their unhappily married master. Even the virtuous Puritan Sir John Forster went to the consistory court at Durham to try to legitimise his son Nicholas, the son of Janet Buickes, after he had married his long-term mistress Isabel Sheppard.[82]

The gentry were apathetic about repairing church buildings, regardless of whether they were Catholic or Protestant. Gentlemen who were lay rectors of parish churches were supposed to keep the chancel (choir) of the church in good repair. Other gentlemen in the parish were supposed to contribute to general repairs, but they were reluctant to do this either because of avarice, the costs involved or recusancy.[83] From 1596 to 1598 the following Protestants refused to contribute to local church repair; Ralph Selby (Chatton), William Selby (Newton and Ilderton chancels), Sir William Reed (Ancroft chancel), Sir John Forster (Alnmouth, Lesbury, Longhoughton, Lucker, Shilbottle, and Warkworth chancels), John Burrell (Newton), William Wallis (Newton chancel), Luke Ogle (Eglingham), Matthew Forster (Tughall curate's house) and William Strother (Newton chancel). Some were even threatened with excommunication for failing to fund repairs.[84] In North Durham the Ords, Mortons and Reveleys all refused to contribute to the repair of Holy Island.[85] The Catholic refusers included Ralph Gray (Chatton and Ilderton chancels, and Belford), Roger Gray (Ilderton) and Thomas Swinhoe (Holy Island and Cornhill chancels). John Craster of Craster was one of the few gentlemen to undertake repairs, as he owed 10s to a local glazier for work in the choir at Embleton in 1601.[86]

Regular services at Newton (Kirknewton) must have been difficult as the local gentry ignored requests to repair it in 1595 and by 1601 the church had 'no church dores glass winedowes nor belles nor pulpitt'.[87] The churches reported to be ruinous in the 1590s must have been usable to some extent as Sir John Forster ordered a letter to 'be openly read and published in the several parish churches' in 1593.[88] If a church stood the gentry could seemingly ignore its needs, but not so leases of monastic and church land or tithes. These were highly sought after for the benefit of themselves rather than the church. Elizabeth I did not help the progress of Protestantism in the diocese by seizing huge land grants from the Dean and Chapter in 1560 to reward her favourites and kinsmen.[89] Lord Hunsdon, as cousin of the Queen, governor of Berwick and warden of the East March gained the tithes of Norham and Islandshire in 1571, which passed to his sons William and Sir Robert Carey.[90] In the 1530s Alnwick Abbey had granted long-term leases to Sir Cuthbert Radcliffe, John Roddam, George Beadnell, John Selby, Sir Roger Gray and Sir Robert Ellerker amongst others.[91] Later, when divisions between Catholic and Protestant were more prominent, the descendants of these leasees still held monastic land. Sir John Forster's rise had begun with his purchase of monastic land in Bamburgh in 1541 and Sir

William Reed was discharged £50 annual payment of the tithes of Holy Island parish, as a mark of favour.[92] Greed did not stop Catholic gentry from taking monastic land and the numerous feuds over tithes show how much they were valued by both Catholic and Protestant families.[93]

Overall, support from the north Northumberland and North Durham gentry for the spread of Protestantism was very poor. Greed, Catholic survival and the lack of Protestant clergy were the major contributors to the slow growth of the Reformation. Bishop Barnes took steps towards establishing majority Protestantism in the diocese of Durham, but he found this a struggle with Catholic gentry and poorly endowed cures. By 1603 Protestantism had presumably taken hold of the church-going population as a whole, but around half of the gentry families north of the Coquet were still Catholic in defiance of recusancy fines and sequestrations. Catholic bravado was found in other northern counties, but the proximity of the Anglo-Scottish frontier makes this situation unusual. Just across the River Tweed the Reformation would take a very different course.

II. Scotland

i. The early days of Reformation

The Reformation in the Eastern Scottish Borders made greater progress, though the spread of Protestantism was still not rapid. At the outset in 1560 many parishes were poorly endowed and served by readers and exhorters rather than ordained ministers. At first readers could only read prayers and homilies whilst exhorters could preach, but were not allowed to administer the sacraments. Catholicism did survive, but not as effectively as in England. It was centred on the nobility and great lairds such as the fifth and sixth Lords Home and Sir Thomas Ker of Ferniehirst. Their kinsmen, however, were overwhelmingly Protestant unlike the kin of the Grays and Collingwoods in Northumberland. As legislation against recusants was tame by comparison with English repression Scottish Catholics had greater freedom. There is no Scottish equivalent of the recusancy rolls, yet there were fewer landed Catholic office holders at local level. The Act of Conformity had contributed to this by insisting that all office bearers subscribe to the 'negative' confession of 1581 that denounced Catholicism.[94] However nobility such as the sixth Lord Home could hold office with scant regard for the reformed church as social position and royal patronage put them beyond the immediate grasp of the General Assembly of the Church of Scotland.

Unlike English wills, Scottish testaments give little indication of post-Reformation Catholicism as the preambles are mostly neutral, although a few are overtly Protestant. The Scots were not ostentatious about death and tended to keep their wills and funerals simple. Lairds who were convinced Protestants are found in the records of the General Assemblies of the Kirk or as commissioners investigating Jesuit activity. Many lairds realised that social and political ascendancy would not be possible without a firm adherence to the reformed kirk. They put their sons into the ministry and outwardly supported the church and its morality, though lairds had illegitimate offspring and fought over church lands and teinds as ferociously as English landed families. Here the lack of church repairs was mostly blamed on Catholics such as the sixth Lord Home, rather than Protestant lairds.

In September 1559 John Knox heralded the arrival of the Reformation in the Borders writing that 'Christ Jesus is begunne to be preached upon the south borders . . . in Jedburgh and Kelso so that the trumpet soundeth over all . . .'[95] The relatively slow progress thereafter must have disappointed Knox. He once thought that a preacher in Berwick would find, 'the favouris of the most part of the gentlemen of the East and Myddle Bordouris . . . yf the hartes of the bordoraris of both partes can be united together in Goddes fear, our victoirie . . . shalbe easy.'[96] This overestimated the legacy of the 1540s English garrisons that had promoted Protestantism in the Scottish Borders. Some of the assured Scots may have feigned Protestantism just to please the English occupiers. Usually when the Borderers were united it was to defy their governments, not their individual faith.[97] The small number of Protestant ministers in the area at the Reformation would have frustrated any laird predisposed to the reformed faith, but there was a crisis in the funding of the new church. Many Merse and Teviotdale parishes generated impoverished stipends as their revenues had been appropriated elsewhere. For instance, in the Merse only five out of thirty-eight parishes were unappropriated and in Teviotdale the figure was ten out of thirty-eight.[98]

TABLE 6.4. THE STATE OF THE MINISTRY IN THE EASTERN BORDER PARISHES, 1563–90

Date	Ministers	Readers	Vacancies
1563	17		
1568	27		
1574	17 including pluralists	36	7
1585	27 including 9 pluralists		
1590	40	7	13

Compared with these statistics, Susan Keeling's estimate of seventy-seven Protestant clergymen in the Scottish Borders by 1574 is striking, yet deceptive. Many were only readers and some either did not adhere to the reformed church, or suspiciously conformed after 1560.[99] By 1574 there were some sixty parishes in the Eastern Borders with only seventeen ministers.[100] As some of these ministers and readers were pluralists the Reformation was still far from completion. The position may have temporarily worsened after 1574 when readers began to die off. By 1585 there were twenty-seven ministers in forty-one churches, nine of whom were pluralists. Linton, Mow, Greenlaw, Legerwood, Earlston and Hownam still had readers, but their powers had been widened. In 1590 there was noticeable improvement as forty churches had ministers and seven had readers, though six of the ministers were still pluralists and the number of vacant churches was consistent.

The General Assembly knew in 1588 that the lack of ministers had promoted recusancy in remote areas, such as West Teviotdale, but the Eastern Borders were relatively unaffected by this. One exception is Greenlaw in the Merse where the reader died in 1590 and was replaced by another who died in 1599. The congregation did not have a minister until 1603, but their patron was the sixth Lord Home, a noted Catholic. Teviotdale churches had a worse record, yet by 1601 there had been a great improvement as most of the parishes had ministers. There were still some pluralist ministers, but the maximum number of their charges was two, in comparison with the multiple pluralism of 1574. Makerstoun was in fact the only parish left with a reader.[101]

In comparison to the Eastern English Borders, where there were only thirteen resident preachers in the late-sixteenth century, Protestantism was seen to have been established as the religion of the majority on the Scottish side. Neither did Scots landed families develop into a religiously divided community like Northumberland. The majority of lairds were probably Protestant by the 1570s, but overall progress was gradual as the shortage of qualified clergy and financial difficulties were a problem throughout Scotland. A 1560 report that noted Homes and Kers as non Protestant is somewhat exaggerated, though there were a few Catholic lairds in Teviotdale. During the 1560s some of the Merse lairds waivered between the old and new faiths, but as the increase in Protestant ministers was more pronounced here most lairds later supported the reformed church.[102] Only the remote upland areas of Teviotdale appear to resemble Northumberland as they had an acute shortage of reformed clergymen and a lingering Catholicism bolstered by Jesuit activity in the 1580s. Calderwood noted that in Teviotdale 'the greatest part of the kirks want ministers, and the word altogether vilipended by the gentlemen of the countrie'.[103] John Knox had not reckoned on the disaffection of so many lairds in the Middle March, but as this report referred to the whole of Roxburghshire it exaggerates Catholicism in East Teviotdale. Here the Kers of Cessford and their allies were all Protestant with the Kers of Ferniehirst being the only Catholic family. Reivers who said 'thair prayeris and pray thair Beides' before raiding were probably from the Western Borders where the progress of Reformation was even slower and violence much more intense.[104] This does, however, prove that upland reivers were Christian, rather than uninstructed. As late as 1598 the archbishop of York noted with surprise that Teviotdale pledges were 'Christian', which certainly makes him look far more ignorant than any Scot![105]

ii. Catholic survival

In the Merse and East Teviotdale a number of priests survived the Reformation and continued to celebrate mass.[106] They were not summoned to appear before the privy council until 1569. This response was much quicker than Durham, yet only a few of those summoned appeared to answer the charge of profaning the sacraments. Five outwardly conformed and were appointed readers in their parishes. Thomas Ker was deposed from Roxburgh and replaced by a minister. However, he remained in the parish and was summoned in 1582 for saying mass. He still persisted there in 1589.[107] James Williamson was deprived from Yetholm, though he also continued there until his excommunication in 1590. That no firm action was taken against these lingering priests proves how slow the reformed kirk could be in enforcing conformity as late as the 1580s. Even Bishop Barnes had taken action across the Border in 1578. Earlier, in 1569, the reinstatement of the five suspected priests as readers showed how critical the regional need for clergymen was during the first decade of reform. Had there had been competent ministers available they would not have been trusted to return. Two other cases of mass still being said after the Reformation at Ettrick (1560) and Fishwick (1563) were at the instance of lairds John Pringle of Galashiels and David Home of Fishwick. They were patrons of these churches, but as they both conformed by the end of the 1560s, these examples are not conclusive proof of post-Reformation Catholicism in these parishes.[108]

The number of Catholics in East Teviotdale would have decreased with so few priests remaining in the region. Teviotdale Catholics referred to in 1588 were mostly in the Western half of Teviotdale, or in the houses of landed families that were visited by Jesuits smuggled across the border by recusant gentry and lairds. Robert Carr of Hetton, for example, had an established contact with William Ker of Linton for conveying Jesuits in and out of Scotland in 1586.[109] This was the kind of Anglo-Scottish co-operation that neither government wanted, yet it was typical of the Borderers to ignore them. Robert Parsons, a leading English Jesuit, visited Scotland using a pseudonym in 1581. His subsequent account of the journey shows how the Reformation had become established in East Teviotdale. He crossed the Border in the Middle Marches and stayed with William Ker of Cessford for a night. Ker and his kin were Protestant, with the exception of his uncle Mark Ker of Newbattle whose children were all Catholic. That evening Cessford had no fewer than three ministers at his table who debated with Parsons without realising his true identity.[110] As the Jesuits had just arrived in the country, little was known of them and no one apprehended Parsons. He then visited the house of James Seton at Greenknowe who reportedly returned to

Catholicism forthwith, but this was an exaggeration as Seton was appointed
a commissioner for papistry in 1589.[111] Subsequent activities by Jesuits in
the Scottish Eastern Borders were noticed around Ferniehirst, though none
were apprehended.[112] Sir Thomas Ker of Ferniehirst and his wife Dame
Janet Scott were probably the only local landed family to be convincingly
reconverted. The Catholic laird of Ednam, was in reality the Midlothian
laird Andrew Edmondston of that Ilk. Priests continued to come across the
Border as Robert Roddam of Roddam brought a suspected priest to Sir John
Ker of Hirsel's house at Spylaw in 1592. Ker may not have been Catholic,
but his concurrent excommunication from the kirk would have made him
sympathetic towards priests.[113]

iii. *Politique* or Protestant?

It is not possible to define lairds as being either Protestant or Catholic at the
time of the Reformation. Political expediency rather than religious persua-
sion was often the priority of those lairds following the Reformers.

TABLE 6.5. EASTERN BORDER LAIRDS SUPPORTING THE REFORMATION IN 1560[114]

William Douglas of Bonjedward
Alexander, fifth Lord Home
Sir John Home of Cowdenknowes
Patrick Home of Polwarth
Sir David Home of Wedderburn
Sir Walter Ker of Cessford
Andrew Ker of Faldonside
George Ker of Linton
Sir John Ker of Ferniehirst
Thomas MacDougal of Makerstoun
George Nisbet of that Ilk
John Rutherford of Edgerston
John Swinton of that Ilk

Most of these greater lairds were seemingly Protestant, with the only
exception being the fifth Lord Home. A 1560 bond 'to set forward the
reformation of religion' had been signed by Cessford, Ferniehirst, Nisbet
and Wedderburn, along with Alexander Home of Manderston, Robin Ker
of Ancrum and John Rutherford of Hunthill, making their first appearance as supporters of the Reformation.[115] The first sign of dissent
amongst the Border lairds happened in December 1560 when Lord
Home, Andrew Home, commendator of Jedburgh, Sir Andrew Ker of
Hirsel, Gilbert Ker of Greenhead, Sir Nichol Rutherford of Hundalee,
James Ormiston of that Ilk and Sir James Cockburn of Langton all

attended a convention at Dunbar to discuss the possible return of the Catholic Mary, Queen of Scots. It was still unclear though exactly who was Protestant or Catholic.[116]

One of the first priorities of the General Assembly of the reformed kirk had been to encourage prominent lairds and nobility to further Protestantism. Andrew Ker of Faldonside proved a strong ally as a signatory of the kirk's *First Book of Discipline* and later as the husband of John Knox's widow. Ker's will was witnessed by no less than three ministers. The socially ambitious Sir James Home of Cowdenknowes and George Home of Wedderburn also helped the General Assembly as they were genuinely committed to the reformed kirk.[117] Teviotdale representatives to the Assembly in 1581 were William Ker of Cessford, Cowdenknowes, Nichol Cairncross of Calfhill and Andrew Rutherford of Hundalee, who, with the exception of Cairncross, had followed their fathers in promoting Protestantism.[118] They were from East Roxburghshire and Lauderdale and supported the Protestant faction in Scottish politics that kidnapped James VI from the allegedly Catholic Lennox faction in the incident better known as the 'Ruthven Raid'.[119] When the problem of Jesuits was noticed 'godlie and weill affected persons' were appointed as commissioners to detain them in the shires. In the Merse Patrick Home of Ayton, Cowdenknowes, John Home of Huttonhall, Wedderburn, Patrick Cockburn of East Borthwick, James Seton of Greenknowe and Thomas Cranston of Morriston were appointed. The Roxburgh (Teviotdale) commissioners included Sir Robert Ker of Cessford, George Douglas of Bonjedward and Faldonside.[120] None of these lairds were Catholic, unlike the church papist commissioners for recusancy in Northumberland.

Many Home and Ker lairds were consistent supporters of the reformed kirk from early days so reports suggesting that the Homes were supporters of the rebel Catholic earls in 1594 are erroneous. Their chief, the sixth Lord Home, was however, intriguing, with the earls at this time, but the Home lairds never followed either the fifth or sixth Lords Home in their return to Catholicism and other Merse lairds remained distant.[121] Alexander Home of Huttonhall, for instance, welcomed the same exiled Presbyterians who dined with Sir John Forster at Alnwick in 1585. They described Huttonhall as 'that maist godlie and comfortable house to all the servants of God'. Other ministers were clearly welcomed there for a family deed of 1594 was witnessed by two local ministers.[122] In 1602 Mr James Home of Eccles spearheaded the parishioners' petition to their synod to find a replacement for their deceased minister. Mr David Home of Godscroft and William Home of Ayton were described as 'two religious and learned gentlemen' in 1598. Godscroft had joined the Protestant eighth earl of Angus, the earl of Mar and the Master of Glamis during their exile in England in the mid 1580s. By 1599 it was obvious that the Homes were justifiably 'reputed religious'.[123]

iv. Counter-Reformation and the elite

In Teviotdale Sir Thomas Ker of Ferniehirst received little support from his kinsmen when he returned to Catholicism, just like the Lords Home in the Merse. As young men Ferniehirst and William Ker of Cessford had been eager reformers. John Knox called them 'two godly and forward young men' for bringing a Protestant preacher to Kelso in 1553, but their friendship deteriorated when Ferniehirst became a Catholic in the late 1560s.[124] His father had supported the Reformation, but died in 1562. Thomas did not sign any Protestant bond or attend the Reformation Parliament. By 1570 he was openly Catholic and sheltered the rebel earl of Westmorland at Ferniehirst after the collapse of the Northern Rising. The fifth Lord Home also returned to Catholicism and sheltered the countess of Northumberland at Hume castle.[125] Home and Ferniehirst were later forfeited for joining the rebels holding Edinburgh castle for Mary, Queen of Scots. When the castle surrendered in 1573 Ferniehirst chose exile and did not return until 1579. He remained a Catholic throughout his exile.[126] He was called before the General Assembly in 1582 for 'going to Mess in France and other ports beyond sea', but he never appeared nor conformed and died ignominiously in 1586.[127] His second wife, Janet Scott of Buccleuch, remained Catholic after his death though the Scotts were Protestant and his daughters all married Protestants. As with some Northumbrian marriages, property may have taken precedence over private faith. Julia Ker, for example, married the notably Protestant Patrick Home of Polwarth. Ferniehirst's heir, Andrew, remained a sincere Catholic. Like his father he had household priests, intrigued with Spain and received Spanish pensions.[128]

Alexander, fifth lord Home, was an unconvincing member of the Reformation Parliament, though he was careful to remain neutral in religion during the early 1560s. By subscribing to the articles of religion in 1567, along with Faldonside, he again did not arouse suspicion. However, Pope Pius IV praised him for remaining Catholic in 1565, so he was undoubtedly a *politique* supporter of reform.[129] By 1570 he was openly Catholic and heard 'two or three masses daily with Lady Northumberland', yet his marriages and children appeared to be Protestant. Home's heir, Alexander, was only ten years old when he died in 1575. His wardship was awarded to his father's friend the very Protestant Lord William Ruthven, later earl of Gowrie,[130] yet his tutor Andrew Home, commendator of Jedburgh, may have been Catholic. This may explain why the sixth Lord Home had become a Catholic as he spent several years within his tutor's household at Jedburgh and may have met Jesuits there as well as later consorting with known Catholics at St Andrews University.

The first indication of Home not supporting Protestantism was in 1582 when a Jesuit declared him to be in the Spanish faction.[131] At this time he was indifferent towards his guardian and refused to marry one of his daughters whilst he was staying with William Pringle, a burgess of Edinburgh. Pringle may have been a Catholic as his apothecary kinsman David Pringle was a known crypto-Catholic.[132] Home was noticeably absent from the bond 'anent true religion' of 1585. The General Assembly sent two ministers to investigate in 1588 and they found him sheltering Mr Andrew Clerk, a priest, but were hopeful that the twenty-three-year old could be reformed.[133] They would be disappointed as Home's conversion proved irreversible.

With Presbyterian organisation established in the East of Scotland by the 1590s Home found his faith an inconvenience. For example he absented himself from Scotland from August 1591 until July 1592 to avoid an investigation by the presbytery of Dunbar. He was also in disgrace for intriguing with the infamous earl of Bothwell. He appeared to have communicated with Spanish agents and may have gone to Italy.[134] When he returned Andrew Clerk was still in his household, and his kinsman and servitor, Thomas Tyrie, was a known Jesuit. Home ignored summons to appear before the General Assembly.[135] James VI valued Home's Border peace-keeping and ignored the rumours about Home's Catholic activities. He sheltered Home and other Catholic nobility from the kirk's wrath, postponing their excommunication for as long as possible.[136] Complications arose when the synod of Fife ignored the king and processed Home's excommunication because he had been a student at St Andrews and subscribed the articles of religion in Fife before marriage.[137] Home could not bear, financially or socially, to be excluded from court as an excommunicant and therefore appeared before the presbytery of Edinburgh, where he 'professed himself a Catholick Roman but desired conference'. Tyrie temporarily left his household to create a good impression. The General Assembly rescinded the synod of Fife's excommunication as Home subscribed the articles of religion anew on 22 December 1593 and appeared before them again in May 1594.[138] Home was as insincere in this endeavour as church papists were to Protestantism in England.

Although Home had sheltered priests, not allowed ministers in his house and obstructed payment of stipends to local ministers, the Assembly now believed his earnestness to conform. Andrew Melville rightly remained sceptical and refused to give Home absolution, making another minister perform it instead.[139] Home was warned that the slightest deviation would result in his immediate excommunication, but this did not deter his Catholicism. The presbytery of Duns cited him for 'sundry faults', but Home rode on the left hand of James VI during a parliamentary procession and avoided excommunication until 1598.[140] Home left the country for another year-long exile, as James VI could not persuade the kirk to change its mind. Ironically this excommunication was prompted by the murder of William Lauder, rather than by his Catholicism, so the journey was not an ostensibly Catholic pilgrimage. Home took his Protestant kinsman, Alexander Home of Huttonhall with him, but Tyrie was also in his company. Lady Home stayed at home, but there is no indication that she was ever

Catholic as a minister witnessed her will in 1604. This religious divide
could account for some of the friction in their marriage.[141] Home sheltered
at court upon his return and refused to accept the godly John Carmichael in
his household. He remained on good terms with the king and was his
ambassador to France in 1602. Home even had an audience with Elizabeth
I on his return journey as his Catholicism was overlooked in favour of his
good Border service. He escaped persecution until 1606, when he was
confined to Edinburgh.[142]

Scottish Catholics were not persecuted with the ferocity prevalent in
England during the later-sixteenth century, but they remained localised and
weak. Both Lords Home were part of a Catholic minority in the Merse, with
only a few kinsmen and their immediate household being Catholic. In East
Teviotdale there were more Catholics, but Ferniehirst failed to convince his
kinsmen to follow his faith so Catholic lairds remained a minority in 1603.
Sir George Home of Spott, a younger son of Manderston was possibly a
recusant in 1595, though he later conformed and rose to great heights. There
was no equivalent of the Collingwoods or Grays here, but Catholicism was
much stronger in the Western Scottish Borders owing to the influence of the
powerful Maxwell family and their support for the counter-Reformation.
Many inhabitants of their nearest burgh, Dumfries, were cited for recusancy
in 1601.[143]

v. Ministry, morality and church property

As the lairds were noticeably more Protestant than the gentry, more of their
younger sons became ministers. John Spottiswoode, a younger son of the
Spottiswoodes in the Merse was a noted pre-Reformation Protestant and
became superintendent of Lothian within the reformed kirk. His son John
Spottiswoode later became archbishop of St Andrews when Episcopalianism
was in government favour. Other younger sons such as Adam Home of
Polwarth at Polwarth, Andrew Home of Wedderburn at Lauder and
William Ker of Ferniehirst at Bedrule all conformed at the Reformation.
Thomas Ker of Cessford became archdean of Teviotdale in the 1560s and
younger sons who became ministers after the Reformation included Robert
French of Thornydykes (Eccles, Greenlaw and Hume), David Home of
Ninewells (Chirnside), John Spottiswoode of Spottiswoode (Mordington,
Nenthorn and Longformacus), Thomas Cranston of Morriston (Leger-
wood), Alexander Home of Fairnieside (Dunbar) and George Home of
Blackadder (Smailholm). John Ker of Faldonside, whose mother was John
Knox's widow, became minister of Prestonpans in East Lothian after the
incumbent minister John Davidson 'solemnly charged him to cast off his
scarlet cloak, lay aside his gilded rapier and take to his book . . .' On the
other hand, William Ker of Linton, a priest at Galashiels and later reader at
Lindean, was deprived for smuggling Jesuits across the Border.[144] Lairds'
sons as seminary priests are difficult to trace though Mark Ker was at the

Scots college at Douai in 1582 and George Ker of Newbattle was a well-known counter-Reformation priest with Border connections.[145]

Lapses in Scottish church discipline resembled those in England as there were many feuds over church lands, ministers' stipends and teinds.[146] Violence flared when John Mow of that Ilk murdered Robert Burr at Mow kirk in 1540 and the Pringles fought amongst themselves in Stow churchyard in 1591. For unknown reasons the Kers of Dalcove and Shaw destroyed Haig of Bemersyde's pew in Mertoun church in 1598 and the Swintons of that Ilk harassed the minister of Swinton in 1588. An attack on the minister of Langton was supported by the Cockburns of Langton, who 'maist cruellie and unmercifullie persewit him for his bodilee harme and slauchter, hurte and woudit him in divers pairtis of his body to the effusion of his blude in grite quantitie . . .' The minister exaggerated somewhat as he only lost a finger, yet this incident demonstrates how otherwise 'godly' men could turn to violence in pursuit of profit from church lands. Ungodly behaviour was not confined to the landed families for in 1576 the parishioners of Hutton and Edrom were remonstrated for breaking the Sabbath and were ordered not to gather the teind grain 'in tyme of sermons or prayers'.[147]

Sir John Ker of Hirsel was excommunicated for adultery in 1589 after his brother-in-law, George Home of Wedderburn, wrote to the ministers of Teviotdale to complain about his 'woman'. He divorced but was not allowed to remarry until his excommunication was absolved in 1603. Ker had remarried in 1590 using an English vicar, but the kirk refused to recognise this ceremony.[148] A few lairds could therefore appear as promiscuous as some of the English gentry, but there was probably a slowing down in immorality as the reformed kirk really began to take control of Eastern Border parishes from *circa* 1580 onwards. Lairds' illegitimate children could be fortunate as James Pringle of Galashiels was born illegitimate and later legitimised to inherit his father's estates, whilst the Lords Home called their bastard sons 'provosts' of Dunglass.[149]

Monastic land in Scotland shared a similar fate to England though the process of secularisation differed as the lairds and nobility grasped monastic lands before and after the Scottish Reformation.[150] The Home lairds held a dominant share of the religious houses of the Merse with Cowdenknowes holding Eccles, Manderston at one time controlling Coldingham, and Lord Home holding Jedburgh, Abbey St Bathans and Coldingham. However the lairds were just as irresponsible as the gentry when it came to repairing local churches or paying ministers' stipends and the thirds of benefices. Andrew Home, commendator of Jedburgh did not pay the minister of Jedburgh's stipend for several years in the 1580s and Lord Home and William Home of Ayton were both ordered to pay stipends during the 1590s. The thirds proved to be an unpopular payment with Protestants and Catholics alike. The Protestant lairds should have willingly paid their thirds to help the reformed kirk, yet avarice made them pay as grudgingly as the Catholic Lord

Home. Home of Cowdenknowes and Home of Wedderburn were also slow to pay their thirds for Eccles and Hutton.[151]

Scottish church repairs were not the responsibility of a patron, though the local lairds were supposed to contribute. English armies had battered the churches of the Merse and Teviotdale in the 1540s and they were still not fixed by the time of the Reformation in 1560. Swinton church was attacked in 1542 as it was used as a shelter. The archbishop of St Andrews was concerned in 1555 that over twenty-five churches were in need of repair, but repairs did not follow as Home of Ayton was lambasted in 1558–9 for letting the choir of Ayton kirk fall into disrepair. It was choked with doves and water dripped onto the altar as five new slates were needed.[152] By the 1590s Merse churches were still not satisfactory for Lord Home was ordered to repair all the 'ruinous' kirks within his newly acquired priory of Coldingham and Cockburnspath's parishioners were ordered to rebuild their church.[153]

Protestantism was established on the Scottish side of the Eastern Borders more rapidly than on the English side, yet progress was hampered by similar problems; a shortage of Protestant clergy, poorly endowed charges, churches in a bad state of maintenance and lingering Catholicism. Catholicism was a greater problem in England, but the few Catholics on the Scottish side were powerful men who could have caused much trouble for the government had they not been deserted by their kinsmen or forced into occasional exile. The greed of landed men surpassed religious constraints everywhere, but the number of disputes over church land in this region was high. Religious loyalty took second place to political allegiance in England but in Scotland they were interlinked. A Catholic laird unless he were of the status of Ferniehirst could not hold office or advance up the social ladder. As the Home lairds were overwhelmingly Protestant this undoubtedly contributed to their success. By 1603 most of the lairds were Protestant, yet the Northumbrian gentry remained divided in one of the most marked differences between the Scottish and English Eastern Borders.

Notes

1 A sample of this debate can be found in P. Collinson, *The Birthpangs of Protestant England* (Basingstoke, 1991), E. Duffy, *The Stripping of the Altars. Traditional Religion in England 1400–1580* (New Haven, 1992), J. Maltby, *Prayer Book and People in Elizabethan and Early Stuart England* (Cambridge, 2000), N. Tyack, ed. *England's Long Reformation* (London 1998), A. Walsham, *Church Papists. Catholicism, Conformity and Confessional Polemic in Early Modern England* (London, 1993), R. Whiting, *The Blind Devotion of the People* (Cambridge, 1991).

2 The diocese covered the counties of Norham and Islandshire (North Durham), Northumberland and County Durham in the sixteenth century.

3 M. H. and R. Dodds, *The Pilgrimage of Grace 1536–7 and the Exeter Conspiracy 1538* (Cambridge, 1915), vols i & ii. See ch. iii.

4 M. A. Clark, 'Reformation in the Far North: Cumbria and the Church, 1500–1571', *NH*, xxxii (1996), 75–89, especially 76, 'Northern light? Parochial life in a "dark corner" of Tudor England', in K. French, G. Gibbs & B. Kumin, eds. *The Parish in English Life 1400–1600* (Manchester, 1997), 56–73 and 'Cross-Border clergy movements in the Reformation West March', *Transactions of the Cumberland and Westmorland Antiquarian and Archaeological Society*, xcviii (1998), 309–12. H. Summerson, *Medieval Carlisle*, ii, 624–32, 640–49. B. Usher, 'Durham and Winchester Episcopal Estates and the Elizabethan Settlement: A Reappraisal', *Journal of Ecclesiastical History*, xlix (1998), 393–406.

5 Based on surviving wills and their preambles in particular (DPRW), exchequer records (PRO E377) and state papers. Those listed without a death date lived beyond 1603. See Meikle. *Thesis*, ch v. app.

6 C. M. Fraser, 'Recusant wives, widows and daughters', *Northern Catholic History*, 33 (1992), 3–8. C. Newman, 'The role of women in early Yorkshire recusancy: a reappraisal', *Northern Catholic History*, 30 (1989), 8–16. M. B. Rowlands, 'Recusant women 1560–1640', in M. Prior, ed. *Women in English Society 1500–1800* (Oxford, 1985), 149–180.

7 BL MS Cotton, Titus, F, xiii, 249.

8 *APC*, xxix, 111–12. *CBP*, ii, 631. B. W. Beckingsale, 'The Characteristics of the Tudor North', *NH*, iv (1969), 76. T. Bowler, 'Some Notes On The Recusant Rolls Of The Exchequer', *Recusant History*, iv (1958), 182–3.

9 *CSPDom Add*, 1580–1625, 231–2. Beckingsale, 'Characteristics', 77.

10 *CSPScot*, x, 630. *APC*, xiv, 15; xxxi, 27.

11 For further details of Tunstall's near deprivation in 1552 see D. MacCulloch, *Thomas Cranmer* (New Haven, 1996), 162, 459, 498–99, 517, 553.

12 *L&P. Hen VIII*, viii, 375. D. M. Loades, *The Last Years of Cuthbert Tunstall, 1547–1559* (Durham, 1973). A. Forster, 'Bishop Tunstall's Priests', *Recusant History*, ix (1968), 175–204.

13 *CSPScot*, i, 488. Robert Selby was vicar there during 1541–65. *CSP For*, 1560–1, 683.

14 *CSP For*, 1560–1, 709. *HMC*, Salisbury, i, 311. *SS*, xxii (1850), 36–41. *L & P. Hen VIII*, xvi, 612. C. M. Fraser, 'Catholic Clergy in the Diocese of Durham, 1563', *Northern Catholic History* 38 (1997), 20–27.

15 *CSP Scot*, ii, 9. *CSPDom Add*, 1547–65, 577. S. M. Keeling, 'The Reformation in The Anglo-Scottish Border Counties', *NH*, xv (1979), 31.

16 J. Raine, 'The injunctions and other ecclesiastical proceedings of Richard Barnes, bishop of Durham 1575–87', *SS*, xxii (1850) 13–23, 36–41, 76–9. *L & P. Hen VIII*, xiv, pt 1, 334.

17 *CSPScot*, ii, 668. *CBP*, ii, 763.

18 *CBP*, ii, 228. G. Carleton, *The Life of Bernard Gilpin* (London, 1629), 19, 26. E. Duffy, 'The Long Reformation: Catholicism. Protestantism and the multitude', in Tyack, ed. *England's Long Reformation*, 38–9. D. Marcombe, 'Bernard Gilpin Anatomy of an Elizabethan Legend', *NH*, xvi (1980), 20–39.

19 *NCH*, i, 95; ii, 285, 491; xiv, 86, 461. *CBP*, ii, 631.

20 BRO B6/11 fo. 12. *HMC*, Salisbury, xv, 351–2. J. Scott, *Berwick Upon Tweed; the history of the town and guild* (London, 1888), 351–2.

21 *NCH*, ii, 70, 163, 391, 444; v, 434; xi, 103, 126, 286, 365; xiv, 364, 570; xv, 319.

22 DDR ii, 4, f. 94. *AA*, 4th ser, xli, 133. *CBP*, ii, 171, 184, 881.

23 DPRW 1551–7.

24 DPRW.

25 DPRW 1596/1.

26 *SS*, ii (1835), xxxviii (1860), cxii (1906), cxlii (1929).

27 DPRW 1602. C. Marsh, ' "Departing well and christianly" will making and popular religion in early modern England', in E. J. Carlson, ed. *Religion and the English People 1500–1640* (Kirksville, Missouri, 1998), 201–44.

28 D. Cressy, 'Death and the social order: the funerary preferences of Elizabethan gentlemen', *Continuity and Change*, v (1990), 99–119. For the costs of gentry funerals see ch. iv.

29 J. D. Alsop, 'Religious Preambles in Early Modern English Wills as Formulae', *Journal of Ecclesiastical History*, xl (1989), 19–27. L. C. Attreed, 'Preparation for death in sixteenth-century England', *Sixteenth Century Journal*, xiii (1982), 37–66. M. C. Cross, 'The Development of Protestantism in Leeds and Hull, 1520–1640: the Evidence of Wills', *NH*, xviii (1982), 230–8. D. Hickman, 'From Catholic to Protestant: the changing meaning of testamentary religious provisions in Elizabethan London,' in Tyack, ed. *England's Long Reformation*, 117–39. R. Houlbrooke, *Death, Religion, and the Family in England, 1480–1750* (Oxford, 1998), chs 4 & 5. C. Litzenberger, 'Local responses to religious changes: evidence from Gloucestershire wills', in Carlson, ed. *Religion and the English People*, 245–70. G. L. Mayhew, 'The Progress of the Reformation in East Sussex, 1530–1559: the evidence of wills', *Southern History*, v (1983), 38–67. M. Spufford, *Contrasting Communities* (Cambridge, 1979), 320–1. M. L. Zell, 'The Use of Religious Preambles as a Measure of Religious Belief in the Sixteenth Century', *BIHR*, l (1977), 246–9.

30 The list in *CRS*, liii 54–61 should be dated 1592 and not 1582, for it closely resembles the first recusant roll, but J. A. Hilton thinks it is 1595–6 in 'Catholicism in Elizabethan Northumberland', *NH*, xiii (1977), 53.

31 *L&I*, ix, 99. *CSPDom Add*, 1580–1625, 355. *CBP*, ii, 631.

32 *APC*, xxxi, 26–7.

33 *CBP*, ii, 1331.

34 PRO SP12/278/53. R. M. Gard, 'Northumberland Recusants, 1592–1601', *Northern Catholic History*, 23 (1986), 13.

35 P. Tyler, 'The Significance of The Ecclesiastical Commission at York', *NH*, ii (1967), 27–44. Watts, *Border To Middle Shire*, 79. A. D. Wright, 'Catholic History, North and South, Revisited', *NH*, xxv (1989), 120–34.

36 PRO C142/227/195. *CBP*, i, 458. *APC*, vi, 254–5. *CSPDom Add*, 1580–1625, 231–2. *SS*, xxxviii (1860), 235. See ch. vii.

37 PRO E377/1, E377/10.

38 *CRS*, liii (1960), 58.

39 *CBP*, ii, 217. *CRS*, liii, 58, 63. *CSPDom*, 1595–7, 354; 1598–1601, 362.

40 PRO ADM 74/85, 75/71, SP23/133/53 (Manor of Cartington), E377/1, E377/11 (Durham), E401/1854, E401/1858, E401/1871.

41 PRO SP59/36 fos 179–80. *CBP*, ii, 862.

42 *CBP*, i. 458. *APC*, xxv, p. 127. M.C. Cross, 'The Third Earl of Huntingdon and The Trials of Catholics in the North, 1581–1595', *Recusant History*, viii (1966), 136–46.

43 *CSPDom Add*, 1580–1625, 342–3. *Sadler Papers*, ii, 204–05.

44 BIHR PR 23a, fos 122–3. PRO E377/1, E377/10. *CSPDom Add*, 1580–1625, 231–2, 365.

45 *CBP*, i, 458. *CRS*, liii (1960), 150. Watts, *Border to Middle Shire*, 79.

46 *CSPDom Add,* 1580–1625, 365.
47 *CBP,* i, 877.
48 DPRW 1602. *CSPDom,* 1591–4, 200. *CSPDom Add,* 1580–1625, 365. *NCH,* i, 158–9. M. M. Meikle, 'A Godly Rogue: the career of Sir John Forster, an Elizabethan Border Warden', *NH,* xxviii (1992), 135–6.
49 *CBP,* i, 126, 458. *APC,* xxii, 482. L. Stone, *The Crisis of the Aristocracy* (Oxford, 1965), 252.
50 DPRW 1604. See ch. v.
51 J. Melville, *The Autobiography and Diary of Mr. James Melville,* ed. R. Pitcairn, (Wodrow Society, 1842), 227. G. Donaldson, 'Scottish Presbyterian Exiles In England, 1584–8', *RSCHS,* xiv (1962), 67–80.
52 *CSPSpain,* 1587–1603, 154.
53 *NCH,* i, 156.
54 *CSPDom Add,* 1580–1625, 367. *CBP,* ii, 631. See ch. iii.
55 *CBP,* i, 458, 515. *CSPDom Add,* 1580–1625, 231–2. *CSPScot,* iii, 84.
56 *APC,* xxvi, 408. *CBP,* ii, 1291.
57 PRO SP15/32/50.
58 *CSPDom Add,* 1580–1625, 193. *CBP,* ii, 351. *NCH,* xiv, 527–8, 537.
59 PRO STAC5 C16/4, E134/23 Eliz/HIL 2, SP13/F/11, SP15/32/59. *CBP,* i, 435.
60 PRO C66/1421 m. 11d, SP13/F/11. R. B. Manning, *Religion and Society In Elizabethan Sussex* (Leicester, 1969), 242–51. See ch. iii.
61 C. Haigh, *Reformation and Resistance in Tudor Lancashire* (Cambridge, 1975), 87. Cliffe, *Yorkshire Gentry,* 167, 210–30, 240–4.
62 *APC,* x, 79–80.
63 *CSPDom Add,* 1566–79, 416. *CSP For,* 1572–4, 472.
64 Beckingsale, 'Characteristics', 73. Hilton, 'Catholicism', 47.
65 Hatfield MS C.P. 235/68. Hilton, 'Catholicism', 46. See ch. iii.
66 S. M. Keeling, 'The Reformation In The Anglo-Scottish Border Counties', *NH,* xv (1979), 41.
67 *AA,* 4th ser, xli (1963), 133.
68 R. G. Usher, *The Reconstruction of the English Church* (New York, 1910), i, 135.
69 Watts, *Border to Middle Shire,* 86. J. A. Hilton, 'Catholicism In Jacobean Northumberland', *Northern Catholic History,* vii (1978), 10–19.
70 *CSPSpain,* 1580–6, 470.
71 T. M. McCoog, *The Society of Jesus in Ireland, Scotland and England 1541–1588* (Leiden, 1996), 129–77.
72 Chillingham Castle, Documents, 6. Raine, *North Durham,* 225.
73 *CRS,* liii (1960), 152.
74 PRO E377/10.
75 A. Morey, *The Catholic Subjects of Elizabeth I* (New Jersey, 1978), 136.
76 *SS,* xxxviii (1860), 268.
77 DDR, Durham Consistory Court Act Book, 1581–2, fos 7–8. *APC,* xi, 291. *CSPDom Add,* 1566–79, 383–4, 416. *NCH,* ii, 432.
78 PRO C66/1340 m. 39. *CSPDom,* 1595–7, 458. Carey, *Memoirs,* 37. See ch. v.
79 DDR iii, 3 fo. 111, iii, 4 unfoliated.
80 See ch. vii.
81 DDR ii, 4, fo. 135; ii, 5, fo. 38.
82 PRO ADM 75/71. DDR iii, 5. unfoliated. 9 July 1596. DPRW 1560–9. DPRW, v, f. 68. M. C. Cross, 'Sin and society: the northern high commission and the

northern gentry in the reign of Elizabeth I', in Cross, Loades & Scarisbrick (eds), *Law and Government under the Tudors* (Cambridge, 1988), 195–209. For a fuller discussion of illegitimacy see ch. i.

83 R. Phillimore, *The Ecclesiastical Law* (London, 1873), ii, 1777.

84 DDR ii, 4, fos 27, 33, 86, 87, 90, 105. DDR ii, 5, fos 11, 13, 14.

85 Raine, *North Durham*, 148.

86 DPRW 1601. DDR ii, 4, fos 26, 86, 90, 95, 102. DDR ii, 5, 12, 14, 22.

87 DDR ii, 5, fo. 33.

88 *CBP*, i, 191, 240. *cf.* A. Foster, 'Churchwardens' accounts of early modern England and Wales: some problems to note, but much to be gained', in French, Gibbs & Kumin, eds. *The Parish in English Life*, 74–93.

89 *CSP Dom Add*, 1601–03, 214. *CPR*, 1560–3, 120. See ch. iv.

90 Raine, *North Durham*, 30–1.

91 G. Tate, *History of the Burgh, Castle and Barony of Alnwick* (Alnwick, 1866–69), ii, 27–8.

92 PRO E318/10/450. *CPR*, 1578–80, 1301. *L & P. Hen VIII*, xvi, 727.

93 e.g. John Carr of Hetton PRO (E318/7/246), Robert Collingwood of Eslington (E318/27/1534), Robert Roddam, Tristram Fenwick, and Sir Thomas Gray (E310/21/107) and Ralph Gray (E310/21/109). For tithe feuds see ch. vii.

94 *APS*, iii, 72.

95 *The Works of John Knox*, ed. D. Laing (Edinburgh, 1846–64), vi, 78.

96 *CSP Scot*, i, 488.

97 See ch. ii.

98 M. H. Merriman, 'The Assured Scots', *SHR*, xlvii (1968), 10–34. Keeling, 'Reformation', 28, 49–50.

99 M. Lynch, 'Calvinism in Scotland, 1559–1638' in *International Calvinism*, ed. M. Prestwich (Oxford, 1985), 229. NLS ADV MS 1/14. fos 50–7.

100 Keeling estimates that there were 83 parishes (cures) in Merse and Teviotdale, Keeling, 'Reformation', 26. In my definition of the Scottish Eastern Borders I estimate there were c. 60 parishes in 1574, viz:- Abbey St Bathans, Ancrum, Ayton, Bunkle and Preston, Channelkirk, Chirnside, Coldingham, Coldstream, Crailing, Cranshaws, Duns, Earlston, Eckford, Eccles, Ednam, Edrom, Ellem, Fishwick, Fogo, Foulden, Galashiels, Gordon, Greenlaw, Hilton, Home, Hownam, Hutton, Jedburgh, Kelso, Langton, Ladykirk, Lamberton, Lauder, Legerwood, Lempitlaw, Linton, Longformacus, Longnewton, Makerstoun, Maxton, Melrose, Mertoun, Mordington and Lamberton, Morebattle, Mow, Nenthorn, Nisbet, Oxnam, Polwarth, Roxburgh, St Boswells, Simprim and Lennel, Smailholm, Sprouston, Stitchill, Swinton, Upsettlington and Horndean (united 1600), Westruther, Whitsome and Yetholm. Figures based on H. Scott, *Fasti Ecclesiae Scoticanae* (Edinburgh, 1916–51), vols ii, viii.

101 NAS E47/3. E47/8. Scott, *Fasti*, ii, 18.

102 I. B. Cowan, *The Scottish Reformation* (London, 1982), 165, 176. HMC, Salisbury, i, 174.

103 Calderwood, *History*, iv, 662.

104 Lesley, *History*, i, 101–02.

105 I. B. Cowan, 'The Reformation in Dumfriesshire', *Transactions of The Dumfriesshire and Galloway Natural History and Antiquarian Society*, 3rd ser, lvi (1981), 82–90. *CBP*, ii, 1031.

106 The priests were sir John Black in Bunkle, sir John Affleck in Greenlaw, Dene Robert Mylne in Mertoun, John Forrest in Swinton, sir Andrew Currie in

Westruther (Bassendean), sir Hew Hudson in Whitsome, William Johnston in Ancrum, sir James Douglas in Crailing, John Brown in Ednam, sir William Ainslie in Maxton, sir Robert Wilson in Morebattle, William Ormiston in Nenthorn (who was a minor laird in his own right at Easter Muirdean), sir Thomas Ker in Roxburgh, and sir James Williamson in Yetholm. NLS MS 17.1.4. fos 50–7. *RPC*, ii, 40. Scott, *Fasti*, ii, 18, 59, 68, 82, 86, 94, 98, 165.

107 *RPC*, iv, 522. Calderwood, *History*, iv, 662. Pitcairn, *Trials*, i, pt 2, 35, 190.

108 *BUK*, i, 6, 40.

109 *CBP*, i, 458, 515, 519. *HMC*, Salisbury, iii, 135.

110 Newbattle's son George was a priest caught with the infamous Spanish Blanks, and two of his children married into the strongly Catholic Maxwell family. PRO SP52/42/27. *SP*, v, 455–6. Spottiswoode, *History*, ii, 425. *The Records of the Synod of Lothian and Tweeddale, 1589–96, 1640–49*, ed. J. Kirk (Stair Society, 1977), 46–7.

111 W. Forbes-Leith, *Narratives of Scottish Catholics* (Edinburgh, 1885), 168–70. *RPC*, iv, 465. McCoog, *The Society of Jesus*, 178–223.

112 *CBP*, i, 457, 760. *CSP Scot*, vii, 19. *CSPDom Add*, 1580–1625, 111. *APC*, iii, 232–3.

113 Calderwood, *History*, iv, 662. *HMC*, Salisbury, iv, 31, 188. See note 148.

114 *APS*, ii, 525–6. G. Donaldson, *All The Queen's Men* (London, 1983), 162.

115 *CSP For*, 1560–1, 792. *CSP Scot*, i, 751. Knox, *History*, i, 316.

116 *CSP Scot*, i, 934.

117 NAS CC8/8/33. *BUK*, 52, 164, 203, 290, 352, 418, 436, 470, 526, 532, 544, 704, 707, 873.

118 *BUK*, ii, 532.

119 Calderwood, *History*, iii, 645. Donaldson, *Queen's Men*, 136–9. (on 162 Donaldson wrongly ascribes Ker of Kersland to the Eastern Borders. Kersland was in Ayrshire).

120 *BUK*, iii, 755. *RPC*, iv, 465. Calderwood, *History*, iv, 44. Spottiswoode, *History*, ii, 381.

121 *CSPScot*, xi, 201, 323. M. H. B. Sanderson, in 'Catholic Recusancy In Scotland In The Sixteenth Century', *IR*, xxi (1970) 99, quotes Cowdenknowes as being hostile to the reformed faith, but he was a noted supporter of the Reformation.

122 NAS RD1/48 fos 199–201. Melville, *Diary*, 219.

123 NAS RH 15/19/14. *CBP*, ii, 1090. *CSPScot*, xiii, 122. Godscroft, *History*, 392–3. *The Miscellany of the Wodrow Society* (1844), 432–3.

124 Knox, *History*, i, 261. *Mary of Lorraine, Corresp*, 368.

125 *CSP Scot*, iii, 84. *CSP Spain*, 1568–79, 172.

126 Forbes-Leith, *Narratives*, 171.

127 *BUK*, ii, 589.

128 BL MS Cotton Caligula, C. VII fo. 341. *SP*, v, 67–72. *CSP Scot*, x, 721. *CSP Spain*, 1587–1603, 746. *HMC*, Salisbury, xi, 168. Calderwood, *History*, iv, 662.

129 *BUK*, i, 110. *CSP Rome*, 1558–71, 280, 340, 803. *CSP Scot*, i, 1010.

130 *CSP Dom Add*, 1566–79, 249. *SP*, iv, 462–3. *RMS*, vii, 1611.

131 Forbes-Leith, *Narratives*, 177. This faction included northern nobility, such as the earl of Huntly.

132 *CSP Scot*, vi, 165. *HMC*, Home, 40. Donaldson, *Queen's Men*, 140–2.

133 *APS*, iii, 423. *CBP*, i, 587. *CSP Scot*, ix, 597; x, 38, 53. *BUK*, iii, 698, 706, 718, 720.

134 *CSP Scot*, x, 607, 647, 655. *Records of the Synod of Lothian and Tweeddale*, 30, 36.
135 *CSP Scot*, x, 713, 720, 776. *Records of the Synod of Lothian and Tweeddale*, 47. The Home-Tyrie kinship was based upon Tyrie's uncle David's widow, who remarried John Oliphant of Oliphant. Lord Home's first wife was the widow of Laurence Oliphant, elder brother of John. James Tyrie was another well known Jesuit. NRAS 859/6/4 859/9/3. *SP*, iv, 283. *CSP Dom*, 1595–7, 27. *HMC, Salisbury*, iv, 30; v, 122; xiii, 341. T. G. Law, ed. *Catholic Tractates of the Sixteenth Century 1573–1600* (Scottish Text Society, 1901), xxx.
136 *BUK*, iii, 834. *CBP*, i, 852. *CSP Scot*, xi, 156–7, 177. *CSP Spain*, 1587–1603, 617. *The Historie and Life of King James the Sext*, (Bannatyne Club, 1825), 279–80. *Records of the Synod of Lothian and Tweeddale*, 54, 66.
137 *CSP Scot*, xi, 135. Melville, *Diary*, 310. *BUK*, iii, 833. *SP*, vi, 373. Calderwood, *History*, v, 263.
138 *CSP Scot*, xi, 186, xiii, 279. Calderwood, *History*, v, 222.
139 BL MS Cotton Caligula. D. II fo. 186. *BUK*, iii, 821, 835–6, 838–42. McCrie, *The Life of Andrew Melville* (Edinburgh, 1819), ii, 44.
140 *CSP Scot*, xi, 289. Calderwood, *History*, v, 329.
141 NAS CC8/8/44. *CSP Scot*, xiii, 299, 329, 356, 359, 797, 811, 816, 825, 841. *HMC, Salisbury*, ix, 151; xi, 73. See ch. i.
142 *CSP Scot*, xiii, 832, 854. *BUK*, iii, 964, 967, 981, 984, 1025. Forbes-Leith, *Narratives*, 374 and Wormald, *Community*, 78. See ch ii.
143 Calderwood, *History*, v, 366. Moysie, *Memoirs*, 67. *RPC*, vi, 326–7, 355. K. M. Brown, 'The Making of a Politique', *SHR*, lxvi (1987), 152–175.
144 NRAS 1100/618. *RSS*, ii, 3838; vi, 718. Scott, *Fasti*, i, 175, 388, 406; ii, 18, 24, 27, 82, 153, 156, 160–1, 176; viii, 135. Spottiswoode, *History*, ii, 336. This proportion of younger sons of lairds as ministers conflicts with the general conclusions of W. Makey, *The Church of the Covenant, 1637–1651* (Edinburgh, 1979), 97–9.
145 *Records of the Scots Colleges at Douai, Rome, Valladolid and Ratisbon*, ed. R. Fraser (New Spalding Club, 1906), 3.
146 NAS RD1/45 fo. 142, RD1/19 fos 417–24. *CSPScot*, vii, 26, 113, 304, 306; x, 730, 749; xi, 186, 637. *RPC*, ii, 56, 596–7; iii, 224–5, 552–3; iv, 115, 274, 284, 352–3, 522, 717, 724; v, 653, 666. *HMC, Home*, 93. See ch. vii.
147 NRAS 859/1/2. *RPC*, iv, 274, 352–3, 574–5, 630, 669, 692, 720; v, 534, 715.
148 NAS GD267/31/6. *HMC, Salisbury*, iv, 31; *Home*, 315; Milne-Home, 128, 130–1. Calderwood, *History*, vi, 205.
149 *SP*, iv, 463, 465. *RMS*, iv, 2982. See ch. i.
150 *Liber S. Marie de Dryburgh* (Bannatyne Club, 1847), 285, 297–9, 324, 338–40, 343–5, 347–8 *etc. Selections from the Records of the Regality of Melrose*, ed. C. S. Romanes, (Scottish History Society, 1917), iii, 275, 329, 348–50. See ch. iv.
151 NAS E48/1/1 fo. 187, E53/8. RD1/24/1 fo. 197. *Records of the Synod of Lothian and Tweeddale*, 77. See ch. iv.
152 NAS CH8/16, CH8/19. *L & P. Hen VIII*, xvii, 1137, 1140.
153 NAS CH8/16. *Records of the Synod of Lothian and Tweeddale*, 77. *BUK*, ii, 720. G. Donaldson, *The Scottish Reformation* (Cambridge, 1979), 23.

7

Feuds, Fights and Disputes: The Nature of Landed Disorder in the Eastern Borders

Feuding was a common disorder in sixteenth-century Scotland and England when 'tempers were short and weapons to hand' and 'loyalty to a friend in a quarrel was a moral duty, regardless of the merits of the case.'[1] The Eastern Border disputes mostly conformed to patterns of bloodfeud and property squabbles found elsewhere, even in so-called civilised societies. Alliances shifted according to the circumstances of the feud and the privy councils of both nations used arbiters, marriages and financial penalties to try to pacify feuds. Settlement could be slow or ineffective until the late-sixteenth century. Government and church abhorred all violence, but contemporary opinion appeared to sanction murder if it was part of a feud. Feuding was fairly constant in landed society, whereas domestic crimes were relatively rare. There was very little cross-border feuding amongst landed families in the East as their ideology was fundamentally different to that of the Western Borders. Rebels were more of a problem in England with the Northern Rebellion enticing a few younger sons, though Scotland had a few insurgent lairds as well. The Northern Rebellion was the only instance where there was anything resembling 'British' polity, as both countries co-operated to quell this rising. Domestic crimes were normally prosecuted through the separate legal pro-cesses of each country, rather than through Border law. Here they concerned petty theft, debts and patricide. Many were later pardoned for their crimes on both sides of the Border, though some of the lairds received far more severe punishment for their wrongdoing than the gentry.

I. Border Feuding

English Border officials could exaggerate the intensity of feuding in order to look successful in a difficult region and boost their standing at court. Lord Grey of Wilton, warden of the East March from 1559–1562, is typical, for in 1560 he boasted that he had pacified the entire March by ending three local feuds.[2] It would have been impossible to end all the local controversies of the English East March this easily. Grey did settle the Forster and Muschamp feud which had shaken the countryside and compelled the local gentry to take sides. However, this was really a non-violent power struggle between the families of Forster and Gray, but true to fashion he reported that

There is daily armour and weapon used both to the church, the market, and the field, as in time of war; as no man here minds to deal in the matter it is needful that some be sent from the Queen and Council to make an end hereof.[3]

Lord Grey failed to mention that ill-feeling still persisted throughout Northumberland over the Heron and Carr feud, whose parties were allegedly more ready to 'overthrow each other than face the enemy'.[4] This was the more likely reason behind the arming of the gentry.

There is little doubt that bloodfeuds were fought with equal vigour on both sides of the frontier, yet Elizabethan courtiers were often reluctant to admit to feuding amongst their own people. They arrogantly criticised the Scots for their disturbances as Sir Robert Cecil informed James VI in 1602 that 'quarrels and feods are here unusual.'[5] This was very hypocritical as there were feuds in Northumberland and elsewhere in England at this time. Only four years previously Cecil had been reprimanded by the dean of Durham for the

> many feuds about our northern borders . . . our neighbours of Scotland have lately composed all theirs among themselves. You could not do a better peace of service than require all three wardens to cause an end of the bloody and horrible murders almost daily committed among us.

The earl of Huntingdon thought that English mischief makers were just copying the Scots in 1593, but his was hardly fair comment. There was no Eastern Scottish Border equivalent of the 1597 feud between the Grays and the Selbies, which had prompted the governor of Berwick to put armed soldiers on every street corner.[6]

Feuds were still designated a 'Border mischief' by contemporaries and past historians have tended to concentrate on Border feuding in isolation. By comparing the Border feuds to a supposedly civil society they appear violent, but this approach is no longer acceptable.[7] Further research has shown that the Borderers should not be singled out for their lawlessness as this region was, for example, little different from the rest of Scotland where feuding was concerned. Keith Brown's research has shown that the Borders accounted for only twenty-three per cent of all feuds in Scotland during 1573–1625, whereas the Lowlands were worst at forty per cent.[8] There were also the usual differences between East and West Borders with fewer cross-border feuds occurring in the more peaceable East. West Border bloodfeuds between the English Grahams and Scots Irvines, or the Fenwicks and the Elliots were a recurrent nightmare for administrators. The four known cross-border feuds in the East between the Kers and the Forsters, Selbies and Stories, or the Burns and the Collingwoods were not prolonged bloodfeuds. Eastern Border authorities therefore had fewer deadly feuds to worry about.[9]

It is highly significant that landed families in the Eastern Borders were able to have a comfortable existence without resorting to cross-border reiving.[10] Underlying poverty was part of Western Border feuding ideology, not the East. This economic division ultimately sets the Eastern Borderers apart from those of the West. However, this did not mean that they were non-violent. Domestic feuds and disputes were commonplace, just as in any other landed community in early modern times.

Definitions of feud vary though the Scottish parliament of 1598 defined 'feud' as involving no slaughter, slaughter on one side only, or slaughter on both sides.[11] In reality feuds were more complicated and extensive as they could range from minor squabbles over lands or teinds to long-lasting, murderous bloodfeuds. 'Deadly feuds' have to be distinguished from lesser property disputes that could be swiftly resolved by arbitration. Surviving evidence about property disputes is more plentiful on the Scottish side with privy council registers recording much civil litigation. English evidence is scant as the local gentry would have taken their disputes to the Council of the North and its records are missing. Only nineteen cases reached the London courts of Exchequer, Requests, Chancery and Star Chamber, but such was the increase in civil litigation after 1540 that there must have been many more cases.[12] Property disputes could be minor boundary squabbles between neighbours or deliberately provoked aggression between political rivals disguised as a territorial feud, but they rarely involved murder. Feuding could also be about local offices or unknown causes that cannot be clearly defined as property disputes or bloodfeuds. The feud alliances of landed families were rarely stable. In major bloodfeuds such as the Herons against the Carrs or the Kers and the Scotts sworn enemies were known to fight on the same side. The lairds and gentlemen therefore determined their priorities in feuds according to the seriousness of the quarrel and their immediate loyalties within the landed community.

Feuding persisted in the Borders until well after the Union of the Crowns, but it was cross-border feuding before 1603 that was feared most by the local population. Both Sir Robert Carey and Lord Eure as wardens of the English East and Middle Marches were horrified at the lack of reprisal against Scottish thieves, as the local gentry dared not kill a Scot 'for fear of feud'. This perhaps contributed to the lack of cross-border feuds in the Eastern Borders, but there were fundamentally better cross-border relations here to begin with.[13] The majority of the thieves Carey referred to came from the Scottish Middle March and not from the more prosperous and peaceable Scottish East March. The Scottish East March was, however, only 'peaceable' in terms of cross-border raiding, for the disorders of feuding and domestic crime were spread throughout the Eastern Borders.

Bloodfeuds were invariably murderous and resulted in the same futile savagery of repeated blood spilling. There were thirty-eight known blood-feuds in the Eastern Borders, one of which confronted the preacher Bernard

Gilpin whilst preaching in Rothbury church in the 1560s. It was between the Ellerkers and Lisles, and the Herons.[14] The feuding parties edged nearer each other and when they drew their swords for a second time Gilpin stopped his sermon and

> commeth downe from the pulpit, and stepping to the ringleaders of either faction, first of all he appeased the tumult. Next he laboureth to establish peace betwixt them, but he could not prevaile in that: onely they promised to keepe the peace unbroken so long as Mr. Gilpin should remain in the Church.

Gilpin returned to the pulpit infuriated and 'spent the rest of the alloted time which remained in disgracing that barbarous and bloody custom of theirs'.[15] Despite this attempt Gilpin could not prevent the numerous feuds in Northumberland from running their fatal course. The Scots prelate John Lesley described Scottish bloodfeuds in an equally disapproving manner as 'this pest albeit it be commoune to the hail Realme and a grevous calamitie . . .'[16] Once started, bloodfeuds could potentially take several generations to settle.

II. Bloodfeud in Scotland

On the Scottish side of the frontier the Ker versus Scott bloodfeud was the most notorious. It persisted from 1526 until 1598. There were several temporary lulls in their fight, but it always rekindled itself. The Kers of Cessford united with their sometime adversaries the Kers of Ferniehirst and the Rutherfords of Hundalee and Hunthill in this controversy. Each generation shelved its private quarrels in order to fight the Scotts. The Kers were also joined by most of their kindred lairds and other lairds of the Eastern Borders, such as Home of Cowdenknowes, Lauder of that Ilk, MacDougal of Makerstoun, Ormiston of that Ilk and Haliburton of Mertoun, who likewise ignored their personal disputes to oppose the Scotts.[17] The feud began with the murder of Sir Andrew Ker of Cessford by an Elliot ally of the Scotts of Buccleuch. There were at least four more murders before the feud was finally pacified. A constant factor here was the pronounced social divide between East and West Teviotdale where these lairds competed for influence in the Scottish Middle March.[18] There were never alliances between lairds from either area, and other east-west bloodfeuds existed between the Pringles and Elliots, and the Kers of Ferniehirst and the Turnbulls.[19]

In 1530 a bond and marriage between the Kers and the Scotts were an attempt to settle the feud, but the rough wooing of the 1540s renewed their vendetta.[20] The Kers of Cessford and Ferniehirst both assured to England and attacked the loyal Walter Scott of Buccleuch's property and tenants on numerous occasions with English assistance.[21] Such was their hatred that the Kers shamefully set fire to Catslak tower with Buccleuch's mother inside, which was all the more shocking as this widow had been a Ker of Cessford before her marriage. The Kers were indicted for this terrible murder, yet none were punished owing to the sensitive nature of this bloodfeud and the turbulence of the times. Buccleuch was rewarded for his loyalty to Scotland during the rough wooing by being made warden of the entire Middle March, rather than just being keeper of Liddesdale. The Kers were infuriated as this struck at the heart of their territory. In 1552 they persuaded a kinsman, John Home of Cowdenknowes, to murder Sir Walter Scott in Edinburgh. The Kers were threatened with exile in France as a punishment, but this never happened as politics intervened. There was no set interval between each outburst of the feud, so both sides were constantly prepared for trouble. During 1568 Sir Thomas Ker of Ferniehirst made a will in the knowledge that Scott of Buccleuch 'be lying in wait to have slaine me', though Ferniehirst lived until 1586.[22]

Marriages and bonds were often adopted during the pacification of Scottish bloodfeuds. The Kers and Scotts were forced into marriage contracts by the privy council on several occasions. Janet, daughter of Sir Andrew Ker of Ferniehirst was married to Sir Walter Scott of Buccleuch in 1530 and George Ker of Faldonside was contracted to marry Janet Scott of Buccleuch in 1565. Thomas Ker, younger son of Sir Walter Ker of Cessford, was likewise contracted to Elizabeth Scott of Buccleuch in 1567 and Sir Walter Scott of Buccleuch married Margaret Ker of Cessford in 1586.[23] Only the latter contract was fulfilled, as the first marriage ended in divorce and the second and third never took place. Elizabeth Scott was then contracted to another Ker in 1569, but this also failed to materialise. In 1569 Janet Scott married Sir Thomas Ker of Ferniehirst as his second wife. She was given 1000 merks in 1577 as compensation for the failure of her 1565 marriage contract.[24] This marriage was a rare success and it stopped Buccleuch from killing Ferniehirst. Marriages were, nevertheless, a fairly ineffective method of ending Border bloodfeuds.

Bonds of assurance, friendship and manrent were also used to pacify feuds, with mixed results. The Kers and Scotts signed bonds of assurance in 1547, 1565 and 1569, but they did not prove binding contracts.[25] In 1589 a new generation fought another running battle on the streets of Edinburgh. The Kers were supporters of the chancellor, Maitland of Thirlestane, and a marriage between his niece Margaret and Sir Robert Ker of Cessford cemented their alliance. The Scotts were supporters of Maitland's rival the troublesome earl of Bothwell, who happened to be Walter Scott of Buccleuch's stepfather. A short peace followed until Sir Robert Ker challenged Buccleuch to combat in 1596. The fight did not take place as James VI intervened and decided to end the feud once and for all. Both parties then competed for royal favour and appeared friendly in public.[26] This pacification held, much to the surprise of contemporaries who expected it to begin afresh. Sadly this peace did not stop their ill-deeds against the English

Marches for by 1597 they were the most wanted men in the Borders.[27] Fortunately the bond of manrent signed by Richard Rutherford of Edgerston and John Stewart of Traquair in 1560 was a more permanent solution to their dispute over the ancestral Rutherford lands.[28]

None of the other bloodfeuds lasted as long as the Ker and Scott enmity, though they were all serious incidents and were often linked to local political rivalries or courtier interference. Punishment could be avoided by powerful connections. Sir Robert Ker of Cessford evaded imprisonment for the brutal murder of William Ker of Ancrum as he had married Chancellor Maitland's niece.[29] Neither was the ascendant Sir James Home of Cowdenknowes punished for murdering Richard Lauder of that Ilk.[30] When there was no political interference there were established procedures for settling bloodfeuds through the privy council. These were sufficient to settle at least half of the bloodfeuds in the Eastern Scottish Borders.[31] The council first required assurance from both sides to keep the peace. This was accompanied by financial sureties given by kinsmen or anyone unfortunate enough to be present at the time. The council then listened to both sides and appointed arbiters to settle claims. Finally the two parties were reconciled before the council and signed a contract awarding financial compensation to the injured party, penance from both sides or marriage between the feuding families.[32] If a bond or a contract was broken the fines became payable by the guarantors. As these men were often kinsmen of the feuding parties their kinship would have been strained by dissenters. Sir James Home of Cowdenknowes was an unwilling guarantor for the Brounfields of the Merse as he knew their feud was unfinished. He later had to pay a £5,000 Scots penalty when trouble flared again. By the early-seventeenth century feuding conventions were changing as central government increased its influence in the Borders. They now began to resolve feuds, like domestic crime, within the normal processes of law. This ended reliance on tenuous assurances given to the privy council from kin groups and put bloodthirsty lairds like the Turnbulls into prison for attacking the Kers of Ferniehirst.[33]

III. Bloodfeud in England

The Herons against the Carrs was the English equivalent of the Ker versus Scott bloodfeud.[34] Their overall feud did not last as long, but it was equally bitter and motivated the local gentry to take sides. It originated with Elizabeth Heron the seventeen-year-old heiress and granddaughter of Sir William Heron of Ford who died in 1535. In 1549 Elizabeth married Thomas Carr, a younger son of the Carrs of Hetton. Elizabeth's widowed mother, a Forster of Adderstone, had twice remarried other Heron kinsmen and was then wife to Sir George Heron of Chipchase who lived fifty miles away to the south of the Coquet. Elizabeth would have been expected to marry one of her relations, but in 1549 she fell in love with Thomas Carr whilst he was defending Ford Castle against the Franco-Scottish army. The incensed Sir George Heron now declared that Ford was his as heir male to Sir William Heron. Alexander Heron of Meldon also put in a claim, but as they had waited fourteen years to do this their intentions seem dubious. The Herons' claims were invalid, but they were persistent and gained sympathy from many of the local gentry during the 1550s.[35] In 1551 Sir Robert Bowes hinted at future trouble over Ford as

> many of the gentlemen of Northumberland be affected and favourable either to one side or the other. Wherfore it were a good deed for the quyetnes of the countery, that clame and traverse were brought to agrement and quyetnes; otherwayse there is like muche trouble to ensue thereof.

Bowes wanted bonds to be taken from both parties to keep the peace as he claimed to have settled a quarrel between the Selbies and the Reveleys in this manner.[36] Violence did not erupt until 1557 when the Carrs had been in possession of Ford for eight years. By then the Herons had good support from many of the gentry of Northumberland and North Durham. The Carrs' assistance came from kinsmen, the Collingwoods of Eslington and Etal, the Horsleys and a few other local families. Cuthbert Horsley referred to Carr as his friend and kinsman and Thomas Carr of Ford had been an executor to Robert Collingwood of Eslington in 1556. This was enough to divide the local gentry into two camps, but the Carrs' support was also linked to local politics.[37]

Thomas Percy, as the restored seventh earl of Northumberland, had few supporters in north Northumberland in 1557. He therefore took up the cause of the Carrs as loyal Percy tenants. Thomas Carr had been warden sergeant in the English East March and became marshal of the Berwick garrison in 1555. Contrary to the views of P. G. Boscher, this appointment was not due to the earl's influence, but it helped the earl as warden of the March to have a loyal supporter in this office.[38] The Carr-Percy alliance antagonised the Herons and their associates, yet the Carrs' best defence had been their possession of Ford. The Herons thus launched an attack on Ford on 27 March 1557 with the help of some Heron allies in the Berwick garrison. Thomas Carr was absent so they expelled his brother Robert and the household servants to take possession.[39] Next day an armed conflict took place near Ford between Robert Carr and his men against Ralph Gray, sheriff of Northumberland, Giles Heron, treasurer of Berwick and Robert Barrow, mayor of Berwick with their men. The mayor was slain and Giles Heron later died of his wounds. Gray's company were allegedly riding peacefully, but another witness said they were armed, so clearly there was provocation on both sides.[40] The scheduled quarter session of the Northumberland J.Ps at Morpeth had to be postponed to prevent both parties appearing and causing more trouble. Sir Robert Ellerker regretted this move and complained that the county had enough problems with the Scots

> wee have god knoweth lytle nedd of any cyvill or demestyque division or defection amongest ourselves . . . wee think this hundreth yeres passed never happed there so perilous a sede of malaefull dissention and hatredd to be sowen in this contrey.[41]

Disruption of domestic justice forced the privy council to intervene to try and settle this bloodfeud. Their methods were not dissimilar to the Scottish privy council as they demanded investigative reports about the title to Ford from the earls of Shrewsbury and Westmorland and the bishop of Durham. They also bound both parties to keep the peace and put Ford in possession of the party that had occupied it for the last three years, namely the Carrs. Arbitration failed, so Thomas Carr and Sir George Heron were ordered to appear before the Council of the North in May 1557.[42] A temporary truce followed, but on 26 January 1558 Thomas Carr was murdered whilst travelling to London on behalf of the earl of Northumberland. Elizabeth Carr had died in 1555 and subsequent *Inquisitions Post Mortem* vindicated the Carr's right to Ford.[43] Their eldest son William, though still a minor, was declared heir. The earl proclaimed the Herons responsible for Carr's death and confiscated their goods. However he failed to apprehend Carr's murderers who were not caught until 1561. In August 1558 the privy council forced the Herons and Carrs to sign a bond of peace, which ceded the manor of Simonburn to the Herons in perpetuity.[44] The privy council had recognised that the Heron's 'kyndred and frendshippe in the said countyes (Northumberland and North Durham) were great' and they stressed that 'dyvers parcells thereof were onlie for quyetnes sake awarded to the said George (Heron)'.[45]

This award was unusually generous and included a marriage agreement akin to Scottish pacifications. This failed to materialise as the Herons were dissatisfied with Simonburn and kept up their claim to Ford. In 1576 John Heron of Chipchase solemnly conveyed Ford to his son and heir Cuthbert. This led to a renewal of the feud in February 1577 when John Heron entered Ford and gave it to Cuthbert. He determined to prove his title by common law, which would have involved a hearing in Newcastle. Here his friends would no doubt have supported him from the bench. William Carr, who had now reached his majority, determined to stop them by peaceful means. He asked the Court of Chancery for an injunction against Heron's proposed case and the Herons used delaying tactics on numerous occasions so that Chancery could not resolve the case until 16 June 1581.[46] Carr's right to Ford was endorsed by the Lord Chancellor, who wondered why there had been no 'traverse tended or challenge made', during the minority of Elizabeth Heron. He also denounced a deed of entail on which the Herons had based their case as a forgery. The seal's back 'was newe waxe and the forepart thereof to be an olde seale of some other evidence'. Indeed one of the 'feofees was deade before the date of the said deede by the space of fyftene yeares'.[47] William was awarded £40 costs, but failed to repossess Ford as the sheriff of Northumberland was none other than John Heron of Chipchase. He refused to carry out orders from London so Carr complained to Chancery, but Heron's allies were still very powerful in Northumberland and he met with more obstruction. In 1583 Carr was forced to go to Star Chamber and accuse the county coroners, Robert Roddam and Ralph Whitfield, of ignoring the writ of Chancery. They did 'uniustly confederate themselves with the saide John Heron aswell further and his contemptuous delinge againste the saide order and decree . . .'[48] The defendants naturally denied the charges against them, but they were probably well founded.

The Carrs were still unpopular amongst the well-established gentry families of Northumberland who opposed the Percies. In 1569 the Carrs proved their continuing allegiance to the earl of Northumberland in the Northern Rebellion as they held Alnwick Castle for him along with the Collingwoods. One of the Carrs of Hetton went south to join the rebels whilst their son-in-law Cuthbert Armorer was another rebel. As few gentry families from Northumberland joined the rebellion this loyalty is significant.[49] The feud can therefore be seen as a political match between those who supported and those who opposed the Percies in Northumberland, as well as being the worst bloodfeud in the sixteenth-century Eastern English Borders.

It would seem that the lairds and gentlemen were able to equate the importance of bloodfeuds to their own standing in the community. If a major rival or upstart younger son threatened to upset the social structure of the local community, then the lairds and gentlemen put loyalty to their leaders before their own private squabbles. Other bloodfeuds were on a smaller scale than the Heron and Carr feud, but they were none the less violent and often had social rivalries as a root cause. The Selbies were involved in at least three bloodfeuds and the Collingwoods in two as they were both rising families and arch-rivals in the competition for Border and county offices. They were also allied to opposing court factions, so it is not surprising that they clashed.[50] These feuds were all typical of a gentry community that had no resident magnate. They were usually pacified by independent arbiters appointed by the privy council, Council of the North, or a London court. They had to try to agree compensation or 'blood' money for the aggrieved party. When there had been murder on both sides settlement was often difficult, but the negotiations were usually kept out of the local law courts in preference for a negotiated solution. As in Scottish settlements, there was a move towards using local assizes when domestic law enforcement became more effective in the late-sixteenth century Borders.[51]

IV. Property Disputes

Property disputes were occasionally connected to national politics, though most were purely local affairs. There is more evidence of property quarrels in the Scottish Eastern Borders, but gentlemen were equally conscious of their property rights and could fight with the same intensity over their estates. A common source of aggravation on both sides of the Border were grain tithes or teinds. On the Scottish side teind disputes were frequently violent such as in the cases of the Homes of Manderston against the Cranstons of Thirlestane and Corsbie over Rumbletonlaw, and Lord Home against the earl of Arran concerning Cockburnspath. There were also many quarrels about the teinds of Duns parish between the Homes of Wedderburn and the Homes of Blackadder.[52] These encounters did not involve intentional murder or injury, rather they were a deliberate show of strength to sway the argument. Kin loyalties could be put to the test during these disputes. At Cockburnspath a Douglas of Jedworth Forest allegedly said to Home of Blackadder, 'now we of the Forrest, will teach you of the Merse to fight . . .' Home was angered by these words and afterwards challenged Douglas. His reply was; 'it is well that ye were (angry) for I was afraid you would not have fought half eagerly, there being so many Homes on the other side'.[53] More usual was the kin support afforded to Sir Robert Ker of Cessford as he carried away Langnewton's teinds in 1595 accompanied by many Kers.[54] Settlement of property disputes usually involved the privy council cautioning the feuding parties with financial guarantors. Therefore in 1591 the cautioners of the Ker of Hirsel and Home of Wedderburn feud were guarantors for 1,000 merks. Patrick Home of Ayton was a typical kinsman cautioner for £1,000 Scots in the Home of Ayton and Home of Tinnis feud.[55] This form of pacification had a reasonable success rate in the Scottish Borders as none of the property disputes were as prolonged as bloodfeuds.

English tithe disputes could involve similar force, such as Ralph Gray's quasi-military formation of men who attacked East Lilburn. His brothers simultaneously attacked Harehope and both took carts with them to carry home the grain. A witness told a subsequent Exchequer commission that

> one Richard Parker, with Thomas Gray constable of Warke in the saide countie with other frends and servants to the said Raphe Gray to the nomber of fortie persons came to the fields of East Lilburn . . . and there and then tooke away thirtie threaves of Rye parcell of the Tythe corne then recewing out of the towne East Lilburn aforesaid, whiche corne was then caryed by the said partie to Chillingham being in value worth six pounds tenn shillings'.

Because this feud involved the use of arms in riotous assembly the privy council used the Court of the Star Chamber to prevent further armed conflict.[56] When arms were used in Scottish feuds the privy council intervened to uphold similar laws against riotous assembly. Settlement of English tithe controversies was slightly different to Scottish teind pacifications. The English government had a variety of law courts available to hear the disputes. Beyond the Council of the North and the consistory court at Durham were the London courts such as the Court of Exchequer which gathered information via a commission held in the locality, or the aforementioned Court of Star Chamber. Exchequer cases concerned tithes that had belonged to monastic foundations before their dissolution. The Holborn tithe case began with confusion as to whether William Reed or Nicholas Holborn held the lease. Nicholas's father held a thirty-year lease of the tithes of Holborn from the Prior of Holy Island dated 5 March 1536. William Selby, acting on behalf of his absent father Sir John Selby of Twizel, found the lease whilst making an inventory of Holburn's deceased father's papers. 'Amonge the wich he founde one Indenture in parchand seal led with a sealle of the pacture of our ladie as he thinketh in whyte wax, which this depositioner supposed to have ben the covent seal of the pryory of the holy Ilande'.[57] Selby was now guardian to Nicholas and wished to protect his interest. However, in 1575 William Reed had been granted a renewal of his 1564 lease for all the tithes of Holy Island by the Crown so he held the better claim.[58] This dispute is illustrative of the confusion known throughout England and Wales in the years after the dissolution of the monasteries. Holy Island Priory was typical of many religious houses that granted long leases to local gentry in advance of their suppression.

In Scotland appropriated monastic lands, teinds or glebelands were also contested by the lairds. The Eastern Scottish Borders were rich in monasteries with houses at Abbey St Bathans, Coldingham, Coldstream, Dryburgh, Eccles, Jedburgh, Kelso, and Melrose. The fight over the priory of Eccles was one of the longest disputes in the area. It began with conflicting monastic charters and was further complicated by forfeiture. There was no victor in this dispute, but the settlement was not amicable either as the Homes of Cowdenknowes used their power and influence to delay any concession to the victorious Hamiltons of Innerwick. The feud over the tithes of Lauder was equally bitter, but it was a Border matter and did not involve outsider lairds.[59] A newcomer settled in the Borders to profit from monastic possession could create tensions among xenophobic local lairds. James Douglas, commendator of Melrose Abbey and second son of William, earl of Morton, had several conflicts with the Kers of Cessford and their allies. His marriage to a daughter of Cessford's rival, Ker of Ferniehirst, in the 1580s only added to the tension. Sir Robert Ker of Cessford, later Lord Roxburgh, certainly kept up the pressure against Douglas as they were still bickering in 1602 over the lands of Lessuden near St Boswells.[60]

The glebelands at Swinton and Langton were a similar source of violent exchange between Robert Swinton of that Ilk, William Cockburn of Choicelee and the parish ministers. Rather than fight themselves the Cock-

burns employed two infamous Kers of Teviotdale to harass William Meth-
ven, minister of Langton.[61] These arguments may well have stemmed from
the post-Reformation shortage of ministers in the Merse. If there was no
resident incumbent to farm the glebe then local lairds probably took
advantage of the situation. As the scarcity of preachers lessened in the
Merse the glebelands would have returned to the ministers' control with
resulting conflict. Resident preachers were sought after by ordinary parishioners, but the lairds' scramble for lands and profits could occasionally
make them unwelcome.

Another feud occurred within the parish kirk of Mertoun. Unlike Swinton
and Langton where the minister was attacked, here part of the fabric of the
church was destroyed. In 1598 the Haigs of Bemersyde had welcomed 'Ane
ordinar and resident pastour, quhairof it wes destitute evir sen the refor-
matioun of religioun within this cuntrey. [Robert Haig] being ane of the
parrochynnaris thairof, for the forder decoiring of the samyn kirk, biggit ane
stall for his mair commodious sitting in the said kirk . . .' The Kers of
Dalcove and Shaw, probably backed by Ker of Cessford (Lord Roxburgh),
maliciously destroyed the new pew in a presumed act of jealousy. This was,
however, a purely local dispute with no outside politics involved and was
thus typical of most Scottish property disputes. Cessford perhaps wanted to
emphasise his social superiority to Haig, so henchmen obliged. The Kers'
anger was not extraordinary as church pews were a common source of
annoyance amongst landed families in England.[62]

Property disputes other than church land disagreements often had a
familiar pattern in Scotland. If a claimant evicted the tenants or farm
servants from lands in dispute by force, or persuaded them by force to
stop sowing or ploughing by loosening the plough, he was staking his claim.
The land was then unprofitable or waste until the dispute was settled. The
Homes were adept at this method, even against their fellow Homes. The
Blackadder Homes came to the lands of Hilton with sixteen armed accom-
plices on 2 October 1584 and chased off Home of Wedderburn's tenants
with 'thair stalffis and speiris'. They kept up their molestation for several
days so that the tenants dared not 'laubour the saidis landis'. The Blackadder Homes were later cautioned for £500 Scots each and were still being
cautioned in 1586.[63] After the Union of the Crowns action to prevent
ploughing remained a popular form of property dispute. For example, Sir
John Ker of Hirsel stopped the tenants of Ralph Gray of Chillingham
ploughing lands he claimed near to the Border in 1605.[64]

Further down the social scale, local farmers and townsfolk were just as
protective of their property and regularly marked their boundaries against
interlopers. The modern-day ceremonial of 'Riding the Marches' in the
Scottish Border burghs owes it origins to the defence of property rights,
particularly the common grazings belonging to these towns. In smaller
communities such as Blainslie the tenants of Over Blainslie and Nether

Blainslie even drew up a formal legal instrument to define their boundaries amicably in 1547. This may have resulted from the land being feued by Melrose Abbey to lairds who were deliberately testing their new boundaries. In 1555 Andrew Haig of Bemersyde had a similar boundary dispute with Melrose Abbey over their respective lands at Redpath and Craig in Lauderdale. This was settled amicably by 'eight discreet men' acting as arbiters.[65]

Before 1603 the bulk of English property disputes would have gone to the Council of the North, so they are now only traceable in the rare cases that reached the London Courts. As the Council's records are lost there are only thirty-six recorded quarrels of English gentlemen disputing lands or tithes, compared to 120 on the Scottish side.[66] These disputes did not involve monetary cautioning as happened in Scotland, but the use of numerous courts seems to have been sufficient to pacify the feuds once they reached them. Other property feuds in the Eastern English Borders concerned the succession of property, such as the Ilderton of Ilderton feud with the greedy Sir Thomas Gray of Chillingham or the Grays' family battle over the Horton estates. Both were eventually settled by the Court of Chancery.[67] Some disputes had political connections, like Sir John Forster's snatching of Thomas Bates's lands in the aftermath of the 1569–70 Rebellion. Others were a device to give a rival the expense of defending an action at a London court. This happened in the Selby and Forster feud over Middleton Hall's tithes and the earl of Northumberland's dispute with Robert Roddam over a demolished house.[68] Local greed was evident in the Strother and Fowberry quarrel, as the Strothers manipulated an advantageous mortgage of Fowberry given by the insolvent Roger Fowberry. Fowberry discovered later that he would lose out financially in the arrangement and lost his ancestral lands as a result. When he tried to revoke the mortgage it was upheld in the Court of Requests, so Fowberry turned to a life of domestic crime.[69]

V. Miscellaneous and Cross-Border Feuds

There were at least fifty-six miscellaneous feuds that do not fit the categories of bloodfeud or property dispute. Sometimes their origins are unknown whilst others can be linked to politics or territorial rivalries.[70] They were often minor feuds or small disagreements between kinsmen or neighbours. If they were serious they were noticed at length, yet most are rarely mentioned. For example, the feuds between the fifth Lord Home and the fourth earl of Bothwell or between the Kers of Cessford and Kers of Ferniehirst were both well-documented territorial rivalries. The Home and Bothwell feud was handed down to the next generation as the sixth Lord Home and the fifth earl of Bothwell (nephew of the fourth earl) continued the feud. Their quarrel ended when Home realised that he would gain financially by discarding Bothwell's allegiance. He was then granted the forfeited commendatorship of Coldingham in 1592, which was the wealthiest monastic property in the Merse. Bothwell was incensed by his forfeiture and swore revenge on Home, giving further fire to their feud, but Home no longer responded. He felt that he had triumphed over a territorial rival who was heading for many years in exile. Ker of Cessford also benefited from Bothwell's downfall by gaining Kelso Abbey, so he triumphed over this territorial carpetbagger as well.[71]

On the English side of the Border there were territorial feuds linked both to local and national politics. The Percies never managed to renew the strong support they had once had in north Northumberland and this left the area open to local rivalries concerning office and status. The long-running feud between Sir John Forster and the Percies discussed in chapter three is typical. Forster never lost an opportunity to squabble with the earls over timber, quarries, cattle and boundaries. The Percies were once forced to go to Star Chamber to recover a mere £16–5s from Forster.[72] Some feuds were caused by marriages for the feud between the Grays of Horton and the Forsters had originated with the marriage of the widowed Lady Dorothy Forster to a Gray in 1526. This feud was little more than ill-feeling, yet Lord Grey de Wilton made it out to be serious when he supposedly pacified both sides in 1560, thirty-four years after the marriage. A feud between George Ord of Longridge and John Collingwood of Etal occurred when a marriage contract was unfulfilled. In 1581 the two parties had agreed to the marriage of Henry Collingwood and Ann Ord with £50 paid to Collingwood and £50 more promised on the wedding day. The nefarious Collingwood then told his son to marry elsewhere as he had only been after the dowry to pay a bribe to secure the office of constable of Etal.[73]

The feud between Sir Cuthbert Collingwood and Sir John Forster was intense despite Forster's senior years. It was a political rivalry similar to the Home and Bothwell feud or the Collingwoods against the Selbies.[74] This was not a bloodfeud, rather it was a high-level slanging match that revealed Forster as a corrupt warden and Collingwood as a jealous power-seeker. When Collingwood did succeed in temporarily toppling Forster he provoked one of the rare cross-border feuds in the Eastern Borders with the Burns of Teviotdale.[75] To prove his efficiency for the post of warden Collingwood stupidly tackled the notorious Burn thieves head on. He led a hot trod against them to recover stolen goods, but they knew his plan beforehand and all he found were empty houses. The next night over a hundred Teviotdale thieves descended on Eslington. A serious skirmish ensued and fifteen foot soldiers of the Berwick garrison were killed. The Burns then challenged the Collingwoods and they accepted. A day and time were arranged for a six a side combat, but James VI forbade the Burns to appear as he feared a bloodfeud would result. Collingwood presented himself at the meeting place with twelve hundred followers, much to the annoyance of the Burns. Such irresponsibility allowed Forster to resume command of the Middle March and to renew his rivalry with Collingwood. The Burns still bore a grudge against the Collingwoods nine years later, for in 1596 they made a point of raiding Collingwood property in Northumberland. Forster, for his part, had earnestly tried to prevent cross-border feuds between the Middle and West Marches as he knew how prolonged and disastrous they could be.[76]

Three other cross-border feuds were short-lived events that were very different from the prolonged and internecine cross-border bloodfeuds of the Western Borders. These disagreements were either settled by the wardens acting on behalf of their respective governments, or were left to quieten without any intervention. They could easily have turned into bloodfeuds as they concerned the murders of Lord Russell and a Ker shepherd, but most landed families in the Eastern Borders preferred to avoid cross-border feuds. The third feud between Sir Robert Ker of Cessford and the Selbies came during the height of his juvenile reiving activities. Cessford was annoyed that the Selbies were pursuing his thieves as part of their Berwick garrison duties. Their dispute did not persist as Cessford was forced to surrender to English Border authorities in 1598 and thereafter reformed his wayward character.[77]

VI. Domestic Crimes

Until the 1980s there had been comparatively little study of crime in the Borders.[78] The Border Laws appear to have taken precedence in the interest of historians, yet towards the end of the sixteenth century domestic justice became more forceful in the Eastern Borders. Many aspects of Border Law were now difficult to enforce so domestic laws were bolstered to take on Border cases, which will be discussed in chapter eight. There were also a few domestic crimes amongst landed society that were prosecuted in the usual manner. They were no different from crimes committed elsewhere in Scotland and England and ranged from petty theft, debt and adultery to treasonable activities related to rebellions. In Scotland there was no equivalent of the rebellious 1536 Pilgrimage of Grace, but some lairds did become involved with the Northern Rebellion of 1569. The fifth Lord Home and Sir Thomas Ker of Ferniehirst sheltered the rebel earls of Northumberland and Westmorland, after the rising collapsed in 1569. They tried to continue the aims of this rebellion with other Marian sympathisers in Scotland until 1573. Home and Ferniehirst were the principal Border lairds involved in this rebellion, but there were more rebel lairds during the 1580s and 1590s as well. Thomas Cranston of Morriston, Patrick Sleigh of Birkinside, Rutherford of Hunthill and Craw of East Reston all joined the fifth earl of Bothwell in his terrorising campaigns against James VI. Rutherford and Craw were not punished as severely as Home or Ferniehirst had been in the 1570s, but Cranstoun was forfeited and Sleigh executed.[79] Their rebelliousness may have been nothing more than youthful high spiritedness for which Sleigh paid dearly, but the allegiance of Sir James Ormiston of that Ilk to the previous earl of Bothwell in the 1560s was far more sinister.

Ormiston was known as 'Black Ormiston' because of his iron colour and should not to be confused with Cockburn of Ormiston in East Lothian. He was a persistent troublemaker from 1547 onwards and turned to treasonable activities in the 1560s. He was a 'principal doer' at the murder of David Rizzio, secretary to Mary, Queen of Scots in 1566 and was involved with the murder of Lord Darnley the following year. His forfeiture followed these acts, yet he was not captured until 1573 when he confessed to placing gunpowder under Darnley's bed and was summarily executed. Ormiston's lands were never restored to his children, owing to the serious nature of his crimes. His downfall was no loss to the laird community of the Eastern Borders as Ormiston had never really belonged there. He had always sided with lairds from the Western Borders and the Scotts of Buccleuch in particular. His uncharacteristic loyalties and criminal intent contrasted with the majority of lairds who lived contentedly within the Eastern Borders without resorting to domestic crime or cross-border reiving.[80]

The involvement of the gentry in rebellions was more pronounced, beginning with the Pilgrimage of Grace of 1536–37. This was a complex protest rooted in northern opposition to an insensitive government. In north Northumberland it became a fight between traditional Percy supporters and the new independent gentry who remained loyal to the crown. This division persisted in the subsequent Heron and Carr feud and the 1569–70 rising, better known as the Northern Rebellion. The minority support for the Percies collapsed after this revolt leaving courtier politics in command of the gentry's loyalty. The only revolt to test the new clientage allegiance occurred in February 1601 when the earl of Essex rebelled.

During the Pilgrimage of Grace local support for the rebel Percy brothers came from the Lisles of Felton, Swinhoes of Goswick and Roddams of Roddam. They were opposed by the Carrs of Hetton, Collingwoods of Eslington, Forsters of Adderstone and Grays of Chillingham and Horton. By the mid 1550s Percy supporters had gained the defection of the Collingwoods and Carrs of Hetton and Ford, as the Heron and Carr feud demonstrates. Late in 1569 the seventh earl of Northumberland thought he would have 'all or most of Northumberland at his devotion . . .' when he rebelled with the earl of Westmorland. The earls supported the restoration of Mary, Queen of Scots to the Scottish throne and the return of state Catholicism in England.[81] Only a handful of gentlemen from the barony of Alnwick joined him in contrast to the beginning of the sixteenth century when the Percies could mobilise 1900 men from Northumberland.

The sporadic Tudor policy to weaken over mighty Northern magnates surely triumphed in the failure of the 1569 Rising.[82] The majority of gentry to the north of the Coquet played no part in this rebellion. S. E. Taylor argues that the earl's tactics were to blame, neither giving his tenants time to assemble at Durham, nor exercising his feudal role as his loyal brother Sir Henry Percy confused the local gentry.[83] M. E. James argues that Percy loyalty was well into decline by 1569 with the advancement of crown client families like the Forsters from the 1530s. Even a personal appearance by the earl in the shire would not have made any difference.[84] James's argument is the more plausible as the Neville tenants of Bywell in Northumberland joined the revolt without a personal appearance from the earl of Westmorland, and they were also geographically distant from the epicentre of the rebellion. By 1569 Percy authority had diminished to mere rent collecting, though they protected their estates by having Sir Henry Percy remain loyal to the crown. The gentry were content to remain independent of the Percies, whom they regarded as absentee landlords. As many of them were still Catholic in 1569 their refusal to join a religiously inspired rebellion is remarkable.[85]

The crushing of the rebellion on both sides of the frontier was left to Lord Hunsdon, Sir John Forster and the earl of Sussex. They pursued rebels into Scotland and took retribution on the houses that had sheltered them without provoking war, owing to the pro-English administration then in power in Scotland.[86] This was, however, Anglo-Scottish co-operation rather than British action. It was with real commendation that the Queen thanked Sir John Forster for his loyalty and service with 'our good subjects the gentlemen and others of Northumberland'.[87] There were further anomalies in support for the rising as the Swinburnes of Edlingham remained aloof despite kinship links with the rebellious Swinburnes of Chopwell.[88] Sir Cuthbert Collingwood held Alnwick castle with the support of several of the Carrs, but they rapidly capitulated after Forster's men pinned a notice to the castle gates. Sir Cuthbert was constable of the castle and probably held it as a gesture of contempt towards his rival Forster. It is doubtful if he was holding the castle for Sir Henry Percy as James suggests, though this story exempted him from forfeiture. If he had genuinely supported the earl he surely could have joined him with 1,000 of his kinsmen and tenants, as he easily raised this number against the Burns in 1586. Collingwood did work for Sir Henry Percy (as eighth earl) in the 1580s, but he was little trusted by his employer who perhaps knew that he was really a client of the earl of Huntingdon.[89]

Robert Collingwood of Abberwick and Robert Carr, a younger son of Hetton took part in the rebellion and fled into Scotland with the countess of Northumberland. S. E. Taylor suggests that they joined because of disappointment at losing a lease of Carham rectory, but this does not equate with the fact that they had been recommended for it by Sir John Forster and the earl of Bedford, sworn enemies of the earl of Northumberland after its collapse. It is more likely that they were remnants of the Percies' meagre support in the locality, who were persuaded by their faith to join a Catholic crusade.[90] John Carr of Boulmer is recorded only as having been pardoned, but was probably a Percy tenant allied with the rest of his Carr kinsmen to the earl. Robert Collingwood, younger of Etal, may have joined as a supporter of the Carrs.[91] Fellow rebel Tristram Fenwick was a tenant of the Percies, but Ralph and James Swinhoe were not.[92] The Swinhoes backed the Percies and went to Durham to join the earls. They may have been employed in the earl of Northumberland's household, but it is more likely that they were protesting about Ralph's imprisonment at Durham in 1568 for murder. Cuthbert Armorer, a younger son of Belford, was definitely a servant of the earl and was married to the pro-Percy Elizabeth Carr of Hetton. He chose exile in the Low Countries to evade punishment.[93]

Another curiosity was the involvement of Sir William Reed on the earl's side. Like Sir Cuthbert Collingwood he was not attainted for his participation in the revolt. Reed deserted his garrison command at Holy Island and travelled to Brancepeth in Durham on the pretext of joining the rebels. He had never been a Percy adherent in the past and held no lands from them. Reed was a staunch Protestant who depended on crown lands and appointments for his livelihood. He presumably intended to spy on the earl's encampment and report their plans. Reed's downfall was that he forgot to inform Lord Hunsdon of his intentions and was thus branded a rebel instead of a hero. Reed had sympathy from Hunsdon and his fellow courtiers Sir Ralph Sadler and Christopher Norton, who believed that he had 'betrayed the earls' and 'opened all their counsel', yet it still took a trip to London to clear his name.[94]

The rebels who joined the earl of Northumberland never returned to his allegiance after they were pardoned in the 1570s. They became crown loyalists and sought patronage from the court. For example, the Swinhoe brothers found employment in the Berwick garrison, with James becoming a gentleman porter and a crown tenant at Berrington.[95] Cuthbert Armorer also joined the garrison and became a cross-border messenger for Lord Hunsdon, often referred to as 'Cuttie Armorer'.[96] Tristram Fenwick was back in favour by 1580 when he received a crown lease. He later emerged in the ranks of the Forster allies as he leased his land from them rather than the forfeited earl. His son George married Dorothy Forster of Newham, a kinswoman of Sir John Forster.[97]

The local gentry did not take part in any other national plots and revolts for the rest of the sixteenth century, but they continued to feud amongst themselves on many occasions. It was not until 1601, when the earl of Essex rebelled, that the gentry response was again overwhelmingly in the crown's favour. The Cecils and the earl of Essex were fierce court rivals during the 1590s, both trying to build up and sustain a gentry clientage in the North. Sir Robert Cecil held a commanding lead north of the Coquet with the powerful Grays and Selbies in his allegiance. It was therefore a surprise when Captain John Selby, younger son of Sir John Selby of Twizel, joined the rebellion. William Selby junior was horrified by his brother's defection and pleaded with Cecil for clemency, stressing his youth, enamour for Mrs Rotherham (a widow and kinswoman of the earl) and the family's good service in the past. John escaped execution, but was fined £100 as part of his pardon. He probably joined the rebellion in defiance of the family's loyalty to Cecil to bring attention to a quarrel within the Berwick garrison. He had clashed with the obnoxious Governor Lord Willoughby and his non-local deputy John Guevara during December 1600. Selby had served with Essex on his ill-fated expedition to the Azores in 1597, but he probably did not join his allegiance until his disaffection over an office in the garrison coincided with a visit of Essex to Northumberland. When Essex rose Selby went absent without leave to join him.[98] John Swinburne of Edlingham was the only other local gentleman connected with Essex's revolt. Why he participated is unknown, but he may have met Essex in December 1600. As he was not fined, his involvement must have been slight. Sir Robert Carey reported that many local gentlemen were openly loyal to the Queen during the rebellion, so there was little overall support for Essex in the locality.[99] There were rumours about Thomas Carr of Ford being involved with Essex, but he never joined the rebellion. Nicholas Forster of Bamburgh's nephew, the earl of Bedford, supported Essex, yet none of the Forsters became involved as their loyalty to the crown was beyond question.[100]

The gentry were fairly law-abiding overall, with the exception of blood-feuds, but some of the lesser gentry were tempted by petty theft when they were in financial difficulties. Sir Robert Carey thought that gentlemen thieves did not exist until he executed two of them at Newcastle in 1598. There were earlier examples of theft and a few gentlemen were murderers as well.[101] In 1562 William Selby of Grindonrig was pardoned for theft of cloth and murder. John Reveley of Berrington, John Reveley of Humbleton and the aforementioned William Selby of Grindonrig stole cloth from an Alnwick merchant in 1565. They may well have been needing resources or perhaps were just greedy, but the process of law caught up with them. Reveley had been charged with murder at a Durham quarter session in July 1555, so his criminal intent was not a temporary aberration. Arthur Ogle of Trewhitt stole from a neighbour in 1600 and Gerard Selby of Pawston was indicted for the lesser offence of not paying a £100 debt to the Queen.[102]

John Carr of Hetton copied a garrison method of raising money quickly to solve his financial shortfall. He acquired, or made, counterfeit money and was caught circulating it.[103] His desperation for money also led him to mortgage Hetton. Roger Fowberry of Fowberry was another financially declining gentleman who turned to crime. He had already lost his ancestral estates when he turned to theft, but he was captured and sent to Durham gaol. It was difficult to find a secure prison in the north east, so this is probably why Fowberry was sent to Durham, though even he escaped in 1596. Fowberry hid in the Middle March after this, probably with the help of sympathetic gentry friends, as he was never recaptured.[104] These financially based crimes are not surprising, as some of the gentry were impoverished and reluctant to lose their ancestral estates. At least they did not resort to cross-border reiving to alleviate their debts. This is why the gentry of north Northumberland and North Durham cannot be lumped together with the notorious reiving surname groups of Tynedale and Redesdale, nor with the Western Borders as a whole.

The few incidents of crime prove that the gentry were not infallible, but their crimes were fairly minor, with the exception of rebellion and murder. The *vetera indictamenta* for 1594–1630 is the first full record of domestic crime and justice to survive for Northumberland and there is a small survival of Durham quarter sessions for 1555–57 and 1602.[105] They contain few references to the gentry, as they mostly concern the crimes of non-landed men and women. Serious criminal matters, such as treason, were always heard at London and pardons were issued from there for most gentry crimes. They were nearly all pardoned or never prosecuted. This contrasts with the severe punishment received by some of the lairds.

On the Scottish side, the lairds' domestic crimes concerned witchcraft, adultery, debt, and murder. Evidence for most of these crimes comes from the records of justice ayres held at Lauder, Jedburgh and Edinburgh.[106] Charges of witchcraft were unusual amongst the lairds, but Ninian Chirnside of Whitsomelaws was indicted because of his connections with the earl of Bothwell, who allegedly conspired to kill James VI by sorcery. Chirnside must have been acquitted of these charges as he was a free man in 1601.[107] The most notorious case of adultery concerned Sir John Ker of Hirsel, who married a daughter of David Home of Wedderburn only to abandon her in 1589. He co-habited with an East Lothian laird's wife, Margaret Whitelaw of that Ilk, who had been married to Alexander Hamilton of Innerwick. Divorces were granted to both parties, but Ker's marriage to Margaret in 1590 was invalid as he was 'continewand in his filthie crime of adulterie'. The kirk took a strong line on immorality and he was not granted absolution from excommunication until 1603.[108]

Debts incurred by the lairds were often evasion tactics rather than serious crimes. Unpaid debts could be linked to feuds if an injured party put the other to the 'horn' for annoyance value or payment of a debt. There were cases unconnected to feuds that reflected the individual debts of the laird. John Haitlie of Mellerstain, for example, borrowed 4,000 merks from two Edinburgh burgesses in 1600, but did not repay the loan before his death in 1602. This caused problems for his heirs as they were summoned for non-payment. Lord Home was similarly summoned for not paying the teinds of Lauder in 1584, though this may be linked to his Catholic faith, and James Pringle of that Ilk was put to horn for not paying his baron's tax in 1591. The payment of ecclesiastical thirds was grudged by Catholic lairds such as Andrew Home, commendator of Jedburgh, during 1569–72 for Jedburgh. Robert Ker of Ancrum refused payment in 1561 for Ancrum parsonage, though this may have been for reasons of indigence.[109] As in the English Eastern Borders, the lairds were not tempted to pay their debts by reiving across the Border.

Local tensions in the Eastern Borders did result in a few murders that were not linked to feuds. For instance, John Mow of that Ilk was responsible for the murder of William Burn in the kirkyard at Mow in 1540, but was pardoned. Gilbert Lauder of Whitslaid was indicted with murdering George Wedderat, a burgess of Lauder, in 1565 and was similarly pardoned in 1566. A less straightforward indictment of a laird occurred when eight non-laird Dicksons were fugitives from justice for killing four neighbouring Gradens in the Merse during 1541. Their kin leader, Robert Dickson of Bughtrig was forfeited even though he may have played no part in the murder. Dickson must have recovered his property as no more is recorded about the case.[110] In 1588 there were tensions within the Dickson of Belchester family when John Dickson killed his father in an infamous case of patricide. John fled to England to evade prosecution, but the case so outraged public opinion that he was repatriated in 1591 to be forfeited, broken at the wheel and executed.

Even amidst violent feuding and general Border violence the crime of patricide was distasteful. Had John fled across the frontier as a debtor, political exile, or even as murderer in a feuding situation, he would probably have been sheltered by landed friends as these were seemingly pardonable offences. Patricide, however, was against all the landed families' sense of consanguine honour. Dickson was the only Eastern Border laird to be executed for domestic murder, whilst Ormiston of that Ilk and Patrick Sleigh of Birkinside were the only lairds to suffer the same fate for treasonable activities with the infamous fourth and fifth earls of Bothwell.[111]

By comparing and contrasting the many bloodfeuds, property disputes, other feuds and domestic crimes of the Eastern Borders from 1540 to 1603, a pattern of violent and criminal disorder emerges. These incidents were often linked to local and national politics through the personal rivalries, alliances and jealousies of the lairds and gentlemen on both sides of the frontier. Their alliances were seldom stable, with the exception of the Ker and Scott, and Heron and Carr feuds. Overall landed families shared everyday interests and problems that were more important to them than the vicissitudes of Border administration. For instance, a local property dispute could merit more attention than attendance at a day of truce.

The Eastern Borders suffered less from cross-border raiding and feuding than the Western Borders, so domestic disputes dominated local society. The settlement of individual feuds was no quicker on the Scottish side than on the English. The proximity of the Scottish privy council to the Borders did not mean that it was more effective than the English privy council in reconciling disputes. Communications did take longer to reach London, but would have reached York fairly quickly if cases were going before the Council of the North. That the council's records are lost is regrettable as it would have been easier and much less expensive to travel to York than take civil litigation to London. Those gentlemen who went south, or were summoned there, are sufficient in number to allow a collation of Scottish and English feuds and serious domestic crimes. Overall, the gentry received pardons or less severe punishment than the lairds for their domestic crimes. Moreover the level of violence in the Eastern Borders was not inconsistent with general disorder between members of the social elite in sixteenth-century Scotland and England. This region's violence should therefore be kept in perspective and not be singled out by historians as being excessive. Finally the reivers, who have often symbolised all Border history, should now be properly placed in the Western Borders and not in the comparatively civilised East.

Notes

1 L. Stone, *The Crisis of the Aristocracy* (Oxford, 1965), 223–4. M. E. James, 'English Politics and the Concept of Honour, 1485–1642', *P&P*, supplement iii (1978), 5–6, 13. K. M. Brown, *Bloodfeud in Scotland* (Edinburgh, 1986), ch. i.
2 *CSP For*, 1560–1, 735.
3 *ibid.* 570/2.
4 *CBP*, i, 41. This is perhaps wrongly dated and should read 1569.
5 *CSP Scot*, xiii, pt 2, 828. *CSP Dom*, 1601–3, 213–14.
6 SP59/33 fos 82–3. *CBP*, i, 893. *CSP Dom*, 1598–1603, 95.
7 *CSP Scot*, vii, 441. Rae, *Scottish Frontier*, 10, 75, and 'Feud and the jurisdiction of the wardens of the Marches', *Transactions of the Hawick Archaeological Society* (1961), 3–9; Tough, *Last Years*, 32–3; Watts, *Border to Middle Shire*, 25–6; G. M. Fraser, *The Steel Bonnets* (London, 1971), xvi–xviii.
8 Brown, *Bloodfeud*, 277. B. W. Beckingsale, 'The Characteristics of the Tudor North', *NH*, iv (1969), 67.
9 *CBP*, i, 571, 646; ii, 77, 80, 431. *CSPScot*, viii, 459–61, 680.
10 See ch. iv.
11 *APS*, iv, 158–9, c. 1. J. Wormald, 'Bloodfeud, Kindred and Government in Early Modern Scotland', *P&P*, lxxxvii (1980), 86n.
12 PRO C1/1023/24–6, C3/71/11, C3/244/42, C142/186/47, E134/12 Eliz/TRIN 3, E134/15 Eliz EAST 2, E178/7353, REQ2/160/62, REQ2/178/25, STAC5 04/39, N10/26, R32/38, S81/2. R. R. Reid, *The King's Council in the North* (London, 1921), 191. C. Muldrew, 'The Culture of Reconciliation: community and the settlement of economic disputes in early modern England', *The Historical Journal*, 39/4 (1996), 915–942.
13 *CBP*, ii, 103, 371, 373. See ch. viii.
14 *CPR*, 1566–9, 261–2; 1569–72, 294. *HMC*, Rutland, i, 86. Meikle, *Thesis*, 558–679. See ch. vi.
15 G. Carleton, *The Life of Bernard Gilpin* (London, 1629), 27–8. D. Marcombe, 'Bernard Gilpin: Anatomy of an Elizabethan Legend', *NH*, xvi (1980), 20–39.
16 Lesley, *History*, i, 101.
17 NAS GD40/2/9/80, GD40/15/2/2–3, GD224/64/5/2, GD224/529/1/108, 114 & 126. *CSPScot*, i, 129; v, 471; x, 156, 280; xii, 26, 212, 224; xiii, 52, 279, 496. Fraser, *Buccleuch*, ii, 185–90, 193–4, 209–11, 222–3, 242–6, 336–7, 445–53.
18 *CSP Scot*, v, 286.
19 NAS GD40/2/10/27. *CSPFor*, 1569–71, 1425. *RPC*, ii, 453–4.
20 Fraser, *Buccleuch*, i, 93, ii, 162–4.

21 M. H. Merriman, 'The Assured Scots', *SHR*, xlvii (1968), 21.
22 NAS GD40/2/9/49. Fraser, *Buccleuch,* 185–94, 209–11. M. M. Meikle, 'Victims, Viragos and Vamps: Women of the Sixteenth Century Anglo-Scottish Frontier', in J. C. Appleby & P. Dalton, eds. *Government, Religion and Society in Northern England 100–1700* (Gloucester, 1997), 174.
23 NAS RD1/7 fo. 131. RD1/26 fo. 34. Fraser, *Buccleuch,* i, 93; ii, 162–4, 222–3, 242–6, 451–3. Brown, *Bloodfeud,* chs. ii & ix. Wormald, 'Bloodfeud', 71–7, 83–7.
24 NAS RD1/11 fo. 75. *RPC,* ii, 643, 665, 671. See ch. i.
25 NAS GD40/15/2/2. Fraser, *Buccleuch,* ii, 185–7, 336–7, 451–3. J. Wormald, *Lords and Men,* ch. vii.
26 *CSP Scot,* x, 156, 280; xii, 26, 212, 224; xiii, pt 1, 52, 279.
27 *CBP,* ii, 783 *et seq.*
28 NLS MS Acc7676/A/IV/12.
29 NRAS 1100/709. NAS GD40/2/11/55. *RPC,* iv, 566, 585–6; v, 273. *CSPScot,* x, 505, 507, 517, 535, 602, 606, 607, 616, 619, 623.
30 *CSPFor,* 1566–8, 1289. *RSS,* vi, 2254.
31 *RPC,* i, 23, 155–6, 327–9, 451–2; ii, 110–11, 117, 266–71, 321–2, 453–4, 534–7, 541, 570–1, 610–11, 684–5; iii, 616; iv, 57–8, 100–01, 140, 478, 497, 566, 574–5, 585–6, 612–14, 616, 630, 633, 669, 677, 679, 692, 694, 697, 706, 720; v, 71, 273, 306, 667; vi, 48, 57; x, 321, 352.
32 Rae, *Scottish Frontier,* 123–6.
33 *CSPScot,* xiii, 745. Pitcairn, *Trials,* ii, 370–5, 378–81, 421, 445.
34 M. Meikle, 'Northumberland Divided: Anatomy of a sixteenth-century bloodfeud', *Archaeologia Aeliana,* 5th ser, xx (1992), 79–89.
35 PRO C78/54/4. LAMB, MS 696 fo. 83.
36 PRO SP15/4/30 fo. 93. BL MS Cotton, Titus, F, xiii, fo. 187.
37 PRO C78/54/4. LAMB, MS 696 fo. 83; MS 3195 fo. 9. *SS,* ii (1835), 148. See ch. iii.
38 PRO SP15/8/66. *APC,* vi, 243. P. G. Boscher, 'Politics, Administration and Diplomacy: The Anglo-Scottish Border 1550–60', unpubl. Ph.D diss. Durham 1985, 291.
39 LAMB, MS 3195 fo. 8; MS 696 fos 83–4.
40 *ibid*, MS 3195 fos 6, 8.
41 *ibid.* fos 5, 9.
42 *APC,* vi, 86–7.
43 PRO C142/131/159, WARD9/438 fo. 54. *CPR,* 1555–7, 116, 373.
44 PRO C142/174/55. *APC,* vi, 284, 360. *CPR,* 1557–8, 112, 250, 365–6. *CSP For,* 1561–2, 221–2.
45 PRO STAC5 C16/4, C78/54/4.
46 PRO C78/54/4. BL MS Lansdowne, 326, fo. 44.
47 PRO C78/54/4.
48 PRO STAC5 C16/4.
49 *CSPDom Add,* 1566–79, 126. See ch. iii.
50 PRO SP15/29/317. *CBP,* i, 521, 601. *CSPDom Add,* 1580–1625, 193–07, 213–14, 249. *SS,* xxxviii (1860), 151. See ch. iii.
51 PRO SP59/3 fo. 221. NRO QS1/1 fos 22, 24–5.
52 *RPC,* ii, 373; iii, 130, 710, 723, 737; iv, 2, 77–8, 779. *CSPFor,* 1572–4, 347, 359. *CSPScot,* iii, 943; iv, 313; vii, 26, 113, 304, 306.
53 Godscroft, *History,* 276.
54 *CSPScot,* xi, 637; xii, 12.

55 NAS GD267/31/6, RD1/45 fo. 142. NRAS 859/6/3. *CBP*, i, 835. *RPC*, iv, 677, 679, 689, 693, 695; v, 589, 666.

56 PRO E134/ 44 Eliz/ EAST 16, STAC5 21/31, 07/25, G5/21, G10/20, G19/29. NRO 1DE/1/123, 1DE/12/35, 650/B/1602.

57 PRO E134 26 & 27 Eliz MICH 20, SC6/Ph & M/222. BL MS Additional, 24,815 fos 216–17.

58 PRO E310/21/113. *CPR*, 1563–6, 200–01; 1578–80, 1301. *CSPDom Add*, 1566–79, 495.

59 NAS CS7/20 fo. 291, RD1/11 fo. 172, RH15/19/3/1. NRAS 859/6/1, 859/7/7, 859/10/2. *CSPScot*, x, 527. *RSS*, v, 3041; vi, 273, 1042, 2320, 2816; viii, 78, 233, 2425.

60 *CSPScot*, xi, 637; xii, 12. *RPC*, iii, 552–3; iv, p. 115; vi, 733.

61 *RPC*, iv, 274, 284, 352–3, 522, 717, 724; v, 653. See ch. vi.

62 *CSPScot*, xiii, 299. *RPC*, v, 534, 715. Stone, *Crisis*, 225. See ch. vi.

63 *RPC*, iii, 707.

64 *HMC*, ninth report, ii, 198. See ch. viii.

65 *Selections from the Records of the Regality of Melrose*, ed. C. S. Romanes (Scottish History Society, 1917) iii, 223–5. J. Anderson & W. Angus, eds. *Protocol Book of Sir William Corbet 1529–1555* (Scottish Record Society, vol xxxix, 1911), no. 35.

66 See Meikle, *Thesis*, 679–711.

67 PRO C3/71/11, C142/158/19, C142/141/31, C142/186/47, REQ2/226/3, SP15/ 19/15.

68 PRO REQ2/178/25, STAC5 N10/26, S6/5. NRO 1DE/1/117.

69 PRO REQ2/270/67, REQ2/64/70, SP15/28/95v. *Laing Chrs*, 1183. See note 104 below.

70 Meikle, *Thesis*, 711–21.

71 NRAS 832/78. *CSPScot*, vii, 138; x, 191, 386, 389, 590–2, 598, 730, 749, 755; xi, 123, 130. See ch. ii.

72 PRO STAC5 N6/21. ALN MS AI/1/b, f, & g., SYON MS NII/6/a – y.

73 PRO REQ2 162/119 & 164/119. *CSPFor*, 1560–1, 735; 1562, 289. See ch. iv.

74 *CBP*, i, 556, 646; ii, 111. *CSPDom Add*, 1580–1625, 268. *HMC*, Salisbury, iii, 290–1; v, 477. See ch. iii.

75 *APC*, xxiv, 53–4. *CBP*, i, 571, 646; ii, 373. *RPC*, iv, 81. *CSPScot*, viii, 452, 459–61, 465, 512; ix, 476.

76 *CBP*, ii, 228. *CSP Scot*, viii, 459. *RPC*, iv, 8l.

77 *CBP*, ii, 77, 80, 431. *CSPScot*, viii, 680. See chs ii & viii.

78 *Cf.* C. M. F. Ferguson, 'Law and Order on the Anglo-Scottish Border, 1603–1707', unpubl. PhD diss. St Andrews 1981. C. J. Neville, *Violence, Custom and Law. The Anglo-Scottish Border Lands in the Later Middle Ages* (Edinburgh, 1998). G. Morgan & P. Rushton, *Rogues, Thieves and the Rule of Law. The problem of law enforcement in north-east England, 1718–1800* (London, 1998). H. Summerson, 'Crime and Society in Medieval Cumberland', *Transactions of the Cumberland and Westmorland Archaeological and Antiquarian Society*, lxxxii (1982), 111–124.

79 *RMS*, vi, 699. Pitcairn, *Trials*, i, pt 2, 270–5; ii, 21–2, 125–7.

80 PRO RD1/7 fo. 131. *APS*, iii, 6, 137. *CSP For*, 1560–1, 792; 1566–8, 205. *CSP Scot*, ii, 490. *A Diurnal of Remarkable Occurrents*, ed. T. Thomson, (Maitland Club, 1833), 333. Pitcairn, *Trials*, i, pt l, 334, 494–9, 511–13.

81 *CSPDom Add*, 1566–79, 129.

82 M. E. James, 'The Concept of Order and the Northern Rising 1569,' *P&P*, lx (1973), 49–83. See ch. iii.

83 S. E. Taylor, 'The Crown and the North of England, 1559–70; a study of the rebellion of the northern earls, 1569–70 and its causes', unpubl. PhD diss. Manchester 1981, 261–71.

84 James, 'Concept', 69–75.

85 See chs. iii & vi.

86 See ch. viii.

87 *CSPDom Add,* 1566–79, 141, 158, 165, 242, 246.

88 NRO ZSW3/35.

89 *CSPDom Add*, 1566–79, 125–6. James, 'Concept', 72. See ch. iii.

90 *Stat*, 13 Eliz c. 16 i. *CPR*, 1572–5, 203, 246, 504. *CSPDom Add* 1547–65, 562–3. Taylor, 'Crown and the North', 122 & app. 124–5.

91 *CPR*, 1569–72, 88. *cf. Stat.*

92 *CPR*, 1569–72, 292; 1575–8, 5–6. *CSPDom,* 1566–9, 187. *CSPDom Add,* 1566–79, 349. *CSP For*, 1568–8, 2524.

93 *CSPDom Add*, 1566–79, 394. *CPR*, 1572–5, 203. *Stat*. 13 Eliz c.16. Sharp, *Memorials*, 272.

94 *CSPDom Add,* 1566–79, 171, 179, 195–6, 261, 273, 495. *CSP For*, 1569–71 216, 790. Sharp, *Memorials*, 15–16.

95 PRO E310/21/107 & 109, SP59/37. *CPR*, 1575–8, pp. 5–6.

96 *CPR*, 1572–4, p. 203. *CSP Scot*, vi, 13, 56, 179, 479, 662, etc. See ch. v.

97 *CSPDom Add*, 1566–79, 164. *CPR*, 1569–72, 407; 1578–80, 1703. *NCH*, vii, 473.

98 *CBP*, ii, 697, 1255–6, 1335, 1338, 1413. *CSP Scot*, xiii, pt 2, 602, 614. *HMC*, Salisbury, xi, 75, 117, 212, 214, 564. Watts, *Border to Middle Shire*, 118.

99 NRO ZSW322B/20. *APC*, xxxi, 473.

100 *CBP*, ii, 1134, 1434.

101 Carey, *Memoirs*, 48.

102 Morpeth Records Centre QS1/1 fo. 12. *CPR*, 1560–3, 323; 1563–6, 254. *SS*, cxix (1991), 77, 79.

103 *CSP For*, 1564–5, 984; 1575–7, 665. CP25/2/192/16 & 17 Eliz/ MICH. See ch. viii.

104 REQ2/270/67 & 64/70, SP15/28/95v. *CBP*, ii, 214, 652. *CSP For*, 1559–60, 449. *Laing Chrs*, 1183.

105 Morpeth Records Centre QS1/1. *SS*, cxix (1991), 77–89, 130–1.

106 Pitcairn, *Trials.*

107 *RPC*, vi, 685. Pitcairn, *Trials*, i, pt 2, 259.

108 NAS GD267/31/6. *RPC*, v, 81, 589. *HMC*, Salisbury, iv, 31. Calderwood, *History*, vi, 205. Pitcairn, *Trials*, i, pt 2, 293. See ch. vi. Divorce was more easily obtainable in Scotland, than in England. *cf.* L. Leneman, *Alienated Affections. The Scottish Experience of Divorce and Separation, 1684–1830* (Edinburgh, 1998).

109 NAS GD239/4/3/26. *RPC*, iv, 669. *RSS*, vi, 211; viii, 2425. *Accounts of the Collectors of Thirds of Benefices*, ed. G. Donaldson, *Scottish History Society*, 3rd ser, xlii (1949), 112. *Formulary of Old Scots Legal Documents*, ed. P. Gouldesbrough (Stair Society, 1985), 21–8. See chs. iv & vi.

110 *RSS*, ii, 3838; v, 2715. Pitcairn, *Trials*, i, pt 1, 256, 257, 467–8.

111 *CSP Scot*, x, 464, 522, 545. R. Chambers, *Domestic Annals of Scotland* (Edinburgh, 1861), 225. Pitcairn, *Trials*, i, pt 2, 241. See ch. viii.

8

Cross-Border Relations

Relations between Scots and English along the Eastern Anglo-Scottish frontier can be classified as both official and unofficial. Official contact was through diplomacy and the administration of Border law. Unofficial communication could entail forays into either realm for the purposes of reiving, burning, ransoming, disputing territory or other general trouble making. Less well known and undeservedly so, are the beneficial cross-border relations that proved to be beyond the control of Border law. These stress how relatively peaceful the Eastern Borders could be in terms of cross-border trade, employment of Scots in England, friendships, marriages and the provision of shelter for fugitives from justice, and these will be the focus for much of this chapter. Cross-border social contacts between the landed families were more marked when James VI looked likely to succeed Elizabeth I but these were long-established Border connections and they cannot be seen as part of any new 'British' phenomenon. The Eastern Borderers could run circles around the officialdom of their nations whenever they chose and this was almost always for their own benefit, rather than that of their respective nations.

I. Official Cross-Border Relations

Official relations usually concerned the endemic violence of the region and subsequent redress needed to correct wrong doing. Accounts for reparations tend to dominate surviving documentation and subsequent Border historical research, so they will only be summarised here.[1] These matters were normally agreed by the wardens of the Marches at their meetings known as 'days of truce'. However these exchanges could also include discussions about debatable lands or even royal visits. Problems facing administrators were the same throughout the Borders, but the records of days of truce and Border commissions have not always survived in sufficient quantity to give precise detail. In 1586 the documentation was said to be 'not so orderly kept' and may only only have been noted in an informal manner. None the less there must have been copious warden correspondence both before and after these meetings. Proof that landed men of the Eastern Borders were less violent than the Western Borders are in the lists of redress, for only a few reiving lairds in Teviotdale and Jedforest are noted for their malevolence. By contrast the antics of Western Borderers fill many pages.[2]

The Western Borders were host to the infamous debatable ground, but it is less well known that the Eastern Borders had their own debatable grounds. They lay between the Scottish Middle March and the English East March consisting of approximately 100 acres at Carham, 300 acres at Haddenrig and forty acres at Wark. These disputed pockets were much smaller than their Western Border counterpart, yet they could still cause friction between the Marches. A 1551 survey of March boundaries recorded the different English and Scottish descriptions of the disputed borderline.[3] After the battle of Flodden in 1513 Scots had pastured and cultivated them. This led to them being called the 'repleynissed grounde' though there was no complaint about this until 1541 when English officials destroyed crops sown there.[4] Efforts made by Border commissioners to arbitrate the disputed lands in 1556 and 1563 failed. They remained contentious for in 1573 the Pringles claimed that Sir Thomas Gray of Chillingham had stolen over 1,000 of their sheep and cattle that were 'feeding within English ground which the Scots affirm was done on Scottish ground.'[5] Sir Thomas produced a boundary agreement to further his claim, but the Pringles rejected this and an international commission was convened again. These arbiters were unsuccessful as the Scots complained that Gray had ploughed their lands in 1590 and the debate continued. In 1604 Ralph Gray of Chillingham granted land in Yetholm parish to Nicol Rutherford of Hundalee 'to give satisfaction'. Gray did not, however, satisfy the claims of Sir John Ker who spoiled ploughed land with 200–300 of his men. Another Anglo-Scottish commission was appointed in 1605, but the controversy continued for decades with neither side prepared to make any concessions. Interestingly Pont's survey of Teviotdale in the 1590s puts the Norhamshire villages of Mindrum and Shotton in Scotland, whilst Armstrong's 1769 map of Northumberland shows there were still patches of 'disputed ground' along the Border.[6]

Tensions between the English East March and the Scottish Middle March were counter-balanced by good relations between the two East Marches.[7] Here the lairds and gentry shared a mutual abhorrence of violent reiving. There were only a few incidents between these Marches, but they were insignificant in comparison to the overwhelming co-operation shown by these men against reivers. For instance, at the swearing of Border bills in 1596–7 Cuthbert Home of Reidheuch, Robert and John Home of Ayton, Mr John Home of Tinnis and Mr James Home of Hilton all helped prove 'foul' (file) English bills for redress against fellow Scotsmen.[8] The English East March gentlemen could also travel freely into the Scottish East March on Border business, such as Ralph Gray of Chillingham's visit to Wedderburn Castle in 1597.[9] The Western Borders would not have been so welcoming before 1603!

Goodwill between the East Marches allowed Scottish royalty to view Berwick on several occasions. For instance in 1566, Mary, Queen of Scots was met at the 'bound road' by Sir John Forster who was deputizing for the absent warden (the earl of Bedford). He conveyed her to Halidon Hill, the nearest vantage point, to witness a cannon volley of welcome. Sir James Melville suggested that Forster's horse reared up in front of the queen injuring her, but as no other report mentions this it was presumably a successful day.[10] James VI also viewed Berwick from Halidon Hill in April 1588 and rewarded the gunners for their half-hour volley from the walls of the town. Lord Home and other attendants of James VI accepted an invitation to witness the cannon fire from Berwick's walls, although the English motive behind this was probably to gather intelligence as well as extend cross-border hospitality. The English firepower used on this occasion was a timely reminder to James VI not to meddle with Spanish interests as the Spanish Armada was expected that summer. In 1595 it was rumoured that James VI and Anna of Denmark wished to see Berwick during a progress through the Merse, but it is unclear if they did so.[11] International events tended to be reflected in the administration of the Borders, for the trial and subsequent execution of Mary, Queen of Scots led to a succession of cancelled meetings between the wardens of the Middle Marches during 1586–87.[12] However, Border incidents could in themselves create international tensions.

II. Cross-Border Incidents

Throughout the period 1540–1603, there was a regular pattern of raiding across the frontier that was particularly intense during the long, dark winter nights. This was inevitably followed by lengthy attempts to gain redress through the wardens. Most forays were so commonplace as to be unremarkable, but there were wars and incidents that severely affected cross-border relations in the Eastern Borders. This began with the severity of the 1540s rough wooing and continued, sporadically, up to the 1590s. Some were short-term incidents related to Anglo-Scots tensions, fishing disputes or even hunting trips that took a wrong turning, but they attracted international attention none the less. This was due to the sensitivity of this frontier in the separate foreign policies of sixteenth-century Scotland and England, rather than any 'British' polity.

The savagery of English attacks during the 1540s soured potential and existing friendships between the lairds and gentlemen for at least a generation. The Kers of Cessford and the Carrs of Hetton should have been on friendly terms considering their mutual, if remote, ancestry. However, Walter Ker had taken John Carr prisoner in 1542 and demanded a ransom that was still unpaid in 1551.[13] This was a small Scottish victory in a decade of devastating English attacks when Borderers were pitched against each other. The majority of these forays were successful, though one English party intent on burning Cumledge and Chirnside 'missed their way in the dark'.[14]

The 1550s were less violent in comparison to the 1540s. On a purely local level there were several Anglo-Scottish disputes over fishings in the River Tweed that had to be settled by arbitrators. To trouble the fishing ground on the opposite side of the Tweed was against Border law, but this merely proved they had been contentious for a long time.[15] There was a conflicting law that fishermen could throw their nets over the whole river as long as they landed their catch on their own side of the Tweed. Tensions were therefore inevitable and trouble arose at Holywell, a fishing ground between Norham Castle and Lord Home's barony of Upsettlington, and between Coldstream (Lennel) and Tillmouth. Lord Home's adversary in this matter was usually the incumbent captain of Norham. Home's nets were cut in 1553, 1561, and 1563 by Henry Percy and Thomas Clavering. Like the debatable ground of the Eastern Borders, there was never any satisfactory or lasting agreement about these fishings as trouble flared again in 1602.[16]

Shipwrecks off the treacherous Northumbrian coastline were another source of international concern, yet as the plunderers were often local gentlemen they were locally important as well. The superior of the land nearest the wreck usually asserted his right to the bounty, as for example the earl of Northumberland at Tughall and Swinhoe in 1567.[17] Sir Ralph Gray of Chillingham claimed a Scottish ship, 'the Marie', at Ross in November 1559 and Thomas Clavering, the captain of Norham, took the Scottish ship 'Bonaventure' at Scremerston in December 1559.[18] In subsequent Anglo-Scottish wrangles for compensation Gray denied his involvement, blaming his water-bailiff and John Horsley of Outchester instead. Thomas Clavering refused to pay £2,000 compensation demanded by Scottish merchants at the English Court of the Admiralty. He claimed that only £44 worth of goods were salvaged. Ultimately these gentlemen were forced to pay small amounts to the unfortunate merchants. George Muschamp of Barmoor and Sir John Forster of Bamburgh were even forced to pay for the plundering activities of their tenantry.[19] However these payments did not deter the local gentry, for in 1568 a Dutch ship was looted at Dunstanburgh by Sir Thomas Gray of Horton and Lancelot Lisle. Another wreck there in 1592 was claimed both by Ralph Gray of Chillingham and the earl of Northumberland's officers.[20]

Shipwreck disputes were initially domestic incidents that could quickly lead to international tension. By contrast, cross-border skirmishes of the later 1550s were international in their origin. The tense alliance extant between England and France broke down in 1557. Neither side wanted full-scale war, so Border conflicts were manipulated instead. The pro-French Scots led a pre-emptive attack in August 1557. This led to a series of counter-attacks that culminated in the battle of 'Blackberye' in November 1557 where 400 Scotsmen were taken prisoner. In 1558 William Swinhoe of Cornhill was murdered when his garrison at Wark was captured by Scots.[21] This attack may have been motivated by the massacre of Scottish prisoners at Wark in 1546, but there were other encounters at Langton, Grindonrig and an episode known as the 'Norham Chase' where more Scottish prisoners were taken. These prisoners included many Ker and Rutherford lairds, as well as Young of Otterburn.[22] They would no doubt have been held for compensation as Borderers were particularly adept at ransoming men of substance. The practice was perhaps more of a game than a serious financial transaction to native Borderers as there is little indication of payment being made. James Home of Cowdenknowes found a way around his predicament by arranging his release in exchange for Rowland Forster of Lucker, who was then a Scots captive.[23]

Anglo-Scottish troubles intensified in 1560 when Queen Elizabeth launched a military campaign to help the Protestant Lords of the Congregation oust French forces from Scotland. This military commitment ended the 1557–59 series of Border skirmishes and would have settled the Eastern Borderers back into more friendly relationships. After nearly a decade of relative Anglo-Scottish tranquillity, cross-border friction arose again in December 1569 when supporters of the failed Northern Rebellion fled into Scotland. Although this did not affect many Eastern Borderers, some did shelter fugitives. This was not a new phenomenon in 1569 as there had always been reciprocal sympathy for some felons in the Eastern Borders, which will be discussed later. In this case, though, an English Catholic minority was sheltered by minority Catholics in Scotland.[24]

Fleeing rebels, led by the earls of Northumberland and Westmorland, were welcomed into Liddesdale by the outlawed James Ormiston of that Ilk. This reception was pre-arranged as Mary, Queen of Scots had long been in correspondence with her loyal supporters in the Borders in anticipation of the rising's success. Now that the uprising had failed the rebels knew where they were guaranteed shelter.[25] The earl of Northumberland was captured, but the others found sanctuary with Sir Thomas Ker of Ferniehirst, Sir Walter Scott of Buccleuch, Sir Thomas Turnbull of Bedrule and the fifth Lord Home. Ferniehirst Castle was visited by Robert Constable, as a well-disguised English spy, and he reported that he had 'waded into trap those who trust in me – as Judas did Christ'. He had been unwittingly escorted there by George Pyle of Millheugh and found Westmorland out walking, oblivious to the danger that Constable posed. With their location now discovered the countess of Northumberland along with Robert Collingwood of Abberwick, Robert Carr of Hetton and Ralph Swinhoe of Cornhill moved to Hume Castle, whilst Tristram Fenwick of Brinkburn stayed at Bedrule.[26]

The rebels took great delight in raiding back into England to cause maximum harassment to their enemies, but ultimate revenge would be carried out by the earl of Sussex and Lord Hunsdon. With a large army they launched a two-pronged attack on the houses of those who had sheltered the rebels. For a moment it seemed as though the savagery of the 1540s had returned to southern Scotland, though the pro-English government in Scotland allowed this to happen. Ferniehirst Castle was razed to the ground and Hume Castle was battered until it surrendered.[27] Westmorland escaped to the Low Countries, through Aberdeen, but lesser men like Ralph Swinhoe remained fugitive in Scotland until 1573. He was finally apprehended by Alexander Home of North Berwick after he had been driven to steal animals and goods from Home's property of Trottingshaw in the Lammermuirs. Obviously this did not endear him to his captor and may well have been the reason behind his betrayal. If exiles caused no trouble they could often stay abroad for years.[28]

The next cross-border incident of consequence was the 1575 Redeswire Fray, but it did not concern the Eastern Borders directly. This fracas arose during a day of truce for the notoriously troubled areas of Tynedale and Liddesdale. It was held near the source of the River Rede, south of Jedburgh. The earl of Huntingdon, as president of the Council of the North, suggested that this incident brought the two realms to the brink of war, but he was over-reacting as usual. The incident offended Elizabeth I as Sir John Forster, Sir Francis Russell, Sir Cuthbert Collingwood and several other gentlemen were apparently taken prisoner by the Scots amidst the mêlée. The Scots maintained that they had only been protecting these gentlemen and this was probably true. The same policy was later adopted by the Homes during a skirmish at Norham Ford in 1597. Proof of the Scots' sincerity was shown the day after when they released most of these men unharmed. David Home of Godscroft blamed the English for causing the initial trouble and singled out Forster's arrogance towards Sir John Carmichael of that Ilk, keeper of Liddesdale, as the main source of tension. This incited the Tynedale men to shoot arrows towards the Scottish delegation, who naturally responded and killed Sir George Heron in the crossfire. The earl of Morton, then regent of Scotland, tried to play down the occurrence by sending falcons to influential Elizabethan courtiers. Their response was that he had given them 'live Hawkes for dead Herons'.[29]

The Redeswire Fray was settled by Border commissioners. It put a strain on Anglo-Scottish relations, but it was not as serious as the death of Sir Francis Russell at a day of truce in 1585. This contributed to the toppling of the Scottish government led by the earl of Arran, yet within a year an Anglo-Scottish league had been agreed. This assured future peace between the realms and made James VI a 'client prince' of Elizabeth I. The strength of this league overshadowed localised cross-border incidents such as the December 1587 pitched battle between Sir Cuthbert Collingwood and the Burns. It was a stupid and avoidable confrontation that left fifteen English soldiers dead, yet did not cause an international furore on the scale of Redeswire or the Russell murder. James VI now took a personal interest in Border problems and began building up a network of loyal Border lairds to try and counter any trouble before it began. However he did not have a great deal of success at first as this incident heralded a period of intensified reiving that worsened after the execution of Mary, Queen of Scots.[30]

March wardens and their deputies varied in their individual response to the persistent problem of cross-border reiving. The main direction of raids was from the Middle and West Marches into the Eastern Borders. Lord Hunsdon, when in residence, was reported to take 'as great pleasure in hanging thieves as other men in hawking and hunting'. Hunsdon was non-resident from 1587 until his death in 1596, so Western Border reivers' attacks on the English East March went largely unpunished. By contrast Sir John Forster made private pacts with notorious reivers that protected him and his kinsmen's property. Being a native Borderer, Forster knew the value of self-protection. His action was contrary to Border law, but many of these laws were openly flouted. Forster was able to keep a modicum of peace in his Middle March, unlike the blatantly antagonistic efforts of Collingwood in 1587 or the over-zealous actions of Hunsdon's sons, Sir Robert and John, in 1596.[31] Impatient for redress of a horse theft, John Carey sent some of his garrison men to the house of one of the principal offenders, John Dalgleish. They hacked John to pieces on his doorstep and retreated to Berwick. Carey expected to be praised for his actions, but received condemnation. Queen Elizabeth referred to it as 'verie barbourous and seldom used emong the Turckes'. Sir Robert Carey remained within the confines of Border law to seek his vengeance on Scottish thieves when he hung a favourite reiver of Sir Robert Ker of Cessford for March treason.[32] Though legal, this was a provocative act at a time of intense reiving and proved to be counter-productive as raiding further intensified.

The bleak reiving years of the mid 1590s culminated in an important meeting of the Border commissioners during 1596–97. Many back-dated bills for redress were heard, but the principal demand of the English commissioners was for the delivery of Sir Robert Ker of Cessford and his brother-in-law, Sir Walter Scott of Buccleuch. They were the two most infamous reivers affecting the Eastern English Borders at that time. Cessford, as an Eastern Borderer, was a disgrace to his more peaceable kinsmen. His family were not known for reiving, so his mafia-like tactics in the late 1580s and 1590s have to be regarded as juvenile rebelliousness.[33] English officials noted that Eastern Border lairds like Sir Andrew Ker of Ferniehirst, William Douglas of Bonjedward and Lord Home were 'good and peaceable neigh-bours to England'.[34] They were far more typical of Eastern Border lairds than Cessford and his mob.

A meeting of the Border commissioners at Norham Ford on 8 October 1597 was supposedly to exchange pledges for unpaid Border bills with Cessford and Buccleuch being the prize Scottish pledges. The English were so conscientious about bringing their pledges that they produced a corpse 'yet was he brought and presented at the place'. Buccleuch gave himself up to Sir William Bowes, the chief English commissioner, but the immature Cessford was reluctant to go into English custody. At dusk one of Cessford's men let off a pistol, knowing that it would create havoc in the half-light.

Soldiers from Berwick garrison panicked and 'bestowed 200 bulletts and yet by the gracious providence of god, slew no man, but forced all men with the speed they could to quitt the place.' This may have been caused by poor light, poor marksmanship, inferior weaponry or a command to fire into the air. In 1591 some Homes caught up in a domestic feud had fired fifty shots across the Tweed without finding their target either.[35] Lord Home and the Homes of Ayton, Huttonhall and Wedderburn saved the Norham débâcle by crowding around the leading English commissioner Sir William Bowes and the local gentry who had accompanied him. They were Ralph, Edward and Roger Gray of Chillingham, Robert Clavering of Callaly and James Swinhoe of Berrington. All were escorted to Huttonhall, about five miles north of the scene, where they dined in more peaceful surroundings. After this the Homes escorted everyone back to Berwick. Lord Home and his kinsmen were praised by both James VI and Elizabeth for preventing a blood-bath, though they had distanced themselves from Border thieves for many years. It was significant that Scottish laird pledges, who were handed over that day, were from the Middle and not the East March. They were mostly disreputable associates of Cessford – Robert Frissell of Overton, Dand Pringle of Hownam, James Young of Feltershaws, Ralph Mow, younger son of that Ilk, Jock Burn of the Coate and his brother Ralph, Rutherford of Littleheuch and William Tait of Cherrytrees.[36]

The exchange of pledges led to a decrease in reiving activities into the Eastern English Borders. Days of truce were certainly more peaceful, but there were still a few cross-border incidents connected with pasturing or hunting. For example, the Redesdale hunting incident of August 1598 was the result of over-zealous retribution by Sir Robert Carey, as warden of the English Middle March. Carey was acting against his long-time adversary Sir Robert Ker of Cessford and had still not learned that it was better to mediate Border problems rather than avenge them. James VI was furious that Carey had attacked his new favourite, Cessford. He was uninjured whereas William Douglas of Bonjedward and his son, Rutherford of Hunthill and Ker of Primsideloch were either injured or imprisoned. The Scots had been hunting along a controversial, yet 'usuall', cross-border route. Game could hardly be expected to recognise an unmarked international boundary, so the Scots continued their chase into English territory before returning to Scotland.[37] Rather than make his protest through official channels, Carey determined to settle the issue with a fight. He therefore took 400 armed men four miles into Scotland to attack the hopelessly outnumbered Scots surrounding Cessford.

Carey's attack was seen as heroic by non-Border Englishmen like Lord Willoughby, warden of the East March, who tried to emulate him in 1599 by hunting very close to the Scottish Border hoping to 'prove things'. Fortunately this time the Scots refused to rise to the challenge.[38] The late-sixteenth century English wardens were all arrogant outsiders who were deliberately provocative towards the Scots. It was fortunate that James VI personally intervened in all Eastern Scottish Border affairs during 1598–1603 to prevent Scots retaliation. He realised that a serious cross-border skirmish could blight his succession to the English throne and jeopardise lucrative cross-border trade, amongst other things.

III. Trade Across The Frontier

The Border was only recognised by local people when it suited them. It was seldom noticed when economics were to the fore as cross-border trade was profitable.[39] The Scots of the Merse commanded the geographical hinterland of the borough of Berwick-upon-Tweed. That Berwick was no longer Scottish did not disturb the natural flow of trade towards this urban centre. Moreover the Merse had no suitable alternative to Berwick for its sixteenth-century trade. There was much illicit trading throughout the Eastern Borders for the frontier was too open to regulate. English horses, for example, made up a good proportion of illegal trade as they were highly valued by the Scots. Legitimate trade tended to centre on Berwick, the largest town north of the Coquet.

After centuries of conflict Berwick-upon-Tweed became an outright English possession in 1482. The borough became a permanent garrison town, run by military men rather than the guild of burgesses. The guild had a voice within the town council, but policy decisions were made by the governor of the garrison. In 1584 and 1593 this arrangement led to confrontation between the mayor and the burgesses on one part, and the governor on the other. The guild's complaints were numerous, but one of the most contentious issues was the number of Scots frequenting and supplying their market. Henry VIII had encouraged Scottish merchants to supply the town in 1532 at the 'Calfhill within the Berwick bounds'. They were never trusted to trade within the walls of the town, but Berwick folk knew they could easily access Scottish merchants just beyond their gates. The large garrison was in perpetual need of victuals and the Scots were willing to oblige them. A 1535 Act of the Scottish parliament prohibiting this trade did not deter the Scots.[40] During the miserable 1540s it was agreed the 'Berwick with its ancient limits shall remain at peace', to facilitate cross-border trade and keep the harbour open for supplies from elsewhere. It even became a legal centre for some Scots in 1548 as a charter was registered in the Guild Book of Berwick between John Edington of that Ilk and George Cockburn of the Woodhead.[41] They probably could see no end to the English occupation and decided to transact their business in the borough, rather than in Edinburgh.

Scots who supplied Berwick were known as the 'victualling Scots' and the garrison men certainly preferred their fresh produce to unappetising victuals sent from the south of England. In 1551 grain was in short supply so the

Scots probably provided some, though Berwick merchants were only supposed to supply the garrison from Newcastle or the South.[42] Scots traded freely in Berwick during the 1550s, but in September 1559 the pro-French Scottish administration tried to ban the trade. They hoped that the Scots merchants would supply French garrisons instead and thus avoid giving intelligence to England. This effort was in vain 'for the Scots come as usual on market day' and Scottish ships also brought in wheat and fish.[43]

The market at Carlisle was similarly patronised by Scots, though the incentives here may not have been so honorable. The goods and livestock sold by notorious West March reivers at Carlisle were likely to have been stolen, rather than genuinely produced for the market. As there was predominantly poor, upland pasture on the Scottish side of the Western frontier, the Scots who brought goods into Carlisle tended to take grain back with them. Traders from more civilised areas such as Kirkcudbright brought English woollen cloth back from Carlisle, proving how important this town was for the economy of south-west Scotland.[44]

Trade into Berwick from the Merse could be lawfully reciprocated when there was a dearth in Scotland and a surplus in the town. This was open to abuse as the treasurer of Berwick was reprimanded in 1561 for selling grain to the Scots when there was no surplus. Berwick burgesses also traded with the Scots in skins, victual, fish and even salmon fishings in the River Tweed, but they had to adhere to strict trading regulations.[45] For instance, a burgess was fined twenty shillings and warded in 1564 for buying 'salmonds of the Scotts in kypper time'. Trade continued undaunted until the autumn of 1565 when Anglo-Scottish friction struck at the heart of the Merse – Berwick supply route. The earl of Bothwell and his men attacked some victualling Scots travelling to Berwick market in December 1565, but the Berwick garrison fought them off and an international row erupted. This temporary curtailment in supplies led to a shortage of flesh in the town, but trade was fully resumed by 1566 when the Scots were noted for 'attending the market without the new works' and buying much bread.[46] There were no other disruptions to this trade after 1565–66, with the exception of two outbreaks of plague in 1579 and 1597.

Supplies were particularly welcome in Berwick during the 1590s when a series of bad harvests threatened the survival of the 900 strong garrison. John Carey praised 'many Scottish men, our good neighbours in the Merse, who supply our markets with beef, mutton, veal, pork and all kind of pullyn . . . without which we could not live'. As dearth and the threat of starvation increased, Carey had good reason to be grateful for good relations between the East Marches. The official garrison victualler proved incompetent and 'if Lord Hume would but keep our neighbours of the Merse from victualling us, wee ned no other seidge, for we should have to starve or leave the town'. Trade continued to be two-way as the traveller Fynes Moryson noted in 1598 that 'the Scots, weekely upon market day, obtained leave in writing of the Governour, to buy Pease and Beanes, whereof as also of Wheate, their

Merchants at this day send great quantity from London into Scotland.'[47]
The Union of the Crowns greatly disrupted Berwick's trade as the garrison
was disbanded. The burgesses petitioned James VI & I for a new charter and
received one in 1604. This gave the town back the independence it had lost
in 1482 and the burgesses were now free to reappraise their relations with
the Scots merchants.[48]

The garrison was on good enough terms with East March Scots to search
there for victuals instead of always relying on them coming to Berwick
market. In 1572 the marshall of Berwick was listed as a debtor in the
inventory of William Craw of Flemington-Fluris for fifteen bolls of oats
worth £12 Scots.[49] Ordinary Berwick burgesses felt safe enough to trade in
the Merse by 1600. This merchandising was unconnected to garrison
victualling as 'furnishing' was mentioned in the inventories of David Home
of Ninewells and the wife of Simon Redpath of Angelrow. Berwick was nearer
than Edinburgh for consumer goods and with the Union of the Crowns
looming these merchants were probably keen to expand their trade into an
area known for its relative peace in comparison to the Western Borders.[50]

Cross-border trade was generally beneficial to local people on both sides
of the frontier, but there was much confusion and argument about Scottish
and English coinage for these transactions. Wardens argued about the
uneven exchange rate of sterling and the falling pound Scots at days of
truce, and Berwick merchants perennially complained about Scots taking
too much English coinage from their market. This created a shortage and
forced merchants to transact their business in Scottish money or even barrels
of salmon.[51] The Scots valued having sterling and seem to have used it for
settling Border bills. Inflation could easily outstrip the agreed value of the
goods in pounds Scots as bills could take years to settle.[52] An additional
problem with Border coinage was the incidence of local forgery. Rowland
Forster of Lucker had a man in his household to 'coin hardheads' in 1568,
but this attempt failed. Others succeeded, as John Carr of Hetton was caught
with counterfeit coin in 1586. The proximity of the realms and the use of
two currencies was evidently an irresistible opportunity for forgery.[53]

Cross-border trade was not confined to Berwick-upon-Tweed, though the
burgesses of the town and the governments of both countries wished it to be.
The custom duty on a boll of victual going from Berwick to Scotland was
four shillings per boll, so customs evasion was commonplace. In 1568 the
burgesses grumbled that

> Yt is of greate hurtt to this comon welthe and hindrance to the
> inhabitants of the same that all or the amoste parte of the corne grayne
> and sundry other comodities . . . beyond tyll water [River Till] ys sold
> and conveyed into the Realme of Scotland all alonge the frontyers.[54]

The wardens were supposed to stop this smuggling, but corruption, lack of
gentry support and ignorance of geography made prevention ineffective.

Interestingly Robert Logan of Restalrig held the rights to the 'customs of Berwick Castle', dating from when it was a Scottish possession. He kept up his claim in charters, but this would not have been practical after 1482.

Smuggling was certainly not just a Border problem, but the geography of this region was conducive to illicit trade. Goods were smuggled in both directions across the landward frontier or through the small ports at Aln-mouth or Holy Island.[55] Regent Morton was so perturbed by this illicit trade that he appointed a 'customer and searcher' for Roxburghshire, Selkirkshire and Berwickshire in 1574. He was to seek out English goods entering Scotland and demand customs duty. Many traders would still have re-mained elusive, but some unfortunate English merchants were arrested at Kelso in 1574 and had their goods confiscated. The grain trade must have continued as there was a curious shortage in 1577, despite there being a good local harvest. Attempts to legislate against this in England proved abortive. Border burghs such as Jedburgh would continue to thrive on cross-border trade until the early-eighteenth century.[56]

Scottish merchants who made illicit use of the natural harbours and bays of the Northumbrian coast were welcomed by the local gentry. This annoyed the Berwick guild as they were supposed to have the monopoly of trade between 'Coquet and Tweed'.[57] The gentry had a well-established supply line to deliver grain to Holy Island which was then uplifted by a passing Scottish merchant ship. In return they probably received luxury goods or money. Scottish merchants traded with other people as well, for Matthew Forster in Bamburgh owed James Coldone, burgess of Edinburgh, £4–10s for a hogshead of wine in 1589. Wine was popular with the elite in the English Western Borders as well, where fishermen landed 'wynes from Scotland' alongside their catches of herring.[58] Numerous attempts to legislate against this trade with Scotland were ineffective. One suggestion to make Holy Island a satellite port of Berwick would have been purposeful if adopted, for this was the principal source of illicit sea trade in the Eastern English Borders.[59]

Horses were an integral part of the landward smuggling network, again despite much legislation against it. This trade was two-way until the Scottish civil wars of the late 1560s created a domestic shortage of horses. This made the direction of trade one-way for the rest of the century.[60] Borderers were renowned horsemen and a smuggled or stolen horse was highly prized. It was far easier to steal horses than buy them and horse theft would remain a cross-border problem until well after 1603.[61] Border horsemanship was even valued by Sir Francis Walsingham, who wanted Scottish and English Borderers recruited to serve in the South in 1581. Andrew Ker of Cessford and William Douglas of Bonjedward brawled over two stolen English horses at a day of truce in 1555. Again in 1600 Steven Brounfield of Greenlawdean and Sir Alexander Home of Manderston argued about whether a horse had been stolen or purchased.[62] A laird wishing to buy a horse from England through official channels had first to acquire a placard from the English privy council. This entailed a long and complicated procedure so placards became highly sought after. It helped if the applicant was on friendly terms with England, but this did not make the process any speedier. For example the sixth Lord Home's application took seven months in 1596, despite his having been granted a placard in 1590. Thomas Cranston of Morriston probably experienced a long wait as well in 1588.[63]

It is notable that Eastern Border lairds opted to go through official channels, rather than resort to theft to acquire horses. Nevertheless the placard system was open to abuse by devious persons. William Selby of Twizel, junior, complained about this in 1601. He stated that seventy-five per cent of Scottish horses came from England because the placards were never surrendered at the time of purchase, allowing sixty horses to be sold with a 'placquett' instead of the official maximum of two. Selby recommended that the placards should be recalled after two months had elapsed to prevent abuse and hoped that this would bring local prices down. Scottish pressure on the English horse market led to sharp increases that reportedly denied horses to all but the gentry and therefore endangered Border defence.[64] Scots sometimes travelled to fairs in Yorkshire to purchase horses or sent an English middleman to buy on their behalf. The unabashed Sir Robert Ker of Cessford decided to go to Yorkshire in person during June 1597, but he had to disguise himself as a servant for he was then one of the most wanted Scottish pledges. He was accompanied by two Englishmen for good camouflage and bought two horses for £55, eluding all trouble. When English Border officials found out about this they were furious, but it demonstrated how easily a Scot could travel to the Yorkshire fairs.[65] English gentlemen were also involved in the sale of horses to Scotland, contrary to laws forbidding this, as it proved too lucrative a trade to be ignored. When Sir John Forster asked for a placard in 1568 to reward Scottish informants with horses, he probably wanted to trade in horses himself. Forster's rival, Sir Cuthbert Collingwood, had a placard in 1577 but he was later accused of selling horses to the Scots illegally.[66]

The overall impression of cross-border trading from 1540 to 1603, whether it concerned grain, meat or horses, is that much of it was illicit or at least unofficial on both sides of the Border. This is not surprising in a frontier region where corrupt officials were either deliberately blind, or actively involved in this trade themselves. Lairds and gentlemen would certainly have profited from this trade, but there was another opportunity for economic advancement in the area with the large settlement of Scots in the Eastern English Borders.

IV. The Scots in Northumberland

The north Northumbrian and North Durham gentry found the settlement of Scots in their area advantageous. They were prepared to lease land that few

Englishmen dared occupy and could pay a higher rental than others could afford. The Scots were also useful craftsmen, colliers, shepherds, servants or entertainers and they were thought to number between 2,500 and 3,000 in the East March in 1568, with another 200 in Berwick.[67] There may not have been as many as this, but Scottish settlement in Northumberland was not a new phenomenon as it was well advanced by 1440. There had been a long standing Scottish migration into England and expulsion measures were never very effective. Scots numbers in the Eastern English Borders increased steadily throughout the sixteenth century. This contrasted with the Western English Borders where resident Scots were far fewer in number. Xenophobic attitudes towards the Scots were more pronounced there, though small numbers were tolerated as servants.[68] The strong Scottish presence in the East was reflected in the local habit of calling some of the gentry who lived near the Border 'lairds', such as Strother of Kirknewton, Selby of Pawston, Morton of Murton and Clennell of Clennell.[69] The Scottish legacy persisted and was noted by Daniel Defoe in 1725. He contrasted a lack of English influence in Berwickshire with the Northumbrian 'abundance of Scotsmen, Scots customs, words, habits and usages'.[70]

It is indisputable that the gentry faced serious problems in 1536 as much of their land near the frontier was 'waste'. Wartime valuations took some account of this predicament as Gavin Selby's Tindall House was worth 13s 4d per annum or '1s in time of war.' Even in peacetime, English tenants were not prepared to farm so near to infamous Scottish reivers. To maintain

> revenue the gentlemen of the country doe rather lette their lands to Scottes then to Englishmen for they will give more then an Englishe man can doe because there cattel shall goe quietlye without stealing, which an englishe manes shall hardley doe.

Lord Eure, warden of the English Middle March in 1541, had even encouraged Scottish craftsmen to settle in his March.[71] By 1568 Lord Hunsdon was complaining about the numbers of Scots in his East March. He claimed that some of the towns were 100 per cent Scottish and that all the late Sir Ralph Gray of Chillingham's tenants were Scots. As none of these Scots were denizens, Hunsdon rightly feared for Border security. However, he may have exaggerated as a late-sixteenth century survey of Gray's lands shows both Scots and English surnames and another report estimated there to be only 443 Scots in the East March.[72] At Ditchburn and North Charlton in the East March there was a mix of English and Scots tenants and cottagers as their names ranged from Forster, English, Blith and Nuton to Sheil, Tailer, Maxwell and Broun. There was even a freehold called 'Scottes Cloose'.[73] The gentry of North Durham had many Scottish tenants and servants as well. In a 1593 survey thirty-seven townships had 247 resident Scots, only one of whom was a denizen. Sir John Selby of Twizel had no English tenants, but had eight Scottish cottagers and four Scots servants.

Robert Clavering of Callaly also had no Englishmen present at Tillmouth, but had six Scots tenants and three Scottish servants. Even crown land had succumbed to this policy as the queen had fifteen Scottish cottagers at Buckton, who were probably placed there by a pro-Scots bailiff. Sir William Reed was alone in refusing to lease his lands to Scots, probably to vindicate his loyalty to Elizabeth I.[74]

Scottish settlement in the area proved irreversible as the wardens failed to remove the Scots from their Marches. Hunsdon made many futile attempts to evict them before he relaxed his anti-Scottish stance in 1587. He then thought that 'sufficient necessarie men as colliours, fysshers, heardes and sheappards' should remain.[75] Though Hunsdon had recognised the economic necessity of having Scots in his March, he still had reservations about their possible collusion with reivers and their lack of English citizenship. He saw no British solution here, as this was truly an English problem. The inventory of Luke Ogle of Eglingham listed three Scottish creditors called Davidson, Dickson and Brounfield. Ogle, like Hunsdon, recognised their usefulness as they were probably craftsmen or servants resident in the locality.[76] The gentry refused to evict Scottish tenants as they were a good source of income in an area that was difficult to settle. The Scots also remained entrenched in towns such as Berwick.[77]

The majority of Northumbrian Scots probably felt like the Scot who 'having lived from his infancy in England . . . knew no other but he was naturalized after the manner of the Border'.[78] Did this mean that he felt English, or was he simply identifying himself as a Borderer? Perhaps the latter is true as Sandy Pringle, a younger son of the laird of Torwoodlee, was the only laird's son to become a denizen of England. He bore no grudge towards England despite the untimely death of his father at Flodden. During the 1540s he and many of his Pringle kinsmen spied for England, though he had been initially forced into this activity to save the life of a kinsman. He then went completely over to the English side and accepted monastic grants and denizenship from Henry VIII. This was regarded as intentional treachery rather than Border craftiness by his fellow Scots. Ostracised by his kin, Pringle had to settle far away from the Border at Fernacres, near Newcastle.[79] His isolation was an exception to the well-established Anglo-Scottish friendships that existed in the Eastern Borders.

V. Unofficial Cross-Border Relations

In contrast to the idiosyncratic view of the sixteenth-century Borders as a region of endemic violence and hatred, the Eastern Border lairds and gentlemen were fairly sociable across their frontier. This has tended not to be recognised, particularly by writers obsessed with disorder, but there is a true sense of these men being Borderers first and foremost when it came to helping friends across the invisible frontier. The River Tweed could be forded as low as Norham and the rest of the frontier could be crossed on land or by boat. The Border was therefore transparent when it came to friendship, as landed families, like any early modern elite, shared interests and pleasures with disregard to any officialdom. Lairds and gentlemen had a good knowledge of their opposite realm's geography, which helped when socialising or chasing stolen goods. Officially they were not supposed to have this knowledge as trysting between Scotsmen and Englishmen was strictly against Border law. In 1550 loyal Scots disapproved of trysting because intelligence could pass to England, but this seldom concerned the Borderers.[80] The only time they recognised the frontier in friendship was when a fellow landed man needed asylum in the opposite realm.

Friendships across the Border were based on familiarity, shared values, neighbourliness, marriage and kinship. These cannot be seen as potentially British links as they were really only Borderers enjoying the company of fellow landed Borderers. These social links did not appear first in the sixteenth century. They probably date back to the time before the frontier was politically defined in the twelfth and thirteenth centuries.[81] Even today there are parts of the Borders 'which some Borderers still consider separate from Scotland and England.'[82] Five centuries ago these contacts were contrary to Border Law, yet could be extremely useful in times of heightened Anglo-Scottish tension when the Borderers hated being in the firing line. For instance in October 1523, when Regent Albany planned Scottish incursions into North Durham, Lord Borthwick 'sent warning to George Urde to put his cattle away, as they would make small forays.' Similar cross-border intelligence had clearly reached Mersemen in December 1532, when Henry VIII threatened to invade Scotland, for they 'had removed with their goods and cattle' to Dunglass in East Lothian.

Again in 1547 during the Scottish defeat at the Battle of Pinkie the Borderers put their self-interest before Scottish or English identity. The English Borderers, who made up a significant part of the English army, were noted for taking prisoners of their fellow Scottish Borderers, rather than killing them. Centuries of tradition had taught them to seek ransom rather than bloodlust from other Borderers on the battlefield. This seemingly treacherous move was certainly not unique in early modern times. It is well known that Danish and Swedish peasants, in contempt of their respective crowns and nobility, used to make private peace treaties before going into battle. These peasants, like the Borderers, knew they were invariably going to be at the forefront of any international battle. This apparent disdain for national patriotism by the Borderers was not a new phenomenon either. In the late-thirteenth century, when cross-border landowners were still common, Borderers 'may have followed their overlords rather than their nation . . .'[83]

The Forsters of Adderstone, Bamburgh and Lucker continued this trend as they were noted as being 'familiar' with Scottish reivers from at least 1559 onwards. The infamous James Ormiston of that Ilk wrote to the Forsters in

1559 asking if he should thresh his corn and put away his goods, in case an invading English army should destroy them. Dispersal of this type of intelligence would have been treasonable in either realm and was certainly against Border law, yet it was acceptable amongst friendly Borderers. This contrasts sharply with later medieval antagonism between Englishman and Scot identified by Cynthia Neville, but this period may just have been an aberration from normally friendly cross-border relations.[84] Sir John Forster kept up his familiarity with Scottish thieves throughout his long career as warden of the Middle March. His livestock near the Border were known to 'feede quyetlye and safelye there. And if any other parson put in his cattell and suffer them to remayne there all night, are they not by Scottishe men taken awaye before the morninge'. When Forster was dismissed from the wardenship he suffered a dramatic loss of prestige and did not keep up his association with these reiving Scots. Some of his sheep were then stolen and a gang of thirty Scots came to Bamburgh Castle to attack him, but fortunately 'his lady gott the chamber doore put to and bolted'.[85]

The Selbies of Twizel were on friendly terms with many Scottish lairds, including the Homes of Huttonhall, Manderston and Wedderburn, and the Kers of Ferniehirst. In 1581 they arranged a meeting by calling across the River Tweed, which was probably their usual method of trysting.[86] The Selbies' association with Scots went back to the early-sixteenth century. In 1540 John Selby of Branxton was noted for being too 'familiar with Scotts'. His continued cross-border friendships led to his being temporarily dismissed from the office of gentleman porter of Berwick in 1556. The English privy council disapproved of his eldest son's marriage to Margaret Douglas, an illegitimate daughter of Sir George Douglas of Pittendreich. He was reinstated when an investigation found this marriage was not a threat to Berwick's security. Margaret Douglas had been born in Berwick and was allowed to keep her father's name as she 'resembled much his other children and carried ever a more then ordinary kindness to the name of Douglas and which hir familiars wald noway refuse hir surname of Douglas'. The Selbies and Douglases remained on good terms as Sir John recommended his kinsman Mr George Douglas to Sir Francis Walsingham in 1582.[87]

There were other cross-border marriages between the families of lairds and gentlemen, again in open defiance of the Border law stating that it was March treason to marry a Scot. These marriages were more numerous in the Western Borders, but there were at least four in the Eastern Borders. A Forster married a Home; a Selby married a Rutherford; a daughter of Thomas Collingwood of Great Ryle married a Hall and Thomas Selby, a younger son of Biddlestone, married a daughter of Rutherford of Little-heuch.[88] The Grays of Chillingham had no marriage links across the Border, but they were friendly with the sixth Lord Home. Home stayed at Chillingham in 1602 on his return journey from France where he had been James VI's ambassador. He may also have stayed there on other unrecorded occasions.[89] The Grays had connections with the frequently exiled Scot, the master of Gray. He stayed at Chillingham in 1592 and 1600 in recognition that they were 'both of one name and arms'. Gray apparently preferred the Northumbrian Grays to 'any cousin german I have within Scotland who is not a Gray'.[90]

Ralph Gray of Chillingham was friendly towards Sir Robert Ker of Cessford, but the 'kindness' between them was seen as 'a bad example to the country' by supercilious Border officials. Their friendship was another example of the disregard held by the local population for the international frontier. Cessford seems to have been able to travel through the English East March in 1595 without being challenged by the warden, soldiers of the Berwick garrison, or local gentry. Local people below the ranks of the gentry were probably too scared to confront him or may have been silenced by his well-established blackmailing network. The gentry seem to have chosen to be on friendly terms with him, either for genuine reasons of amity or simply to protect their property. For example, Cessford was known to have stayed with the avaricious Collingwoods of Etal in 1595 and to have drunk with Selby of Pawston.[91]

There are examples of landed men crossing the Border for short visits to hunt or dine with one another, but these visits are rarely documented.[92] Cross-border visits probably occurred with frequency in the Borders, but would have been kept fairly secret so as not to alarm panicky Border officials. D. Nobbs has suggested that the Scots were unable to maintain the rank and resources necessary to reciprocate English hospitality, but this is blatantly untrue for the Scottish Border lairds made a good living from their lands.[93] An outstanding example of friendship and goodwill between the Marches occurred in October 1594 when the sixth Lord Home came into the English East March to buy hounds and hunt with his gentry friends. He stayed with Sir William Reed, dined with Sir John Forster at Alnwick and hunted with the Forsters in Bamburghshire. The local gentry thought nothing amiss in this Anglo-Scottish hospitality, but John Carey typically refused to believe that Home's visit was purely sociable and accused the gentry of treachery. The outsider Carey's confusion is understandable for Home's visit coincided with the traditional start of the reiving season. As relations were good between landed families in the East Marches he should not have been so alarmist. Carey was renowned for being apprehensive as he once called out the garrison to evict a group of carousing Scots from Carham though, in truth, they would have been too intoxicated to cause serious trouble. Ironically the garrison men were known to cross the Border themselves for sociable activities. For instance, in 1588 some prominent members of the garrison dined with the earl of Bothwell at Coldingham.[94]

Sporting challenges between Borderers were not unknown because of their mutual interests in the chase. Sir Robert Ker of Cessford hunted with Thomas Percy, the constable of Alnwick and they arranged a hare coursing challenge during the winter of 1597–98. Cessford confessed 'for as God witness me I am so drowned with the love of that game the care of all other things is from me'.[95] This event was certainly a distraction from the pressure of English Border commissioners to have him handed over as a key Scottish pledge. It would appear that Ker's love of hunting was respected by the gentry in their accustomed defiance of Border law, even at this critical time in Anglo-Scottish relations.

This familiarity and friendship across the Border was equally valued by fugitives seeking asylum from the justice of their respective countries. This was one of the rare occasions when the Border was recognised as an international frontier and it had ancient roots.[96] In 1557 three supporters of the besieged Carrs of Ford made use of their alleged mutual ancestry with the Kers and sheltered at the house of Robin Ker of Ancrum. Interestingly, the Kers of Ferniehirst and the Carrs of Ford were both left-handed, as staircases at Ferniehirst and Ford Castles are both designed for sinistral defence on a dextrogyrous spiral.[97] Perhaps they were related, but there were many other cases of landed and non-landed rebels sheltering in the Eastern Borders.[98] Scottish exiles in the English Eastern Borders included Thomas Cranston of Morriston and Ferniehirst. Cranston sought refuge in the East March in 1588 and during the 1590s; firstly for being involved in a feud and secondly for allying with the infamous earl of Bothwell. Walsingham allowed him to stay with the Selbies of Twizel in 1588 as they had mutual Douglas kinship. (Cranston's mother was a Douglas and Sir John Selby had married a Douglas.) Cranston moved around the March and probably went back and forth across the Border to receive shelter from his Cranston kinsmen as well.[99] Sir Thomas Ker of Ferniehirst was exiled in the 1570s and again in the 1580s for reasons of political expediency. After an initial exile in the English Middle March, where he stayed with his friends Sir John Forster and Sir George Heron of Chipchase, Ferniehirst went to France. Forster later regretted this kindness towards him as Ferniehirst was probably involved with the death of his son-in-law, Sir Francis Russell, and never repaid the money Forster lent him. Ferniehirst must have played upon local rivalries in England as Sir Cuthbert Collingwood also advanced him money.[100] Forster was still trying to recover this debt by way of a Border bill against Ferniehirst's widow in 1590, but his chances of success were slender as Ferniehirst also left debts in France.[101]

By 1590 the traditional system of gaining redress for cross-border grievances via Border law was ineffective and it continued to deteriorate. Many pledges were handed over in 1597, yet few of them had been redeemed by payment of the original bills by 1601. Many ordinary Scottish Borderers could simply not afford to pay the amounts due because of inflation and currency devaluation. Their custody meant that they were no longer able to work or steal for a living. In their frustration for compensation some Northumbrian gentry decided to circumvent the authority of the wardens of the Middle Marches and the Border commissioners to try and gain redress through private English bonds. Sir John Forster had used similar techniques during his wardenship to protect his kin, so perhaps the gentry were copying him now that he was out of office. These bonds first surfaced in 1596, a year after Forster was dismissed, though the majority date from 1601–02. They were negotiated directly between the gentry and reivers who owed them compensation, probably because newer, non-local, wardens refused to co-operate with the scheme. They certainly undermined the authority of the wardens and left the gentry's neighbours more vulnerable to attack, but the gentry were desperate to stop further loss or damage to their property. They were also anxious to recover reimbursements awarded to them by the Border commissioners.

The Delavals of Seaton Delaval, for example, made an agreement with the Frissells of Overton in June 1601. This doubled the original £40 bill to £80 in return for the laird's freedom and the handing over of his brother Thomas as a new pledge.[102] William Swinburne of Capheaton followed the Delavals' example and forced a bond of good behaviour out of the Ainslies of Falla in February 1602 by taking one of their sons hostage. Thomas Selby of Biddlestone succeeded in forcing a bond from Dand Elliot of Redheuch.[103] Another bond was probably transacted between the Fenwicks and the Turnbulls as lands near Hawick in Scotland were put up as surety. This transaction was even registered in a Feet of Fine at the Court of Common Pleas in London in 1601.[104] Surprisingly the use of private bonds was declining within Scotland at this time. Nevertheless, as this chapter has demonstrated, bonds were used as Border laws were clearly unworkable in many areas by the 1590s.

A further indication of the decline in Border law occurred when mischievous younger sons of lairds and gentlemen were called before the Newcastle assizes in 1596 and 1601, instead of being summoned by the warden. For example Robert Selby, a younger son of Biddlestone, was indicted for stealing Scottish cattle in 1596.[105] The weakness of using domestic justice and private bonds was that culprits still had to be apprehended. When the Selbies took James Young hostage in 1596 to extract a bond, the plan backfired. Sir Robert Ker of Cessford rescued him before the document could be signed. In 1602 Thomas Carr of Ford had to hand back some of the Liddesdale men he had taken because of warden complaints, which proved that Border law was not yet defunct.[106] These bonds enhance the overall impression of familiarity between landed men in the Eastern Borders, though the principal offenders were younger sons of Jedwater and Teviotdale lairds, not the lairds themselves. The prospect of dynastic union between Scotland and England was probably not linked to these bonds. The criminal and civil legal systems of Scotland and England would always be separate, so these cannot be seen as quasi-British transactions. They were simply an enforcement of domestic English law

upon Scots causing trouble within England to compensate for the weak-
nesses of Border law.

The years immediately preceding the Union of the Crowns witnessed a
heightened interest in Anglo-Scottish affairs and with cross-border familiarity in particular. There had not been a sudden increase in the long-
established Border habit of trysting; it was just receiving far more attention
than before. Trysting still evoked the wrath of the ever-complaining John
Carey, who persistently refused to believe that it could be harmless. He
moaned of 'too great familiarity and intercourse between our English and
Scottish borders: the gentlemen of both countries crossing into either at their
pleasure, feasting and making merry with their friends'. Carey chose to
ignore evidence that Lord Home had been trysting like this since at least
1594 and that he was highly regarded by Elizabeth I for his cross-border
friendship.[107] It was perhaps Elizabeth's disapproval of anyone trying to see
James VI without her permission that prompted Carey's disgust on this
occasion. Thomas Carr of Ford had secretly visited James VI at Cessford's
house of the Friars, near Kelso, in March 1601. Gentry reaction was typified
by Ralph Gray of Chillingham's letter of complaint to Cecil in July 1601. He
objected to Carey's ban on meeting with Scots as it was upsetting traditional
cross-border friendships.[108]

The friendship between Lord Home, as warden of the Scottish East March
and Sir Robert Carey, as warden of the English Middle March, proved
beneficial to Carey in 1603. He hurried north to break the news of
Elizabeth's death to James VI and after seeing the king, Carey lodged with
Lord Home in Edinburgh. He remained there until James VI began his
journey southwards on 5 April 1603.[109] The royal entourage stayed the first
night at Lord Home's house of Dunglass and travelled to Berwick the next
day. James VI had already been presented with the keys of Berwick on 27
March when William Selby of Twizel visited Holyrood, and he knighted him
in gratitude. James now formally entered the town and the guns that had
welcomed him to Halidon Hill in 1588 were fired again. Many people had
gathered in Berwick to witness his entrance and James stayed there for two
days surveying the fortifications and visiting the church several times. He left
Berwick on Friday 6 April, knighting Ralph Gray of Chillingham as he went,
near the Tweed bridge. Nicholas Forster of Bamburgh as high sheriff of
Northumberland waited on the other side of the bridge to welcome him
officially to England as the liberties of Berwick were independent from both
North Durham and Northumberland. James then made a detour in his
journey to honour Sir William Reed with a visit, 'who being blind with age,
was so comforted with the presence and gracious speeches of the king that
his spirits seemed . . . to feele the warmth of youth stirre in his frost-nipt
bloud'.[110] James then rode thirty-seven miles to Sir Robert Carey's house at
Widdrington, south of the Coquet, in only four hours.

The royal party reached London on 7 May 1603, but the Eastern Border lairds and gentlemen had accepted that a new era was upon them from the moment the king left Edinburgh. They would henceforth be able to socialise without the scrutiny of the Berwick garrison or the wardens. The rapid anglicization of the greater lairds that followed 1603 made many lairds from north of the Borders willing to meet their English gentry counterparts for the first time. They were encouraged by James VI & I's proclamation of the 'Middle Shires' to enforce pacification on the frontier region and emphasize his belief in the possibilities of fuller union between the kingdoms. Whilst this was fashionable for a while, few people living in the early-seventeenth century were really convinced by the idea of full constitutional union or the designation Middle Shires. James may well have succeeded in pacifying the immediate problems of the frontier, but his desire to extinguish the name 'Borders' was frustrated. The Borders and the Borderers with their centuries of tradition could not be abolished that easily. Indeed a Border mentality still thrives in the present day Scottish and English Borders.[111]

Notes

1 Rae, *Scottish Frontier*, Tough, *Last Years* and C. A. Coulomb, *The Administration of the English Borders* (New York, 1911). For Border law see W. Nicolson, ed. *Leges Marchiarum* (London, 1747), C. Neville 'Keeping the Peace on the Northern Marches in the Later Middle Ages', *EHR*, cix (1994), 1–25 and H. Summerson, 'The Early Development of the Laws of the Anglo-Scottish Borders, 1249–1448', in *Proceedings of the Ninth British Legal History Conference at Glasgow 1989*, 29–42.
2 NAS GD40/2. APS, iii, 461–6. CBP, ii, 1310. CSP Scot, viii, 60, 739. Calderwood, *History*, iv, 171. Fraser, *Douglas*, iv, 176–216.
3 PRO SP15/4/30 fo. 67. This document also gives an insight to the format of a day of truce and the warden's court (fos 82–93).
4 *Hamilton Papers*, i, 73, 304. *L & P. Hen VIII*, xvi, 990, 1206, 1263, 1399.
5 CBP, i, 6, 77. CSP For, 1572–4, 1193.
6 NAS GD6/648. CSP Scot, x, 354. HMC, Ninth Report, 198; Salisbury, x, 47; xvii, 168–9, 394.
7 PRO STAC5 G4/27. APC, xix, 442. CSP Scot, xiii, pt 1, 83.
8 PRO SP59/33 fos 135–142, SP59/34 fos 262–8. For a description of the unique Border terminology such as 'foul' see *CBP*, ii, 1310.
9 BL MS Cotton, Caligula, D, ii, fo. 337.
10 R. Keith, *History of the Affairs of the Church and State in Scotland*, Spottiswoode Society (1844–50), ii, 469–71. J. Knox, *History of the Reformation in Scotland*, ed. W. C. Dickinson (Edinburgh, 1949), ii, 191–2. Melville, *Memoirs*, 173.
11 BL MS Cotton, Caligula, D, i, fos 336–7. CSP Scot, ix, 455. HMC, Salisbury, v, 192. Moysie, *Memoirs*, 67.
12 CBP, i, 470, 473, 475, 476, 485, 489, 493. W. Ferguson, *Scotland's Relations with England: a Survey to 1707* (Edinburgh, 1978), chs iv & v.
13 APC, i, 27. SS, ii (1835), 38.
14 *L & P. Hen VIII*, xix, pt 2. 33; xx, pt 2,456; xxi, pt 1, 1279. See ch. ii.

15 Tough, *Last Years,* 104. For a detailed description of the Tweed fisheries see V. E. Watts, 'Some Northumbrian Fishery Names IV: The River Tweed', *Durham Archaeological Journal,* xiii (1997), 89–98.

16 PRO SP15/4/30 fo. 71. *APC,* iii, 439; iv, 352. *CBP,* ii, 1484. *CSP For,* 1553–8, 53, 66; 1560–1 1039; 1563 93. *CSP Scot,* i, 401. *RPC,* i, 148.

17 ALN MS AI/1 fo 15.

18 *CSP For,* 1559–60, 248, 268–9, 276, 310, 532, 533. *Sadler Papers,* i, 593–4, 672–3.

19 *CSP For,* 1561–2, 200, 574, 630; 1562, 288; 1563 279, 916, 993, 1280. *CSP Scot,* i, 1034.

20 SYON MS EIV/3/h. *CSP For,* 1566–8, 2242.

21 PRO CS6/29 fo 95. LAMB, MS 3195, fos 72, 270, 278. NRO 1DE/7/109. *CSP For,* 1558–9, 139. Ferguson, *Scotland's Relations,* 67–70, & Rae, *Scottish Frontier,* 187–8.

22 *APC,* i, 399; vi, 318, 396. *CSP Dom Add,* 1547–65, 464–5, 468, 470, 474, 482. *CSP For,* 1559–60, 35. *Sadler Papers,* i, 453–4, 483. R. Holinshed, *The Scottish Chronicle* (Arbroath, 1806), i, 362–3.

23 NAS CS7/2 fo. 64, CS7/16 fo. 56, CS7/42 fo. 59, CS7/63/1 fo. 94. *ADCP,* 546, 550, 566. *CSP For,* 1559–60, 35. *TA,* viii, 193.

24 LAMB, MS 3195 fo. 6. *CSP For,* 1563, 112, 224, 273. See chs. vi & vii.

25 NAS GD40/2/19/1/1A. NLS MS 7103. *CSP Dom Add,* 1566–79, 126, 164. *CSP For,* 1569–71, 555, 556, 565. *CPR,* 1572–5, 513. *HMC,* Salisbury, i, 390, 459. *Sadler Papers,* ii, 110–123. See ch. vii.

26 *CSP Dom Add,* 1566–79, 179 (which wrongly states that Robert Collingwood and Ralph Swinhoe were taken captive in 1570). *CSP For,* 1569–71, 603, 627, 686, 715, 840, 858. Camden, *The History of Princess Elizabeth,* ed. W. MacCaffrey (Chicago, 1970), 122–4. Pitscottie, *Historie,* 220–2, 226–7. *A Diurnal of Remarkable Occurrents,* ed. T. Thomson (Maitland Club, 1833), 154–5. R. Pollitt, 'The Defeat of the Northern Rebellion and the Shaping of Anglo-Scottish Relations', *SHR,* lxiv (1985), 1–21.

27 PRO SP59/20 fo. 107. *CSP For,* 1569–71, 686, 841, 858. *CSP Scot,* iii, 960.

28 *CSP Scot,* iii, 290. *RPC,* ii, 245.

29 *CSP For,* 1575–7, 216, 218, 220, 222–3, 234, 245, 275, 309, 332–4, 432. *CSP Scot,* v, 166. Godscroft, *History,* 339–40. J. Spottiswoode, *History of the Church of Scotland,* ed. M. Russell & M. Napier, Spottiswoode Society, (1847–51), ii, 198. M. C. Cross, *The Puritan Earl* (London, 1966), 202–04. J. Reed, *The Border Ballads* (London, 1973), 118–123.

30 *CBP,* i, 570–7, 582. G. Donaldson, *James V – James VII* (Edinburgh, 1965), 182–83. K. M. Brown, 'The Price of Friendship: The well-affected and English Economic Clientage in Scotland before 1603', in R. A. Mason, ed. *Scotland and England, 1286–1815* (Edinburgh, 1987), 139–162. Rae, *Scottish Frontier,* 220. See ch ii.

31 *CBP,* ii, 279–80, 329, 351, 375. *CSP For,* 1575–7, 438. *L & P. Hen VIII,* xviii, pt 1, 141, 207, 237, 567. *HMC,* Third Report, 50. See ch. iii.

32 PRO SP59/32 fo. 4. *CBP,* ii, 298, 329, 337. *CSP Scot,* xii, 272 (p. 330), 437. Carey, *Memoirs,* 33–42. John Carey's attack was not in revenge for the daring escape of Kinmont Willie Armstrong from Carlisle Castle as Watts suggests in *Border To Middle Shire,* 117.

33 *CBP,* ii, 507. *CSP Scot,* xii & xiii pt 1 (in which there are numerous references to Cessford and Buccleuch's reiving activities). *The Egerton Papers,* ed. J. P.

Collier (Camden Society, 1840), 226–239, 276–281. *HMC*, Milne-Home, 140. Knox, *History*, i, 124.

34 *CSP Scot*, xiii, pt 1, 50.

35 BL MS Cotton Caligula, D. II fo. 293. Godscroft, *De Familia*, 79–80.

36 PRO SP59/35 fos 257–60. *CBP*, ii, 783–6. *HMC*, Salisbury, vii, 226–7, 238–41; ix, pp. 16–17, 28–9, 107.

37 PRO SP59/37 fo. 306. *CBP*, ii, 410, 975, 986–9, 992. *CSP Scot*, xiii, pt 1, 303, 313, 315, 318–20. *HMC*, Salisbury, xii, 115. Carey, *Memoirs*, 55.

38 *CBP*, ii, 1085.

39 A. Cardew, 'A Study of Society in the Anglo-Scottish Borders, 1455–1502'. unpubl. Ph.D diss. St Andrews 1970, 194. Rae, *Scottish Frontier*, 225. S. G. E. Lythe, *The Economy of Scotland, 1550–1625* (Edinburgh, 1960), 215–231. Cross-border trade continued to be significant after 1603. See T. Barrow, 'Corn, carriers and coastal shipping. The shipping and trade of Berwick and the borders 1730–1830', *The Journal of Transport History*, 3rd ser. xxi (2000), 6–27.

40 BL MS Cotton, Titus, C, xii fos 56–62. BRO B1/2 fo. 1. *APS*, ii, 346–7. *CBP*, i, 240, 806–07, 810. *CSP For*, 1558–9, 600; 1575–7, 1432. *L & P. Hen VIII*, xvi, 120. *HMC*, Salisbury, xv, 351. Pitcairn, *Trials*, i, pt 1, 181–2, 379, 476. H. M. Wallace, 'Berwick in the Reign of Elizabeth', *EHR*, xlvi (1931), 79–88. P. C. Waite erroneously suggests that the loss of Berwick was a disaster for Berwickshire's trade, *The Land of Britain* (London, 1941), xiv, 18.

41 BRO B1/1 fo. 2. *L & P. Hen VIII*, xviii, pt 1, 804, 200. For a map of the Berwick bounds see Hatfield MS CPM I /24.

42 *APC*, iii, 206. *CPR*, 1550–3, 106; 1553, 408. *HMC*, Talbot, 351 (P. fo. 319)

43 *CSP For*, 1560–1, 548. *CSP Scot*, i, 544. *CSP Spain*, x, 180. *Sadler Papers*, i, 440.

44 Summerson, *Medieval Carlisle*, ii, 568–74.

45 BRO B1/1 fos 113, 114, B1/3 fo. 40. B1/4 fo. 39. *CBP*, i, 807; ii, 77. *CSP For*, 1561–2, 654, 939; 1566–8, 1677; 1575–7, 1432.

46 BRO C1/1 fo. 2. *CSP For*, 1564–5, 1462, 1589, 1625, 1665, 1720; 1566–8, 9, 45, 525, 1017, 2133.

47 P. Hume Brown, ed. *Early Travellers in Scotland* (Edinburgh, 1978), 89.

48 *CBP*, ii, 77, 178, 743/2. *CSP For*, 1575–7, 1432. *HMC*, Salisbury, xi, 139–40; xv, 351. *RPC*, iii, 229. Raine, *North Durham*, 145–54.

49 NAS CC8/8/2 fo. 177.

50 NAS CC8/8/40 fos 36–7, 42–4.

51 BRO B1/1 fo. 105, B1/4 fo. 85, C1/2 fos 147, 149. *CSP For*, 1561–2, 939. *CSP Scot*, i, 1035. See ch. iv.

52 NAS CC8/8/1 fo. 368, CC8/8/10 fos 131–3, CC8/8/29 fos 8–9, SC62/2/1, SC62/2/5.

53 NAS GD16/37/69. *CSP Dom Add*, 1566–79, 182. *CSP For*, 1575–7, 665, 670. See ch. vii.

54 BRO C1/1/ fo. 2. *CSP For*, 1562, 289. *SS*, xxxviii (1860), 256n.

55 BL MS Cotton, Caligula, C, iii, fo. 113. *CSP For*, 1575–7, 931. *RPC*, vi, 791. *NCH*, xiv, 332n.

56 *APC*, ix, 288–9, 299. *CSP Scot*, i, 409. *RSS*, vi, 2359. G. Elton, *The Parliament of England, 1558–81* (Cambridge, 1986), 248. G. Hilson, *Jedburgh 100 Years Ago* (Kelso Mail, 1897), 7.

57 *CSP For*, 1563, 224; 1575–7, 1432. Watts, *Border to Middle Shire*, 51.

58 *CBP*, i, 825, 841. *CSP For*, 1575–7, 931. *SS*, cxii (1906), 147. Summerson, *Medieval Carlisle*, ii, 575.

59 *APC*, xiv, 245; xxv, 153; xxxii, 400, 431–3. *CSP Dom Add*, 1547–65, 421.

60 PRO SP59/20 fos 196–7. *APC*, iii, 191. *CBP*, i, 104. *CPR*, 1547–8, 247. *Stat*, 23 Hen VIII, c. 16; 1 Eliz, c. 7.

61 P. Edwards, *The Horse Trade of Tudor and Stuart England* (Cambridge, 1988), 135–9.

62 LAMB, MS 3194 fo. 99. *HMC*, Hastings, 17. *RPC*, vi, 150–1.

63 *CSP Scot*, x, 464 (p. 381); xii, 141, 172, 231, 286. *HMC*, Salisbury, iii, 319.

64 *CBP*, ii, 1368.

65 *CBP*, i, 168; ii, 672, 764, 841.

66 *CBP*, i, 601. *CSP For*, 1566–8, 2151. Fraser, *Douglas*, iv, 216.

67 *HMC*, Salisbury, i, 374.

68 J. A. Galloway & I. Murray, 'Scottish Migration to England, 1400–1560', *Scottish Geographical Magazine*, 112/1 (1996), 29–38. Pollard, *Wars of the Roses*, 17–18. Summerson, *Medieval Carlisle*, ii, 568, 570. J. A. F. Thomson, 'Scots in England in the Fifteenth Century', *SHR*, lxxxix (2000), 1–16.

69 NAS GD40/2/9/85, SP15/32/76, SP59/34 fos 262–8. *CBP*, ii, 77. *HMC*, Talbot, 40. *RPC*, vi, 408. *SS*, cxii (1906), 161.

70 D. Defoe, *A Tour Through The Whole Island of Great Britain*, ed. P. Rogers (Harmondsworth, 1986), 563–4. G. Donaldson, 'Foundations of Anglo-Scottish Union,' in S. Bindoff, J. Hurstfield and C. Williams, eds. *Elizabethan Government and Society* (London, 1961), 312.

71 PRO SP59/20 fos 196–7, WARD7/8/42. *Hamilton Papers*, i, 120–1.

72 NRO 2088. *CSP For*, 1566–8, 2015, 2524. *L & P. Hen VIII*, x, 1260. *HMC*, Salisbury, i, 374, 397.

73 NRO 399.

74 PRO SP15/32/76.

75 *CBP*, i, 571; ii, 881. *CSP For*, 1575–7, 554. *L & P. Hen VIII*, xviii, pt 1, 800; pt 2, 540. *CSP Scot*, vii, 483.

76 DPRW 1596 (2).

77 PRO SP59/17 fos 144–5, SP59/33 fos 82–3. BRO C1/1 fos 44, 114. C1/3. *CSP Scot*, vii, 483.

78 *HMC*, Salisbury, vii, 240.

79 *APC*, ii, 222. *CPR*, 1547–8, 319; 1548–9, 81; 1549–51, 293. *Hamilton Papers*, ii, 38–41. *L & P. Hen VIII*, xiv, pt 1, 723; xviii, pt 1, 58, 978. *RSS*, iii, 841.

80 *CBP*, ii, 129. *CSP For*, 1566–8, 525. *The Complaynt of Scotland*, ed. A.M. Stewart (Scottish Text Society, 1979), 84–5.

81 P. G. B. McNeill & H. L. MacQueen, eds. *Atlas of Scottish History to 1707* (Edinburgh, 1996), 450.

82 R. McCann, 'In Search of the Border Reivers', *The Scots Magazine*, new ser., 149/3 (1998), 235.

83 *L&P. Hen VIII*, iii, pt 2, 3456; v, 1635. D. H. Caldwell, 'The Battle of Pinkie', in N. Macdougall, ed. *Scotland and War AD79–1918* (Edinburgh, 1991), 61–94. A. J. MacDonald, *Border Bloodshed. Scotland, England and France at War, 1369–1403* (East Linton, 2000), 207. I would like to thank Prof. Thomas Riis for giving me the Scandinavian comparison.

84 *CSP For*, 1559–60, 216. *Sadler Papers*, i, 559–60. C. J. Neville, *Violence, Custom and Law. The Anglo-Scottish Border Lands in the Later Middle Ages* (Edinburgh, 1998), 152, 168 and 'Local Sentiment and the "National" Enemy

in Northern England in the Later Middle Ages', *Journal of British Studies*, 35 (1996), 419–37. *cf.* T. Thornton. ' "The Enemy or Stranger, that shall invade their country": Identity and community in the English North', in B. Taithe and T. Thornton, eds. *War. Identities in Conflict 1300–2000* (Stroud, 1998), 57–70.

85 PRO SP59/32 fos 4–11, STAC5 F2/34. *CBP*, i, 535; ii, 763, 815. *CSP For*, 1566–8, 2497. *CSP Scot*, iv, 32. *L & P. Hen VIII*, xviii, pt 1, 800.

86 *CBP*, i, 104, 134, 258, 285. *CSP Dom Add*, 1580–1625, 368. *HMC*, Salisbury, iii, 100. Godscroft, *De Familia*, 37.

87 BL MS Cotton, Caligula, B, vi, 2 fo. 519. NRAS 2177/2690 fo. 140. NLS ADV MS 31.2.1. LAMB, MS 3194 fo. 241. *APC*, v, 342. *CBP*, i, 134. *HMC*, Talbot, 45.

88 PRO SP59/31 fos 35–7. BL MS Cotton, Caligula, C, iii, fo. 120. *CBP*, i, 893; ii, 211, 746 (p. 392). *CSP Dom Add*, 1580–1625, 335. *NCH*, xiv, 545–6.

89 *CBP*, ii, 1505.

90 *CSP Scot*, x, no 732; xiii, pt 2 no 572. *HMC*, Salisbury, x, 368–9.

91 *CBP*, ii, 77, 881. See ch. iv.

92 *CBP*, ii, 861. *HMC*, Salisbury, iii, 188. Fraser, *Douglas*, iv, 177.

93 D. Nobbs, *England and Scotland* (London, 1952), 24. See ch. iv.

94 *CBP*, i, 987. *CSP Scot*, ix, 467. *HMC*, Salisbury, x, 47–8.

95 *HMC*, Salisbury, vii, 452; viii, 2–3, 498, 520–2. G. R. Batho, 'The Percies and Alnwick Castle', *AA*, 4th ser, xxxv (1957), 57–8.

96 MacDonald, *Border Bloodshed*, 214.

97 LAMB, MS 3195 fo. 6. See ch. vii.

98 *CBP*, i, 285. *CSP Dom Add*, 1566–79, 340. *CSP For*, 1562, 282. *CSP Scot*, x, 464, 522, 545. Calderwood, *History*, iv, 33, 72. J. Melville, *The Autobiography and Diary of Mr James Melville*, ed. R. Pitcairn, Wodrow Society (1842), 119–120, 134.

99 *CBP*, ii, 487, 518, 620. *CSP Scot*, x, 653; xi, 355, 366. *HMC*, Salisbury, iii, 246, 250, 319. See chs ii & vii.

100 NAS GD40/2/9/71. *CBP*, i, 145, 155, 678. *CSP For*, 1572–4, 719, 791, 1564; 1575–7, 1140. *CSP Scot*, iv, 567. See chs. ii & iii.

101 NAS GD40/6/1/1–4, RD1/20/1/1. See ch. iv.

102 NRO 1DE/8/114, 1DE/8/115. Wormald, *Lords and Men*, 161.

103 NRO 1DE/8/143, ZSW6/16.

104 PRO CP 25/2/192/43 & 44 Eliz/MICH.

105 Morpeth Records Centre QS1/1 fos 24, 31, 38.

106 *CBP*, ii, 255, 321, 353. *HMC*, Salisbury, xii, 89.

107 *CBP*, ii, 1537. *CSP Scot*, xi, 26; xiii, pt 1,370; pt 2, 854.

108 *CBP*, ii, 1434. *CSPScot*, xiii, pt 2, 684. *HMC*, Salisbury, xii, 11–12.

109 Carey, *Memoirs*, 64–5.

110 *Fragments of Scottish History*, ed. J. G. Dalyell (Edinburgh, 1798), ii, 58–9. T. Middleton, *A True Narration of the Entertainment of his Royal Maiestie, from the time of his departure from Edenbrough* (London, 1603).

111 B. Galloway, *The Union of England and Scotland 1603–1608* (Edinburgh, 1986), 16, 142–43. A. D. Nicholls, *The Jacobean Union. A Reconsideration of British Civil Policies Under the Early Stuarts* (Westport, 1999), chs i & ii. Watts, *Border to Middle Shire*, 133–34, 204.

Conclusion

Before 1603 the affinity of many lairds and gentlemen was to their families
and the Borders, with little regard as to whether they were Scots or English.
This Border allegiance should, however, not be misread to argue that Anglo-
Scottish frontier was part of a British frontier. When the loyalties of the
lairds were sorely tested by aggressive English imperialism in the 1540s, they
responded with a mixture of greed, fortitude, opportunity and defiance.
They never thought of this as British polity and were reluctant to accept any
state building at this time be it English, or French, in origin. As the century
progressed and various Scottish administrations took a more pro-English
stance, there was still no basic change in the Borderers' attitudes. Landed
men in the Eastern Borders knew who their friends were across the frontier,
but did not necessarily wish to share one nationality with them. They were
all happy to regard themselves as Borderers, but any thought of having
notorious Western Border thieves as fellow nationals in a British state would
have horrified them. If any British state existed in some parts before 1603,
localism ensured that it was not in the sixteenth-century Eastern Anglo-
Scottish Borders.

The landed families' shared values of kinship, tradition, education and
field interests show how their society was developing with the times. It was
not unique as landed societies held similar interests in Scotland, England,
Ireland and Wales during this period. However, the existence of draconian
Border laws made their friendship stand out for its illegality and cunning. To
these families the Border was a mere political boundary coming between
them which could be ignored, or occasionally recognised, at their pleasure.
Their friendships are exemplary at a time when enmity between Scot and
Englishman was commonplace, but to label their association as British is
dubious. The cross-border friendships that were noticed before the Union of
the Crowns were not just a flurry in anticipation of the Union. They were the
result of established fraternisation across the frontier which stretched back
through many decades, and perhaps even centuries, of illegal trysting.
Defiance of the dictates of Border law was the Borderers way of snubbing
authority whether it be in London or Edinburgh. They did not seek to be
ruled by any administration and though they dallied with courtier faction,
they preferred to keep overall control of their localities to themselves
throughout 1540–1603.

These Border families, like landed communities anywhere else, were not slow to take advantage of political changes and readily accepted upward social mobility when it was proffered. The rise of the gentry was typified by the achievements of Sir John Forster in north Northumberland and North Durham. Lairds and their younger sons took advantage of similar changes in the magnatial power structure of the Scottish Borders, but their traditional kin chiefs were not as sidelined as the Percies, earls of Northumberland. The sixth Lord Home revived much of his family's power, though in a changing world he had ultimately to acknowledge the spectacular advance of men like Sir George Home. The lairds asserted their rise in the creation of a fourth estate of the Scots Parliament in 1587 and took a more direct interest in national politics than most of the gentry. They also had a much higher profile at the Scottish Court that checked much outsider interference from the centre to the Borders by the 1590s. Geographically the lairds were much nearer their centre of government than the gentry and they were not restricted in their movements, so along with the spread of Protestantism, this probably accounts for their more direct interest in politics. The gentry dabbled with various courtier factions, but collectively they did not visit London as much as the lairds visited Edinburgh. Northumbrian sheriffs were also notoriously absent when accounts were due in London. Unlike the Scottish lairds, the gentry had obligations of Border service and the fact that they were not directly governed by parliament were excuses for this lack of communication. Recusancy may latterly have been a stronger reason for their relative political isolation, particularly after 1585.

The landed families of the Eastern Borders were detached from the poverty of the Western Borders by their ability to make a reasonable living from their more fertile lands. Although comparisons of wealth are tricky, they appear to have had comparable lifestyles, accepting additional income when and where they were given the opportunity. The confidence of the lairds' housebuilding and the small, subtle changes made by the gentry mark a change in direction from the traditionally defensive nature of Border architecture. If defence was the critical element against housebuilding in the Borders then the lairds would surely not have built on such a wide scale, nor with such aesthetic consideration. However, the gap between laird and gentry levels of housebuilding cannot be adequately explained. It would appear that the gentry were being as devious about their true wealth levels as they were in illegally letting their lands to Scots. They feared that open displays of affluence would attract too much official attention, whereas the lairds delighted in doing just this.

Landed families in the Eastern Borders were not ignorant and backward in the sixteenth century, though this myth keeps being perpetuated. When scrutinised they were found to be educated at a much higher level than had previously been recognised. By the later-sixteenth century the majority of lairds and gentlemen were literate and well educated, though the lairds attended universities at home and abroad in far greater numbers than the gentry. David Home of Godscroft is an outstanding example of how advanced and sophisticated some of the Border lairds could be. He surely proves how false the violent and uncivilised image of the Borders is.

The effects of Reformation highlight more interesting comparisons within the Borders. Protestantism did not take hold in the English Eastern Borders until after 1577 and recusancy was not punished until 1585. This was remarkable, yet not surprising when the poor coverage of Protestant preachers in the area and the survival of Catholicism are considered. Recusancy was entrenched in the landed families and the government found conformity difficult to enforce. The Reformation made better progress in the Eastern Scottish Borders, but the advancement of Protestantism was still not rapid as there was a lack of ministers in the years immediately following the 1560 Reformation. Recusancy was not such a problem to the authorities in Scotland, so Catholics were not treated as punitively as in England.

The general level of violence and crime in the Eastern Borders was not excessive compared with other sixteenth-century landed communities in England and Scotland. Gentlemen bearing arms were as susceptible to moments of rashness as any other man and the defence of honour by whatever means was thought to be a virtue. The lairds were more severely punished for their domestic crimes than the gentry, but criminal and civil laws were different in each country. Incidents such as that at Norham Ford in 1597 vindicated the good relations between lairds and gentlemen of the East Marches. Eastern Borderers knew that mediation was better than revenge in Border affairs, but few Western Border reivers appreciated this. There were, of course, valued trading links to preserve in the East as well as their cross-border friendships.

Comparing and contrasting landed families across the Eastern Anglo-Scottish Border has highlighted the importance of a neglected region that was to become part of early modern Britain in 1707, not 1603. Their similarities can make the international frontier seem irrelevant, though their differences invariably reinforce the duality of the Borderland. The divide between the Eastern and Western Borders was pronounced throughout 1540–1603, but more work needs to be done on the West to probe their differences from the East. For instance there may well be Western Borderers who have been incorrectly included as violent men in standard Border histories. Perhaps sophisticated and relatively peace loving gentlemen were not just confined to the Eastern Borders?

Finally, it is worth noting that when James VI & I tried to obliterate the term Borders by renaming this region in 1606 as his 'Middle Shires', there was widespread reluctance to accept this new British label.[1] The king liked to use the term Great Britain, but his ambition for a full parliamentary union after 1603 was universally opposed by Scot and Englishman alike. Not surprisingly when James died in 1625 the concept of the Middle Shires died with him. No one could really change centuries of tradition and the terms English or Scottish Borders are still with us today in spite of the Union of the Parliaments in 1707.

Note

1 *RPC*, vii, p. 286.

THE HOME CONNECTIONS

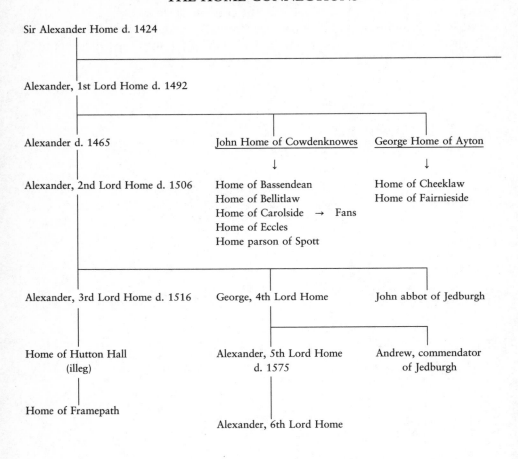

Sir Alexander Home d. 1424

Alexander, 1st Lord Home d. 1492

Alexander d. 1465   John Home of Cowdenknowes   George Home of Ayton

Alexander, 2nd Lord Home d. 1506   Home of Bassendean   Home of Cheeklaw
                                      Home of Bellitlaw   Home of Fairnieside
                                      Home of Carolside → Fans
                                      Home of Eccles
                                      Home parson of Spott

Alexander, 3rd Lord Home d. 1516   George, 4th Lord Home   John abbot of Jedburgh

Home of Hutton Hall   Alexander, 5th Lord Home   Andrew, commendator
     (illeg)   d. 1575   of Jedburgh

Home of Framepath   Alexander, 6th Lord Home

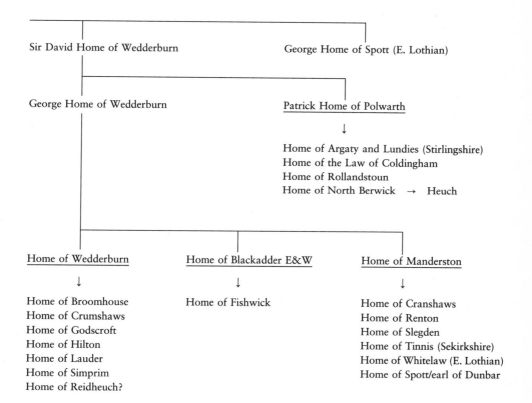

Sir David Home of Wedderburn   George Home of Spott (E. Lothian)

George Home of Wedderburn   Patrick Home of Polwarth

↓

Home of Argaty and Lundies (Stirlingshire)
Home of the Law of Coldingham
Home of Rollandstoun
Home of North Berwick → Heuch

Home of Wedderburn   Home of Blackadder E&W   Home of Manderston

↓   ↓   ↓

Home of Broomhouse   Home of Fishwick   Home of Cranshaws
Home of Crumshaws   Home of Renton
Home of Godscroft   Home of Slegden
Home of Hilton   Home of Tinnis (Sekirkshire)
Home of Lauder   Home of Whitelaw (E. Lothian)
Home of Simprim   Home of Spott/earl of Dunbar
Home of Reidheuch?

FORSTER OF ADDERSTONE AND BAMBURGH

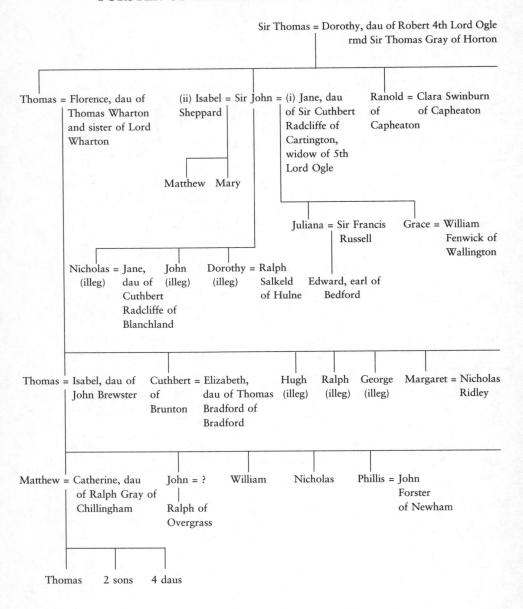

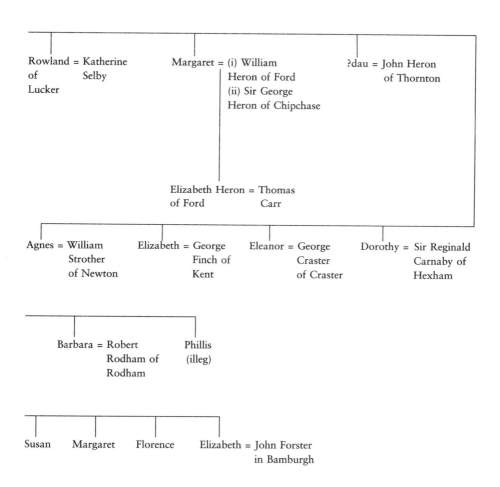

Rowland = Katherine   Margaret = (i) William   ?dau = John Heron
of   Selby   Heron of Ford   of Thornton
Lucker   (ii) Sir George
                                           Heron of Chipchase

                        Elizabeth Heron = Thomas
                        of Ford   Carr

Agnes = William   Elizabeth = George   Eleanor = George   Dorothy = Sir Reginald
          Strother   Finch of   Craster   Carnaby of
          of Newton   Kent   of Craster   Hexham

        Barbara = Robert   Phillis
                  Rodham of   (illeg)
                  Rodham

Susan   Margaret   Florence   Elizabeth = John Forster
                                                  in Bamburgh

Bibliography

MANUSCRIPT SOURCES[1]
(–) indicates multiple references in one class of records.

Alnwick: Alnwick Castle.
Alnwick MS (AI/1 -, AII/1, CIV -, DI/1, JV/14, MI/2)
Syon MS (AI/5/c, AI/6 -, AII -, CI -, CIV -, CVI/8/b, CVIII/1/1, EII/7, EIV -, MII/11/a -, NII/6, Q/XI/1, RII/9/a)

Berwick-upon-Tweed: Berwick Record Office.
Berwick Garrison Rule Book (637)
Crossman (Cheswick) MS (683)
Ford Estates Deeds and Papers (1216)
Blackburn & Price MS (1697/1)
Guild Minute Books (B1/1 –)
Enrolment Memoranda Books (B6/1, B6/11)
Bailiff Court Books (C1/1 –)
Court of Rolls Books (C3/1 –)
Haggerston (Harelaw) MS (ZHG –)

Duns: Berwickshire County Library.
Folio 3/5/6.

Durham: Durham Chapter Archives, 5 The College.
Dean and Chapter Registers (1–6) [Now DCD/B/BA/1–6]
Consistory Court Proceedings: 16th century tempus bishops Tunstall and Pilkington. (Now DCD/D/EPB/1)

Durham: Durham Chapter Library.
MS. C.III.20.
MS. Hunter.23.
MS. Raine.3. (formerly vol 6)

Durham: Durham County Record Office.
Clayton and Gibson Collection (D/CG/7/15, D/CG/7/16)

Durham: University of Durham Library, Archives and Special Collections, Palace Green.[2]
Durham Probate Records: Wills (1540 –)

Durham Probate Records: Probate Act Books (I-IX)
Durham Probate Records: Register of Wills (I, IV-VI)
Durham Diocesan Records: ii, Visitation Books (1–5)
Durham Diocesan Records: iii, Consistory Court Act Books (2–5)
Durham Diocesan Records: v, Consistory Court Depositions Books (1–7)
Durham Diocesan Records: vii, Acts before a Commissary for Northumberland (1–2)
Durham Bishopric Halmote Court Records: Miscellaneous Volumes M.64 (195566a) II.
Mickleton & Spearman MS.6.

Edinburgh: National Archives of Scotland (formerly the Scottish Record Office).[3]
Edinburgh Commissary Court: Testaments (CC8/8/1 –)
Edinburgh Commissary Court: Minute Book (CC8/9/1)
Lauder Commissary Court: Testaments (CC15/5 –)
Lauder Commissary Court: Miscellaneous Documents (CC15/16/1)
Acta Dominorum Concilii (CS5)
Acta Dominorum et Concilii et Sessionis (CS6)
Register of Acts and Decreets of the Lords of Council and Session: 1st series (CS7)
Cartulary of Jedburgh (CH6/6/1)
Miscellaneous Ecclesiastical Documents (CH8)
Accounts of the Treasurer 1488–1635 (E21/76)
Thirds of Benefices (E45)
Register of Assignations and Modifications of Stipends (E47)
Book of Assumption (E48/1/1)
Books of Assignations and Superplus of Thirds (E48/3)
Benefices, Teinds and Stipends (E53/8)
Gifts and Deposits:-
   Miss Heiton of Callendar (GD1/146)
   Home of Hirsel (GD1/180)
   W. L. Ferguson, Edinburgh (GD1/200)
   J. S. Richardson (GD1/220)
   Captain George Swinton (GD1/239)
   Logan Home of Edrom (GD1/384)
   The Chartered Accountant's and Estate Agent's Institute (GD1/411)
   John Kelman, Edinburgh (GD1/420)
   J & F Anderson, W.S., Edinburgh (GD1/453)
   William Brockie, Edinburgh (GD1/461)
   D. S. Bowser, Doune (GD1/540)
   Biel MS (GD6)
   Swinton Charters (GD12)
   Airlie MS (GD16)

Hay of Yester (GD28)
Shairp of Houstoun Muniments (GD30)
Elibank MS (GD32)
Lothian MS (GD40)
Dalhousie Muniments (GD45)
Harwood Writs (GD53)
Melrose Charters (GD55)
Wilkie of Foulden (GD59)
William Douglas, Bookseller, Edinburgh (GD98)
Hamilton-Dalrymple of North Berwick (GD110)
Curle MS (GD111)
Mar and Kellie MS (GD124)
Morton Papers (GD150)
Scott of Harden (GD157)
Hume of Polwarth, earl of Marchmont (GD158)
Ogilvy of Inverquharity (GD205)
Dunglass Muniments (GD206)
R. K. Hannay's Papers (GD214)
Cockburn of that Ilk MS (GD216)
Messrs Tods, Murray & Jamieson, W.S. (GD237)
Don of Newton Don (GD239)
Wilkie of Foulden, Thomson & Baxter, W.S. (GD241)
Shepherd and Wedderburn, W.S. (GD242)
Mackenzie, Innes & Logan, W.S. (GD245)
Messrs Hope, Todd & Kirk, W.S. (GD246)
John C. Brodie, W.S. (GD247)
Scott of Ancrum (GD259)
Home of Wedderburn MS (GD267)
Blackadder Deeds (GD362)
Ranken and Reid Collection (GD384)
Register of Deeds: 1st series (RD1 –)
Register of Deeds: Minute Books (RD6 –)
Register of Deeds: Warrants, 1st series (RD11 –)
Register House: Miscellaneous Papers (RH9)
Register House: Home of Prenderguest (RH15/16)
Register House: Home of Eccles Papers (RH15/19)
Register House: Haddington Papers (RH15/39)
Jedburgh Sheriff Court: Diet Books (SC62/2 –)

Edinburgh: National Library of Scotland.
Rutherford of Edgerston Charters (Acc 7750)
Nisbet (Ker) Charters (CH5122–643)
Nisbet Charters (CH4775–810)
Spottiswoode of Spottiswoode Papers (CH1492–568)

Advocates MS (17.1.4, 30.5.22–23, 31.2.1, 35.2.4.i)
Marquis of Tweeddale MS (MS 7103)

Edinburgh: National Register of Archives Scotland.[4]
Scott-Ker of Sunlaws (NRAS 182)
Pringle of Torwoodlee (NRAS 482)
Maitland of Thirlestane (NRAS 832)
Home of The Hirsel (NRAS 859)
Roxburghe Muniments (NRAS 1100)
McEwen of Marchmont (NRAS 1351)
Duke of Hamilton (NRAS 2177)
Palmer of Manderston (NRAS 2405)

Edinburgh: University of Edinburgh Library, Special Collections.
Laing. Additional 1 & 2.

Hatfield: Hatfield House.
Hatfield MS (CP 235/68. C.P. Petitions 991)

Jedburgh: Jedburgh Castle Jail Museum.
Miscellaneous Manuscripts (JEDJM 506–517)

London: British Library.
Cotton MS: Augustus (1/ii/14)
Cotton MS: Caligula (B v, B vi, B viii, C iii, D i, D ii)
Cotton MS: Titus (F xiii)
Lansdowne MS (326)
Additional MS (24815, 32646–32657, 33262, 33256)

London: Lambeth Palace Library
Talbot MS (3192, 3194, 3195)
Shrewsbury MS (696)

London: National Register of Archives.
Bedingfield MS (NRA 5522)
Crosswood Deeds (NRA 11468)
Tollemache (Dysart) MS (NRA 23003)

London: Public Record Office.
Greenwich Hospital Deeds (ADM74, ADM75)
Early Chancery Proceedings (C1/1023/24)
Chancery Proceedings Series II (C3 –)
Patent Rolls (C66 –)
Chancery Decree Roll (C78/54)

Chancery Inquisitions Post Mortem, Series II (C142 –)
Chancery Crown Office: Miscellaneous Books (C193/32)
Court of Common Pleas: Feet of Fines Series II (CP25/2 –)
Duchy of Lancaster: Pleadings (DL1 –)
Duchy of Lancaster: Draft Leases (DL14/6/69)
Duchy of Lancaster: Ministers' Accounts (DL29/360/5956)
Duchy of Lancaster: Court Rolls (DL30/107/1540)
Duchy of Lancaster: Miscellanea (DL41/14/11)
Palatinate of Durham: Inquisitions Post Mortem (DURH3 –)
Exchequer, Treasury of the Receipt: Miscellaneous Books (E36/40)
Exchequer, King's Remembrancer: Accounts (E101 –)
Exchequer, King's Remembrancer: Depositions, Northumberland (E134 –)
Exchequer, King's Remembrancer: Estreats (E137)
Exchequer, King's Remembrancer: Miscellanea (E163/14/8)
Exchequer, King's Remembrancer: Special Commissions of Inquiry (E178 –)
Exchequer, King's Remembrancer: Subsidy Rolls of Northumberland (E179 –)
Exchequer, King's Remembrancer: Sheriffs' Accounts (E199 –)
Exchequer, Augmentation Office: Particulars of Concealments (E302/1/36)
Exchequer, Augmentation Office: Deeds of Purchase and Exchange (E305 –)
Exchequer, Augmentation Office: Particulars for Leases (E310 –)
Exchequer, Augmentation Office: Original Letters Patent (E313 –)
Exchequer, Augmentation Office: Miscellaneous Books (E315/399)
Exchequer, Augmentation Office: Particulars for Grants (E318 –)
Exchequer, Augmentation Office: Particulars for Grants to Schools (E319/1/20)
Exchequer, Lord Treasurer's Remembrancer and Pipe Offices: Particulars and Warrants for Leases (E367–978)
Exchequer, Lord Treasurer's Remembrancer: Recusant Rolls (Pipe Series) (E377 –)
Exchequer, Receipts, Enrolments and Registers (E401 –)
Miscellaneous Index to Border Papers (IND/6887)
Exchequer, Office of the Auditors of Land Revenue: Miscellaneous Books (LR 2/118)
Exchequer, Office of the Auditors of Land Revenue: Northumberland (LR10/24)
Exchequer, Office of the Auditors of Land Revenue: Receivers' Accounts, Series III (LR12 –)
Obsolete Records (OBS1/1058)
Court of Requests: Proceedings (REQ2 –)
Special Collections: Ministers' Accounts (SC6/Hen VIII, SC6/Edw VI, SC6/Ph & M, SC6/Eliz I, SC6/Jas I)
Special Collections: Rentals and Surveys (SC11/959)
Special Collections: Rentals and Surveys (SC12/13/66)
State Paper Office: Letters and Papers: Henry VIII (SP1 –)

State Paper Office: State Papers Domestic: Elizabeth (SP12 –)
State Paper Office: State Papers Domestic: Elizabeth (SP13/F)
State Paper Office: State Papers Domestic: Addenda (SP15 –)
State Paper Office: State Papers Domestic: Docquets (SP38 –)
State Paper Office: State Papers Scotland (SP52 –)
State Paper Office: State Papers Borders (SP59 –)
State Paper Office: State Papers Foreign (SP70 –)
Court of Star Chamber: Elizabeth I (STAC5 –)
Court of Star Chamber: James I (STAC8 –)
Court of Wards and Liveries: Deeds and Evidences (WARD2 –)
Court of Wards and Liveries: Feodary's Surveys (WARD5/31)
Court of Wards and Liveries: Inquisitions Post Mortem (WARD7 –)
Court of Wards and Liveries: Miscellaneous Books/ Feodary's Accounts
  (WARD9 –)
Court of Wards and Liveries: Miscellaneous (WARD11/3)

Longleat House, Wiltshire.
Dudley MS 1.

Maidstone: Centre for Kentish Studies (formerly Kent Archives Office).
Selby MS (U947)

Morpeth: Morpeth Records Centre.
Berwick Parish Registers (EP38, EP171)
Holy Island Parish Registers (EP136)
Vetera Indictamenta (QS1/1)

Newcastle-upon-Tyne: Northumberland Record Office.
Lord Crewe's Charity (452)
Delaval (Hastings) MS (650)
Wharton Letter Book (1228)
Blackett-Ord (Whitfield) MS (324 –)
Collingwood (Lilburn) MS (1147 –)
Butler-Ewart MS (ZBU/H/1)
Craster (Craster) MS (ZCR –)
Carr-Ellison (Hedgeley) MS (ZCE/2/1)
Delaval (Horsley) MS (1DE –)
Society of Antiquaries of Newcastle-upon-Tyne, Lambert MS and J. Raine
  Testamenta Dunelmensia (ZAN M15 –)
Loraine (Styford) MS (ZLO –)
Riddell (Whitefield) MS (ZRW –)
Swinburne (Capheaton) MS (ZSW –)
Waterford Charters (1DE Delaval MS-Waterford Chrs)

Newcastle-upon-Tyne: Tyne and Wear Archives Service.
Records of the Merchant Adventurers of Newcastle (988 –)

Northallerton: North Yorkshire Record Office.
Lawson of Brough MS (ZRL –)

Oxford: University of Oxford, Bodleian Library.
Dodsworth MS (45)
Northumberland Rolls no 2.

York: Borthwick Institute of Historical Research.
Cause Papers (CPG –)
Probate Registers, vols 18, 23.

PRINTED PRIMARY SOURCES

Accounts of the Collectors of the Thirds of Benefices, 1561–72, ed. G. Donaldson (Scottish History Society, 1949).

Acta Facultatis Artium Universitatis Sanctiandree, 1413–1588, ed. A. I. Dunlop (Scottish History Society, 1964), 2 vols.

Acts and Proceedings of the General Assemblies of the Kirk of Scotland from 1560 to 1618 (Booke of the Universall Kirke) (Bannatyne Club, 1839–45).

Acts of the Lords of Council in Public Affairs, 1501–1554, ed. R. K. Hannay (Edinburgh, 1932).

Acts of the Parliaments of Scotland, ed. T. Thomson & C. Innes (Edinburgh, 1814–75).

Acts of the Privy Council of England, ed. J. R. Dasent (London, 1890–1907).

Admissions to the Honourable Society of the Middle Temple, ed. H. A. C. Sturgess (London, 1949).

Ancrum, earl of., *Correspondence of Sir Robert Kerr, first Earl of Ancram*, ed. D. Laing, (Bannatyne Club, 1875), 2 vols.

The Bannatyne Miscellany; containing original papers and tracts, chiefly relating to the history and literature of Scotland, ed. W. Scott & D. Laing (Bannatyne Club, 1827, 1836, 1855), 3 vols.

Birrel, R., 'Diary of Robert Birrel, 1532–1605', ed. J. G. Dalyell, *Fragments of Scottish History* (Edinburgh, 1798), part ii.

Biographical Register of Christ's College, 1505–1905, ed. J. Peile (Cambridge, 1910), 2 vols

P. C. D. Brears, ed., 'Yorkshire Probate Inventories, 1542–1689', *Yorkshire Archaeological Society*, record ser, cxxxiv (1972).

Brown, P. Hume., *Early Travellers in Scotland* (Edinburgh, 1891).

Calderwood, D., *History of the Kirk of Scotland by Mr. David Calderwood*, ed. T. Thomson & D. Laing (Wodrow Society, 1842–49).

Calendar of Letters and Papers relating to the affairs of the Borders of England and Scotland, ed. J. Bain (London, 1894–96).

Calendar of the Laing Charters 854–1837, ed. J. Anderson (Edinburgh, 1899).

Calendar of the Patent Rolls Edward VI, Philip and Mary and Elizabeth I (London, 1924–).

Calendar of State Papers Domestic, ed. R. Lemon et al (London, 1856–72 & 1992–).

Calendar of State Papers Domestic Addenda, ed. M. A. E. Green, 2 vols (London 1870–72).

Calendar of State Papers Foreign, ed. W. B. Turnbull et al (London, 1861–1901).

Calendar of the State Papers relating to Scotland and Mary, Queen of Scots, ed. J. Bain et al (Edinburgh, 1898–1969).

Calendar of the State Papers Rome, ed. J. M. Rigg (London, 1916–26).

Calendar of State Papers, Spanish, ed. G. A. Bergenroth et al (London, 1862–1954).

Calendar of Writs preserved at Yester House, 1166–1625, ed. C. C. H. Harvey & J. MacLeod (Scottish Record Society, 1930).

Camden, W., *Britain, or a chorographical description of the most flourishing Kingdomes, England, Scotland and Ireland, and the ilands adioyning, out of the depth of Antiquitie . . .* (London, 1586). Also published as *Britannia* (London, 1610).

Camden, W., *The History of Princess Elizabeth*, ed. W. T. M. MacCaffrey (Chicago, 1970).

Carte Monalium de Northberwic, ed. C. Innes (Bannatyne Club, 1847).

A Catalogue of the Graduates in the Faculties of Arts, Divinity and Law of the University of Edinburgh, ed. D. Laing (Bannatyne Club, 1858).

Carey, R., *The Memoirs of Sir Robert Carey*, ed. F. H. Mares (Oxford, 1972).

Chambers, R., *Domestic Annals of Scotland from the Reformation to the Revolution*, second edition (Edinburgh, 1861), 3 vols.

The Chartulary of the Cistercian Priory of Coldstream, ed. C. Rogers (Grampian Club, 1879).

Collier, J. P. ed., *The Egerton Papers*, Camden Society, 12 (1840).

Colville, J., *Original Letter of Mr John Colville, 1582–1603*, ed. D. Laing (Bannatyne Club, 1858).

Commissariot Record of Edinburgh: Register of Testaments, ed. F. J. Grant (Scottish Record Society, 1897–98), vols 1 & 2.

Commissariot Record of Lauder, ed. F. J. Grant (Scottish Record Society, 1903).

The Complaynt of Scotland c. 1550, ed. A. M. Stewart (Scottish Text Society, 1979).

Compota Thesauriorum Regum Scotorum: Accounts of the Lord High Treasurer of Scotland, ed. T. Dickson & J. Balfour Paul (Edinburgh, 1877–1916).

Dalyell, J. G. ed., *Fragments of Scottish History* (Edinburgh, 1798), 2 vols.

Depositions and other Ecclesiastical Proceedings from the Courts of Durham, ed. J. Raine (Surtees Society, 1845 & 1850), vols 21 & 22.

A Diurnal of remarkable occurrents, that have passed within the country of Scotland, since the death of King James the Fourth, till the year 1575, ed. T. Thomson (Maitland Club, 1833).

Early Records of the University of St Andrews, ed. J. M. Anderson (Scottish History Society, 1926).

Extracts from the Records of the Burgh of Edinburgh, 1403–1603, ed. J. D. Marwick & M. Wood (Scottish Burgh Record Society, 1869–92 & 1927), 5 vols.

Extracts from the Records of the Merchant Adventurers of Newcastle-upon-Tyne (Surtees Society, 1895 & 1899), vols 93 & 101.

Forbes-Leith, W. ed., *Narratives of Scottish Catholics under Mary Stuart and James VI* (Edinburgh, 1885).

Forbes-Leith, W., *The Scots Men at Arms and Life Guards in France, 1418–1830* (Edinburgh, 1882).

Foster, J., *Pedigrees Recorded at the Herald's Visitation of Northumberland in 1615 and 1666* (London, 1891).

Foster, J., *The Register of Admissions to Gray's Inn 1521–1889* (London, 1889).

Foster, J., *Alumni Oxonienses 1500–1714* (Oxford 1891–92), 4 vols.

Fraser, W., *The Annandale Family Book of the Johnstones* (Edinburgh, 1894).

Fraser, W., *The Scotts of Buccleuch* (Edinburgh, 1878).

Fraser, W., *The Douglas Book* (Edinburgh, 1885).

Fraser, W., *Memorials of the Earls of Haddington* (Edinburgh, 1889).

The Hamilton Papers: Letters and papers illustrating the political relations of England and Scotland, ed. J. Bain (Edinburgh, 1890–92).

Heraldic Visitation of the Northern Counties by Thomas Tonge, ed. W. H. Dyer Longstaffe (Surtees Society, 1862), vol 41.

The Historie and Life of King James the Sext, ed. T. Thomson (Bannatyne Club, 1825).

Holinshed, R., *The Scottish Chronicle* (Arbroath, 1806), 2 vols.

Home, A., *The Poems of Alexander Home*, ed. A. Lawson (Scottish Text Society, 1902).

Home, A., *Hymnes and Sacred Songs*, ed. J. G. Kinnear (Bannatyne Club, 1832).

Home of Godscroft, D., *De Familia Humia Wedderburnensi Liber* (Abbotsford Club, 1839).

Home of Godscroft, D., *The History of the House and Race of Douglas and Angus* (London, 1657).

Ilderton, W., 'Poetry', *Harleian Miscellany*, x (1813), 266–71.

Inquisitionum ad Capellam Domini Regis Retornatarum, quae in publicis archivis Scotiae adhuc servantur, Abbreviatio, ed. T. Thomson (Edinburgh, 1811–16).

Keith, R., *History of the Affairs of the Church and State in Scotland, from the beginning of the Reformation to the year 1568. By the Right Rev. Robert Keith, primus of the Scottish Episcopal Church,* ed. J. P. Lawson & C. J. Lawson (Spottiswoode Society, 1844–50), 3 vols.

Knox, J., *The Works of John Knox,* ed. D. Laing (Edinburgh, 1846–64), 6 vols.

Knox, J., *John Knox's History of the Reformation in Scotland,* ed. W. Croft Dickinson (Edinburgh, 1949), 2 vols.

Law, T. G. ed., *Catholic Tractates of the Sixteenth Century 1573–1600* (Scottish Text Society, 1901).

Laws, A. R., *Schola Novocastris. Volume One 1545–1699* (Newcastle, 1925).

Lesley, J. *The Historie of Scotland, wrytten in Latin by the most reverend and worthy Jhone Leslie, Bishop of Rosse,* ed. E. G. Cody & W. Murison (Scottish Text Society, 1888–95), 2 vols.

Le livre du recreur de L'Academie de Genève, 1559–1878 (Geneva, 1959 & 1966), 2 vols.

Letters and Papers, Foreign and Domestic, of the Reign of Henry VIII, ed. J. S. Brewer et al (London, 1862–1932).

Liber Sancte Marie de Calchou, ed. C. Innes (Bannatyne Club, 1846), 2 vols.

Liber Sancte Marie de Dryburgh, ed. W. Fraser (Bannatyne Club, 1847).

Liber Sancte Marie de Melros, ed. C. Innes (Bannatyne Club, 1837), 2 vols.

Lindsay of Pitscottie, R., *The Historie and Chronicles of Scotland by Robert Lindsay of Pitscottie,* ed. J. G. Mackay (Scottish Text Society, 1899–1911).

Mary of Lorraine, *The Scottish Correspondence of Mary of Lorraine,* ed. A. I. Cameron (Scottish History Society, 1927).

Melville, J., *The Autobiography and Diary of Mr James Melville, minister of Kilrenny, in Fife, and professor of theology in the University of St Andrews,* ed. R. Pitcairn (Wodrow Society, 1842).

Melville, J., *Memoirs of his own life by Sir James Melville of Halhill,* ed. T. Thomson (Bannatyne Club, 1827).

The Miscellany of the Maitland Club. Consisting of original papers and other documents illustrative of the history and literature of Scotland, ed. J. Dennistoun & A. Macdonald et al (Maitland Club, 1833, 1834, 1840, 1843, 1847), vol i (2 pts); vols ii – iv.

The Miscellany of the Wodrow Society, ed. D. Laing (Wodrow Society, 1844).

Moysie, D., *Memoirs of the Affairs of Scotland by David Moysie, 1579–93*, ed. J. Dennistoun (Bannatyne Club, 1830).

Munimenta Alme Universitatis Glasguensis: Records of the University of Glasgow till 1827, ed. C. Innes (Maitland Club, 1854), 4 vols.

Newcastle-upon-Tyne Records Committee Series: vol ix. Miscellanea, including selections from the Delaval papers (Newcastle, 1930).

North Country Wills, ed. J. W. Clay (Surtees Society, 1908 & 1912), vols 116 & 121.

Pitcairn, R., *Criminal Trials in Scotland, 1488–1624* (Maitland Club, 1833), 3 vols in 7 parts.

Protocol Book of Sir William Corbet, ed. J. Anderson & W. Angus (Scottish Record Society, 1911).

The Records of the Honourable Society of Lincoln's Inn, 1420–1799 (London, 1896).

Records of the Scots Colleges at Douai, Rome, Valladolid and Ratisbon, ed. R. Fraser (New Spalding Club, 1906).

Records of the Synods of Lothian and Tweeddale, 1589–96, 1640–49, ed. J. Kirk (Stair Society, 1977), vol xxx.

Recusant Roll no 1. ed. M. M. C. Calthrop (Catholic Record Society, 1916), vol xviii.

Recusant Roll no 2, 1593–1594, ed. H. Bowler (Catholic Record Society, 1965), vol lviii.

Recusant Roll no 3 (1594–5) and 4 (1595–6), ed. H. Bowler (Catholic Record Society, 1970), vol lxi.

The Register of Apprentices of the City of Edinburgh, 1583–1666, ed. F. J. Grant (Scottish Record Society, 1906).

The Register of the Privy Council of Scotland, ed. J. H. Burton & D. Masson (Edinburgh 1877–1898), vols i – vii & xiv.

Registrum Honoris de Morton, ed. T. Thomson, A. Macdonald & C. Innes (Bannatyne Club, 1853), 2 vols.

Registrum Magni Sigilli Regum Scotorum, ed. J. M. Thomson et al (Edinburgh, 1882–1914).

Registrum Sancte Marie de Neubotle, ed. C. Innes (Bannatyne Club, 1849).

Registrum Secreti Sigilli Regum Scotorum, ed. M. Livingstone et al (Edinburgh, 1908–).

Reports of the Royal Commissioners of the Historical Manuscripts Commission, Third Report (London, 1872).

Reports of the Royal Commissioners of the Historical Manuscripts Commission, Fourth Report (London, 1874).

Reports of the Royal Commissioners of the Historical Manuscripts Commission, Fifth Report (London, 1876).

Reports of the Royal Commissioners of the Historical Manuscripts Commission, Sixth Report (London, 1877–78).

Reports of the Royal Commissioners of the Historical Manuscripts Com-

mission, Seventh Report (London, 1879).

Reports of the Royal Commissioners of the Historical Manuscripts Commission, Ninth Report (London, 1883–4).

Reports of the Royal Commissioners of the Historical Manuscripts Commission, Tenth Report (London, 1885).

Reports of the Royal Commissioners of the Historical Manuscripts Commission, Eleventh Report (London, 1887).

Reports of the Royal Commissioners of the Historical Manuscripts Commission, Manuscripts of the marquis of Bath, preserved at Longleat (London, 1904–80).

Reports of the Royal Commissioners of the Historical Manuscripts Commission, Manuscripts of the duke of Buccleuch and Queensberry, Drumlanrig I (London, 1897).

Reports of the Royal Commissioners of the Historical Manuscripts Commission, Manuscripts of Lord and viscount De L'Isle and Dudley, ii (London, 1933).

Reports of the Royal Commissioners of the Historical Manuscripts Commission, Manuscripts of Reginald Hastings (London, 1928–47).

Reports of the Royal Commissioners of the Historical Manuscripts Commission, Manuscripts of the duke of Hamilton (London, 1887).

Reports of the Royal Commissioners of the Historical Manuscripts Commission, Manuscripts of the earl of Home. Twelfth Report, appendix viii (London, 1891).

Reports of the Royal Commissioners of the Historical Manuscripts Commission, Manuscripts of Hope-Johnstone of Annandale (London, 1897).

Reports of the Royal Commissioners of the Historical Manuscripts Commission, Laing Manuscripts, University of Edinburgh (Edinburgh, 1914–25).

Reports of the Royal Commissioners of the Historical Manuscripts Commission, Manuscripts of H. Hume Campbell, Fourteenth Report, appendix iii (London, 1894).

Reports of the Royal Commissioners of the Historical Manuscripts Commission, Manuscripts of the earl of Mar and Kellie (London, 1904 & 1930).

Reports of the Royal Commissioners of the Historical Manuscripts Commission, Manuscripts of David Milne-Home of Wedderburn (London, 1902).

Reports of the Royal Commissioners of the Historical Manuscripts Commission, Pepys Manuscripts, Magdalen College, Cambridge (Cambridge, 1911).

Reports of the Royal Commissioners of the Historical Manuscripts Commission, Manuscripts of the duke of Roxburghe, Fourteenth Report, appendix iii (London, 1894).

Reports of the Royal Commissioners of the Historical Manuscripts Commission, Manuscripts of the duke of Rutland (London, 1888–1905).

Reports of the Royal Commissioners of the Historical Manuscripts Commission, Manuscripts of the marquess of Salisbury (London, 1883–1930).

Reports of the Royal Commissioners of the Historical Manuscripts Commission and the Derbyshire Archaeological Society, Manuscripts of the earl of Shrewsbury, Lambeth Palace Library (London, 1966).

Reports of the Royal Commissioners of the Historical Manuscripts Commission and the Derbyshire Archaeological Society, Talbot Manuscripts, College of Arms (London, 1971).

Reports of the Royal Commissioners of the Historical Manuscripts Commission, I. Corporation of Berwick-upon-Tweed (London, 1903).

Reports of the Royal Commissioners of the Historical Manuscripts Commission, Various Collections V. Hay of Duns Castle (London, 1909).

Rogers, C. ed., *Estimate of the Scottish Nobility during the minority of James the sixth* (Grampian Club, 1873) vol vi.

Roll of Alumni in Arts of the University and King's College of Aberdeen 1596–1860, ed. P. J. Anderson (Aberdeen, 1900).

Roll of the Edinburgh Burgesses and Guild Brethren, 1406–1700, ed. C. B. B. Watson (Scottish Record Society, 1929).

Rotuli Scaccarii Regum Scotorum: The Exchequer Rolls of Scotland, ed. J. Stuart et al (Edinburgh, 1878–1908).

Sadler, R., *The State Papers and Letters of Sir Ralph Sadler*, ed. A. Clifford (Edinburgh, 1809), 2 vols.

Selections from the Records of the Regality of Melrose 1547–1706, vol iii, ed. C. S. Romanes (Scottish History Society, 1917).

Selkirk Protocol Books 1511–1547, ed. T. Maley & W. Elliot (Stair Society, 1993).

Speed, J., *The Theatre of the Empire of Great Britaine: Presenting An Exact Geography of the Kingdomes of England, Scotland and Ireland and the Iles adioyning: with the Shires, Hundreds, Cities and Shire-townes, within the Kingdome of England divided and described by John Speed* (London, 1611).

Spottiswoode, J., *History of the Church of Scotland, beginning the year of our Lord 203, and continued to the end of the reign of King James VI, By the Right Rev. John Spottiswoode, Archbishop of St Andrews, and lord chancellor of Scotland*, ed. M. Russell & M. Napier (Spottiswoode Society, 1847–51), 3 vols.

Statutes of the Realm, ed. A. Luders et al (London, 1810–28).

Students Admitted to the Inner Temple, 1547–1660, ed. W. H. Cooke (London, 1878).

Sterry, W., *The Eton College Register, 1441–1698* (Windsor, 1943).

Teulet, J. A. B., *Relations politiques de la France et de l'Espagne avec l'Ecosse au XVe siècle* (Paris, 1862), 5 vols.

Venn, J. & J. A., *Alumni Cantabrigienses* (Cambridge, 1922–27), 4 vols.

Venn, J. & J. A., *Book of Matriculations and Degrees, Cambridge. 1544–1659* (Cambridge, 1913).

Visitations of the North, ed. F. W. Dendy & C. H. Hunter-Blair (Surtees Society, 1912–30), vols 122, 133, 144, 146.

Walter Mason Trust, *The Protocol Book of John Haw and John Chepman c. 1536–60*, unpublished transcript (Selkirk, n.d.).

Walter Mason Trust, *The Protocol Book of Robert Wedderop notary public 1543–53*, unpublished transcript (Selkirk, n.d.).

The Warrender Papers, ed. A. I. Cameron (Scottish History Society, 1931–32).

Waus, R., *The correspondence of Sir Patrick Waus of Barnbarroch*, ed. R. V. Agnew (Edinburgh, 1887), 2 vols.

Wills and Inventories from the Registry at Durham, ed. J. Raine et al (Surtees Society, 1835–1929), vols 2, 38, 112, 142.

Wilson, T., 'The State of England, 1600', ed. F. J. Fisher, *Camden Miscellany XVI*, 3rd series, lii (1936).

SECONDARY SOURCES

Adam, F., *The Clans, Septs and Regiments of the Scottish Highlands* (Edinburgh, 1952).

Adams, S., ' "Because I am of that countrye & mynde to plant myself there": Robert Dudley, earl of Leicester and the West Midlands', *Midland History*, 20 (1995), 21–74.

Alsop, J. D., 'Religious Preambles in Early Modern English Wills as Formulae', *Journal of Ecclesiastical History*, xl (1989), 19–27.

Anderson, M. ed., *The James Carmichael Collection of Proverbs in Scots* (Edinburgh, 1957).

Asch, R. G. ed., *Three Nations – a common history? England, Scotland, Ireland and British History c. 1600–1920* (Bochum, 1993).

Armstrong, R. B., *History of Liddesdale, Eskdale, Ewesdale, Wauchopedale and the Debateable Land* (Edinburgh, 1883).

Attreed, L. C., 'Preparation for death in sixteenth-century England', *Sixteenth Century Journal*, xiii (1982), 37–66.

Aytoun, A., *The Aytons of Ayton in the Merse* (privately printed 1887).

Baptie, D., *A Lairdship Lost. The Mowats of Balquholly, 1309–1736* (East Linton, 2000).

Barrow, G. W. S., 'The Aftermath of War', *TRHS*, 5th ser, xxviii (1978), 103–126.

Barrow, T., 'Corn, carriers and coastal shipping. The shipping and trade of Berwick and the borders 1730–1830', *The Journal of Transport History*, 3rd ser. xxi (2000), 6–27.

Bates, C. J., *The Border Holds of Northumberland* (Newcastle, 1891).

Batho, G. R., 'The Percies and Alnwick Castle 1557–1632', *AA*, 4th ser, xxxv (1957), 48–63.

Bawcutt, P., 'The Art of Flyting', *Scottish Literary Journal* x (1983), 5–24.

Bean, J. M. W., *The Estates of the Percy Family, 1416–1537* (London, 1958).

Beckingsale, B. W., 'Characteristics of the Tudor North', *NH*, iv (1969), 67–83.

Bell, G. M., *A Handlist of British Diplomatic Representatives 1509–1688* (London, 1990).

Bell, H. E., *An Introduction to the History and Records of the Court of Wards and Liveries* (Cambridge, 1953).

Bernard, G. W., ed. *The Tudor Nobility* (Manchester, 1992).

Blackwood, B. G., *The Lancashire Gentry and the Great Rebellion, 1640–60* (Manchester: Chetham Society, 1978), third series, vol xxv.

Bonner, E., *The French Reactions to the Rough Wooings of Mary, Queen of Scots,* (Journal of the Sydney Society for Scottish History, vi, 1998).

Bonner, E., *The Politique of Henri II: De Facto French Rule in Scotland, 1550–1554* (Journal of the Sydney Society for Scottish History, vii, 1999).

Boothroyd, G., 'The Birth of the Scottish Pistol', in D. H. Caldwell, ed. *Scottish Weapons and Fortifications 1100–1800* (Edinburgh, 1981), 315–38.

Bossy, J., *The English Catholic Community 1570–1850* (London, 1975).

Bouch, C. M. L. & Jones, G. P., *A Short Economic and Social History of the Lake Counties, 1500–1830* (Manchester, 1961).

Bowden, P. J., 'Agricultural Prices, Wages, Farm Profits and Rents', in J. Thirsk, ed. *Agrarian History*, v, pt 2, 1–118.

Bowler, T., 'Some Notes On The Recusant Rolls Of The Exchequer', *Recusant History*, iv (1958), 182–3.

Braddick, M., *State Formation in Early Modern England c. 1550–1700* (Cambridge, 2000).

Bradley, P. J., 'Social Banditry on the Anglo-Scottish Border during the late Middle Ages', *Scotia*, xii (1988), 27–43.

Bradshaw B. & Morrill, J. eds., *The British Problem, c. 1543–1707* (Basingstoke, 1996).

Brander, M., *Scottish and Border Battles and Ballads* (New York, 1975).

Broce G. & Wunderli, R. M., 'The Funeral of Henry Percy, sixth earl of Northumberland', *Albion*, xx (1990), 199–215.

Brooks, F. W., *The Council of the North* (London, 1953).

Brown, K. M., *Bloodfeud in Scotland 1573–1625* (Edinburgh, 1986).

Brown, K. M., 'The Making of a Politique: The Counter Reformation and the Regional Politics of John, Eighth Lord Maxwell', *SHR*, lxvi (1987), 152–75.

Brown, K. M., 'Burghs, Lords and Feuds in Jacobean Scotland', in M. Lynch, ed. *The Early Modern Town in Scotland* (London, 1987), 102–24.

Brown, K. M., 'The Price of Friendship: The well-affected and English Economic Clientage in Scotland before 1603', in R. A. Mason, ed. *Scotland and England, 1286–1815* (Edinburgh, 1987), 139–162.

Burke, J. B. et al., *A Dictionary of the Dormant, Abeyant, Forfeited and Extinct Peerages* (London, 1840).

Burke, J. B., et al. *A Dictionary of Landed Gentry*, sixth edition (London, 1882).

Burke, P. Harrison, B. & Slack, P. eds., *Civil Histories Essays presented to Sir Keith Thomas* (Oxford, 2000).

Burnett, J., *Riot, Revelry and Rout: Sport in Lowland Scotland Before 1860* (East Linton, 2000).

Bush, M. L., *The Pilgrimage of Grace* (Manchester, 1996).

Bush, M. L. & Bownes, D., *The Defeat of the Pilgrimage of Grace* (Hull, 1999).

Bush, M., 'The Pilgrimage of Grace: Reactions, Responses and Revisions', *The Historian*, lx (1998), 16–20.

Bush, M. L., 'The Problems of the Far North and the Crisis of 1537', *NH*, vi (1971), 40–63.

Bush, M. L., 'Tenant Right under the Tudors: a revision revised', *Bulletin of the John Rylands Library*, lxxvii (1995), 161–188.

Butlin, R. A., 'Field Systems of Northumberland and Durham', in A. R. H. Baker and R. A. Butlin, eds. *Studies of Field Systems in the British Isles* (Oxford, 1973), 93–144.

Butlin, R. A., 'Enclosure and improvement in Northumberland in the sixteenth century', *AA*, 4th ser, xlv (1967), 149–160.

Caldwell, D. H., 'The Battle of Pinkie', in N. Macdougall, ed. *Scotland and War AD79–1918* (Edinburgh, 1991), 61–94.

Carleton, G., *The Life of Bernard Gilpin* (London, 1629).

Carmichael, C. H. E., *Additions and Corrections to The Rutherfords of that Ilk by Thomas [Cockburn-] Hood* (Kelso, 1899–1903).

Carr, R. E. and C. E., *The History of the Family of Carr* (London, 1893–99).

Clark, M. A., 'Reformation in the Far North: Cumbria and the Church, 1500–1571', *NH*, xxxii (1996), 75–89.

Clark, M. A., 'Northern light? Parochial life in a "dark corner" of Tudor England', in K. French, G. Gibbs & B. Kumin, eds. *The Parish in English Life 1400–1600* (Manchester, 1997), 56–73.

Clark, M. A., 'Cross-Border clergy movements in the Reformation West March', *Transactions of the Cumberland and Westmorland Antiquarian and Archaeological Society*, xcviii (1998), 309–12.

Clarkson, L. A., *The Pre-Industrial Economy in England* (London, 1971).

Cliffe, J. T., *The Yorkshire Gentry* (London, 1969).

Cockburn, R. & H. A., *The Records of the Cockburn Family* (Edinburgh, 1913).

Cockburn-Hood, T. H., *the Cockburns of that Ilk* (Edinburgh, 1888).

Cockburn-Hood, T. H., *The Rutherfords of that Ilk* (Edinburgh, 1884).

Cokayne, G. E., ed. *The Complete Baronage, vol one* (Exeter, 1900).

Cokayne, G. E. et al., *The Complete Peerage* (London, 1910–59), 13 vols.

Coleman, D. C., *The Economy of England, 1450–1750* (Oxford, 1977).

Collinson, P., *The Birthpangs of Protestant England* (Basingstoke, 1991).

Connolly, S. J. ed., *Kingdoms United? Great Britain and Ireland Since 1500* (Dublin, 1999).

Cooper, J., *Land, Men and Beliefs* (London, 1984).

Cooper, N., *Houses of the Gentry 1480–1680* (New Haven 1999).

Cormack, A. A., *Teinds and Agriculture* (Oxford, 1930).

Coulomb, C. A., *The Administration of the English Borders* (New York, 1911).

Cowan, I. B., *The Scottish Reformation* (London, 1982).

Cowan, I. B., 'The Reformation in Dumfriesshire', *Transactions of The Dumfriesshire and Galloway Natural History and Antiquarian Society,* 3rd ser, lvi (1981), 82–90.

Cowan, I. B. & Easson, D. E., *Medieval Religious Houses, Scotland*, second edition (London, 1976).

Cox, N. & J., 'Probate Inventories: the legal background', *The Local Historian*, xvi (1984), 133–45 & 217–27.

Craig-Brown, T., *The History of Selkirkshire* (Edinburgh, 1886).

Craster, E., 'The Early History of the Craster Family', *AA*, 4th ser. xxx (1959), 118–48.

Cressy, D., *Education in Tudor and Stuart England* (London, 1975).

Cressy, D., *Literacy and the Social Order* (Cambridge, 1980).

Cressy, D., 'Social Status and Literacy in North East England, 1560–1630', *Local Population Studies,* xxi (1978), 19–23.

Cressy, D., 'Kinship and Kin Interaction in Early Modern England', *P&P*, xiii (1987), 38–69.

Cressy, D., 'Death and the social order: the funerary preferences of Elizabethan gentlemen', *Continuity and Change*, v (1990), 99–119.

Crockett, W. S., *Minstrelsy of the Merse* (Paisley, 1893).

Cross, M. C., *The Puritan Earl: the life and times of Henry Hastings, third earl of Huntingdon, 1536–1595* (London, 1966).

Cross, M. C., 'Sin and society: the northern high commission and the northern gentry in the reign of Elizabeth I', in C. Cross, D. Loades & J. Scarisbrick (eds), *Law and Government under the Tudors* (Cambridge, 1988), 195–209.

Cross, M. C., 'The Third Earl of Huntingdon and The Trials of Catholics in the North, 1581–1595', *Recusant History*, viii (1966), 136–46.

Cross, M. C., 'Berwick upon Tweed and the neighbouring parts of Northumberland on the Eve of the Armada', *AA*, 4th ser. xli (1963), 123–34.

Cross, M. C., 'The Development of Protestantism in Leeds and Hull, 1520–1640: the Evidence of Wills', *NH*, xviii (1982), 230–8.

Davis, K. R., *The Rutherfords in Britain* (Gloucester, 1987).

Defoe, D., *A Tour Through The Whole Island of Great Britain*, ed. P. Rogers (Harmondsworth, 1986).

Devine, T. M. and Lythe, S., 'The economy of Scotland under James VI – A revision article', *SHR*, l (1971), 91–106.

Dibben, A. A., *Title Deeds* (London, 1968).

Dickinson, W. C., 'Freehold in Scots Law', *Juridical Review* (1945), 135–51.

Dickinson, W. C., 'The Death of Lord Russell, 1585', *SHR*, xx (1922–3), 181–6.

Dictionary of National Biography, eds. L. Stephen & S. Lee, et al (Oxford, 1917 –), multi-volumed.

Dilworth, M., 'The Commendator System in Scotland', *IR*, xxxvii (1986), 51–72.

Dilworth, M.,. 'The Border Abbeys in the Sixteenth Century', *RSCHS*, xxi (1981–3), 233–245.

Dixon, P., 'Towerhouses, Pelehouses and Border Society', *Archaeological Journal*, 136 (1979), 240–52.

Dodds, M. H. & R., *The Pilgrimage of Grace 1536–7 and the Exeter Conspiracy 1538* (Cambridge, 1915), 2 vols.

Dodgshon, R. A., *The Origin of British Field Systems* (London, 1980).

Dodgshon, R. A., *Land and Society in Early Scotland* (Oxford, 1981).

Donaldson, G., *James V to James VII* (Edinburgh, 1978).

Donaldson, G., *All The Queen's Men: Power and Politics in Mary Stewart's Scotland* (London, 1983), 102–112.

Donaldson, G., *The Scottish Reformation* (Cambridge, 1979).

Donaldson, G., 'The Legal Profession in Scottish Society in the sixteenth and seventeenth centuries', *Juridical Review* (1976), 1–19.

Donaldson, G., 'Scottish Presbyterian Exiles In England, 1584–8', *RSCHS*, xiv (1962), 67–80.

Donaldson, G., 'Foundations of Anglo-Scottish Union,' in S. T. Bindoff, J. Hurstfield and C. H. Williams, eds. *Elizabethan Government and Society* (London, 1961).

Douglas, R., *The Baronage of Scotland* (Edinburgh, 1798).

Dowling, M., *Humanism in the Age of Henry VIII* (London, 1986).

Duffy, E., *The Stripping of the Altars. Traditional Religion in England 1400–1580* (New Haven, 1992).

Duffy, E., 'The Long Reformation: Catholicism. Protestantism and the multitude', in N. Tyack, ed. *England's Long Reformation 1500–1800* (London, 1998), 33–70.

Drury, J. L., 'Inventories in the Probate Records of the Diocese of Durham', *AA*, 5th ser. xxviii (2000), 177–91.

Durkan, J., 'Education in the Century of the Reformation', in D. M. Roberts, ed. *Essays on the Scottish Reformation, 1513–1625* (Glasgow, 1962), 145–168

Durkan, J., 'Education: the laying of fresh foundations', in J. MacQueen, ed. *Humanism in Renaissance Scotland* (Edinburgh, 1990), 123–60.

Durkan, J., 'The French Connection in the Sixteenth and Early Seventeenth Centuries', in T. C. Smout, ed. *Scotland and Europe, 1200–1850* (Edinburgh, 1986), 14–44.

Easson, D. E., 'The Reformation and the monasteries in Scotland and England: Some Comparisons', *Transactions of The Scottish Ecclesiological Society,* xv (1957), 7–23.

Edwards, P., *The Horse Trade of Tudor and Stuart England* (Cambridge, 1988).

Ellis, S. G., *Tudor Frontiers and Noble Power. The Making of the British State* (Oxford, 1995).

Ellis, S. G. & Barber, S. eds., *Conquest and Union, Fashioning a British State 1485–1725* (Harlow, 1995).

Ellis, S., 'Crown, Community and Government in the English Territories, 1450–1575', *History,* lxxi (1986), 187–206.

Ellis, S. G., 'Tudor Northumberland: British History in an English County', in Connolly, ed. *Kingdoms United?* 29–42.

Ellis, S. G., 'The English State and its Frontiers in the British Isles, 1300–1600', in D. Power & N. Standen, eds. *Frontiers in Question. Eurasian Borderlands 700–1700* (Basingstoke, 1999), 153–81.

Ellis, S. G., 'Tudor state formation and the shaping of the British Isles', in Ellis & Barber, *Conquest and Union,* 40–63.

Ellis, S. G., 'Civilizing Northumberland: Representations of Englishness in the Tudor State', *Journal of Historical Sociology,* 12/2 (1999), 103–27.

Ellis, S. G., 'A Border Baron and the Tudor State: The rise and fall of Lord Dacre of the North', *Historical Journal,* 35 (1992), 253–77.

Elton, G. R., *England Under The Tudors,* second edition (London, 1974).

Elton, G. R., *The Parliament of England, 1558–81* (Cambridge, 1986).

Emsley, K., 'North Durham', *Tyne & Tweed,* 46 (1991–92), 17–23.

Erickson, A. L., 'Common law versus common practice: the use of marriage settlements in early modern England', *Economic History Review,* 2nd ser, xliii (1990), 21–39.

Everitt, A., *The Community of Kent and The Great Rebellion, 1640–60* (Leicester, 1966).

Fawcett, J. W., 'Early Schools in Northumberland', *Proceedings of The Society of Antiquities of Newcastle,* 3rd series, ix (1921), 264–66.

Fenwick, H., *Scottish Baronial Houses* (London, 1986).

Fleming, A., *The Medieval Scots Scholar in France* (Glasgow, 1952).

Ferguson, J., *Papers illustrating the history of the Scots Brigade in the Service of the United Netherlands,* (Scottish History Society, 1899).

Ferguson, W., *Scotland's Relations with England: a Survey to 1707* (Edinburgh, 1978).

Fergusson, J., *Lowland Lairds* (London, 1949).

Ferne, J., *The Blazon of Gentrie,* (London, 1586).

Fischer, E. L., *The Scots in Germany* (Edinburgh, 1902).

Fischer, E. L., *The Scots in Eastern and Western Prussia* (Edinburgh, 1903).

Fleming, P. Gross, A. & Lander, J. R. eds., *Regionalism and Revision. The Crown and its Provinces in England 1200–1650* (London, 1998).

Ford, W., 'The problems of literacy in Early Modern England', *History*, lxxviii (1993), 22–37.

Foster, A., 'Churchwardens' accounts of early modern England and Wales: some problems to note, but much to be gained', in K. French, G. Gibbs & B. Kumin, eds. *The Parish in English Life 1400–1600* (Manchester, 1997), 74–93.

Forster, A. M. C., 'Bishop Tunstall's Priests', *Recusant History*, ix (1968), 175–204.

Fox, A., *Oral and Literate Culture in England 1500–1700* (Oxford, 2000).

Franklin, T. B., *A History of Scottish Farming* (Edinburgh, 1952).

Fraser, C. M., 'Catholic Clergy in the Diocese of Durham, 1563', *Northern Catholic History* 38 (1997), 20–27.

Fraser, C. M., 'Recusant wives, widows and daughters', *Northern Catholic History,* 33 (1992), 3–8.

Friedman, A. T., 'The Influence of Humanism on the Education of Girls and Boys in Tudor England', *History of Education Quarterly* (1985), 57–70.

Fraser, G. M., *The Steel Bonnets* (London, 1974).

French, A. D. W., *Notes on the Surname of French* (Boston, 1893).

Gard, R. M., 'Northumberland Recusants, 1592–1601', *Northern Catholic History*, 23 (1986), 3–14.

Galloway, B., *The Union of England and Scotland 1603–1608* (Edinburgh, 1986).

Galloway, J. A. & Murray, I., 'Scottish Migration to England, 1400–1560', *Scottish Geographical Magazine*, 112/1 (1996), 29–38.

Gaunt, P., *The British Wars 1637–1651* (London, 1997).

Gilbert, J., 'The usual money of Scotland and exchange rates against foreign coin', in D. M. Metcalf, ed. Coinage in Medieval Scotland, *British Archaeological Reports,* 45 (1977).

Gilbert, J. M., *Hunting and Hunting Reserves in Medieval Scotland* (Edinburgh, 1979).

Girouard, M., *Life in the English Country House* (London, 1980).

Gleason, J. H., *The Justice of the Peace in England, 1558–1640* (Oxford, 1969).

Goodman, A. E., 'The Anglo-Scottish Marches in the Fifteenth Century: A Frontier Society?' in Mason, R. A. ed., *Scotland and England, 1286–1815* (Edinburgh, 1987), 16–33.

Goodare, J., *State and Society in Early Modern Scotland* (Oxford, 1999).

Goodare, J., 'Parliamentary Taxation in Scotland, 1560–1625', *SHR*, lxviii (1989), 23–52.

Gordon, J. F. S., *Monasticon* (Glasgow 1868).

Gouldesbrough, P. ed., *Formulary of Old Scots Legal Documents* (Stair Society, 1985), vol. xxxvi.

Grant, A. & Stringer, K. J. eds., *Uniting the Kingdom? The Making of British History* (London, 1995).

Grant, A. & Stringer, K., 'The enigma of British History' in their *Uniting the Kingdom*, 3–11.

Guy, I., 'The Scottish Export Trade, 1460–1599', in T. C. Smout, ed. *Scotland and Europe* (Edinburgh, 1986), 62–82.

Guy, J. ed., *The Tudor Monarchy* (London, 1997).

Haig, C. E., *Haig of Bemersyde* (Edinburgh, 1907).

Haigh, C., *Reformation and Resistance in Tudor Lancashire* (Cambridge, 1975).

Hodgson, J., *A History of Northumberland* (Newcastle, 1820–58), 7 vols.

Hassell Smith, A., *County and Court, Government and Politics in Norfolk 1558–1603* (Oxford, 1974).

Hardie, R. P., *The Roads of Medieval Lauderdale* (Edinburgh, 1942).

Havinden, M., 'The Increase and Distribution of the Resident Gentry of Somerset, 1500–1623', *Southern History*, xx-xxi (1998–99), 68–107.

Hay, D., 'The Dissolution of the Monasteries in the diocese of Durham', *AA*, 4th ser. xv (1938) 69–114.

Heal, F. & Holmes, C., *The Gentry in England and Wales 1500–1700* (Basingstoke, 1994).

Heslop, D. & Harbottle, B., 'Chillingham Church, Northumberland: the South Chapel and the Grey Tomb', *AA*, 5th ser. xxvii (1999), 123–34.

Hewitt, G. R., *Scotland Under Morton, 1572–80* (Edinburgh, 1982).

Hickman, D., 'From Catholic to Protestant: the changing meaning of testamentary religious provisions in Elizabethan London,' in N. Tyack, ed. *England's Long Reformation 1500–1800* (London, 1998), 117–39.

Hicks, M., 'Cement or Solvent? Kinship and Politics in Late Medieval England: The Case of the Nevilles', *History*, 83 (1998), 31–46.

Hilson, G., *Jedburgh 100 Years Ago* (*Kelso Mail*, 1897).

Hilton, J. A., 'Catholicism In Jacobean Northumberland', *Northern Catholic History*, vii (1978), 10–19.

Hilton, J. A., 'Catholicism in Elizabethan Northumberland', *NH*, xiii (1977), 44–58.

Hodgson, J., *A History of Northumberland* (Newcastle, 1820–58), 7 vols.

Hodgson, J. C., 'Barmoor and the Muschamps', *HBNC*, xxii (1912–15), 98–117.

Hodgson, J. C., 'Fowberry and its Ancient Owners', *HBNC*, xxii (1912–15), 325–30.

Hodgson, J. C., 'An Attempt to Elucidate the Descents of the Family of Alder of Prendwick', *AA*, 3rd ser. v (1909), 16–39.

Hodgkin, T., *The Wardens of the Northern Marches* (London, 1908).

Hollinshead, J. E., 'The gentry of south-west Lancashire in the later-sixteenth century', *NH* xxvi (1990), 82–99.

Houlbrooke, R. A., *The English Family 1450–1700* (London, 1984).

Houlbrooke, R. A., *Death, Religion, and the Family in England, 1480–1750* (Oxford, 1998).

Houston, R. A., *Scottish Literacy and the Scottish identity: illiteracy and Society in Scotland and Northern England, 1600–1800* (Cambridge, 1985).

Hoyle, R. W. ed., *The Estates of the English Crown* (Cambridge, 1992).

Hoyle, R. W., *The Pilgrimage of Grace and the Politics of the 1530s* (Oxford, 2001).

Hoyle, R. W., 'Faction, Feud and Reconciliation amongst the Northern English Nobility, 1525–1569', *History*, lxxxiv (1999), 590–613.

Hoyle, R. W., 'An Ancient and Laudable Custom: The Definition and Development of Tenant Right in north-western England in the sixteenth century', *P&P*, cxvi (1987), 22–55.

Hoyle, R. W., 'Lords, Tenants, and Tenant Right in the Sixteenth Century: Four Studies', *NH,* xx (1984), 38–63.

Hoyle, R. W., 'Henry Percy, sixth earl of Northumberland, and the fall of the House of Percy', in G. Bernard, ed. *The Tudor Nobility* (Manchester, 1992), 180–211.

Hull, S. W. ed., *Chaste, Silent and Obedient: English Books for Women 1475–1640* (Pasadena, 1988).

Hume-Brown, P., *Early Travellers in Scotland* (Edinburgh, 1978).

Hunter Blair, C. H., 'Scottish Borderers of the Sixteenth Century', *HBNC*, xxvii (1932–4), 87–100.

Hunter-Blair, C. H., 'Wardens and Deputy Wardens of the Marches of England toward Scotland in Northumberland', *AA*, 4th ser. xxviii (1950), 18–95.

Hunter-Blair, C. H., 'M.Ps for Northumberland, 1399–1558', *AA*, 4th ser. xii (1935), 82–132.

Hunter-Blair, C. H., 'M.Ps for Northumberland and Newcastle-upon-Tyne, 1559–1831', *AA*, 4th ser. xxiii (1945), 102–155.

Hunter-Blair, C. H., 'M.Ps for Berwick-on-Tweed, 1529–1558', *AA*, 4th ser. xiv (1937), 63–66.

Hunter-Blair, C. H., 'M.Ps for Berwick-upon-Tweed and Morpeth, 1558–1831', *AA*, 4th ser. xxiv (1946), 71–112.

Hunter-Blair, C. H., 'The Sheriffs of Northumberland to 1603', *AA*, 4th ser. xx (1942), 11–90.

Hurstfield, J., *The Queen's Wards* (London, 1958).

Jack, R. D. S. ed., *The History of Scottish Literature: Volume One, Origins to 1660* (Aberdeen, 1988).

Jack, R. D. S., *The Italian Influence on Scottish Literature* (Edinburgh, 1972).

James, M. E., 'The Concept of Order and the Northern Rising', *P&P*, lx (1973), 49–83.

James, M. E., Family, Lineage and Civil Society (Oxford, 1974).

James, M. E., 'Change and Continuity in the Tudor North', *Borthwick Papers*, 27 (1965).

James, M. E., 'Estate Accounts of the Earls of Northumberland, 1562–1637', *SS*, clxiii (1948).

James, M. E., 'English Politics and the Concept of Honour, 1485–1642', *P&P,* supplement iii (1978).

Jeffrey, A., *The History and Antiquities of Roxburghshire* (Edinburgh, 1855–64), 4 vols.

Jewell, H. M., ' "The bringing up of children in good learning and manners": a survey of secular educational provision in the north of England, *c.* 1350–1550', *NH,* xviii (1982), 1–25.

Johnson, G., *The Natural History of the Eastern Borders* (London, 1853).

Jones, J. G., *The Wynn Family of Gwydir: origins, growth and development c. 1490–1674* (Aberystwyth, 1995).

Jones, J. G., *The Welsh Gentry 1536–1640. Images of Status, Honour and Authority* (Cardiff, 1998).

Joyce, M. B., 'Catholic Education in Sixteenth-Century Northumberland,' *Northern Catholic History*, ii, (1975), 9–15.

Kaufman, G., 'Juan Lius Vives on the education of women', *Signs,* 3 (1978), 891–96.

Keeling, 'S. M., The Reformation In The Anglo-Scottish Border Counties', *NH,* xv (1979), 24–42.

Kerr, A., *The Genealogie of the Trotters* (Edinburgh, 1704).

Kerridge, E., *Agrarian Problems in the Sixteenth Century and After* (London, 1969).

Kitching, C., 'The Disposal of Monastic and Chantry Lands,' in F. Heal and R. O'Day, eds. *Church and Society in England: Henry VIII to James I* (London, 1977), 119–136.

Lamb, H. H., *The Changing Climate* (London, 1966).

Larminie, V., *Wealth, Kinship and Culture. The seventeenth-century Newdigates of Arbury and their world* (London, 1995).

Larner, C., *Enemies of God. The Witch Hunt in Scotland* (London, 1981).

Laslett, P., *The World We Have Lost* (London, 1983).

Lawrence-Archer, J. H., *An Account of the Surname of Edgar* (London, 1873).

Le Hardy, W., *History of the Family of Ridpath* (London, 1927).

Lee, M., *John Maitland of Thirlestane* (Princeton, 1959).

Leneman, L., *Alienated Affections. The Scottish Experience of Divorce and Separation, 1684–1830* (Edinburgh, 1998).

Lithgow, S. A., 'Mellerstain and the Haitlies thereof', *HBNC,* xv (1894–95), 122–43.

Litzenberger, C., 'Local responses to religious changes: evidence from Gloucestershire wills', in E. J. Carlson, ed. *Religion and the English People 1500–1640* (Kirksville, Missouri, 1998), 245–70.

Lloyd, H. A., *The Gentry of South-West Wales, 1540–1640* (Cardiff, 1968).

Loades, D. M., *The Last Years of Cuthbert Tunstall, 1547–1559* (Durham, 1973).

Logan-Home, G. J. N., *History of the Logan Family* (Edinburgh, 1934).

Lomas, R., *A Power in the land: the Percies* (East Linton, 1999).

Lomas, R., 'The Impact of Border Warfare: The Scots and South Tweedside, c. 1290–c. 1520', *SHR*, lxxv (1996), 143–67.

Lynch, M., *Edinburgh and the Reformation* (Edinburgh, 1981).

Lynch, M., 'The Crown and the Burghs 1500–1625', in M. Lynch ed. *The Early Modern Town in Scotland* (London, 1987), 55–80.

Lynch, M., 'Calvinism in Scotland, 1559–1638' in *International Calvinism*, ed. M. Prestwich (Oxford, 1985), 225–55.

Lythe, S. G. E., *The Economy of Scotland, 1550–1625, in its European setting* (Edinburgh, 1960).

Lythe, S. G. E., 'The Economy of Scotland under James VI and I,' in A.G.R. Smith, ed. *The Reign of James VI and VI* (London, 1973), 57–73.

Maag, K., 'Education and training for the Calvinist ministry: the Academy of Geneva, 1559–1620', in A. Pettegree, ed. *The Reformation of the Parishes* (Manchester, 1993), 133–52.

McAlpine, K., 'Proude Armstrongs and Border Rogues: History in Kinmont Willie, Jock o the Side and Archie o Cawfield', in E. J. Cowan, ed. *The Ballad in Scottish History* (East Linton, 2000), 73–94.

McCann, R., 'In Search of the Border Reivers', *The Scots Magazine*, new series, 149/3 (1998), 234–6.

Macaulay, T. B., *History of England from the Accession of James the Second* (London, 1849–55), 4 vols.

McCrie, T., *The Life of Andrew Melville* (Edinburgh, 1819), 2 vols.

McCoog, T. M., *The Society of Jesus in Ireland, Scotland and England 1541–1588* (Leiden, 1996).

MacCulloch, D., *Suffolk and the Tudors: Politics and Religion in an English County, 1500–1600* (Oxford, 1986).

MacCulloch, D., *Thomas Cranmer* (New Haven, 1996).

MacDonald, A. J., *Border Bloodshed. Scotland, England and France at War, 1369–1403* (East Linton, 2000).

MacGibbon, D. & Ross, T., *The Castellated and Domestic Architecture of Scotland* (Edinburgh, 1887), 5 vols.

MacIvor, I., 'Artillery and Major Places of Strength in the Lothians and East Border, 1513–1542', in D. H. Caldwell, ed. *Scottish Weapons and Fortification 1100–1800* (Edinburgh, 1981), 94–152.

McKean, C., *The Scottish Chateau. The Country House of Renaissance Scotland* (Stroud, 2001).

McKean, C., ' "Castle-wise" country houses', in D. Howard, ed. *The Architecture of the Scottish Renaissance* (Edinburgh, 1990), 17–18.

Mackenzie, G., *The Works of Sir George Mackenzie of Rosehaugh* (Edinburgh, 1716).

McMullen, N., 'The education of English Gentlewomen 1540–1640', *History of Education*, 6 (1977), 87–101.

Macpherson, R., 'Francis Stewart, Fifth Earl Bothwell, and James VI: Perception Politics', in T. Brotherstone & D. Ditchburn, eds. *Freedom and Authority. Scotland c. 1050–c. 1650* (East Linton, 2000), 155–64.

McNeill, P. G. B. & MacQueen, H. L. eds., *Atlas of Scottish History to 1707* (Edinburgh, 1996).

Madden, C., 'The Feuing of Ettrick Forest', *IR*, xxvii (1976), 79–81.

Maltby, J., *Prayer Book and People in Elizabethan and Early Stuart England* (Cambridge, 2000).

Makey, W., *The Church of the Covenant, 1637–1651* (Edinburgh, 1979).

Manning, R. B., *Religion and Society In Elizabethan Sussex* (Leicester, 1969).

Marcombe, D., 'Bernard Gilpin Anatomy of an Elizabethan Legend', *NH*, xvi (1980), 20–39.

Marks, R., *Burrell* (Glasgow 1983).

Marsh, C., ' "Departing well and christianly" will making and popular religion in early modern England', in E. J. Carlson, ed. *Religion and the English People 1500–1640* (Kirksville, Missouri, 1998), 201–44.

Maxwell-Irving, A. M. T., *The Border Towers of Scotland: Their History and Architecture. The West March* (Blairlogie, 2000).

Maxwell-Irving, A. M. T., 'Early Firearms and their influence on the military and domestic architecture of the Borders', *Proceedings of the Society of Antiquaries of Scotland*, ciii (1970–71), 194–224.

Mayhew, G. L., 'The Progress of the Reformation in East Sussex, 1530–1559: the evidence of wills', *Southern History*, v (1983), 38–67.

Meikle, M. M., 'The Invisible Divide: The Greater Lairds and the Nobility of Jacobean Scotland', *SHR* lxxi (1992), 70–87.

Meikle, M. M., 'A Godly Rogue; The Career of Sir John Forster, an Elizabethan Border Warden', *NH* xxviii (1992), 126–63.

Meikle, M. M., 'Northumberland Divided; Anatomy of a sixteenth-century bloodfeud', *AA* 5th ser. xx (1992), 79–89.

Meikle, M. M., 'The sixteenth-century Border Lairds: a study of the links between wealth and house building', *HBNC*, xlvi (1993), 9–36.

Meikle, M. M., 'Victims, Viragos and Vamps: Women of the Sixteenth Century Anglo-Scottish Frontier', in J. C. Appleby & P. Dalton, eds. *Government, Religion and Society in Northern England 100–1700* (Gloucester, 1997), 172–184.

Meikle, M. M., 'The Homes and the East March', in R. Oram & G. Stell, eds. *Family Fortunes: Architecture and Patronage in Scotland from the twelfth to the seventeenth centuries* (Tuckwell Press) forthcoming.

Merriman, M. H., *The Rough Wooings Mary Queen of Scots 1542–1551* (East Linton, 2000).

Merriman, M. H., 'The Forts of Eyemouth: Anvils of British Union', *SHR*, lxvii (1998), 142–155.

Merriman, M. H., 'The assured Scots', *SHR*, xlvii (1968), 10–34.

Merriman, M. H., 'War and Propaganda during the Rough Wooing', *Scottish Tradition*, ix (1979–80), 20–30.

Middleton, T., *A True Narration of the Entertainment of his Royal Maiestie, from the time of his departure from Edenbrough till his Receiving in London* (London, 1603).

Mingay, G. E., *The Gentry: The Rise and Fall of a Ruling Class* (London, 1976).

Moore, J. S., 'Probate Inventories: Problems and Prospects', in P. J. Riden, ed. *Probate Records and the Local Community* (Gloucester, 1985), 11–28.

Moran, J. H., 'Literacy and Education in Northern England, 1350–1550: A Methodological Inquiry', *NH*, xvii (1981), 1–23.

Morey, A., *The Catholic Subjects of Elizabeth I* (New Jersey, 1978).

Morgan, G. & Rushton, P., *Rogues, Thieves and the Rule of Law. The problem of law enforcement in north-east England, 1718–1800* (London, 1998).

Morgan, H., 'British Policies before the British State', in Bradshaw & Morrill, *The British Problem*, 66–88.

Morgan, V., 'The Cartographic image of "the country" in early modern England', *TRHS*, xxix (1979), 129–54.

Morrill, J. S., 'The Northern Gentry and the Great Rebellion', *NH*, xv (1979), 66–87.

Muldrew, C., 'The Culture of Reconciliation: community and the settlement of economic disputes in early modern England', *The Historical Journal*, 39/4 (1996), 915–942.

Murray, P. J., 'The Lay Administrators of Church Lands in the Fifteenth and Sixteenth Centuries', *SHR* lxxiv (1995), 26–44.

Neale, J. E., *Elizabeth I and her Parliaments* (London, 1953).

Nef, J. U., *The Rise of the British Coal Industry* (London, 1932), 2 vols.

Neilson, G., *Peel: its meaning and derivation* (Edinburgh, 1894).

Neilson, G., 'The Feuing of Drygrange from the Monastery of Melrose', *SHR*, vii (1910), 355–63.

Nesbitt, A. & C., *History of the Family of Nisbet* (Torquay, 1898).

Nesbitt, R. C., *Nisbet of that Ilk* (London, 1941).

Neville, C. J., *Violence, Custom and Law. The Anglo-Scottish Border Lands in the Later Middle Ages* (Edinburgh, 1998).

Neville, C. J., 'Local Sentiment and the "National" Enemy in Northern England in the Later Middle Ages', *Journal of British Studies*, 35 (1996), 419–37.

Neville, C. J., 'Keeping the Peace on the Northern Marches in the Later Middle Ages', *EHR*, cix (1994), 1–25.

Newman, C., 'The role of women in early Yorkshire recusancy: a reappraisal', *Northern Catholic History*, 30 (1989), 8–16.

Newton, R., *The Northumberland Landscape* (London, 1972).

Newton, R., 'The Decay of the Borders: Tudor Northumberland in transition', in C. W. Chalkin and M. A. Havinden, eds. *Rural Change and Urban Growth, 1500–1800* (London, 1974), 2–31.

Nichols, J. G., *The Herald and Genealogist* (1873), vol vii.

Nicholls, A. D., *The Jacobean Union. A Reconsideration of British Civil Policies Under the Early Stuarts* (Westport, 1999).

Nicholls, M., *A History of the Modern British Isles 1529–1603* (Oxford, 1999).

Nicolson, W., *Leges Marchiarum or Border Laws* (London, 1747).

Nicolson, J. and Burn, R., *The History of Westmorland and Cumberland* (London, 1777).

Nobbs, D., *England and Scotland, 1560–1707* (London, 1952).

Northumberland., *A History of Northumberland*, ed. E. Bateson, et al (London, 1893–1940), 15 vols.

O'Day, R., *Education and Society 1500–1800* (London, 1982).

Orme, N., *From Childhood to Chivalry* (London, 1984).

Orme, N., *English Schools in the Middle Ages* (London, 1973).

Ormiston, T. L., *The Ormistons of Teviotdale* (Exeter, 1951).

Overton, M., 'Estimating crop yields from probate inventories: an example from East Anglia 1585–1735', *Journal of Economic History*, xxxix (1979), 363–78.

Palliser, D. M., *The Age of Elizabeth* (London, 1983).

Palmer, W., 'High Officeholding, Foreign Policy, and the British Dimension in the Tudor Far North, 1525–1563', *Albion* 29 (1998), 579–595.

Petre, *Notices of the English Colleges and Convents Established on the Continent* (Norwich, 1849).

Pevsner, N., *The Buildings of England – Northumberland* (London, 1957).

Phillimore, R., *The Ecclesiastical Law* (London, 1873), 2 vols.

Phillips, G., *The Anglo-Scots Wars 1513–1550* (Woodbridge, 1999).

Phillips, G., 'Strategy and its limitations: the Anglo-Scots Wars 1480–1550', *War in History,* vi (1999), 396–416.

Pocock, J. G. A., 'British History: A Plea for a New Subject', *Journal of Modern History*, 47 (1975), 601–28.

Pocock, J. G. A., *The Limits and Divisions of British History* - Studies in Public Policy 31 (Strathclyde, 1979).

Pocock, J. G. A., 'The Limits and Divisions of British History: in search of the unknown subject', *American Historical Review,* 67 (1982), 311–36.

Pocock, J. G. A., 'Two Kingdoms and Three Histories? Political Thought in

British Contexts', in R. A., Mason, ed. *Scots and Britons: Scottish Political Thought and the Union of 1603* (Cambridge, 1994), 293–312.

Pocock, J. G. A., 'British History: the pursuit of the expanding subject', in W. Prest, ed. *British Studies into the 21st Century. Perspectives and practices* (Melbourne, 1999), 58–72.

Pollard, A. J., *North-Eastern England during the Wars of the Roses* (Oxford, 1990).

Pollard, A. J., 'The Characteristics of the fifteenth-century North', in J. C. Appleby and P. Dalton, eds. *Government, Religion and Society in Northern England 1000–1700* (Stroud, 1997), 131–143.

Pollard, S. and Crossley, D. W., *The Wealth of Britain, 1085–1966* (London, 1968).

Pollitt, R., 'The Defeat of the Northern Rebellion and the Shaping of Anglo-Scottish Relations', *SHR*, lxiv (1985), 1–21.

Pollock, L., 'Younger Sons in Tudor and Stuart England', *History Today* (June 1989), 23–9.

Prest, W. R., *The Inns of Court Under Elizabeth I and the Early Stuarts* (London 1972).

Prest, W. R., 'Legal Education of the Gentry at the Inns of Court, 1560–1640', *P&P*, xxxviii (1967), 20–39.

Prest, W. R., *The Professions of Early Modern England* (Sydney, 1987).

Pringle, A., *The Records of the Pringle Family,* Edinburgh 1933.

Public Record Office, 'List of Sheriffs for England and Wales', *List and Index Society*, ix (1898).

Purvis, J. S., *An Introduction to Ecclesiastical Record* (London, 1953).

Rae, T. I., *The Administration of the Scottish Frontier, 1513–1603* (Edinburgh, 1960).

Rae, T. I., 'Feud and the jurisdiction of the wardens of the Marches', *Transactions of the Hawick Archaeological Society* (1961), 3–9.

Raine, J., *The History and Antiquities of North Durham* (London, 1852).

Reed, J., *The Border Ballads* (London, 1973).

Reid, C. L., *Pedigree of the Family of Ker* (Newcastle, 1914).

Reid, R. R., *The King's Council in the North* (London, 1921).

Reid, R. R., 'The Rebellion of the Earls, 1569,' *TRHS,* 2nd series, xx (1906), 171–203.

Richardson, W. C., *History of the Court of Augmentations 1536–54* (Baton Rouge, 1961).

Ridpath, G., *The Border History of England and Scotland* (Edinburgh, 1776).

Robson, R., *The English Highland Clans,* (Edinburgh, 1989).

Rollins, H. E., 'William Elderton: Elizabethan Actor and Ballad Writer', *Harvard University Studies and Notes in Philogy and Literature,* xviii (1920), 199–245.

Rowse, A. L., *The Expansion of Elizabethan England* (London, 1955).

Rowlands, M. B., 'Recusant women 1560–1640', in M. Prior, ed. *Women in English Society 1500–1800* (Oxford, 1985), 149–180.

Royal Commission on Ancient Monuments, County of Berwick (Edinburgh, 1915).

Royal Commission on Ancient Monuments, County of Roxburgh (Edinburgh, 1955).

Royal Commission on Ancient Monuments, County of Selkirk (Edinburgh, 1957).

Russell, J., *The Haigs of Bemersyde* (Edinburgh, 1881).

Sanders, J., ' "A true man minded to justice" Robert Collingwood (*c*. 1490–1556) of Eslington, Northumberland', *AA*, 5th ser, xxvi (1998), 87–104.

Sanderson, M. H. B., *Scottish Rural Society in the Sixteenth Century* (Edinburgh, 1982).

Sanderson, M. H. B., 'The Edinburgh Merchants in Society, 1570–1603; the Evidence of Testaments', in Cowan & Shaw, eds. *The Renaissance and Reformation in Scotland* (Edinburgh, 1983), 182–199.

Sanderson, M. H. B., 'Manse and Glebe in the Sixteenth Century', *RSCHS*, xix (1975–7), 81–92.

Sanderson, M. H. B., 'Catholic Recusancy In Scotland In The Sixteenth Century', *IR,* xxi (1970), 87–107.

Sanderson, R. P. ed., *Survey of the Debateable and Border Lands, 1604* (Alnwick, 1891).

Sayer, M. J., *English Nobility* (Norwich, 1979).

Scott, H. ed., *Fasti Ecclesiae Scoticanae* (Edinburgh, 1915–61), 9 vols.

Scott, J., *Berwick Upon Tweed; the history of the town and guild* (London, 1888).

Scott, W., *The Minstrelsy of the Scottish Border* (Edinburgh, 1802).

Scott, W., *The Border Antiquities of England and Scotland* (London, 1814), 2 vols.

Scott, W., *Memorials of the Haliburtons* (Edinburgh, 1824).

The Scots Peerage, ed. J. P. Balfour-Paul (Edinburgh, 1904–14), 9 vols.

Sharp, C. ed., *Memorials of the Rebellion* (London, 1840).

Sharpe, J. A., *Early Modern England* (London, 1987).

Sharpe, J. A., *Crime in early modern England* (Harlow, 1990).

Shire, H. M., *Song, Dance and Poetry of the Court of Scotland under King James VI* (Cambridge, 1969).

Signet, Writers to. *A History of the Society of Writers to Her Majesty's Signet with a list of Members 1594–1890* (Edinburgh, 1890).

Simpson, A., *The Wealth of the Gentry* (Cambridge, 1961).

Simpson, G. G., *Scottish Handwriting* (Aberdeen, 1983).

Simpson, G. G., *The Scottish Soldier Abroad 1247–1967* (Edinburgh, 1991).

Simon, J., *Education and Society in Tudor England* (Cambridge, 1966).

Slack, P., *From Reformation to Improvement. Public Welfare in Early Modern England* (Oxford, 1999).

Smith, S., 'Bordering on Identity', *Scotlands*, iii (1996), 18–32.

Smith-Bannister, S., *Names and Naming Patterns in England 1538–1700* (Oxford, 1997).

Smout, T. C., *A History of the Scottish People, 1560–1603* (London, 1969).

Somerset, A., *Unnatural Murder* (London, 1998).

Southworth, J., *Fools and Jesters at the English Court* (Stroud, 1998).

Sowards, J. K., 'Erasmus and the education of women', *The Sixteenth Century Journal*, xiii (1982), 77–89.

Spence, R. T., 'The Backward North Modernized? The Cliffords, Earls of Cumberland and the Socage Manor of Carlisle', *NH*, xx (1984), 64–87.

Spratt, A., 'The Cistercian Nunnery of North Berwick and the Hume Family', *East Lothian Life*, xxxv (Spring 2001), 28–9.

Spring, E., *Law, Land and Family*, (Chapel Hill, 1993).

Spufford, M., *Small Books and Pleasant Histories: Popular Fiction and its Readership in the Seventeenth Century* (Cambridge, 1985).

Spufford, M., *Contrasting Communities* (Cambridge, 1979).

Stanford Reid, W., 'Clerical Taxation: The Scottish Alternative to Dissolution of the Monasteries, 1530–60', *Catholic Historical Review*, xxxv (1948), 129–153.

Stevenson, A., 'Taxation in medieval Scotland', in P. G. McNeill & H.L. MacQueen, eds. *Atlas of Scottish History* (Edinburgh, 1996), 298–305.

Stevenson, J. H., 'The Usher of the White Rod', *Scot Antiq*, x (1897), 158–161.

Stodart, R. R., *Scottish Arms* (Edinburgh, 1881).

Stone, L., *The Crisis of the Aristocracy, 1558–1641* (Oxford, 1965).

Stone, L. & J. C. F., *An Open Elite? England 1540–1880* (Oxford, 1984).

Storey, R. L., 'The Wardens of the Marches of England towards Scotland, 1577–1489', *EHR*, lxxii (1957), 593–616.

Stoyle, M. J., 'The Last Refuge of a Scoundrel: Sir Richard Grenville and Cornish Particularism, 1644–6', *Historical Research*, lxxi (1998), 31–51.

Summerson, H., *Medieval Carlisle: The City and the Borders from the late eleventh to the mid-sixteenth century* (The Cumberland and Westmorland Antiquarian and Archaeological Society, Kendal, 1993), 2 vols.

Summerson, H., 'Crime and Society in Medieval Cumberland', *Transactions of the Cumberland and Westmorland Archaeological and Antiquarian Society*, lxxxii (1982), 111–124.

Summerson, H., 'The Early Development of the Laws of the Anglo-Scottish Borders, 1249–1448', in *Proceedings of the Ninth British Legal History Conference at Glasgow 1989*, 29–42.

Swinburne, H., *A Treatise of Testaments and Last Wills, 1591* (London, 1743).

Swinton, A. C., *The Swintons of that Ilk and their Cadets* (Edinburgh, 1883).

Tancred, G., *The Annals of a Border Club*, second edition (Jedburgh, 1903).

Tate, G., *History of the Burgh, Castle and Barony of Alnwick* (Alnwick, 1866–69), 2 vols.

Tawney, R. H., *Religion and the Rise of Capitalism* (Harmondsworth, 1980).

Tebeaux, E., 'Women and Technical Writing, 1475–1700: Technology, Literacy and Development of a Genre', in L. Hunter & S. Hutton, eds. *Women, Science and Medicine 1500–1700* (1997), 29–62.

Thirsk, J. ed., *The Agrarian History of England and Wales* (Cambridge, 1967), vol iv.

Thirsk, J., 'The Fashioning of the Tudor-Stuart Gentry', *Bulletin of the John Rylands Library*, lxxii (1990), 69–85.

Thirsk, J., 'The limitations of the probate inventory', in J. Chartes and D. Hey, eds. *English Rural Society, 1500–1800* (Cambridge, 1990), 139–74.

Thomson, G. H., *Some Influences of the Geography of Northumberland upon it's History* (London, 1912).

Thomson, J. A. F., 'Scots in England in the Fifteenth Century', *SHR*, lxxxix (2000), 1–16.

Thornton, T., ' "The Enemy or Stranger, that shall invade their country": Identity and community in the English North', in B. Taithe and T. Thornton, eds. *War. Identities in Conflict 1300–2000* (Stroud, 1998), 57–70.

Thornton-Kennedy, C., *Bonnet Lairds* (Montrose, 1972).

Tomlinson, W. W., *Life In Northumberland During The Sixteenth Century* (London, 1897).

Tough, D. L. W., *The Last Years of a Frontier* (Oxford, 1928).

Tranter, N. G., *The Fortified House in Scotland* (Edinburgh, 1962), 5 vols.

Trevelyan, G. M., 'The Middle Marches,' in *Clio, A Muse and Other Essays* (London, 1930), 19–41.

Tuck, R. F., 'The Origins of the Royal Grammar School Newcastle Upon Tyne', *AA*, 4th ser, xlvi (1968), 229–271.

Tyack, N. ed., *England's Long Reformation* (London 1998).

Tyler, P., 'The Significance of The Ecclesiastical Commission at York', *NH*, ii (1967), 27–44.

Usher, B., 'Durham and Winchester Episcopal Estates and the Elizabethan Settlement: A Reappraisal', *Journal of Ecclesiastical History*, xlix (1998), 393–406.

Usher, R. G., *The Reconstruction of the English Church* (New York, 1910), 2 vols.

Vale, M., *The Gentleman's Recreations, 1560–1630* (Cambridge, 1977).

Waite, P. C., *The Land of Britain*, xiv – Berwickshire (London, 1941).

Wallace, H. M., 'Berwick in the Reign of Elizabeth', *EHR*, xlvi (1931), 79–88.

Walsham, A., *Church Papists. Catholicism, Conformity and Confessional Polemic in Early Modern England* (London, 1993).

Watts, S. J., *From Border to Middle Shire: Northumberland 1586–1625* (Leicester 1975).

Watts, S. J., 'Tenant-Right in early Seventeenth Century Northumberland', *NH*, vi (1971), 64–87.

Watts, V. E., 'Some Northumbrian Fishery Names IV: The River Tweed', *Durham Archaeological Journal*, xiii (1997), 89–98.

Whiting, R., *The Blind Devotion of the People* (Cambridge, 1991).

Whittington, G., 'Field Systems of Scotland', in A. R. H. Baker and R. A. Butlin, eds. *Studies of Field Systems in the British Isles* (Oxford, 1973), 530–579.

Whyte, I. D., *Agriculture and Society in Seventeenth Century Scotland* (Edinburgh, 1979).

Whyte, I. D. and Whittington, G., *An Historical Geography of Scotland* (London, 1983).

Williams, P., *The Council in the Marches of Wales* (Cardiff, 1958).

Williams, P., 'The Northern Borderland Under The Early Stuarts', in Bell & Ollard, *Historical Essays Presented To David Ogg* (London, 1963), 1–17.

Williams, P., 'The Crown and the Counties', in C. Haigh, ed. *The Reign of Elizabeth I* (London, 1985), 126–46.

Williamson, A. H., *Scottish National Consciousness in the Age of James VI* (Edinburgh, 1979).

Williamson, A. H., 'A Patriot Nobility? Calvinism, Kin-Ties and Civic Humanism', *SHR*, lxxii (1993), 1–21.

Williamson, E., 'Horse-racing in Scotland in the sixteenth and earlier seventeenth centuries: Peebles and beyond', *Review of Scottish Culture*, 14 (2001–02), 31–42.

Wilson, C. and Parker, G., *An Introduction to the Sources of European Economic History*, (Cornell, 1977).

Woodward, J., *The Theatre of Death* (Woodbridge, 1997).

Wormald, J., *Court, Kirk and Community, 1470–1625* (London, 1981).

Wormald, J., *Lords and Men in Scotland: Bonds of Manrent, 1442–1603* (Edinburgh, 1985).

Wormald, J., 'Lords and Lairds in Fifteenth Century Scotland: Nobles and Gentry', in M. Jones, ed. *Gentry and Lesser Nobility in Late Medieval Europe* (Gloucester, 1986), 182–200.

Wormald, J., 'Bloodfeud, Kindred and Government in Scotland', *P&P*, lxxxvii (1980), 54–97.

Wright, A. D., 'Catholic History, North and South, Revisited', *NH*, xxv (1989), 120–34.

Wright, L. B., *Middle Class Culture in Elizabethan England* (Chapel Hill, 1935).

Wrightson, K., 'The Social Order of Early Modern England: Three approaches', in Bonfield, Smith and Wrightson, eds. *The World We Have Gained* (Oxford, 1986), 177–202.

Young, J. ed., *Notes and Historical references to the Scottish family of Lauder* (Glasgow, 1884).

Young, M. D. ed., *The Parliaments of Scotland. Burgh and Shire Commissioners* (Edinburgh, 1992), 2 vols.

Zell, M. L., 'The Use of Religious Preambles as a Measure of Religious Belief in the Sixteenth Century', *Bulletin of the Institute of Historical Research*, 1 (1977), 246–9.

THESES

Bardgett, F. D., 'Faith families and faction: the Scottish Reformation in Angus and the Mearns'. unpubl PhD thesis. Edinburgh 1987.

Boscher, P. G., 'Politics, Administration and Diplomacy: The Anglo-Scottish Border 1550–1560', unpubl. PhD diss. Durham 1985.

Brown, J. J., 'The economic, political and social influences of the Edinburgh merchant community, 1600–38', unpubl. Ph.D diss. Edinburgh 1985.

Cardew, A. A., 'A Study of Society in the Anglo-Scottish Borders. 1455–1502', unpubl. PhD diss. St Andrews 1974.

Dixon, P. J., 'The Deserted Medieval Villages of North Northumberland: A Settlement History From The Twelfth to the Nineteenth Century', unpubl. PhD diss. University of Wales 1985.

Dixon, P. W., 'Fortified Houses on the Anglo-Scottish Border. A Study of the Domestic Architecture of the Upland area in its Social and Economic Context', unpubl. D.Phil diss. Oxford 1977.

Ferguson, 'C. M. F., Law and Order on the Anglo-Scottish Border, 1603–1707', unpubl. PhD diss. St Andrews 1981.

Goodare, J. M., 'Parliament and Society in Scotland, 1560–1603', unpubl. PhD diss. Edinburgh 1989.

Johnson, P. A., 'A Synchronic and Historical View of Border Area Bimoric Vowel Systems', unpubl. Ph.D diss. Edinburgh 1985.

Keeling, S. M., 'The Church and Religion in the Anglo-Scottish Border Counties, 1534–1572', unpubl. PhD diss. Durham 1976.

Knowles, A., 'Customary tenure on the northern estates of the Percy earls of Northumberland in the sixteenth century', unpubl. MA diss. Manchester 1983.

Meikle, M. M., 'Lairds and Gentlemen: a study of the landed families of the Eastern Anglo-Scottish Borders, c. 1540–1603'. unpubl. PhD diss, Edinburgh 1989.

Parry, M. L., 'Changes in the Upper Limit of Cultivation in South East Scotland, 1600–1900', unpubl. Ph.D diss. Edinburgh 1973.

Pollard, H., 'Some aspects of the History of Education in the area of Northumberland, 635–1600'. unpubl. M.Ed. Durham (Newcastle) 1952.

Taylor, S. E., 'The Crown and the North of England, 1559–70; a study of the rebellion of the northern earls, 1569–70 and its causes', unpubl. PhD diss. Manchester 1981.

White, A. J., 'Religion, Politics and Society in Aberdeen, 1543–93.' unpubl PhD thesis. Edinburgh 1985.

Wilson, B. N., 'The Changes of the Reformation Period in Durham and Northumberland'. unpubl. PhD diss. Durham 1939.

Zulager, R. R., 'A Study of the middle-rank administrators in the government of King James VI of Scotland, 1580–1603', unpubl. PhD diss. Aberdeen 1991.

Notes

1 Many archives have been reorganised since I did my original research. I have attempted to update the locations for these references, but some archive collections listed may have been reclassified or rehoused.

2 The Durham Diocesan Records have been recatalogued. DDR ii, 1–3, are now DDR/EV/VIS/1/1–3. DDR iii, 2–5, are now DDR/EJ/CCA/1/2–5. DDR v, 1–7, are now DDR/EJ/CCD/1/1–7. DDR vii, 1–2, are now DDR/EJ/CCA/3/1–2.

3 Some collections in the NAS are now outhoused in Thomas Telford House. Records from Chancery, the Court of Session, Exchequer, Register of Deeds and Privy Seal, amongst others, were moved to West Register House, Charlotte Square in 2000.

4 NRAS lists are periodically updated. These references therefore may have changed.

Index

Unless otherwise stated men listed below are the heads of household. Likewise the females are their daughters, unless specified as their wives or widows.